PROJECT MANAGEMENT FOR BUSINESS PROFESSIONALS

PROJECT MANAGEMENT FOR BUSINESS PROFESSIONALS

A COMPREHENSIVE GUIDE

Edited by

Joan Knutson

John Wiley & Sons, Inc.

New York • Chichester • Weinheim • Brisbane • Singapore • Toronto

Copyright © 2001 by PMSI = Project Mentors, a part of the Provant Solution. All rights reserved.

Published by John Wiley & Sons, Inc.

Published simultaneously in Canada.

This publication is designed to provide accurate and authoritative information in regard to the subject matter covered. It is sold with the understanding that the publisher is not engaged in rendering legal, accounting, or other professional services. If legal advice or other expert assistance is required, the services of a competent professional person should be sought.

Designations used by companies to distinguish their products are often claimed as trademarks. In all instances where the author or publisher is aware of a claim, the product names appear in Initial Capital letters. Readers, however, should contact the appropriate companies for more complete information regarding trademarks and registration.

Library of Congress Cataloging-in-Publication Data:

Knutson, Joan.
    Project management for business professionals : a comprehensive guide / Joan Knutson.
        p.   cm.
    Includes bibliographical references and index.
    ISBN 0-471-38033-4 (cloth : alk. paper)
    1. Industrial project management.   I. Title.
    HD69.P75 K65 2001
    658.4'04—dc21   00-043695

Printed in the United States of America.

10 9 8 7 6 5 4 3 2 1

Grateful acknowledgement is hereby given for permission to reprint the following works:

Figure 1.1 is reprinted with the permission of the Project Management Institute Headquarters. Four Campus Boulevard, Newtown Square, PA 19073-2399 USA. Phone: (610) 356-4600, Fax: (610) 356-4647. Project Management Institute (PMI) is the world's leading project management association with over 50,000 members worldwide. For further information contact PMI Headquarters at (610) 356-4600 or visit the web site at www.pmi.org.

Chapter 7 copyright © Frank Toney.

Chapter 9 copyright © Rita Mulcahy, PMP.

Chapter 15 is adapted from Carl N. Belack, "Computer-Aided Project Management," in *Handbook of Industrial Engineering, Third Edition,* Gavriel Salvendy, ed., New York: John Wiley & Sons, forthcoming. © copyright Carl N. Belack and John Wiley & Sons.

Chapter 16 reprinted with the permission of ABT Corporation.

Figures 17.1 through 17.4 are reprinted with the permission of the Project Management Institute Headquarters. See PMI citation above. The data in Chapter 17 is reprinted with the permission of Hewlett-Packard.

Chapter 19 reprinted with the permission of Robert Storeygard and 3M.

The Case Study accompanying Chapter 21 is copyright protected by SPMgroup Ltd. and Performance Support Tool 21.1 Preliminary Assessment of the Ethical Dimensions of a Situation and 21.2 The Ten-Step Method of Decision Making are © Jon Pekel and Doug Wallace.

Chapter 24 is reprinted from the Proceedings of the 1996 PMI Annual Seminar/Symposium with the permission of Vijay K. Verma and the Project Management Institute Headquarters, Four Campus Boulevard, Newtown Square, PA 19073-2399 USA. Phone: (610) 356-4600, Fax: (610) 356-4647. Project Management Institute (PMI) is the world's leading project management association with over 50,000 members worldwide. For further information contact PMI Headquarters at (610) 356-4600 or visit the web site at www.pmi.org.

Chapter 27 copyright © Management Strategies, Inc.

Chapter 28 copyright © AT&T. All rights reserved. Reprinted with the permission of AT&T. Adapted from Daniel P. Ono and Russell D. Archibald, "Project Team Planning and Project Start-Up," presented at the Second National Forum, PMI Mexico, November 25, 1998, Mexico City; and from Russell D. Archibald, *Managing High-Technology Programs and Projects (Second Edition),* New York: John Wiley & Sons, 1992, Chapter 11, pp. 236–256.

Portions of Chapter 30 are excerpted from Chapter 18, J. K. Pinto and O. P. Kharbanda, *Successful Project Managers,* New York: Van Nostrand Reinhold, 1995.

First and foremost, to Linda Nietlisbach, whose focus, professionalism, and persistence made this book happen.

Secondly, to the Provant organization and its Project Management Group, PMSI-Project Mentors, who allowed me the time to pull together this anthology.

And, thirdly, to my son, David, who lost his mom for more hours than I would like to admit.

Contents

ACKNOWLEDGMENTS

Grateful acknowledgment and the sincerest gratitude are extended to all of the contributors to this book, who are the most professional people with whom I have had the pleasure to work and whose thoughts, ideas, and insights will add immeasurably to the evolution of project management in the business community.

I also wish to express my heartfelt thanks to each and every project management practitioner who today and over the past lifetime of project management has made project management a recognized and respected discipline.

Finally, on behalf of PMSI-Project Mentors; a part of the Provant solution, and John Wiley & Sons, Inc., grateful acknowledgment is given to the Project Management Institute, for permission to reprint work that appears in three of the chapters in this book, and to the other organizations and publishers that have kindly granted permission to reprint previously published material. Details of previous publications are given on the copyright page of this book.

PREFACE

Project Management for Business *Professionals: A Comprehensive Guide* is an anthology of chapters written by a cadre of recognized project management practitioners. It is designed to provide need-to-know information for the business professional on a topic that is seeping into the broader business community, the topic of project management.

For many years, the engineering and construction industries have been recognized for using the project management discipline to plan, organize, and manage their jobs. The spectrum of the project management discipline has broadened and expanded with each ongoing year. What was once called project management is now evolving into "the managing of projects." What was a part-time job carried out by a technician is now a full-time job fulfilled by a person possessing a host of project management competencies. What was once accomplished on an ad hoc basis is now being performed by applying structured project management methodologies and processes.

The organizations that employ you, the reader, are evolving into project-driven organizations which conduct much if not all of their business in a project mode. Projects are those endeavors with a discrete beginning and end, producing a discrete deliverable. Various skilled personnel carry out this unique process in order to meet an expected time frame, resource utilization, and specified cost. Considering this definition, it is obvious why construction and engineering would employ the discipline of project management.

If you think about it, you'll recognize that many other industries also utilize project management. For example, the development of a new drug in the pharmaceutical industry is a project. So is the release to the marketplace of a new piece of high-technology hardware or software. In the service industry, a rollout of a new checking account service, a modification to an airline reservations system, or a response to new governmental insurance regulations are also projects.

Project management has become a driving, irreplaceable, here-to-stay discipline within organizations. It is not now nor will it ever be a "flavor of the month." Project management is a way of doing business that will continue to be inculcated and ingrained into each of our organizations.

The methods, systems, and processes related to project management are not cut and dried. They need to be dynamic, scalable, and repeatable. But more important, they need to take every possible creative twist to make them amenable to the people who are required to use them day in and day out.

Project Management for Business Professionals is designed for the reader who is searching for advanced material that deals with a wide spectrum of business-oriented subject matter as it relates to project management. This text addresses the practical application of the project management discipline in today's business world. It provides a wide range of perspectives on the discipline by allowing 33 subject matter experts to share their unique areas of expertise all under one cover.

These subject matter experts were carefully chosen because of their prestige and positions within the project management discipline. Not only are these authors seasoned practitioners of the discipline of project management, but they have over the years added value to the growth and evolution of project management in the business community. These 33 authors have been drawn from the three following areas:

1. *Academia.* This group of authors consists of professors and educators who not only teach the discipline but also practice it in their consultations with various clients.
2. *Suppliers of training, consulting, and software.* Here we have found prominent consultants, authors, and software creators.
3. *Private industry.* These professionals manage significant projects and/or manage project offices within their organizations.

SOCIO-TECHNICAL MODEL

Project Management for Business Professionals is designed around a socio-technical model. The role of the project manager has become not only one of coordinating the tangible data around the project but also one of becoming proficient at dealing with the intangible, human behavioral condition as it relates to the discipline of project management. The book therefore has been divided into two parts, The Technical Track and The Human Dimensions Track. Let me explain the logic flow of the book.

Project management's role has traditionally been in administering schedule, cost, and resource data. That view is still correct. The planning, monitoring, and tracking of the start and end dates of tasks, the hours of commitment for human and nonhuman resources, and the dollars allocated to the commitment of those resources over time still comprise a major part of the project manager's job. The managing of this type of data has been categorized in the first part of this text, entitled The Technical Track. This track consists of 14 chapters, and it represents half of the socio-technical model.

The other half deals with the human behavioral aspect of the model and explores the management of the team/group dynamics within the project. These organizational and team perspectives of project management are becoming more and more important to the success of projects and of project management. The Human Dimensions Track explores more people-oriented subjects. This track contains 13 chapters that look at the interpersonal relations, the team dynamics, and the political as well as organizational considerations impacting project management. The second part of this handbook has been designed to focus on these people-related aspects of project management.

In addition, this text is book-ended with three contributions that assume broader outlooks. Chapter 1 presents an overview of the evolution of project management, including insightful perspectives on the history of the discipline. Following the overview, Chapter 2 describes the current condition of project management, as it becomes more visible and recognized throughout the business community. The anthology concludes, in Chapter 30, with a discussion of the influences on project management as we move into the twenty-first century.

TECHNICAL TRACK

The Technical Track consists of 14 chapters that address the methods, procedures, and processes required to plan and manage projects. These process-related topics map the work efforts needed in order to initiate and define; plan; execute and control; and close out a project endeavor.

Every project management environment requires a set of rules by which the game is to be played. These are the policies and procedures that delineate who is to do what and when it is to be done.

Project management processes may be managed with varying degrees of rigor and structure. If a project management culture in an organization requires a high degree of structure, these policies and procedures can be documented at a level of detail that affords no possible chance of misinterpretation. In other project management environments, formalized policies and procedures may not be considered appropriate.

The rules are conveyed more as guidelines that are flexible and left open to interpretation.

Project management methodologies of either type are available off-the-shelf, ready to be customized to each unique organization. Yet some organizations develop their policies and procedures on the fly, and these ad hoc guidelines are handed down from one project generation to the next by word of mouth. In whatever fashion these policies become inculcated into the culture, they provide the project players with the technical direction to get the job done.

Much of what is proposed by our contributors in this track can be supported by automation. The software of today and the upcoming software of tomorrow will make it easier for all of us to build project-related databases, to deal with the enterprise allocation of resources, and to generate a myriad of customized reports for all audiences. It is the job of the business professional to explore the types of software available, to pick and to choose those products that will make their project organizations more effective, and to use these products in an intelligent manner.

Here is an outline of the chapters in The Technical Track, as they are presented.

The first 10 chapters describe selected (not all-inclusive) processes needed in order to conduct the four phases of the project management life cycle. They are:

1. *Initiation and Definition* (Chapters 3, 4, and 5)
   - Portfolio Management
   - Scope Management
   - Requirements Management
2. *Planning* (Chapters 6, 7, and 8)
   - Schedule Management
   - Accounting and Financial Management
   - Risk Management
3. *Execution and Control* (Chapters 9, 10, and 11)
   - Contracts and Procurement Management
   - Earned Value Management
   - Information Management
4. *Closeout* (Chapter 12)
   - Project Closeout Management

This series of selected processes ends with a chapter discussing how to work within an environment that deals with more than one project at the same time.

   - Multiple Project Management (Chapter 13)

Note: These chapters are sequenced according to when the work effort begins in the project life cycle. However, please keep in mind that project management is an iterative process. The documents and plans generated from the initiation, definition, and planning phases are monitored, tracked, and managed during the execution and control phase. And the actual results as compared to the plans from the execution and control phase are reviewed during closeout.

The remaining three chapters in The Technical Track take a look at how these processes can be automated to be more efficient and effective. This automation option is explored from the following three perspectives:

1. Today (Chapter 14)
2. Tomorrow (Chapter 15)
3. The Future Is Today (Chapter 16)

HUMAN DIMENSIONS TRACK

Decorating our office in early PERT network will never ensure a successful project management initiative within any organization. People—not charts, graphs, and numbers—drive projects. The success of a project is dependent on the people involved. The project community is widespread. It extends from those people who are vested in the outcome of the project to those folks who have little or no vested interest, but whose skills and buy-in are needed in order to get the job done. The second track in this text is dedicated to exploring the people side of project management.

The people side of project management addresses what it takes for the project players to support and contribute to the project management discipline in the most professional manner possible. The writing and distribution of policies and procedures does not necessarily make this a reality. The human considerations are the "socio" aspect of the model. People who are asked to use the project management processes discussed in The Technical Track need to be part of the development and upgrade of the processes, so that they believe in the rules enough to follow them. Furthermore, the management and the culture need to support adherence to these guidelines and rules for the good of the organization as well as for the success of the project and the project players. This occurs through active team management.

In today's project management world, the project manager may have all the responsibility and accountability for the success of the project, but on the other hand have no authority over some, if any, of the project players with whom he or she must interact. Therefore, there are project political/people skills that must be understood and applied.

The obvious challenge is to match the correct people with the correct talents to the appropriate tasks. Each task on the work plan has the need for particular technical skills. These skills may be those acquired at the university or in vocational training. They may be skills learned through advanced adult education or on-the-job training. It is great when the project has the most technically qualified people assigned. But what if there are not enough people with the competencies needed by all of the multiple projects being run within the organization? Or what if these perfect technical people can't get along with each other? Then the "politics of projects" rears its ugly head. The business professional must see to it that the proper interpersonal tone is set within the culture.

This includes establishing clarity around the roles and responsibilities of all the project players and the criteria upon which rewards will be given. Who is in charge? That question is first and foremost. Each project player needs to know what he or she is authorized to ask of others, what dollars they are allowed to spend, what changes they can commit to without asking permission. Knowing one's boundaries is part of the battle. The other part of the battle is knowing "What's in it for me?" What tangible and intangible motivations make it worthwhile to play the game by the rules? The "socio" side of this issue revolves around the awareness of the business professional to address the benefits and hurdles that exist within the project management discipline. Business professionals need to be aware so that they can understand their own boundaries and successfully influence the project scenarios revolving around them. In addition, the project players must have the competencies to assume the roles and responsibilities discussed above.

The outline of the chapters in The Human Dimensions Track is designed to go from the strategic to the tactical. Of the 13 chapters in this track, the first three explore the strategic positioning of the project management discipline within the organization as a whole.

Strategic, Organizational Perspective of the Project Organization (Chapters 17, 18, and 19)
- Concept
- Design
- Deployment

The remaining 10 chapters focus on the more tactical issues of establishing and managing a viable team environment in which projects can be run. These chapters consider the project players individually, interacting with one another, and coalescing as a team.

Individual Project Players (Chapters 20 and 21)
- Professional and Personal Development Management
- Ethics Management

Interpersonal Interactions (Chapters 22, 23, 24, and 25)
- Conflict Management
- Role Management
- Culturally Diverse Management
- Expectations Management

Team Dynamics (Chapters 26, 27, 28, and 29)
- Participative Management
- Virtual Team Management
- Team Infrastructure Management
- Team Management

SUMMARY

Abilities, both technical and human behavioral, are key to getting the job done. This handbook is positioned as the guiding text for the business professional who is being asked to include project management in his or her day-to-day work. The new awareness that organizations are becoming project driven has heightened the visibility of project management within the business community. This greater visibility brings with it an increasingly larger audience of people who are interested in learning how to work within a project environment.

In fact, many organizations are instituting internal project management implementation initiatives for a variety of reasons, including these:

- Project management is necessary for continued competitive growth within the marketplace.
- Project management is a core competency that has been recognized as critical to support an organization's internal infrastructure.

The discipline of project management has established itself to the point where there is now a trade association, the Project Management Institute (PMI), that specifically addresses the needs of the project management community. The library of books being published in the field of project management is increasing, as are alternative modes of training technology, such as CD-ROMs, Webcasts, and knowledge-based systems. Much of the current literature addresses basic project management relative to planning and controlling a project. Some books focus on a specific topic within the project management discipline, such as risk management or project planning. There is also literature specific to project management as it is being applied in various industries such as information systems, construction, and high technology. The newest wave of project-related books deals with the human side of project management—in other words, interpersonal skills and team dynamics. However, very few books address the discipline of project management in as comprehensive a manner from as advanced a perspective as *Project Management for Business Professionals: A Comprehensive Guide.*

Many readers looking for project management information have already read the basic books, or they have been in the business long enough to be looking for something that is more advanced. This need for more advanced content is not directed at the technical, mathematics-based project charts and graphs, but at a higher business orientation. The content of this book focuses on how to apply the project management discipline in a normal day-to-day business environment within any function within any industry.

Whether you read this guide from cover to cover or choose only those topics of special interest to you, you will find that the contributions in this text are superior in every sense of the word. The topics are definitely beyond the basics. They are steeped in solid, practical, use-it-tomorrow information.

I have been in the field of project management for over 30 years, and during that time I have never seen as much solid business acumen articulated from such a clear and fresh business perspective as is presented in this volume. I hope that you enjoy reading this book as much as I have while editing it, and that you appreciate, as I do, the willingness of these subject matter experts to share their insights with all of us.

JOAN KNUTSON
PMSI-Project Mentors,
a part of the Provant solution

About the Contributors

Joan Knutson, editor, is president of PMSI-Project Mentors, a part of the Provant solution, which has been providing training and consulting to diverse organizations for 23 years. Joan presently devotes her time to writing, speaking at conferences and symposia, and working with management in implementing project management. She has developed courseware and computer-based training products that address the full spectrum of project management. The editor of the "Executive's Notebook" column in the Project Management Institute's magazine *PM Network*, she is the author of five books, including *Succeeding in Project-Driven Organizations* (2001, John Wiley & Sons).

Russell D. Archibald, Fellow PMI, PMP, has held senior management positions with the Bendix Corp., ITT Corp., and Hughes Aircraft Co. For over 40 years, he has consulted in 12 countries on four continents to companies in telecommunications, information technology, industrial engineering, construction, consumer products, and service, as well as federal and local governmental agencies and international development banks. He is the author of *Managing High-Technology Programs and Projects* (Second Edition, 1992, John Wiley & Sons) and is an original trustee of the Project Management Institute.

Richard Bauhaus served as project manager in manufacturing and research and development at Hewlett-Packard from 1961 to 2000. He was manager of HP's Project Management Initiative and developed and delivered courses and consulted in project management as part of the PMI team in the HP Product Processes Organization. He is now a partner in The Bauhaus Group, consultants and trainers of global project teams.

Carl N. Belack, PhM, PMP, is a founding partner of Oak Associates, Inc. Since 1979, when he was program manager for a Trident Submarine Navigation Subsystem program, he has worked in project and program management for diverse companies, from small to Fortune 500. He is a past director of education for the New York City Chapter of the Project Management Institute.

Danek Bienkowski is cofounder of ABT Corporation (recently merged into Niku Corp.), providing enterprise project management solutions. He has more than 40 years of business, project management, and IT experience, including positions at Philips NV, Rank Xerox, Hoskyns PLC in England, and Price Waterhouse in New York.

David I. Cleland, PhD, often described as the "Father of Project Management," is professor emeritus in the School of Engineering at the University of Pittsburgh and the author/editor of 31 books in project management, engineering management, and manufacturing management. An active member of PMI and cofounder/codirector of the University of Pittsburgh Manufacturing Assistance Center, he has been honored internationally for his original and continuing contributions to the discipline. In 1997, he was honored with the establishment of the David I. Cleland Excellence in Project Management Literature Award.

Terry Cooke-Davies, PhD, is the founder and managing director of Human Systems Limited, UK, which creates and supports interbusiness project management knowledge networks through which corporate members, typically global organizations, share data and resources. Dr. Cooke-Davies's client members recognize project management as a key corporate capability and represent a broad range of industries, including aerospace, pharmaceuticals, financial services, telecommunications, electronics, information systems, energy, transport, utilities, and manufacturing.

J. Kent Crawford, PMP, is chief executive officer of Project Management Solutions, Inc., a consulting, training, and research organization that provides total solutions for corporations implementing or enhancing their project management systems and processes. As a former president and chair of the Project Management Institute (1994-1995), he worked to implement innovative programs and establish productive relationships with other national and international associations in order to advance the state of the art and practice of project management.

Catherine Daw, PMP, is a principal of SPMgroup, Ltd., a project management consulting and training firm focusing on project process and performance improvement. In a career spanning more than 20 years of business, technology, and project management experience, she has managed a wide range of complex multimillion-dollar projects in IT and business.

Quentin W. Fleming, senior staff consultant of Primavera Systems, has 30 years of industrial project management experience, including having served in various managerial roles at the Northrop Corporation from 1968 to 1991. Past president of the Orange County chapter of the Project Management Institute, he has developed and taught courses in scope, cost, time, and procurement management and is the author of seven textbooks on subjects related to project management, including, with coauthor Joel M. Koppelman, *Earned Value Project Management.*

J. Davidson Frame, PhD, is Academic Dean at the University of Management and Technology and was on the faculty and chairman of the Department of Management Science at George Washington University for 19 years. He has served as director of certification and director of educational services at the Project Management Institute and was elected to PMI's board of directors in 2000. He has written six books on project management and has trained more than 30,000 managers in such organizations as Morgan Stanley Dean Witter, Donaldson Lufkin & Jenrette, Lucent Technologies, AT&T, IBM, Motorola, Hewlett-Packard, Fannie Mae, the White House, the World Bank, and Roche Diagnostics.

Shlomo Globerson, PhD, PMP, professor in the Graduate School of Business Administration at Tel Aviv University, is a researcher and consultant in project and operations management and a frequent visiting professor at universities and institutions around the world. He develops new courses and workshops for MBA students, project managers, and executives and has published more than 70 refereed articles and seven books.

Martha Haywood is senior consulting partner at Management Strategies, specializing in the management of geographically distributed teams for companies such as Oracle, Lockheed Martin, Hewlett-Packard, and Amdahl, as well as Infoseek, Cisco, and Conductus Corporation. She is the author of *Managing Virtual Teams* (1998, Artech House), teaches project management at the University of California Berkeley Extension, and developed the online Project Management Certificate program for Santa Clara University.

Martin D. Hynes III, PhD, is director of the Pharmaceuticals Management Center of Excellence at Lilly Research Laboratories, Eli Lilly and Company. He has authored more than a hundred articles, abstracts, chapters, and patents in subjects/products related to program and project management.

Joel M. Koppelman is president of Primavera Systems, which offers a family of project management software products. Before cofounding Primarvera in 1983, he planned, designed, and managed major transportation projects as vice president/chief financial officer of Transportation and Distribution Associates, Inc. He is a registered professional engineer and a frequent speaker at universities and international management organizations.

Paula Martin is cofounder of Martin Tate, a global project management training and consulting firm specializing in project management as a core competency. She is coauthor, with Karen Tate, of the bestselling book *Project Management Memory Jogger™* and is a columnist for the Project Management Institute magazine *PM Network*.

Margery Mayer has served as program manager for complex, mission-critical projects for a variety of industries, including high-tech manufacturing, information technology, electric utility, banking, and aerospace. She teaches strategic decision-making and project management at San Francisco State University and managing an ebusiness at Golden Gate University, as well as seminars on project management and the project office. Her book *The Virtual Edge: Embracing Technology for Distributed Team Success* (Project Management Institute, 1998) introduces the concept of managing remote work teams.

Rita Mulcahy, PMP, is the author of *PMP Exam Prep*, (2000, Beavers Pond Press) and a columnist for the Project Management Institute magazine *PM Network*. A former contracts manager, she is the founder of RMC-Project Management, a project management training, consulting, and speaking firm in Minneapolis and has appeared as a speaker at annual PMI conferences.

John M. Nevison, PMP, is a founding partner of Oak Associates, Inc. He is the author of six books and many articles on computing and project management, including the classic *Executive Computing* (1980, Addison-Wesley). He has served as internal and external management consultant to Fortune 100 companies, has been featured in articles in *The Wall Street Journal*, and has been quoted by *US News and World Report*, *Time*, and *Science*. He is past president of the Massachusetts Bay Chapter of the Project Management Institute and past chair of the Greater Boston Chapter of the Association of Computing Machinery.

Daniel P. Ono, PMP, has over 30 years of experience in project management, including 12 years as global project director of the business communications systems groups of such corporations as AT&T, Lucent Technologies, Inc., and Cisco Systems. He received the PMI Distinguished

Contribution Award in 1994, the PMI Presidential Citation for Outstanding Contribution in 1991, and the PMI Award for Showcase Project of the Year in 1990 and has authored numerous papers and chapters and lectured extensively on project management.

Jeffrey K. Pinto, PhD, is Samuel A. and Elizabeth B. Breene Fellow and Professor of Management in the School of Business at Pennsylvania State University at Erie. He is the author of 12 books and numerous articles on project management. A former editor of *Project Management Journal,* he has consulted widely in the US and internationally on a variety of project management topics. Dr. Pinto has won a number of awards for his work in the field.

George Pitagorsky, PMP, is director of product development for the International Institute for Learning, for which he developed several courses and multimedia products for implementing professional project management in IT and other environments. He is the author of numerous articles on project management and leads seminars in project management, problem solving, and other organizational development issues. He has created systems development and project management procedures for the New York Metropolitan Transportation Authority, Dean Witter Financial Service Group, Consumer Union, and the Bank of Bermuda.

Carl Pritchard, PMP, is principal and founder of Pritchard Management Associates in Frederick, Maryland. He lectures to and trains project managers around the world and is the architect of several key programs in distance learning. He has authored several articles and is published regularly in *Project Manager Today,* a leading UK project management journal.

Vickey Quinn, PMP, has served as a project manager with PMSI-Project Mentors, a part of the Provant solution, and in several successful software application development and launch projects and as organizational strategist for the Base Realignment and Closure Committee in the San Francisco Bay Area. A consultant in project management to Fortune 1000 companies, she has presented numerous seminars at national conferences and is the author of *Teach Yourself Microsoft Project* (2000, IDG Books).

James J. Schneidmuller, PMP, is a district manager at AT&T, where he created a successful professional project management organization for its Information Technology Services group and managed the group from 1991 through 1997. As part of the AT&T Solutions unit, he later was a member of the Global Transition Team for the Citicorp engagement, the largest networking outsourcing agreement at that time. He assumed leadership of the Solutions Project Management Center of Excellence in 1998 and today leads the AT&T Corporate Project Management Center of Excellence.

Aaron J. Shenhar is the institute professor of management and director of the project management program at Stevens Institute of Technology. He has published over 150 articles on project management, is consultant to leading high-tech organizations, including 3M, Honeywell, and the US Army, and was selected Engineering Manager of the Year by the Engineering Management Society of the IEEE in 1999. With 20 years of experience in leading high-tech organizations in the defense industry in Israel, he is presently devoting himself to teaching, research, and consulting.

Robert Storeygard, PMP, is project leadership specialist in the 3M Corporate Learning Center. He is author of the 3M Project Leader Curriculum and teaches project management at 3M and in the PMP Certification Program of the Project Management Institute. He has helped to deploy 3M's best project management practices and methods throughout 3M's Latin American and Asian subsidiaries and has worked with plant departments in St. Paul and Austin to deploy project management in business and technology areas.

Karen Tate, PMP, is cofounder of Martin Tate, a global project management training and consulting firm specializing in project management as a core competency. She is coauthor, with Paula Martin, of the bestselling book *Project Management Memory Jogger™* and is a columnist for the Project Management Institute magazine *PM Network*.

Hans J. Thamhain, PhD, PMP, is professor of management at Bentley College in Waltham, Massachusetts. Well-known for his research and writings on project management and team building, Dr. Thamhain is a frequent speaker at major conferences and consults in all phases of project management.

Frank Toney, PhD, is past chair of the finance faculty at the University of Phoenix. Having served as chief financial officer of several corporations, Dr. Toney leads and administers the Top 500 Project Management Benchmarking Forum, a group of large corporations that meet to identify best practices in project management. He is past chair of the Project Management Institute Research Committee and served on the PMI Standards and Education Committees. He is also lead author of *Accounting and Finance for Project Management*, coauthor of *Implementation of Project Manage-*

ment in Large Functional Organizations, and author of the two-volume work of *Global Project Manager and Project Organizations Standards and Best Practices* (forthcoming, Marcel Dekker, Inc.).

Vijay K. Verma is a group leader in the Planning Department of TRIUMF, a Canadian National Research Laboratory at the University of British Columbia for which he provides. project management services. He has taught seminars and workshops on project management in the US, Canada, South America, Europe, Asia, and South Africa. He authored a three-volume series on the Human Aspects of Project Management: *Organizing Projects for Success, Human Resource Skills for the Project Manager*, and *Managing the Project Team* (PMI, 1995, 1996, 1997). For the third volume, he was awarded the 1999 PMI David I. Cleland Project Management Literature Award. He also received the PMI Distinguished Contribution Award in 1999.

Richard E. Westney, PE, PMP, is chief executive officer of Westney Project Services, a Houston-based project management consulting, training, and outsourcing firm, which he founded in 1978. He is also the author of five books on project management and has served as faculty for executive programs at Texas A&M University and Stanford University.

R. Max Wideman, FCSCE, FEIC, FICE, FPMI, is a fellow of the Project Management Institute, of which he is past president and chair and for which he developed the 1987 version of the *Project Management Body of Knowledge*. He is also a fellow of the Institution of Civil Engineers (UK), the Engineering Institute of Canada, and the Canadian Society of Civil Engineering. A retired engineer and professional project manager, with experience in systems, social, environmental, design, and engineering projects, he has lectured in 11 countries and contributed to numerous books on the subject of project management.

INTRODUCTION

CHAPTER 1

OVERVIEW: THE DISCIPLINE OF PROJECT MANAGEMENT

DAVID I. CLELAND

Despite its importance, project management (PM) is not fully understood; at the same time it is one of the most ubiquitous activities in modern societies, being found in homes, in churches, and in government, military, and economic undertakings of all societies. It has become the strong right hand of leaders as they deal with the changes that buffet all societies today. The truly great leaders of history were also managers—managing countries, explorations, wars, and economic and social challenges. Project management, although not recognized in antiquity as an emerging and distinct field of study and practice, was used, at least in an informal sense, in the construction of infrastructures and to facilitate social and political change. Early managers did not recognize the discipline of project management as an activity of importance; as a result, their references to it are few. Yet in reviewing the infrastructures of antiquity it becomes clear that a form of project management played a key role.

EVOLUTION OF PROJECT MANAGEMENT

The project management discipline emerged in an unobtrusive manner in the 1950s in the construction field, and in more recent times in military systems development businesses. In an informal sense, project management had appeared in building antiquities such as the Great Pyramids of Egypt, the old cathedrals of Europe, and the many infrastructure improvements such as aqueducts, roads, canals, and castles.

The building of cathedrals in Europe after the year 1000 is an example of early infrastructure projects. In France alone, between 1050 and 1350 over 500 large churches and 1,000 parish churches were built, so that there was a church or chapel for about every 200 people. The cathedrals became focal points of community life. The building of some of these cathedrals had an extraordinarily long life cycle. For example, Cologne Cathedral's foundation stone was laid in 1248. By 1437, one of its towers was finished to one-third of its present height, but at the time of the Reformation its roof was still covered with boards. When the original plans of the cathedral were discovered in the nineteenth century, the completion of the cathedral became a national undertaking. The cathedral was finally completed in 1880, over 630 years after construction first began.[1]

The Panama Canal project was far more than a vast and unprecedented feat of project engineering and management. It was a profoundly important historic event and a sweeping human drama not unlike that of war. Apart from wars, it represented the largest, most costly single effort ever mounted anywhere on earth up until that time. It held the world's attention over a span of 40 years. It affected the lives of tens of thousands of people at every level of society and of virtually every race and nationality. Great reputations were made and destroyed. For numbers of men and women it was the adventure of a lifetime.[2]

A true and comprehensive description of the evolution of project management would be a history of change. It is not possible in this short chapter to say much about the history of project management. Instead, I have tried to select and to bring together the characteristics of the framework of a *discipline* of project mangement.

In ferreting out the characteristics of project management as a discipline, one has to focus on what has been written in recent times. Although project management has been practiced in some form for centuries, it is only since the 1960s that there have been increasing descriptions of this field in the literature—as well as in organizational documentation. A research project sponsored by the Project Management Institute (PMI) directed to identifying the research that has been carried out in this field has found over 500 books and over 5,000 articles in periodical literature published in the past 40 years. The publication of both scholarly and pragmatic works in the field of project management is an idea whose time has come.

Major Characteristics

Some of the major characteristics of project management described in the literature during its evolution include:

- Projects are ad hoc endeavors and have a defined life cycle.
- Projects are building blocks in the design and execution of organizational strategies.
- Projects are the leading edge of new and improved organizational products, services, and organizational processes.
- Projects provide a philosophy and strategy for the management of change in the organization.
- The management of projects entails the crossing of functional and organizational boundaries.
- The traditional management functions of planning, organizing, motivation, directing, and control are carried out in the management of a project.
- Both leadership and managerial capabilities are required for the successful completion of a project.
- The principal outcomes of a project are the accomplishment of technical performance, cost, and schedule objectives.
- Projects are terminated upon successful completion of the cost, schedule, and technical performance objectives—or earlier in their life cycle when the project results no longer promise to have an operational or strategic fit in the organization's future.

CONTRIBUTIONS OF PROJECT MANAGEMENT

During its evolution, project management contributed to a theory and practice in its own right as it matured as a discipline. Major changes that have come about in project management since its emergence include:

1. Recognition that project management is a discipline in its own right, as a branch of knowledge and skills springing from general management theory and practice
2. Discovery and establishment of the legitimacy of the matrix organizational design as a means for delegating authority, responsibility, and accountability for the management of project resources
3. Stimulation and propagation of growth of professional associations in the field
4. The "strategic pathway" for the emergence and use of alternative teams in the operational and strategic management of the organization

5. The principal means for the management of ad hoc activities in organizations
6. The concept of the influence of project stakeholders, and the importance of their management
7. Creation and definition of a new career path for managers and professionals

During the emergence of project management, it modified the management discipline. These modifications include:

- Acceptance and growing institutionalization of the matrix organizational design.
- Acceptance of the interdependence of project plans with higher-level organizational plans.
- Recognition of the legitimacy of using alternative project teams as key organizational design units in the management of operational and strategic initiatives in the organization.
- Acceptance of the importance of stakeholders in the management of the organization, and the design and execution of strategies to manage such stakeholders.
- Greater involvement of professionals and hourly paid workers on teams, and through such involvement making significant contributions to the effectiveness and efficiency of the organization.
- Broadened opportunities for more people to participate in the management and leadership of teams, thus enhancing their mobility to move to higher-level management positions in the organization.

When the general business literature recognizes growing forces in contemporary management thought and practices, it usually keynotes these forces in business publications. Such has been the case of project management, where a landmark article in the prestigious *Fortune* magazine[3] gave impetus to the notion of project management as a discipline by sending several key messages about what was happening in this field. These key messages were:

- Mid-level management positions are being cut.
- Project managers are a new class of managers to fill the niche formerly held by middle managers.
- Project management is the wave of the future.
- Project management is spreading beyond its traditional uses.
- Managing projects is managing change.

- Expertise in project management is a source of power for middle managers.
- Job security is elusive in project management, as each project has a beginning and an end.
- Project leadership is what project managers do.

Given this brief background, can project management be described as a discipline?

THE DISCIPLINE OF PROJECT MANAGEMENT

A dictionary definition of "discipline" is: a subject that is taught: a field of study; training that corrects, molds, or perfects the mental faculties or moral character; . . . a rule or system of rules governing conduct or activity.[4] Some related terms are: system of knowledge; department of knowledge; doctrine.[5] Given these definitions of a "discipline," is project management in fact a discipline?

Characteristics of a Discipline

For a subject to qualify as a discipline, the following conditions must be met:

- A body of knowledge exists that is generally recognized as providing guidelines for practice by professionals in the field.
- Professional organizations have been formed with the mission of providing a forum for those people interested in the theory and practice in the field.
- Substantial research initiatives exist that are directed to the advancement of the state of the art of the body of knowledge.
- Graduate and undergraduate programs have been developed in the curricula of leading universities and colleges.
- Continuing education and specialized training courses have been developed and are offered to practitioners in the field.
- A substantial number of books have been published by leading publishers—and there is a growing number of periodical journal articles that appear on a regular basis.
- Users of the discipline recognize the value in the use of informed practice of the discipline to successful performance in contemporary organizations.

- A distinct career path has opened up for people who wish to progress in their ability to practice the discipline.
- Experience in the field is required of those individuals who wish to progress to higher levels of responsibilities in their professional lives—and in their organizational assignments.
- Both art and scientific methodology are carried out in the theory and practice of the discipline.

Breadth of the Discipline

During its evolution, a discipline such as project management develops a substantial breadth in its topic context. The typical topic contents of project management include the following:[6]

Project success and failure
Project management: a distinct discipline
Project management: profiles of change
A project management philosophy
Benefits of project management
Ethics in project management
Professional associations
Project management body of knowledge
Project management process
Project life cycle
Organizing for project management
Project organization charting
Authority—responsibility—accountability
Project management training
International projects
Working in projects
Project office
The project team culture
Alternative project teams
Reengineering through project teams
Concurrent engineering
Management of small projects
Managing multiple projects
Self-managed production teams
Benchmarking teams
Managing change by project management
Selling project management to senior managers

Project partnering
Project strategic issue management
Project stakeholder management
Strategic management of teams
Senior management and projects
The board of directors and capital projects
Overviews—another perspective
Leadership in projects
Coaching project team members
Managing conflict in projects
Project selection considerations
Legal considerations in project management
Project start-up
Developing winning proposals
Selecting and using PM software
Project contract negotiations and administration
Quality in projects
Project termination
Project planning—an overview
Project planning—revisited
Project scheduling
Project monitoring, evaluation, and control
Risk management
Project auditing
Scheduling standards
Outsourcing project management
Decision making in project management
Establishing a project management system (PMS)
Managing costs in projects
Project work breakdown structure
Understanding the team culture
Positive and negative aspects of teams
Motivating the project team
Project team building and development
Role and responsibilities of the project team
Project manager capabilities
The political process in project management
The project management information system
Communication in project meetings
Project communications
Negotiations

The "new managers"
Project management maturity
Project recovery for the project team
Project recovery for the challenged project
Project stability
Certification in project management

Note: A key characteristic of a discipline is its philosophical foundation.

EMERGENCE OF A PHILOSOPHY

One key characteristic of a discipline is providing a philosophy that guides the thinking and practice of users. A philosophy is defined as "a system of thought based on some logical relationships between concepts and principles that explains certain phenomena and supplies a basis for rational solutions of related problems."[7]

A philosophy, taken in its most basic sense, is simply a way of thinking about a field of endeavor. A sound philosophy of project management is necessary for the continuance of success in dealing with product, service, and organizational process change. An effective and efficient project manager is one who has developed a broad, fundamental basis for effective thinking in the solution of project management problems and opportunities—and in providing the leadership of the project stakeholders.

When an area of work specialization gains maturity it can be defined as a discipline. An important consideration in the emergence of the discipline is the appearance of a philosophy describing that discipline.

A PHILOSOPHY OF PROJECT MANAGEMENT

An expression in the literature of a philosophy of project management has come about only in the past couple of decades. Some of the key characteristics of this philosophy include:

- The theory and practice of project management have reached a level of maturity that entitles it to a rightful place in the field of general management.
- Project management is the principal means for dealing with product, service, and process change in contemporary organizations.

- Project management has laid down the pathway for the emergence of alternative forms of teams, such as reengineering, benchmarking, concurrent engineering, and self-managed production teams.
- Specialized processes and techniques have been developed by the project management community to deal with the challenges of planning for, organizing, and motivating team members; leading project teams; and monitoring, evaluation, and control of the use of project resources.
- A rapid growth in the membership of professional associations is strong evidence of the popularity and use of project management in the management of operational and strategic change in today's organizations.
- A distinctive descriptive literature has developed in the field of project management, which has provided performance standards for professionals to develop their requisite knowledge, skills, and attitudes essential to the successful practice of project management. The philosophy of project management has been influenced by the principal project management professional organization, the Project Management Institute (PMI).

Influence of Professional Association

The Project Management Institute (PMI) made a major contribution to the project management discipline literature in 1996 through the development and propagation of the *PMBOK Guide*,[8] with its knowledge areas that comprise the elements of project management:

Project integration management
Project scope management
Project time management
Project cost management
Project quality management
Project human resources (HR) management
Project communications management
Project risk management
Project procurement management

The *PMBOK Guide* has become a universal force in shaping the discipline of project management.

Certification Program

Another force developed and unleashed by PMI has been its certification program. Starting in 1984, this program has facilitated the development of professional project managers around the world. Other project management professional associations worldwide have their unique certification processes, based on an established body of knowledge and experience, education, and service criteria. Collectively, all of these associations have done excellent work in furthering the project management discipline.

Another major force in project management has been the broad view of the discipline in the systems context.

THE SYSTEMS CONTEXT

A key characteristic of project management has been its systems context. This context is best described as a project management system (PMS). The principal subsystems of a PMS include the following:

- Facilitative organizational subsystem
- Project control subsystem
- Project management information subsystem
- Techniques and methodologies subsystem
- Cultural ambiance subsystem
- Planning subsystem
- Human subsystem

The Facilitative Organizational Subsystem

This is the organizational design used to provide a focal point for the use of resources to support the project purposes. The key characteristics of such a subsystem include:

- Superimposing the project teams on the existing functional structure of the organization
- The creation of a matrix organization that provides a paradigm on how complementary authority, responsibility, and accountability are assigned and allocated among the project team, the supporting functional elements, the work package managers, and the general and senior managers of the organization
- A definition of how individual and collective roles are assigned in the matrix organization

Project Control Subsystem

This provides for the philosophy and process for selection of performance standards for the project, the design of feedback mechanisms, the comparing of planned and actual performance, and the initiation of corrective action as required to keep the project on track. The key requirements for such a control system include:

- Regular and ongoing review of project progress by relevant stakeholders to provide intelligence regarding how well work is going on in the project
- The commitment of all project stakeholders to provide accurate and timely reporting of key matters involving the use of project resources

Project Management Information Subsystem

This contains the information essential to effective planning and oversight of the project. Both formal and informal information useful in managing the project include, but are not necessarily restricted to:

- Information required to develop project plans and relate those plans to the strategic management initiatives of the organization
- Formal and informal information required to provide intelligence for the ongoing review of project progress
- Identification and assessment of information required to make and implement decisions in the management of the project

Techniques and Methodologies Subsystem

This contains the techniques and methodologies such as Program Evaluation and Review Technique (PERT), CPM (Critical Path Method), and related scheduling techniques as well as specialized techniques for estimating project costs, technical performance assessments, and other management science methodologies. The use of quantitative methodology to evaluate risk and uncertainty in the use of project resources is included in this subsystem.

Cultural Ambience Subsystem

This is the general cultural environment in which project management is practiced. This subsystem typically entails:

- The social context of the perceptions, attitudes, prejudices, assumptions, experiences, values, mores, and behavior patterns of the people associated with the project
- Influence on how people act and react, how they think and feel, and what they do and say—all of which affects the behavioral norms of the people associated with the project
- Education, training, team building, and similar techniques to enhance the interpersonal skills of all the project stakeholders. If effectively developed and applied, these can improve the cultural ambience of the project

Planning Subsystem

This provides for the means to identify and develop strategies relative to what resources will be required to support the project, and how these resources will be utilized during the course of the project. Some of the principal elements of project planning include:

- Development of the work breakdown structure (WBS), which shows how the project is broken down into its component parts
- Development of project schedules and budgets, selection of technical performance goals, and stipulation of the organizational design for the project
- Creation of an integrated project plan that can become the performance standard against which project progress can be monitored, evaluated, and controlled

Human Subsystem

This includes most of everything associated with the human element. This subsystem includes:

- Some knowledge of sociology, psychology, anthropology, communications, semantics, leadership, and motivation theories and applications
- A management and leadership style on the part of the project and supporting managers that engenders trust, loyalty, and commitment among the managers and professionals associated with the project
- The artful management style that the project manager/project leader develops, demonstrates, and encourages with the project team, which will have a marked impact across the project stakeholders

Figure 1.1 depicts a project management system (PMS) in the context of a public utility organization. It shows how the existence and operation of a PMS approach cuts across the strategic management and the functional levels of the organization. As such it can be used as a fundamental philosophical model of how a project should be managed.

One of the major characteristics of the management discipline is the

Figure 1.1
The Project Management System

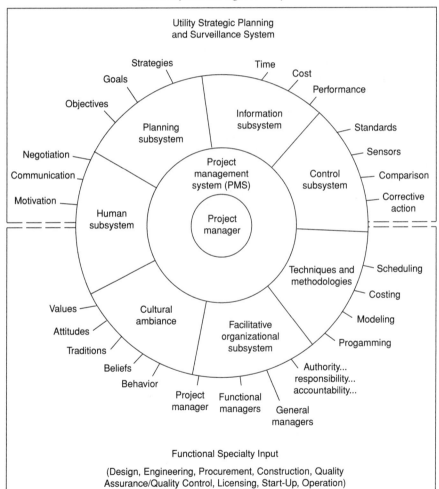

Source: Adapted from David I. Cleland, "Defining a Project Mangement System." *Project Management Quarterly,* Vol. 10, No. 4, p. 39. Reprinted with permission.

pervasiveness of the major activities or functions involved. It is no different in project management.

PROJECT MANAGEMENT FUNCTIONS

Project management is carried out through a distinct management process consisting of the core functions of management. These core functions, shown in Figure 1.2, are:

Planning—Development of the objectives, goals, and strategies to provide for the commitment of resources to support the project

Organizing—Identification of the human and nonhuman resources required for the project, providing a suitable layout for these resources, and the establishment of individual and collective roles of the members of the project team

Figure 1.2
The Core Functions of Project Management

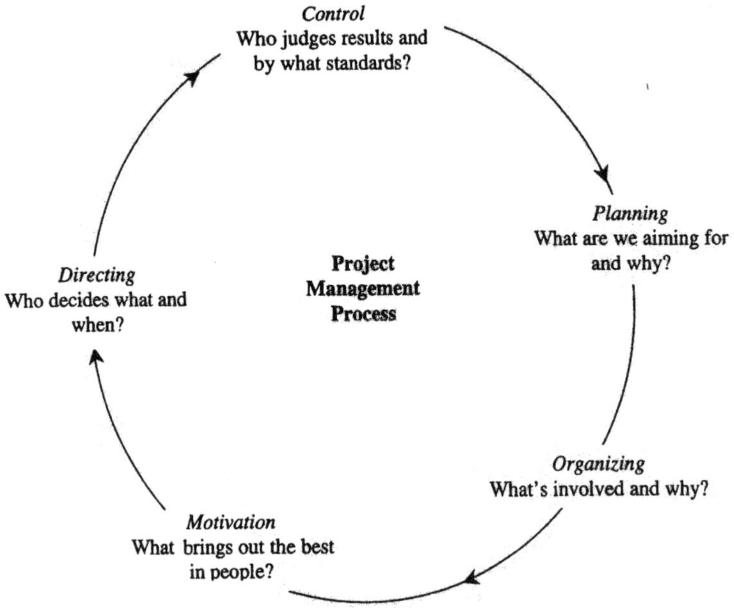

Source: Adapted from David I. Cleland and Lewis R. Ireland, *Project Manager's Portable Handbook*, New York: McGraw-Hill, 2000, p. 17. Reproduced with permission of The McGraw-Hill Companies.

Motivation—The process of establishing a cultural system that brings out the best in people in their project work

Directing—Providing for the leadership competency necessary to ensure the making and execution of decisions involving the project

Control—Monitoring, evaluating, and controlling the use of resources on the project consistent with project and organizational plans

Growing evidence of the maturity of project management is found in its alignment with higher strategic purposes in the organization.

STRATEGIC LINKAGES

As the discipline of project management has matured, there has been a growing awareness of the essential linkage between strategic management and project management. The essence of strategic management is that you manage the enterprise as if its future mattered. Product, service, and organizational process projects play a crucial role in the future of the enterprise. It is through such projects that the enterprise is able to change its strategy to meet changing environmental conditions.

In today's enterprises, projects provide the means for bringing about realizable changes in the future of the enterprise. Once enterprise managers realize the importance of project management as the principal means for dealing with change, the theory and practice of project management take on strategic importance in the enterprise.

The linkage of strategic management and the theory and practice of project management attests to the importance and the maturity of project management as it is used in nontraditional teams.

NONTRADITIONAL PROJECT TEAMS

Project teams have provided remarkable means for dealing with many of the elements of change facing an enterprise. Some of the areas in which such teams have proved useful include:

Market assessment
Competitive assessment
Organizational strengths and weaknesses
Benchmarking
Establishing performance standards
Vision quest
Stakeholder evaluation

Market research
Product-service-process development
Business process reengineering
Crisis management
Self-managed production initiatives
Resolution of organizational issues
Quality improvement
Audit processes
Senior-level decision making
New business development initiatives

The teams used for the preceding purposes have many of the characteristics of the traditional project teams. There are, however, some singular characteristics:

- The organizational element with which these teams deal is already in existence, usually in the form of organizational processes rather than physical entities.
- The teams are directed to improve the efficiency and effectiveness of an organizational process. The work of the team begins immediately in dealing with a problem or opportunity.
- Although hardware is involved, the teams deal principally with the identification and use of resources in meeting organizational objectives and goals.
- The deliverables of these teams many times are reports that outline recommendations for the improvement of the use of resources.
- The teams are used in many diverse enterprise purposes.
- The teams have direct vital links with the design and execution of operational and strategic initiatives in the enterprise.
- Many times the recommendations of these teams bring about significant changes in the individual and collective roles carried out by the members of the enterprise.
- These nontraditional teams deal with and cause changes in the way the enterprise uses resources to support mission, objectives, and goals.
- The teams, and the results of their use, can have a major impact on the culture of the enterprise.

The emergence of these teams—as expressed in the project management literature and in their use in helping to deal with the many changes that impact today's organizations in a changing world—adds further strength to the claim that project management is indeed a discipline in its own right!

As a discipline grows in maturity it tends to develop a distinct culture.

THE PROJECT CULTURE

Culture is a set of behaviors that people have and strive for in their society. In the project management society in an organization, unique cultures have emerged and grown that portray the manner of behavior characteristic of the project ambience. As the theory and practice of project management have grown, buttressed by the growing abundance of literature, a distinct project-related culture has emerged. This culture has added credibility to the claim that project management is indeed a unique discipline. Some of the distinguishing characteristics of a project management culture that has become endemic to the discipline are shown in Table 1.1.

One outcome of the development of a project management culture

Table 1.1
Project Management Culture

- There is an excitement about project management in the enterprise as the principal way of dealing with product, service, and process change.
- There is a proven track record in the organization in using projects as drivers of change in the organization.
- Appropriate project management organizational strategies, policies, procedures, and resource allocation initiatives have been developed and are being used as the hallmark of project management.
- Extraordinary efforts have been undertaken and continued in the clarification of authority, responsibility, and accountability for the project team members and other stakeholders.
- Full support of the use of project management has been recognized and fostered by the senior members of the organization.
- Appropriate merit evaluation and reward systems are in place which fully consider the contribution that team members are expected to make in the project.
- Project management has reached a level of maturity in the organization where it is recognized as "simply the way we do things around here."
- Experience as a project manager is a requirement for promotion to higher level management positions in the organization.

Source: David I. Cleland & Lewis R. Ireland, *Project Manager's Portable Handbook*, New York: McGraw-Hill, 2000, p. 2.48. Reproduced with permission of The McGraw-Hill Companies.

has been an interest in the roles of "managership" and "leadership" in the field.

MANAGERS OR LEADERS

As project management has matured, it has sparked a debate about whether the person in charge of a project is a manager or a leader. Some of the arguments for each side of the debate are:[9]

Leadership
- Develops and sells a vision for the project
- Copes with operational and strategic change on the project
- Builds reciprocal networks with relevant stakeholders
- Develops a cultural ambience for the project team that facilitates commitment and motivation
- Sets the general direction of the project through collaboration with project stakeholders
- Perceives broad issues that are likely to impact the project, and then works with the team members in accommodating these broad issues
- Becomes a symbol of the project and its purposes
- Does the right things

Managership
- Copes with the complexity of developing and implementing a management system for the project
- Maintains oversight of the efficient and effective use of project resources
- Designs and develops the management functions of planning, organizing, motivating, directing, and controlling within the context of a project management system (PMS) for the project
- Reprograms resources as needed to maintain a balance for supporting the project
- Monitors the competence of project team members to include guidance to these individuals for the improvement of their knowledge, skills, and attitudes
- Ensures that the communication processes involving the project work effectively
- Maintains oversight to ensure that project monitoring evaluation and control are carried out
- Does things right

Project managers must both *lead* and *manage*. In carrying out these two roles, competency in the following is required:

- Having a general understanding of the technology that is involved in the project
- Having those interpersonal skills that facilitate building a cultural ambience for the project team and its stakeholders that reflects trust, loyalty, commitment, and respect
- Understanding the management processes and its application to the project
- Being able to see the systems context of the project
- Being able to make and implement decisions involving the project
- Being able to produce results

The competency to serve as both a project leader and a project manager is dependent on the individual's knowledge, skills, and attitudes.

SUMMARY

The origin of project management appeared in antiquity, and is represented in the infrastructure relics of historical periods. Today, project management is recognized as an idea whose time has come. Its origins may be nebulous, but the results that it has produced are clear. The continued evolution of project management adds strength to the claim that it is a distinct discipline, derived from general management theory and practice. Project management is a major player in the management of change in contemporary organizations.

REFERENCES

1. *Glimpses*, Christian History Institute, Issue #117.
2. Paraphrased from David McCullough. 1976. *The Path between the Seas*, New York: Simon & Schuster.
3. Stewart, Thomas H. "The Corporate Jungle Spawns a New Species." *Fortune*, July 10, 1995: 179–180.
4. *Webster's New Collegiate Dictionary (Eighth Edition)*. Springfield, MA: G. & C. Merriam Company, 1977.
5. *Roget's International Thesaurus (New Edition)*, New York: Thomas Y. Crowell Company, 1946.
6. The listing of topic areas in project management is taken from the table of contents of the *Project Manager's Portable Handbook*, by David I. Cleland and Lewis R. Ireland, New York: McGraw-Hill, 2000.

7. Davis, Ralph Currier. 1951. *The Fundamentals of Top Management*, New York: Harper & Brothers, p. 6.
8. PMI Standards Committee. 1996. *A Guide to the Project Management Body of Knowledge (PMBOK)*. Upper Darby, PA: Project Management Institute.
9. From Cleland and Ireland, *Project Manager's Portable Handbook*, pp. 5.1–5.1.22.

CHAPTER 2

TRANSITION: THE PROJECT-DRIVEN ORGANIZATION

JOAN KNUTSON

What do Main Street and Wall Street have in common? Among other things, both Wall Street and Main Street are measuring success relative to speed, teamwork, and customer focus. These three critical success factors ultimately equal earnings per share. A manufacturing company in Ohio is pushing forward an entire initiative to sensitize its management to this premise. Roll-up companies are gambling their futures and those of their acquired companies on earnings per share. A technology corporation in Silicon Valley has reduced cycle time by more than 50 percent.

Some of these companies are our clients, and some are our competitors. These clients and these competitors have latched onto a discipline that will help them reach the earnings per share goal that is expected by both Main Street and Wall Street. And that discipline is project management.

As we move into the next millennium, growing behemoths and smaller emerging concerns are touting project management as a vehicle to success. They will use project management not only to plan and manage new revenue-generating initiatives, but also to facilitate containment of expenses, assuring the desired earnings per share. In addition, the discipline of project management will aid us in our efforts to positively differentiate ourselves from our competitors. Therefore, project management will be the most important management technique available to ensure competitiveness as we move into the twenty-first century.

This chapter will address the ways in which project management has become a tool for improving shareholder value for our clients while helping us to differentiate ourselves from our competitors. This chapter covers

23

the following topics: where we have been, where we are going, how we are going to get there, and how we know that we've been successful.

WHERE WE HAVE BEEN
Through an Era of Recognition and Exponential Growth

It is time to celebrate an era of recognition. Project management has been recognized in the United States and globally as an essential discipline used within corporate business and government agencies alike. The planning, organizing, and tracking of projects has become a core competency within small and large organizations, profit and nonprofit. As an article in *Fortune* magazine predicted on February 19, 1994, "Jobs as we know them will disappear." Instead of being a jobholder, a person will become "a package of capabilities, drawn upon variously in different project-based situations." Such packages will coalesce into teams around emerging issues, deal with the issues, and then regroup into other team configurations around other issues.

Consider the Paradigm Shift in the Nineties

In the last decade of the twentieth century, the momentum of cultural change has increased within companies. Let me share several examples. Organizations in the past have been very hierarchical, which often meant bureaucratic. Individuals performed work as part of a self-sufficient unit. As we move into the new millennium, organizational success is based on networking and maximizing resources, which often means sharing resources. Functional departments are no longer self-sufficient but are compelled to be interdependent. Now teams from various functional areas must come together to accomplish a goal. As envisioned by *Fortune* magazine, individuals will coalesce into teams around different project-based situations, accomplish their goals, and then be reformulated into new teams around the next goals. The advantage for organizations as we move into the twenty-first century will be minimizing costs and reducing time to market or time to money.

WHERE WE ARE GOING
Applying Project Management to Revenue-Generating and Cost-Containment Initiatives

Projects have become a way of doing business. A project is initiated and justified with the goal of either creating a product or a service to be sold (thus increasing revenue) or reducing costs. The process of justifying new projects must become more rigorous as more potentially enticing projects enter the portfolio mix of projects to be considered by top management. Our organizations cannot afford, literally, to fund the resources needed to accomplish every "good idea." Therefore, top management must require the justification and selection of projects based on solid business premises.

Is the project compatible with our organization's short- and long-term strategies? Is the project feasible with the resources and the knowledge base that we possess? Are the risks associated with this project worth taking? But most important, will this project generate large enough revenues and/or reduce costs enough to financially justify the expenditures necessary to fund the project? And how does the justification of this project compare to the multitude of other projects in the queue for consideration?

As we move into the next millennium, management is going to be concerned not only about whether we are conducting projects correctly, but also with whether we have chosen the right projects.

Positioning Project Management as a Sales Differentiator

Using project management as a sales differentiator became more prevalent as we ended the twentieth century. Imagine the scenario in which you are assigned to choose a vendor from between two competing companies. Both vendors appear to have similar features and functionalities within the products that they are offering. They both say that they provide the best implementation/installation support possible. What will be the differentiator that will influence you to pick one vendor over the other? I suggest that it will be how the winning vendor proposes to *define*, *plan*, *execute*, and *control* the work effort—in other words, what project management processes, reports, and tools it is going to use when interacting with your organization. I would suggest that the vendor that appears to be better organized and better in control of the effort would be the one that you would pick.

As we move into this millennium, our prospective clients will be asking us what our project management approach will be. They will have within their request for proposals (RFPs) specific questions concerning what we will and will not be offering. They will be expecting us to plan, organize, and manage the assignment using project management techniques. They will expect that the project will be done on time and within budget, and be of the quality expected—with as little upheaval as possible. They will want to see the project management discipline in evidence during the sales process, during the launch of the effort, and during the entire evolution of the engagement, until the last bill is submitted and paid. And by the way, I suggest that these prospective clients will be willing to pay for this project management capability.

HOW WE ARE GOING TO GET THERE
Heighten Awareness
The more the business community becomes familiar with the process of project management and aware of its benefits, the more companies will encourage and even require its application. The project management process according to PMI's *Project Management Body of Knowledge (PMBOK)* includes four phases:

1. Initiation and definition
2. Planning
3. Execution and control
4. Closeout

The inputs into this project management process are business needs. The business community will need to understand, accept, inculcate this. These business needs include meeting mandated government or legal regulations, creating products or services to stay competitive, and upgrading systems and technology to become more efficient and effective. As these business needs pass through the project management process, business results and added customer value are the output. The deliverable out of each and every project will be a solution to a business problem or opportunity, thus a business result, that provides added value to our internal and/or our external customers.

There are limitless ways to heighten the awareness of the business community. Let me suggest several ways that are face-to-face approaches and some that are nonpersonal.

Face-to-face approaches are events orchestrated to address the subject of project management. These can be formal one-, two-, or three-day symposia combining speakers from both inside and outside the organization. They can be designed to put a spotlight on project management as well as to provide a learning forum for the participants. More informal brown-bag lunches or one-on-one coaching and mentoring provide a continual stream of information and insights on how to better maneuver within the project management discipline.

Other forms of communication can be equally productive. Some examples would be to create a monthly newsletter, offer access to a project's updated web site, or set up a centrally located project management library of books and internal best-practice documents. Ultimately all these options will need to be combined into an automated, knowledge-based system. This knowledge-based system will be a database repository of standards, procedures, templates, just-in-time training information nuggets, and best-practice samples from completed projects, to name only a few. This type of performance support tool is technologically feasible and cost justifiable. It is only as far away as our creativity and imagination.

Solidify Infrastructure

Even with all the heightened awareness gained through the varied techniques just described, we are not going to get to a fully accepted and functioning project management discipline without an infrastructure of support. This infrastructure must consist of systems made up of policies, standards, procedures, and/or guidelines for defining how the project management work is to be performed. There are four key systems:

1. A portfolio management system
2. A process management system
3. An organizational management system
4. A performance management system

Portfolio Management

A portfolio management system ensures that the initiation of the project management process is grounded in sound strategic business decisions. In brief, a portfolio management system consists of four subsystems:

1. A solicitation process (prepare the business case)
2. A selection process (eliminate the wrong projects)
3. A prioritization process (do them in the right order)
4. An enterprise resource planning process (involve the right people)

Let me describe the portfolio management system in more detail. First, a solicitation process provides a consistent model for all requesters of projects to follow. This model defines how they, as requesters, are to prepare business cases that will be evaluated by the organization's decision makers. Next comes the selection process where the decision makers approve those projects that add value to the organization, and reject those that do not. After certain projects are approved, this same group of decision makers prioritizes all projects relative to predefined business criteria. Those projects with a higher priority are given greater visibility and support. Lastly, those prioritized projects will be staffed (or resourced) relative to all the projects within the portfolio mix and relative to where each project sits within the prioritization.

Process Management
A process management system takes the approved and prioritized project through the definition, planning, execution/control and closeout phases. The approved project goes into the definition process, which creates a project charter. The project charter becomes the input to the planning phase, which creates a work plan (i.e., schedule, staffing plan, project budget, etc.) The charter and the work plan then become the baseline during the execution/control phase of the project process. During this phase, the project team creates performance reports, keeps logs, issues change requests, and generates product deliverables. And once the project is over, these outputs from the execution/control phase are the input into the closeout phase from which lessons learned are documented and archived for reference when starting the project management process all over again.

Organizational Management
An organizational management system is the governance structure defining roles, responsibilities, authorities, and reporting relationships. Today the project office is the strongest version of the alternative project organizational structures. This autonomous department staffed by project management subject matter experts becomes the focal point for the project management discipline. I would suggest that the project office evolves from an advisory, consultative staff role to an enterprise-wide information dissemination and evaluation role and ultimately to a line role that provides project managers with the resources to run large initiatives within the organization. As time evolves, the project office gains credibility, builds expertise, grows in self-confidence, and simultaneously increases its responsibility within the organization.

Performance Management
The performance management system supports all three of the systems just described. It is a process that sets project management performance objectives for project managers and for project team members. It ensures that team members are rewarded for their successes and given development plans to improve areas of deficiencies. The performance management system consists of a performance improvement process in which

performance expectations and personal developmental plans are established and agreed upon.

During the typical 12-month appraisal review cycle, the project managers have interim dialogues with their functional managers with input from the project sponsor. At the same time, the project team members are having interim dialogues with their functional managers, in this case with input from their project managers. The interim dialogues focus on whether the project players are attaining their performance objectives and whether they are working toward their developmental plans. If they are not, either the objectives and/or the plans need changing or the project players need to step it up.

As the performance management system comes to a close, the performance appraisal review process takes over. In this process, the functional manager of the project players prepares an official review document with final input from the appropriate project sponsor or project manager. The functional manager then executes the performance appraisal and the cycle begins all over again.

HOW WE KNOW THAT WE'VE BEEN SUCCESSFUL

Establish and Track Attainment Metrics

Measuring the success of project management is not easy, but it is not impossible. Easy or not, the project management discipline is expending corporate/agency dollars; and at some point in time, someone with power is going to ask the following questions: Is project management worth it? Have we done a cost/benefit analysis? How do we know that project management is successful? We need to be prepared to respond.

Answer the following five questions:

1. Do people comprehend what project management is and its benefits? (Comprehension.)
2. Do people accept project management as a value-added discipline within the organization? In other words, do they speak well of the concept? (Acceptance.)
3. Are project management tools and techniques being used? For example, are updated Gantt charts pinned onto people's bulletin boards or are project kickoff meetings being held with representation from all appropriate cross-functional departments? (Application.)

4. Are projects, as a composite, being more successful? Are they better meeting time, cost, and quality commitments? (Business Results.)

5. Is there a financial return to the implementation of project management–related initiatives? For example, did it cost less to implement the change control process as compared to how many dollars are being saved? (Return on investment.)

For every question that was answered yes, you can add one more positive score to the success of project management. These are the metrics that need to be established within the culture. Some of them are measured by observation and listening. Others are measured by quantifiable tracking of time, cost, and quality results.

CONCLUSION

Being profitable is an expectation of both Main Street (our management and our employees) and Wall Street (our shareholders).

Where have we been? Through a gradual but observable paradigm shift, project management has been recognized as one of the management disciplines that will drive higher profitability.

Where are we going? Organizations are applying project management to endeavors that generate revenue and/or contain or save costs. In addition, project management is being presented to potential clients and customers to differentiate us from our competition.

How are we going to get there? Project management will become a more recognized and respected business discipline as we heighten its awareness and build an infrastructure to support it.

How will we know that we've been successful? We will measure comprehension, acceptance, application, business results, and possibly return on investment.

The bottom line is, *businesses and governmental agencies are transitioning into project-driven organizations using project management as a tool for improving value for our clients and for our organizations while differentiating ourselves from our competitors.*

PART I

THE TECHNICAL TRACK

CHAPTER 3

PORTFOLIO MANAGEMENT: OVERVIEW AND BEST PRACTICES

J. KENT CRAWFORD

INTRODUCTION

Once the basics of managing individual projects are mastered, an organization must provide a system for selection, prioritization, and oversight of all the projects in which the enterprise engages. This level of project management differs as much from standard single-project management as single-project management does from ordinary ongoing operational management. Making the conceptual leap from the tool-and-technique-focused variety of project management to *portfolio management*, with its broader focus on business strategy and enterprise-wide integration, is a special challenge and one that many organizations now face with little in the way of standards, best practices, or other generally accepted knowledge to guide them. The object of this chapter is not to offer a single solution for portfolio management or to describe all the possible solutions, but to steer the reader to the many sources of information on this topic and establish the common themes in the array of ideas about portfolio management ideas and practices.

DRIVERS OF PORTFOLIO MANAGEMENT

Internally, the leap to managing the organization as a portfolio of projects is an important step in an organization's project management maturity. But in the global sense, the idea of organizations as portfolios of projects is even more important, as it reflects a significant change in the way companies are organized and managed. Let's look at some of the reasons why refocusing corporate management from the old-style "pyramid of depart-

33

ments/functions" mind-set to the "portfolio of projects" mind-set is a must for companies to thrive in the emerging business environment.

1. *Time to market.* The reduction in product cycle times in the past decade is stunning. In some industries, products are now obsolete in the marketplace in half the time it once took for research and development (R & D) alone. This pressure on companies to innovate and bring out new products faster will continue. Time-consuming, bureaucratic processes for identifying opportunities and moving projects through to completion spell disaster.

2. *Working smarter (and cheaper).* Most companies are laboring under a shortage of qualified staff, in part the legacy of unbridled downsizing a decade ago; competition for resources, especially in information technology (IT), is intense. Companies are being forced to find new ways to make the most of the knowledge possessed by the staff they do have. Thus the flattened organization, in which project personnel communicate directly across old functional boundaries instead of up and down the chain of command, is becoming commonplace. Such communication speeds up decision making.

3. *Stakeholder response-ability.* The focus on quality and customer satisfaction in recent years has caused organizations to become more inclusive of and responsive to stakeholders. In the old silo paradigm, customer requirements or feedback could easily get stuck behind departmental firewalls. Interdisciplinary teams, such as those project management specializes in, are now being conceptualized to include not only internal organizational players but also members of other stakeholder groups, including vendors, customers and the community. This becomes more crucial as, in response to the "working smarter and cheaper" imperative, companies rely more on outsourcing for many functions once performed in-house.

Interestingly, these three market imperatives roughly correspond to the old project management triumvirate of time-cost-quality—the triple constraint—proving what some management gurus have said: that all the world's a project.

EVOLUTION: FROM PROJECT MANAGEMENT TO PORTFOLIO MANAGEMENT

To backtrack just a little, the basic definition of a project is provided by *A Guide to the Project Management Body of Knowledge* (PMI 1996)—a temporary, unique endeavor undertaken to create a product or service within defined parameters. On the individual project level of project management, the focus is on planning and controlling the various activities that go into the single project.

For many years, this focus sufficed organizations because the nature of most project endeavors was to be large-scale, long-duration, single projects: a bridge, an airplane, a legacy computer system. Recently, however, the world economy has made a dramatic shift to information-based wealth creation. With that shift, the projects that create value for companies have both proliferated and changed in nature. Software and hardware development—indeed, almost any kind of new product development projects—necessitate short-cycle, rapid, and flexible project management. And the cultural change permeating the workplace—which has abandoned rigid departmental divisions in favor of a multidisciplinary team approach—has meant that project management is no longer concentrated in nuts-and-bolts areas like construction, engineering, and research.

Today, members of an organization from finance to marketing participate on project teams, value project management concepts, and view their own function-area endeavors as projects in themselves. Once a company might have seen itself as having one or a few major "projects" and many supporting operational functions. Now it is more common for companies to define themselves in terms of the projects they are engaged in—projects that may involve all areas of the organization and often people outside the organization as well, in the form of outsourcing, contract labor, consulting firms, or public stakeholders.

This increased fluidity has occurred as an organic response to market conditions and has outpaced companies' development of methods for managing under these new conditions. As a result, there has been a disconnect between companies' ability to manage projects on the project level and their ability to manage them collectively on the organizational or enterprise level. The business of selecting which project to invest in, when to change priorities from one project to another, and how to align the projects a company does with one another and with organizational strategy and mission must be carried out at the executive level—at the level of *managing by projects*, rather than of *project management*.

Proper portfolio management results in bottom-line yields—another reason why it's important for the executive level to champion this process. Research by Robert Cooper, Scott Edgett, and Elko Kleinschmidt reveals that, for R&D portfolios, the top 20 percent of companies, in contrast to poorer performers, had an explicit, established method of portfolio management, with top management buy-in and support, which was consistently applied across the organization. Of those in the top 20 percent, nearly 70 percent had used the portfolio management method for more than two years. So, even though most of the businesses in their sample were relatively new to portfolio management, their research seems to show that a rigorously followed process will begin to yield positive results very quickly.

In addition, Frank Toney and Ray Powers found that for large functional organizations that implement a project management group and its corollary practices (including portfolio management), time to market has been reduced by up to 60 percent, development costs have declined, quality has improved, and forecasting accuracy has increased. Companies without good portfolio management are prone to a welter of problems (see Table 3.1).

Clearly, there are compelling reasons for the executive level to take an interest and a leadership role in this aspect of the project management process.

ELEMENTS OF PORTFOLIO MANAGEMENT

Project portfolio management seeks to answer the questions, *What should we take on? What should we drop?* It often requires determining what is possible and what is needed. Thus the analytical tasks involved in portfolio management are more akin to higher-level business management than to the traditional planning and controlling functions of project manage-

Table 3.1
Is This Your Company?

Cooper, Edgett, and Kleinschmidt developed the following checklist of common problems in portfolio management. If this sounds familiar to you, you aren't alone; nearly all the firms in their study reported at least some of these problems:

- Projects have poor linkage to business strategy. Too many are "off strategy"; there are disconnects between spending on projects and strategic priorities.
- Portfolio quality is poor; there are too many unfit, weak, or mediocre projects.
- Go/kill decision points for new projects are weak; poor projects are often not terminated in a timely manner, and take on a life of their own.
- Resources are scarce, but unfocused. Cycle times and success rates suffer as a result.
- There are too many trivial projects—updates, modifications, and so on—and not enough major breakthroughs. This is the result of overemphasis on cycle time reduction coupled with staff shortages.

ment. Portfolio management is the way in which decision makers align projects with the organizational strategy, just as strategy is the way the organization aligns itself to the wider marketplace. While most decision making on the project level is concerned with tactical issues (*How can we do this thing right?*), decision making on the portfolio level is concerned with strategic issues (*How can we be sure to do the right things?*).

While there is no universal method, dominant theme, or generic model for effective portfolio management, a few basic assertions can be made about its challenges:

- There are three main goals in portfolio management (according to Cooper et al.):
  1. Maximizing the value of the portfolio against objectives
  2. Seeking the right balance or mix of projects (see Table 3.2)
  3. Linking projects to business strategy
- Portfolio management must consider all types of projects that compete for resources.

Table 3.2
Questions to Ask of Your Current Project Mix

- Do all your projects fit strategically? That is, are they consistent with your business's strategy?
- Does the breakdown of your project spending reflect your strategic priorities?
- What is the quality of your portfolio? Are most of the projects solid ones? Are they of high value to the business?
- Have you ever determined the economic value or worth of your business's project portfolio? If so, is it considerably higher than what you've spent on it?
- Once projects start, do they drag on indefinitely?
- Are projects being completed in a time-efficient manner?
- Are your success rates and profit performance results consistent with expectations?
- Is your project portfolio heavily weighted to low-value, trivial, small projects?
- How does your current portfolio of projects rate against these three goals: maximizing the value of the portfolio, optimal balance, and strategic alignment?
- Has your business consciously considered the various goals it seeks for its project portfolio?
- How are opinions of senior people and key decision makers in your business captured in order to make project decisions?
- Have you considered the question of what is the right balance of projects for your new product portfolio?

- Gate decisions for individual projects must be integrated with portfolio decisions.
- Information overload can be a problem in portfolio management; continual focus must be maintained on improving the quality of information inputs.

In pursuit of the three main goals, various approaches have been developed to address the issues of quality of information, integration of decision making, and so on. These approaches vary widely on a detail level, but share a general pattern of progressing through six basic steps: strategic planning, identification, selection, prioritization, tracking, and reprioritization. Dianne Bridges suggests that almost every organization uses a framework based on considering three aspects of project mix: fit, utility, and balance (see Figure 3.1).

In general, fit is determined in the identification stage; utility is assessed quickly during identification, but more thoroughly explored in the selection process; and balance is achieved in the selection and prioritization (and reprioritization) of projects.

THE SIX-STEP PROCESS
Step 1: Strategic Planning
This is more of a pre–portfolio management step, and it may seem too obvious to be included here. However, many organizations still make project

Figure 3.1
Fit, Utility, and Balance Paradigm

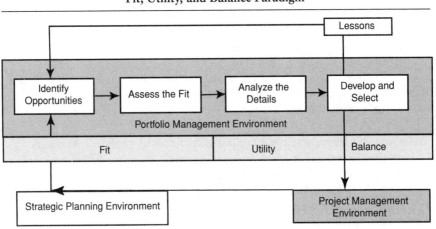

decisions without first having thought through their long-term goals. At this level, such activities as environmental scanning, market research, and development of mission and vision statements must be carried out in order for an organization to express any rationality or coherence in its project selection process. "Groups and individuals that conduct strategic planning," say Toney and Powers, "are consistently more successful at achieving goals than those who don't utilize it."

Since strategic focus becomes the foundation for selecting projects, the strategic direction and business goals must be clearly established. These may be reflected in the vision statement, mission statement, statement of principles, organization objectives, and/or strategic plan(s). Even something as basic as traditional SWOT planning (strengths, weaknesses, opportunities, and threats), suggests Paul Dinsmore, can provide an analytic framework for selecting and prioritizing projects.

Step 2: Identification (or Solicitation) of New Project Ideas and Opportunities

Where do projects come from? Joan Knutson has suggested two categories: *strategic* or top-down projects that are imposed on the organization by upper management and *bottom-up* projects, ideas that are generated by the people "in the trenches." There may be a third category, projects pressed on an organization by its customers. In any case, the step of opportunity identification is a critical one. Bridges offers a set of procedural tips for the identification process:

- *Develop a process to identify opportunities that is easy to follow.* Many people are averse to complex processes and bureaucratic paperwork. Establish an avenue for communicating ideas that is easy to use. Identify a team to review the opportunities and assess the fit within the strategic direction and business goals.
- *Establish a template for project justification.* The ideas must be supported by some substance; otherwise it will be difficult to screen the proposed initiatives. The template may include things such as the link to business goals and a top-level description of the project's costs, benefits, and risks.
- *Establish minimal acceptance criteria.* Individuals submitting ideas and the review team should both understand the minimal acceptance criteria a project must meet before being considered for further analysis. Such requirements may include the link to strategic direction, business threshold minimums (e.g., return-on-investment or

cost/benefit ratio minimums), compliance with organizational constraints (e.g., existing technology architecture), and completion of
the project justification paperwork.
- *Reward ideas and suggestions.* People love recognition. Take the
time and interest to acknowledge formally the ideas that meet the
"fit" test and always give credit where credit is due.

Another perspective on identifying opportunities is offered by Preston
Smith and Donald Reinertsen in their discussion of the "fuzzy front end."
Their research indicated that even otherwise well-managed companies can
fail abysmally at opportunity management, due to the complexity of established companies' processes for dealing with new ideas. In one example cited in their book, the fuzzy front end at a start-up company was 500
times faster than it was at the Fortune 500 company where well-inten-
tioned planning and budgeting processes guaranteed defeat.

Their recommendation: Capture opportunities frequently and early and
make it simple to submit an idea—for example, a one-page form that can
be submitted by any employee. The objective of the idea-capture process,
they remind us, is to achieve visibility, not to filter out bad ideas. They
recommend soliciting and evaluating new project ideas frequently—even
as often as once a month.

Steps 3 and 4: Selection and Prioritization

In any company, multiple projects vie for resources and funding, and
somehow a decision has to be made on which ones to select. As nearly
everyone is aware, the statistics on project failure are dismal. The latest
CHAOS Report, released by the Standish Group in 1998, noted that 28
percent of IT projects fail, while another 46 percent are "challenged."
Even projects that succeed in meeting their requirements can be failures if
the project requirements don't match up to the business realities faced by
the company. For project management to live up to its promise, projects
must be preselected with care.

Project selection and prioritization are the heart and soul of portfolio
management, and much has been written about these hard-to-separate
steps. Many models exist to choose from. The following tips are offered
to assist you in first selecting a model, then refining the procedures that
make up that model, and, finally, carrying out those procedures.

Selecting a Model
In selecting a model, Jack R. Meredith and Samual J. Mantel propose the
following criteria:

- *Realistic*: It must take into account the realities of facilities, capital, resources, and risks.
- *Capable*: The model must be capable of dealing with multiple time periods and with situations both internal and external to the project (strikes, interest rate changes, etc.). It should be an optimizing model, one that makes comparisons based on criteria important to management, considers risks, and then selects the best overall mix of projects.
- *Flexible*: The model must be able to take into account the range of conditions that company might experience. It should be easily updated or modified with changing times.
- *Easy to use*: A model that is not overly complex will be more widely used and take less time to generate results, with obvious benefits.
- *Cost-effective*: The expense of data gathering and analysis must be kept low, relative to the cost of a project.
- *Easily automated*: It should be easy to input, store, and work with the data in a standard computer program.

Developing Procedures
Bridges offers some additional tips on developing a selection process:

- *Establish criteria.* Establish common decision criteria and measure each project against the criteria. Since most decisions *are* based on multiple factors, weight each criterion to establish the relative importance of each item. This will be important in the prioritization step.
- *Make sure accurate data is available.* Information from the accounting system (expenditures, revenues, and manpower) will be necessary to forecast project costs and benefits. Your organization should have reliable, up-to-date market, technical, and manufacturing information. Since project portfolios include both new projects and ongoing projects, your organization should have a system to track the status of ongoing project activity.
- *Establish a process to analyze the project information.* The purpose of this is to ensure data validity and consistent application of the decision criteria. It is important to go through this process before selecting the portfolio to eliminate any controversy over the data and key assumptions.
- *Uniformly apply the methodology across the organization.* The criteria and weights should be completely documented. An analogy can be made to performance reviews: Different managers may have different definitions of an "excellent" rating. In order to ensure fairness for all

employees, it is imperative that the organization clearly defines all performance criteria so managers consistently interpret and apply them.

- *Optimize the portfolio, not just the individual projects.* Industry approaches for developing portfolios range from simple ranking based on individual project financial returns to more complex methodologies that take into account the interrelationships between projects. When developing and selecting the portfolio, the organization needs to make relative comparisons between types of projects such as research, new product development, information technology, and business improvement.
- *Establish portfolio decision meetings.* Separate decision meetings and teams should be established to make portfolio decisions using the validated project information. Typically, senior leadership makes portfolio decisions.

Carrying Out the Procedures

J. Davidson Frame has suggested five behaviors that support a good selection and prioritization process:

1. *Be explicit about what's important.* Selection criteria must be clearly defined—Frame even suggests printing them out in bold type and taping them to the walls in the room where selections are made. It's important, he says, not to get distracted by "the wealth of interesting possibilities" that confront organizations. The selection criteria should capture organizational needs, and project selection occurs in accordance with those needs.

2. *Stick to explicit procedures for selection of projects.* Decisions become less arbitrary and more rational when there is rigid adherence to a defined approach.

3. *Challenge all assertions.* Statements about possible benefits or costs of a project must be subjected to detailed scrutiny. Neither champions nor critics of a project are objective, so the veracity of their statements should be validated by as much data as is available.

4. *Include a broad array of stakeholders on the project selection team.* The typical team should include members who reflect the varying perspectives of all the functional units of an organization. (To this we would add those stakeholders associated with but perhaps not internal to an organization: customers, key vendors or alliance partners, and so on.)

5. *Involve key project personnel in the selection process.* Frame notes that only 20 percent of project managers, according to his research,

have input into selection decisions. Without the input and buy-in of project personnel, it will be difficult to maintain continuity between the selection and execution phases.

Finally, Renee Sommer suggests that all projects under consideration should be screened initially by whether they are *survival* projects—those that *must* be completed for the health of the business, such as Y2K projects—or *growth* projects—projects that, while they don't necessarily produce revenue, have business value for the organization. Once projects have been triaged into these two categories of "must-do" and "discretionary," the process she recommends looks at how projects are allocated among the various areas of organizational concern such as infrastructure, new product development, and so on. Then, within each area, projects are selected. Having some projects identified up front as survival projects simplifies both the prioritization process as well as the allocation of resources enterprise-wide.

Note: A description of the many techniques employed in the selection and prioritization process is beyond the scope of this chapter: for an excellent overview of these, see Norman Archer and Fereidoun Ghasemzadeh's article, "Project Portfolio Selection." See also Table 3.3.

Steps 5 and 6: Tracking (or Registration) and Reprioritization

The organization must have some way to track the progress of approved projects so that final step 6, reprioritization, will be conducted with accurate performance data. These steps are more along the lines of traditional project management; however, the development of enterprise project management software means that it is becoming easier for organizations to store and access the metrics they need to make good decisions. Harvey Levine, former "Software Forum" editor of *PM Network* magazine, devised this list of the functionalities that companies should look for in software they plan to use as part of their portfolio management system:

- *Electronic time sheets, supporting the collection of actual time spent on project tasks and auxiliary work.* These must allow the posting of time to all projects in the system, and should support various means of remote entry. These tools should also provide for management review and control of time reporting. In some environments, the time entry tools must also support progress of the work, including revised estimate-to-complete data.
- *Posting and retention of project data in an open, SQL-type database.* This database acts as a repository for the data produced by various

Table 3.3
A Review of Industry Practices in Portfolio Management

- Hoechst-AG uses a scoring portfolio model with 19 questions in five major categories to rate projects. The five categories are: probability of technical success, probability of commercial success, reward to the company, business strategy fit, and strategic leverage (ability of the project to leverage company resources and skills). Within each of these five factors are a number of specific characteristics (or measures) which are scored on 1–10 scales by management (e.g., strategic impact, synergy with other operations within the corporation, absolute contributions to profitability). The criteria and scoring approach comprise a particularly effective model, purported to be one of the best.

- The Royal Bank of Canada uses a scoring model to rate projects (almost 200 projects competing for the same pool of resources). The criteria for portfolio scoring include project importance (strategic importance, magnitude of impact, and economic benefits) and ease of doing (cost of doing, project complexity, and resource availability). Expected annual expenditure and cumulative spending are added to this rank-ordered list to evaluate resource availability. The bank also uses a risk-reward bubble diagram to analyze the balance of projects. Ease of execution is plotted against importance on x-y axes, and circles representing the bank's projects are placed in the appropriate quadrants. Decision rules are set up (e.g., projects of low importance that are difficult to execute get a no-go decision). The circle sizes show current annual funding per project. Also, the bank categorizes product groups and defines strategic missions for each, which then become major inputs to the allocation of resources in the portfolio selection exercise. Concurrently projects are also prioritized using a scoring model. Results from the two methods are reconciled via several iterations of this process.

- Procter & Gamble claims an 85 percent predictive ability using its computer-based scoring model.

- The Weyerhaeuser corporate R&D program has put new processes into place to align and prioritize R&D projects. The program has three types of activities: technology assessment (changes in external environment and impact to the company); research (building knowledge bases and competencies in core technical areas); and development (development of specific commercial opportunities). Four key inputs are considered when establishing priorities: significant changes in the external environment; long-term future needs of lead customers; business strategies, priorities, and technology needs; and corporate strategic direction. Lessons learned are: Be patient, as it takes time to engage company business leaders; get the project leaders involved so they understand the criteria and rationale; and put processes in place that encourage staff across technical areas to be involved.

- At Eli Lilly, strategy tables are used to develop alternative portfolios and compare alternative strategies. The strategy table represents different combinations of projects and different courses of action for each project, thus providing an array of portfolios for selection. The benefits of examining multiple portfolios versus simply ranking projects are: (1) the focus is on the

Table 3.3 *(Continued)*
A Review of Industry Practices in Portfolio Management

portfolio of opportunities versus individual opportunities; (2) relationships between opportunities are considered; and (3) alternative courses of action are determined and evaluated.

- SmithKline Beecham examines a range of alternatives for each candidate project before assessing the value of each project. In doing so, the organization has gone away from a single plan of action with one viable option to four project alternatives with four viable options. Each project team must develop at least four alternatives: the current plan (follow existing activity), a "buy-up" option (have more to spend); a "buy-down" option (have less to spend); and a minimal plan (abandon project but preserve as much as possible). The benefits to creating project alternatives include: (1) the formation of new ideas, (2) the creation of new chances for projects that would not survive under their current plans, and (3) the help to teams to understand the elements of their development plans (they have to think it through to determine options).

- At 3M, bubble diagrams are used to visually depict project portfolios. Generally two axes are drawn dividing the space into four quadrants. Each axis stands for a key characteristic that describes the portfolio. The most popular diagram is a risk-return diagram (such as the probability of technical success and reward). In this case, the separate quadrants stand for different combinations of the risk-return (low risk, low return; high risk, high return; low risk, high return; high risk, low return). Each project is assessed and placed within a quadrant, resulting in a visual depiction of the portfolio. There is really no prioritization of projects, but more a display of information to help in the portfolio decision. 3M uses bubble diagrams and adds another level of complexity to portray uncertainty and probabilities. The size and shape of each "bubble" on the diagram is adjusted to reflect project uncertainties. The bubble diagrams help decision makers visualize the total portfolio.

- Mobil Chemical uses six categories of projects to determine the right balance of projects: (1) cost reductions and process improvements; (2) product improvements, product modifications, and customer satisfaction; (3) new products; (4) new platform projects and fundamental/breakthrough research projects; (5) plant support; (6) technical support for customers. Senior management reviews the spending split across these six types—the *what is*—and compares this to the target breakdown—the *what should be*.

- Rohm and Haas defines areas of strategic thrust of the business (e.g., to grow via product development of products aimed at Germany). Then the leadership team defines how much effort it wishes to spend against each area of strategic thrust.

- At Exxon Chemical, management begins with a good understanding of the business unit's strategy and strategic priorities; target spending is decided according to a project newness matrix. As the year progresses, all projects are prioritized using a scoring model. Imbalances in the targeted spending versus prioritized portfolio become evident, and adjustments are made for the upcoming year.

project management tools, as well as connectivity to other data of the enterprise.

- *For some applications, integration with corporate accounting systems.* For seamless integration, look for "Projects" modules provided by enterprise resource planning (ERP) vendors as part of their financial packages, coupled with integration engines provided by your project management software vendor.
- *Analysis engines, or other means of prearranging the data for rapid access.* Also, for the analysis capabilities, the enterprise project management software must have robust project classification systems (coding) with support for hierarchical structures.
- *Earned value computation to support schedule and cost variance analysis.*
- *Mid- and high-level resource loading and budgeting, with discrete spreading capabilities.* These are to allow analysis of proposed projects without requiring planning at the detailed level.
- *Risk assessment capabilities.* These should include ranking of project risks, determination of risk possibility, and impact of the risk events.

A few more words about reprioritization: In a 1998 interview in *PM Network* magazine, Jim Johnson, chairman of the Standish Group, noted that, even though they are still too high, the 1998 Standish Group project failure figures represented an improvement over previous surveys—an improvement that he largely credited to the companies' ability to know when to kill unproductive projects. This is exactly the kind of decision the reprioritization stage is designed to encourage.

CONCLUSION

Futurist John Naisbitt has said, "The most reliable way to anticipate the future is by understanding the present." Currently, a typical company's level of understanding of the projects that make up its business is not good enough to manage the ongoing endeavors, much less be able to anticipate future opportunities. Following good portfolio management processes can ameliorate this in many ways. For example, Frame notes that currently project selection frequently is driven by people whose performance is measured by generating revenue, so they promise more than they can deliver. His research shows that only 20 percent of project managers have any input into project selection. Including the right people in project selection will have an effect on project outcomes.

What's ahead for portfolio management? Some signs of evolution as theory begins to meld with business realities include newer, more dynamic portfolio management techniques. One example is Option Space Analysis, proposed by Timothy Luehrman, which takes uncertainty into account through using active strategic planning rather than passive. Also, companies like Northwestern Mutual Life are now consolidating planning and project execution at the corporate level—merging strategic planning with traditional project office roles in the areas of defining strategy, maintaining the corporate portfolio, helping project managers and sponsors maintain alignment with strategic plans, and identifying the implications of the project portfolio. "We have found that the placement of the Project Office in conjunction with the corporate planning function is key to successful alignment of strategy with project priorities," says Northwestern's Margaret Combe. "The Project Office at Northwestern Mutual Life plays the following roles in driving strategy through projects: leads strategy-defining projects; maintains the company's project portfolio; helps project sponsors and managers to maintain alignment; identifies implications of project portfolio; and supports good project management."

As the project-level management and strategic-level management players draw closer together through a shared, documented process, the historic disconnects between strategic management and individual projects will increasingly fade away. Then—watch out, world.

REFERENCES

Archer, Norman, and Fereidoun Ghasemzadeh. 1999. "Project Portfolio Selection," in *Project Portfolio Management*, J. Pennypacker and Lowell Dye, eds. West Chester, PA: Center for Business Practices (CBP).

Bridges, Dianne N. 1999. "The Art of Project Portfolio Managementa: Selecting the Right Projects," in *Project Portfolio Management*, J. Pennypacker and Lowell Dye, eds. West Chester, PA: Center for Business Practices (CBP).

Cabanis, Jeannette. 1998. "A Major Impact: The Standish Group's Jim Johnson on Project Management and IT Project Success." *PM Network*, September: 7. Newtown Square, PA: PMI.

Combe, Margaret W. 1998. "Project Prioritization in a Large Functional Organization," *Proceedings of the 29th Annual PMI Seminars & Symposium*. PMI.

Comstock, Gilbert L., and Danny E. Sjolseth. 1999. "Aligning and Prioritizing Corporate R&D." *Research Technology Management*, May–June: 20.

Cooper, Robert G., Scott J. Edgett, and Elko J. Kleinschmidt. 1998. *Portfolio Management for New Products*. Reading, MA: Perseus Books.

Dinsmore, Paul. 1998. *Winning in Business with Enterprise Project Management*. New York: AMACOM.

Frame, Davidson, J. 1999. "Selecting Projects That Will Lead to Success," in *Project Portfolio Management*. J. Pennypacker and Lowell Dye, eds. West Chester, PA. Center for Business Practices (CBP).

Knutson, Joan. 1999. "A Portfolio Management System." *PM Network*, June: 22–23. Newtown Square, PA: PMI.

Levine, Harvey. 1999. "Project Portfolio Management: A Song without Words?" *PM Network*, July: 25–27. Newtown Square, PA: PMI.

Luehrman, Timothy A. 1998. "Strategy as a Portfolio of Real Options." *Harvard Business Review*, September–October: 91–93.

Meredith, Jack R., and Samuel J. Mantel Jr. 1995. *Project Management: A Managerial Approach* (Third Edition). New York: John Wiley & Sons.

Miller, Bruce. 1997. "Linking Corporate Strategy to the Selection of IT Projects." *Project Management Institute 28th Annual Seminars & Symposium Proceedings*: 56.

PMI Standards Committee. 1996. *A Guide to the Project Management Body of Knowledge*. Upper Darby, PA: PMI.

Smith, Preston G., and Donald G. Reinertsen. 1998. *Developing Products in Half the Time*. New York: John Wiley & Sons.

Sommer, Renee. 1999. "Portfolio Management for Projects: A New Paradigm," in *Project Portfolio Management*, J. Pennypacker and Lowell Dye, eds. West Chester, PA: Center for Business Practices (CBP).

Spradlin, C. Thomas, and David M. Kutoloski. 1999. "Action-Oriented Portfolio Management." *Research Technology Management*, March–April: 27.

Toney, Frank, and Ray Powers. 1997. *Best Practices of Project Management Groups in Large Functional Organizations*. Upper Darby, PA: PMI.

CHAPTER 4

SCOPE MANAGEMENT: DO ALL THAT YOU NEED AND JUST WHAT YOU NEED

SHLOMO GLOBERSON

INTRODUCTION AND INITIATION

The objective of this chapter is to briefly review, explain, and demonstrate the issues involved in scope management. The structure of the chapter is similar to that of Chapter 5 in *A Guide to PMBOK* (Project Management Institute, 1996), which defines the content and processes included in scope management. An example is used throughout the chapter in order to demonstrate the application of the various concepts, but let us first define some of the major concepts of scope.

Project scope defines the work that must be done in order to deliver a product, with its specified features and functions. It should include *all* the work required, since otherwise not all the deliverables will be executed. Moreover, it should include *only* the work required, since otherwise items that were not planned and budgeted for will be executed and violate the project's objectives.

Project scope management involves the processes required to ensure that the project *includes* all the work required, and only the work required, to complete the project successfully.

The issue of scope is a major one in the execution of any given project. It has to be dealt with in different stages of a project, starting with the initiation stage, continuing with introducing changes, and ending with the approval of project deliverables. The following is a list of the scope-related concepts that arise throughout the project life cycle and their deliverables, which will be discussed later in more detail.

- *Scope in the initiation stage.* Initiation of a project may be the result of a need, a feasibility study, or a preliminary plan. It may also be a result of informal efforts that do not yet have any formal account number (e.g., internal service or new product development projects). Informal effort before formal initiation of a project is very common in many organizations, although it is not formally budgeted. Typically, a limited amount of work is informally done in order to secure the approvals needed for formal initiation. The end result of the initiation stage is a project charter that gives a general and short description of the project content, the project sponsor, and the way that it will be managed. A project charter for an internal project is similar in nature to signing a contract with an outside vendor.

- *Scope planning.* This includes a short description of the project scope, called a scope statement, and list of guidelines concerning the way the scope will be managed. It starts during the final phase of project initiation and commonly ends before the start of any significant planning efforts.

- *Scope definition.* This detailed description of the project content (the work breakdown structure or WBS) is one of the significant tasks, if not the most significant one, for which the project manager has full responsibility. It is performed after scope planning.

- *Scope change.* This involves mechanisms governing the ways that scope changes are introduced and operate throughout the entire project.

- *Scope verification.* This consists of comparing the planned project scope to the actual result, and either accepting, requiring corrections to, or rejecting the result. It should be performed throughout the project on partial components, and at the end on the project as a whole.

Figure 4.1 presents the changing relevance of the scope concepts over time.

From the figure it can be seen very clearly that scope is an issue of concern throughout the whole life cycle of the project. For demonstration purposes let us start right now with the example given in Figure 4.2.

During the initiation phase, the need is identified, possible alternatives for a solution are explored, the feasibility of each is evaluated, and a decision is made concerning go-no-go and the selected alternative. It is beyond the scope of this chapter to deal with the methods used to select a preferred alternative.

SCOPE PLANNING

Scope planning includes two major deliverables: a scope statement and a scope management plan.

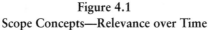

Figure 4.1
Scope Concepts—Relevance over Time

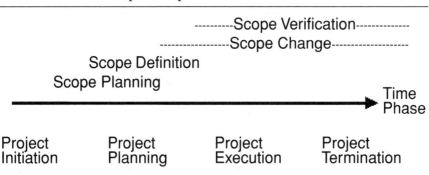

The *scope statement* is a short description of the project scope. It is used as the basis for future project decisions and the criteria used to determine if major phases of the project and the project as a whole have been completed successfully. The scope statement forms the basis for an agreement between the project team and the project customer by identifying:

• The justification for the project
• Project objectives
• Major project deliverables
• Success criteria

If a request for proposal (RFP) has already been issued, it may serve as the basis for the scope statement document, since it includes most of the required information.

Figure 4.2
The Need and Possible Alternative Solution

The need: There is a regional shortage of qualified managers able to lead companies effectively in the new competitive and international environment.

Possible alternatives:
1. Attract managers from other places around the globe.
2. Send present regional managers abroad for additional training.
3. Open a regional school specializing in top management training programs.

Figure 4.3 shows a possible scope statement and supporting material for our example.

The *scope management plan* consists of set of documents describing how the project scope will be identified, classified, documented, and managed, and the expected stability of the scope.

Scope stability is an expression of the extent of expected scope changes during the project life cycle. Thus, an original scope of a project that is repetitive in nature—say, building a new transformer house—is expected to undergo very few changes. However, an original scope of the installation of an Internet purchasing system for a company is expected to undergo more changes. This is so because of the greater number of problems in getting accurate customer requirements at the initial stage, as well as the changing environment of Internet technology during project execution. The less the scope stability the more important is the issue of scope management. A sample scope stability description is given in Figure 4.4.

Scope management planning is similar in nature to configuration

Figure 4.3
Scope Statement and Supporting Details

Scope statement:
To design a regional Top Management Program (TMP) school equipped with advanced communication and teaching systems, and prepare it to start functioning within a year. The school will run two major programs, an executive MBA program, and TMP executive programs. TMP will serve managers who wish to take selective workshops on advanced management issues. The school will use an existing building that will be renovated to fit the needs.

Sponsor of the project:
The regional governor, who is also the fund-raiser. As such, he is also a major stakeholder.

Major stakeholders:
The regional university, an internationally known university, situated in the region, which will be responsible for the MBA program. Dr. Kite has been nominated to be the coordinator on behalf of the university.

The RMA—Regional Management Association, which will be involved in identifying managers' needs, and help in promoting the program. Ms. Carter has been nominated to be the coordinator on behalf of the Association.

The regional industry—organizations that wish to upgrade the managerial abilities of their employees and potential employees. There is an emerging high-tech concentration in the area.

The project manager:
The regional governor has nominated Mr. Jones as the project manager. Mr. Jones, who has 10 years of project experience in the communication industry, has recently gained an MBA degree at one of the leading schools.

Figure 4.4
Scope Stability Expectation

Scope stability:
Although an identical project has not been executed before in the region, it appears that the scope will be relatively stable after a baseline is established, and not too many changes are expected to take place. This is so since programs of a similar nature exist in other places in the country and around the globe. Also, establishing the infrastructure (building, equipment, etc.) does not seem to present any unusual difficulties since the intention is to follow an infrastructure design similar to the one used for the regional university.

management, which has relatively well defined working procedures, as described in ISO 10007. The following concepts are the backbone of such a system:

- *Configuration*: the functional and physical characteristics of a product, or service, as defined in technical documents. That is, configuration of all the project work packages (defined later) should be established and documented in a prespecified manner.
- *Configuration baseline*: an agreed-upon plan, which serves as reference for future activities, whether work packages or plans. When the designer, or planner, is satisfied with the configuration, it is "frozen" and used as the baseline. A scope baseline may be "unfrozen" as a result of a change request. Change is introduced according to a specified procedure and a new baseline is generated as a result of the approved change. The final product is compared to the latest scope baseline.
- *Configuration item*: the definition of an entity for which the configuration management process should be applied. If configuration of every single item, regardless of its size and complexity, is formally managed, the scope management work content may be too complex to handle. Typically, only entities executed by the company should be identified as those whose configuration should be managed. For example, there is no need to manage the configuration of standard parts.
- *Configuration board*: the group of technical and administrative experts with the authority and responsibility to make decisions on the configuration of a part. This board reviews and approves/disapproves the original configuration and future changes.

Figure 4.5 presents brief scope management plan guidelines for the project example.

SCOPE DEFINITION

Scope definition involves subdividing the major project deliverables into smaller, more manageable components, called work packages (WPs). The end result structure of the subdivision is the work breakdown structure (WBS). According to *PMBOK*, "WBS is a deliverable-oriented grouping of project elements which organizes and defines the total scope of the project. Each descending level represents an increasingly detailed definition of a project component. Project components may be products or services." The concept "WBS Dictionary," widely used, means a set of documents that consists of the WBS, as well as a detailed description of each work package included in it.

The WBS provides a common language for describing the work content of the project. This common language, expressed by the work package definitions and the hierarchical coding of the WBS, enables all project stakeholders such as customers, suppliers, and other participants to communicate effectively throughout the whole life of the project.

The resources required to execute a project equal the sum of the resources required to execute each of the WPs, plus the level of effort (LOE) resources used for maintaining the infrastructure required to support the project. Typical LOE resources are project management, quality assurance, and data processing.

Figure 4.5
General Guidelines for the Scope Management Plan

Scope Management Plan
1. A seed configuration board was established, consisting of Mr. Jones—the project manager, Dr. Kite—the university coordinator, and Ms. Carter—the RMA coordinator.
2. Mr. Jones is the head of the configuration board.
3. Mr. Jones will nominate additional, or other, board members, as the need arises.
4. It was decided to adopt *PMBOK* and ISO 10007 as the standards for managing the scope and the configuration of the project.
5. Every work package will be treated as a configuration item, carrying its WBS code as an identification code.
6. The project manager, Mr. Jones, with the WP owner, will decide whether subcomponents of the work package require treatment as separate configuration items.
7. Baseline documents will be managed in a single archive.

Appropriate development, maintenance, and use of the WBS contributes significantly to the probability of successful completion of a project. For example, Hall (1993) reports on the successful completion of a large-scale project in the range of $225 million, claiming that a major contributor to its success was the appropriate use of WBS.

There is not just one unique WBS structure for each project. As shown by Globerson (1994), a variety of different WBS structures may be generated for the same project, each being preferable under different conditions. The structure of the WBS is determined by the meanings of the levels within the WBS hierarchy. Normally, the first level of the WBS represents the entire project. Subsequent levels represent subdivisions, according to a number of possible criteria, such as product components, organization functions, or life cycle stages. Different WBSs are obtained by applying the criteria at different levels of the hierarchy.

Figure 4.6 demonstrates a WBS for the example. As can be seen from the figure, the nature of the components was used as the guidelines for the second-level breakdown: the administration, the academic part, the building, and management.

Each work package requires a certain amount of planning, reporting, and control. Although division of the project into smaller work packages seems to increase the workload on the project manager and on the project team, it supports better planning and control. As shown by Raz and Globerson (1998), organizations use general guidelines for the recommended size of work packages. These guidelines are typically expressed in terms of effort (e.g., person-hours, person-days, dollar value) or in terms of elapsed time (e.g., days, weeks). For example, a work package (WP) should last not more than four weeks.

Ideally, the project manager should ensure that each WP is assigned to a single responsible person or organizational unit, and that this unit has the ability to properly execute it. Smaller work packages mean more frequent deliveries to the customer and earlier payments, if applicable, reducing finance charges to the contractor and increasing them for the customer.

Since a WP is the smallest manageable unit of a project, the success of the project depends to a large extent on the ability of the project manager to properly deal with each WP. A powerful tool for this purpose is the Work Package Description Form, which serves to describe all relevant attributes of the WP. It is also used as the basis for a contract, either formal or informal, between the project manager as a client and the supplier (internal or external) of the WP. Figure 4.7 presents such a sample form for the example.

Figure 4.6
Work Breakdown Structure (WBS) of the School Project

```
1. THE SCHOOL OF MANAGEMENT PROJECT
    1.1 THE ADMINISTRATION PART
            1.1.1 THE REGISTRATION PROCESS
            1.1.2 THE SCHEDULING PROCESS
            1.1.3 THE ACADEMIC SUPPORT
            1.1.4 STAFF SELECTION
            1.1.5 PROMOTION OF THE TWO PROGRAMS
    1.2 THE ACADEMIC PART
            1.2.1 THE MBA PROGRAM
            1.2.2 THE "TOP" PROGRAM
            1.2.3 STAFF SELECTION
    1.3 THE BUILDING
            1.3.1 ESTABLISH OVERALL REQUIREMENTS
            1.3.2 SELECT A SITE
            1.3.3 GET APPROVAL OF THE AUTHORITIES
            1.3.4 REMODEL THE BUILDING
            1.3.5 PREPARE PARKING SPACES
            1.3.6 OFFICE FACILITIES
            1.3.7 THE LIBRARY
            1.3.8 THE CLASSROOMS
            1.3.9 THE COMPUTER FACILITY
                    1.3.9.1 ESTABLISH REQUIREMENTS
                    1.3.9.2 DESIGN THE SYSTEM
                    1.3.9.3 PURCHASE OFF-THE-SHELF SYSTEM
                    1.3.9.4 INSTALL THE SYSTEM
                            4.1 THE ADMINISTRATION PART
                            4.2 THE ACADEMIC PART
                            4.3 THE COMPUTER LABORATORY
                    1.3.9.5 TEST THE SYSTEM
                            5.1 THE ADMINISTRATION PART
                            5.2 THE ACADEMIC PART
                            5.3 THE COMPUTER LABORATORY
                    1.3.9.6 PREPARING FOR OPERATION
                            6.1 LOADING THE SYSTEMS
                            6.2 TRAINING THE STAFF

    1.4 MANAGEMENT
```

The form is generic in nature and may be used for different work packages. For example, type of required resources will obviously change from one WP to another. The attachments noted in Figure 4.7 are not included in this chapter as they do not add value to the subject matter.

There are general guidelines that may be used when structuring a WBS. They refer to both the general structure and the specific definition of its work packages, as summarized here:

Figure 4.7
Work Package Description

Work Package Description Form

<u>WP identification:</u>
Project name: *School of Mgt.*   **Project code:** *PUB5*   **Project manager:** *Jones*
WP name: *Loading the systems*   **WP code:** *PUB5-1.3.9.6.2*   **WP owner:** *Ms. Hepner*
WP deliverables: *Installed programs (see attachment PUB5-1.3.9.6.2-A1 for details)*
Revision no.: *2*   **Date:** *10.10.99*   **Previous revision:** *1*

<u>Resources required:</u>

<u>labor</u>		<u>other resources</u>		
<u>type</u>	<u>labor days</u>	<u>type</u>	<u>quantity</u>	<u>cost</u>
hardware technician	3	software A	2	$6,000
software technician	3	software B	8	$4,000
subcontractor	......	equipment		
programmer	......	facility	......	....
others	......	other	......	....

<u>Required prerequisites:</u> *tested systems – Work Packages 1.3.9.5.1/2/3*
<u>Acceptance tests:</u> *test of each terminal on each program, and combined tests*
(see attachment PUB5-1.3.9.6.2-A2)
<u>Number of working days required for completing the WP:</u> *20*
<u>Possible risk events, which may impair the successful completion of the WP:</u> *incompatibility of the software packages*

TO BE COMPLETED AFTER SCHEDULING THE PROJECT:

Earliest start of the WP: *6.5.00*   **Earliest finish of the WP:** *6.30.00*
<u>Review meeting according to milestones:</u>

Name of milestone	**deliverables**	**meeting date**	**participants**
Sample installation	*one functional terminal*	*6.8.00*	*Jones, Hepner, Forman*
Complete installation	*functional terminals*	*6.30.00*	*Jones, Hepner, Forman*
....	....	....	....
....	....	....	....

<u>Design approval of the WP:</u>
WP owner: **Name:** *Ms. Hepner*   **Signature:** .... **Date:** ....
WP customer: **Name:** *Mr. Forman*   **Signature:** .... **Date:** ....
Project manager:Name: *Ms. Jones*   **Signature:** .... **Date:** ....
<u>Completion approval of the WP:</u>
WP owner: **Name:** *Ms. Hepner*   **Signature:** .... **Date:** ....
WP customer: **Name:** *Mr. Forman*   **Signature:** .... **Date:** ....
Project manager:Name: *Mr. Jones*   **Signature:** .... **Date:** ....

Points to Remember When Structuring a WBS

- The WBS represents work content and not an execution sequence.
- The second level of the WBS may be components, functions, and geographical location.
- Managerial philosophy impacts the structure.
- The WBS and its derived WPs should be compatible with organizational working procedures.
- The WBS should be generic in nature so that it may be used in the future for similar projects.

- The WBS is *not* a product structure tree (PST), or bill of materials (BOM). Both refer to the hierarchy of components that are physically assembled into a product.

Points to Remember When Defining a Work Package (WP)
- The WP is the lowest level in the WBS.
- A WP has a deliverable result.
- A WP should have one responsible party, called the WP owner.
- A WP may be considered by the WP assignee as a project in itself.
- A WP may include several milestones.
- A WP should fit organizational procedures and culture.
- The optimal size of a WP may be expressed in terms of labor hours, calendar time, cost, report period, risks.

It is important to emphasize that since a company operates within a certain line of business, its projects are fairly similar in nature. Therefore, it is essential for the company to develop a generic approach to these projects. Although one project is not identical to the other, they are similar enough to use a template structure for the WBS as a starting point, and later adjust it to the specific project. Using this approach will enable a company to improve its performance and survive the competition.

SCOPE VERIFICATION

Scope verification is the process of comparing the actual performance of the products, with their scope baseline, in order to ensure that all have been completed correctly and satisfactorily. If discrepancies are found between the scope baseline and the actual product, the product should be changed to fit the baseline. The end result of the verification process is either a formal acceptance or a rejection of the project by the stakeholders (sponsor, client, customer, etc.).

The verification process requires execution of a battery of tests on those project components which have a scope baseline that defines their configuration. The results of the tests are then compared to the features stated in the baseline.

The verification process is relatively easy if there is a section in the scope baseline that defines those tests, called acceptance tests. If project requirements are not sufficiently detailed, it is impossible to execute the verification process in a reliable way. For example, let us say that the major deliverable of a project is a new type of tent that has to remain standing in a storm. If maximum storm intensity is not specifically stated in the requirements, it is impossible to verify that the project has been completed properly. Therefore, testing must be carefully planned at a very early stage. A valid testing program relates to the following phases and issues:

- *A list of the components to be tested.* Only components identified as items in the configuration identification list should be tested.
- *The test measures.* The criteria that will be used for evaluating the performance and the desired results will relate to physical measures (dimensions, etc.) and performance measures (ability to withstand temperature, shocks, etc.).
- *Testing location.* Testing may be performed in a laboratory, on the company's site (then called the alpha site), or on the customer's site (then called the beta site). Needless to say, a customer site gives the most reliable result. However, it is of great value to have pilot tests on the company's site before trying it on the customer's premises.
- *Who should carry out the tests?* They can be carried out by people who are responsible for executing the components, by the customer, or by an organization certified for carrying out such tests.
- *Specifying the testing procedures.* The testing results depend to a large extent on the testing procedures. For example, if you wish to check the maximum weight that may be carried by a seat before it breaks down, you should specify how the weight should be loaded and distributed on the seat—for example, whether the weight should be dropped on the seat, and, if so, from what height.
- *Specifying the test support equipment.* Support equipment required for the execution of the tests may be standard or designed specifically to carry out the test.

Figure 4.8 demonstrates an example of the verification process for a work package.

Although a project manager does not have the professional responsibility for carrying out the tests, he or she does have the responsibility to make sure that the tests are properly planned and executed. Many projects fail due to lack of proper advanced test planning. The test planning should be done at a very early stage, so that the work package assignee knows in advance how the verification process of the work package is to be carried out and plan to work accordingly.

SCOPE CHANGE

Very few projects, if any, are executed according to their original design and execution plan. That is, design and planning changes occur all the time.

Figure 4.8
Verification Process of a Work Package

Work Package Verification Form

WP identification:
Project name: *School of Mgt.*   **Project code:** *PUB5*   **Project manager:** *Jones*
WP name: *loading the systems*   **WP code:** *PUB5-1.3.9.6.2*   **WP owner:** *Ms. Hepner*
WP deliverables: *Installed programs*
Revision no.: *1*   **Date:** *10.1.99*   **Previous revision:**
Items to be tested:
Installation of all agreed-upon programs
Proper functioning of all programs
Ability to integrate the programs with each other
Backup in case of a need to reload the programs
Ability to deal with large database
Individuals involved in the testing: *A team consisting of one designated employee from the computer laboratory and Ms. Hepner, the WP owner.*
Testing procedure: *Testing each program by using a relatively complicated sample of the work that is to be performed on it. Leave three programs active while testing each of them.*

Any changes should be considered in relation to a baseline (i.e., an original plan that was approved as the base for execution of the project). For example, an original project scope includes the work package "writing an operations manual." Although nothing was said about it during the initial scope definition, it was understood that it should be written in English. At a later stage of the project it became clear that a significant portion of the customer's employees are fluent not in English, but in Spanish. The new information was considered and it was decided to deliver two manuals, one in English and one in Spanish. This change should now be coordinated into the old baseline in order to generate the new one.

Changes may be required with regard to adding or dropping a work package, as well as design changes. Since a design change alters the work content of the project, it is considered a scope change as well. For every entity/component/item/program that has a baseline configuration, introduction of a change in its features should be done in a specific manner.

The following are the major reasons for a need to change the original scope:

- Lack of sufficient information during the early stage of planning
- Increase of customers' ability to specify their requirements, resulting from a better understanding of their real needs
- Change in environmental conditions
- Improper original planning
- New technology that may improve the project's performance

Figure 4.9 demonstrates the introduction of a change in the example project.

A well-managed change process enables the following:

- Proposed suggestions can be compared to previous ones, in order to avoid repetitions.
- The potential impact on all relevant components can be evaluated.

Figure 4.9
Evaluating the Impact of Introducing a Change to a Work Package

---

Change Request Form

WP identification:
Project name: *School of Mgt.*   **Project code:** *PUB5*   **Project manager:** *Jones*
WP name: *Loading the systems*   **WP code:** *PUB5-1.3.9.6.2*   **WP owner:** *Ms. Hepner —IT*
WP deliverables: *Installed programs*
Change no.: *2*   **Date:** *10.1.99*   **Requestor:** *Prof. D. Hunt*

Nature of requested change: *To add a generic simulation software, similar to GPSS, to the available packages.*
Change Control Board:
Mr. Jones, the project manager
Ms. Hepner, the WP owner
Mr. March, computer analyst
Benefits of the change: *Ability to support courses, such as Operations Management and Project Management, in which analysis of systems requires simulation.*
Required analysis:
Impact on the work package: *The impact of increasing the number of loaded programs.*
Impact on other work packages: *Since the software is relatively large, there is a need to check the ability of the present hardware configuration to effectively deal with the requested software. There is a need for adding training on that program.*
Impact on cost: *If hardware has to be upgraded, estimate the additional cost. Find the price of the requested program. Estimate the additional training costs.*
Results of analysis:
Impact on the work package: *It will require two more hours for installation. No software related problems are expected (Mr. March _____, Date _____).*
Impact on other work packages: *There will be a need to upgrade the computer hardware and to add memory. Since the requested program is not a common one, there will be a need to train the laboratory staff. The additional training may take around a day (Mr. March _____, Date _____).*
Impact on cost: *Additional software installation will not carry additional cost. Memory upgrade will cost $50 per computer. Software training cost is expected to be around $2,000 (Mr. Young _____, Date ____).*
Impact on project completion time: *No delays are expected if the change is approved, since the additional activities can be performed simultaneously (Mr. Jones _____, Date_____).*
Decisions made and additional financial sources:
To install the software on just one group of computers (10 computers).
The additional budget will come out of the Dean's discretionary fund.
Functions to be notified:
Prof. Hunt   *Computer laboratory*
Purchasing   *Dean's office*
Authorized By:
Name: *Mr. Jones*   **Signature:**   **Date:**
Name: *Ms. Hepner*   **Signature:**   **Date:**
Name: *Mr. march*   **Signature:**   **Date:**

- The benefits and costs of the changes can be evaluated, taking into consideration the impact on time, cost, and technical performance.
- Changes can be accepted, or rejected, by relevant stakeholders.
- All relevant parties can be notified of the changes.
- The previous baseline of the scope is updated.
- Execution can be compared to the most recent scope baseline.

From the material presented in this chapter it becomes obvious that the project scope is a very crucial and complicated issue. In spite of its complexity, it is possible to manage it properly since the proper processes exist; they just need to be executed without shortcuts. Proper scope management is a major step toward the successful planning and execution of a project.

REFERENCES

Globerson, S. 1994. "Impact of Various Work Breakdown Structures on Project Conceptualization." *International Journal of Project Management*, Vol. 12, No. 3: 165–171.

Globerson, S., and A. Shtub. 1995. "Estimating the Progress of Projects." *Engineering Management Journal*, Vol. 7, No. 3: 39–44.

Hall, W. 1993. "Scope Management through a WBS." *PM Network*, Vol. 7, No. 5 (May).

ISO 10007. 1995 *Quality Management—Guidelines for Configuration Management*. Geneva: International Organization for Standardization.

Luby, R. E., D. Peel, and W. Swahl. 1995. "Component-Based Work Breakdown Structure." *Project Management Journal*, Vol. 26, No. 4: 38–43.

Matthews, M., 1993. "Introducing Networks to an In-Progress Project." *Project Management Journal*, Vol. 24, No. 2 (June).

PMI Standards Committee. 1996. *A Guide to the Project Management Body of Knowledge (PMBOK)*. Upper Darby, PA: Project Management Institute.

Raz, T., and S. Globerson. 1998. "Effective Sizing and Content Definition of Work Packages." *Project Management Journal*, Vol. 29, No. 4: 17–23.

Shtub, A., J. Bard, and S. Globerson. 1994. *Project Management: Engineering, Technology and Implementation*. Englewood, NJ: Prentice Hall.

CHAPTER 5

REQUIREMENTS MANAGEMENT: ADDRESSING CUSTOMER NEEDS AND AVOIDING SCOPE CREEP

J. DAVIDSON FRAME

$\mathbf{I}$n project management, the concept of *requirements* is an important one. Requirements describe conditions that must be met in order to produce a satisfactory deliverable. Typically, they are divided into two broad categories: business requirements and technical requirements.

Business requirements define business conditions that the deliverable must achieve. Examples of business requirements include:

- To produce a widget for less than $25,000
- To develop a new database that costs 20 percent less to operate than the current database
- To use the project to strengthen the organization's technological capabilities by adding three new engineers to the staff
- To carry out the project solely by means of contract workers

In project management today, most experts believe that projects should be led by business considerations rather than purely technical ones. This stands in contrast to the prevailing view just a few years ago that project management (including the development of requirements) should be left in the hands of technical experts. Various problems were generated by the old approach. For example, technical experts often developed technically competent deliverables that customers did not want. Or the technically adept solutions that were created did not make economic sense. Or the drive for technical perfection led to unacceptable schedule slippages.

Technical requirements describe what the deliverable should look like and what it should do. More formally, they define the physical and functional characteristics of the deliverable. Technical requirements can be broken down into two categories: *functional requirements* and *specifications*.

Functional requirements serve two roles. First, they are an attempt to rough out what it is that we hope to create. You need to learn to crawl before you walk, and to walk before you run. Similarly, you need to scope out functional requirements before delving into the creation of detailed specifications.

Second, they provide customers with insights into what they will be getting. While it is unrealistic to suppose typical customers are able to read and understand blueprints (specifications), it is reasonable to assume they can make sense out of an artist's conceptual drawing (functional requirement). Customer satisfaction is largely tied to managing customer expectations. And to the extent that well-developed functional requirements provide customers with a realistic understanding of what they will be getting out of the project, they contribute to the achievement of customer delight. If customers don't like what they see in the functional requirements, they can request adjustments. It is better to have these adjustments addressed at an early stage of the project than during the project implementation stage or, worse yet, after the deliverable has been produced.

Specifications define precisely what the deliverable should look like and do. In designing a project solution, the technical team members use the specifications to guide them in their work. Whatever it is that they are developing—a new building, software code, a novel advertising campaign—should, ultimately, "meet the specs."

THE PLACE OF REQUIREMENTS IN THE PROJECT MANAGEMENT PROCESS

The place of requirements in the project management process is illustrated in the following flow diagram:

Needs → Requirements/Specifications → Design →
The Project: Build-to-Design

Requirements are the concrete embodiment of needs. They in turn form the basis of designing a deliverable. Ultimately the project effort centers on creating a deliverable that satisfies the design, which in turn is a reflection of requirements, which are built on an assessment of needs. We are dealing with a chain here, and clearly the old adage holds: "A chain is no stronger than its weakest link." If any link in this chain is deficient, then the whole process is weakened. Consequently, if we haven't done a good job managing requirements, then the deliverable will be flawed.

Needs → Requirements

Getting the needs right, and then converting them to requirements, can be a perilous journey. Are we focusing on the right customers? They appear to have conflicting needs—which should we address? The needs seem to be evolving—how insistent should we be that the customers stick to the statement of needs that they authorized? How should we deal with changing needs?

The single most important skill set in developing requirements from needs is the *communication* skill set. The people who are expected to develop an excellent deliverable—that is, the project team—must understand what is in the heads of the people who want the deliverable to be developed—that is, the customers. If customers are unable to express their needs and wants intelligibly, then it is unlikely that a deliverable will be developed that will satisfy them. Similarly, if the project team lacks the capacity to capture the nebulous needs and wants of customers and to express them in meaningful terms, then it is unlikely that they will be able to produce a satisfactory deliverable. The challenge of communicating and capturing requirements is covered later.

Requirements → Design

Transforming requirements into a well-designed solution is largely a mechanical issue that does not pose major project management challenges. If the design team is competent, they should have little difficulty transitioning from a well-stated requirement to the creation of a good design. The obvious point here is that if the requirements are shaky, then the resulting design will be off center.

Design → The Project: Build-to-Design

The most significant requirements-related challenge facing the project team during the "build" phase (i.e., implementing a project solution) is the challenge of *scope creep*. The term refers to the propensity for requirements to change once the project is underway. There are many reasons why requirements change: New players come on the scene, budgets are altered, government regulations shift, people change their minds, and so on. The pressure for scope creep is inevitable. Consequently, it is important that projects are carried out in an environment where change control processes have been established and communicated to all project players. Currently, the prevalent methodology for change control on projects is *configuration management*, which will be discussed later.

THE NEEDS-REQUIREMENTS LIFE CYCLE: UNDERSTANDING HOW REQUIREMENTS ARE BUILT ON NEEDS

Requirements do not spring out of thin air. A little reflection shows that they are the concrete embodiment of people's needs. For example:

> *Need:* "I need to get to work by 8:00 A.M. each morning."
> *Requirement:* "I must catch the 7:15 A.M. commuter train into the city."

In general, the connection between needs and requirements can be expressed through the needs-requirements life cycle. This life cycle reflects the fact that the well-defined efforts we carry out in our lives have their origins in vague sentiments that initially are difficult to express. At the outset, we have a sense that something needs to be addressed, although we are not sure what this is. Upon further thought, we begin to get a handle on this feeling and through a course of refinement we express this sentiment with increasing precision. Through a process like this, what starts off as a vaguely intuited need eventually is transformed into a precise requirement.

The stages that comprise the needs-requirements life cycle are:

- *Stage 1*: Needs emerge
- *Stage 2*: Needs are recognized
- *Stage 3*: Needs are articulated
- *Stage 4*: Functional requirements are expressed
- *Stage 5*: Detailed specifications are developed

It is important to understand and appreciate the link between needs and requirements. Too often we treat these two concepts as if they were entirely separate entities, when in fact they are parts of a continuum. The significance of their connection is obvious when we discover—to our dismay—that despite our brilliant formulation and management of requirements, customers reject our deliverable because it is built on a foundation of poorly formulated needs. If you have not captured needs properly, the subsequent requirements will inevitably be flawed.

Stage 1: Needs Emerge

Needs are highly dynamic. There are limitless reasons why they change—why new needs emerge and old ones wax. For example, changes in technology create new opportunities, which in turn alter people's perceptions of their needs and wants. In an age when communications were based on posting letters that were carried to their destinations by letter carriers riding horseback, nobody actually expressed a *need* to be in touch with other people continually and instantly. Such a need was never articulated because it could never be met given the technological limitations that humans lived with at the time. Today, cell phones, satellite phones, and beepers make it possible to reach others and be reached instantly, 24 hours a day. Now a whole range of people—from teenagers to businesspeople—express a strong need to be accessible via the new technology.

Stage 2: Needs Are Recognized

It is not enough for a need to emerge. People must perceive its emergence if it is to assume any meaning or form. When I was a child, I puzzled over the query: "If a tree falls in the forest and no one hears it fall, has there been any sound at all?" A corresponding needs recognition analog is: "If a need emerges and no one recognizes that it has emerged, has it really emerged at all?" The point is simple: If people are going to address a need, they must recognize that it exists in the first place.

In order to expedite the recognition of unknown needs, many organizations support market research activities. A primary function of market research specialists is to identify emerging needs before the competition does, in order to be first to market with new products and services.

Stage 3: Needs Are Articulated

Good ideas are a dime a dozen. A man may find that great ideas come to him while he is shaving his whiskers in the morning. A woman might develop great ideas while relaxing in the bathtub. However, it is not enough to recognize that a new need exists. It must be articulated clearly and convincingly if anyone is going to act to address it.

The whole point of project proposals is to develop a convincing argument that we have identified a need that we can address and profit from, provided we have access to the right resources and do the right things. To a large extent, articulating needs effectively is tantamount to a sales job—saying what needs to be said in order to get support to move ahead to transform an abstract need into an actual product or service.

Stage 4: Functional Requirements Are Expressed

A beautifully articulated statement expressing the need for a new shopping mall will not enable engineers to build the mall. Needs must be converted into requirements, which when expressed in detailed form (i.e., when they appear as specifications) provide the basis for designing and building solutions. In general, requirements define what a deliverable will look like and what it will do. Functional requirements do this in lay terms. They are expressed in understandable language and can be augmented with visual displays that clarify them. They help technical people to visualize what they will be producing before they get bogged down in complexity; and they enable customers to understand what they will be getting.

Sticking to our shopping mall example, an artist's conceptual drawing of the mall is one tool to express the functional requirements associated with building the mall.

Step 5: Detailed Specifications Are Developed

Functional requirements are imprecise and will not provide the level of detail and precision needed to produce nontrivial goods and services. Ultimately, they must be converted into detailed technical requirements. When these requirements are highly detailed, they are often referred to as *specifications*. On technical projects, these detailed technical requirements provide technical personnel with the information they need to develop and implement good solutions, but they are incomprehensible to most customers, who lack the technical insights to understand them.

In our shopping mall example, blueprints and engineering drawings are expressions of the technical requirements.

DIFFICULTIES IN IDENTIFYING AND MANAGING NEEDS

The needs-requirements life cycle shows how needs and requirements are part of a continuum. If we do not have the needs right, then the resulting requirements will be flawed, no matter how beautifully formulated and managed they are. Clearly, project success demands that customer needs be properly identified and managed.

Regrettably, it is not easy to identify and manage needs for a number of reasons. Problems in defining needs include the following.

Addressing Needs of the Wrong Customers

An example is seeing one individual (usually a powerful player) as *the* customer. For the most part, the concept of a single customer is a fiction. The old adage "The customer is always right" applies only in the retail sector, where a purchaser of a product can be clearly identified. In other arenas, we find that invariably there are *multiple* customers. This is particularly true in the project environment. Consider, for example, a project to develop a new management information system that enables an array of players to access information on the availability of people to carry out project assignments. If we expand our view of customers to include *anyone who will be affected by a project or who can affect the project*, then *data entry clerks* can be viewed as customers—the system we are developing must be configured in such a way that they can do their jobs properly. Their *bosses* are customers—they want a system that makes their workers (and by extension, themselves) look good. The *managers* who "own" the resources are customers—they are concerned that these resources are employed effectively. And so on.

Confusing Wants and Needs

The difference between wants and needs can be significant. For example, I *want* a Mercedes-Benz 600 SEL. However, I really *need* a mechanism to get from point A to point B, and a sturdy pair of walking shoes might be the solution I should pursue. The gap between wants and needs—between the Mercedes-Benz and the walking shoes—can be substantial!

To achieve customer satisfaction, needs analysts must address both wants and needs. First, they must take wants seriously, because in the customers' view, these wants express their needs. If these wants are ignored, customers feel that the needs analysts are insensitive to their needs and they may turn to someone else for help.

Needs analysts must also address the customers' *true* needs. If they work with only customer wants, they will gain temporary satisfaction from customers, who initially are pleased to have their wants filled. However, when it becomes apparent that the wants do not satisfy true needs— that the deliverable is only marginally useful—the customers may feel that the project team did not serve them well.

Defining Needs Prematurely—Ready, Fire, Aim!

Highly capable technical people may feel frustrated dealing with customers who clearly do not know what they are talking about. It may be tempting to offer a solution to their needs as soon as a viable need appears to arise. The solution may, in fact, be good. However, it may not. We won't really know, because the needs analysts have jumped on a solution before conducting an adequate assessment of customer needs and wants.

Encountering Changing Needs

Needs continually change. One of my colleagues once expressed his frustration in dealing with this aspect of managing needs by stating that getting a handle on needs is similar to trying to nail Jell-O to the wall. Sources of changing needs include: changing players, particularly in a time of corporate reengineering; budgetary instability, where ample funds are made available one day and then taken away the next; technological change; a changing business environment (for example, when a competitor introduces a new product into the market that makes the product we are developing look shabby); and people changing their minds as the deliverable moves from the realm of the abstract to the realm of the concrete. We will address this matter of changing needs later, when we discuss the need for change control in managing needs and requirements.

COMMUNICATING AND CAPTURING REQUIREMENTS

One of the greatest challenges facing any project is to have customer needs captured effectively. If the needs are poorly understood, the resulting requirements will be deficient, and customer satisfaction will be low. The problem is this: Customers typically have only the remotest sense of their needs and wants and have no idea of how to communicate these meaningfully to the project team. Project team members, in turn, generally lack the knowledge and skills needed to capture customer needs and to convert them into requirements. They often take a narrow technical approach to doing their jobs and are not interested in dealing with customer confusion as to what their real needs are.

Clearly, work must be done on both the customer and developer side to improve communication between customers and developers. Customers must be made to realize that their vague formulation of needs results in a misunderstanding of what ought to be produced to satisfy them. They should do their homework to discover what they should know in order to articulate their needs and wants clearly. For their part, developers must be made aware of the fact that an important component of their jobs is to capture customer needs meaningfully. They should be sensitized to common pitfalls associated with defining requirements. To illustrate this point, consider the sources and implications of the following three requirements definition problems: stating requirements imprecisely, selective filtering of requirements, and inattention to business requirements.

Lack of Specificity

Most people are not very good at conveying their needs and wants clearly. A boss might tell an assistant: "My office looks a bit dowdy. It really needs a fresh paint job. Why don't you contract a painter to come in and paint it a pleasing color?" This "statement" of a requirement is so ambiguous that it is a disaster waiting to happen. There are many ways it can be interpreted. In specifying the requirement this way, the boss is assuming that the assistant can read the boss's mind. Of course, the assistant is not a mind reader and is likely to carry out the directive in a way that ultimately will disappoint the boss.

For this requirement to be stated properly, the following issues must be addressed:

- What is meant by "pleasing color"? Certainly, this is a subjective concept that can be interpreted in a myriad of ways. To reduce ambiguity, the paint manufacturer and the paint color number should be stated.
- When should the painting occur? Without this specified, the painters can arrive at any time. It would be a good idea to have them arrive at a time that does not interrupt work activity (e.g., painters should begin their work at 6:00 P.M. on the night of the 16th of this month).
- Precisely what should be painted? Walls? Ceilings? Trim? Theoretically, the painter can paint window glass and carpets as the requirement is currently specified!
- Are there additional requirements that should be enunciated? For example: Should fixtures (e.g., door handles, light switch plates) be removed before the painting commences? Should special precautions be taken to protect furniture? Are there specific rules for cleanup?

On serious projects, the possibility for misinterpretation of vaguely specified requirements is enormous. Following are some ambiguous requirements stated on actual projects:

- "Make sure on the monthly statement report generated for customers that computation of tax liability reflects the new processes we have adopted." Stating requirements in this fashion leaves a number of significant questions unanswered: Which new processes are being referenced? If we have multiple formats for reporting monthly statements, which format(s) should be revised? By when should the changes be made? Will there be some sort of testing procedure established to make sure that implementation of the requested changes will lead to the desired results?
- "We want the system to access information on a real time basis." While intuitively the concept of "real time" is obvious, in practice it can be interpreted in different ways since there is no such thing as instant access to live data. One major financial services company defines real time explicitly as follows: "Real time access to data is defined as response times from query to answer in three seconds or less during business hours, and one second or less during off-hours." By specifying requirements reasonably precisely, developers have a good idea of what they should be striving to achieve.

- "The new system should double throughput of key data." Again, this statement of a requirement is fraught with ambiguity. What is the baseline the development team should employ to establish what doubling of throughput means? (In this case, an absolute standard should be set—say, throughput should occur at a 56K baud rate.) Which "key data" should the development team focus on?

There are several steps that can be taken to reduce problems of ambiguity in the statement of requirements. First, customers should be trained on the principles of phrasing requirements clearly. They should learn how poorly stated requirements can lead to undesired results. They should be given opportunities to practice stating requirements clearly.

Second, the recipients of the requirements—the project team that will be charged to implement them—should devise a form that customers need to fill out when requesting work be done, forcing them to articulate their requirements clearly. The form should be fairly easy to fill out and should address the following items:

- Name of requester, with other pertinent information (e.g., department affiliation, phone number, e-mail address)
- Date of request
- Description of the nature of the request, emphasizing the need for precision (in particular, the request should have measures built into it—dimensions of a product, performance characteristics, etc.)
- Description of impacts of the request on budget, schedule, and performance of the system
- Date by which the request should be fulfilled

Third, the recipients of the requirements should know something about the customers' businesses. Only by knowing the businesses can they put the requirements into their proper context. Also, by knowing the businesses and the customers themselves, they can detect when a given requirement doesn't quite smell right, enabling them to follow up with the customers to clarify the ambiguity.

Fourth, employing a rapid prototyping methodology might help in developing requirements. With this approach, customers are asked to review an evolving prototype of the deliverable periodically (e.g., once a week or once a month—whatever is appropriate). The first version of the prototype is very rough. For example, in developing a new display at a natural history museum, the first iteration may entail the museum professionals creating 10 drawings of possible displays. A panel of customers is then brought in to review the drawings and offer their reactions. As a result of this review, the museum's display developers may reduce the alternative displays to four, corresponding to the four most appealing drawings.

Subsequent versions of the prototype entail gradual refinements. For example, in round two, the museum professionals may create four plaster of paris models corresponding to the four selected drawings. The review panel would then be brought in to review the physical models and comment on them. Then the museum team may select two of the four models for further work, creating fully developed, realistic scale models of each. A review panel would be brought in to examine the scale models. Based on this final review, a decision will be made to proceed to build the display associated with the more attractive model. Note that the display's requirements are embedded in the scale model. Requirements have been collected by enabling customers to see what they will get! They are not expected to articulate them verbally, a rather perilous exercise in view of the fact that customers seldom can articulate their needs, wants, and requirements effectively.

Selective Filtering

It is difficult for people to make judgments about things that lie outside their realm of knowledge and understanding. Consequently, they tend to organize information inputs into a context that they comprehend, even when this context may be off base. This tendency leads to selective filtering of requirements. It is best captured in the observation "If your only tool is a hammer, every problem is a nail."

We experience this phenomenon daily. A Freudian psychoanalyst may interpret all human behavior within the Freudian paradigm. An engineer may approach understanding a political action using systems analytical procedures. Fundamentalist religious folks may view all events in accordance with a literal reading of scripture. What occurs in each of these cases is that people's perceptual filters allow them to see and hear only what they are perceptually equipped to handle. Information that does not conform to the filter gets rejected.

In the realm of developing requirements, selective filtering of needs and wants is a common occurrence. For example, when customers state that they need a better way to organize information, what the Sybase database expert likely hears is that they need a Sybase solution to their problems. The problem with selective filtering of needs, wants, and requirements is that it severely constrains the range of options available to dealing with issues.

The best way to handle this problem is to enable a cross-functional group to participate in the requirements development effort. By cross-functional, we mean that people from different functional areas should be involved. For example, when dealing with broad business issues, it is always helpful to solicit inputs from players coming from engineering, operations, finance, marketing/sales, legal, and IT departments. If only one group is charged with developing requirements, with no input from outside, then a solution colored by tunnel vision is likely to occur. This cross-functional group can be recruited to work directly on the requirements-definition team, or they can be brought in later to review various versions of the requirements as they evolve.

Inattention to Business Requirements

An interesting development occurred in project management during the 1990s. Traditionally, technical staffs were expected to play the lead role in driving projects forward, because they had the technical knowledge needed to implement viable solutions. Business staff played a secondary role, providing guidance to the technical staff from the sidelines. As mentioned earlier, this approach led to a number of unfortunate consequences. For one thing, technical staff developed solutions that were not pertinent to the true needs and requirements of customers. For another, because technical staff did not operate according to a business discipline, they would develop deliverables that lacked business sense (e.g., they would spend $100,000 to create a deliverable whose market value was $80,000). Finally, with technical staff in the driver's seat, there was a tendency to look for technically perfect solutions, when good enough solutions were all that were needed. The search for perfection often led to cost overruns and schedule slippages.

In the 1990s, however, it became clear that projects should be driven by the business, and the role of the technical team should be to enable the business requirements to be achieved in an effective fashion. The problem with this new approach is that businesspeople seldom know how to identify their needs and wants and to formulate them as requirements. Consequently, even with businesspeople leading the project effort, difficulties with translating business requirements into technical requirements continued to prevail.

One approach to dealing with this issue has been to employ co-managed project teams, where a business manager and a development manager work together to carry out the project function. The co-managed team acknowledges that neither the businessperson nor the technical person has enough insights to manage the project effort effectively, so why not tap into the collective wisdom of both players? The obvious difficulty with this approach is that its success rests on getting the two managers to work together seamlessly. For example, one question that frequently arises when co-managed teams are formed is: So who is the real project manager of the effort? This is the wrong question. What the two players should ask is: How can we collectively carry out the project management function?

Experience shows that after initial confusion about who's the real boss, co-managed teams can lead projects successfully, providing a balance between technical and business requirements. The trick is to find two managers who are willing to work collaboratively and who will take the time to develop skills enabling them to build on each other's strengths.

MANAGING CHANGING REQUIREMENTS (CONFIGURATION MANAGEMENT)

Scope creep is an acknowledged evil in project management. It occurs when requirements are changed without adequate review and discipline. While the intent of a project team may be to build a horse, what emerges through scope creep is development of a camel. Not only has the deliverable itself undergone dramatic change in appearance and function, but also typically it is produced with substantive schedule slippages and cost overruns.

As a project is implemented, it is likely that its requirements will experience some measure of change. This is not necessarily bad. For example, technological change, or a shift of regulations, or budget cutbacks may force us to reconsider the scope of what is being produced. If requirements are adjusted through a conscious and deliberate approach, we are managing change. If they occur through haphazard means, we face scope creep.

The most heavily employed technique for controlling change today is called *configuration management*. This is a change control technique that arose in the 1950s in the U.S. defense community. At that time, defense contractors were changing the configurations of various weapon systems in response to customer requests, but they were doing so without much discipline. So once a new version of a weapon system emerged, it was difficult to maintain, because no one knew exactly how the system worked, owing to a lack of effective documentation. In response to this messy situation, the Department of Defense declared in the mid-1950s that defense contractors would need to demonstrate that they had in place a change control process to manage changes to the evolving configurations of their products.

While a fully developed configuration management system can be quite complex and can vary dramatically from project to project, it has two features that are universal. The first is that it demands the discipline of *traceability*. The second is that it establishes a formal mechanism for reviewing change called the *change control board* (or CCB). Each of these features will be discussed in turn.

Traceability

As a part of a newly developed product morphs from a specification to a general design element to a detailed design element to a built product, it is important that we are able to trace precisely how we stepped from one developmental stage to the next. We do this by maintaining traceability. Practically speaking, traceability is carried out by employing a coding system. The specification for a part may be given the code number 1234. When the specification becomes a general design element, the code may be GD1234. When the general design component in turn becomes a detailed design element, the new code may be DDGD1234. And when the designed part becomes an actual physical component, it may carry the code PCDDGD1234. By reviewing the code number for a physical component, we are able to trace its whole history.

Employment of this coding system helps suppress scope creep during the development process. As an evolving product moves from specification to general design stage, tests of traceability are conducted on all of its elements. With backward tests of traceability, we start with a general design element and attempt to find its corresponding specification. If no corresponding spec is found, then the general design element is tossed out, because it reflects a feature that has been added, even though it does not appear in the specifications. Should this be an attractive feature, then whoever wants it incorporated into the deliverable must go before a change control board and request that it be adopted. Only the change control board is authorized to change baselines.

With forward tests of traceability, we begin with the spec and trace forward to see if a corresponding general design element has been defined. If it has not, then we must add it.

As we go from the general design to the detailed design stage, and from the detailed design to the build stage, we repeat these tests of traceability. By pursuing this disciplined approach, it is unlikely that new features are accidentally added to our deliverable, or that desired features are left out.

Change Control Board

The change control board, or CCB, is a "murder board" designed to resist unwarranted change. The composition of the CCB is cross-functional. For example, in a business organization, the CCB might have members representing the perspectives of the marketing/sales, finance, IT, engineering, and legal departments. Board members review change requests in terms of their impact on budgets, schedules, and quality. Their job is to treat change requests skeptically. When a change is desired, the burden of demonstrating its desirability rests with the individual requesting the change.

In an organization whose deliverables are substantially technological, a parallel *engineering review board* (ERB) may be established. The ERB's job is to review the technical impacts of change requests. Is the proposed change technically viable? What impact might it have on the integrity of the whole product?

If both the CCB and ERB approve a change request, then it will be granted. If both agree that the change request lacks merit, then it will be killed. If there is a mixed review, then the two boards need to get together to see whether they can agree how to proceed.

Project managers should view CCBs and ERBs as their friends. These bodies are in a better position than project managers to say "no" to powerful players who demand the execution of a particular change. Furthermore, they can view change requests from a multifunctional perspective and can develop a richer sense of the effects associated with adopting a change request than can a single project manager.

CONCLUSION

Requirements define what a deliverable should look like and what it should do. For requirements to be meaningful, they must capture customer needs and wants. Consequently, in order to develop good requirements, we must have good skills in identifying customer needs and wants and in conveying them to the project team. If we don't get the requirements right, then the subsequent project effort is a sham.

Once requirements are created, they face another challenge—there are tremendous pressures at work to change them. Each time a new player comes on board, or customers change their minds on what they need, or technology creates new opportunities, or competitors challenge us with new products, then someone will attempt to change the requirements to reflect the new realities. While by itself change is not bad, if it is introduced unchecked it will lead to scope creep, and this in turn will contribute to cost overruns, schedule slippages, and the creation of jerry-built deliverables.

Today special attention addresses developing requirements at breakneck speed. After all, we live in the Internet era and we must operate at Internet speed. Software developers in particular are trying to create approaches to developing requirements and implementing software solutions quickly. Consider the plight of one software group that operates in the financial sector: "Right now we find that we have to develop a reasonably sophisticated software routine in four weeks for a product that may be on the market only six months!" The general tack taken to develop software quickly is covered under the title *rapid application development* (RAD). Within RAD, a promising approach employed by developers working in the Internet industry is called *time-boxed scheduling*, a technique based on the premise that "you can't have it all." With time-boxed scheduling, customers and developers must work together to identify what subset of their wish list of requirements they should focus on in order to develop a product quickly. Items dropped from the list might be addressed later as enhancements to future editions of the software.

Of course, a danger we face in developing deliverables quickly is that we do not allot sufficient time to understanding needs and converting them to effective requirements. It does not make sense to create products quickly if the products address the wrong set of requirements. To assure that rapidly developed requirements are on target, many software houses wed RAD with another methodology called *joint application development* (JAD). With JAD, developers and customers work closely together to establish requirements that reflect both technical and business sensibilities.

When reviewing requirements and their role in project management, the bottom line is that *requirements must be managed.* There is nothing automatic about establishing them. At the outset, we must be certain that we are addressing the right requirements. Once they are articulated, we must be prepared to control pressures to change them. Projects where requirements are treated as an afterthought are projects that will travel on troubled waters.

CHAPTER 6

SCHEDULE MANAGEMENT: SEEING THE FUTURE BY MAPPING OUT THE PRESENT

CARL PRITCHARD

More often than not, building a schedule is something that's done from the inside out—it's constructed in reverse. As project managers, we are given a deadline and we ultimately work to serve that deadline. Ideally, schedules are constructed in precisely the opposite fashion. We identify the work to be done, put it in its proper sequence, and that becomes the schedule. Both approaches have merit, but both have their shortcomings as well. To better understand the nature and issues associated with both, we will work from the ideal and then examine the more common approach.

The key to success in scheduling is the same no matter the approach. Know the dates when work is to be performed, know which activities drive other ones, and know when the work is due. These simple elements of knowledge have extraordinary power in the hands of an effective project manager. With this information, the effective project manager can guide the right resources to the right tasks, communicate free time and shortfalls, and identify areas of potential risk.

To build an effective schedule, the triple constraint is another important concept. When looking at the three constraints of projects (time, cost, and requirements), we see that each influences the other. No single constraint stands alone. As such, the network schedule cannot be constructed in a vacuum. It reflects the budget and the work to be performed.

BASICS OF NETWORK SCHEDULING

Network scheduling derives its name from its nature—it is a network of activities. It is the act of "hard-wiring" or connecting all of the work that has to be performed. It operates from the premise that all work is, in one way or another, connected to all other work. Nothing is done in isolation. We develop networks so that we know which activities precede others and which activities have to wait. We develop networks to preclude work from being done out of sequence.

Networking is often done by rote or by habit. In washing windows, one doesn't wipe a dry window with a paper towel. Windows are wiped only after the cleaning solvent has been applied. There is an implied network of activity. The actions are done in a sequence that encourages the best practice in ensuring clean windows.

In projects, sequence plays a critical role. Demolition must occur before debris may be hauled away. Computer systems must be backed up before an upgrade can be installed. There is a logical approach to doing the work. In some cases, it *could* be done in other ways, but it wouldn't make good sense. Network logic tells those performing the work, "This is how we do it, and this is the order in which the work should take place."

Back in Chapter 1, the basic nature of projects was discussed. Projects are unique. Thus, the sequence for different projects will be inherently different. While some work will be performed in the same fashion time and again, some of the work must be done in a different sequence to accommodate the shifting needs of different clients. These differences are accounted for in the process of network scheduling. The needs of a project are reflected in the work breakdown structure (WBS), which the *PMBOK Guide* describes as a "deliverable-oriented grouping of project elements." At the lowest level of the WBS is the work package, the smallest deliverable, component, or subcomponent in the structure. Those deliverables may then be broken down into activities, from which a network diagram is organized. Activities are the actual work to be done. They can be assigned costs and resources, and they can be put in their proper order. This is where the actual work of a project is conducted. In some project management references, activities may be further broken down into tasks. In others, the two terms are used synonymously. For the sake of this discussion, "task" and "activity" may be used interchangeably.

Schedule management is built on arranging the activities in a logical fashion from the start to the end. While some project managers leave the end date or end product undefined, such an act is antithetical to the concept of effective schedule management, because the end date frequently drives the nature and the approach to the schedule. Work drives the network. The project's outcome will, in many ways, determine the overall project duration.

For the remainder of this discussion, we'll examine schedule management using the example of a project to create system documentation.

What's the final output? What is the project supposed to deliver? Documents. Systems documents. But what's the form? What's the format? It's going to make a huge difference if the documents are supposed to be leather-bound rather than spiral-bound. It's much quicker to build a three-ring binder than it is a glossy, graphics-intensive brochure. This addresses a fundamental premise associated with schedule management. The other two sides of the triple constraint (cost and requirements) are going to determine the nature of the schedule. If we seek very simple project documentation in a three-ring binder, the project can probably be achieved with minimal headaches. If we want a heavily edited, graphics-intensive, four-color, management-approved document, the effort may take significantly longer. The work to be performed will determine the nature of the activities in the WBS. And the activities within the WBS will ultimately determine the schedule.

Initially, we'll examine this project from the perspective of an ideal environment. That's an environment where resources are unlimited and there are no significant schedule constraints. Later, we'll take a look at the impact of those types of constraints.

RESOURCE-AVAILABLE, UNCONSTRAINED NETWORK SCHEDULES

Even in environments where network schedules are constrained, effective schedule analysis begins from this perspective. In an unconstrained environment, the project manager and the team examine activities in depth for all of their predecessors and successors. Specifically, what has to happen first? What will the activities produce? Who is waiting for the outputs? A simple system documentation project might incorporate the following 10 tasks:

1. Generate initial outline
2. Get outline approval from management
3. Write technical system chapters
4. Write user system chapters
5. Edit technical chapters
6. Edit user chapters
7. Purchase bindings and paper
8. Finalize reproduction schedule
9. Proofread edited copy
10. Print document

Different people will visualize the list in different ways. Some will look at it and see a linear progression of activity. Others will readily identify tasks and responsibilities that can overlap. The differences in perspective are born out of different experiences in documentation and publication. In building effective schedules, a key is to remove as much personal bias from the process as possible. Without personal bias, the schedule may take on a shape or form that saves time or that recognizes perspectives that hadn't been considered in the past.

START NODES AND START MILESTONES

The first step in building a schedule is to generate a *Start* node. While this may seem like an artifice, it is actually an essential element. The *Start* node provides a point to which all other efforts can be linked. In the project management software applications, the *Start* node also makes it much easier to conduct what-if analyses involving a change in the project's calendar start date. Because the *Start* node is a milestone, the graphics programs frequently represent it as a diamond (see Figure 6.1).

It's important to examine the nature of a milestone here. Milestones are activities of zero duration. They have no resources, no costs, and no work associated with them. They either happen or they don't. There is no halfway point on a milestone. The start milestone is not the kickoff meeting. It is not a management approval cycle. It is an event of no duration. The project has either started or it has not. This basic premise applies not only to the start milestone, but also to all milestones within a project. They all require some clear pass-or-fail criterion.

A project's start milestone is frequently associated with management activity, approvals, specific dates, or external performance goals. No matter the driver behind it, it is crucial to remember that the start milestone itself is an instantaneous flash in time. It has either passed or it has not.

All initial work begins immediately after the start milestone, which serves as the initiation point for all other work. In the example of the system documentation project, the next activity would be the first task listed—generate initial outline. Because we don't know the size or scope of the document until we know what it will contain, purchasing bindings

Figure 6.1
Start Milestone

or performing other work would be premature at this point. The diagram now looks like Figure 6.2.

The relationship here allows the migration of start dates based on the preferences of the scheduler. Rather than artificially moving the first day of outline generation, the start milestone becomes the impetus for all other project activity. The Generate Outline task will not begin until the project itself has formally begun.

Once the activities are clearly defined, they can be placed in sequence. Different managers will have different approaches to the work, so the sequence may vary based on individual or professional preference. Initial network schedule development is an exploratory and evolutionary process. As an example, the schedule may evolve as in Figure 6.3. In another instance, it could take on a significantly different look, feel, and shape, as in Figure 6.4.

The seemingly modest variation in appearance can make all the difference in the world in terms of achieving objectives, meeting schedule, or satisfying organizational demands—because the change represents a change not only in the appearance of the network, but also in the way in which individuals will interact, in which deliverables will be prepared, and in which assumptions must be made.

In the first figure, there are assumptions that once management approves, we'll have a sense of the general size and scope of the document,

Figure 6.2
The Initial Work

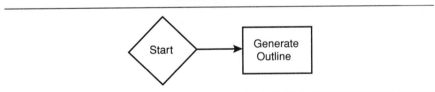

Figure 6.3
One Schedule Perspective

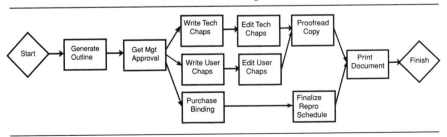

Figure 6.4
An Alternate Schedule Perspective

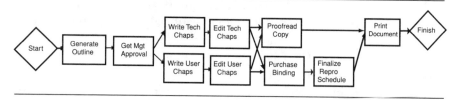

which will enable us to purchase the binding. This may or may not be the case. In order to move forward on this particular approach, we need to validate our plan against the experience of those who have gone before us. Anytime we modify the network, we are modifying the logic that drives the project in a particular direction. Such changes can't be taken lightly.

These diagrams represent two approaches, and as with any project there are other approaches as well. They will be examined later in the chapter. Before we can look at other approaches to the network logic, it's important to examine how this logic drives the project's duration.

DURATION ESTIMATING

No discussion on schedule management can avoid the issue of how to estimate duration at the task and project levels. In many instances, project duration is preordained, either by contract, by management fiat, or by resource availability. For example, resources will be available only through June 1st. The customer has a business need for October 6th. The boss wants it by January 10th. This kind of broad estimate on project duration is rarely rooted in the details. More often than not, it stems from a general overview of the project, a broad assessment of objectives, and a cursory examination of the resources available. That doesn't make it a bad estimate, but it does make it an estimate that needs to be validated.

Validation of such estimates is rooted in the detailed logic and duration estimating at the task level. Only by knowing the duration of the individual tasks can project managers effectively determine the duration of the overall project.

Individual task duration is normally established using the average duration for the task. This means that it is based on the performance of the mythical average worker. If special resources are required to perform a task or to perform it within project specification, such resource requirements should be identified early in the project to ensure they become part of the overall schedule and time management plan. Such information, if lost, becomes the driver for delays. Estimates at the task level can be derived from experience, from those who will actually perform the task, or from others with familiarity with the task and the organization. The estimates are then cataloged as the projected duration for the activity.

The concept of time becomes a major issue in these estimates. If time is recorded as calendar days, then that assumption needs to be documented. A calendar month has 28 to 31 days in it, while a work month has 20 to 23. An elapsed day has 24 hours in it, while a workday has eight hours in most cultures. These measurements become critical in sharing schedule information and in calculating overall project duration.

They also become critical when there is waiting time in the schedule associated with external activities such as procurement. For example, if a contracting staff member says, "The contract should be final in 30 days," there could be a half-month window of difference in interpretation. If the project manager hears "The contract should be final in a month," but the contracting team member believes "There will be 30 days of work until this is cleared," there's a world of difference. When in doubt, ask. And no matter the approach used to do the calculations, document, document, document.

In some cases, building the duration estimate will be a simple function of personal know-how and experience. Question after question must be asked. How long does it take to generate a systems documentation outline? How much experience does the person performing the task have? How detailed is the outline supposed to be? How many levels down should it go? Are there any midterm approvals before it is submitted? What format does it have to be presented in? In many instances, establishing the duration estimate will lead to a refinement of the work to be performed and the approaches to be used. And if such information isn't available in advance, the assumptions used to establish the estimate need to be thoroughly, exhaustively documented. That way, when several minor issues lead to a delay, it becomes easier to understand why the original assumptions were in error, and what could have been done to resolve the situation before it became a problem.

For the sake of this discussion, the estimate on the *Generate Outline* activity comes from an editor who has worked extensively on systems documentation. She says an effective outline should take about 10 hours of effort by a single, skilled individual. Even in that simple statement, there are assumptions. First, it assumes that a single individual will be working on the task. That's very important because some organizations thrive on teams and put teams to work on any task that seems even remotely appropriate. Using a team might cause some problems and some delays in this network. The law of diminishing returns argues that for every activity there is a point at which adding more resources is no longer cost-effective. Four writers would slow down this process, rather than speed it up. Two would indicate a certain level of efficacy.

Furthermore, the editor says an effective outline should take 10 hours of effort by a "skilled" individual. Skill levels and productivity are highly variable. One person's perspective on "skilled" versus another's will be radically different. Skill levels vary not just from organization to organization, but from individual to individual.

PRODUCTIVITY CONCERNS

Productivity is a topic that many organizations avoid because of the social and political implications. They fear discussing productivity in a frank and open manner because some team members inherently feel they are more productive than they are in actuality. Organizations also fear discussions on productivity because of the potential for legal action relating to any system that labels individuals based on action or performance.

Still, productivity is something that should be, at the very least, acknowledged, as it has a direct influence on an organization's capacity to complete a project on time, according to schedule. Take the very simple task of assembling a table from a large discount furnishings store. The package comes with all of the essential parts, as well as clear direction on the tools to be used. In some instances, the package may also cite an average completion time for the effort.

For the individual putting together a table of this type for the very first time, several issues will play into his or her level of productivity. Does the person perform this type of assembly often? Are the recommended tools readily available? Does the individual understand the construction and the nature of the finished product? All of these considerations will contribute to the duration of the project. The more productive individual will be the one who knows the work, has the tools, and understands the finished product. It's common sense. Even so, many organizations do not allow managers to take these considerations into account when establishing duration. It becomes an exercise in political sensitivity.

If such sensitivity can be overcome, and if some common metrics can be established for the implementation of the practice, there are basic formulas for factoring productivity into task duration estimates. At its simplest, it is a function of dividing the total number of hours at 100 percent productivity by the percentage of productivity being applied. A 10-hour task performed by someone who is 70 percent productive would be calculated as:

$$\frac{10}{.7} = 14.3 \text{ hours}$$

This calculation perspective provides a more realistic expectation associated with the individual performer responsible for the task, but from a schedule development perspective, it can become an administrative nightmare. This type of calculation is an asset to the project in that it renders the estimate more accurate and precise. It is a detriment to the project plan in that the estimate is now tied solely to the performance of a single individual. If the team member assigned to the task changes, then the performance expectations may also change. It's clearly a trade-off, and a decision has to be made as to which issue is more important to those building the schedule.

If productivity measures or metrics are applied on a regular basis within the schedule, the foundation information for those metrics needs to be maintained consistently with the rest of the schedule information. Such documentation becomes a vital link back to the understanding on which the schedule is constructed. It also allows future project managers to either incorporate the information or discount it from their considerations.

Ultimately, the duration of the activity must be determined. How long will it take? If the activity starts on Monday, when will it actually end? What is the elapsed time? Whether or not productivity factors are applied, whether or not availability is taken into consideration, some clear duration must be assigned to the activity. In the project management software applications, there is often an option to select the duration either as work time or elapsed time, as discussed earlier. But ultimately, a single piece of information must be assigned as the activity's duration.

Once that bit of data is assigned to every activity, it's possible to assess the schedule as a whole and to determine how reasonable it may be.

PROGRAM EVALUATION AND REVIEW TECHNIQUE (PERT)

In some instances, schedule duration will not be based on a single data point. The Program Evaluation and Review Technique (PERT) was developed as a risk tool, with the intent of ensuring that estimates are built on the best possible information. Managers often use "PERT chart" as a colloquial term for the project network diagram. A PERT chart is not synonymous with a network diagram. More specifically, a PERT chart refers to a network diagram that incorporates PERT data, and very few of them actually do.

To develop the PERT estimates for any given activity, three data points must be evaluated:

1. Best case, or optimistic
2. Worst case, or pessimistic
3. Most likely scenario, or simply most likely

In the PERT formula, those three data points are weighted and then averaged. The most likely estimate is given the heaviest weight (four times the value of either of the others) because it is most representative of the duration that will probably occur. The formula for PERT is:

$$\frac{\text{Optimistic} + 4\text{Most Likely} + \text{Pessimistic}}{6}$$

The PERT formula tends to drive activity durations that are slightly longer than the duration as established by the most likely estimate. In large part, that's because there is a limit to human capability and optimism, but there are few boundaries on our ability to perceive how poorly a given endeavor can turn out. Thus, PERT tends to yield more negative (conservative) estimates than single data point estimates.

DATA ENTRY AND NETWORK CALCULATION

Whether the project manager decides to use PERT, productivity and availability factors, or just plain single data point (most likely) estimates, the information needs to be incorporated into the network diagram. In the best case, this is done as a team, with team members reaching consensus on the duration for each activity. In the worst case, it is done in total isolation, with team members only receiving their assignments and duration as they prepare to begin their tasks. Duration estimates are integrated into the network as shown in Figure 6.5.

With those estimates in place, it's now possible to get an accurate picture of how long the project might take. There are a variety of ways to do

Figure 6.5
Network with Duration Estimates

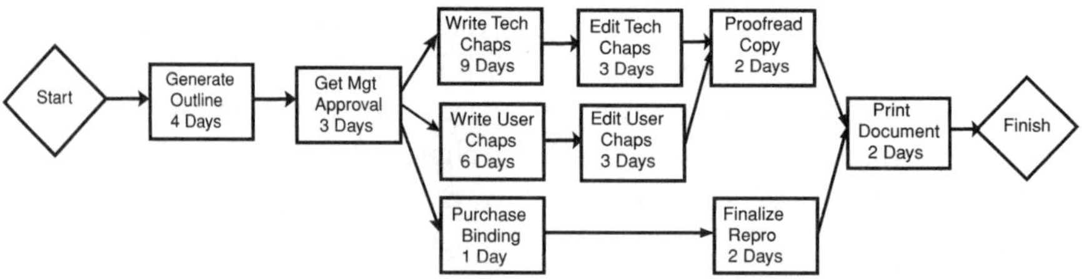

the network calculations, but the first and simplest is to follow the various paths within the network, looking for the highest numbers. By tracing the single path with the highest aggregate number, it's possible to get a quick assessment of the total project duration. In this instance, that path is relatively easy to identify: The longer duration of the *Write Technical Chapters* activity signals the project's longest path (as highlighted by the bold arrows in Figure 6.6). Even so, given that most networks are not this simple and that there is other information that should be derived, it's important to work through the math to affirm which activities occur at which times.

The easiest way to calculate the math is to establish the Early Start and Early Finish based on a 24-hour clock. This assumes that a day begins at 8:00 A.M. and ends the following day at 8:00 A.M. While most tools do project managers the service of calculating to an eight-hour clock, the 24-hour clock makes manual calculation significantly easier to accomplish.

Calculating Early Start (ES) and Early Finish (EF)

Early Start (ES) times are established based on the Early Finish (EF) of their predecessors. If there is no predecessor (except the *Start* milestone), the ES is 0. With the ES established, it's possible to calculate the EF of an activity by simply adding its duration to the ES. Thus, ES + duration = EF. The *Generate Outline* task has an ES of 0 and an EF of 4, based on its four-day duration. *Get Management Approval* is the next task in the network. Since *Generate Outline* finishes at 8:00 A.M. on Day 4, *Get Management Approval* can begin at 8:00 A.M. on Day 4. The ES of *Get Management Approval* is the same as the EF of *Generate Outline*.

For the first seven or eight activities, the calculations are rather simple (see Figure 6.7). The trick, or challenge, comes in dealing with calculations where multiple paths feed a common node. Both *Edit Technical Chapters* and *Edit User Chapters* must be completed before the *Proofread Copy* ac-

Figure 6.6
Network with Critical Path Highlighted

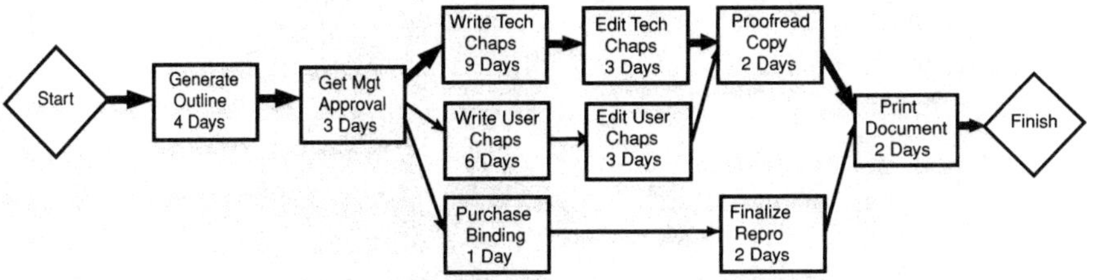

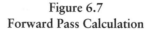

Figure 6.7
Forward Pass Calculation

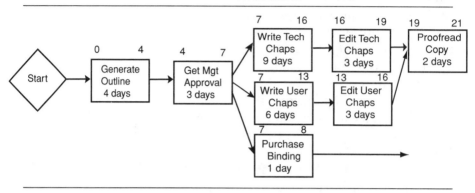

tivity can get under way. As a result, the proofreader must wait until *all* of the editing is done. (There may be other approaches, but for the sake of this discussion, the network as documented currently calls for all editing to be completed before the proofreading begins.) As the network is currently developed, the technical chapters will be complete on Day 19. The user chapters will be complete on Day 16. Because both have to be done before the proofreading activity can begin, proofreading will start on Day 19. At that point, *all* of the predecessors will be complete. Similar logic drives the *Print Document* activity to an early start of Day 21 (see Figure 6.8).

Using this technique, known as the forward pass, we're able to establish the Early Start (ES) and Early Finish (EF) for each activity. We're also able to identify where there is a particular type of free time available, known as *free float*. Free float is the time available after the completion of one activity until the Early Start of its successor. With these activities, for example, there is free time between the completion of the *Edit User Chapters* activity and the *Proofread Copy* activity. There are three days of free float. If a team member is assigned for the duration of the project, an awareness of those three days becomes critical. With staff billing full-time (or even part-time) to a project, the identification of free float gives the project manager something specific to manage—the free time of team members who might otherwise not be engaged in project activity. The *Finalize Reproduction* activity also has a lot of free float. From the time that activity is complete until the next one begins, there are 11 days of free float. Given this volume of free float, the project manager may decide to release that team member back to the organization, rather than pay for his or her time.

Note that free float addresses the amount of time from the EF of one ac-

Figure 6.8
Forward Pass Calculation *(Continued)*

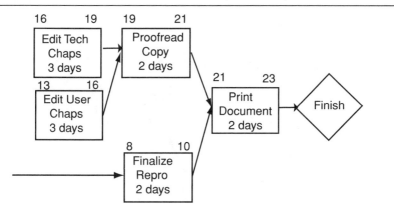

tivity to the ES of its nearest successor. As a result, *Edit Technical Chapters* and *Proofread Copy* have no free float. As soon as those two activities are complete, the next activity will begin. The proofreader is waiting for that editor. The printer is waiting for the proofreader. This distinction is important, because there is another type of float that may still afford the project manager options in terms of schedule management. To determine how much of that float exists, the project manager must perform a "backward pass." A backward pass is an analysis to derive the Late Finish (LF) and Late Start (LS) of each activity by working backward through the network.

Calculating Late Start and Late Finish

From the end date of the project, it's possible to ascertain how late each activity can be completed and still get the project done on time. The process is very similar to that done for the ES and EF, just in reverse, and starting from the *Finish* node of the project. Here, however, the calculations are done from right to left, and the information is cataloged below the activity (see Figure 6.9).

Now the activities have Late Start (LS) and Late Finish (LF) times. Note that the Late Finish of *Proofread Copy* is Day 21. That's the same as its Early Finish, which is indicative that the task is critical. That's because it has no *Total Float*. Total float differs from free float in that it is derived by subtracting the Early Finish of an activity from its Late Finish.

For most of the activities in Figure 6.9, the total float mirrors the free float. However, on some of the earlier activities, there's a differ-

Figure 6.9
Backward Pass Calculation

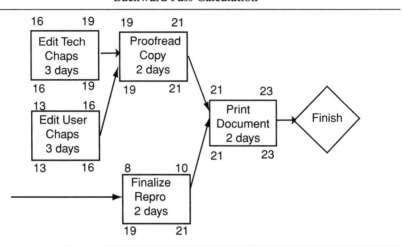

ence. In Figure 6.10, *Write User Chapters*, for example, has no free float. If it were delayed by a day, the next activity would be delayed (from its Early Start) by a day. But it does have total float. The Late Finish is 16. The Early Finish is 13. That means there are three days of total float. In some circles, total float is colloquially referred to as network float or path float because it is a function of the path within the network. *Write User Chapters* can be delayed by as much as three days without having an impact on the overall duration of the project. Because it has no *free* float, even the smallest delay will have an impact on the next activity. But in terms of extending the total project duration, there are three days of leeway.

The two approaches just discussed are known as the forward pass and the backward pass, and are fundamental concepts in network diagramming. The forward pass is an analysis of the network beginning from its start date to establish the Early Start and Early Finish of each activity. The backward pass analyzes the network beginning with its completion date and working from the last activities to the first to determine the Late Finish and Late Start of each activity.

In precedence diagramming, however, there are additional concepts that have to be considered to take more advanced relationships into account. Specifically, those alternative relationships need to account for

Figure 6.10
Backward Pass Calculation *(Continued)*

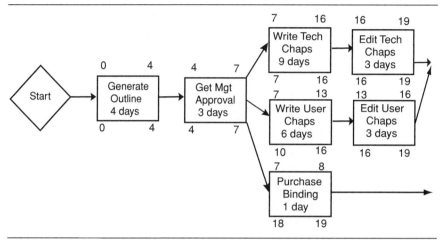

some of the overlapping activities inherent in modern project management.

All of the relationships discussed up to this point have been linear in nature—finish to start. *Generate Outline* finishes, and then *Get Management Approval* may start. In many projects, particularly those that involve multiple functions and numerous resources, there are some activities that inherently have a degree of overlap. Those relationships are, primarily, Finish-to-Finish and Start-to-Start.

FINISH-TO-FINISH RELATIONSHIPS

A Finish-to-Finish relationship ties the completion of one activity to the completion of another. In a tree-trimming project, for example, the work crew cannot finish grinding the trimmed branches into mulch until the trimming crew has finished trimming the tree. The two tasks may run concurrently for the most part, but in the end, the finish of the grinding relies on the completion of the trimming.

It is the finish of the activities that drives the relationships. No matter how efficient the grinders may be, they must still wait until the last branch falls before they can finish mulching the last branch and thus finish their work.

Finish-to-Finish relationships are driven exclusively by the finish, rather than the start of an activity. Suppose grinding mulch was a three-day activity that included generating mulch from other yard waste. If trimming the tree was scheduled for two days, and the two were to finish simultaneously, grinding mulch would start *before* trimming the tree. Even so, the completion of grinding mulch would *still* be driven by the finish time of the tree work.

START-TO-START RELATIONSHIPS

A Start-to-Start relationship dictates that one activity starts and then its successor may start. Other relationships are driven by the start rather than the finish of their predecessors. One activity starts and then another may start. Some start concurrently, but one is more important than the other is. In some regulatory settings, for example, the regulatory process *must* begin before any other work of a particular nature begins. The approvals don't have to be complete, but the process must be initiated. In other cases, however, some lag is applied between the activities to allow for a time-phased approach.

In myriad business situations, a process merely has to get under way to begin a cascade of other activities. Approvals processes begin and meetings begin. A move begins and materials shipping begins. A reorganization begins and job application cycles begin. In all of these instances, it is the start of one activity that initiates others.

LAG

Lag is the amount of waiting time that is applied between precedence relationships. Two tasks in sequence might be *Mail Invitations* and *Review Responses*. While the two are in sequence and no other work must be performed between them, it is unreasonable to expect that they can be done without some waiting time in between. That waiting time is lag time. Lag time allows the project manager to take the waiting time into account without assigning it as part of the overall project duration. If the *Mail Invitations* activity involves a day at the mailing house for one administrative resource, it should cost the organization one day of that administrator's time. However, there is a propensity among some managers to assign the wait time as part of the overall duration of the *Mail Invitations* activity. As such, the activity would need to have a duration of roughly two weeks. In most of the popular project management software packages, the tools would account for that same administrator's cost for every day during those weeks, even though the work really only occurs on the first day.

Lag time is the avenue to avoid that problem. Lag is assigned on the relationship between activities, rather than to the activity itself. Thus, after *Mail Invitations* finishes, the project manager could apply nine days of lag (to account for the remaining business days in the overall two-week duration), and then start the *Review Responses* activity. The administrator will be properly charged to the project, and if there is a change in the lag time (for example, mail strike or new express mail service), the changes will affect only the schedule, not the cost of the activities involved.

Lag is normally (in the project management software packages) expressed as a supplement to the relationship. Finish-Start plus four days (FS + 4d), for example, would indicate that the predecessor activity must finish and four days must pass before the successor can begin. Lag is an undervalued element of many schedules, and because of project managers' failure to apply it properly, resources are sometimes mischarged to a project or important schedule waits are overlooked.

In some situations, there is the opportunity to jump ahead, rather than fall behind. That's known as lead time.

LEAD

Lead time allows project managers to massage the precedence relationships by shifting the time frame ahead by a few days or a few hours. Lead time indicates that while the relationship between two activities is important, there is still a little bit of time in which the team can get a head start on the work to be performed. In the conventional, serial, Finish-to-Start relationship, for example, lead time can be applied when the project manager knows that most of the work must be finished before the next activity can start, but a few loose ends may be outstanding when the successor activity gets under way.

Lead is normally (in the project management software packages) expressed as a subtraction from the relationship. FS – 3d would indicate that the predecessor activity must finish, but three days before it does, the successor may begin.

PUTTING IT ALL TOGETHER

While project management software packages have the tools to present all of this information in a host of different ways, the best approach is often still the classic calendar view. Working through the network schedule and translating the days into a calendar reduces confusion for team members (and for the manager). The translation process is relatively simple.

A traditional calendar might look something like the one in Figure 6.11. The numbers in the upper left are the conventional calendar dates. The numbers in the center are the project workdays.

It then becomes a simple matter of transposing data from the network diagram to the calendar as shown in Figure 6.12. And from this format, conventional management practices can readily apply. The information is easily communicated to the team, and potential resource overloads and conflicts can be easily visualized.

MANAGING THE SCHEDULE

Once in place, the schedule is not a monolithic document. It flexes with time and change. It is affected by the vagaries of business. Fortunately, such change does not mean that the manager's efforts are for naught. Earlier, free float and total float were identified. During times of change, these notions become all the more critical, as float is frequently the only

Figure 6.11
Conventional Calendar with Project Workdays

Monday	Tuesday	Wednesday	Thursday	Friday
1	2	3	4	5
0	1	2	3	4
8	9	10	11	12
5	6	7	8	9
15	16	17	18	19
10	11	12	13	14

Figure 6.12
Schedule in Calendar Format

Monday	Tuesday	Wednesday	Thursday	Friday
1 Generate Outline	2 Generate Outline	3 Generate Outline	4 Generate Outline	5 Get Mgt Approval
8 Get Mgt Approval	9 Get Mgt Approval	10 Write Tech Chaps Write User Chaps Purchase Binders	11 Write Tech Chaps Write User Chaps Finalize Repro	12 Write Tech Chaps Write User Chaps Finalize Repro
15 Write Tech Chaps Write User Chaps	16 Write Tech Chaps Write User Chaps	17 Write Tech Chaps Write User Chaps	18 Write Tech Chaps Edit User Chaps	19 Write Tech Chaps Edit User Chaps

schedule element that a project manager actually gets to manage. By knowing where the schedule has some modest flexibility (courtesy of float), the manager can draw down resources from those more flexible areas and apply them to more time-sensitive elements. These scheduling approaches also encourage the involvement of team members in the development of the schedule, and increase their understanding of how and when the schedule may be forced to change.

To keep the schedule dialogue alive, the project manager needs to constantly and consistently communicate the current schedule status to the team. Even the simple calendar view can provide this level of documentation, as shown in Figure 6.13.

Team members can see their progress. Those facing delays can get a sense of what other tasks are moving forward (or pending) related to their delay. The key is communication. Calendars and other similar vehicles (e.g., Gantt charts, action item lists) facilitate schedule understanding. They open the door for a better appreciation of what work needs to be done and when it's going to be accomplished.

BEYOND THE MECHANICS

While these are the fundamental mechanical issues of building networks and planning schedules, the issues addressed extend well beyond the mechanics. Schedules involve the most precious element of individuals' lives. While fortunes may be made or lost in the course of projects, time slips away inexorably. There is no recovery. To squander time is the most wasteful act of all, and most people are acutely attuned to when and how well their energies are being applied. By drawing in team members to participate in the scheduling process and by ensuring they have the opportunity to identify alternative ap-

Figure 6.13
Updated Schedule in Calendar Format

Monday	Tuesday	Wednesday	Thursday	Friday
1 ~~Generate Outline~~	2 ~~Generate Outline~~	3 ~~Generate Outline~~	4 ~~Generate Outline~~	5 ~~Get Mgt Approval~~
8 ~~Get Mgt Approval~~	9 ~~Get Mgt Approval~~	10 ~~Write Tech Chaps~~ ~~Write User Chaps~~ ~~Purchase Binders~~	11 ~~Write Tech Chaps~~ ~~Write User Chaps~~ ~~Finalize Repro~~	12 ~~Write Tech Chaps~~ ~~Write User Chaps~~ ~~Finalize Repro~~
15 ~~Write Tech Chaps~~ ~~Write User Chaps~~	16 ~~Write Tech Chaps~~ ~~Write User Chaps~~	17 ~~Write Tech Chaps~~ ~~Write User Chaps~~	18 Write Tech Chaps Edit User Chaps	19 Write Tech Chaps Edit User Chaps

proaches and relationships, project managers can improve the team's understanding of the work to be performed, as well as their own.

Getting the team involved is not an easy feat. Given the opportunity, team members will challenge schedule approaches, argue over dependency relationships, and quibble about the need for particular activities. Encourage it. Foster it. Post the network diagram in a room and let them have at it with pencils, Post-it Notes, and whatever other creative tools may be at your disposal. The arguments settled over a whiteboard in a conference room are far preferable to heated discussions in the field over concept and approach.

And while management often perceives the schedule to be a fixed, monolithic document etched in granite, project managers need to see it as a living, breathing, *changing* document that acknowledges the realities of professional, procedural, technological, and methodological change.

CHAPTER 7

ACCOUNTING AND FINANCIAL MANAGEMENT: FINDING THE PROJECT'S BOTTOM LINE

FRANK TONEY

$\mathbf{I}$t is broadly recognized within industry and supported by a body of research data that the knowledge of accounting and finance tools is critical to project and associated career success. Superior project managers of the most successful project groups critically analyze alternatives and opportunities and control the performance of their organization by relying heavily on accounting and financial tools. Consequently, the objective of the chapter is to address accounting and finance topics that will assist project managers and project groups to speedily, efficiently, and effectively achieve the project's goals.

Topics are addressed in a sequential or methodological order much in the same manner they would be encountered on an actual project. Specifically, the chapter outlines the financial tools used to *select* a single project from a portfolio of projects. It discusses the type of decision making information that is used and details how projects are ranked based on forecasted financial return and expected risk factors, and then evaluated in light of pertinent subjective factors. Once a project is selected, it is necessary to address the accounting and financial factors that are used during the *project-planning phase*. The chapter explores financial forecasting and budgeting, identifies risk elements specific to an individual project, describes mitigation plans, and explains the effective leverage of funds, personnel, and equipment.

Once the project is underway, a new set of financial techniques and tools is used for *monitoring and controlling* the project. Topics covered include cost and schedule tracking using earned value and other industry costing techniques; the use of variance analysis as a control tool; and asso-

101

ciated subjects such as make or buy, leasing versus purchase, and effective stewardship of project assets. As the project reaches maturity, it is necessary to plan for *project termination*. Pricing strategy and termination planning are covered. Finally, the process of *following up* the project's results includes warranty estimation and measurement, project performance evaluation, and lessons learned.

BENEFITS FOR THE PROJECT MANAGER

The superior project manager needs to be thoroughly versed in project accounting and finance. These disciplines benefit the superior project manager in five ways. They:

1. Are core elements resulting in project goal achievement.
2. Constitute key entrepreneurial skills.
3. Help make the *right* decision.
4. Maintain project control.
5. Increase project manager credibility.

Each factor is discussed in detail in the following sections.

Core Elements Resulting in Project Goal Achievement

Figure 7.1 is the result of over 10 years of research conducted by the Fortune 500 Project Management Benchmark Forum. The Forum is a group of 60 large companies that meet every quarter to address project management problems, identify best practices, and support project management-related research. The group supports increased emphasis on accounting and finance as a core knowledge area for superior project managers. In support of this judgment, the figure summarizes factors that have a scientifically validated positive impact on project goal achievement. The influence of the use of accounting and financial tools and analytical techniques permeates every area. Project goal achievement is impacted by several large groups of factors. The factors are categorized in order of importance as follows:

- Superior project manager
- Project office organization
- Host organization
- External environment

Figure 7.1
Factors Impacting Project Goal Achievement

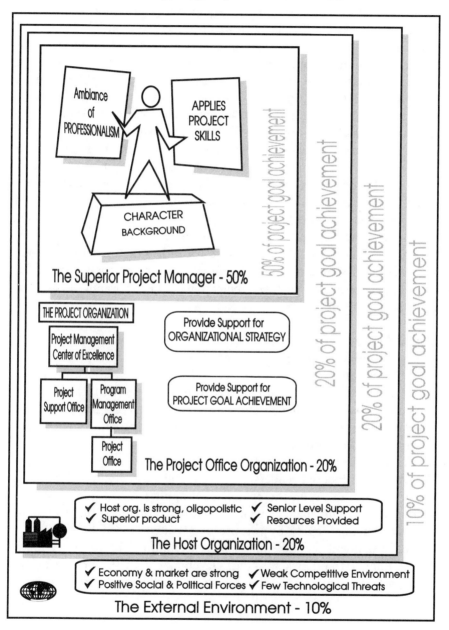

Superior Project Manager

To obtain the highest degree of potential project success, the single most important element is the selection of a superior project manager or leader. Various studies conclude that the leader is directly responsible for 45 to 75 percent of an organization's success. Experienced project executives testify that a superior project manager has the ability to overcome almost any obstacle to project success. The project office organization might be nonexistent; the host organization could be weak; and adverse conditions could be encountered in the external environment. Nevertheless, the superior project manager will give the project the highest probability of success.

To achieve the project's objectives, the superior project manager relies on a large tool kit of accounting and financial analysis aids and managerial approaches. He or she assists in setting the budgets that ensure the project meets its cost and performance targets. Use of analytical problem-solving methods results in correct decisions being made. Truthfulness is substantiated by empirically supported proposals and project control reports. Accounting and financial tools lend themselves to the structured methodologies that are a key to project success. They make possible the pragmatic evaluation of project risks as well as the ability to measure the overall successes and failures of the team's efforts.

Project Office Organization

The project office organization increases the probability of project success by providing direct support to the project manager. Although the project office organizational structure varies from one company to another, it generally consists of a single element or combination of a project management center of excellence, project support office, program management office, and project office.

The project office organization supports the project manager by providing project-focused leadership within the host organization. All of the activities depend on the professional application of accounting and financial tools and management techniques. Portfolios of projects are managed predominately by the use of accounting and finance performance measurements and summarizing techniques. Project selection involves financial and risk ranking. Development of the project group's strategy often focuses upon the financial contributions of the group and its portfolio of projects.

The Host Organization

Project goal achievement is impacted by the host organization. The relationship of the host organization with the project office organization and/or specific projects is generally strategic and financial in nature. Specifically, the projects being performed have been approved primarily because they achieve financial and strategic objectives. Typically, the view of the host organization to specific projects is heavily biased toward bottom-line performance. The ability to use and communicate financial and accounting conclusions is paramount when making presentations or preparing reports for executive offices.

External Environment

There are many remote forces outside the influence of the organization that impact project success. It is the duty of the superior project manager to be cognizant of factors in the external environment and their possible impact on the project. From this knowledge base, modifications can be made to budgets and financial forecasts. Reports and recommendations can be submitted to project stakeholders.

Key Entrepreneurial Skills

Superior project managers essentially perform the same role as the entrepreneurial chief executive officer. In fact, many organizations use the project manager role as a training ground for future executives. As project leaders progress higher within the functional organization, or through larger projects, they will be required to rely increasingly upon accounting and finance.

Making the *Right* Decision

The most successful organizational leaders rely on analytical processes to make the right decisions. The superior project manager strives to *make the right decision rather than simply to build support for a preconceived opinion*. The analytical decision-making approach is heavily dependent on accounting and finance tools.

Maintaining Project Control

There is an old saying in the world of finance that the person who controls the project budget controls the project. If the project manager professes no knowledge of accounting and finance, there is an inclination to delegate these critical leadership functions to other people.

Increasing Project Manager Credibility

Evidence of accounting and finance knowledge can be as simple as understanding the language of accounting and finance. This is particularly important when making presentations to executive-level boards that are focused on the bottom line. There is a tendency to assume that if a person is speaking accounting and finance terminology that the speaker's data is founded on more solid decision-making principles.

ACCOUNTING COMPARED TO FINANCIAL MANAGEMENT OF PROJECTS

Financial management is concerned with the creation and maintenance of monetary value or wealth. Accounting is generally defined as the process of identifying, measuring, and communicating monetary information. With these definitions setting the stage, it is timely to note that many people approach the discipline of accounting with the visual image in mind of the stereotypical bookkeeper. Their view of the discipline is often dominated by mechanical tasks such as record keeping and number crunching. The emphasis of project management is on the managerial aspects of accounting and finance.

There is a danger in that the financial and accounting tools can become an end in themselves, and the project manager can ignore the personal management aspects of the role. An extreme mode of this behavior occurs when the project manager starts thinking that the project plan or budget represent reality and that somehow the project and team members should be conforming to this artificial perception.

BASIC ACCOUNTING CONCEPTS

The world of project management is permeated with accounting and financial factors and variables. The superior project manager must understand the finances of the project itself as well as how the project financially interfaces with the host organization and other stakeholder groups. The fundamentals of accounting are necessary to ensure the project manager is familiar with common accounting and finance terminology and financial statements, such as the income statement, balance sheet, and cash flow statement. Of these, the income statement is most appropriate to project management. The income statement represents the basic approach used by most project managers to develop project forecasts. By modifying the income statement approach to show cash flow coming in at the top of the page and cash expenses below, the income statement effectively is converted to a cash flow projection, budget, or forecast.

The balance sheet is used to show what an organization possesses (assets) and where the money came from to purchase those assets (liabilities and owners' equity). Normally it has fewer applications to projects than the income statement.

ACCRUAL VERSUS CASH ACCOUNTING

In accrual accounting, transactions are recorded in the period in which the revenue or expense occurred. Cash accounting records transactions when money is received or spent. Most people enter the world of project management with an accrual accounting mind-set. Particularly if they have taken accounting courses in school, there is a tendency to think the world is measured by accrual accounting procedures. In reality, project management follows the premise that "cash is king." Virtually all project management and accounting is cash-based. The world of accrual accounting is primarily focused on external reporting in the form of financial statements and for the Internal Revenue Service. For the purposes of project management selection processes, planning, implementation, control, and evaluation, cash flow is the method of choice.

WHY FINANCIAL STATEMENTS RARELY PRESENT AN ACCURATE PICTURE

The superior project manager assumes that financial statements rarely if ever perfectly depict the organization they represent. This surprises many people new to the study of accounting and finance. Many view the discipline of accounting and finance as rigidly controlled with tight guidelines and a highly structured reporting format. In fact, the United States has the most flexible accounting and financial guidelines in the world. Inversely, the least flexible systems are found in socialistic and communistic countries.

The advantage to management of a flexible accounting system is that since every organization is different, a flexible system is needed to present the appropriate portrait. On the other hand, government accounting systems are accused of existing simply to satisfy various legal reporting requirements by "filling in the blanks."

The flexible accounting approach has the advantage that it can be applied to different organizations and projects. Its major disadvantage is that a higher degree of knowledge is needed to apply and to interpret the accounting knowledge and information. In addition, it is easy to present a biased picture or to flavor the presentation with a slanted view. Consequently, the superior project manager soon learns to view any accounting or financial statement with a critical eye.

ETHICS

The major reason to be ethical from a financial viewpoint is that ethical organizations and people are consistently more profitable than unethical organizations and people. Ethics have a direct impact on project success and efficiency.

The cornerstone of ethics is truthfulness. There is a high correlation between honesty and goal achievement. Studies indicate that honesty is so important that it compensates for other major shortcomings in project leadership. When interviewing team members, one hears statements such as, "My project manager has shortcomings, but I am always given an honest answer! I admire that!"

Ethical project teams are consistently more successful, efficient, and effective for several reasons. For example, if sales are associated with the project product or service, they will be higher on the average than those attained by unethical means. The reason is that people like and prefer to deal with ethical people. Inversely, many customers refuse to buy from companies considered unethical.

In terms of efficiency, costs are reduced. The project group and host organization can expect to pay fewer fines and have lower legal expenses. Less time is spent handling disputes. Codes of ethics also give people guidelines for behavior, and the amount of supervision required is reduced. Employees don't have to ask, "What should I do?" so much.

Other benefits accrue from ethical and honest behavior. More durable relationships result. It isn't necessary to start constantly from scratch. The strength of personal networks is increased. Top-quality employees are attracted to ethical companies, and it just plain makes life simpler. Being ethical makes it easier to stay out of trouble.

TERMINOLOGY

As project managers ascend the organizational ladder, an increasing amount of time is directed toward accounting and finance topics. Research data discloses that the board of directors spends from 60 to 80 percent of a typical board meeting on finance and accounting analysis and matters. To be accepted as knowledgeable, it is necessary to understand the terminology of accounting and finance. Some projects involve raising of funds, dealing with public stock offerings, provision of operating credit, and any number of other tasks that involve dealing with accounting and finance experts.

INTERNATIONAL PROJECT FINANCE AND ACCOUNTING

The professional management of international projects is more similar than different in most global locations. After all, the study of project management methodology is an ancient endeavor dating at least to the time of the pyramids. Over the millennia a reasonably universal approach to building a project has evolved. In addition, most project management texts take a generally common approach to managing projects.

There is a much less universal approach to the financial and accounting management of projects in the international arena. Virtually no two countries have the same accounting system and financial reporting requirements. Currencies differ in value, and inflation rates vary wildly. There is an impact on project budgeting, control, procurement, and performance evaluation. Variations in cultural views about secrecy affect public availability of the financial details of a project. It may be difficult or even impossible to remove funds and equipment from some countries after the project is terminated. Generally, the sophistication and education of the users of the information have a direct impact on the quality of information.

APPLICATION OF FINANCIAL MATH TO PROJECTS

Understanding the time value of money is crucial for the superior project manager. This concept is used in all forms of debt and equity project financing. It applies to the evaluation of various project cash flows that occur at differing periods of time, and it enables projects to be ranked using a common standard of money measurement.

Many people fear that time value of money calculations are difficult to master and understand. Luckily, the availability of inexpensive financial calculators has resolved these learning dilemmas.

SELECTING THE PROJECT
Project Portfolio Analysis

To the upper management in most large organizations the projects selected and approved simply represent financial investments. In the early stages of the selection process, all prospective projects are analyzed and ranked according to financial return, risk, and subjective factors. Constraints are always a factor. Rarely is sufficient money available to accept every project proposed.

The trend in many large best-practice organizations is to include the project management team in the project selection process; this is termed end-to-end project team involvement. There is a higher probability of project success as well as financial return to the organization when the project team is aware of the relative importance of each project and how it helps achieve the company's strategic objectives.

Project portfolio analysis falls under the general financial subject area of capital budgeting. The subject is particularly appropriate to the project management of large projects. Capital budgeting involves large amounts of money. Its direct and indirect impacts affect the organization for years. Finally, a poor capital budgeting decision can be a career buster because of the high visibility of the results.

The decisions inherent in capital budgeting will sound familiar to experienced project management executives. Common capital and project budgeting questions are as follows:

- Whether to purchase labor-saving equipment or to perform operations manually.
- How to evaluate projects that have cash flows varying in duration.
- How a cutoff can be implemented to eliminate marginal projects.

The project selection process generally involves the evaluation of three sets of criteria:

1. Financial return
2. Risk
3. Subjective factors

Financial Return

People tend to rank all investment opportunities intuitively by how much money the project will earn. Financial return analysis involves calculating how much money the project will generate compared to its cost. Techniques that are commonly used involve the calculation of net present values (NPV), internal rates of return (IRR), and payback periods. From these calculations, the projects can be ranked according to those generating the most revenue down to those generating the least.

To evaluate a portfolio of projects necessitates ranking them according to expected financial return. Problems arise because rarely do any two projects have the same timing of cash flows. The three project opportunities shown in Table 7.1 serve as a good example. All three projects require a $1,000 investment. In return, Project A receives relatively small amounts of return in the early years but expects a large payoff later in its life. In actual dollars, it forecasts a return of $1,700 or the largest amount of any of the three prospects. Project B has sizable funds coming early in the project life, but its total return at $1,500 is the least of any option. Finally, Project C forecasts a steady flow of funds over its life and records the second best lifetime return in actual dollars at $1,625. From the standpoint of financial return, Project A would appear to offer the greatest potential.

Present Value—NPV and IRR. Intuitively, most businesspeople express uneasiness with the timing of returns associated with Project A. The returns are minimal until the fifth year, at which point a sizable payoff is forecasted. Many things can go wrong in five years, so risk is higher than for Projects B and C, where the payoff is faster. To level the field of evaluation, present value techniques are used. Present value calculations have become easy as a result of numerous inexpensive financial calculators that eliminate the math. Applying the math to the three alternatives results in the data in Table 7.2, assuming a minimum of 10 percent return is required.

Adjustment of all the cash flows to current values results in a different

Table 7.1
Expected Financial Return

Year	Project A	Project B	Project C
0 Investment	($1,000)	($1,000)	($1,000)
1	300	1,500	525
2	300	250	525
3	300	250	525
4	300	250	525
5	1,500	250	525
Total	$1,700	$1,500	$1,625

Table 7.2
Net Present Value, Internal Rate of Return, and Payback Methods

Ranking Method	Project A	Project B	Project C
NPV	$882.34	$1,084.06	$990.16
IRR	20%	79%	44%
Payback	3 years, 4 months	8 months	2 years

view of the project alternatives. Now Project B would appear to be the most financially favorable project. Its net present value is highest, at $1,084.06. Net present value is interpreted as the profit the project will earn *over and above* its 10 percent minimum rate of return. The internal rate of return for Project B is a whopping 79 percent per year. Project A now becomes the least favorable project, with the lowest net present value at $882.34 and lowest internal rate of return at 20 percent.

Payback. The payback method measures the period of time it takes to recover the initial investment of the project. In this case, payback for Project A would be approximately three years and four months; for Project B it would be eight months, and for Project C, approximately two years. Another example would be that if a truck were required for moving dirt on the project, its cost might be $50,000 and it might be projected to save $5,000 per month. Its payback would be 10 months.

Until the advent of computers, the payback method was the most popular one used to evaluate the financial return of investments. It is simple to calculate and easy to understand. It reflects conventional investment wisdom because it encourages fast returns. Its disadvantages compared to present value calculations are that no cash flows are considered after the initial payback period and it fails to consider the time value of money.

Portfolio Risk

It could be tempting to simply select the projects with the highest return. Unfortunately, high-financial-return projects are often saddled with corresponding high rates of risk. Consequently, the superior project manager evaluates the risk elements associated with each project. These are then compared with the expected financial returns. Risk analysis is more difficult than the process of financially ranking projects because there are few well-accepted, simple, and easy-to-understand project risk ranking tools.

Project management involves two types of risk analysis. The first occurs during the project selection process and involves the overall risk inherent in one project when compared to another. The second application of risk analysis occurs during the project planning process. It involves a detailed risk analysis of a specific project. Project portfolio risk analysis is much more difficult than the process of estimating and ranking projects according to their amount of financial returns. Various methods of ranking portfolio risk are as follows.

High-Medium-Low. The most common and easily understood method of risk ranking consists of estimating whether the project is high-risk, medium-risk, or low-risk. Projects can then be grouped into categories.

Weighted Risk Factors. Various key project portfolio risk elements can be listed and given a numerical value. For example, the projects might require new, unproven technology, capital investment could be large and stretch the company's resource base, or there could be stringent delivery time constraints. Each of these factors can be listed on a grid as shown in Table 7.3.

In this example, Project C has the lowest number of risk points. This information would be compared with the amount of potential financial return as well as the subjective factors in making the decision whether to select the project.

Company Project Portfolio Beta. The mathematical average risk for all the projects in the organization's portfolio is called the "company project portfolio beta." The beta is used as a baseline to evaluate the risk of new projects and to diversify the risk of the overall portfolio. For example, if a company has the majority of its project investments focused on the domestic market, it could choose to diversify and reduce overall portfolio risk by focusing new project investments on the foreign market.

Table 7.3
Weighted Risk Factors

	Unproven Technology	High Investment	Stringent Delivery	Total
Project A	5	5	5	15
Project B	4	4	5	13
Project C	3	3	3	9

Note: 5 is highest risk; 1 is lowest risk.

Probability. Although most organizations evaluate project risk by estimating "high-medium-low," it is also possible to apply probabilities of success to various alternatives and subalternatives. An example in the world of project management would be to develop a probability decision tree with each branch of the tree showing the expected probability of occurrence and the expenses or gains associated with the occurrence. This method is particularly appropriate for complex projects with numerous options unfolding at various project phases.

Simulation. An easy way to think of simulation is "change one thing at a time," typically using spreadsheets such as Lotus and Excel. For example, suppose an income statement or cash flow is developed for a new product and the impact of a pending recession is to be evaluated. The team could estimate the impact (say, a 20 percent reduction in sales), plug that into the spreadsheet, and then observe and evaluate the results.

Subjective Factors
Numerous factors other than financial return and risk impact the project selection decision process. For example, the opportunity might not be directly associated with the organization's core competency, or a new product development might be mandatory to fill in a product line. Often the subjective factors are more important than financial and risk factors in the decision processes. Respondents to surveys reveal that some projects are so obvious that there is little need for detailed evaluations. At the other end of the spectrum, some projects offer so little appropriateness and benefit to the organization that further evaluation is pointless.

Relationship to Capital Budgeting

Project portfolio management is constantly faced with the constraint that there is rarely, if ever, sufficient money to initiate every project desired. Consequently, some form of selection process must be implemented. Its objective is to maximize the potential returns of the portfolio of projects, while minimizing portfolio risk and optimizing subjective factors such as the attainment of organizational goals.

Project Selection and the Need for Relevant Information

The information available to assist in making the selection decision ranges from almost nonexistent to nearly infinite. Consequently, the seasoned participant in the selection process will be selective in analyzing only relevant information.

Minimize Sunk Cost as a Factor

Sunk cost is represented by money already spent or invested in a project. In project management as well as financial management, sunk cost is not considered when evaluating future project investments or additional investment in a continuing project. The objective of the approach is simple. It is to protect against the human tendency to "pour good money after bad." It is particularly appropriate in project evaluations where scope has changed numerous times and it is difficult to evaluate future returns related to past targets and investments. In those cases, the evaluators ignore sunk cost, and evaluate the potential future returns related to forecasted costs.

Include Opportunity Cost

When evaluating project alternatives, opportunity costs are pertinent considerations. They represent opportunities sacrificed by making one project investment related to another. For example, if funds are limited, the selection of one project means that another must be sacrificed. It is valid to evaluate the impact of the opportunity lost when comparing more than one project.

Think Incrementally

The selection of projects often becomes confusing. For example, it is common in high-technology projects for a new product to cannibalize or take away from the sales of existing products. In those situations, the recommended approach is to evaluate the incremental sales expected from the project selection.

Include Interest Payments

An occasional misconception in the world of business is that interest payments are not a business expense. The misconception arises because finance texts teach that interest payments are already included in present value calculations and should not be shown as a separate item. Unfortunately, some have interpreted this to mean that they are not a direct cost of doing business. Some companies even show interest payments as a nonbusiness expense on their financial statements. The reality is that interest expenses are a direct cost of doing business and conducting projects and have been a predominate factor in the failure of various enterprises. Consequently, interest expenses should always be included in cash flow projections and project performance evaluations.

PLANNING THE PROJECT

Financial Forecasting: Its Impact on Project Success

Financial forecasting and budgeting are accounting and financial activities shared by most project managers. The manner in which the tasks are performed can have a significant impact on the project. Effective financial forecasting impacts and is used by each of the areas that affect project goal achievement. If the forecast is biased, it will cloud stakeholders' views of the project leader's integrity and the overall knowledge base. For the project organization, it can alter the selection of projects. For the host organization, it could impact the bottom line as well as the attainment of organizational goals. Forecasting should reflect the external environment and expected changes to attain the highest probability of project success.

Methods of Forecasting

Numerous methods of forecasting are used in the project management profession. Almost all involve an estimation of project inflows and outflows of cash. Most experienced forecasters avoid applying accrual accounting concepts to forecasts. This is because the timing lags of the associated cash flows tend to complicate and confuse the process.

Budgeting

Forecasting specific and detailed expenditures is budgeting. The budget ensures that adequate funds are available to perform operations. Typically, budgets involve forecasts of cash expenditures rather than accrued expenses and revenues.

Flexible versus Fixed Budgets. Many organizations prepare a yearly budget. Almost as soon as the budget is completed, the working environment and economic situation change. Inflation may occur, sales may increase or decrease, or a myriad of other events may take place. The result is that the budget is no longer valid. For this reason, many organizations use a flexible budgeting process that involves modifying the budget as conditions change.

Progressive Budgets. A common way to adjust the budget for changing economic conditions is to utilize the rolling budget process. For example, a rolling 12-month budget would involve updating the budget monthly. Each month, the prior month's activities are dropped, and a new estimate is made of month 12. The process is relatively easy, as the only changes made are those dictated by changing conditions.

Leverage and Project Management

Financial planning for projects always involves various types of expenditures. A fixed expenditure remains constant over the life of the project. Examples are machines and interest paid on loans. Variable costs change as the project requirements vary. The most common example of a variable cost is labor. The selection of the balance between fixed and variable expenses has a significant impact on risk and is entitled "leverage." Basically, the more fixed expenses incurred, the more leverage or risk. The reason is simple. If the project falters or the economy enters a recession, the interest and payments on the machines still must be paid. On the other hand, variable expenses such as labor can be modified to fit the situation. Specifically, in time of recession the labor force can be reduced.

Financial Leverage

When organizations or individuals borrow money and make more return than the interest paid, they are using financial leverage. For example, if money is borrowed at 8 percent and earns a return of 15 percent, a gross profit of 7 percentage points is earned. As more and more money is borrowed, risk increases. The payments must always be made even if there is an economic recession or discontinuance of revenues.

Operating Leverage

The concept of operating leverage is similar to financial leverage except that machines and equipment are used to increase financial return. For example, if a task currently being performed by humans can be executed less expensively by a machine, the purchase of the machine represents operating leverage. Risk is increased because the cost of the machine is a fixed cost and must be paid no matter what. Humans, on the other hand, are considered variable costs and can be removed from the project.

Risk Specific to Individual Projects

The prior discussion related to *portfolios* of projects. This section delves into the specific elements of risk associated with *each project.*

Superior project managers rely on empirical support for risk assessment and evaluations. They formally seek ways to mitigate or reduce risk. There is a growing research base of specific actions that affect projects and increase the probability of project success, or, inversely, increase the risk of failure. During the planning stage, a formal effort should be made to define answers to the questions, "What can go wrong?" and "What is the effect of the risk?" If these actions can be further identified, quantified, and combined into a predictive model, the probability of achieving project goals can be measurably improved. Most importantly, contingency plans can be developed to minimize the risk.

Checklists

There are checklists of generic project risks that affect the probability of project goal achievement. (For an example, see the evaluation form in *Best Practices of Project Management Groups in Large Functional Organizations* by Frank Toney, published by the Project Management Institute. Every factor on the form has been scientifically correlated with project success or failure.) Most risk templates list the risk event, estimated probability of occurrence, and financial magnitude of the event. The risk checklist provides a structured way to ensure that all project risks are recognized and evaluated.

Project managers and host companies can supplement the risk evaluation form with items from their own companies and specific situations. A user of the risk evaluation form would complete the chart and fill in risk categories and checklist items. The end product gives a visual picture of the various risk categories and items. Risk events with high probability of occurrence and large financial magnitude would receive the most scrutiny and planning effort to minimize the risk, although a risk mitigation, diversion, or minimization plan would be developed for all items on the checklist that represent significant risk to the project.

The risk analysis evaluation should be a periodic and ongoing process, and would be reviewed at each project milestone. At each review, the relative risk of various factors should be evaluated and updated.

Breakeven Analysis

The point at which a project becomes profitable is its breakeven point. It occurs when all the project's fixed costs have been paid as well as the variable costs related to the productive output of the product. The breakeven point is particularly important to project managers because once it is reached, the project or enterprise becomes much more profitable. Above breakeven, all the fixed costs have been paid. Profit is greater because the only cost is the variable cost of each unit of production.

Make or Buy

Numerous considerations affect the decision to make or buy productive inputs or components for the project. The organization may have excess capacity, the needed item might not be available elsewhere, or there may be concern about security of technology. Usually factors other than cost impact the decision whether to make or to buy.

Lease versus Purchase Analysis

When acquiring assets for the project, payment can be in the form of leasing or an outright purchase. Leasing represents a viable option and often is competitive in price with purchasing. Because the experience of most people with leasing is through automobiles, it is important to note that often automobile leasing represents a sales opportunity on the part of the dealer to get incremental revenue out of the customer. On the other hand, equipment leasing is generally an alternative financing medium. As a result, the rates are more competitive with other funds sources.

MONITORING AND CONTROLLING THE PROJECT

Once the project is underway, the attention of the project team shifts from emphasis on planning to monitoring and controlling the project. Specifically, project control includes all the formal and informal methods of ensuring that the project proceeds as planned. The control process is often compared to a temperature thermostat that detects ambient temperature, assesses the significance of change, and then makes appropriate adjustments. The control process has any or all of the following financial objectives:

- Determining project progress related to goals, schedules, and budgets
- Identifying problems
- Evaluating management
- Making decisions about continuing
- Rewarding management
- Ranking performance

One of the most important control tools in project management is the use of milestones and go-no-go decision points. Both establish a discipline for evaluating the project before proceeding to the next step and incurring additional expenses. It is important to note that project control pertains to both project strategy as well as project tasks.

Cost Accounting for Projects

Conventional costing concepts from the world of accounting are directly applicable to project management. Use of cost accounting techniques is the primary method of tracking project spending. It is as simple as comparing the amount budgeted with the amount actually spent. The result is the variance. Project management software packages have greatly simplified the cost accounting process. An estimate of the cost of each work package is entered. As the actual costs are incurred they are also entered in the work package information. The computer calculates variances from that information.

Even without computers and software, cost accounting is simple to implement. For example, in an automobile service shop it consists of the service ticket that the car owner fills out when bringing the car in for repair. In a factory environment, the service ticket would be titled a job tracker, cost sheet, or similar term. The purpose of the document is to track two basic groups of costs: material costs and labor costs. In the case of the automobile service shop, the mechanic takes the service ticket to the parts department and obtains the parts needed to make the repair. Generally, the price of the parts is noted on the service ticket when they are issued to the mechanic. At this point the material costing portion of the process is complete. The mechanic then completes the job and notes the time taken. The service ticket is then given to accounting where the price of the mechanic's time (usually a standard or flat rate) is calculated and added to the material costs. Finally, the bill is presented to the customer.

The process is similar in a manufacturing environment. The parts department issues the materials needed, and these are noted on the job tracker. The job tracker then accompanies the materials to the assembly line where all the different manufacturing processes commence. Generally the manufacturing stages are listed on the tracker with an estimated standard time for each. As the materials pass each stage of the process, a notation is made on the tracker. The process is simple and easy to manage. The manufacturing status and cost of work in process of several assembly lines can be determined by walking out to the lines and noting the stage of production on each of the job trackers.

In a project environment, the service ticket and job tracker are replaced by the project schedule, which is most commonly represented by a software-driven Gantt chart. If the information on the project schedule has been maintained, it is a simple matter of pushing a button on the computer to determine the status and variances related to the project.

The various types of costing systems detailed in cost accounting texts all start with estimated costs that are then compared with actual costs. There are two types of variances commonly used: the *amount* of any resource used (for example, the number of people) and the *per unit cost* of each resource (for example, the estimated cost per hour of a person). The difference between the costing systems is the type of measurement performed.

Job Order Costing Applied to Project Management

Job order costing applies costing concepts to jobs that have a specific beginning and end and include clearly definable units of production. In a project environment, it could pertain to the activities or segments between each milestone, individual work packages, or even the total project.

Job order costing measures the cost to produce a group of products or services. For example a batch in a sporting goods factory might be 50 baseball bats. Total material and labor costs to build the batch of bats would be recorded. To determine the cost of one bat would entail dividing the total cost recorded by 50.

Process Costing

The difference between job order and process costing is that job order costing measures the cost of a group of *units of production*, and process costing measures units produced in *a specific period of time*. Process costing is used in operations such as mining and petroleum production. Over a period of time, projects that have few milestones take on the attributes of a process flow operation. The earned value method of costing summarized next is a derivation of process costing. The schedule-related calculations apply more to projects with continuous flows rather than those with many small, segmented milestones.

Earned Value Costing

Earned value costing consists of two basic elements. The first is to compare estimated total work package costs with actual total work package costs. No distinction is made between number of resources or unit costs of each resource. The second element is to measure time with dollars. It is somewhat analogous to a percentage complete calculation where the amount of money to be expended or work packages to be completed at any point are compared with the number actually completed.

Earned value is emphasized by the Project Management Institute's Project Management Professional (PMP) certification exam. It is also an integral part of many government project management-related contracts. A survey of 60 corporate participants in the Fortune 500 Benchmarking Forum concludes that *none* use earned value to measure time in the same format as that promoted by PMI or utilized by the government. The complaint is that earned value is complicated and difficult to understand. In particular, the conversion of schedule time delays into dollars and cents is a troublesome concept to visualize.

Most companies resolve the schedule control problem by planning projects with numerous milestones and measurement points. Upon arriving at the milestone, it is a simple matter to observe whether the project is ahead or behind schedule. Where milestones are impractical or project status is required between milestones, earned value or some other form of percentage complete calculation represents a logical costing approach.

Activity-Based Costing

Most large projects lend themselves to activity-based costing. The cost of an entire activity is measured over the period that the activity is underway. It is particularly appropriate if a project spans multiple accounting periods. Traditional accounting is geared toward closing the books at the end of major periods such as at year-end. With activity-based costing, the costs and revenues would continue to be recorded over the life of the project.

Life Cycle Costing

The entire life of a product is the measurement standard for life cycle costing. It is often encountered in the project management environment, particularly in association with new product evaluation. Life cycle costing differs from other costing methods because it normally includes revenue as well as material and labor costs. Life cycle costing can have dramatic impact on new product selection and strategy. Numerous products have greater cash flows after the product has been sold than before. For example, some computer printers are sold at low prices with the company planning to make their lifetime profit from the sale of toner. When evaluating the life cycles of capital goods and machinery, there are sizable cash flows after the sale of the product, including such items as repair parts, maintenance, potential to move up to larger models, added features, trade-in potential, and salvage value.

Standard Costs Related to Project Costs

During the project planning process, the costs for each of the tasks comprising project work packages are estimated. These estimated costs become the standard costs of the project. They have counterparts in nearly every industry. In the auto service business they are termed flat rates. They are used primarily because it is easier to use an estimate than to calculate actual rates, and actual costs are not known. After the project starts, actual costs begin to be accumulated. Comparing the actual costs with the estimated or standard costs results in "variances."

Variance Analysis and Performance Evaluation

Once the project is underway, the *actual* expenses and bills related to each work package are paid. These are then compared with the *estimated* work package costs using any of the costing techniques described in the previous paragraphs. The difference between the estimated and the actual costs are the variances.

Project Value Analysis

Value analysis refers to the formal process of eliminating cost from the project or the project's product and service. Value analysis is a goals-oriented method for improving project, product, or service value by comparing elements of project, product, or service value or worth with their corresponding elements of cost. The objective of value analysis is to accomplish the goals of the project, product, or service at the minimal cost.

This process is necessary because often cost is not the major consideration during the project planning process. Generally planners focus on including every element, work package, and activity. The emphasis is on establishing time and budget definitions. If a new product is being designed, the perspective is usually on performance and meeting specifications. During all these activities, cost is a secondary element. If the project is of long duration, say several years, the constant influence of external economic factors encourages higher labor rates and more expensive materials, and increases in the overall cost of doing business.

There is a tendency for costs to increase even more as unforeseen events occur and schedules change. Often in the haste to get under way or to design a product against a deadline, quality features and activities may be added that do not contribute to the product or overall project suitability.

From this view, the extra quality, detail, and features represent wasted expenditures. More so, the cause of the cost may result in continuation of the problem. The value analysis is a formal process to review the project and/or its associated product or service with the objective of reducing costs without impairing efficiency, effectiveness, or suitability of the product or service.

Pricing Considerations

The process of setting prices on products associated with projects involves many disciplines including psychology, costing, market evaluations, and organizational strategy. When global pricing implications are included, the considerations impacting pricing are expanded. Included are international tax regulations, restrictions on expatriation of funds, intercompany costs and transfer considerations, specific country competitiveness, and many other factors.

Asset Turnover

One of the fastest and easiest ways to generate cash is to increase asset turnover. Inventory turnover is the most common example. If a company has a $1 million inventory and it takes a year to sell it, there is an inventory turnover of one time per year. By buying only one month's worth of inventory at a time, inventory turns increase to 12 times per year. Since the inventory is sold in one month, only one-twelfth as much cash is required ($83,333) as when a year's supply of inventory was on hand. The excess of $916,667 is made available for other applications.

The same principle applies to multifunctional project management. Completion time is much faster when projects are executed in parallel rather than sequentially. Hence asset turnover is increased, more projects are completed, and each project is completed at a faster rate.

Asset Stewardship

Project managers are entrusted with sizable amounts of assets and funds. The concept of stewardship recognizes the fiduciary responsibility of the project manager to protect those assets. Most commonly in the world of finance and accounting, asset stewardship includes protecting the project's assets against theft. There are numerous accounting controls that serve notice that the assets are being monitored and protected.

Audits

An audit involves performing an arm's-length and objective evaluation of the project. Its objective is to serve as a financial and accounting quality control evaluation. Acquisition, uses, and disposition of funds are reviewed. Many project groups expand the role of auditing to include an evaluation of the project's objectives, schedules, and status of deliverables.

PROJECT TERMINATION AND FOLLOW-UP

One of the most overlooked activities in planning for a project is the termination process. Many project plans fail to include termination costs or even the steps necessary to terminate the project. The manner in which the termination process is handled directly impacts the residual attitudes of stakeholders about the project and the project team. Although many human emotional elements dominate the termination process, the financial and accounting aspects of the termination impact the perception of success or failure.

To ensure that the project is terminated in an orderly fashion, most best-practice project managers prepare a checklist of termination activities to perform. Plans are developed to transfer assets back into the host organization or to another project. Accounts are closed, all monies are accounted for, and property and equipment are inventoried. Contracts and agreements with vendors are concluded, and purchasing and other functional areas are notified of the project's termination. Many project organizations require an audit of the accounting and financial records.

The termination phase of the project also includes making plans for project follow-up. The project follow-up planning process includes consideration of such items as setting up new accounts for the goods or services generated by the project and the development of a project follow-up budget.

Premature Termination

Occasionally a project goes astray. In an ideal situation, the decision to terminate will be made on a timely basis. The judgment to terminate any project is generally subjective, although financial performance is invariably a critical element in the decision process. Financial and accounting analysis and supporting data are important tools in answering the following questions:

- Is the project meeting its original goals?
- Is organizational resource support adequate?
- Could the project be contracted to outside vendors?
- Could the project's product or service be purchased or subcontracted?
- Is the project profitable?
- Is the project cost-effective?
- Could the project be integrated with an ongoing operation of the host organization?
- Are there more profitable applications of the funds being expended on the project?
- Have any profitability or return-on-investment elements of the project changed?

Lessons Learned

Superior project managers evaluate the project's successes and failures. From these, lessons learned are recorded for the benefit of future projects. Some best-practice companies review lessons learned from prior projects at the kickoff meetings for new projects.

The lessons-learned document is the method of transferring knowledge and learning from project to project. Some project groups use a generalized lessons-learned template to guide a structured review of the project. Others wait four or five months after completion to ensure all information is available. At that point, they can draw arm's-length conclusions and more accurately identify things that went wrong. They also look at factors that can't be changed. Lessons learned can be tied to the project assessment process and should be prepared at each milestone.

The financial management approach to lessons learned is to quantify or convert to dollars and cents each of the lessons. The review team can start with an overview comparison of total project costs with estimated costs. Reasons for the variances can be discussed and recorded. The variances can be ranked in terms of financial impact on the project. The team can then attempt to identify the costs of errors and problems. All of this information is used to place a price on future risk items. The transfer-of-knowledge process results in a more precise risk-weighting process.

Communication of Project Contributions

Superior project managers and best-practice project organizations measure the impact of the project on the host organization's bottom line. Measurement of the project group's performance is crucial to ensure that the benefits of project groups are recognized and that continuous improvements are made. To project managers, the benefits and positive results of the project effort seem clear; but the portrait is often opaque to senior executives and others in the organization. The situation is accentuated because, historically, project management groups have not always quantified and measured the bottom-line benefits of implementing cross-functional project management groups in their organizations.

Warranty Preplanning

Many projects produce a product or service. Companies often agree to provide free service on units that are defective or fail to perform properly. When these costs or warranties are expected to be minor in nature, the project team will need to allocate little attention to their implications. However, if the warranty costs are expected to be sizable, it is necessary to estimate the size of the obligation. It is not uncommon for excessive warranty costs to have an impact on the perception of stakeholders about the overall success of the project.

Warranty costs are usually estimated based on past experience. In situations involving a totally new product or service, the warranty estimate can be based on an analysis of individual components and experience gained during the project development process.

Preplanning for warranty cost often gives the company time to develop a mitigation strategy. Customers can be sold a service contract that results in shifting some of the financial burden. In effect, the service contract is an insurance contract executed with the customer. Warranty preplanning also gives the company time to develop education programs to prepare customers for the expected result. Finally, warranty preplanning provides information needed to budget the cost into future financial statements.

CHAPTER 8

RISK MANAGEMENT: MAXIMIZING THE PROBABILITY OF SUCCESS

RICHARD E. WESTNEY

THE HIGH COST OF PROJECT RISK MISMANAGEMENT

If done well, project risk management will reduce costs and schedule. It stands to reason, then, that project risk management, if done poorly or not at all, is likely to increase the cost and time required to complete a project. Let's begin by examining the causes and effect of project risk *mis*-management.

Profits Require Successful Projects

Projects are vital to the success of any enterprise. From a management perspective, a project can be defined as the work required to take an *opportunity* and convert it to an *asset*. A business usually has many opportunities, and, if its projects are successful, these become assets such as manufacturing facilities, information systems, new technologies, or new products. Whether a project results in the creation of a new asset, the improvement of an existing asset, or simply maintaining the value of an existing asset, it clearly has a direct impact on the bottom line.

The importance of the project portfolio is illustrated by comparing a corporation's annual investment in projects to its net after-tax income. It is not uncommon to find an organization's investment in projects to be two to three times its net after-tax income!

Successful Projects Require Project Risk Management

We all know that many projects are completed with costs and completion dates that exceed their targets considerably. Of course, this has a direct and deleterious impact on profitability as well as the achievement of business goals such as market penetration and competitive advantage. *Clearly, to be competitive, an organization must be proactive in managing the risks to successful achievement of the cost and schedule objectives for its projects.*

So the critical issue is, simply, *How well does an organization perform project risk management?* For most organizations today, the answer is, surprisingly, *Not very well!*

Project Risk Management Is Seldom Done Well

Most leading companies today are recognizing the importance of a disciplined, professional approach to project management. Many now consider project management to be a core competence, and they provide the organizational structures to facilitate its effective application company-wide (as discussed in other chapters in this book). To achieve profitability, they focus on critical project variables such as:

- Quality/customer satisfaction
- Cost
- Schedule
- Safety, health, and environmental impact

It is fair to say that enormous improvements have been made in project performance in each of these areas. Most organizations have methods, systems, procedures, and trained professionals to manage them. But there is one remaining project variable, a variable that is geared directly to profitability and yet has, so far, received little attention. Of course, that variable is *project risk.*

Risk is a project variable just like quality, cost, schedule, safety, health, or environmental impact. And risk can be managed using good project management methods, similar to these other variables. This is the essence of project risk management.

When project risk management is done ineffectively, or (as is often the case) not at all, we can call this project risk mismanagement.

Characteristics of Project Risk Mismanagement

There are 10 key indicators characteristic of an organization that suffers from project risk mismanagement. (Use this checklist to evaluate your organization!)

1. *Projects are authorized primarily based on financial criteria such as profitability, with little quantitative consideration of relative risk.*

   We are accustomed to the idea that investment decisions (for example, the purchase of a stock or mutual fund) must always balance risk and return. However, project investments, although of critical importance to the corporation, are often made with little regard for risk. When risk is introduced into the funding discussion, it is usually in a general way with little if any genuine risk analysis to back it up. Is it any wonder that so many projects fail to achieve the profitability objectives that created them?

2. *The corporate culture encourages project "champions" whose perceived priority is to "sell" the project to management.*

   Although we accept that the purpose of a project is to create an asset that achieves its business goals, we often find it hard to accept the idea that projects that will not do so should be dropped from the portfolio. The successful project manager is often viewed as the one who can get a project approved—and this is considered unlikely when risks are discussed openly, fully, and realistically.

   Paradoxically, although those in corporate management are the biggest beneficiaries of a realistic and thorough discussion of risks, they are sometimes uncomfortable with such a discussion (because it makes decision making that much harder). As a result, they consciously or unconsciously discourage project managers from incorporating risk and uncertainty into the project decision-making process.

3. *Management seeks to minimize project cost and time by punishing project managers and teams whose projects overrun their budget or schedule.*

   It is rare to find an organization whose management does not operate with this philosophy. After all, what better way to assure that budgets and schedules are met than to reward those who do so and punish those who do not? Most managers intend for this practice to reduce project costs and durations, and would be surprised to find that it actually had the opposite result!

   Every experienced project or resource manager knows that the best way to avoid the career damage often associated with cost or schedule overruns is to assure that the budget and schedule have sufficient padding to create a very low probability of being exceeded. Of course, this has a number of harmful effects to the profitability of the organization's project portfolio:

- Project budgets and schedules are unnecessarily high and long, so projects inevitably cost more and take longer than they need to. Once the money has been authorized, it generally gets spent!
- Profitable projects will be rejected from the portfolio, either because they appear to be uneconomic (due to the apparent high cost or long schedule) or because the budget is taken up by the swollen estimates for the projects that have been approved.
- A culture of dishonesty, distrust, and lack of communication is formed around the critical subjects of estimates, budgets, and performance appraisal.

4. *Management rejects the concept of cost or schedule "contingency" and forbids it to be included in estimates and schedules (or will accept only a nominal amount).*

   Like the practice of punishing overruns, this practice often has the opposite of the desired effect. Project managers, resource managers, and team members know they need a certain amount of time, money, and resources to do the project. They will inevitably bury contingency in their estimates, in order to gain the confidence they need that they will not have to be embarrassed by asking management for more time, money, or resources.

   A significant drawback to this approach is that everyone contributing to the plan and estimate tends to bury some contingency, so that the total amount of buried contingency is impossible to determine. What is clear is that it is excessive; when organizations eliminate hidden contingencies and adopt formal methods for setting contingency, they often find that project costs are reduced. Once again, a management practice that is intended to reduce cost, time, and resources needed actually results in a culture that increases them.

5. *Projects are managed and judged individually and not as a portfolio.*

   Every project has a probability of success and a risk of failure. It is inevitable that some projects will meet their cost and schedule objectives, and some will fail to do so—some will be profitable, and some will not. Once again, project investments are analogous to our personal investments. In both cases, we know we will have some winners and some losers; what is more important is how well the overall portfolio performs. Placing more focus on the project portfolio means that risks are shared and better performance metrics used. When a project experiences a cost overrun, instead of "fixing the blame" we do better by "fixing the process" by which budgets are set and risks managed.

6. *There is no common language for project risk management. Terms such as "contingency," "risk," "uncertainty," "management reserve," "estimate accuracy," and "probability of success" are not defined, understood, or used in a consistent way.*

One of the reasons corporate and project managers feel uncomfortable discussing risk and uncertainty is the association of these concepts with fear. Knowing that the budget and schedule for the project are uncertain and that there are risks that may cause it to fail makes it rational to be uncomfortable with the uncertainty and fearful of the risks.

Of course, no one likes to be uncomfortable or fearful, so most organizations resist focusing on risk and uncertainty, and on the terms that define them. However, once the terminology is clarified, risk becomes just another variable to be controlled, and the discomfort fades away.

7. *There is no common, consistently applied method for setting or administering cost and schedule contingency. All project managers, planners, resource managers, and cost estimators have their own ways of determining how much contingency they require and their own ways to incorporate it into the schedule or budget.*

As noted earlier, the common practice of motivating project teams by punishing cost and schedule overruns has the effect of project participants padding estimates with hidden contingencies. This problem is made worse by the fact that most organizations lack a common method for setting cost and schedule contingency on a project. As a result, teams eventually learn what levels of contingency their management is likely to accept (usually from zero to 10 percent). They then show that amount in their budgets, and hide the rest.

8. *There is no common, consistently applied method for determining or communicating estimate accuracy.*

Estimates of time or cost are, by definition, certain to be wrong. In fact, cost estimators and schedulers often say that the only thing they can be absolutely sure of, with respect to their estimates of cost or time, is that they are wrong! And of course this is true. So the real question about an estimate of time or cost is not whether it is right (we know it is not) but rather by how much it is likely to be wrong.

The question is answered by how we express estimate accuracy. Without a common, consistent definition of estimate accuracy and a method to calculate it for each project, it is impossible for management to make project investment decisions and optimize the project portfolio.

9. *There is no common, consistently applied method for identifying, assessing, and analyzing risks.*

In the many organizations that lack a formal process for project risk management, project managers tend to address risks in whatever way their experience suggests is best. As a result, experienced project managers who have lived through the problems many projects encounter are likely to recognize the need to cover risks with contingency, as well as to be circumspect about how openly risks are discussed. Of course, less experienced project managers are likely to be too optimistic.

Once again, without a consistent approach, management's attempts to manage the investment in the project portfolio are severely hampered. Decision making often involves selecting which projects go ahead and which are rejected. It may be misguided because some weak projects may look more attractive than they should, while some strong projects, having more realistic estimates, look less so.

10. *There is no common, consistently applied method for risk mitigation.*

Of course, when any of the aforementioned indicators are present, it is unlikely that there will be any effective plans for risk mitigation. Yet this is one of the most important things a project team can do: Maximize the probability of success.

Many of these indicators of project risk mismanagement are the result of attempts to control project risks, and the rest are essentially the result of ignoring them. Yet they all contribute to the reverse of the desired result: Risks are increased, and projects cost too much and take too long. Yet the solution is not that difficult. It simply requires that we move from project risk mismanagement to an effective program of project risk management.

PROGRAM FOR PROJECT RISK MANAGEMENT

Effective project risk management requires that an organization have a well-defined program including standard terminology, work processes, tasks, and training.

Definitions and Basic Concepts

Effective project risk management is inevitably hampered by the general lack of understanding of relevant concepts and terminology. Although many of these terms are defined in different ways, the following definitions work well in the project risk management application. Basic concepts are provided as part of the discussion of the definitions. Terms for which definitions are provided are shown in italics.

Base Estimate

The *base estimate* of cost or duration represents the most likely outcome if everything on the project happens exactly in accordance with the given information and assumptions on which the estimate was based. Since experience shows us that the actual execution of the project will vary from the base estimate, and since such variations (e.g., design changes) are more likely to add time and cost than to reduce them, the *cumulative probability* of the base estimate is usually quite low. The base estimate should be devoid of all forms of *contingency*.

Contingency

Contingency is the provision made for variations to the basis of an estimate of time or cost that are likely to occur, and that cannot be specifically identified at the time the estimate is prepared. Contingency is not meant to cover scope changes or extraordinary random events. Most corporate managers agree that contingency should be the amount required to bring the estimate to the point at which it has a 50/50 chance of overrun or underrun. (See Figure 8.1.)

Cumulative Probability

Cumulative probability is usually expressed as the probability that the project's final cost or duration will be equal to or less than a given value. For example, a project manager might advise management that there is an 80 percent probability that the project's final cost will be equal to or less than $2.5 million. When expressed graphically, a cumulative probability curve usually looks like an S, since it is simply the familiar normal distribution or bell curve expressed a different way. (*Note*: Some practitioners prefer to express cumulative probability as the probability that the final cost or duration will be equal to or *greater* than a given value.) The cumulative probability curve is the result of integrating the *frequency distribution*. Figure 8.1 shows cumulative probability increasing as the estimate of

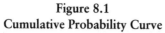

Figure 8.1
Cumulative Probability Curve

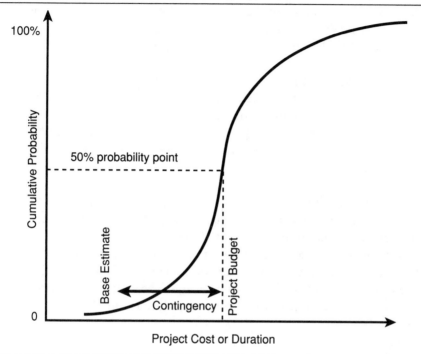

cost or duration increases. The project budget, including contingency, is set at the 50/50 probability point.

Decision Tree

Decision trees are used for evaluating the impact on project success of different choices or events. A probability and consequence are attached to each branch of the decision tree, and expected outcomes calculated for each decision or event.

Estimate

An *estimate* is a prediction of the final cost and duration of the project. The purpose of the estimate is usually to make a decision to approve funds, although detailed estimates are also used for cost control. Because all estimates contain significant *uncertainty*, it is important that the *estimate accuracy* be expressed clearly.

Estimate Accuracy

Estimate accuracy describes how likely the final cost or duration is to be within a specified range of the estimate. To properly express estimate accuracy, one must state both the range (for example, plus or minus 10 percent) and the probability of being within that range.

Frequency Distribution

A *frequency distribution* (often shown as a bell curve) displays the relative frequency or probability of any value of cost or duration. The area to the left of a given value expresses the *cumulative probability* that the final cost or duration will be equal to or less than the given value. (See Figure 8.2.)

Management Reserve

Management reserve is the additional funding that management may wish to set aside in order to be able to fund the project at a higher level of confidence than the budget provides. For example, using the *cumulative probability* curve, the management team might decide to set aside (or assure access to) funds sufficient to have an 80 percent probability that the final cost will exceed the available funding. (See Figure 8.3.)

Mean

The *mean* is the average of all the points in the probability distribution. If the distribution is symmetrical, the mean, *median*, and *mode* are the same.

Median

The *median* is the value for which there is a 50 percent chance that the actual outcome will be higher and a 50 percent chance that it will be lower. It represents the value used for the project budget. (See Figure 8.4.)

Mode

The *mode* is the most likely (that is, most probable) value in the distribution. It is the value of cost or duration that corresponds to the highest point on the *frequency distribution* curve. If the curve is asymmetrical (that is, *skewed*), the mode will be at a lower value of cost or duration than the median (that is, budget) value. The *base estimate* should be the mode of the frequency distribution. (See Figure 8.4.)

Monte Carlo Simulation

Monte Carlo simulation is a well-known method for performing *probabilistic project analysis* of cost and schedule. The goal of Monte Carlo

Figure 8.2
Frequency Distribution Curve Showing Contingency

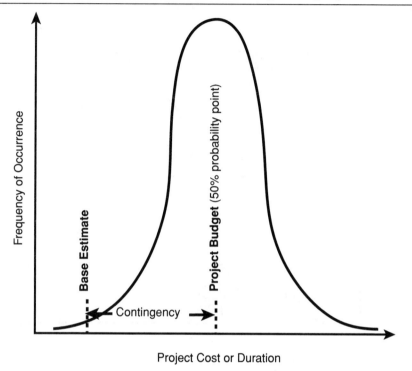

simulation is to produce the *frequency distribution* for the project cost or schedule. Once we have the distribution, we have all the information we need to calculate *contingency, estimate accuracy, management reserve,* and the *cumulative probability* curve.

Monte Carlo simulation works by using a random number generator to operate on a model of the project cost or schedule. The result is the generation of thousands of possible project outcomes (that is, a simulation) with a cost or duration associated with each one. The program analyzes the data to provide the frequency distribution and associated information. Popular software for Monte Carlo simulation operates on a spreadsheet.

PERT
The Program Evaluation and Review Technique (*PERT*) is a shortcut method for determining the *contingency* for an estimate of cost or

Figure 8.3
Cumulative Probability Curve Showing Management Reserve

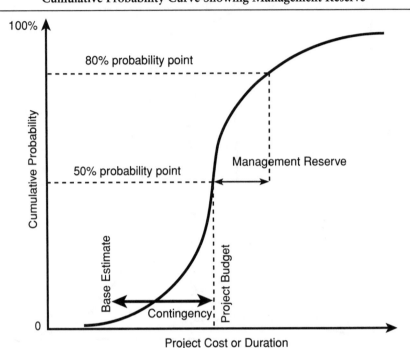

duration. The following PERT formula can be applied to each cost or schedule element:

$$50/50 \text{ value} = \frac{\text{minimum value} + 4(\text{most likely value}) + \text{maximum value}}{6}$$

- The 50/50 value is the *median*, or project budget value.
- The minimum value is the lowest possible value (usually the most optimistic).
- The maximum value is the highest possible value (usually the most pessimistic).
- The most likely value is the *mode*, and is usually the *base estimate*.

Once the 50/50 values have been calculated for each cost element, these can be simply added to determine the 50/50 value for the total project

Figure 8.4
Skewed Distribution Curve for a Typical Cost or Schedule Element

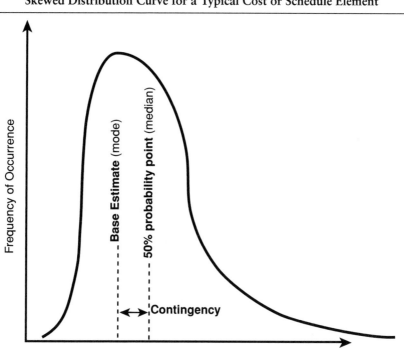

cost. The difference between this value and the *base estimate* is the required cost contingency.

Once the 50/50 values have been calculated for each schedule element, the critical path should be recalculated using the 50/50 values. The sum of the 50/50 durations along the critical path is the 50/50 value for total project duration. The difference between this value and the base schedule is the required schedule contingency.

Probabilistic Project Analysis
Probabilistic project analysis is the process of determining the relationship between project cost and probability and/or project duration and probability. The purpose is to set reasonable levels of cost and schedule *contingency*, determine *estimate accuracy*, improve decision making by the use of the *cumulative probability* curve, and provide the basis for a *risk mitigation* plan.

Project Risk Management

Project risk management is the process of optimizing the relationship of risk and reward. It consists of four steps:

1. Risk identification
2. Risk assessment
3. Risk analysis
4. Risk mitigation

Each of these steps will be discussed in detail later in this chapter.

Range Estimating

Range estimating is the process of determining the minimum and maximum values for each cost and schedule element. The range is the difference between the maximum and minimum values. The purpose of range estimating is to provide the basis for *probabilistic project analysis* using *Monte Carlo simulation* or *PERT*.

Risk

A project *risk* is a potential development or event that can impact a project's ability to achieve its objectives. A risk has a probability of occurring. Risks are generally thought of as having an undesirable outcome.

Risk Analysis

Risk analysis, in this context, is the performance of *probabilistic project analysis* of cost and schedule. It is based on the results of the *risk assessment* and provides the basis for decision making and developing a *risk mitigation* plan.

Risk Assessment

Risk assessment is determining the impact of risks on cost and schedule elements. The cost and schedule elements are the components of the *base estimate* of time and cost, and the impact of risks on these elements is usually expressed as a range. This range serves as the basis for *risk analysis* using *Monte Carlo* or *PERT* for the calculation. It is based on the results of *risk identification*.

Risk Identification

Risk identification is determining the risks that are likely to impact project success.

Risk Mitigation
Risk mitigation is taking steps to reduce the probability of the most severe risks occurring, to reduce the impact of those risks if they should occur, or both. These steps are summarized and tracked using a risk mitigation plan.

Skewness
Skewness is an attribute of the *frequency distribution* curve often associated with project cost and schedule in which the curve is asymmetrical (that is, "skewed"). Since many project cost or duration variables can (in a worst-case scenario) be double the estimate, it is common to find the maximum value of the range to be much further from the *base estimate* (typically the *mode*) than is the minimum value. Such a distribution is said to be skewed. The *median* value, used to set the budget, will be higher than the base estimate, and the difference between them is the required *contingency*. This relationship is shown in Figure 8.4.

Standard Deviation
The *standard deviation* represents the accuracy of the estimate. If the standard deviation is large, the *estimate accuracy* is poor and the probability is great that values of cost or duration will be experienced at significant variations from the *base estimate*. Conversely, if the standard deviation is small, the estimate accuracy is high, and there is a small probability that significant variations from the base estimate will be experienced.

In general, as a project progresses through the phases of the project life cycle, its scope of work, design, and plan become better defined. As a result, the accuracy of an estimate of time or cost becomes greater, and this is reflected by the standard deviation becoming smaller.

These concepts are illustrated by Figure 8.5.

Uncertainty
Uncertainty is an expression of confidence or lack of confidence in the basis of the estimate of cost or duration. It is expressed by using ranges. Clearly, if the project manager or estimator is very uncertain about a cost or duration, this will be expressed with a large range. When an estimate is uncertain, we will see a large *standard deviation*, low accuracy, large *contingency*, and a high probability of significant overruns. The *risk mitigation* plan is often a good way to reduce uncertainty.

Implementing a Project Risk Management Process

It is important to remember that the goal of a project risk management process is to gain competitive advantage by increasing the return on in-

Figure 8.5
Estimate Accuracy and Standard Deviation

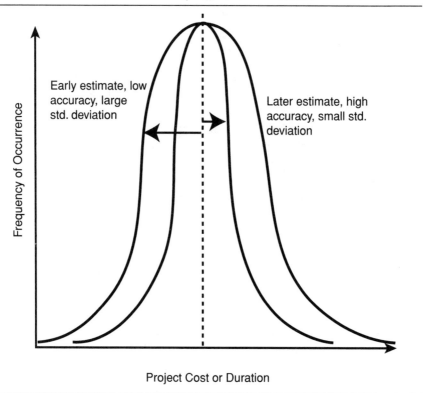

Early estimate, low
accuracy, large
std. deviation

Later estimate, high
accuracy, small std.
deviation

Frequency of Occurrence

Project Cost or Duration

vestment from the project portfolio. To accomplish this goal, the project
risk management process must achieve the following three objectives:

1. Reduce project costs and durations by:
   - Eliminating the use of hidden contingencies
   - Reducing the required contingency through effective risk mitigation
   - Improving project manager and team effectiveness by replacing an atmosphere of distrust with open communication on the subject of risk and uncertainty
2. Increase the probability of success by:
   - Identifying and mitigating risks in all phases of the project
   - Providing a method to manage risk as effectively as other project variables such as cost, schedule, quality, and safety

3. Improve portfolio performance through better investment decision making resulting from better information for optimizing project risk and return.

To accomplish these objectives, a project risk management process is required, as well as organizational changes to ensure the process is successful.

The recommended project risk management process is illustrated by the flowchart in Figure 8.6. The project risk management process provides a feedback loop such that the beneficial results of risk mitigation are reflected in the updated risk assessment.

Let's now discuss each step in the project risk management process. The preferred way to carry out these steps is in a project team setting with all project participants contributing and exchanging information.

Risk Identification
The objectives of risk identification are as follows:

- Encourage an open dialogue about the risks to project success.
- Get the input of all project participants about their perceptions of risks.
- Identify and categorize project risks.
- Provide a basis for risk assessment.

To accomplish this, the project team and other stakeholders are asked, in a group setting, to brainstorm possible risks to project success. The most efficient way to do this has proven to be to provide the team with risk categories and have them develop risks in each one. For

Figure 8.6
Project Risk Management Process

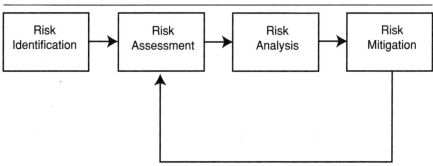

example, a table such as Table 8.1 can be used. This risk identification table organizes the risks identified through brainstorming. Sample categories and risks are shown as they might be developed during a risk identification session.

Risk Assessment

The objectives of risk assessment are as follows:

- Establish the range of each cost and schedule element due to each risk category acting alone.
- Provide a basis for risk analysis.

To accomplish this, the same team members who participated in risk identification now assess the impact of each risk category on each cost or schedule element, as if that risk category were acting alone. This is done using a risk assessment matrix as shown in Table 8.2.

Table 8.1
Sample Risk Identification Table

Eternal Risks	Technical Risks	Project Management Risks	Site-Related Risks
Unfavorable market conditions raise prices and decrease availability of critical equipment.	Current systems-design architecture proves incompatible with new developments.	Lack of strategic project planning results in unresolved issues that delay the schedule.	Customer changes existing systems prior to implementation of the project.
Labor shortages delay the schedule.	Customer requirements changes.	Scope proves to be poorly defined, and extensive changes cause delays.	Existing infrastructure proves inadequate to handle the demands of the new system.
Changes in legislation require significant design revisions.	Late changes are caused by difficulties in rollout and implementation.	Contract planning and administration problems cause delays, disputes, and cost overruns.	Inference from other projects in the same time frame and location causes disruption and delays.

Table 8.2
Sample Risk Assessment Matrix

Cost Element	Base Estimate ($000)	External Risks	Technical Risks	Project Management Risks	Site-Related Risks
Equipment	750	−10$/+50%	−25%/+75%	−15%/+50%	−5%/+30%
Design and development	450	−5%/+10%	−10%/+25%	−10%/+40%	−5%/+25%
Testing	140	−5%/+10%	−10%/+50%	−5%/+20%	−10%/+10%
Documentation	75	−5%/+10%	−0%/+50%	−5%/+25%	NA
Installation	375	−5%/+10%	−5%/+50%	−5%/+15%	−10%/+10%
Training	300	−5%/+10%	−0%/+20%	−5%/+15%	NA
Total base estimate	2090				

Note that this approach overcomes the traditional problem associated with range estimating: People find it very difficult to set ranges. If we ask a project team how much higher or lower the $750,000 estimate for equipment might be, they might well say, "We have no idea." But if we ask how much higher this cost might be due to the external risks they just defined on the risk identification table, they will begin to describe scenarios and attach cost implications to them, thereby setting the range shown in the risk assessment matrix.

The risk assessment matrix presents a project cost model as reflected in the row headings of the matrix. The project cost model will provide the basis for Monte Carlo simulation. Note that it is a simple model based on the following idea:

$$\text{Total Project Cost} = \Sigma \text{ (cost elements)}$$

To satisfy the need of the Monte Carlo analysis that the variables (that is, cost elements) be independent, it is best to keep the number of cost elements small (fewer than 20) and ensure that they will vary fairly independently.

Risk assessment for schedule is done in much the same way. My preferred approach is to break the schedule into a series of key milestones, such that the total project duration is the sum of the durations between these milestones. The project schedule model, which will provide the basis for the Monte Carlo simulation of schedule, will look like this:

$$\text{Total Project Duration} = \Sigma \text{ (schedule elements)}$$

The risk assessment matrix for the schedule then looks just like the cost matrix, and uses the same risk categories.

Risk Analysis

The objectives of risk analysis are as follows:

- Establish the cost and schedule contingency required for the total project as well as for each cost and schedule element.
- Define the contingency associated with each cost and schedule element as well as with each risk category.
- Define the cost and duration cumulative probability curves.
- Establish the basis for the risk mitigation plan.

Monte Carlo simulation is generally the preferred method to accomplish these objectives. A number of relatively easy-to-use software packages are available to perform the Monte Carlo simulation. The steps in Monte Carlo simulation are as follows:

1. The cost and schedule risk assessment matrices are prepared in a spreadsheet format.
2. The Monte Carlo software is set up to operate on each cell in the matrix that contains a range. This setup requires that a type of probability distribution be selected. Most software provides a selection of distributions. I recommend a triangular distribution, as it more closely reflects the variation in typical project data. In the triangular distribution, a straight-line relationship is assumed from the minimum value (at which the probability is zero) up to the most likely value (at which the probability is greatest), and from the most likely value down to the maximum value (at which the probability is zero).
3. The Monte Carlo software is then triggered to run the simulation. At this point the software produces the frequency distribution curve for total project cost and duration. It does this by using the probability distributions in each cell of the risk assessment matrix together with a random number generator to simulate thousands (I recommend at least 6,000) of possible outcomes of the project. When these values are analyzed, the result is the desired frequency distribution.
4. The output of the simulation is presented in the formats described in Figure 8.7. From this information, contingency, accuracy, and other decision-support information can be gained.

Figure 8.7
Cumulative Probability Curve from Simulation

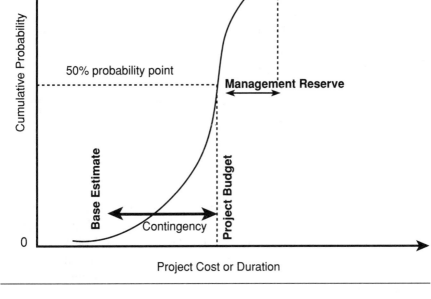

The output from the software will also indicate which cost or schedule elements require the most contingency and which risk categories contributed the most to contingency. This information will be used in the risk mitigation plan.

If proper preparation is done, it is often possible to run the risk analysis during the same meeting after the risk identification and assessment. (The participants can take a break during the 15 minutes or so it takes to run the simulation.) This gives results right away while the team is still assembled. The meeting participants can then proceed directly to develop the risk mitigation plan.

Risk Mitigation
The objectives of risk mitigation are as follows:

- Increase the likelihood of success by reducing the probability that high-probability risks will impact the project and/or by reducing the impact if they should occur.
- Address the most critical risk categories and cost or schedule elements.
- Provide a path forward plan, including steps to be taken, responsibilities, and dates, for mitigating risks.

Risk mitigation planning begins by reviewing the results of the risk analysis to determine what the highest-priority risks are for mitigation. The risk identification table will also be helpful in this regard. The project team should then proceed to develop a risk mitigation plan as shown in Table 8.3, which involves developing mitigation steps and assigning them to project team members.

The resulting risk mitigation plan can usually be implemented immediately and should be periodically updated.

SUMMARY

In order for the project risk management process to succeed, it is critically important to address the organizational and corporate cultural issues described earlier in this chapter under "The High Cost of Project Risk Mismanagement." Having a formal process, definitions, and team activities for risk management will be helpful. Some additional recommended steps include the following:

- Incorporate the results of project risk analysis into the procedures used to select and authorize funding for projects.
- Reward project managers who communicate openly about project risks and uncertainties, and who recommend killing projects whose risks are not commensurate with returns.
- Increase management awareness of project risk management and gain visible support for its application.
- Change the punishment/reward paradigm from one based on punishment for overruns to one based on how well a project team implements the project risk management process and other project management best practices.
- Ensure consistent, uniform use of the project risk management process across all projects in the portfolio.

Table 8.3
Risk Mitigation Plan

Risk	Action to Mitigate	Cost to Mitigate (H/M/L)	Probability Mitigation Succeeds (H/M/L)	Do Mitigation? (Y/N)	Who Is Responsible?	Date to Complete
Equipment pricing could exceed estimate due to supplier shortages.	Accelerate orders for critical equipment (reduces probability of occurrence).	L	H	Y	Hy Price	May 15
System design experiences changes due to ambiguous customer requirements.	Set up configuration management program and expedite kickoff meeting (reduces both probability and impact).	M	M	Y	Natalie Attired	April 10
Resource shortfalls could result from demands from other projects.	Develop a program-level plan showing the resources required for each project from the shared resource pool (reduces both probability and impact).	L	H	Y	Justin Tyme	April 30

Note: H is high; M is medium; L is low; Y is yes; N is no.

When all these things are done, project risk mismanagement becomes effective project risk management. As a result the following benefits will be realized:

- Projects cost less and take less time.
- More projects are completed on time and on budget.
- Communication between project teams and management is improved. Risks are discussed more openly, and high-risk projects can be eliminated early, before there is no turning back.
- Better decisions are made, increasing the value of the project portfolio.

In summary, it can be seen that project risk management offers a great opportunity to improve project performance dramatically. The amount of work needed to implement the project risk management process is considerably less than that devoted to other project variables such as cost, schedule, or quality, yet the benefits are equally great. Like quality management, the greatest challenge to implementing project risk management lies in changing the corporate culture. However, once this is done, and risk management becomes routine, significant performance benefits to the project portfolio will be achieved.

CHAPTER 9

CONTRACTS AND PROCUREMENT MANAGEMENT: WHY SHOULD YOU CARE?

RITA MULCAHY

Procurement, the acquiring of goods or services, is sometimes called contracting. When the word "contract" is mentioned to people, the first question that comes into many people's heads is, Why should I care? In many companies the contracts, purchase orders, and other agreements are handled by the legal, purchasing, or contracts area. With that expertise around, people wonder why the project manager must have an understanding of contracts.

This chapter is written in the form of questions and answers. The questions come from two sources: the most common ones people ask me about procurement, and the most important areas of understanding required by business professionals and project managers. I have intended them to be interesting and thought-provoking, but mostly I have tried to convey some critical ideas to make your projects successful.

There are many different words used to refer to one party or another in the contract. These include *owner, contractor, prime contractor, supplier, vendor, consultant,* and *seller.* Yet, companies are frequently both buying services and selling services at the same time. This adds confusion to many discussions about the procurement process. Therefore, I will use the terms *buyer* and *seller* only and try to give you a sense of both sides of the fence.

WHY UNDERSTAND CONTRACTS AND PROCUREMENT?

No matter the title, one could say that a project manager or business professional should understand procurement and contracts because they

151

comprise one of the nine knowledge areas in the Project Management Institute's *Guide to the Project Management Body of Knowledge (PMBOK)*. Because this is now the international standard for project management, that alone would make it a very good reason to know procurement. There are more important reasons, however. What are they?

Exercise: Why should a project manager have an understanding of contracts and the procurement process?

Answer:

First, when one person is working on a project, he or she has control over the project; the success of the project depends on that individual. When a team of people is completing a project within one company, the project manager has less control but everyone is working with the same procedures, company culture, and project purpose. The success of the project now depends on the actions of a team.

However, when a project involves a contract (either the work is contracted or part of it is being done by someone outside the company), you are working with two companies with different agendas, procedures, and cultures. Not only are each company's procedures and cultures largely unknown to the other side, but the sellers are not even working to meet your company's project objectives—they are working to make money.

There are many instances recorded in articles, papers, and even some books where multimillion-dollar projects were unsuccessful because of the impact of the failure of a small-dollar contract. More frequently, the effect is delays, cost increases, and decreases in quality. In a contracting environment, the success of the project does not depend on the project manager or the team, but on the procedures, culture, and people from a whole different company. This is the first reason for a project manager to understand contracts.

In a contract or procurement environment, the success of the project may depend on a whole other company.

There are many other reasons to understand contracts. These are described in the rest of this chapter and are outlined in the conclusion.

WHAT IS A CONTRACT?

When I first began teaching project managers how to understand contracts I discovered something interesting. In general, what project managers *think* is a contract and what it actually is are two different things.

Exercise: What is a contract?

Answer:

_____

_____

When you think of the word *contract*, what comes to mind? If you are like many others, you will think of all the legal words such as indemnification, intellectual property, and other legal small print. Others think of the preprinted or standard contract—boilerplate contracts—supplied to them from the contracts or legal departments. They are all incorrect.

The word *contract* actually refers to the entire agreement between both parties. Therefore, it includes legal language, but it would also include business terms regarding payments, reporting requirements, marketing literature, the proposal, and the scope of work—all the requirements of the project.

Many project managers and business professionals think that the only relevant part of a contract is the scope of work because they are naturally most familiar with that aspect of the contract. However, the scope of work does not include all the requirements. In fact, some of the legal language can be more relevant than the scope of work. For example, think of a project to develop new software. Who owns the resulting program? Who owns the resulting program if it contains modules or pieces of programs previously used and planned for future reuse? How do you protect your rights and ensure that all source code is delivered? The ownership clause in a contract for such services might be more relevant than the scope of work itself.

The following is a list of some common clauses in a contract:

- *Acceptance*—How will you know specifically if the work is acceptable?
- *Agent*—Who is an authorized representative of each party?
- *Authority*—Who has the power to do what?
- *Breach*—When a part of the contract is not performed (remember that the contract consists of the scope of work and legal terms)
- *Changes*—How will they be made? What forms will be used? What is the time frame for notice? What is the turnaround?
- *Confidentiality*—What information must not be given to third parties?
- *Copyrights*—Who owns the tangible components?
- *Force majeure*—An act of God, such as fire or freak electrical storm
- *Incentives*—What benefits can the seller receive for aligning with the buyers' objectives of time, cost, quality, risk, and performance?
- *Indemnification*—Who is liable for such things as personal injury, damage, and accidents?
- *Independent contractor*—States that the seller is not an employee of the buyer.
- *Inspection*—Does anyone have a right to inspect the work during execution of the project? If so, under what circumstances?
- *Intellectual property*—Who owns the intangibles?
- *Invoicing*—When, to whom, and what attachments or supporting documents are required?
- *Liquidated damages*—Estimated damages for specific breaches, described in advance
- *Material breach*—A breach so large that the work under the contract may not be able to be completed
- *Notice*—To whom should certain correspondence be sent?
- *Patents*—Who will own any patents or rules governing the use of existing patents?
- *Payments*—When will they be made? When will late payment fees be applied? What are the reasons for nonpayment?
- *Reporting*—What reports are required, at what frequency, and from and to whom?
- *Retainage*—An amount of money, usually 5 or 10 percent, withheld from each payment. This money is paid when all the final work is completed and helps ensure completion
- *Scope of work*—May be included in the contract or attached to the contract as a separate document
- *Site access*—Any requirements for access to where the work will be performed

- *Termination*—Stopping the work before it is completed
- *Time is of the essence*—Delivery is strictly binding. Seller is on notice that time is very important and that any delay is a material breach.
- *Waiver*—Intentionally or unintentionally giving up a right in the contract due to lack of oversight. If you don't require that the scope of work or other legal requirements be fulfilled, you could waive your right to get them.

Project managers manage the accomplishment of the requirements of the project. Therefore, they need to understand all the requirements, not just the scope of work.

> A contract is not just legal language but also business terms and the scope of work—all the requirements of the project.

WHAT IS THE PURPOSE OF THE CONTRACT?

> *Exercise:* What is the purpose of a contract?
>
> *Answer:*
> _____
> _____

Unfortunately, many people think of a contract as a necessary evil—something for the lawyers to put together and then never use again. Considering previous comments defining the term, you can see that they are designed to describe requirements and allocate roles and responsibilities between both parties. Therefore, the focus of the contract is not to place blame or to tie one's hands; it is to allocate risks properly. In fact, the benefits of proper attention to creating a clear, complete, and concise contract result in the following:

- Decreased changes
- Decreased conflict

- Decreased time to complete
- Better pricing
- Higher project success rates

Contracts are risk mitigation tools.

WHEN SHOULD PROJECT MANAGERS BE INVOLVED IN THE CONTRACT PROCESS?

Exercise: When should project managers be involved in the contract or procurement process?

Answer:

_____

_____

If the project manager must do a risk analysis before a contract is signed, this must mean that a project manager is assigned before a contract is signed. However, if yours is like many companies, this comes as something of a shock. In companies where projects are created through winning a contract from an outside client, sales and marketing will have handled the whole proposal process and signed a contract before the project manager is assigned. The project manager then is handed a project that is already in trouble because the contract, its terms and conditions, and even the scope of work are not appropriate.

Many such companies bid on many contracts to win only one of them. It is not possible, under these circumstances, to assign a project manager to every project when the company is not sure if the project manager will be needed to manage the project. A solution that many companies have adopted is to have a project manager, usually a senior project manager, assist in proposal creation using work breakdown structures, risk assessments, and other tools and techniques of project management. If the project is won, the actual project manager—the one who will manage it—is assigned and receives the work breakdown structure, risk analysis, and other high-level plans in order to plan the project in enough detail to manage its completion.

A project manager must be assigned before a contract is signed.

WHAT IS THE PROJECT MANAGER'S ROLE IN THE CONTRACTING OR PROCUREMENT PROCESS?

Exercise: What is the project manager's role in the contracting or procurement process?

Answer:

In a recent situation, a consultant was asked to provide technical assistance on a project for a project manager the consultant knew and respected. The company had a contracts department that used standard boilerplate contract forms, which is common practice. To execute the work of hiring the consultant, the project manager simply turned the contracting component over to the contracts department to handle. The consultant received a boilerplate contract not applicable to the work and spent two days negotiating the contract for two days' worth of work.

Can you think how this situation might have impacted the project? If you had to spend two days negotiating two days' worth of work, would you want to work on the project? Would your performance on the project be less than it could be? Would the project be as successful as it could be? Would your objectives be to complete the project, or might you have an ulterior motive to try to get even? This problem is actually very common and is usually an unperceived threat to the project. It puts the project at risk before it starts. If the project manager is accountable for the project, he or she must also be involved during the precontract stage in protecting the relationship between both parties signing the contract.

During the contracting process the project manager must protect the relationship between buyer and seller in order to protect the project.

In another situation, a project ran into some difficulties that caused schedule and cost impacts. At a meeting, one of the team members stated that they had known the problem was going to happen all along, but "No one asked us." The contract had been signed before the project manager and team were designated and therefore before a risk analysis could be done. As a result, the contract did not describe responsibilities for some problems that the team fully expected. The team and the contractor were consequently spending more time in meetings talking about who was going to do what to solve the schedule and cost problems than actually solving the problems.

A contract must be tailored to the needs of the project. This tailoring can be achieved easily with teamwork between the project manager and the contracts, legal, or purchasing department. The result is a contract that includes the risk allocation that needs to be there without any irrelevant details. Without such tailoring, the project can fail before it even gets started. What should you consider in this type of tailoring? Take into account the specific risks of the project, and the terms and conditions that can be added or changed to mitigate or allocate them properly.

> A contract must be tailored to the unique needs of the project.

The main complaints of project managers regarding the contracts, procurement, or legal department are that they take too long; they are bureaucratic; they are roadblocks for the project. Sometimes, these comments are delivered with an extreme amount of anger and frustration. However, when I ask why this is so, I usually receive comments such as, "They just are!" After a few moments, it is apparent to me that these project managers do not understand the role of the contract manager and, interestingly, contract managers do not understand the project management process.

Curiously enough, most project managers have never had training in project management and most contract managers have never had training in contract management, let alone training in each other's fields. Yet, the project manager and contract manager must work together to have a successful project. The project manager also needs to understand the contracting process in order to manage the project around the time the contracting process takes.

Project managers must understand the process of contract and procurement management.

WHAT IS THE CONTRACTING PROCESS?

Exercise: What is the contracting process?

Answer:

_____

_____

The contracting or procurement process consists of the six following steps:

- Step 1: Procurement planning
- Step 2: Solicitation planning
- Step 3: Solicitation
- Step 4: Source selection
- Step 5: Contract administration
- Step 6: Contract closeout

Step 1: Procurement Planning

To start the procurement process, someone must answer the question, "Do we do it ourselves or do we need assistance?" and make a decision based on the answer. This step is called procurement planning in the Project Management Institute's *Guide to the Project Management Body of Knowledge.* Also included here is a decision on the form or type of contract to be used.

The seller has the tough job of discovering what services the buyer will need before the buyer knows this himself or herself. If the seller does this successfully, he or she can begin to inform the buyer why it would be better to use outside help.

The project manager can influence the success of the project during this step by making sure all the relevant people have bought into the decision to use outside help.

> Step 1—Determine if you need help.

Step 2: Solicitation Planning

Once the decision is made to use outside assistance, the buyer will begin to formulate his or her requirements into a cohesive whole. These requirements will take the form of a *scope of work* (a description of what needs to be accomplished), evaluation criteria, and specific terms and conditions for the contract. The evaluation criteria will tell the seller what is important to the buyer and therefore help the seller respond to the procurement document appropriately.

These requirements will be put in the form of a procurement document. Depending on how well the buyer can describe what needs to be done, the procurement document may take the form of a *request for proposal* or *RFP* (called a *request for tender* in some parts of the world), *invitation for bid* (*IFB*), or *request for quotation* (*RFQ*).

A proposal is requested if the buyer is buying technical expertise that will be required to determine the complete scope of work (as in research, or in many information systems or information technology projects). A bid is requested if the buyer has determined in advance the exact scope of work (as in construction). A quote is requested for the purchase of commodities or services that are priced on an hourly basis.

The requirements are sent out to prospective sellers and the buyer waits for a response. This is a key area of complaint from project managers. They often want it now! But take a moment to understand what is going on here. The requirements take time to create. Once they are ready and are sent out, the sellers need time to analyze the requirements and to respond. For some types of projects, a whole month is required for the seller to respond. There are some things that can be done to decrease the waiting time, but it can not be decreased very much. Impatience during the waiting stage will lead to poorer proposals and therefore a higher-risk project with less probability of success. It is important here to be patient and to know that the process takes time. Good project managers will keep this time requirement in mind when planning their projects.

If sellers become aware of the potential procurement, they can offer to assist in the creation of the scope of work, or simply make a good impression for winning the work to come. They can also gain an understanding of the timing of the project and the procurement, and start to prepare their teams for the receipt of the procurement documents from the buyer.

The project manager can influence the success of the project during this step by working hard to make the scope of work absolutely complete. The more complete the scope of work, the cheaper and less risky will be the project. The project manager should also be involved in the creation of the terms and conditions of the contract, and in the creation of the evaluation criteria.

Step 2—Put your requirements together.

Step 3: Solicitation

Once the seller has had some time to review and analyze the buyer's requirements, the buyer will usually allow the seller to ask questions about the requirements. This is a very important step in decreasing risk and getting better proposals. Often, such questions are asked at a *bidders' conference* (a meeting of all the bidders), but it is sometimes done through written requests. In any case, the project manager for the buyer must make sure that all questions and answers are conveyed to all those who may respond to the procurement documents.

This is a tough step for sellers. They need to ask as many questions as necessary in order to get a good understanding of the project yet not give away anything to other sellers. Discovering and understanding the risks or potential risks of the project are critical here in order to respond properly to the procurement documents.

The project manager can influence the success of the project during this step by leading the technical parts of the bidders' conference. Often, smart project managers will take the time to walk the sellers around their facilities. Project managers can also encourage sellers to ask all their questions and to make sure the answers are clear and complete.

Step 3—Answer questions.

Step 4: Source Selection

This is the toughest part—picking a company with which to do business. The selection is made by comparing the responses to the requirements. In the case of a proposal, the selection may be made through interviews, presentations, and negotiation. A team may be formed to perform such an evaluation. It may contain the contracts manager, project manager, and technical people. If a bid is used, the selection may be made by picking the lowest-priced bidder.

The selection process can also take time. In some instances, evaluating the proposals can take three weeks and then there may be a two-week wait to arrange everyone's schedules in order to hold meetings with the sellers. Then, once a selection is made, the contract must be discussed and more time will be needed for the seller to start up. Therefore, the whole procurement process can take from three to 18 months, depending on the nature of the project.

The seller will be trying to make a good impression during this step as well as trying to make sure to win the work. The seller's team will be attending presentations, meetings, and negotiations. Often, the seller's team is made up of salespeople as well as the project manager and financial, technical, and quality experts. Discovering risks for the project is important here as well as protecting the relationship with the buyer.

The project manager can influence the success of the project during this step by making sure the evaluation team is made up of people from all relevant areas of the company, and that the seller is being evaluated fairly. I have often seen an administrative member of an evaluation team discover important reasons for not selecting sellers.

The project manager can also help with the schedule of this step by making sure things are scheduled in advance, if possible, and that all parties have the schedule then. Project managers must also participate in negotiations by protecting the relationship between the buyer and the seller and making sure any negotiations result in a win-win situation.

It is important to realize that this step sets the stage for how the buyer and seller will work together, what they think of each other, and what they expect from the people involved in the project and from the project itself. If the atmosphere is one of working together, both sides will expect to be able to focus on producing the project and not protecting themselves, fighting back, or any other potential problems.

Step 4 —Pick one!

Step 5: Contract Administration

After the contract is signed, work on the project can begin. Issues to be handled include conflicts, meetings, changes, and reporting, just like any project. Depending on the nature of the company, the project, and the industry, there are many different ways the contract manager and project manager may be involved during this step. In some organizations, the contract manager will be in charge of managing performance as it pertains to the contract, while the project manager will handle completion of the scope of work. In other organizations, the project manager must manage the contract.

In a contracting environment, project management activities must be more formal than may be the case without a contract. Changes must be in writing, communications must be documented, and formal approval of performance and progress must be given. The contract should include a description of how changes will be made and managed and what types of detailed records must be kept.

The project manager is often caught up with scope management, determining if work is in or out of scope and if all the work is being done. In managing such issues, there will be a need to interpret the contract. Therefore, the project manager should maintain a good relationship with the contract manager in order to learn contract interpretation skills and to gain the contract manager's assistance when such issues arise.

During this step, the seller will not only be performing the work but can also be performing other activities to make sure the project is successful. Some of these activities include looking for anything different about the project or the buyer than what was expected, and understanding how the project fits into the buyer's business strategies.

The project manager can influence the success of the project during this step by keeping in mind that problems will not be so easy to see as when a project is done in-house. Building good relationships with the seller and carefully communicating can have a profound impact on the project. In most instances, the project is placed in the project manager's hands during this step and the project manager gains more control over the success of the project.

Step 5—Perform and control the work.

Step 6: Contract Closeout

Finally, the project is finished! During this step final approvals are received, final payments made, and a lessons-learned document is completed. Keeping in mind that a contract environment requires more formality, files will also be documented.

A lessons-learned document can be very valuable to the company. Created by the team and the seller, it addresses what went right and wrong on the project (or contract) and makes recommendations on what should be done differently next time. It not only improves quality but also helps ensure future success. To gain the most from each project, lessons learned are written down and shared within the whole company.

The seller should be performing these same activities, also creating a lessons-learned document for their own company from the point of view of only the seller's team. Such a document can change the seller's project participation from simply a moneymaking venture to a way to gain valuable experience for the entire company.

The project manager can influence the success of the project during this step by making sure that all loose ends are tied up and that the project actually finishes. The tendency for management and other managers to add work to a project will prevent it from ever being completed and therefore hinder its success.

Project managers can also help the project by advertising within the company the successes of the project, and making sure the lessons-learned document is complete and distributed to other project managers. Imagine a company where a project manager has access to the good ideas and mistakes from every project the company has ever done.

Step 6—Finish!

CONCLUSION
Why understand contracts?

- Contracts can have a profound impact on the project. When a project involves contracts or some other form of procurement the success of the project may depend on the seller and not the project manager.

- A contract is not just legal language but also business terms and the scope of work—all the requirements of the project. The work of the project manager is to manage all the requirements of the project, more than just the scope of work.
- Contracts are risk mitigation tools. The project manager must be able to contribute to the creation of contract terms and conditions in order to properly assign and mitigate risk on the project.
- The contract should be a useful tool to help manage the project. The project manager needs to be able to help tailor the contract to the needs of the project.
- The relationship between the buyer and the seller is fragile. The project manager must protect the relationship so that he or she is not handed a project that starts out with major problems.
- The contracting process takes time. The project manager must be able to fit the contracting process into the project schedule effectively.

In order to perform these functions, the project manager must be assigned before the contract is signed.

Projects are hurting because of the lack of knowledge and understanding of the contracting process and the lack of proper and efficient coordination between the contracts and project management functions. Precious time is wasted, conflict is increased, and much more time is spent in meetings related to contract issues than should be occurring. Hopefully you have gained some insight into the issue as well as ideas on making the contracting process an asset to the project instead of a detriment.

CHAPTER 10

EARNED VALUE MANAGEMENT: AN INTRODUCTION

JOEL M. KOPPELMAN and QUENTIN W. FLEMING

You've heard it a hundred times, maybe a thousand: "We're doing fine on that project, boss. We had to postpone that last deadline for a few days, but we're making it up now and we're right on budget." You know they're telling you what you want to hear.

But is good news always what you want to hear? Only if it's the truth. What you really want to know is exactly when a critical project will be done, and exactly what it will cost. You want a pinpoint-accurate view of a project whose completion is still a moving target. You can get it, by using some simplified calculations called "earned value" to help you quantify the true status of any kind of project and to predict realistic completion times and final costs. Forecasts based on earned value are remarkably accurate almost as soon as work begins, enabling you to make minor course corrections early in the project rather than attempting heroic salvage efforts later.

Sound too good to be true? Well, it's not.

Let's say you're three months into a yearlong development project for a theater-quality HDTV (high-definition television) system. Most of the project is on schedule, except that the prototype fails resoundingly—the controls are too difficult for customers to use. Looking ahead to the completion of the HDTV development project, you want to schedule a factory shutdown to prepare for production, but that requires an exact and accurate forecast of the project completion date.

Perhaps you expect to approve a new prototype one month late. Minor trouble? Or the catalyst for a crisis? The project manager assures you that this is a slight but recoverable delay, and that's good news—for now. But the extra time and money required to solve the problem could combine to leave the HDTV project further behind than it appears to be when the project manager describes a minor delay or accounting notes a small cost overrun.

If you accept the project manager's optimistic assurances, you're leaving yourself vulnerable to a shock when, months later as you approach the factory shutdown date, you suddenly learn that the project is significantly over budget and irrecoverably behind schedule. The project somehow shifted from minor trouble to deep difficulty. Neither you nor the project manager saw it coming. Production start-up is delayed, some desired features must be sacrificed, a competitor beats you to the marketplace, and overrunning the budget means you have to cut funds for another promising product development effort.

Or perhaps you don't accept those optimistic projections at face value. Perhaps you direct the project manager to report to you on the project's earned value each month. You use it to extrapolate from the project's current status—inevitably affected by unforeseen delays and minor overexpenditures—to an accurate final forecast, so that you can rectify any serious slippage or overrun before the money's all spent and the delivery date is looming overhead.

But, you say, your project manager continually reforecasts the project's schedule and expenses. That's what you pay the manager to do. Well, if adjusting schedules and expenses was enough, then nasty end-of-project surprises wouldn't be so common. You need a more powerful tool, a more accurate way to view the project as soon as it's really underway.

That tool is called earned value. It's not a new tool, just an underutilized one. Earned value integrates schedule and cost data that project managers already use to achieve milestones, meet intermediate deadlines, and stay within budget. It was first developed as a simple part of factory-floor cost engineering, then grew into an intimidating set of calculations as complicated as the huge government projects it was designed to measure. But you can get the benefits of earned value without investing in a complex measurement system, by using a simplified form of earned value that can provide illumination of the real status of a project, at every stage from 15 percent complete through 100 percent, to ensure its success.

A Brief History of Earned Value

Earned value measurements started simply and became overwhelmingly complex. It's helpful to understand these two extremes in order to understand how to apply the simplified form to your own projects.

The original concept was developed by industrial engineers in the factories of the early 1900s. They used two factors to assess the factory's cost performance in a production cycle: *planned units* (the physical items they originally planned to produce by any point during the production cycle) and *earned units* (the physical items produced at the time of measurement). Comparing the planned units to the earned units produced told them whether they were ahead of or behind schedule. But like you, they soon learned that this was not enough information.

So these engineers figured out how to integrate schedule and cost information to get a more accurate picture of the project's status. They used three monetary figures: the *planned cost* (the total cost of the planned units, spread over the delivery cycle); the *actual cost* (the amount of money spent as of a particular date); and the *earned value* (the money originally budgeted to produce the number of units manufactured as of that date). Because they may have paid more than they planned for labor or materials, their actual cost per unit manufactured might exceed the earned value (the planned cost per unit manufactured).

Now they could compare planned costs to earned value to identify *schedule variance*, and they could compare earned value to actual costs to identify *cost variance*. If planned cost minus earned value was negative, they had a schedule variance, which meant they'd produced less units than specified in their plan. If earned value minus actual cost was negative, they had a cost variance, which meant they had spent too much money for the work produced. You can use the same techniques to identify the same variances in your own projects—to learn whether the milestones accomplished to date are in proportion to the time and money spent to achieve them.

Converting these measurement techniques from the ongoing assembly line to finite projects, the U.S. Navy in 1957 introduced a Program Evaluation and Review Technique (PERT), in which managers created a network of logical, sequential events and used it to schedule the Polaris missile project. Five years later, the government started requiring cost information as well, enabling project managers to calculate earned value on these projects.

Over the next four decades, the U.S. Department of Defense added more and more requirements, culminating in an enormously complicated performance measurement technique called the Cost Schedule Control Systems Criteria or C/SCSC. Eventually deciding that earned value was the most valuable aspect of that system, the government in 1996 scaled it down to a 32-requirement Earned Value Measurement System (EVMS). The fact that government monitors consider earned value to be worth the cost of fulfilling all those requirements indicates just how much trust they put in the ability of earned value to predict final cost and schedule results.

But what do those notoriously cumbersome government projects have in common with the necessarily more nimble, flexible projects undertaken by private companies? Companies benefit from using earned value for the same reason the government does—many of their projects are internal efforts, meaning that the company carries the risk of cost growth. Management is highly motivated to eliminate end-of-project surprises, but no one wants to make an EVMS-sized investment in the measurement system itself. You need the same kind of information, but faster and with less number crunching—less diversion from the primary task, the project itself.

It may appear that you have a difficult choice: traditional nonintegrated cost and schedule information that lulls you into complacency, or accurate but burdensome earned value measurement. However, we have suggested a simplified earned value approach that returns to the commonsense concept used on the factory floor, adding only enough requirements to apply it to finite projects rather than ongoing production cycles. There are exactly 10 requirements.

TEN ELEMENTS NECESSARY FOR MEASURING EARNED VALUE ON ANY KIND OF PROJECT

Your project managers probably already collect most of the information they'll need to calculate earned value: Specific tasks required, a schedule by which to accomplish them, and estimates of the resources needed to accomplish those tasks. These are summarized in Steps 1 to 5, and covered in detail in many texts on project management. Steps 6 to 10 describe specific earned value calculations and how you can use them to get a far more realistic view of your project's past and future than either schedule or cost data alone can provide.

Step1: Define the Scope of Work

Definition of the pieces of work to be accomplished is the first step, and one of the most critical ones, in project planning of any kind. This kind of bottom-up, details-first planning is a difficult task for any project, especially when it seems that the ground is always moving underneath the project plan. However, detail-level planning is absolutely necessary. If you do not define what constitutes 100 percent of the work, how can you ascertain whether you have completed 10 percent, 20 percent, or 50 percent of a job?

Realistically, no one can define a project's work with absolute precision. However, the person you assign to manage a particular project must be familiar enough with this type of project to be able to estimate the required work with some degree of certainty. Anything less and you are in practical terms authorizing a blank check for the project.

How does a project manager estimate the types and amounts of work required when specific details are often lacking before the project starts? There are no absolutely foolproof methods when so much depends on the competence of the person or people doing the estimating, but one of the most useful tools available is the work breakdown structure (WBS), a hierarchical diagram of the work scope of the project.

The WBS is to the project manager what the organization chart is to the executive—it allows the project manager to define a new endeavor by breaking out the broad categories of work to be done (usually the individually deliverable parts of the project), dividing each of those deliverables into products, and then subdividing each product into specific tasks. When you can measure the cost of each specific task in time or money, it's defined narrowly enough.

The process of creating a WBS greatly reduces the chance that some significant portion of the work is left out of the plan entirely. It also offers oversight at different levels of the project without duplication of effort: a high level for senior management, a more specific level for project managers, and a detailed level for task managers. (See Figure 10.1.)

When a project is divided into measurable pieces, the WBS becomes a reasonable portrayal of the scope of the project itself. It can be used to take the next steps in the project planning process, including scheduling, estimating, make-or-buy analysis, risk assessment, and the authorization to proceed.

If you've never used a WBS before, start by identifying the various deliverables of your project. For our HDTV, these might include prototype design, engineering, manufacturing, and a marketing campaign. Then break down each of these deliverables into products. The prototype deliverable might include exterior design, component selection, wiring, assembly, and patent application. The marketing campaign deliverable might include a web site, press releases, brochures, magazine reviews, advertising, and dealer incentives.

Then break down each of these products into tasks: Individual items of work that are accomplished collectively to produce the product. For example, component selection might involve specifications, vendor quotes,

Figure 10.1
Work Breakdown Structure

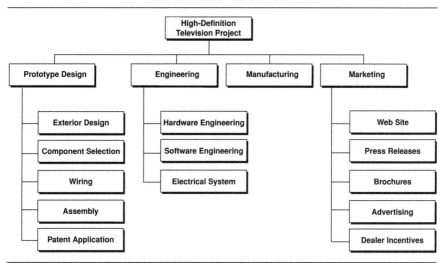

purchase orders, and inventory management. Dealer incentives might involve targeted mailings, factory rep appearances at consumer electronics shows, sales quotas, and rewards.

The WBS gives management an overview of the progress on each deliverable. The project manager tracks progress on the next level of detail, the products. And department managers track detailed tasks in their own work areas.

Step 2: Integrate the WBS Work Packages into Subprojects

Once the details of the project's work scope have been diagrammed at the bottom level of a WBS, the project manager moves up the hierarchy from these detailed tasks, combining them to form control account plans (CAPs). There may be several work products in one CAP, depending on the size and complexity of the project and the number of managers available.

For example, a technical CAP might include most of the tasks from the prototype deliverable except the artistic design, all of the tasks in the engineering deliverable, and some manufacturing tasks. A legal CAP might include competitor research, patent application, independent safety audit, and review of marketing materials.

Each CAP is essentially a subproject that is managed, measured, and controlled by a CAP manager, who is responsible for scheduling and estimating resource requirements for each of the detailed tasks in that CAP. Establishing these CAPs will enable you to integrate cost and schedule information. This contrasts with the way many projects are monitored in which the project manager uses a schedule that can't be examined by cost center, and accountants use a cost-coding system that shows only budget margins without relating them to the amount of work being accomplished.

Each CAP's performance will be measured independently, and the master (total) project's performance is the summation of the performance of its CAPs. Thus the project manager can—at any stage of the project—evaluate the earned value of the project as a whole, and, more importantly, identify which CAPs are underachieving—producing less work product than what should have been produced by the resources expended at that point.

Step 3: Schedule the CAPs

Earned value incorporates two metrics: money and time. As you probably do when planning a project, we'll start with time. In order to measure performance in time, you must create a project schedule, a plan that specifies what is to be done when.

All projects require a scheduling system, and it's crucial to the success of the project that you use project scheduling software. Choose software that will support you in listing tasks for the project, assigning resources to those tasks (in hours or monetary values), scheduling them in sequence using dates or dependencies, establishing key milestones in the project, identifying deadlines, recording progress on the tasks, and making adjustments to the plan.

The more complex the project, the more demands you'll make of the scheduling system. For example, a project spread over several sites requires more flexibility for recording progress. A complex project requires the ability to observe and report progress at several levels, from the master project to the CAPs to department group tasks.

If you haven't used scheduling software before, you'll want to consult your system's manual for advice on where to start. In general, though, you'll want to list the tasks required for each product and how much time you expect each one to take. Then you'll connect them in sequential order (some are likely to overlap), and end each sequence in a milestone that represents the completion of that product. You'll probably assign deadlines to many of the milestones. (See Figure 10.2.)

Figure 10.2
Project Master Schedule

Qtr 1, 2000			Qtr 2, 2000			Qtr 3, 2000			Qtr 4, 2000			Qtr 1, 2001		
Jan	Feb	Mar	Apr	May	Jun	Jul	Aug	Sep	Oct	Nov	Dec	Jan	Feb	Mar
◆ Award														
	◆ Design													
		◆ Parts specifications												
		◆ Factory plans												
			◆ Vendor quotes											
			◆ Tool design											
				◆ Tool fabrication										
				◆ Purchase orders										
					◆ Parts fabrication									
						◆ Receive materials								
								◆ Assembly: sub & final						
									◆ Test & checkout prototype					
										◆ QC acceptance				
											◆ Article shipment			

When all the tasks at the bottom level of the WBS have been linked up to their end products, you have a project schedule baseline. This is the planned work, the baseline against which you will later measure work accomplished to calculate schedule performance. Later you will assign resources (hours and monetary values) to the tasks to create another baseline for planned costs.

In our example, three units of work are scheduled to be completed in the first three months of the HDTV project: parts specifications, and factory preparation plans, prototype, and so on.

Step 4: Assign Each CAP to an Executive Responsible for Its Performance

You must assign each CAP to a permanent functional executive and hold that executive accountable for that CAP's performance. This sounds obvious, but it's often overlooked in situations a company regards as temporary—like projects. By their very nature, projects are transient within a firm's permanent organizational structure. They are planned, authorized, worked on, accomplished, and then cease to exist.

Some companies are more fluid than others in project assignments—functional employees are temporarily assigned to one or several projects in matrix fashion, without much regard to the company's permanent organizational structure. Because of this fluid organization, a person managing a CAP might not carry the formal title of "manager" within a firm's organizational structure. For example, the corporate counsel might use his or her own legal staff for patent application, work with marketing staff for competitor research, review written materials with engineering staff, and contract out the safety audit.

The reverse can also be true: a CAP "manager" may be doing some of the actual work in that CAP, and possibly in other CAPs as well. For example, in our HDTV project, the technical CAP manager might design the quality assurance (QA) procedures and provide technical specs to marketing, as well as supervise all engineering tasks.

To secure a firm commitment from the functional executives, who have the authority and resources to turn the project plan into reality, it is wise to have each of the CAPs adopted by a senior functional executive, such as a vice president, director, or formally titled manager.

Step 5: Establish a Project Measurement Baseline

The next essential step is to create a project baseline of estimated work to which actual costs and earned value will eventually be compared. To accomplish this, each CAP manager loads every task in the CAP with an estimate of the resources required to accomplish it. It's simplest to measure these resources in monetary values, but if you're using reasonably sophisticated software, you can estimate hours required and the software will convert these estimates to costs for each task.

For example, on our HDTV system project, the engineering CAP manager calculates most of that CAP's expenses as labor: the number of engineer hours times the cost per hour. The marketing CAP manager calculates some labor hours, but also adds direct costs for brochure printing, media buys for advertising, and contract costs for the web site.

After resource-loading the tasks, you can see how resources will be used across the schedule. This generally necessitates some adjustments to the schedule, as you may find key people working 60 hours some weeks and others, not yet hired or trained, working on activities scheduled at the beginning of the project.

Once the schedule is adjusted to make realistic use of the available resources, you have a baseline for expenditures that represents expected costs for the entire project. It is made up of the planned expenses of the separate CAPs plus any other projected expenses or funding. For an in-house project, the project baseline may be the sum of the CAPs' planned expenses plus any contingency reserves. (If management holds contingency reserves, not within the discretionary power of the project manager, they should be excluded from the baseline.) On a commercial-type contract, the project baseline may also include indirect costs, profits, fees, and other line items leading up to the total amount of money authorized for the project.

With the schedule baseline from Step 3 and this cost baseline, you can measure planned value, the first set of earned value calculations. Planned value requires two data points: work scheduled for completion and budgeted value of work scheduled. Work scheduled for completion comes directly from the project master schedule. In our example, the first three units (prototype, parts specifications, and factory preparation plans) were scheduled to be finished by the 25 percent completion point (three months into a 12-month project).

Let's say that this project has 15 units of work, each budgeted at $100,000. To determine the budgeted value of work scheduled, we add the budgets for the three units of work that were scheduled to be completed, so the budgeted value of work scheduled is $300,000. This is the planned value: how much the work accomplished so far should be worth.

Step 6: Measure Schedule Performance

One of the simpler measurements of the successful management of a project is its adherence to the original schedule. But the work you've put into the plan so far provides you with a more sophisticated measurement of progress—earned value. To measure earned value, we need to measure the amount of work accomplished and the budgeted value of work performed.

Checking our master project schedule, we find that three units of work should have been accomplished, but only two of them have been. No work has been done on the third unit. Next, we check the budgeted value of the work performed. The two units that have been accomplished were budgeted to cost $100,000 each, so the budgeted value of the work performed is $200,000—and that's the earned value of the project at this point.

At any point in the project, you can compare the planned value of the project to its earned value, for any CAP or for the project as a whole. The result is the schedule variance—the difference between how much the project *should be* worth at this point (based on what your company planned to spend on it) and how much the project *is* worth (based on what has been earned).

A negative schedule variance means that the value of the work accomplished does not match up to the value of the work scheduled (i.e., the project is falling behind in the planned schedule). In our example, we planned to accomplish $300,000 worth of work, but only accomplished $200,000, so we have a negative schedule variance of $100,000. If that doesn't sound like a crisis, consider that we have accomplished only 67 cents' worth of work for every dollar's worth we planned to do.

It's important to realize that negative schedule variances can occur even if work is being accomplished on schedule or if money is being spent at the rate planned, because earned value integrates the measurement of time and costs to show the true value of the work produced to date in comparison to the expected value to date—in other words, making it a more accurate indicator of project performance than either schedule or cost information alone could possibly be.

Our original schedule called for us to accomplish another 12 units of work (worth $1,200,000, budgeted at $100,000 each) in the remaining nine months of the project. If we continue to work at this same level of schedule efficiency where we complete only two units of work for every three units we have scheduled, we will have accomplished only eight of those units by the projected completion date, and we'll have a negative schedule variance of $400,000 at the scheduled completion date for the project.

Step 7: Measure Cost Performance

Now that we have established earned and planned values, we will compare them to actual costs—the amount of money actually spent on the project so far. In our example, let's say we've spent $300,000. That seems right on target; it matches the planned value, the budgeted amount for work scheduled. That's the comforting figure that might have misled us into thinking the project was progressing satisfactorily if we weren't tracking earned value.

However, we now calculate cost variance by comparing earned value to actual costs. Three months into our project, the earned value is $200,000 and the actual costs to complete two units of work are $300,000. Now we see that we spent $300,000 to accomplish $200,000 worth of work. This means that for every dollar we have spent, we have earned only 67 cents of value in the project. We have a 67 percent cost efficiency rate.

Even though the dollar value is small, this is a serious overrun, because it has occurred on a part of the project that's already accomplished. That means it is irrecoverable—the money has already been spent to accomplish less work than it should have paid for. No amount of creativity or effort can change the past. However, overruns identified at early stages of the project, when they can still be expressed in terms of cost efficiency percentage values, can be mitigated if management takes aggressive action on the remaining work.

The cost efficiency rate has been found to be a reliable and stable indicator of a project's adherence to the time and cost baselines, starting at about the 15 percent completion point of a project. It gets progressively more stable as the project goes from the 20 to 30 to 40 percent completion point, making it an important metric for any executive to monitor.

Step 8: Forecast Final Costs Based on Performance to Date

Management at all levels must continually reforecast the project's final cost. Almost as soon as work begins on a project, the originally budgeted total cost ceases to be the most accurate assessment. A far more accurate predictor related to earned value—the cost efficiency rate just described— replaces it.

Simply put, you can use the cost efficiency rate of the completed work to realistically predict the cost of the remaining work, under the valid assumption that the project continues to perform at about the same efficiency. This calculation deploys a sanity check against the more comfortable but less quantifiable idea that "we can make up the difference as we go along."

We have 13 units of remaining work budgeted at $100,000 each for a total of $1,300,000. At our current cost efficiency rate of 67 percent, the remaining work will cost us about 50 percent more than our budget provides. At this efficiency rate, rather than $1,300,000 to complete the remaining 13 units of work, it will cost about $1,950,000. This project is facing a significant overrun of costs, but with an early-warning signal we might have a chance to mitigate the remaining costs. While the project manager and the CAP manager may be assuring you that they can hustle to complete their subprojects on time and on budget, you have a more objective, earned-value–based assessment. In this project, it's clearly time for a senior management person to step in and reconcile the professional difference of opinion. This warning flag for management is one of the most beneficial aspects of earned value measurement.

Step 9: Manage Remaining Work

The work accomplished to date, costs accrued, cost efficiency rate, and earned value achieved to date are in effect sunk costs—gone forever. Any improvements in performance must come from future work, so managing a project means continually monitoring and managing the project's remaining work.

After using earned value to quantify the value of the work achieved, you can quantify what will be required for the rest of the project to stay within the project's, and management's, objectives. If progress and efficiency to date is falling short, the project manager can exert more pressure on future work, and can focus on the most at-risk CAPs within the project.

Step 10: Continually Adjust the Baseline—Manage Changes

In most real-world projects, the performance baseline—the original plan for the project—is subject to change. Calculations involving earned value remain accurate only to the extent they reflect those changes over the duration of the project, no matter when they occur. For example, if the project manager fails to incorporate into the baseline such changes as increased or reduced work, the original baseline will no longer be a valid point of comparison to the work accomplished to date, throwing off subsequent earned-value–based calculations.

Keeping the baseline updated is as important, and sometimes as challenging, as the initial definition of the project scope. However, the payoff is the ability to predict the effects of changes to the plan and understand their implications in a quantifiable manner.

CONCLUSION

A simplified form of earned value can be extraordinarily valuable to anyone responsible for the success of a project. You probably already employ its basic requirements of work breakdown, task scheduling, and resource loading. Using the resulting data points to calculate earned value and the cost and schedule variations will pay for itself in virtually any project where cost growth affects profit, anytime funding is in the form of a lump sum or fixed-price contract, and on all internally funded projects. Why? Because no matter what causes project delays or cost overruns, earned value calculations provide early and accurate warning signals about risks while there's still time to affect the outcome of the project.

CHAPTER 11

INFORMATION MANAGEMENT: FOR THE PROJECT MANAGER IN AN INFORMATION AGE

MARTIN D. HYNES III

The amount of information generated in our society has grown exponentially in the latter part of the twentieth century. Information is bombarding us at an ever-increasing rate enabled by e-mail, voice mail, cell phones, pagers, laptop computers, and personal digital assistants (PDAs). Cellular phones are now so sophisticated that they are Web enabled, allowing one to receive e-mail, voice mail, stock prices, current weather conditions, and so on anywhere at any time. This dramatic increase in information flow is illustrated by the observation that our parents received in one week the amount of mail our grandparents got in one year, while we are receiving in just one day the amount of mail our parents received in that one week.

It is within this context that the project manager manage today's projects. There are at least two important ramifications of this situation for the project manager and those in the project office as they attempt to manage and communicate project-related information. First, people want to receive the specific information they need in a timely manner. An example that illustrates this point is the observation that people are no longer content to wait for the morning paper to check the prices for their stocks. Now they can log on to the Internet at any time of day to obtain the most current stock prices. Additionally, the challenge for the project manager is to communicate project-related information effectively within a society that is on the verge of information overload. This information overload is not only a result of today's technology but more importantly a result of the fact that knowledge is cumulative and the growth of science exponential. This situation presents a significant challenge and opportunity for today's project manager.

This chapter will review project and portfolio information from a general perspective and then offer several examples of information management tools that have been utilized at Eli Lilly and Company to communicate project-related information.

A great deal of information is generated during the course of working on a project. This accumulation starts during the phases of initiating, planning, and developing a detailed scope statement and project plan. Once the project team has been assembled and begins the execution of the plan, there are results of the work performed to report. The team must also be aware of the overall status of the plan with respect to time, cost, and specifications. Potential changes would need to be reported and justified as well. The volume of information that exists for each project is then multiplied by the total number of projects a given organization has in its overall project portfolio, thus resulting in a significant volume of project-related information in many organizations.

For an organization to be successful, this wealth of project-related information needs to be managed and effectively communicated. The communication of this information may span the gamut from internal stakeholders to people external to the organization. This project-related information must be meaningful, reliable, and current to be appreciated, valued, and utilized by the various stakeholders.

TYPES OF INFORMATION

The amount of project-specific information, to some extent, will depend on the scope, complexity, and duration of the project. The typical types of information that exist for a project are scopes, plans, costs in dollars and full-time equivalents (FTEs), time lines, lists of team members, quality requirements, risks, issues, and change-control logs. These types of project information should be included in the project communication plan. However, all projects are unique and, as such, each should have its own well-thought-out communication strategy that is individualized to reflect the project's uniqueness.

Most organizations expect to have an initial burst of communication based on the initiation of the project. Another important expectation exists around the routine communication of project status. In many organizations, status is updated on some regular basis—that is, monthly or when there is a significant change in the project's scope, cost, or schedule. This is frequently accomplished through some type of standardized status reporting format. These status reports provide current information relating to the execution of the project plan.

The major piece of information that stakeholders are most interested in is whether the team is "on plan." This can be determined by assessing variance from the planned schedule. Thus, the majority of attention is focused on plan versus actual for both schedule and cost.

Additionally, status reports can provide the framework for the team to resolve issues that require management attention. For example, if a function has not provided the required resources, this issue can be raised within the context of a status report. Where possible, it is desirable to use a common format for status reports as these can be circulated to a large number of stakeholders. This commonality allows readers of the report to find key pieces of information easily, as well as make comparisons among teams.

Information for a Portfolio of Projects

Most organizations conduct a number of projects simultaneously, making it important for the organization not only to know the status of each individual project, but also to know on an aggregated basis how all of the projects in its portfolio are performing. This assessment can be based on analyzing cost and cycle time performance for the entire portfolio of projects. For example, it may be important to know how many of the projects in the portfolio are on schedule. If they are not on schedule, how many are ahead and how many are behind schedule? Additionally, the organization may want to have performance metrics on cycle time to major milestones. Current cycle time values can then be compared to historical data to assess if the organization is getting better or worse.

Cost is another important factor that organizations track at the portfolio level. The degree of cost variance from plan is an important performance indicator for individual projects as well as the portfolio. Cost variance can be assessed by looking at dollars, as well as people assigned to the project in terms of FTEs. Given that some projects may be above plan while others below it, the aggregate spent for the organization becomes important to ensure that the organization does not over- or underspend its project budget within a fiscal year.

Portfolio value is another typical portfolio indicator. The value of a typical project can be measured in a variety of ways, including expected yearly sales figures or net present value (NPV). Because these value indicators exist for individual projects, they can be summed up across all of the projects in the portfolio, thus allowing an organization to determine if the value of its project portfolio is increasing or decreasing. This information will enable the organization to assess whether the value of its portfolio will meet its business needs and stakeholder expectations for future revenue growth.

INFORMATIONAL NEEDS

One of the most important jobs of the project manager is communication. This is supported by the fact that the Project Management Institute's *Project Management Body of Knowledge (PMBOK)* identifies communication as one of the fundamentals of project management. The *PMBOK* chapter on this fundamental, Chapter 10, outlines communication as a major process with the following four steps:

1. Communication planning.
2. Information distribution.
3. Performance reporting.
4. Administrative closure.

Additionally, within our organization we have identified communication as one of the core competencies for our project managers (Hynes et al. 1999; Kerzner 2000). The operational definition we have utilized is *the ability to listen well and provide information that is easily understood and useful to others.* On a behavioral level, we are looking for project managers who will demonstrate this competency by doing the following:

- Presenting technical and other complex issues in a concise, clear, and compelling manner
- Targeting or positioning communication to address needs or level of understanding of recipient(s) (for example, medical, senior management, and so on)
- Filtering data to provide the mose relevant information (for example, doesn't go over all the details but knows when and how to provide an overall view)
- Keeping others informed, in a timely manner, about decisions or issues that may impact them
- Facilitating and encouraging open communication among team members
- Setting up mechanisms for regular communications with team members in remote locations
- Accurately capturing key points of complex or extended discussions

- Spending the time necessary to prepare presentations for management
- Effectively communicating and representing technical arguments outside one's own area of expertise

Project Managers who do *not* demonstrate this competency will do the following:

- Provide all the available details
- See multiple reminders or messages as inefficient
- Expect team members to understand technical terms of each other's specialties
- Reuse communication and briefing materials with different audiences
- Limit communication to periodic updates
- Invite only to meetings those who (are presumed to) need to be there or who have something to contribute
- Rely on technical experts to provide briefings in specialized technical areas

The selected consequences of *not* demonstrating this competency are

- Individuals outside the immediate team have little understanding of the project.
- Other projects are disrupted by "fire drills" or last-minute changes in plans.
- Key decisions and discussions are inadequately documented.
- Management briefings are experienced as ordeals by team and management.
- Resources/effort are wasted or misapplied.

The goal in identifying communication as a core competency is to help project managers in our organization understand the importance of appropriate communication and to provide direction on how to do this well. The ultimate goal is improving our capability to manage projects that will enable the flow of new medicines to those in need (Hynes et al. 1999). The importance of communication on the project to the success of the project manager has been noted in other studies of project management core competencies (Toney 1999).

Given the sheer wealth and volume of information that is generated within the context of a project and the additional impact on those organizations where there is more than one project being worked on, there is a critical need for an information infrastructure to support the project managers. The need for some type of well-thought-out infrastructure is supported by both the project volume as well as its complexity. The larger a project, the more components it tends to have, thus increasing its complexity. The more complex a project, the more difficult it tends to be to comprehend. Additionally, large and complex projects tend to have large numbers of people working on them, and the more people, the greater the number of connections that exist. The following example from J. Davidson Frame (1994) provides an illustration of the number of connections in relation to team size:

Team Size	Number of Connections
2	1
3	3
4	6
5	10

As the team size grows, the number of connections also grows dramatically. This serves to underscore further the need for a well-thought-out communication plan that is supported by both business and computer systems.

The infrastructure to support project communication must be comprised of both business processes and computer systems. Additionally, it must be designed to assist the project manager in the management of team-based information, as well as its dissemination to the appropriate stakeholders. This would include stakeholders both internal as well as external to the organization.

Team Members

The project manager has the responsibility to communicate with a number of internal stakeholders. The larger the project team and organization, the greater the communication challenge as illustrated by the number of connections in Frame's example.

This responsibility starts with communication to the core and extended members of their teams, as well as line, senior, or executive management. These internal project stakeholders have their unique information needs. It is best if these needs are identified early in the life cycle of a project, therefore allowing the construction of an appropriate communication plan for that team. This will help ensure that these important stakeholders get the project information they need in a timely manner. It is important to understand these needs so that the stakeholders get the correct amount of information they require, not too little or too much, thereby reducing the potential for information overload.

The needs of the core and extended team members can be quite different. For example, team members need to have a detailed level of understanding of what work needs to be done, when it must begin, and when it must be completed. The interrelationship between tasks in the team's project plan, especially those that are on the critical path, is another key piece of information needed by team members. The extended team members need more detailed information relating to their functional jobs and less detailed information on the overall cross-functional project plan.

Non-Team Members

The roles of line management, senior management, and external stakeholders are discussed next.

Line Management
One of the most important internal stakeholders that a project manager needs to communicate with is his or her line management. It is within line organizations that the project team's plans get executed—that is, the function does the work specified in the project plan. Therefore, it is critical that the line management and line organization know what work needs to be performed and when it needs to be completed. This is especially true if the work is on the critical path, *the series of activities which determines the earliest completion of the project (PMBOK, 1996)*. In the event the work is not on the critical path, it may be important for the line organization to know the amount of float it has to deal with. Float is defined as *the amount of time that an activity may be delayed from its early start without delaying the project finish date (PMBOK, 1996)*.

Additionally, the line organization needs a clear understanding of the project manager's and team's quality expectations. This communication process must be a two-way street so there is a flow of information from the team to the function and back. The importance of communicating with the team on the line organization's ability to deliver on time, on specification, and on budget can't be overemphasized.

Senior Management
The needs of senior management in those organizations where there are a number of projects underway are greater than just simply understanding

the status of a particular project. Will a covert project achieve its milestones on time, on specification, and on budget? Senior management generally also wants to know about the overall performance of the portfolio of projects within their organization. Are all the projects progressing according to plan? Will there be a steady flow of new projects to support the economic growth of the organization? Thus their information needs are at both the project and portfolio levels.

Additionally, they will want to know if the organization is improving its ability to execute projects, and if not, what can be done to improve the situation. They may also want to know how they are doing relative to the competition. This may apply to specific projects where another company has a competing project. Therefore, they are keenly interested in monitoring who will be first to market. An aggregate look at the performance of a project portfolio versus the rest of the industry provides an assessment of the firm's ability to remain competitive in the long term. Given the variety of information required by different stakeholders, a well-thought-out communication strategy needs to be designed, developed, and implemented to disseminate and manage the wealth of project-related information. This strategy should be developed very early in the project's life cycle.

External Stakeholders

There may be a need to communicate with people outside of the organization, ranging from contractors who will execute project-related work to stockholders who invest in the organization. In the case of contractors, they are for all intents and purposes acting like an internal line organization; that is, they need to know what work to execute and when, as well as the quality standards. Stockholders or potential investors may consider project-related information key to evaluating the soundness of their investments. This is particularly true for the development and launch of new products, which have the potential of generating significant income.

Investors want to be kept informed on the status of all key projects that will affect the organization's future income and financial viability. In many cases, project-related information is provided by the project team to investor relations by public affairs groups that have the expertise and experience in dealing with external stakeholders.

Additionally, as this project information may be material to the organization/company, its public release may be subject to the U.S. Securities and Exchange Commission (SEC) oversight.

INFORMATION MANAGEMENT

In light of the amount of information that needs to be communicated on a large portfolio of projects, it is critical that both sound business processes and computer systems exist.

Business Systems or Business Processes

The project office should play a strong role in building the business process that supports the dissemination of information. The business process will describe what information should be shared, when it should be communicated, and how it should be shared.

What Information Should Be Shared

The information management strategy should define what information is going to be shared with each of the stakeholders. The project office can facilitate this process by first understanding the stakeholders' information needs. Once these needs have been made explicit, then templates can be built to assist in the formal communication process. For example, templates can and should be developed for project plans, status reports, time lines, and so on. These templates serve two important purposes. One, they ensure that the information key stakeholders want is in fact provided. Additionally, they provide a degree of standardization. This is useful in an organization when more than one project is being conducted, and it allows stakeholders relatively easy cross-project comparison. The creation of the common templates should facilitate the creation of metrics that can be used to assess the performance of the portfolio of projects currently being worked on. For example, organizations not only will want to know how their projects are doing relative to their plans, times, costs, and quality standards, but they will also want to be able to summarize these metrics for all those projects being worked on.

When Information Should Be Communicated

Once the informational needs of key stakeholders have been identified, the frequency with which that information is updated needs to be determined. There are two important drivers for updating key project information: the occurrence of a major change in a project and, secondly, elapsed time. Key stakeholders will want to know when there is a major change or event in the life cycle of the project. These major changes can be related to things such as modification of scope, slippages in time, and cost overruns, to name a few.

Additionally, achieving significant project milestones may prompt the need for a project and/or portfolio update. While it is important to communicate these major events in a timely manner, not all projects have these types of significant events in a given period of time. Therefore, there is a need to have a business process that facilitates the updating of projects and portfolio data on a regular or routine basis. For example, monthly status reports may be the correct frequency for routine project updates. The frequency of these reports can be driven by the stakeholders' need for updated information.

How the Information Should Be Shared

Once the informational needs have been established and it has been determined how frequently this information needs to be updated, the next major task is to define how to provide this information to key stakeholders. This is a particularly daunting task in the information-based society in which we live. In the past, the tradition has been to copy key reports and mail them to key stakeholders. "Snail" mail, whether it be mail handled by the post office or interoffice mail, will in all likelihood not provide the timely updates that will meet stakeholders' needs in this fast-paced society.

Additionally, the risk of paper status reports landing in an in basket and sitting there unnoticed for some period of time is very real. The information technology revolution can be useful in the dissemination of project/portfolio information. Tools such as voice mail, e-mail, the Internet, and the corporate intranet can be valuable to the project manager as he or she tries to communicate key information to team members, line managers, and senior management.

Electronic Tools

The projects management workbench and team-based Web tools will be discussed in this section as examples of electronic communication tools.

Projects Management Workbench

Over the past several years, we have been able to develop and deploy a number of electronic tools to assist project managers in communicating with the global organization, as well as with team members. One of the first electronic tools that we constructed was the *projects management workbench* (Hynes et al., 1999). The workbench was designed to make three types of information available to the global organization:

- Project-specific information.
- Data on the performance of the portfolio.
- Project-management tools.

A screen shot of the workbench is shown in Figure 11.1.

Internal business processes call for a standard set of documents to be available for each project, or, in our case, each new drug under development. This standard set of documents includes the detailed project plan, status reports, draft package insert, project team directory, project team assumptions, and project time line. Additional documents can be added at the discretion of the project manager. A search function is available to help users locate compound-specific information based on the compound identifier, therapeutic class, project leader, and/or indication, as well as the project description. Data on the performance of all of the projects in the portfolio is also available. A vast amount of information on the performance of all the drug development projects in the portfolio is available in this section of the workbench.

A variety of different types of reports have been designed to summarize the aggregate performance of the portfolio. This includes a history of those compounds under development, high-level Gantt charts for those molecules currently being worked on, and milestone reports that

Figure 11.1
Projects Management Workbench

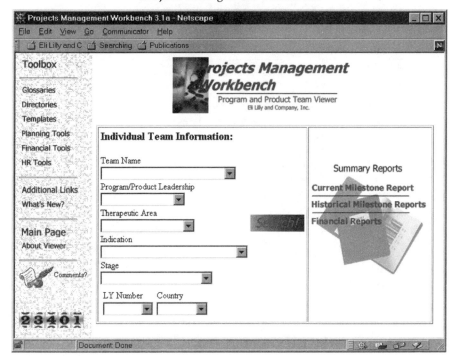

chronologically show all of the projects under development that will achieve that major milestone within the next 12 months. An example of the Gantt chart showing all compounds under development is provided in Figure 11.2. These charts are color coded by phase of development to indicate the duration of each phase of the drug development process. The data depicted are for real projects; however, the names of the compounds have been replaced with the appropriate therapeutic class for confidential purposes.

Figure 11.3 shows all of the compounds that will achieve their first human dose milestone, which marks the start of Phase I safety trials in volunteers in the next year. Similar reports exist for each major milestone; all of these reports are updated on a monthly basis and posted to the workbench. Financial information is also available on the workbench. Data on actual project expense versus planned expense for individual projects, functional areas, and therapeutic classes is also available. Financial information is updated on a quarterly basis.

Brief status reports are provided by the project leader on a monthly ba-

Figure 11.2
Gantt Chart Showing All Compounds under Development

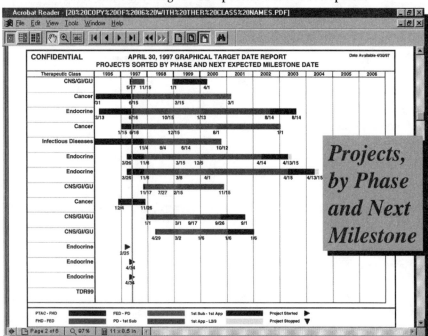

Figure 11.3
Compounds That Will Achieve Their First Human Dose Milestone

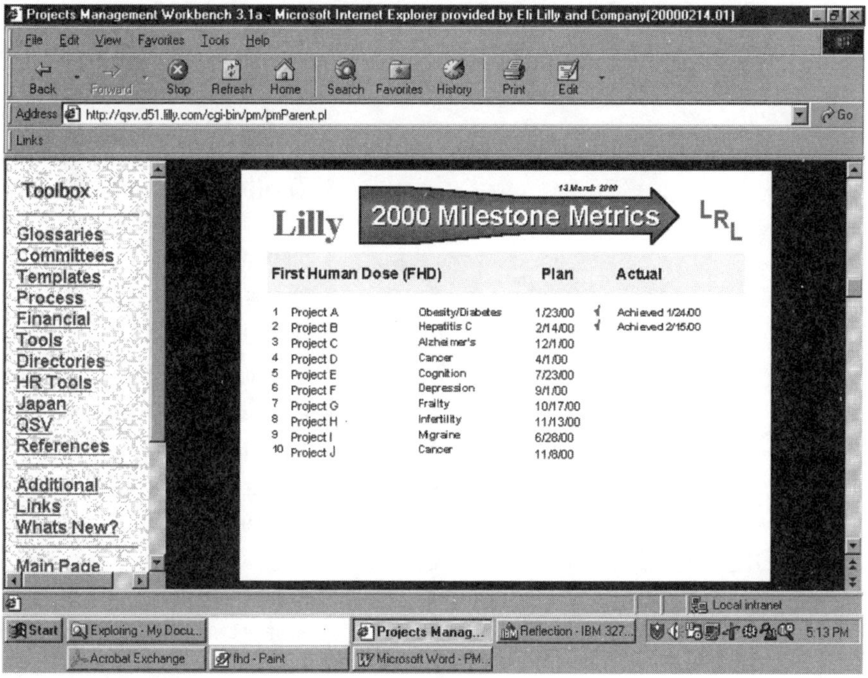

sis. Standard templates exist for these status reports so that uniform data is available for each project. These status reports contain brief summaries on the current status of the project and any issues that could potentially delay the project.

Given that all of this information is updated on a monthly basis, the workbench provides one central site for all drug development information, thus helping to ensure rapid communication of project status and issues. The availability of these issues supports their identification at a time when corrective action to maintain the current schedule, scope, and budget is still feasible.

The third major type of information that is made available on the workbench relates to projects management tools and techniques as seen in Figure 11.4. This section of the workbench contains a dictionary of drug development terms, planning templates, and a variety of project management tools. Within this section of the workbench there are links to external references as resources on best practices in project management and

Figure 11.4
The Project Managment Tools and Techniques Section of the Workbench

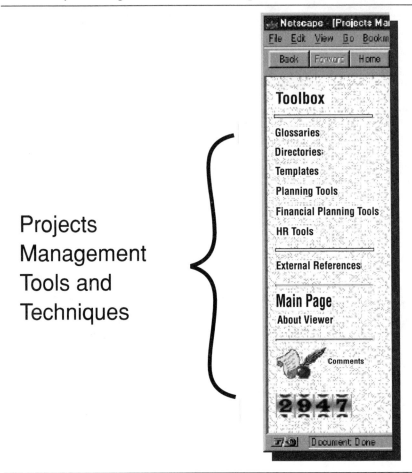

Projects
Management
Tools and
Techniques

drug development. These links include the web sites of the Project Management Institute, the Food and Drug Administration, and the Drug Information Association.

The workbench has been a key tool in the management of project information. However, the level of detail, particularly on the projects under development, is extremely helpful to those people who support the project. Additionally, we have found that it is extremely helpful to those in a functional area or those who are distant from the centralized research site where the vast majority of projects are managed.

A Team-Based Web Tool

To meet the information management needs of project teams, a team-specific electronic communication tool was then created. This is a tool that is accessible only to team members. Access is not provided to line or senior management. This team-based tool was designed to provide a consistent means of creating, circulating, storing, and retrieving team-based information (McElwain et al. 1999). Additionally, this team tool has the capacity to store as much detailed information as the team desires.

The following is a list of the types of information that the team can place in their tool:

- Team agendas.
- Team minutes.
- Team plans.
- Functional plans.
- Time lines.
- Competitive analyses.
- Discussion database.

This information management tool has helped teams by greatly reducing the time required to manage information. For example, in the past, team minutes were published, duplicated, and sent to relevant parties by e-mail or interoffice mail. After receipt, the team members would then have to file them. Now, the team minutes are directly posted to the minutes section of the tool where they exist with all of the minutes from past team meetings in chronological order.

Additionally, the tool is extremely helpful in transitioning new members to an existing team. The database can be loaded onto their desktop computers so that they have all team-based information in one place at one time, thus achieving a high degree of consistency in information storage, access, and retrieval. An example of this type of tool is shown in Figure 11.5.

COMMUNICATION TOOLS TO FOSTER SHARED LEARNING

The tools that have been described so far have been designed, developed, and deployed to help manage team-based performance information, thus meeting the informational needs of many stakeholders relative to project and portfolio performance. It is important to recognize that as

Figure 11.5
Team-Specific Electronic Communication Tool

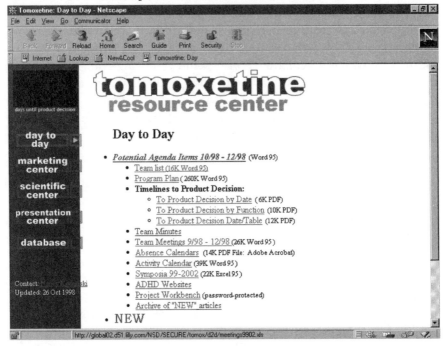

project-related work progresses, many lessons relevant to the conduct of projects are learned. These lessons could potentially help others as they manage and guide their projects through the product development process. These lessons can frequently help others achieve excellence in how they manage their projects. Therefore, it is important that the project management organization or project office have methods or procedures in place that allow for the capture and dissemination of this type of information.

A routine practice should be the completion of a lessons-learned exercise, or an *after-action review* as they are known in the military, at the completion of projects or the achievement of major project milestones. Once these lessons learned have been captured, it is critical that a mechanism for their dissemination be in place. This mechanism can range from a discussion at a shared learning forum or a staff meeting to creating a central repository for these lessons-learned documents. Such a repository would provide project managers important reference material that could be utilized when needed, such as prior to planning a certain type of project, or while trying to deal with certain types of development issues or problems. This central repository could take the form of hard-copy documents, web sites, or Lotus Notes folders. In our experience, the creation of a Lotus Notes folder has proven to be a viable method for sharing learning across teams (Stephens 1999).

INFORMATION MANAGEMENT VERSUS KNOWLEDGE MANAGEMENT

In recent years, there has been a growing focus on knowledge management. As a result, many organizations have started knowledge management initiatives in the hope of improving their business results. Knowledge management initiatives have at least five major dimensions (Perez and Hynes 1999):

1. Technology
2. Process
3. Context
4. People
5. Content

The technology dimension encompasses the tools utilized in the knowledge management initiative, which can range from pencils to computers. The flow of information, its use, and governance are the key elements of the process dimension. The context of a knowledge management initiative is the environment in which it exists, from both a cultural and a climatic standpoint. Content represents the data, its definitions, accuracy, and relevance.

The fourth dimension of knowledge management is people, which includes the psychology of how information is taken in, absorbed, and made into new knowledge. This integrated model assumes that information leveraged or acted upon is central to knowledge management. Information can be collected, organized, managed, and disseminated, but it is not considered knowledge unless it is actionable. Without causing or enabling a change relative to a business problem, any information may have great value but it does not qualify as knowledge.

It is only when technology, process, context, people, and content are integrated in a meaningful fashion does one move from information management to knowledge management. Each of these five knowledge management dimensions is intertwined with the others, as can be seen in Figure 11.6. All five of these dimensions must be addressed in a high-

Figure 11.6
The Integrated Five-Dimensional Knowledge Management Model

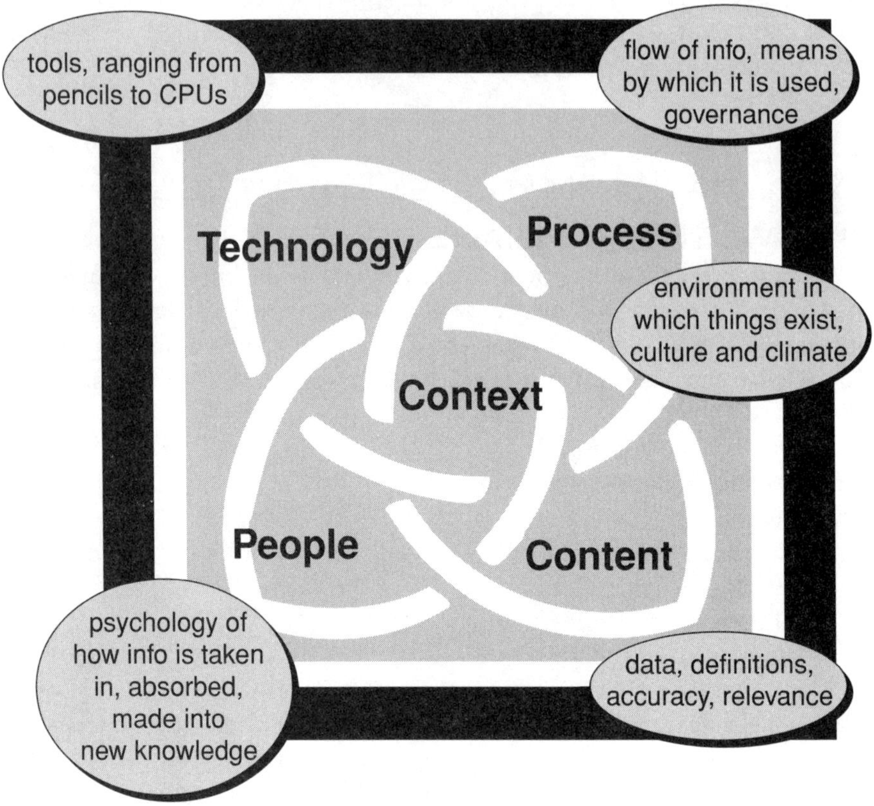

quality way in order to have maximum impact on an organization. No one dimension is regarded as inherently more important than the others nor should one dominate the others. Thus, with a consideration of each of these five knowledge management dimensions, an organization can change information into actionable knowledge that can lead to improved business performance.

CONCLUSION

The management of project information is key to the success of project managers and the projects they have responsibility for. Managing information well is a particularly challenging task given the exponential growth of information in the twentieth century. This challenge results from the wealth of information that is available, as well as expectations surrounding availability. In this age of cell phones, e-mail, the World Wide Web, and voice mail, people demand that information be delivered in a timely manner.

The issue of information volume is exacerbated in a project environment by the fact that each project can generate a significant amount of information. Typically, a project will have a scope statement, plan, budget, time line, list of team members, quality requirements, risks, issues, and change-control logs. This is not even an exhaustive list of information elements because as the project starts, there is status to communicate on all of these dimensions as well as on the results of the work conducted. Further compounding the issue is the fact that most organizations are working on multiple projects. So one just needs to take the information on a given project and then multiply it by the total number of projects ongoing within the organization's portfolio.

Given the sheer volume and complexity of information for a given portfolio, it is important for the project manager to construct a well-thought-out communication plan. This plan not only needs to take into consideration the project-specific information that the manager wants to communicate but the people with whom the manager will be communicating. Understanding the informational needs of the people with whom you will be communicating is extremely important, as a typical project has multiple stakeholders, many of whom have very different informational needs as well as expectations around the frequency of communications. Therefore, the communication plan needs to be built with an understanding of these unique needs. At a minimum, the project manager needs to have a full appreciation for the informational needs of the core and extended team members. Additionally, the communication plan needs to take into consideration the informational needs of non-team members, most importantly line and senior management.

Once the types of project-related information that need to be communicated to the various project stakeholders have been determined, the frequency of communication can be established. The project manager can then address how this all-important communication task will be accomplished. Within the chapter, several examples of electronic tools that we have built at Eli Lilly and Company have been described. These electronic tools have greatly aided in the communication of drug development information within our organization.

A project management organization not only has the role of managing projects; it also has the responsibility of improving the methods utilized in the management of projects. These improvement activities can be aided by conducting a lessons-learned analysis on each project at a major milestone or termination. To store this information, a Lotus Notes database has been developed at Lilly. This allows the storage and retrieval of important reference material for project managers. Given that this information is electronically available, it can be retrieved when needed by a project manager.

The goal of any organization in this competitive economy is to turn information into knowledge that provides a competitive advantage. This is the objective of the myriad knowledge management initiatives that have been undertaken by industry.

There are at least five important dimensions to knowledge management. They are technology, process, context, people, and content. It is only when each one of these dimensions is carefully considered that information can be turned into knowledge. This actionable knowledge can be used to drive improvements at the project and portfolio level to provide a sustainable competitive advantage.

REFERENCES

Frame, J. Davidson. 1994. *The New Project Management*. San Francisco: Jossey-Bass.

Hynes, M. D. III. 1999. "The Assessment of Several Knowledge Management Tools Implemented to Accelerate Drug Development." Drug Information Association's 35th Annual Meeting, Baltimore, MD (June 27–July 1).

————. 1999. "The Development of a Core Competency Model for Pharmaceutical Project Managers." PMI '99 30th Annual Seminars and Symposium, Philadelphia, PA (October 10–16).

Hynes, M. D., S. A. Getzin, L. McQuaid, C. M. Seward, N. L. Miller, and R. R. Field-Perez. 1999. "Creation of a Knowledge-Based System to Accelerate Drug Development." *Drug Information Journal*, Vol. 33, (November 2): 641–648.

Hynes M. D. and R. R. Perez. 1999. "Assessing Knowledge Management Initiatives." *Knowledge Management Review*, Issue 8 (May/June).

Kerzner, Harold. 2000. *Applied Project Management*. New York: John Wiley & Sons.

McElwain, K., N. A. Kowinski, and M. D. Hynes III. 1999. "The Use of Web-Based Communication Tools to Facilitate the Drug Development Process." Drug Information Association's 35th Annual Meeting, Baltimore, MD (June 27–July 1).

Project Management Institute Standards Committee. 1996. *A Guide to the Project Management Body of Knowledge (PMBOK)*. Upper Darby, PA: Project Management Institute.

Stephens, C. 1999. "How to Transfer Innovations, Solutions, and Lessons Learned across Product Teams: Implementation of a Knowledge Management System." PMI '99 30th Annual Seminars and Symposium, Philadelphia, PA (October 11).

Toney, F. 1999. "Competencies of Superior Project Managers and Project Organizations That Result in Project Goal Achievement." Fortune 500 Project Management Benchmarking Forum, Scottsdale, Arizona, June 1999.

CHAPTER 12

PROJECT CLOSEOUT MANAGEMENT: MORE THAN SIMPLY SAYING GOOD-BYE AND MOVING ON

TERRY COOKE-DAVIES

Nobody gets excited about project closeout management. That isn't to say that nobody wants to complete their projects, or that people don't want to judge how successful projects have been. It's just that the associated routine (or process) and paperwork never seem as important as the myriad of other things that a project manager and his or her team must do as a project, or a stage of one, is being closed. The work has been done, the customer has what it wants, and everybody's mind is moving on to the next project or challenge. Project managers, project sponsors, and project team members alike will readily acknowledge the importance of project closeout management. The logic is unassailable.

If adequate product records are not kept, whole-life costs of the product are likely to increase. If there is no deep and thorough understanding of where reality has diverged from plans, there is little hope of making better plans next time. If time is not taken to reflect on the lessons of the past, the likelihood is that similar mistakes will be made in the future. If project relationships are not brought to a satisfactory closure, unresolved issues and resentments may smolder beneath the surface, ready at any time to erupt with unpleasant consequences. And yet none of these arguments is enough to change people's attitudes toward and responses to project closeout management.

In the course of the next few pages we will review the following:

- The activities that project managers generally advocate should be a part of project closeout management.

- Why project closeout management is vitally important to every organization that undertakes projects.
- Factors that prevent organizations from managing project closeout effectively.
- A new perspective on project closeout management—its function as a part of a knowledge management system.
- Steps that organizations can take to improve the practice of project closeout management.

PROJECT CLOSEOUT
MANAGEMENT ACTIVITIES

Although each of the different project management "bodies of knowledge" refer to "closeout," "commissioning," or "handover," the general lack of interest in project closeout is typically mirrored in textbooks about project management. Look through the index of a project management book for the words "closeout," "project completion," or "post-implementation review," and there is a good chance you will come up with a blank.

Where reference is made, however, there is general agreement on the kinds of activities that should be undertaken. In this section, we will consider them under the seven following topics (see Figure 12.1):

Figure 12.1
The Seven Elements of Project Closeout Management

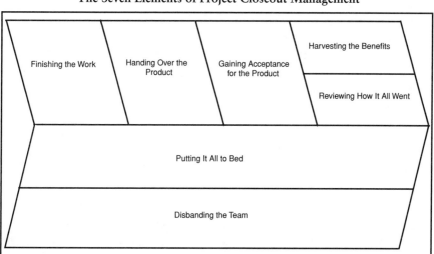

1. Finishing the work
2. Handing over the product
3. Gaining acceptance for the product
4. Harvesting the benefits
5. Reviewing how it all went
6. Putting it all to bed
7. Disbanding the team (ending relationships)

It is perhaps worth mentioning that not all of these activities are equally important to all kinds of projects. Therefore, the project manager and other members of the leadership team should consider between them which activities deserve more attention for their specific project.

Finishing the Work

As the project nears completion, there is a natural tendency for members of the team to do sufficient work to meet time and de facto quality standards, while leaving a number of small elements of the work outstanding. There may also be issues that have emerged at various times during the life of the project and have yet to be resolved. An orderly closeout requires that some kind of checklist of these tasks and issues be prepared and used as a control mechanism. Such short-term activity lists are sometimes referred to as *punch-lists.*

Rodney Turner advocates that this control should be more frequent during project closeout than during the main execution phase of the project (possibly daily rather than weekly), and at a lower level of work breakdown structure—that is, they should be detailed tasks.[1] It can also be particularly useful to make use of 360-degree feedback to ensure that all the tasks and issues are identified. Anyone who has moved into a new house when the builders have already left and moved onto their next project will be able to attest to the fact that users (in such a case) are much more aware of unfinished tasks than are the project team members whose attention is by now elsewhere.

Handing Over the Product

Whatever the nature of the project, some form of handover will be required. In the case of large items of capital equipment, it would be unthinkable to let the handover take place without careful planning, and this same care is actually required on projects of all types. The managers or end users of the product (or providers of the service) that has been created or modified in the course of the project won't share the same insights and knowledge about it that the project team has generated in that time. The activity of handover includes not simply the transfer of the physical deliverables, but also the training of users, the sharing of technical designs and important design concepts, the provision of drawings and specifications, and much more besides.

If there is a formal warranty period or an informal equivalent, the handover time frame extends for several weeks or months after acceptance, and needs to be controlled and resourced appropriately.

The quality of the handover has a major influence on the extent to which the anticipated benefits are maximized from the newly created product or service. The handover plan should include activities designed both to allow the end user to understand how to obtain optimum performance and to build up the necessary motivation to accomplish that goal.

Gaining Acceptance for the Product

There is a routine between two pilots flying the same airplane that is designed to ensure that there is never any ambiguity about who is actually at the controls. The one passing over control says something like "You have control," and the other replies, "I have control." It is this second element in the interaction that represents the actual passing of control. Projects need a similarly clear cutoff to signal the end of handover and the transfer of full operational responsibility from the project team to the customer.

Gaining acceptance is not as simple or straightforward as it might appear at first. One aspect of this activity involves having the customer who is signing the acceptance certificate (or its equivalent) now accept full control for managing the new product or service. This might feel scary for all kinds of reasons, such as:

- The customer may lack confidence in his or her ability to manage the product or service effectively without the ongoing help and support of the project team.
- The customer may doubt his or her ability to deliver the benefits from the product or service on which the business case was built, and there will no longer be anyone else with whom to share the blame.
- The customer may be receiving adverse comments from end users who were never convinced of the merits of the project in the first place.
- The customer or end users may have come to realize in the course of the project that what they really want isn't the product or service that the project has delivered, and as long as no acceptance has been signed, it might be possible to improve the match.

For these reasons, planning for project acceptance needs to start much earlier in the life of the project—ideally during project initiation. The problems listed, as well as many not mentioned, can all be taken care of if two preconditions apply: the problems have been foreseen and remedies planned, and the relationship between the customer and the project manager/team is sufficiently strong to have built the confidence that is necessary to gain acceptance.

Harvesting the Benefits

Opinion is divided as to whether it should be the responsibility of the project manager to deliver the benefits or the responsibility of the sponsor or client, with the project manager simply delivering the product or service as specified within budget, time scale, and quality criteria. To an extent, the debate is academic and irrelevant; regardless of whether the responsibility lies with the project manager or the project sponsor, the project will be successful only when the intended benefits are harvested. This means that the project team has a genuine interest in the product or service being managed in such a way that the full benefits are obtained.

Benefits come in many shapes and sizes. Some of them are easy to quantify and measure, such as sales and revenue from a new line of products. Others are easy to quantify but less easy to measure, such as cost savings from an improved interdepartmental business process. Still more are difficult both to quantify and to measure, such as the benefits of company-wide education in risk management.

Many words have been written about the importance of measurement. Techniques such as the "balanced scorecard" are increasingly seeking to present a rounded view of the different measures needed to assess the overall health of a business enterprise. There is no room here to add significantly to these words. The important point to make for project close-out management is that the project manager and sponsor need to ensure that three conditions exist before the project is finally put to bed:

1. The criteria by which benefits of the product or service will be measured or assessed are clear.
2. The points in time at which the measurement or assessment will be carried out are established.
3. A named person has accepted responsibility for carrying out the measurement or assessment in the agreed way at the agreed points in time.

Reviewing How It All Went

Project success is a very elusive concept. A project that appears to have been successful from the point of view of one set of stakeholders might appear to have failed when seen from another viewpoint. A project that is completed on time and within budget might look splendid at the time of project closeout, but a year later, with the benefit of hindsight, it might appear to have been a big mistake. For this reason, it is important that the different groups of stakeholders all agree at the outset precisely what will constitute "project success."

These same groups of stakeholders should then, as far as possible, be involved in reviewing at the close of the project the degree of success that was actually achieved. Because many of the benefits will not be harvested until after the project is complete, the post-implementation review is best carried out in two stages—a lessons-learned review while members of the project team have the actual events of the project fresh in their minds, and a post-implementation review some months after the product has been in operation, when the benefits can be more accurately assessed.

The object of the lessons-learned review is to reflect on the events that took place in the course of the project and to consider what might have been done differently to improve the results obtained. The review may well be led by the project manager or the project sponsor, and will be attended by representatives from all significant parties that contributed to the project. The review is likely to be based on a comparison between the actual results and conduct of the project, and the project charter and project plan.

A frequently encountered problem is how to create the right climate for an honest review. Lessons learned are unlikely to be of real and lasting value if they are tainted by the need for participants to present what happened in a light that is favorable to themselves. Unfortunately, there is no easy answer to this. The skills of creating an atmosphere of trust within a group are subtle and complex, but some pointers for the conduct of the review meeting can be helpful:

- Establish clear and explicit ground rules about the quality of openness and communication that is expected. For example, each person should speak for himself or herself, and everyone will have their say. It is not important that everyone agrees about everything; participants will listen to others respectfully.
- Focus the meeting's attention on describing what happened, and

move on to interpreting what it might mean only after perceptions of what happened have been clearly established.

• Concentrate on extracting lessons for the future, rather than establishing blame for what is now in the past.

The results should be communicated to everyone who needs to know what happened. This group is likely to include the project sponsor, future project sponsors, members of the present project team (including suppliers and subcontractors), potential managers of similar future projects, and the person or group responsible for the conduct of projects throughout the organization. (See Figure 12.2.)

The post-implementation review has a somewhat different focus. Its purpose is to establish the extent to which the product of the project is delivering the anticipated benefits. The review is likely to be based on a comparison between actual operating benefits being harvested and those predicted in the business case for the project. Although it is desirable for the project manager to be present, some person or group that was not intimately involved in the project itself ideally, such as an internal auditor or a specially appointed reviewer conducts the review. The focus is on the

Figure 12.2
The Hidden Complexity of Project Closeout Management

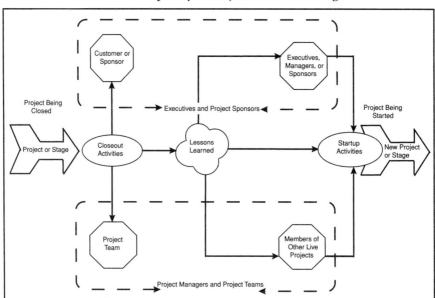

product in operation and the impact on benefits of decisions made during the establishment and execution of the project.

Similar to the lessons-learned review, the results should be communicated widely to the appropriate audience.

Putting It All to Bed

Completing the documentation and archiving the project records are perhaps the most monotonous and least exciting parts of project closeout management, which is in itself hardly the most glamorous part of project management (although it is arguably one of the most important ones).

At least one telecommunications infrastructure company during the early 1990s was very far behind with updating the drawings of switch houses after upgrade projects. When engineers would routinely arrive to upgrade the system, they would find that there was no room to install the specified upgrade because previous upgrades had already utilized all the available space, but the drawings had not yet been updated to reflect the true situation.

In addition to drawings and technical documentation, there are other project records to complete and archive, including financial records, personnel records, and essential records of meetings, reviews, contracts, and so on.

If the project has had the use of dedicated resources, such as offices or technology, then these need to be returned or passed on.

Anticipated benefits need to be included in business plans, and in the operating plans and budgets of all departments that are the beneficiaries of the product or service.

Ending Relationships

The seventh and final element of project closeout management is ending relationships, or disbanding the project team. As tasks come to an end, resources can be released in an orderly fashion. In the case of people who work for the same organization as the project manager, they can return to their own line or functional department in order to take on other tasks. In the case of contractors and suppliers, it is important that contracts are closed to prevent unnecessary work being charged to the project after it has formally ended.

Two aspects of saying good-bye are important—celebrating and providing feedback. At some time when the memories of the project are still fresh in the minds of the project team, some form of celebration such as a party can help team members move on from the past to their future assignments with a sense of closure regarding the completed project. This is an important social dynamic.

The second aspect is equally important, and just as often ignored—people need to understand their own contributions to the project's results. Appraisals with each team member are the means by which members' own perceptions of their contributions can be checked against the project manager's perceptions. In an organization where much of the work is carried out in projects, this can be the only feedback available to the line or functional manager on which development plans and career opportunities can be assessed.

WHY PROJECT CLOSEOUT MANAGEMENT MATTERS

The seven sets of activities just discussed all relate to closing a single project. They are important to each and every project. But that is far from the whole story. Project team members will go on to work on other projects; project clients will initiate other projects on behalf of their businesses; new projects will be established; and suppliers and subcontractors will be employed on future projects.

When this broader perspective is considered, project closeout management becomes the springboard for a whole set of future value-creating activities in an organization, and is a pivotal activity in the context of organizational learning. (See Figure 12.2, earlier in this chapter.)

Project closeout management carried out well will give people the chance to learn lessons while they are still fresh in the memory and while the context is well understood. Conversely, the lack of effective project closeout management can lead to the demotivation of team members, who can easily feel that their contribution was not valued and that the organization has no interest in learning from their experience.

While survey after survey points to the high social and economic cost of project failures, project closeout management becomes the focal point for understanding the particular circumstances that led to success and/or failure on each specific project. Yet, in spite of this, project closeout management remains one of the least well executed of project management activities.[2]

How can this be? As the philosopher George Santayana said, "Those who cannot remember the past are condemned to repeat it." What prevents organizations from applying common sense in such an important area? The next section will examine possible answers to this question.

WHAT PREVENTS EFFECTIVE PROJECT CLOSEOUT MANAGEMENT?

What has just been described is common knowledge and common sense, but is far from common practice. This is what actually happens all too often:

- Getting paid, or getting closure, drives all closeout actions. Unresolved issues and incomplete tasks that frustrate customers and end users drag on while the project manager hopes they will eventually go away.
- Acceptance becomes acrimonious, with the project team doing the minimum they have to in order to get the signature, the customer signing an acceptance certificate (or its equivalent) only grudgingly, and relationships ultimately being soured or severed.
- Companies feel that they don't have time to complete postproject reviews correctly. The project team is busy on the next urgent project, and there just never seems to be the time to fit the meeting into a crowded schedule.
- The task of completing project records is assigned such a low priority that drawings are never completely finished, archives are never closed off, and so on.
- Lessons learned may be noted, recorded, and even filed, but they aren't *learned*. Sometimes a politically correct story about the project gains acceptance in corporate folklore.

Why it should be this way becomes understandable when the following formidable array of barriers to effective project closeout management is considered:

- Completing records is a distraction. There are already too many important activities that obviously add value and that clamor for attention.
- Closeout activities cost money, and in the final stages it is easy to see that money can be saved simply by not doing them. If the project lost money or cost more than expected, why should good money be thrown after bad? If the project went well, there probably isn't much to be dealt with, anyway.
- There is a widespread myth that learning is a personal activity, and so the lessons to be learned from the project will be available to the organization informally through the experience of the project manager and project team members.

- While most project organizations pay lip service to the importance of project closeout management, there are rarely any tangible or emotional/psychological rewards given to people who pay particular attention to this aspect of project management. The folly of "asking for X while rewarding Y" may be acknowledged, but instances of it abound.

- Effective project managers tend to be very task-oriented people with a strong commitment to the project and a desire to deliver results. They tend to prefer to organize tasks for action rather than sitting in meetings reflecting on events that they can no longer influence. Preferring practice to theory, they tend to know what they have concluded from the recent project and have now moved on, in their thinking, to their next challenge.

- While many organizations acknowledge the importance of projects and their success, they frequently underestimate the extent of the difference necessary between thinking about projects on the one hand and either operations (repetitive processes) or tasks (simple activities) on the other hand. Because operations are by their very nature repetitive, they do not require specific closeout; a philosophy of continuous improvement is more relevant. Because tasks, which may or may not be repetitive, lack the complexity of projects, they often lend themselves to simple and straightforward analysis and a philosophy of "just do it." Consequently, there is often insufficient attention paid to the unique difficulties of creating organizational learning in a project environment, where circumstances guarantee that every experience contains unique elements.

This latter point will now be explored in depth.

A MISSING PERSPECTIVE— KNOWLEDGE MANAGEMENT

The essential tasks of project closeout management can be seen as two quite distinct types of activities. On the one hand, there are the tasks associated with completing the project in all its aspects, and on the other hand, there is the qualitatively different set of tasks associated with learning all that the project has to teach. This second set of tasks can be characterized as *knowledge management.*

People use the word *knowledge* to mean many different things, and a whole field of management activity known as knowledge management is emerging. Much of this development seems to be in response to the challenge of creating a truly "learning organization."

Unfortunately, many terms are used loosely in this connection, and there is no commonly accepted definition for many of them. As a result, there is a tremendous potential for "woolly thinking" and miscommunication. It helps to make a distinction between knowledge and information. *Knowledge* cannot exist outside of a "knower," whereas *information* can have an independent existence. Information can be written down, stored on a computer, or even transmitted by videotape. On the other hand, information only becomes knowledge when it is internalized by somebody or some group of people and becomes available to them for practical application.

With this distinction in mind, it is clear that learning lessons on projects is much more about knowledge than it is about information. Consequently, the process often adopted by organizations to capture and transmit what has been learned on projects (see Figure 12.2, earlier in this chapter) is a process for transmitting information rather than knowledge. This is true regardless of whether the files containing the records of lessons learned are paper-based, stored in computerized databases, or distributed throughout the organization on an intranet.

Knowledge has a large tacit element and is applied selectively. In other words, when people possess high know-how, they are very careful to apply what they know only when it is appropriate to do so, and the greater the degree of mastery of the subject, the greater the finesse they display in applying their knowledge.

In terms of the process of transferring lessons from one project to another, this has major implications. On closer examination, it is clear that a fault line runs down the center of the process—between capturing lessons learned on the project being closed and applying them on the project being started (see Figure 12.3). The first part is the responsibility of an outgoing project team, whereas the second part occurs toward the beginning of a project and is the responsibility of an incoming project team.

Why should the second team learn from the first one? It can be tempting to dismiss the experiences of the first project due to specific circumstances that don't apply to the new project. There is also little incentive to learn unless the second team has a high degree of respect for the first one, and its members are anxious to learn what their predecessors have discovered. This is much more likely if both project teams see themselves as members of a higher-level community, with accountability to all members of the community as well as to the organization that employs them. This suggests that the role of the project-management community

Figure 12.3
Disconnects in the Lessons-Learned Process

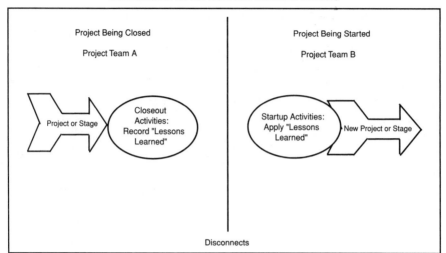

within an organization is much more significant than has been previously recognized.

Support for this suggestion comes from a completely separate source that is in no way connected with the world of project management—the study of communities of practice[3]:

> Communities of practice are emerging in companies that thrive on knowledge. The first step for managers now is to understand what these communities are and how they work. The second step is to realize that they are the hidden fountainhead of knowledge development and therefore the key to the challenge of the knowledge economy. The third step is to appreciate the paradox that these informal structures require specific managerial efforts to develop them and to integrate them into the organization so that their full power can be leveraged.[4]

The final section in this chapter will consider what steps an organization can take to use this new perspective to give effective project closeout management the emphasis in practice that it currently receives only in theory.

OPPORTUNITIES TO MAKE FUNDAMENTAL IMPROVEMENTS

Unlike any other project management activity, project closeout management is more important for future projects that will be undertaken by an organization than it is for the current project to which it is being applied. Unless this is recognized from the outset, it will continue to languish in the twilight world of "worthy activities that we never quite get around to."

The people who need to do the recognizing are not, in the first instance, the project managers but rather the beneficiaries of an effective and efficient project management system. They are the people who are responsible for the efficient implementation of the project portfolio—senior management. This recognition requires making the following three decisions, supported by follow-through at the executive level of the organization.

First, the learning-lessons element of project closeout management needs to be seen not as a part of the bundle of activities associated with completing the project; it should be given its rightful place as an essential input to the organization's collective wisdom about project management practice. It should be perceived as an input to the knowledge-management process.

For example, this element should include the recognition that the application of lessons learned during project start-up is a continuation of the process of knowledge transfer that starts during project closeout. Executive actions might then include the refusal to sanction new projects unless the project team can demonstrate that they have applied all relevant lessons from past projects to their thinking about the current project.

Second, the importance of the organization's project managers as a community of practice should be recognized, and steps taken to encourage it to flourish in spite of the pressures on individual project managers.

Finally, every effort should be made to enable performance data to be compared between projects in such a way that the relevance of lessons learned on one project is clear to other project teams. Practical steps toward doing this might include categorizing projects into different types, and maintaining common sets of performance data with clear definitions that are understood by all project managers.

None of these decisions are easy or obvious, and the payoff will come from an improvement in the performance of the whole portfolio of projects undertaken by an organization rather than from any individual project.

As the project model increases in importance for all organizations (as it surely will) and as organizations seek to reduce the social and economic costs of poor project performance (as they surely must), project closeout management will emerge as what it truly is—the gateway to an organization's knowledge about what constitutes excellence in project management practice.

NOTES

1. J. Rodney Turner. 1993. *Handbook of Project-Based Management*. London: McGraw-Hill.
2. This assertion is based on proprietary benchmarking data.
3. Etienne Wenger. 1998. *Communities of Practice: Learning, Meaning, and Identity*, New York: Cambridge University Press.
4. Etienne C. Wenger, and William M. Snyder. January–February 2000. "Communities of Practice: The Organizational Frontier." *Harvard Business Review*.

CHAPTER 13

MULTIPLE PROJECT MANAGEMENT: RESPONDING TO THE CHALLENGE

JOHN M. NEVISON

"When I use a word," Humpty-Dumpty said in a rather scornful tone, "it means what I choose it to mean—neither more nor less."
Lewis Carroll
Through the Looking Glass

INTRODUCTION

In the world of white-collar work, the term "multi-project management" means different things to different people. To the chief executive officer, it means six-sigma process improvement efforts, accelerating cycle time, competitive products in a strong strategic portfolio, and increased profits. To the engineering vice president in charge of new product development, it has overtones of strategic portfolios, production ramp-ups, market projections colliding with manufacturing costs, and break-even time analysis. To the chief information officer, it means internal customers quarreling about whose need is the most urgent. To the head of the marketing department, it means staff members being asked to split time between the corporate-sponsored process improvement efforts and their regular work demands. To the project manager, it's a noisy, contentious environment where other projects steal your key people.

To the individual white-collar professional who is dividing time between two projects, multi-project management means juggling appearances to keep two bosses happy at the same time. The closer you get to multi-project management, the more difficult it looks. It challenges everyone in the organization, and those actually splitting their time between

215

several projects have the biggest challenge. The most common form of divided time management for the individual professional is not even "multiproject"; it is "multi-assignment" management—dividing time between a regular, functional job and a special, temporary project.[1] A work assignment can be either a regular job activity or a project task. The project work usually extends beyond the boundaries of the regularly defined job.

In order to respond to the challenge of multi-project management we will dedicate the first half of the chapter to solving this most common problem, multi-assignment management. We will begin with the *knowledge worker assigned to both a regular job and a temporary project*. The solution to the simple form of this common problem should point the way to the solution of the more complex cases of multi-project management. If we can solve the problem for the knowledge worker, we can specify the minimum requirements for what the white-collar organization must do to support the worker's needs. In the second half of the chapter we will explore how these minimum requirements may be turned into "just enough process" to meet the challenge of multi-project management. So just how does the individual knowledge worker successfully balance a regular job and a temporary project?

THE CHALLENGE TO THE INDIVIDUAL

We ought to give the whole of our attention to the most insignificant and most easily mastered facts and remain a long time in contemplation of them until we are accustomed to behold the truth clearly and distinctly.

Rene Descartes
Rules for the Direction of the Mind

From Interruption to Work Assignment

For this discussion, we will adopt a simplifying rule of thumb and say that a small project, one that requires less than 20 percent of your time, can be handled as an interruption in the normal give-and-take of a regular job.[2] (If you find 20 percent too large, supply your own boundary for when assignments become "interruptions.") Our knowledge worker's balancing problem begins when the project's work grows larger than four days a month. (If several small fragments of projects are being worked on, then they can be bundled together under the heading of "small projects" and treated like a single project of some size.)

If a month contains 20 workdays, a large project might, in an extreme case, claim as many as 16 days. If the project's demands grow even larger, then the balancing problem disappears and the month transforms itself into a "project month" with a few "interruptions" from the regular job. By using the 20 percent rule of thumb we can focus the problem of balancing two assignments on a month where each work assignment takes between 4 and 16 days.

So, for the moment, our knowledge worker begins with a pile of work that totals no more than 20 days of work for the month. The work is split between days of project tasks and days of regular job activities.

Pick-Up-Sticks Planning

If you are a knowledge worker, planning your work can be like playing a grown-up game of pick-up-sticks. You circle the pile of work, sizing up the pieces, looking for a good piece to start with. After the first piece, you may choose to pick up other, similar pieces to achieve some efficiencies with what you learned from the first piece. You also consider the size of each piece and compare how long it will take to finish with what remains of the day or of the week. You will try to pick up pieces that make your work schedule efficient.

You also consider what must be done first, what piece precedes what other piece, so that you progress in a natural order through the work. So you circle the pile of sticks, grouping pieces where they give you efficiencies, being careful not to pick up a piece out of order.

The pieces in this pile may be either regular activities for the office or special tasks for the project. The interplay between the two is hard to predict and depends heavily on the nature of the actual work itself. In general, the regular work is more familiar and more predictable (because you have done it before). The project work is less familiar and less predictable (because, by definition, the result is unique, so some of the work must be new). As you walk around the pile you can clearly see the outlines of the regular work while the outlines of the project work remain somewhat obscured.

The Whole Week

What guidelines for balance does the pick-up-sticks approach suggest if you are a white-collar professional? Let's begin with smallest details and begin by *scheduling the whole week*. The seven-day week is large enough to provide a degree of flexibility, yet small enough to be clearly understood. Many time-management methods recommend weekly planning.[3] A week allows for balancing professional and personal commitments, as well as for balancing long-term and short-term professional activities. And most importantly, a week allows you to balance office activities and project tasks.

Imagine a table with columns headed "Monday," "Tuesday," and so on, through "Sunday." The rows are the hours of the day labeled in 30-minute increments from 6:00 A.M. to 9:00 P.M. Enter pieces of work on this table. Begin with personal activities, then turn to the project-office mix of work lying in a pile. (See Figure 13.1.)

We are assuming you do not need to schedule time to learn how to do your assignment. Even on projects, the evidence is that people often have adequate technical talent to perform the task.[4]

First Things First

What's next? A skilled worker seeks to achieve a good balance by *doing the most important work first*. When the departmental schedule is most important, you pick up any regular activities that must be completed before a deadline. When the project's schedule is in jeopardy, you pick up project tasks that lie on the critical path. When two assignments both need your immediate attention, you get help or push out the less important deadline.

When the schedules have been attended to, you do the next most important work. As you arrange the work in declining order of importance, wherever you can you bundle the pieces of work in the most efficient

Figure 13.1
Mornings a Week at a Time

Monday	Tuesday	Wednesday	Thursday	Friday	Saturday	Sunday
6						
7						
8						
9						
10						
11						

manner. This may mean bundling project work together, then bundling office work together, or it may mean bundling similar work (both office and project) together.

The way you "pick up" work here is by placing it on your weekly personal calendar. You begin by placing the "big bundles" on the calendar before the "smaller bundles" and finally the individual pieces. You try to arrange your work so that if the big bundles shift you can gracefully rearrange the smaller bundles and individual pieces. You allow for the variation inherent in the estimates of the work, especially the project work.

Reduce Risks Early

A second rule of thumb says *do risky assignments early*. When you have a choice, and one assignment has a higher risk factor than another (in terms of either likelihood of problems, impact if there is a problem, or uncertainty about the estimate of how big it is), you should do the risky assignment first. This lets you find out whether you have a problem early, when you still have the maximum flexibility to respond to the problem. Do the well-known and safe work later to avoid having last-minute crises.

"Schedule-Driven" Work

A third rule of thumb says *limit schedule-driven work*. Avoid filling more than 85 percent of your workweek with schedule-driven work.[5] That's 34 hours of schedule-driven work in a 40-hour week. Scheduling 34 hours of schedule-driven work does not mean you will work less than 40 hours; it means you will at least *plan* for six hours of "work that can be delayed." The six hours may actually be spent on a variety of options: on slips in the schedule-driven work, on helping others with their work, on unexpected risk events, or on the originally planned "work that can be delayed" itself.

If you plan 40 schedule-driven hours, allow yourself 47 hours, following the 85 percent rule, to complete them. Also, remember that when working more than 50 hours, you will lose efficiency and you should allow for that loss in your planning.[6]

How Big Are the Pieces?

While work that comes from the regular job may be familiar, work from the project is probably less so. It's wise to keep the less familiar project tasks under control by keeping them relatively small. A well-formed project task should take the worker *no more than two weeks* to finish. The upper boundary when you are full-time on the project is 10 workdays, or 80 hours. Office activities may be allowed slightly larger boundaries because they can be more reliably predicted.

A work assignment has two opposing sets of forces pushing on its size and duration. Pushing to make it larger and longer is the worker's desire for autonomy and the manager's desire to lessen the overhead of reporting. Pushing to make it smaller and shorter is the worker's need to see progress and the manager's need to minimize the impact of a missed deadline. (If the deadline were eight days, you could take corrective action sooner than if the deadline had been 15 days.) An old rule in software development says never let a task exceed two weeks.[7]

From Hours per Week to Days per Month

Our knowledge worker needs to balance work over days of the month as well as hours of the week. At any one time, a project task can range in size from 4 to 10 days, with complementary job activities filling the schedule. If you are a skilled knowledge worker, how many project tasks can you complete in a month?

In the best case, by skillfully balancing your time between the regular job and the temporary project, you can finish several small project tasks ahead of schedule and manage to log *four* completed milestones during the month. (Remember, at least four days were reserved for your regular job.)

In the worst case, you could fail to complete a single milestone. For example, you have only four days available for project work and a task planned for nine days. If the project work was limited to four staff days during the month, the project task should have been split into two smaller pieces.

There are a number of ways to break up a task into subtasks. When faced with the worst-case schedule, you should take the initiative to break up the work in such a fashion that the project manager can expect *a deliverable within two calendar weeks*.

So in the worst case, after you split the task into pieces, you get one completed milestone in a month. If you started just before the beginning of the month, completed the first task in a little longer than the expected two weeks, you could still be working on the second task when the month runs out.

The result? Our individual worker, by skillfully balancing the regular job and the temporary project, can, in one month, accomplish some regular job activities and *one to four project tasks*.

Ongoing Work

The new work assignments come to our knowledge worker from the job supervisor or the project manager, from the regular needs of the job, or from the posted plan for the project. The assignments often arrive with embedded challenges and attached urgency.

On the regular job, you handle work activities in the routine way. You report your work according to the defined operations of the office. Communications are governed by office policy.

On the project, new work can arrive when a predecessor task is completed, when a co-worker needs a hand, when a change of plan intervenes, or when a risk event occurs. You deliver completed tasks as soon as they are finished and report their delivery in the weekly or biweekly project progress meetings. Communications are governed by the project communications plan.

As a skilled knowledge worker you constantly juggle your plans for the week and for the month. Business value drives each assignment's priority. As special needs arise, you fluidly rearrange the activities of the job and the tasks of the project to optimize your delivered business value for the week and for the month. You use the work that can be delayed to safeguard the schedule-driven work and keep things moving according to plan. In short, you successfully balance your regular job and your temporary project.

Balancing Skills

Our knowledge worker can successfully meet the challenge of balancing a regular job and a temporary project by exercising skills that include:

- Obtaining a good estimate of both the size and the schedule of every job's activities and of every project's tasks
- Intelligently grouping small pieces of work (parts of both regular job activities and project tasks)
- Managing personal and professional hours on a seven-day week
- Doing the most important work first
- Doing the risky assignment before the safe assignment
- Committing to no more than the total real calendar days available in the month
- Limiting schedule-driven work to 85 percent of the calendar and scheduling work than can be delayed to the remaining 15 percent
- Defining, or redefining, a project task to finish within a two-week duration

- Understanding the business goals of both the regular job and the temporary project, and being able to choose between them

From Multi-Assignment to Multi-Project

Now that we understand how a knowledge worker can balance the demands of a regular job and a temporary project (the problem of multi-assignments), how does our knowledge worker apply these skills to more than one project (the problem of multi-projects)? The answer, it turns out, is simple.

Our white-collar professional can handle at most five assignments, activities, or tasks, a month. If each task comes from a different project, our knowledge worker can balance up to five multi-project obligations across the four weeks of the month. With reasonably sized tasks, the number will usually be between two and four.

Remember that the month's assignments should include three days of "work that can be delayed." Such work can be either job activities or project tasks not on the critical path (and with sufficient slack to avoid affecting the critical path). So by applying multi-assignment balancing skills an individual knowledge worker can solve the multi-project problem. The next pressing question is what must the white-collar organization do to allow the individual knowledge worker to exercise these balancing skills?

THE CHALLENGE TO THE ORGANIZATION

A man is rich in proportion to the number of things which he can afford to let alone.

Henry David Thoreau
Walden

Just Enough Process

We will begin with the minimum requirements needed to help our knowledge worker and expand our list only under duress. Our goal is to understand what are the few critical organizational actions necessary to meet the multi-project management challenge. Looking at the knowledge worker's list of balancing skills in the previous section we see that, at a minimum, the organization must:

- Provide good estimates of both the size and the schedule of every job's activities and of every project's tasks.

- Avoid committing any person to more than the month's total calendar days.
- Be sure that work plans limit schedule-driven work to 85 percent of the calendar and allow work that can be delayed to fill the remaining 15 percent.
- Encourage skillful individual time management.
- Be sure every assigned project task has a two-week (or less) duration.
- Be sure that everyone understands the business goals of both the regular job and the temporary project(s) in a way that enables them to choose among them.

While the list is obvious, these minimal requirements may provide a real challenge to many organizations. For starters, how does an organization provide good estimates for both job activities and project tasks?

Good Estimates

Regular job activities may not always be easy to estimate, but they should be easier than the unfamiliar tasks of the average project. Project estimating has received a lot of attention over the years and experienced-based ranges of values will do the trick in most circumstances.[8] Range estimates can capture what total-quality experts call "common cause variation" and will reliably estimate both the individual tasks and the project's overall size and schedule.[9]

An organization with elementary project planning skills should have no trouble providing our knowledge worker with estimates for the work assignments he or she is being asked to undertake. The functional departments can do the same. Our knowledge worker can use the estimates to fit the work into the days of the month. If the total plan exceeds the days available, the knowledge worker must renegotiate the work.

Monthly Fit

Organizations that fail to understand their role in supporting good project management usually fail the "monthly fit" test of adequacy. The leading symptom of this failure is that the responsible senior line manager cannot say how many staff days of project work are budgeted for the upcoming month.[10] A related symptom is that the project and department managers do not know the total work the people on their projects have been asked to do. Another symptom of this problem is that the project managers complain that their projects are understaffed. Such symptoms are all too common.[11]

Sometimes department managers assert that their staff is 100 percent dedicated to the department work, but cannot supply any supporting details. Sometimes the list of department work totals well over 100 percent to show that no member of the staff can possibly do any additional work. In both cases, the senior line manager must insist on better tracking of time spent. Only when the departmental work is held to the same standards as the project work can rational trade-offs be made.

When even the heads of the individual departments and the managers of the active projects have no idea what their group's total staff day budget for the upcoming month is, the first thing the organization must do is:

- Have each department manager submit a budget in staff days for everyone in the department.
- Have each project manager submit a budget in staff days for everyone on the project.
- Have both (or all) the parties agree on the number of staff days for each staff person involved, so that *everyone's budget is within the calendar month's available staff days*.
- Have everyone adjust the plans' schedules to reflect the monthly agreement.

This agreement among the projects and the departments is the responsibility of the senior line manager overseeing both. The agreement must be reviewed monthly and probably should look ahead two or three months. Best-practice companies have this meeting at least monthly and sometimes more frequently.[12] Software tools exist to track these agreements in a practical way with a minimum of overhead to either the department heads or the project managers.[13]

At a strategic level, best-practice organizations practice quarterly (or semiannual) long-term resource planning, to be sure the multiyear goals of the organization can be factored into the monthly decisions. Successful project managers know they must be prepared for both the monthly and the quarterly meetings.

Project Managers of Part-Time Resources

In order to be effective during the monthly meeting, a project manager needs to have reviewed the project's planned budget for each part-time staff member. The project manager must first know *how much* time will be required of each individual. Only after that question is answered should the project manager explore what the detailed *schedule* will be.

An emerging best practice in many companies is to leave working out the details of the schedule to the individual knowledge worker in consultation with the project managers, cooperating fellow workers, and department heads. This can work if everyone's monthly total fits within the month and no one is grossly overworked. Software that supports the individualized scheduling has proven quite successful in practice.[14]

The watchword for successful managers of part-time project resources is, "Don't level your resources, *budget* your resources." Part-time white-collar resources frequently have such volatile schedules that traditional resource leveling is a waste of time. It's a waste of time because the resources' constantly shifting schedule requires constant releveling. And the new answers are no more lasting than the old answers. A skillful manager will recognize when overplanning is a waste of time and back off.

What can the skillful project manager do to ensure his or her project will get completed in this multi-project environment with part-time resources?

1. Be sure to fight for monthly allocations of the appropriate resources.
2. Adjust the plan's schedule to reflect the result of these resource fights.
3. Be sure everyone knows the business value (priority) of the project (and each assigned task).
4. Be sure that a schedule-driven task is highlighted to the individual who will be working on it.
5. As you negotiate the work plan with each individual, make sure that no task exceeds the two-week boundary. (Redefine the work if necessary.)
6. Make sure each of your resources has scheduled at least three days of "work that can be delayed" during the month.

Deciding Who Gets the Critical Resource

Multi-project management grows more complex when a person with a unique skill is needed for two different assignments at the same time. The decision rules are well known (but difficult to apply):

1. Do the assignment with the bigger business value first.
2. If the assignments are close in business value and one is schedule-driven, do the schedule-driven one first.
3. If both are schedule-driven, translate the schedule effects into business value and do the one with the bigger business value first.
4. If both are schedule-driven and have the same business value, do the one that has the earliest project deadline (higher risk) first.

When a critical resource becomes a constraint across several projects, the projects should be arranged to provide the most overall business value. When value is synonymous with schedule, well-known methods can be applied to scheduling the critical resource.[15]

The first and third rules are often violated because the organization has failed to make, or to make widely known, an assessment of the business value of the work. But how, exactly, does the organization arrive at the business value of the work?

Business Value

When a project is undertaken to provide a unique service, the business value is the expected net profit that the project earns by completing the effort. When a project is undertaken to produce a product, the business value of the project is entwined in the fortunes of the product.

A basic understanding of the business value of the products produced by the projects is critical to the organization wrestling with the challenges of multi-project management. Business value determines whether the project should be done at all, and whether, after it has been started, it should be continued. Business value determines who gets the organization's scarce resources first. Business value affects the value of a day of schedule, the value of a product feature, the value of a dollar of cost. Finally, business value allows everyone on the project to make intelligent trade-offs in their day-to-day work decisions.

The business value of a project is best expressed in two dimensions, profit over time—not only *how much* profit, but *when it will occur*. Two of the many ways to view such business value are shown here.[16] Figure 13.2 is a six-year business model of the product that includes the investment (mostly the project cost) and the return (the product's cumulative profit). Figure 13.3 graphs the monthly cash flow for the same six-year model.

Every project should have such a business model. (In fact, every project does have a model, but many remain *implicit* because no one has written the model down and made it *explicit*.) If the organization fails to provide an explicit business model to the project, the project team should construct its own and publish it to the organization.

Exploring Figures 13.2 and 13.3

Figures 13.2 and 13.3 have several features. First, they insist that the product of the project, the project's deliverable, be considered in terms of economic costs and benefits. The economic gross benefits are often sales,

Figure 13.2
A Business Model of the Value of a Project's Product

	Year					
	−1	0	1	2	3	4
Gross economic benefits (sales)			143	257	463	625	375
Economic cost (expenses)			105	194	369	530	335
Project cost	130					
Net benefits (profit)		(130)	38	63	94	95	40
Cumulative benefits		(130)	(92)	(29)	65	160	200

the economic costs are often business expenses plus the one-time project costs, and the economic net benefits are often profits. Second, they show how these forces are expected to play out over time. We can see the full life of the idea (or at least its future for the next six years).

Note that this economic cost-benefit analysis can work even in not-for-profit organizations. Coming into compliance with a new regulation, trying to reach a new audience, upgrading to meet a competitive challenge, instituting a new departmental process, or capitalizing on a new discovery are all projects whose results have economic gross benefits, costs, and net benefits over time.

A third feature of Figures 13.2 and 13.3 is that they require advice from

Figure 13.3
Business Model Cash Flow

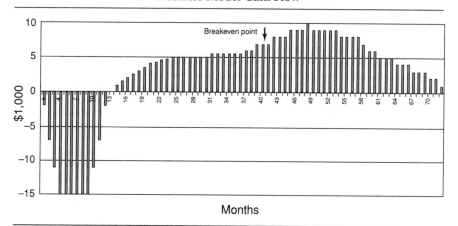

the relevant experts in the organization. Relevant experts might include marketing, sales, manufacturing, legal counsel, R&D, development engineering, support engineering, or representatives from a particular user community.

A fourth feature of the two figures is that they allow the project team to illustrate how a marginal change (say, plus or minus 10 percent) might affect the overall business value. By comparing marginal changes in project schedule, product features, and project cost, the organization can make critical trade-offs both during the planning and during the execution of the project.[17] These discussions of marginal value necessarily require seeking advice from the relevant experts.

With the business value derived from a business model, our project team can allocate business value down through its work breakdown structure to the individual tasks.[18] After completing its detailed planning, our project team is prepared to manage its resources flexibly and to defend itself against the onslaughts of other projects.

With a clear concept of each project's business value, the project managers and the department managers have some hope of resolving their monthly negotiations over constrained resources. Schedules must yield to business value.

The individual project business models can be assembled into a strategic portfolio analysis of the organization's many projects (especially new product projects) and allow the senior management to adjust the projects to reflect the strategic objectives of the corporation.[19]

With the individual knowledge worker balancing the day-to-day work and with the organization engaged in just enough process to coordinate multiple projects, the multi-project management challenge has been substantially met. What remain are a few considerations about full-time work—when the individual is completely dedicated to one project, but the organization is still doing many projects.

CHALLENGES OF FULL-TIME PROJECT WORK

What of architectural beauty I now see, I know has gradually grown from within outward.

Henry David Thoreau
Walden

Full-time project work has disadvantages as well as advantages. The stability and efficiency of the assignments of a regular job are transformed into the higher-risk, volatile tasks of the project. Safeguarding long-term functional expertise is subordinated to supporting the short-term, ad hoc needs of the project. However, organizations often decide, after carefully weighing the alternatives, to launch a full-time project.

Full-Time Work for the Individual

By focusing on the needs of the individual knowledge worker, we see clearly that our multi-project solutions for part-time work also apply to full-time work on projects. Full-time project work is simply the management of a series of one to five tasks in a given month. The same intelligent grouping of work details that occurs in the multi-project world occurs when our worker is engaged in a variety of tasks on a single project. The level of contention for an individual's services may be less, and time may be more focused on the work at hand and less on switching contexts between projects. So in general a skilled worker with a supportive organization will find the full-time environment easier to manage than the multi-project environment.

Full-Time Work for the Project

A project manager with a full-time staff is much happier than a manager with a part-time staff. With the competition for staff removed, the project's schedule and cost become much easier to manage. Dates can be met, costs can be contained, and the product appears as planned.

Full-Time Work for the Organization

At the organizational level, the full-time environment usually results in an increased emphasis on project organizations and decreased emphasis on functional departments. The alternative organizational structures are well understood and documented in the literature as "functional, weak matrix, strong matrix, and project."[20]

Organizational structures strongly influence the role of a project office (or even whether one exists). Traditionally "project" and "strong matrix" organizations have sponsored project offices to select computer tools, define processes, audit practices, and manage the career development of project managers. Today some "functional" and "weak matrix" organizations have project offices that provide part-time project managers with basic administrative support, such as scheduling or financial reporting. In almost all cases, a project office can offer critical coordination and support for the monthly resource meeting.

CONCLUSION

By focusing on the individual knowledge worker in a white-collar organization, we have arrived at the individual skills necessary to balance work
in a multi-project environment. From these individual skills, we have derived a minimum set of business imperatives for an organization that
wishes to enable its members to be successful in this environment. In particular, we have derived effective practices for project managers and for
line managers. One critical element of these practices is an explicit model
of the business value of each project.

As an organization gets better at multi-project management, it will
achieve more business value with less difficulty. "Multi-project management" will mean the same thing to all parties. Everyone will understand
that as they move to meet the challenge of multi-project management they
can expect to see job satisfaction increase, business productivity rise,
strategic focus sharpen, and bottom-line profits increase.

NOTES

1. Of 226 respondents doing project work in eight companies, over 75 percent spent significant amounts of time on regularly assigned nonproject
   work. Specifically, only seven respondents (three percent) worked exclusively on project work and only 66 (25 percent) spent more than 80 percent of their time on project work. Overall, 64.5 percent of their time was
   spent on project work and 34.5 percent on office work (the numeric aver-
   ages don't necessarily add to exactly 100 percent) (Nevison 2000).
2. The figure 20 percent is a handy place to begin a discussion of splitting
   time between two assignments that both demand attention. It was suggested by Heinz Scheuring, a veteran of 18 years of project management
   consulting (Scheuring 1999).
3. Time management is about balancing the many goals of an individual. It is
   especially relevant to the particular problem of balancing different work
   assignments. The most ardent proponents of the week-at-a-time management are Covey (1989) and Covey, Merrill, and Merrill (1994). Oncken
   (1984) and Webber (1972) have additional valuable insights.
4. In a recent Oak Associates study, 280 respondents doing project work in
   eight companies answered "In our organization, people who work on our
   current projects have adequate technical skills," a heartening "Often." (See
   Nevison 2000.)
5. The 85 percent figure is a rule of thumb that comes from skilled senior
   project managers. One of my most experienced partners, Carl Belack, uses
   85 percent (Belack 1999). A current client uses 6.5 hours per 8-hour day
   for scheduled activity. Another client's senior project manager reported in
   confidence that he scheduled all his projects using a four (not five) day
   workweek. The 85 percent figure is cited as an upper bound on the value-

added work of development engineers on projects at several clients (Smith and Reinertsen 1998; Wheelwright and Clark 1992).

6. A personal study of 30 white-collar professionals suggested the "Rule of Fifty," which says, "On the average, no matter how many hours per week people are at work, they each return only 50 productive hours." Blue-collar productivity studies of the past 50 years confirm this statistic (Nevison 1992, 1997; *Winning Project Management* 1998).

7. An early reference to the two-week rule is in Metzger (1973). Since then, numerous software clients have confirmed its critical utility.

8. An easy-to-read introduction to the mechanics of estimating can be found in Durrenberger (1999). See also *Winning Project Management* (1998).

9. Simple explanations of how to add up estimates are in the *PMBOK Guide*, page116. See Duncan (1996) and Durrenberger (1999). For additional details on advanced scheduling, see Nevison (1999).

10. Marvin Patterson, former vice president for new product development at Hewlett-Packard, says, "Even though it is counterintuitive, booking every resource to the limit usually results in a huge waste of effort. If everyone is always busy on urgent tasks, people are not available when they are needed to resolve a bottleneck, and critical cross-functional talent is not at hand to get the next project started in the right direction." See Patterson with Lightman (1993).

11. When 300 managers across the country were asked for factors causing problems on their projects, the most common answer was "inadequate resources." These managers are not just whining; they are genuinely and chronically understaffed (Taylor 1998). In a recent Oak Associates study, 278 respondents doing project work in 10 companies said that only "seldom" was it true that "In our organization we have an adequate number of people to work on our current projects." See Nevison (2000).

12. When asked if his firm allocated resources monthly, a recent client laughed and said, "Right now, we are doing it weekly." This may be a little too frequently, but it can occur in a crunch.

13. ResSolution is successfully used by over 100 companies to perform this monthly budgeting. These companies combine the computer tool with monthly resource management meetings among the managers of active projects (*Scheuring ResSolution 3.1* 1999). For an excellent introduction to the whole subject of computer aided project management see my colleague's summary (Belack 2000).

14. Scheuring Project 98 Plus allows an individual to collect a to-do list and assignments from one or more Microsoft Project 98 files, to sort all the tasks in order of their due date, and to print out the list for the month. The individual has the responsibility to contact any project managers whose work may require rescheduling and negotiate an acceptable solution. The individual can practice the pick-up-sticks qualitative arrangement of the work, because his or her quantitative boundaries were set by the organization (*Scheuring Project 98 Plus* 1999).

15. Methods to develop a resource-constrained critical path for the whole portfolio of projects are well known. The methods are all trial-and-error heuristics because no analytical method exists to arrive at the one true answer to this resource-leveling problem. Some recent approximations have been labeled a "critical chain" and discussed in Newbold (1998). The helpful concept of DRAG on the critical path is defined and explained in Devaux (1999). For a simple discussion of the traditional view, see Nevison (1981).

16. Many models exist in the literature. Figures 13.2 and 13.3 trace their origins to Smith and Reinertsen (1998), to Patterson (1993), and to the "return map" of House and Price (1991).

17. Recently the author has developed a new diagram to help project teams make the trade-offs among scope, schedule, and cost, called "The 10 Percent Chart" (Barker and Nevison 2000.)

18. Assigning value to the branches and sub-branches of a work breakdown structure all the way down to the level of the work assignments is a useful skill for all project managers. (See Devaux 1999).

19. Portfolio management is a familiar idea to those engaged in strategic planning. A sound approach to portfolio fundamentals includes a preliminary allocation of project resources for the next business year (Gill, Nelson, and Spring 1996; *Scheuring ResSolution 3.1* 1999).

20. Traditional discussions on the organizational implications of projects are well known (Kerzner 1998; Kezsbom, Schilling, and Edward 1989; Frame 1987).

REFERENCES

Barker, Michael D., and John M. Nevison. 2000. "How Much Is 10 Percent Worth?" In *PM Network*, Vol. 14, No. 4 (April).

Belack, Carl N. 1999. Private communication (November).

————. 2000. "Computer-Aided Project Management." Chapter 43, to appear in Gavriel Salvendy, ed., *Handbook of Industrial Engineering (Third Edition)*. New York: John Wiley & Sons.

Covey, Stephen R. 1989. *The Seven Habits of Highly Effective People*. New York: Simon & Schuster.

Covey, Stephen R., A. Roger Merrill, and Rebecca Merrill. 1994. *First Things First*. New York: Simon & Schuster.

Devaux, Stephen A. 1999. *Total Project Control*. New York: John Wiley & Sons.

Duncan, William R. 1996. *A Guide to the Project Management Body of Knowledge*. Newtown Square, PA: Project Management Institute.

Durrenberger, Mark. 1999. "True Estimates Reduce Project Risk." *PM Network*, Vol. 13, No. 5 (May).

Frame, J. Davidson. 1987. *Managing Projects in Organizations: How to Make the Best Use of Time, Techniques, and People*. San Francisco: Jossey-Bass.

Gill, Bob, Beebe Nelson, and Steve Spring. 1996. "Seven Steps to Strategic New Product Development." In Milton D. Rosenau Jr., Abbie Griffin, George

Castellion, and Ned F. Anschhuetz, *PDMA Handbook of New Product Development*. New York: John Wiley & Sons.

House, Charles H., and Raymond L. Price. 1991. "The Return Map: Tracking Product Teams." *Harvard Business Review* (January–February).

Kerzner, Harold. 1998. *Project Management: A Systems Approach to Planning, Scheduling, and Controlling (Sixth Edition)*. New York: John Wiley & Sons.

Kezsbom, Deborah S., Donald L. Schilling, and Katherine A. Edward. 1989. *Dynamic Project Management: A Practical Guide for Managers and Engineers*. New York: John Wiley & Sons.

Metzger, Philip W. 1973. *Managing a Programming Project*. Englewood Cliffs, NJ: Prentice-Hall.

Nevison, John M. 1981. *Executive Computing: How to Get It Done on Your Own*. Reading, MA: Addison-Wesley. (Especially Chapter 6, "Project Planning, Scheduling and Control.")

———. 1992). *Project Management Questionnaire Report*. Internal working paper. Maynard, MA: Oak Associates, Inc. (March).

———. 1997. *Overtime Hours*. Internal working paper. Maynard, MA: Oak Associates, Inc. (December).

———. 1999). *Understanding Scheduling: How to Build a Robust, Probabilistic Schedule*. Internal working paper. Maynard, MA: Oak Associates, Inc. (September).

———. 2000). *Snapshot Assessment Data*. Internal analysis. Maynard, MA: Oak Associates. (February).

Newbold, Robert C. 1998. *Project Management in the Fast Lane: Applying the Theory of Constraints*. New York: St. Lucie Press.

Oncken, William, Jr. 1984. *Managing Management Time*. Englewood Cliffs, NJ: Prentice-Hall.

Patterson, Marvin L., with Sam Lightman. 1993. *Accelerating Innovation: Improving the Process of Product Development*. New York: Van Nostrand Reinhold.

Scheuring, Heinz. 1999. Private communication (October).

Scheuring Project 98 Plus®, User's Guide. 1999. Maynard, MA: Oak Associates.

Scheuring ResSolution® 3.1: Multi-project Management Resource Tool for Line and Resource Managers, User's Guide. Maynard, MA: Oak Associates.

Smith, Preston G., and Donald G. Reinertsen. 1998. *Developing Products in Half the Time: New Rules, New Tools (Second Edition)*. New York: Van Nostrand Reinhold.

Taylor, James. 1998. *A Survival Guide for Project Managers*. New York: Amacom.

Webber, Ross A. 1972. *Time and Management*. New York: Van Nostrand Reinhold.

Wheelwright, Steven C., and Kim B. Clark. 1992. *Revolutionizing Product Development*. New York: Free Press.

Winning Project Management. 1998. Program Notebook, Vol. 4.1. Maynard, MA: Oak Associates.

CASE STUDY 13.1

Manager Brown's January Work

John M. Nevison

INTRODUCTION

To better understand what work planning might look like in detail, consider, for the moment, Manager Brown's January work. Manager Brown runs a generic department. Like many senior line managers in white-collar companies, he must meet the multi-project challenge. Brown wants to make sure that the regular work of the department gets done. At the same time, Brown has two winter projects going on, Generic Project Apple and Generic Project Pear. His success next year depends on completing both of these projects as soon as possible. His problem is how to coordinate his regular work with the work of his two projects.

(The actual work details in this example have been "abstracted" to provide a generic model that fits many different work situations.)

Brown runs a small department. Working for him are Red, White, Blue, Yellow, Black, and Green. Black and Blue will manage the two winter projects: Black, the Generic Project Apple, and Blue, the Generic Project Pear. It's late December and Brown is getting ready to sit down with Black and Blue and lay out their January work.

Before the meeting each constructs a list of work. The three lists look like those shown in Figure 13.4. Let's explore each of the three lists.

BROWN'S LIST

Brown is in charge of the department's regular work. From experience, he knows how long most jobs take by the hour, day, week, or month, and he knows who has the skills to do them. He jots down some of those thoughts in his activity description and sketches the number of staff days that each will require for the month.

Brown supports his estimate with some background numbers. As you look at these figures you are reminded that some activities require considerable, even full-time, work. Other activities are special monthly activities that need to be done at a certain time of year. For these special activities, Brown notes what kind of skill is needed. (Skills are represented here as geometric shapes such as circle, triangle, and so on. Each individual

Figure 13.4
Work List of January Days of Work: First Detailed Thoughts

Work Description — Regular Department Work	Monthly Staff-Day Budget	Background	Brown	Red	White	Black	Yellow	Blue	Green	Later	Check
Activity A, an hour a day	2.5	= 1*5*4/8	2.50								OK
Activity B, two hours, twice a day	10.00	= 2*2*5*4/8		10.00							OK
Activity C, two people, four hours a day	20.00	= 2*4*5*4/8			10.00	10.00					OK
Activity D, two hours, three times a week	15.00	= 2*3*5*4/8	7.50	7.50							OK
Activity E, one person, full-time	20.00						20.00				OK
Special monthly activity F, Circle or Square	6.00	3, 5, 10	6.00								OK
Special quarterly activity G, two days this month, Circle	2.00		2.00								OK
Special one-time activity H, 20 hours, Triangle	2.50	= 20/8						2.50			OK
Special one-time activity I	5.00	2, 4, 9			5.00						OK
Total Regular Dept.	**83.00**		18.00	17.50	15.00	10.00	20.00	2.50	0.00	0.00	OK

Generic Project Apple	Staff-Day Budget	Background	Brown	Red	White	Black	Yellow	Blue	Green	Later	Check
Activity AA, an hour a day	2.5	= 1*5*4/8				2.50					OK
Activity AB	2.00	1, 2, 3				2.00					OK
Activity AC, Square	8.00	5, 8 ,11				3.00			5.00		OK
Activity AD, Square	7.00	4, 6, 11			2.00	2.00				3.00	OK
Activity AE	7.00	4, 6, 11								7.00	OK
Activity AF, Circle	7.00	3, 6, 12								7.00	OK
Activity AG, Circle	7.00	3, 6, 12								7.00	OK
Activity AH, Circle or Ellipse	6.00	4, 5, 9								6.00	OK
Activity AI, Circle or Ellipse	4.00	2, 4, 6								4.00	OK
Activity AJ, Circle	8.00	7, 8, 9								8.00	OK
Total Generic Project Apple	**58.50**		0.00	0.00	2.00	9.50	0.00	0.00	5.00	42.00	OK

Generic Project Pear	Staff-Day Budget	Background	Brown	Red	White	Black	Yellow	Blue	Green	Later	Check
Activity PA, an hour a week	2.00	= 4*4/8						2.00			OK
Activity PB, Square	2.00	1, 2, 3						2.00			OK
Activity PC, Square or Triangle	7.00	5, 7, 9						7.00			OK
Activity PD, Square or Triangle	8.00	7, 8, 9							8.00		OK
Activity PE, Triangle	8.00	7, 8, 9						4.00	4.00		OK
Activity PF	10.00	4, 6, 20								10.00	OK
Activity PG	7.00	3, 6, 12								7.00	OK
Activity PH, Circle	8.00	7, 8, 9								8.00	OK
Activity PI	8.00	5, 8 ,11								8.00	OK
Activity PJ	9.00	7, 8, 12								9.00	OK
Activity PK, Circle or Square	8.00	7, 8, 9								8.00	OK
Activity PL, Circle, Square, or Ellipse	7.00	3, 6, 12								7.00	OK
Activity PM, Triangle	8.00	7, 8, 9								8.00	OK
Activity PN, Square or Ellipse	8.00	5, 8, 11								8.00	OK
Activity PO, Circle or Square and Triangle	8.00	4, 8, 12 (4)								8.00	OK
Activity PP, Triangle	7.00	5, 7, 9								7.00	OK
Activity PQ, Triangle	8.00	7, 8, 9								8.00	OK
Activity PR, Triangle	9.00	8, 9, 10								9.00	OK
Activity PS, Triangle	6.00	3, 6, 9 (3)								6.00	OK
Activity PT, Triangle and Square	8.00	4, 8, 12 (4)								8.00	OK
Activity PU	5.00	3, 5, 7								5.00	OK
Activity PV	7.00	5, 7, 9								7.00	OK
Activity PW, Circle	9.00	7, 8, 12								9.00	OK
Activity PX	8.00	7, 8, 9								8.00	OK
Activity PY, Circle, Square, and Triangle	6.00	3, 6, 9 (3)								6.00	OK
Total Generic Project Pear	**181.00**		0.00	0.00	0.00	0.00	0.00	15.00	12.00	154.00	OK
Total Monthly Work Assigned	**126.50**	Staff Days	18.00	17.50	17.00	19.50	20.00	17.50	17.00	196.00	
Remaining Work	**196.00**	Staff Days									

worker may possess one or several skills.) As it turns out, every activity that Brown puts on his list for the meeting needs to be completed in January.

Brown assigns the department's regular work to himself, Red, White, and Yellow. He goes light on Black and Blue, who will be leading the projects, and frees up Green, who will be helping on the projects.

BLACK'S LIST

Black makes a preliminary list of tasks for Generic Project Apple. She sizes the project tasks by using three-point estimates of the staff days of work involved. (The formula for a three-point estimate with an assumed underlying triangular distribution is: mean = [low + likely + high]/3).[1] She lists activities in the order she thinks they should be done. She lists the required skills that certain activities require, be it "circle" or "square" ("ellipse" is optional). She assigns Green where she can best use her. As she assigns the work she realizes not all of it will get done in January, so she stops and comes to the meeting prepared to adjust her draft list.

BLUE'S LIST

Blue goes through similar thinking as he builds the list for Generic Project Pear. Several tasks can benefit by lots of help and a few tasks require several people (noted in parentheses). The tasks, like Black's, are estimated in staff days of work and placed in the order they need to be done. Blue also specifies required skills for certain tasks. He knows that several activities may be performed in parallel, but that even so his project will continue for several months. He comes to the meeting prepared to be flexible.

THE MONTHLY RESOURCE MEETING

By the time Brown, Black, and Blue get together they have boiled their lists down to the summary categories in Figure 13.5. They quickly see that they have more work than they can do in January. With 67.5 + 255 = 322.5 staff days of work and seven workers it is easy to see that the projects will go on for several months. The three make the work assignments for Brown's regular departmental work. They distribute the work so that everyone is under the 20-day limit except for Yellow, who is working full-time.

After they complete the regular work, the group turns its attention to

Figure 13.5
Budget of January Days of Work: Summary Version before the Meeting

Work Description **Regular Department Work**	**Monthly Staff-Day Budget**	Background	Brown	Red	White	Black	Yellow	Blue	Green	Later	Check
Regular Activities (A–E)	67.5		10.00	17.50	10.00	10.00	20.00				OK
Special Activities, Circle, Square (o), Triangle	15.50	4 Activities								15.50	OK
Total Regular Dept.	83.00		10.00	17.50	10.00	10.00	20.00	0.00	0.00	15.50	OK

Generic Project Apple	**Staff-Day Budget**	Background	Brown	Red	White	Black	Yellow	Blue	Green	Later	Check
Activity AA, an hour a day	2.5	Mgt.								2.50	OK
Milestone AE, Square	24.00	4 Activities								24.00	OK
Milestone AJ, Circle, Ellipse (o)	32.00	5 Activities								32.00	OK
Total Generic Project Apple	58.50		0.00	0.00	0.00	0.00	0.00	0.00	0.00	58.50	OK

Generic Project Pear	**Staff-Day Budget**	Background	Brown	Red	White	Black	Yellow	Blue	Green	Later	Check
Activity PA, an hour a week	2.00	Mgt.								2.00	OK
Milestone PE, Square, Triangle	25.00	4 Activities								25.00	OK
Milestone PJ, Circle	42.00	5 Activities								42.00	OK
Milestone PO, Circle, Triangle, Square, Ellipse (o)	39.00	5 Activities								39.00	OK
Milestone PT, Triangle, Square	38.00	5 Activities								38.00	OK
Milestone PY, Circle, Square, Triangle	35.00	5 Activities								35.00	OK
Total Generic Project Pear	181.00		0.00	0.00	0.00	0.00	0.00	0.00	0.00	181.00	OK

Total Monthly Work Assigned	67.50	Staff Days	10.00	17.50	10.00	10.00	20.00	0.00	0.00	255.00	
Remaining Work	255.00	Staff Days									

Black's project. Black is not only managing the Apple project; she is its chief worker. (Both Black and Blue possess all the skills needed on their projects.) White and Green have "square" skills and can help a little. Black can expect to have half of Milestone AE done by the end of the month with the rest of the work put off until February.

Blue's project is similar to Black's. With Green's help he will manage to complete Milestone PE by the end of the month. Green has both "square" and "triangle" skills.

By the time they are done they have revised their work assignments to look like those in Figure 13.6. The "Later" column reveals work for the next month. The "OK" is a spreadsheet check to be sure that the assigned work adds up to the monthly budget.

THE HIGH-LEVEL CRITICAL AGREEMENT: MONTHLY DAYS OF WORK

Brown, Black, and Blue try to stop when they have reached the point where each individual is in the 17 to 19-day range (Yellow is a little over). They have reached a critical agreement on the monthly days of work. They have figured out how to work within their resource constraints.

Figure 13.6
Budget of January Days of Work: Summary Version after the Meeting

Work Description	Monthly Staff-Day Budget	Work Assignments									
Regular Department Work		Background	Brown	Red	White	Black	Yellow	Blue	Green	Later	Check
Regular Activities (A–E)	67.5		10.00	17.50	10.00	10.00	20.00				OK
Special Activities, Circle, Square (o), Triangle	15.50	4 Activities	8.00		5.00			2.50			OK
Total Regular Dept.	83.00		18.00	17.50	15.00	10.00	20.00	2.50	0.00	0.00	OK
Generic Project Apple	Staff-Day Budget	Background	Brown	Red	White	Black	Yellow	Blue	Green	Later	Check
Activity AA, an hour a day	2.5	Mgt.				2.50					OK
Milestone AE, Square	24.00	4 Activities			2.00	7.00			5.00	10.00	OK
Milestone AJ, Circle, Ellipse (o)	32.00	5 Activities								32.00	OK
Total Generic Project Apple	58.50		0.00	0.00	2.00	9.50	0.00	0.00	5.00	42.00	OK
Generic Project Pear	Staff-Day Budget	Background	Brown	Red	White	Black	Yellow	Blue	Green	Later	Check
Activity PA, an hour a week	2.00	Mgt.						2.00			OK
Milestone PE, Square, Triangle	25.00	4 Activities						13.00	12.00		OK
Milestone PJ, Circle	42.00	5 Activities								42.00	OK
Milestone PO, Circle, Triangle, Square, Ellipse (o)	39.00	5 Activities								39.00	OK
Milestone PT, Triangle, Square	38.00	5 Activities								38.00	OK
Milestone PY, Circle, Square, Triangle	35.00	5 Activities								35.00	OK
Total Generic Project Pear	181.00		0.00	0.00	0.00	0.00	0.00	15.00	12.00	154.00	OK
Total Monthly Work Assigned	126.50	Staff Days	18.00	17.50	17.00	19.50	20.00	17.50	17.00	196.00	
Remaining Work	196.00	Staff Days									

The have also wisely left a little slack in their plan to *increase* their efficiency. They know that the department team works well together and that they need some time to help each other out, rearrange schedules, and deal with the many small emergencies of work life. As a second check on their slack, both Blue and Black will assess their project schedules to be sure that the schedule-driven tasks total less than 16 staff days for their team members. As a third check, each individual will also examine his or her own personal monthly calendar.

DETAILED PROJECT SCHEDULING
During the January meeting Brown, Black, and Blue have made a number of staffing decisions without fully understanding their detailed scheduling implications. Brown knows how the regular work looks because it changes little from month to month. But after the meeting Black and Blue will set up their detailed project plans to see how their staffing constraints will affect the projects' completion dates.

Black's Generic Apple Project

Black's project's work breakdown structure, resource assignments, and Gantt chart (with its implied network logic) are shown in Figure 13.7.

Figure 13.7
Black's Generic Apple Project (Microsoft Project 98 Plus)

Stru	Task	Resp	Asst	Duration	Dec. 27, '99	Jan. 10, '00	Jan. 24, '00	Feb. 7, '00	Feb. 21, '00	Mar. 6
1	Generic Apple Project			50 d	1/3					3/1
1.1	Phase Deliverable I			21 d	1/3		1/31			
1.1.1	Jan Activity AA, an hour a day	Bla		21 d			1/31			
1.1.2	Activity AB	Bla		4 d	1/6					
1.1.3	Activity AC, Square	Bla	Gre	6 d	1/14					
1.1.4	Activity AD, Square	Bla	Whi	4 d		1/20				
1.1.5	Activity AE			4 d		1/26				
1.1.6	January Buffer			3 d		1/31				
1.1.7	Jan and Del I Milestone			0 w		1/31				
1.2	Phase Deliverable II			29 d		2/1				3/1
1.2.1	Feb Activity AF, an hour a day			21 d					2/29	
1.2.2	Activity AF, Circle			14 d				2/18		
1.2.3	Activity AG, Circle			14 d						3/9
1.2.4	Activity AH, Circle or Ellipse			12 d				2/16		
1.2.5	Activity AI, Circle or Ellipse			7 d					2/25	
1.2.6	February Buffer			2 d					2/29	
1.2.7	February Milestone			0 d					2/29	
1.2.8	Mar Activity AA, an hour a day			1 d					3/1	
1.2.9	Activity AJ, Circle			8 d						3/1
1.2.10	Activity AA, an hour a day			7 d						3/9
1.2.11	Project and Del II Milestone			0 d						3/

Black has adjusted her schedule to reflect the budget constraints on her January activities. She schedules what she knows is possible within the month and hopes that a little extra can be worked in. She has extended each task's duration to reflect the staffing that it will receive. She has added dependencies to reflect how the work must be ordered and she has added milestones to signal the completion of significant events. She has added a buffer task to explicitly manage her schedule slack. She reviews what it would take to hire an extra hand to help with the project activities if they run long.

Green can look at the project schedule and see that her work will fall in the early part of the month. Black hopes Green can plan her schedule to meet the project's schedule. The details will be worked out between Black and Green.

Blue's Generic Pear Project

Blue's project's work breakdown structure, resource assignments, and Gantt chart (with its implied network logic) are shown in Figure 13.8. He has planned five days of schedule buffer to be sure that he gets the first deliverable completed in January. He has tentatively scheduled his project all the way to its end in June.

Figure 13.8
Blue's Generic Pear Project (Microsoft Project 98 Plus)

Stru	Task	Resp	Asst	Duration
1	**Generic Pear Project**			**127 d**
1.1	**Phase Deliverable I**			**21 d**
1.1.1	Jan Activity PA, an hour a week	Blu		21 d
1.1.2	Activity PB, Square	Blu		2 d
1.1.3	Activity PC, Square or Triangle	Blu		8 d
1.1.4	Activity PD, Square or Triangle	Gre		8 d
1.1.5	Activity PE, Triangle	Blu	Gre	5 d
1.1.6	January Buffer			5 d
1.1.7	Jan and Del I Milestone			0 d
1.2	**Phase Deliverable II**			**44 d**
1.2.1	Feb Activity PA, an hour a week			21 d
1.2.2	Activity PF			10 d
1.2.3	Activity PG			7 d
1.2.4	Activity PH, Circle			8 d
1.2.5	February Buffer			4 d
1.2.6	February Milestone			0 d
1.2.7	Mar Activity PA, an hour a week			23 d
1.2.8	Activity PI			8 d
1.2.9	Activity PJ			9 d
1.2.10	March Buffer			6 d
1.2.11	March and Del II Milestone			0 d
1.3	**Phase Deliverable III**			**20 d**
1.3.1	April Activity PA, and hour a week			20 d
1.3.2	Activity PK, Circle or Square			8 d
1.3.3	Activity PL, Circle, Square, or Ellipse			7 d
1.3.4	Activity PM, Triangle			4 d
1.3.5	Activity PN, Square or Ellipse			8 d
1.3.6	Activity PO, Circle or Square, and Ellipse			2 d
1.3.7	Deliverable III Milestone			0 d
1.4	**Phase Deliverable IV**			**43 d**
1.4.1	Activity PP, Triangle			7 d
1.4.2	Activity PQ, Triangle			8 d
1.4.3	Activity PR, Triangle			3 d
1.4.4	April Buffer			1 d
1.4.5	April Milestone			0 d
1.4.6	May Activity PA, an hour a week			23 d
1.4.7	Activity PS, Triangle			2 d
1.4.8	Activity PT, Triangle and Square			2 d
1.4.9	Deliverable IV Milestone			0 d
1.5	**Phase Deliverable V**			**38 d**
1.5.1	Activity PU			5 d
1.5.2	Activity PV			7 d
1.5.3	May Buffer			7 d
1.5.4	May Milestone			0 d
1.5.5	June Activity PA, an hour a week			19 d
1.5.6	Activity PW Circle			9 d
1.5.7	Activity PX			8 d
1.5.8	Activity PY, Circle, Square, and Triangle			2 d
1.5.9	End of Project and Del V Milestone			0 d

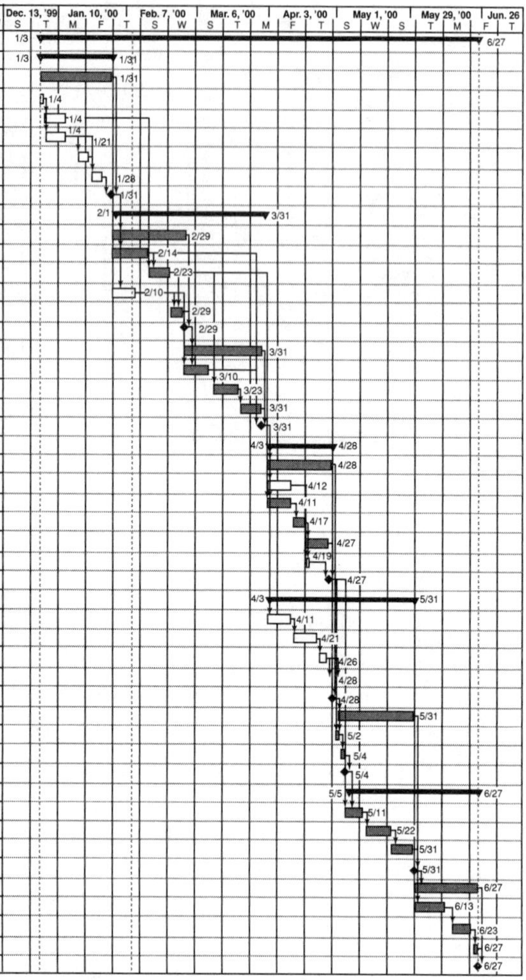

BROWN'S LIST

Brown lists the special monthly department assignments. The details are familiar to all. He makes a note to talk to White about some concerns about her special assignment. Brown expects the team to understand the regular work and sort out the details among themselves.

After completing their plans, Black and Blue attach Brown's list of special departmental activities and publish a consolidated list with each individual's work highlighted. Figure 13.9 combines the monthly regular

Figure 13.9
January Combined Work, with Green's Work Underlined
(Microsoft Project 98 Plus)

Stru	Task/ToDo	Resp	Assist	Date (in ToDo)	Prio	Sta	Notes
1.1.2	Activity PB, Square	Blu		1/4/00			
1.1.2	Activity AB	Bla		1/6/00			
1.1.3	Activity PC, Square or Triangle	Blu		1/14/00			
1.1.4	Activity PD, Square or Triangle	Gre		1/14/00			
1.1.3	Activity AC, Square	Bla	Gre	1/14/00			
1.1.4	Activity AD, Square	Bla	Whi	1/20/00			
1.1.5	Activity PE, Triangle	Blu	Gre	1/21/00			
1.1.5	Activity AE			1/26/00			
1.1.6	January Buffer			1/28/00			
1.1.1	Jan Activity PA, an hour a week	Blu		1/31/00			
1.1.7	January and Del I Milestone			1/31/00			
1.1.1	Activity AA, an hour a day	Bla		1/31/00			
1.1.6	January Buffer			1/31/00			
1.1.7	Milestone Deliverable I			1/31/00			
1	Special monthly activity F, Circle or Square	Bro		1/31/00			
2	Special quarterly activity G, two days this month, Circle	Bro		1/31/00			
3	Special one-time activity H, 20 hours, Triangle	Blu		1/31/00			
4	Special one-time activity I	Whi		1/31/00			

work with all the project work. Each member of the department gets a copy of this sheet with his or her activities highlighted. In Figure 13.9, Green's activities are highlighted.[2]

Green's Personal Schedule

Green makes sure that her assignments will fit into her work calendar. She notes that she should focus first on Black's project, then on Blue's. She warns Blue that she will not be able to finish activity PD when it is scheduled, and after Blue discusses the schedule with her they decide that the five days of schedule buffer will cover it. Finally, Green notices she is doing schedule-driven work for 17 days. She knows she cannot say yes to any other schedule-driven work.

The rest of the team will do what Green has done. They will create their own personal schedules and fit their work to the calendar month with particular attention to the first week. They will line up all the schedule-driven work and move the rest of the work around to accommodate the schedule. If anyone has difficulty with a scheduled date, the conflict will be worked out between the person and the appropriate manager or, as a last resort, in a meeting of Brown, Black, and Blue. This personal detailed scheduling works because the management team is committed to maintaining the budgeted monthly days of work.

PERSONAL SCHEDULING

This personal self-scheduling works extremely well in the world of quickly changing priorities where limited resources juggle many assignments. By limiting the overall monthly work budget for each member of the department, the three leaders, Brown, Black, and Blue, can expect the individuals to work out their own scheduling details to get the work done. This places the fine details of planning where they belong: with the individual doing the work.

The formal scheduling technique known as "resource leveling" becomes worthwhile when priorities are stable, when the number of full-time project workers increases, when a few scarce talents are required on several projects, and when the projects' business value exceeds the business value of the departmental work. Only when the resource-leveled schedule has the expectation of being both valuable and stable is the benefit of resource leveling worth its cost.[3]

CONCLUSION

For a great number of companies meeting the multi-project management challenge, Manager Brown's January work illustrates a practical solution with just enough process: The management team budgets the monthly days of work, the project managers schedule their projects within the budgeted constraints, and each team member arranges a personal schedule to get the work done in a timely fashion.

AFTERWORD: ONGOING MONTHLY PLANNING TOOLS

While Brown and his small team worked out the month of January on a spreadsheet, larger groups have found that a mature resource scheduling tool such as ResSolution permitted them greater flexibility in their decision making.

Imagine that Manager Brown's department has grown to 20 people. Seven Yellows (with a variety of skills) are all working full-time in the expanded department, while a total of eight Greens (also with a mix of skills) are working mostly on projects. Black and Blue are each managing two projects. The ResSolution view of the year might look something like that shown in Figure 13.10.[4]

Before the regular monthly meeting, Black and Blue review their Microsoft Project 98 Plus project plans for the needed skills, the schedules, and the total amount of work. Brown lists any special departmental activ-

Figure 13.10
A ResSolution Screen of Brown's Department for the Year

	Start	End	Total	Brown	Red	White	Black	Blue	YlGrp	GnGrp
Planned Absences										
Reserved Dates										
Vacations										
Operations				128.0	212.0		120.0		1640.0	
Regular Department Work	1/1/2000	12/31/2000		120.0	212.0	120.0	120.0		1640.0	
Special activities	1/1/2000	1/31/2000		8.0		5.0		2.5		
Projects			1725.5			2.0	46.5	63.0		1614.0
Project Apple			46.5			2.0	6.5			38.0
Activity AA	1/1/2000	1/31/2000	2.5				2.5			
Milestone AE	1/1/2000	2/15/2000	12.0			2.0	2.0			8.0
Milestone AJ	2/1/2000	12/31/2000	32.0				2.0			30.0
Project Pear	1/1/2000	6/30/2000	179.0					23.0		156.0
Activity PA	1/1/2000	1/31/2000	2.0					2.0		
Milestone PE	1/1/2000	1/31/2000	25.0					13.0		12.0
Milestone PJ	2/1/2000	3/31/2000	40.0					2.0		38.0
Milestone PO	2/1/2000	4/27/2000	39.0					2.0		37.0
Milestone PT	2/1/2000	5/4/2000	38.0					2.0		36.0
Milestone PY	5/5/2000	6/27/2000	35.0					2.0		33.0
New Project A	3/1/2000	7/31/2000	515.0				20.0			495.0
New Project B	5/1/2000	9/30/2000	360.0					20.0		340.0
New Project C	7/1/2000	11/30/2000	275.0				20.0			255.0
New Project D	8/1/2000	12/31/2000	350.0					20.0		330.0

ities for the month. At the meeting, ResSolution makes it possible to search for special talent, to juggle people between projects and, once again, to achieve a budget for the monthly days of work.

After the meeting the project plans are revised and then collated. Each person gets a list of individual activities and due dates. Everyone assembles a personal calendar for the month and resolves any remaining conflicts.

With a mature resource-scheduling tool, the Brown management team plans out the regular departmental work for the year and the four projects' work in full. The team reserves time for the easily anticipated seasonal work, and blocks out time for much-needed vacations. They filter their list of people to find any combination of required talents. In addition, they track the work to see how the month's days were really spent, so they can improve their future planning.

Many companies have found that a mature resource-scheduling tool provides a convenient, practical way to support the critical agreement on monthly days of work. This essential picture of who's working on what assignments has helped some senior managers to achieve for the first time a realistic monthly fit of their total resources.

NOTES

1. The three-point estimate is based on the triangular distribution from the
   PMBOK Guide. It was selected instead of the beta distribution because it is
   an exact formula and provides a more conservative estimate. See Duncan
   (1996), page 116.

2. Scheuring Project 98 Plus allows an individual to collect a to-do list and assignments from one or more Microsoft Project 98 files, to sort all the tasks in order of their due date, and to print out the list for the month. The individual has the responsibility to contact any project managers whose work may require rescheduling and negotiate an acceptable solution. The individual can practice the pick-up-sticks, qualitative arrangement of the work, because his or her quantitative boundaries were set by the organization (*Scheuring Project 98 Plus User's Guide* 1999).

3. No method exists to arrive at the one true answer to the resource-leveling problem. Some recent approximations have been labeled a "critical chain" and discussed in Newbold (1998). For a simple discussion of the traditional view, see Nevison (1981).

4. Over 100 companies successfully perform this monthly budgeting using ResSolution. These companies combine the computer tool with monthly resource management meetings among the managers of active projects (Scheuring 1999; *Scheuring ResSolution 3.1* 1999).

REFERENCES

Duncan, William R. 1996. *A Guide to the Project Management Body of Knowledge.* Newtown Square, PA: Project Management Institute.

Nevison, John M. 1981. *Executive Computing: How to Get It Done on Your Own.* Reading, MA: Addison-Wesley. (Especially Chapter 6, "Project Planning, Scheduling and Control.")

Newbold, Robert C. 1998. *Project Management in the Fast Lane: Applying the Theory of Constraints.* New York: St. Lucie Press.

Scheuring, Heinz 1999. Private communication (October).

———. 1998. *Winning Project Management.* Program Notebook, Vol. 4.1. Maynard, MA: Oak Associates.

Scheuring Project 98 Plus®, User's Guide. 1999. Maynard, MA: Oak Associates.

Scheuring ResSolution® 3.1: Multi-project Management Resource Tool for Line and Resource Managers, User's Guide. 1999. Maynard, MA: Oak Associates.

CHAPTER 14

PROCESS AUTOMATION IN PROJECT MANAGEMENT: TODAY

VICKEY QUINN

Project management process automation: That's a phrase I have heard tossed around for years. Frequently, clients tell me that they have automated their project management process and what they really mean is that they are using a scheduling software package. Yet, others tell me that they have automated their processes and what they mean is that they have dumped all project schedules into a database. If you look up the word *automate* in the dictionary, you will find the definition "to make automatic." The definition of *automated* is "designed to function without human intervention." Based on these definitions, the end state of an automated project management process might appear to be like a manufacturing assembly line: Project ideas go in one end, and results come out the other. (Oh, that life was actually like that; but then where would the challenge lie?) In reality, we can probably never "automate" the project management process as defined by the current usage of *automate*, nor would we probably ever want to. Human intervention—the ability to think critically, respond, negotiate, problem solve—these are skills valuable for running projects. So, where does that leave the myriad of software tools on the market today?

The most effective project managers I know harness the software tools at their disposal into a system that stores and helps manage data, allowing the manager in turn to use the data to make decisions that impact project success. The system also assists in meeting the communication demands of today's teams and work groups. Our definition of project management process automation then becomes: *to design a system of integrated tools that assist with data management needs of project managers, team mem-*

245

bers, and other project stakeholders. In other words, if the goal is to increase the chances of having a successful project, then certain tools help us in reaching that goal.

For those unfamiliar with classes of software tools, let's review the following basic definitions prior to discussing software systems:

- *Scheduling software* allows for the development of a project schedule with calculated critical path and start and finish dates for tasks, and the ability then to track progress against those dates.
- *Databases* are "storage bins" that hold project data; they allow for queries and respond with database entries that match your questions. Databases are great tools for resource capacity planning, pooling resources, and collecting multiple project information.
- *Spreadsheets* are tables of columns and rows that easily allow for calculations and data viewing.
- *Word processing software* eases the task of physically putting words to paper (or screen).
- *Notes software* allows rapid message sending and receiving among project stakeholders and is extremely useful for distributed teams that are not in the same physical location.
- *Multimedia tools* capture visual images and sound bites so that project stakeholders get the feeling of "being there" during important project events.
- *Web-authoring tools* help create Web pages for access by project stakeholders.
- *Accounting software* performs project bookkeeping functions.
- *Software development tools* assist in creating interfaces between software packages, customizing software, and automating data flow needs.
- *Charting software* creates wonderful graphics from data you input.

Numerous software packages on the market today combine two or more of these classes of tools to ease the burden of creating your own system. These combination packages already have the appropriate interfaces (or connections) between types of software tools.

In this chapter, we will explore the following areas of designing and implementing a project management software system:

- Design and implementation pitfalls
- Developing a design and implementation plan
- Design and implementation methodology
- Popular software tools

DESIGN AND IMPLEMENTATION PITFALLS

I worked for a number of years as a trainer for a developer of project management software scheduling and tracking tools. During my four years with the organization, I taught thousands of users in Fortune 1000 companies throughout North America how to use the tools. My biggest learning during this experience was seeing how little difference the tools made in a project manager's ability to manage projects more effectively. In fact, introducing these tools often seemed to cause irreparable harm to the project management implementation process or to the project's results. (Those of you wishing to find suggestions about implementing software tools in your organizations, please don't stop reading. I, too, find these tools invaluable if used properly. Please read on.)

Pitfall 1: Substituting Tools for Process

Many less-than-successful organizations elevate software tools above process. In almost all cases, this misalignment is unintentional. Tools produce tangible products and easily become the focus of the undisciplined. In fact, I was often asked to help organizations implement a project management scheduling and tracking tool throughout the organization as a means of improving project performance. When I asked to review the groups' project management processes, as a rule—rather than the exception—I was told that they had not been developed yet, but would be as soon as projects ran more smoothly! Readers, this is known as "putting the cart before the horse," as my grandmother was fond of saying. From an observer's vantage point, it is easy to see why these efforts fail in the medium and long term, as there is no foundation upon which to build.

Pitfall 2: Not Considering Project Performance Improvement as a Process

In an article by Ron Remy in *PM Network* (July 1997, "Adding Focus to Improvement Efforts with PM³," according to quality expert Dr. W. Edwards Deming, process improvement is not an event, but rather a journey. Often over my 15 years as a project manager and consultant I have observed individuals and organizations attempt project process improvement as an event—a one-time ordeal to bring control to otherwise chaotic projects. More often than not, these efforts have had short-lived improvements. This observation was most evident in the use and distribution of project management software support tools. The tools were introduced as the event, brief training occurred, and long-term results were erroneously anticipated.

Pitfall 3: Lack of a Design and Implementation Strategy

Because introducing project management support tools was viewed as an event, often there was an inadequate or nonexistent implementation strategy. Usually, the implementation stopped with training and users were expected to apply the tools to existing projects without much assistance.

Pitfall 4: Lack of a Comprehensive Design

Introducing any system into an organization requires a comprehensive design. The design phase requires a thorough look at user requirements, and both a conceptual design (what the system will do) and a technical design (what software and hardware will be used and how the data will move from one to another). This process helps ensure that requirements are translated into a system that works now and in the future. The nondesigned implementations often failed because the end states were not envisioned prior to tool introduction, and after several years there was still no integrated system, but rather a collection of software tools.

Pitfall 5: Designing the Project Management Process Based on Tool Capability

On numerous occasions, clients told me that they changed their project management process because "the tool doesn't let us do that easily." To me, this seems to be a dangerous road to tread. Some of the most significant advancements in construction and engineering have resulted from innovative tool development because the right one did not currently exist.

Pitfall 6: Forgetting That These Are Tools

For the technically inclined, it is easy to see how we become enamored of software tools. It is a very impressive collection, and new ones seem available almost daily. It is important to remember that tools should serve the project management process, and the system design and implementation should reflect that concept. A good question to ask is: After the user is efficient with the tool, does it assist with decision making or the success of the project, or did I just add another layer of bureaucracy?

DEVELOPING A DESIGN AND IMPLEMENTATION PLAN

One approach to creating a project management system for your organization is to treat the implementation as a project. During development of a scope for this project you will design the end state or goal for the system. Due to the ever-changing nature of software and hardware, it is typically a good idea to plan out maybe three years in advance for user needs. Although you may create a user requirements document that spans three years, typically you will break the actual implementation or project into 12-month increments. This fits nicely into budgeting cycles as you decide what projects or parts of the implementation can be accomplished each year. Looking at the system from a three-year perspective helps assure that each element selected or added fits into the overall design.

After the system is designed, you will decide what benefits you are looking for from each design component and prioritize these into an order list for implementation. You might start with the easiest ones to implement, or the ones that will give you the greatest benefit for the money spent, or the ones that will benefit project results most dramatically.

Next, you will create a technical design where you will actually select which component software tools to use or you will develop your own. Fortunately, there are many knowledgeable consultants available who can provide guidance as to the best choice of tools for your system design. As previously mentioned, many vendors are currently creating system parts by combining tools such as scheduling software and a database repository to address multiple project needs developed by the same company.

After purchasing or developing the tools, work up an implementation plan complete with tasks and milestones. The most important aspect of implementation is to remember that you are introducing what will likely be a cultural change. The bigger the change, the more time users need to adjust.

The implementation does not stop with tool training; rather, you will need to supply mentoring assistance as project stakeholders try to apply the tools in their unique project environments. This means that the standards and guidelines, for both project management and tool use, are already documented and available.

The implementation typically becomes like a rolling wave. After the first set of tools is introduced and support is underway, you will begin to plan the next wave of implementation while closely monitoring and adjusting the tools in use. It is important to remind project stakeholders frequently that tool use is an evolutionary process, just like project management practices within the organization.

DESIGN AND IMPLEMENTATION METHODOLOGY

The following project management software system design and implementation methodology is based on two principles: introduction and use of software tools follows introduction and implementation of project management process, and the development of an implementation strategy is done prior to tool release. This methodology provides a conceptual framework around which your system design and implementation can be structured.

The foundation for this framework uses the project management maturity model concept as the base. Much like Carnegie Mellon University's capability maturity model for software development, Micro-Frame Technologies of Ontario, California, proposes a framework for analyzing project management capability. (This registered and trademarked model is discussed in detail of *PM Network* in the July 1997 issue.) Project management maturity describes the evolutionary process of changing from a chaotic, disorganized project environment into a results-oriented organization where project success is the norm.

The concept of project management maturity serves as a valuable springboard for our discussion of software tool use to improve project results. Using the maturity model concept, as the maturity of an individual project manager or organization increases, so does the ability to utilize project management software tools. Furthermore, in my experience, there is a direct correlation between the maturity level of the group and the ease of use and success of tool implementation. The key to implementation seems to be to allow tool use to follow the project management maturity level and to "grow" both together.

Let's consider the following five maturity levels developed by Micro-Frame Technologies Inc., of Ontario, California:

1. Ad hoc
2. Abbreviated
3. Organized
4. Managed
5. Adaptive

If you think of moving from level to level as an evolutionary path, the path can be followed by an individual project or in larger terms by an organization as a whole. The cultural changes alone make evolution on an organizational scale a much more daunting task. Our further discussion centers around the maturity of a multi-project group such as a department, division, or organization. Based on our previous discussion of tool implementation failure, it becomes easy to understand why failure occurs when an ad hoc group (every project is autonomous) tries to use enterprise-wide databases to track project costs and resource usage. (Resource tracking is much more appropriate at the managed or adaptive levels.) Your implementation plan should address moving from one maturity level to another.

Therefore, prior to implementing software tools, it is important to evaluate the maturity of the project group. Keep in mind that although an individual project team may be able to mature rapidly, given the nature of cultural change for a group, moving from one maturity level to another takes on average about 12 to 18 months, and that is with a project management advocate! For a group to claim a particular level, all participants in the group must be able to perform at that level.

Project Management Maturity Level 1: Ad Hoc

At this level, each project is viewed as having a great deal of autonomy. Furthermore, each project is seen as unique and separate from other projects. There is little or no consistency in the project management practices being used, and typically no standards are yet developed. In this stage, most project constraints are established in a top-down method with little or no bottom-up verification. The project management environment is typically disorganized, maybe even chaotic. Results usually depend on individual heroic efforts.

Software Tool Implementation Suggestions (Ad Hoc Level)

Given the unavailability of project management process guidelines or methodology, probably the best that can be hoped for is to introduce the concept of evolving the project management process and the software system. This can start the cultural change process. It is also appropriate to introduce the use of both a scheduling tool and a tool for distributing notes, and to allow for adequate training and practice. The use of the scheduling tool should concentrate on developing a schedule (no resource allocations) and tracking progress. Again, given the nature of the ad hoc stage, schedules are created for individual projects with no attempt made to consolidate projects (lack of standards in developing project plans). Project schedules are typically treated as practice schedules in this stage with the real goal being understanding of the application of the tool to real-world projects.

Project Management Maturity Level 2: Abbreviated

In the abbreviated stage, planning is still predominately top-down, and software tools are too often erroneously chosen as solutions to process problems. In the abbreviated stage, project management standards and guidelines are starting to be documented but are not applied consistently, mainly because they are not understood. Typically, scheduling software is used to plan projects to too low a level of detail while other projects may be overly simplified. No data integration is yet visible. Project success is still unpredictable.

Software Tool Implementation Suggestions (Abbreviated Level)
As in the ad hoc stage, the payoff for software tool use is low in the abbreviated stage. However, to further implementation for future growth, begin documenting software standards and guidelines that mirror the automated parts of the documented project management standards and guidelines. For example, standards for scheduling software might include the storage and naming of project files, the use of WBS (work breakdown structure) numbers, the number of hours in a standard workday, standard levels of task detail, and the use of task documentation (task descriptions and estimating methodology). A goal for the abbreviated stage might typically be that every project has a project schedule that is updated periodically according to the project management process guidelines. At this point, users begin to see that tools are actually helpful in applying the processes outlined.

Most software tool implementations seem to stall or terminate during maturity levels 1 and 2. Be prepared for steep learning curves, often dramatic cultural changes, and not a lot of visible payoff. However, if these tendencies are anticipated during the evolution of the project management process within the group, they can be planned for and handled well with an implementation plan. Often, the most difficult part of the implementation is the recognition by corporate executives and managers that reaching the level of project management that produces the benefits they seek takes time, planning, encouragement, and an effective implementation strategy and execution.

Project Management Maturity Level 3: Organized

In this level, projects typically undergo a thorough scope identification and documentation process. Project management processes are standardized and integrated into an end-to-end system. More credible plans are developed as milestones, resource requirements, budgets, and schedule constraints are integrated. A great deal of time is usually spent in maintaining the automated versions of the plan such as scheduling tools, databases, and spreadsheets, and not enough time is spent in analyzing project information, risk assessment, and problem solving. There is still not much evidence that information between projects is shared in any meaningful way. The focus is still typically at the individual project level as opposed to the group level or management level. The "roll-up," or summarized, data seen as useful or necessary for upper management decisions is typically not yet available or is so inaccurate as to be not useful. Project success is more predictable.

Software Tool Implementation Suggestions (Organized Level)
Word processing document templates support standards in project scope definition. If a project office is established, this office can maintain and disseminate form templates.

Likewise, the beginnings of a simple project database that contains summary information about each project is a great tool for cross-referencing project ideas. Typical information contained in this database includes project name, project manager's name, project sponsor and/or client name, project objective statement, list of main project deliverables, business need addressed, anticipated budget, FTE (full-time equivalent) resource count, and anticipated completion date.

More robust scheduling is attempted as milestones are included in the schedules and resources assigned. The schedules are updated periodically, but resource expenditures are probably not entered as there may not be a convenient way to collect this data. As projects occur, a historical database can be created to archive estimating guidelines and risk factors for common tasks.

Notes software is introduced as an automated means of keeping team members informed about project issues and information, especially if the team is a distributed team (not in the same physical location).

Project Management Maturity Level 4: Managed

Project success is more consistent at this level because the project management process is understood and controlled. At the managed level, projects consistently use the scope definition templates, schedules are created to the appropriate level of detail, and what-if scenarios can be analyzed during constraint balancing. Work breakdown structure (WBS) task templates are created and can be reused with new projects.

At the managed level, an estimating methodology is documented. At this level, actual project performance data is collected and archived in a database, and also is available for new project planning. An added element at the managed level is the ability to perform basic resource capacity planning and forecasting through the use of a consolidated project database.

The managed level returns several benefits that many organizations aspire to—although their expectations might have been that they would reach them at the ad hoc level. Your implementation strategy should address the anticipated benefits for each maturity level in regard to software tool implementation and plans for reaching these goals.

Software Tool Implementation Suggestions (Managed Level)
At the managed level, tool users go beyond the basics. Users use scheduling and tracking software consistently not only to assist in executing a project plan but also in analyzing what-if scenarios. Customizations to the software may occur so that project personnel can easily mirror their custom project management process using consistent terminology and steps.

Spreadsheets may be introduced to assist in analyzing project trends or collect resource expenditure information. Databases continue to grow as project data is archived from completed projects. A database is in use to serve as a data repository or warehouse to view resource usage across projects. This information can also be used to forecast future resource needs.

A front-end database, spreadsheet, or a combination of the two is introduced to allow upper management the ability to begin to select, approve, and prioritize project ideas that are sanctioned as real projects. These projects are then planned and added to the data repository to give the enterprise view demanded by most executives today.

Project communications and information sharing takes place routinely via the company intranet or the Web.

Project Management Maturity Level 5: Adaptive

There is an abundance of historical information available on which to base new project plans, and the information is available online.

Enterprise-wide project management is evident by capacity planning, resource allocation analysis, and review. At the adaptive level, budgeting and expenditures tie into the corporate accounting system, and cross-project query capability is available to executives. Project success is expected at this level and the focus is on continuous improvement through analysis of the processes that are in place.

Software Tool Implementation Suggestions (Adaptive Level)

At the adaptive level, information is readily available and shared throughout the enterprise. This usually means that most or all of the project management methodologies, forms, templates, guidelines, databases, spreadsheets, and other general information is available online.

The following table summarizes the maturity levels and the software tool introductions at each level:

Maturity Level	Software Tool Introduction
Ad hoc	Training is provided on a scheduling tool.
	Training and general guidelines for using a communication tool for distributing notes are available.
Abbreviated	Document software use standards and guidelines are available.
	Use of scheduling software to schedule each project and track progress periodically is begun.
	Mentoring support is provided as users apply the software tool to a real project.
Organized	Word processing document templates and forms are introduced for project documentation.
	A project summary database is created.
	Milestone tasks are added to project schedules.
	Resources are assigned to projects and/or project tasks.
	An historical database is created.
	Notes distribution software use is expanded.
	A shared drive or directory is created and accessible by project team members.
Managed	Project managers use what-if scenarios.
	Project data is accurate enough that analysis can occur and decisions can be reached based on the analysis.
	Software customizations occur.
	Spreadsheets are introduced for trend analysis or data capture.
	A project repository database is created to store information from all active projects.
	Project communication is possible through the intranet or the Web.

Adaptive   Historical databases are expanded.
                  Databases and spreadsheets are created to allow for
                  capacity planning, and project selection and
                  prioritization.
                  Interfaces are created to tie project accounting
                  information to the corporate accounting process.
                  Project management process information is available
                  online.
                  Project data is available to the enterprise online.

SOFTWARE TOOLS

There is an abundance of tools available on the market today. For example, at last count, I noted over 400 scheduling packages! Consider conducting informational interviews with software users to determine what they like and don't like about their selected packages. The Web is another wonderful source of information about various packages available. Searching for project management software, software, or project management will yield numerous valuable software sources.

The value of a software implementation strategy is that you will determine the end results or goals before buying your first package. This way, you can determine what to buy and what to develop to create a seamless automated system as opposed to the patchwork collection of software in evidence in many organizations. Even though you may not be ready for anything sophisticated at the moment, design your system for future considerations so that it is not outdated before it is even implemented.

The following is a brief listing of some packages and their Internet addresses to give you a running start toward developing your project management process software system.

Scheduling and Tracking Software

Artemis	www.artemispm.com
Microsoft Project	www.microsoft.com
Open Plan	www.wst.com
PlanView	www.planview.com
Primavera	www.primavera.com
Project KickStart	www.experienceware.com
Project Scheduler	www.scitor.com
SureTrak	www.primavera.com
TimeLine	www.tlsolutions.com
Workbench	www.abtcorp.com

Spreadsheets
Lotus   www.ibm.com
Microsoft Excel   www.microsoft.com

Databases
Informix   www.informix.com
Oracle   www.oracle.com
Sybase   www.sybase.com

Word Processing
Microsoft Word   www.microsoft.com
Word Perfect   www.corel.com

Project Repositories
ABT Corporation   www.abt.com
Allegro Group, Inc.   www.allegrogroup.com
IMS Corporation   www.imscorp.com

Web-Based Enterprise Project Management
jeTech Data Systems   www.jetechdata.com
Journyx   www.journyx.com
MESA Systems Guild   www.mesasys.com
Scitor PS Suite   www.scitor.com
Systemcorp   www.systemcorp.com

Team Groupware
Inovie   www.inovie.com
IntraPlan   www.intraplan.com
Netmosphere Inc.   www.netmosphere.com

Timekeeper Software
Advanced Management Solutions, Inc.   www.amsusa.com
HMS Software   www.hmssoftware.com
TimeWizard   www.timewzrd.com

Project Office Software
Pacific Edge Software   www.pacific-edge.com
Systemcorp   www.systemcorp.com

Presentation Graphics
Deneba Software   www.deneba.com
Lightware   www.lightware.com

Risk Assessment Tools

Monte Carlo	www.primavera.com
Risk+ (C/S Solutions, Inc.)	cs–solutions.com

In conclusion, I would like to restate that most projects are not technology driven. Instead, most projects are driven by business need. With that stated, it is equally important not only to understand but to believe that thorough design and implementation planning often means the difference between successful implementation and failure. Although design planning often seems tedious or even painful for some (usually the *integrative* thinkers, who compile information pieces into meaningful blocks, as distinguished from *holistic* thinkers, who break the big picture view into meaningful pieces), the benefits are easily recognized by all during implementation.

To put this entire conversation into perspective, please remember that the technology decisions that you make today can and probably will affect others for several years to come. Use the tools wisely and with forethought; in the wrong hands the same technology becomes a weapon!

CHAPTER 15

COMPUTER-AIDED PROJECT MANAGEMENT: TOMORROW

CARL N. BELACK

INTRODUCTION

Although the art of managing projects has been with civilization for thousands of years, it is only relatively recently that modern project management techniques were developed, codified, and implemented in any consistent, methodological manner. Perhaps it is not totally coincidental that these techniques came about during the same period as did the beginning of the commercial availability of computers, as we know them today. As of the writing of this book, we have arrived at a point where hundreds of commercial software applications that address various aspects of the project management processes are available for purchase. For one who is unfamiliar with the wide variety of these applications on the market, the process of selecting and implementing these tools can be a daunting task. The purpose of this chapter is to help make that process somewhat more manageable.

The reader should note that the subject of this chapter, computer-aided project management (CAPM), is specifically intended to allow for the discussion of the different types of tools available to facilitate the entire process of project management. To many people, the consideration of project management tools is unfortunately limited to what has become known as *project management software*. Granted, this type of tool was among the first applications developed with project management in mind, and it does address an important aspect of project management, namely scheduling and tracking. This author believes, however, that such a tool is but one among many in what we will refer to as a *computer-aided project management platform*. A CAPM platform is one that includes applications that automate many of the project management processes, not just scheduling and tracking, and it is this platform that will be discussed here.

The following pages will address:

1. The historical development of computer-aided project management (CAPM)
2. The set of processes involved in or surrounding project management (the Project Concentric Circle Model)
3. The tools or platform to automate the concentric circle processes
4. Implementation of CAPM platforms in business organizations
5. What we might expect of these tools in the years to come

It is hoped that this examination will help the reader better understand the use of CAPM tools while facilitating their selection and successful implementation.

HISTORY OF COMPUTER-AIDED PROJECT MANAGEMENT

While it may be difficult for some to believe (particularly those to whom the slide rule is merely a curious artifact from an ancient civilization), modern project management techniques were at one time employed by those who did not have the advantage of using computers. In fact, there are some companies that still don't use computers for project management in any organized fashion. And, as laborious as the work is, it is perfectly possible to put together a good project plan without the use of computers. However, having spent some time doing just that, the author can attest to the enormous amount of time and resources such an undertaking consumes. And, once changes are introduced to the initial project plan, the incremental use of time and resources expands exponentially.

In the late 1950s and early 1960s, a few companies began to develop their own internal software tools for managing projects, some of which are still in use today. With the apparent increasing need for such tools, commercial applications began to appear in the marketplace. Most of these tools were initially used by U.S. government contractors (who were required by the Department of the Energy or the Department of Defense to adhere to rules for managing government contracts) and were implemented on mainframe computers—the only computers commercially available at that time. These applications were the predecessors to tools that are still available today (although in a much different form), such as Artemis and Primavera. At the time, these tools were both difficult to learn and cumbersome to use. Since graphical user interfaces did not yet exist, command language was used to interface with the application. Nonetheless, since they enabled some automation of scheduling, tracking, and reporting activities, they were a welcome change for most project managers who were used to performing these same tasks by hand.

The advent of commercially available personal computers brought about the development of project management tools specifically aimed at the PC market. These tools (which we will refer to as "low-end" tools, as distinguished from the "high-end" tools that run on mainframes and mini-computers) were much less expensive than their high-end counterparts, and were much easier to learn and to use, but also had far fewer capabilities. These tools also allowed the user to interface with the application through a rudimentary graphical user interface (GUI). These tools included software applications such as Harvard Project Manager, SuperProject, Project Workbench (originally known as Project Manager's Workbench, and now called Niku Workbench), and Microsoft Project. These tools were primarily aimed at the IBM-compatible marketplace. There were fewer tools available for Apple Macintosh computers, such as MacProject.

Over the past few years, the manufacturers of the high-end tools have incorporated GUIs and other devices to make their tools user-friendly. At the same time, the makers of the low-end tools began building into their applications more capabilities that had, prior to that time, been available only in the high-end tools. Some formerly low-end tools, such as Project Workbench, have migrated into the realm of high-end tools. And a number of high-end tool manufacturers have produced low-end tools for managing individual projects whose files can then be integrated into the high-end tools (such as SureTrak for Primavera). As confusing as this all sounds, all of these software manufacturers have been trying to achieve the same end: to develop a tool that balances ease of learning and use with ever-increasing capabilities.

As the profession of project management began to gain acceptance in the workplace, additional applications became commercially available. These range from tools that automate other project management processes (such as risk management tools like @Risk) to tools that help manage areas that are ancillary to, but that have a direct impact upon, project management (such as multi-project resource management tools like ResSolution). With the availability of all of these different types of tools, it is often a difficult proposition deciding which tools, if any, are appropriate for a specific organization. The next sections will discuss the processes that are involved in, or have an impact upon, project management and will examine how the use of computer tools can facilitate these processes.

PROJECT CONCENTRIC CIRCLE MODEL

In any given organization, there are generally two types of work activities that take place. The first type, the one with which most people are familiar, is *operations* work. The activities in operations work have the following characteristics:

- They are repetitive (they occur over and over from fiscal quarter to fiscal quarter, and from fiscal year to fiscal year).
- Their end result is essentially the same (production of financial reports, operations reports, etc.).

The second type, which we are addressing in this chapter, is *project* work. As one might expect, project work is characterized by work that (1) is not repetitive, but rather time-limited (it has a specific beginning and end), and (2) produces a unique product or service. Project management is the set of activities involved in managing project work.

When looking at the set of processes involved in or surrounding project management, it is useful to use a framework that the author has called the Project Concentric Circle Model.[1] This model is depicted in Figure 15.1.

The model consists of three concentric circles. Each circle represents a level at which project management processes, or processes affecting the project management processes, take place.

Project Management Core Processes

The center circle represents the project management core processes, or processes that function within individual projects. The reader can find a detailed description of these processes in *A Guide to the Project Management Body of Knowledge* (Project Management Institute, 1996), also referred to as the *PMBOK Guide*. In brief, these are areas that address the following project management activities at the individual project level:

- Time management
- Scope management
- Cost management
- Risk management
- Quality management
- Human resources management
- Procurement management
- Communications management
- Integration management

Figure 15.1
Project Concentric Circle Model

SENIOR MANAGEMENT

PROJECT MANAGEMENT

PROJECT
MANAGEMENT
CORE
PROCESSES

SUPPORT PROCESSES

LEADERSHIP

The *PMBOK Guide* also describes the five project management processes throughout which activities in each above-noted area of management need to be performed. These processes are portrayed in Figure 15.2.

It is these management areas and processes that most organizations associate with project management. And some assume that attending to these alone will assure successful organizational project work. That, however, is a fatal error for many organizations. In order to achieve a high level of competence in project management, two other levels must also be addressed.

Project Management Support Processes

The second circle represents the project management support processes level and includes processes that occur outside of the day-to-day activities of the individual project teams. The activities within these processes generally comprise operational activities, not project activities, that support project work and project teams. In fact, these can best be described as processes that establish and maintain an environment in which project work can be successfully performed.

Figure 15.2
Project Management Process

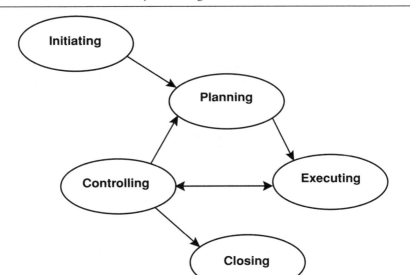

These processes can be grouped into two categories:

- *Organizational development.* Activities that occur in these processes include: assessing organizational and individual competency; development and updating of job descriptions for people at all levels of the project team; design of career paths for project managers and project team members; project manager selection and competency development; project team member selection and support; and training and mentoring.
- *Communications and knowledge systems.* Activities that occur in the development and maintenance of these systems focus on: interproject and intraproject communications; project reporting systems (for project team members, customers, and senior management); in-progress and post-project reviews and audits; development and maintenance of historical activity and estimating databases; capacity planning; project scope management; and project and technical document/software configuration management.

Senior Management Leadership

The outermost circle represents processes that senior management must undertake in order to promote project-friendly corporate environments. This involves:

- *Championing project management within the organization.* This is done by: understanding project management and project work within the organizational context; leading the change effort to enhance the role of projects and project management; prioritizing project work (to enable effective resource management); and managing the portfolio of projects to ensure alignment with corporate goals.
- *Creating and enabling the culture of project success.* This includes: fostering open and honest communication; promoting rational risk taking; supporting the need for project planning; valuing the differences of project and functional management; and encouraging "quiet" projects (and discouraging "heroic" projects).

Now that we have constructed a framework for the processes that need to work effectively in order for projects to be successful, let us look at the types of software applications that could automate many of these processes.

THE CAPM PLATFORM

An organization needs to have available for project managers, project teams, line managers, and senior managers a tool set that facilitates the activities of the management processes noted in the previous section. An example of one type of tool frequently used in project management is a list of items which, when completed, would signify the completion of a project deliverable; a "punch list" is one such list that is regularly used to this day in construction projects. More and more, these tools are being incorporated into computer applications. In this section, we will take a look at tools that are available, or are being constructed, to automate the concentric circle processes.

Automating the Project Management Core Processes

Before proceeding, a brief word of caution is in order. It is the mistaken belief of many that in order to manage projects effectively, one merely needs to purchase a project management tool and become trained on use

266 THE TECHNICAL TRACK

of the tool (the "buy 'em a tool and send 'em to school" approach). This is possibly the worst approach that could be taken to improve the effectiveness of project management in an organization. As has already been noted, project management predated the commercially available tools to aid that endeavor. So we know that it is possible to manage projects effectively without the use of automation. The single most important thing to remember about these tools is that it is not the tool, but rather the people using the tool, that manage the projects. *In order for people to use the tools properly, they must first master the techniques upon which these tools are based.*

As an example, to develop useful data for scope, time, and cost management, the successful tool user must have a working knowledge of the following: scope statement development; work definition (through work breakdown structures or other such techniques); activity estimating: precedence diagramming method (also known as project network diagramming); and progress evaluation techniques (such as earned value). Expecting success through the use of a tool without a thorough prior grounding in these techniques is like expecting someone who has no grounding in the basics of writing (grammar, syntax, writing technique) to use a word processing application to produce a novel. Some novels on the market notwithstanding, it just does not happen that way. With this firmly in mind, let's look at the types of tools one might use in modern project management.

Scope, Time, Cost, and Resource Management
The preponderance of tools on the market today are those that aid project managers in time and cost management (commonly called schedule and budget management). In addition, many of these tools include resource management. These tools can be helpful in:

- Developing activity lists (project scope) and displaying work breakdown structures (Figure 15.3)
- Noting activity estimates (in some cases, calculating "most likely" estimates for three-point estimating techniques)
- Assigning dependencies (precedence structure) among activities
- Calculating and displaying precedence diagrams (PERT charts—Figure 15.4)
- Calculating and displaying project schedules (Gantt charts—Figure 15.5)
- Assigning individual or group resources

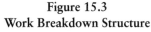

Figure 15.3
Work Breakdown Structure

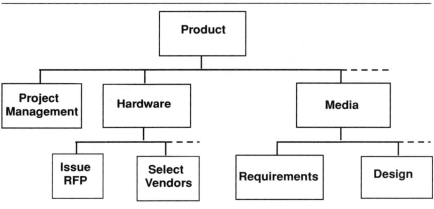

- Setting and displaying calendars (both for the project and for individual resources)
- Calculating project costs (for various types of resources)
- Entering time card and resource usage data
- Tracking project cost, schedule, and resource data
- Rescheduling and recalculating schedule and cost data after input of actual activity data
- Calculating and displaying project progress (Figure 15.6).

Figure 15.4
Precedence Diagram

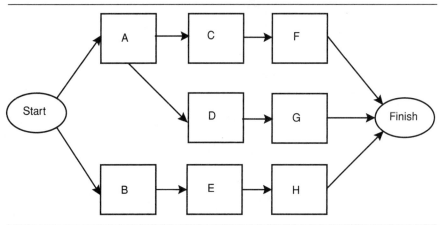

Figure 15.5
Gantt Chart

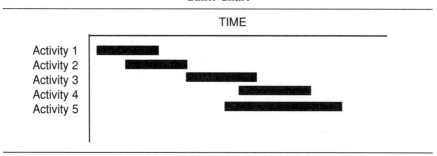

Figure 15.6
Earned Value "S" Curves

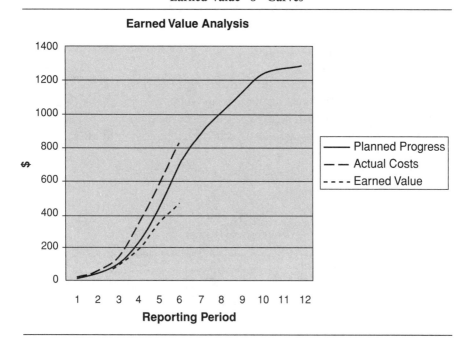

- Leveling resources
- Displaying resource histograms
- Sorting and filtering for various scenarios
- Report generation for use by various project stakeholders

These are just some of the capabilities that can be found in these tools. The tools that can be used for such efforts are too numerous to list. Examples are Microsoft Project 98, PS7, and Artemis. For some of the low-end tools (particularly for MS Project 98), there is an after-market of tools that can be used in conjunction with the primary tool to help it do its job more effectively. These range from tools like GRANEDA Dynamic (which provides an excellent graphical interface to print professional-looking precedence diagrams, Gantt charts, and work breakdown structures), to tools such as Project 98 Plus (which provides a very user-friendly interface for sorting and filtering for MS Project 98).

Risk Management

Since two characteristics that we have attributed to project work are its unique nature and its time limitations, projects are inherently risky. Many projects run into problems or fail altogether because an inadequate job was done around risk management. Project risk management is a three-step process that involves:

1. Identifying, assessing, and documenting all potential project risks
2. Developing risk avoidance and mitigation plans
3. Implementing these plans when the risks occur

Clearly, this is not a process that ends once the project planning activities have been completed. Rather, project managers need to monitor and assess potential project risk throughout the entire conduct of the project.

One type of risk that all project managers face is that associated with project schedules. A typical method for handling this risk is to run Monte Carlo simulations on the project precedence diagram (PERT chart). This is done by (1) assigning random durations (within predefined three-point activity estimates) to individual activities, (2) calculating project duration over and over for hundreds (sometimes thousands) of repetitions, and (3) analyzing the distribution of probable outcomes of project duration. There are a number of tools on the market that perform these tasks. Two of the most popular are @Risk and Risk+. There are also other fine tools available that perform similarly. These tools can perform simulations on practically any project calculations that lend themselves to numerical analysis. The output of these tools is the analysis of probable project durations in both numerical and graphical formats (see Figure 15.7).

Why is it important to use tools like these to help us manage risk? Quite simply, single-point project estimates are rarely, if ever, met. Project managers need to understand the probable range of outcomes of both project cost and duration so they can make informed decisions around a host of project issues (e.g., setting project team goals, deciding when to hire project personnel). They also need this information to set proper expectations and to conduct intelligent discussions with the project team members, senior managers, and customers. The correct use of such tools can help project managers do just that.

In addition to these tools, other tools are available to help track the status of potential risk events over the course of a project. One such tool, Risk Radar, was designed to help managers of software-intensive development programs. Regardless of the intended target audience, this tool can be quite helpful for any type of project risk tracking effort. With the proper input of risk data, it displays a graphic depicting the number of risk events with similar risk exposure and lays them out on an easily un-

Figure 15.7
Project Outcome Probability Curve

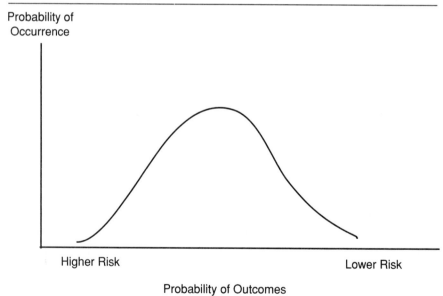

derstood grid. This is a common way to track risk. An example of a similar grid is shown in Figure 15.8.

Change Management

As noted earlier, there are two types of changes with which project managers need be concerned. The first is a change in the scope of work of the project. Most projects encounter scope changes during the evolution of work on the project. Since scope changes almost always result in budget and schedule changes, it is very important to track them accurately. Using the scope, time, cost, and resource management software discussed earlier can usually do this.

The second type of change is one that addresses changes in technical project documentation. Technical drawings, quality documents, and electrical wiring diagrams are examples of such documents. There are a number of tools available for these efforts, and they are as diverse as the technical functions that might employ them. They are generically known as configuration management tools. While these will not be addressed in this chapter, project functional teams should make every effort to select

Figure 15.8
Project Risk Grid

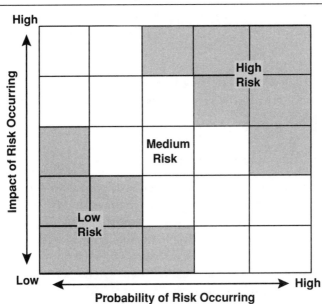

tools like these that will help them manage these documents so that current versions are available to all project members who need them.

Communications Management
Communications skills are arguably the most important skills of project management. Similarly, communications tools can be considered among the most important project tools. As noted in the *PMBOK Guide*,

> Project Communications Management includes the processes required to ensure timely and appropriate generation, collection, dissemination, storage, and ultimate disposition of project information. It provides the critical links among people, ideas, and information that are necessary for success. Everyone involved in the project must be prepared to send and receive communications in the project "language" and must understand how the communications they are involved in as individuals affect the project as a whole.

Tools that aid managers in project communications are not terribly different from those that are used in operations communications. They include:

- Word processors (e.g., WordPerfect, MS Word)
- Presentation tools (e.g., MS PowerPoint, Corel PRESENTS)
- Spreadsheets (e.g., Lotus 1-2-3, MS Excel)
- Individual and work group communications tools (e.g., e-mail, Lotus Notes)

With the availability of Internet communications and the advent of tools similar to those noted, tool sets such as these should be readily available for use by project teams.

Automating the Organizational Support Processes

Like the communications tools just discussed, applications that are useful in the organizational support processes are those that have been used for some time in operations management. Operations management processes are, after all, operations work (line management), as opposed to project work (project management). Since operations management has been taught in business schools for decades, there are tools on the market that can aid in various aspects of these endeavors. While these tools are too numerous to discuss here, some have been designed with the express purpose of supporting project management activity. Among them are:

- *Multi-project resource management tools.* These tools help line managers manage scarce resources across the many projects in which their organizations are involved. They include tools such as ResSolution[2] and Business Engine.
- *Project portfolio management tools.* These are tools that help senior managers balance the accomplishment of their organizational goals across the range of projects, both ongoing and potential, in their organizations. They address issues such as budget, benefits, market, product line, probability of success, technical objectives, return on investment (ROI), and the like in order to help them prioritize and undertake projects. One such tool that does this is the project portfolio module of Portfolio Plus.
- *Activity and project historical databases.* These are tools that help a project team and all managers more accurately estimate the outcomes of their projects. Among the many problems that arise in projects, an unrealistic expectation about project outcomes is one of the most flagrant. One reason for these unrealistic expectations is the poor quality of activity-level estimates. One way to increase the accuracy of these estimates is to employ three-point estimating techniques, which have been referred to earlier. An even better way of increasing the accuracy of estimates is to base them on historical data. Were one to examine the activities that are performed over time in an organization's projects, it would become apparent that many of the same types of activities are performed over and over from one project to another. In some cases, nearly 80 percent of these activities are repeated from one project to another. Unfortunately, in many organizations such historical data is rarely available for project team members to use for estimating. Consequently, three-point estimating techniques need to be universally employed, project after project. Once organizations develop, maintain, and properly employ accurate activity historical databases, the need for the relatively less accurate three-point estimates (remember that single-point estimates are much less accurate than three-point estimates) will be reduced, thereby resulting in more accurate estimates at both the activity and project levels.

Finally, we should mention that while integration of all the types of tools discussed is probably technologically possible, it is not always either necessary or desirable. In fact, it is the author's belief that in some instances, particularly in the case of multiple-project resource management, it is better to do detailed management of project resources within the context of the center circle, and less detailed management at a higher level within the context of the outer circles without daily integration of the two activities.

IMPLEMENTING CAPM

The selection, implementation, and use of these tools are not tasks to be taken lightly. And while the process may at first seem daunting, there are ways to make it easier. A number of sources can aid in the selection process. At least two publications at present do annual software surveys in which they compare the capabilities of various project management tools. Many of these tools perform the functions discussed earlier. These publications are *IIE Solutions*, a monthly publication of the Institute of Industrial Engineers, and *PM Network*, a monthly publication of the Project Management Institute. The National Software Testing Laboratories (NSTL) also tests and compares software programs. It makes these comparisons in over 50 categories of tool capabilities for project management software. The major areas of comparison include:

- Performance
- Versatility
- Quality
- Ease of learning
- Ease of use

Individuals responsible for such selection need to ask the following types of questions:

- What is my organization trying to accomplish with this software? Will the software tools being considered meet those needs?
- How many people will be using the software—one person, a group of people, or an entire organization?
- Have the users of the software previously used any other type of project management software? If so, what were the tools, and were they similar to any of the tools being considered at present?
- Have the users of the software been trained in project management methods, tools, and techniques?
- Are the tools being considered both easy to learn and easy to use?
- Can the tool be used as is or are modifications required?
- What type of post-installation support is required? Will the vendor do the support, or does it require an in-house support group?
- Does the tool need to be integrated with other tools being used in the organization? If so, how difficult will that integration be?

- What are the implications of introducing software of this sort into my organization? Do I need to develop a formal plan to get organizational buy-in for its introduction and use?

The answers to all of these can have a profound impact on the success of the tool in an organization. One needs to be especially careful in considering the last question. The human implications of introducing software tools in an organization are frequently underestimated. This underestimation has caused organizations to be unsuccessful in the introduction and implementation of these tools, resulting in wasted effort and dollars, and in the frustration of those project stakeholders who were affected by the failed effort.

For many reasons, tool section processes can at times resemble religious wars. Participation in the process is not for the fainthearted. Anyone contemplating the introduction of these tools into an organization would be well advised to develop a detailed project plan. Included in this project plan should be a plan to ease the introduction of the tool into the organization, thereby allowing for the greatest probability of a successful introduction and implementation.

As with any project, a competent project team needs to be assembled with a specific individual assigned responsibility to manage the project. There should be senior management support and involvement appropriate to the effort.

Expectations of all organizational stakeholders need to be set and met throughout the conduct of the project. These expectations should include (1) a detailed description of what will be done during the project, (2) who needs to be involved, and (3) how the implementation of the tool will affect members of the organization.

Once project execution has begun, and throughout the course of the project, frequent progress reviews need to take place to ensure that the implementation is on schedule, is on budget, and meets the needs of the project stakeholders. These efforts will go far in aiding in the integration of the tool into regular use in project and operations work.

CAPM IN THE TWENTY-FIRST CENTURY

One important thing for the reader to note is that, with the rapid development and introduction of software into the marketplace, some of what has been described here may soon be out of date. One thing that will surely not vanish, however, is the ever-increasing need by project managers and organizations for tools to help them accomplish their complex and difficult jobs. While once just nice to have, these tools are now a necessity. So, what does the future hold for computer-aided project management?

More and more tools are expanding from those aimed at individual use to those available for work groups. Projects are, after all, team endeavors. Microsoft Project 2000 includes an Internet browser module called Microsoft Project Central, which is aimed at allowing the collaborative involvement of project stakeholders in planning and tracking projects, as well as access to important project information.

With the increasing demand for accurate project information, coupled with the cross-geographical nature of many project efforts, Web-based project communications tools will surely also become a requirement and not just a convenience. The author has worked with a few companies that have already developed these tools for their internal use.

It is also inevitable that, at some point in the not too distant future, complete tool sets that incorporate and integrate many of the varied capabilities described in the previous paragraphs will also become available for commercial use. It is only a matter of time before such software applications will be developed and appear on the shelves of your electronic shopping sites.

However, despite the advances in technology that will inevitably lead to this availability, the age-old problems of successful selection, introduction, and implementation of these tools will remain. If organizations take the time to accomplish these tasks in a cogent and supportive way, the tools will continue to be a significant benefit in the successful implementation of the project management processes.

NOTES

1. The reader is advised that the Project Concentric Circle Model is a copyright product of Oak Associates, Inc. Any reproduction or use of the model without the express consent of Oak Associates, Inc., and the publisher is strictly prohibited.

2. In the interest of fairness and full disclosure, the author must acknowledge that the organization in which he is a principal is a reseller of both ResSolution and Project 98 Plus software, both of which are cited in this chapter.

REFERENCES:

Graham, Robert J., and Randall L. Englund. 1997. *Creating an Environment for Successful Projects*. San Francisco: Jossey-Bass.

Kerzner, Harold. 1995. *Project Management: A Systems Approach to Planning, Scheduling, and Controlling (Fifth Edition)*. New York: Van Nostrand Reinhold.

Martin, James. 1984. *An Information Systems Manifesto*. Englewood Cliffs, NJ: Prentice-Hall.

National Software Testing Laboratory (NSTL). 1990. "Project Management Programs." *Software Digest*, Vol. 7, No. 16. Plymouth Center, PA: NSTL.

Project Management Institute Standards Committee. 1996. *A Guide to the Project Management Body of Knowledge*. Upper Darby, PA: Project Management Institute.

Trademark Notices

Artemis is a registered trademark of Artemis Management Systems.

Business Engine is a registered trademark of Business Engine Software Corp.

GRANEDA Dynamic is a registered trademark of Technology Associates.

Harvard Project Manager is a registered trademark of Harvard Software, Inc.

Macintosh and *MacProject* are registered trademarks of Apple Computer Inc.

Microsoft Project, *Microsoft Project 98*, and *Microsoft Project 2000* are registered trademarks of Microsoft Corp.

Portfolio Plus is a registered trademark of Strategic Dynamics, Ltd.

Primavera and *SureTrak* are registered trademarks of Primavera Systems, Inc.

Project Workbench is a registered trademark of Applied Business Technology Corp.

PS7 is a registered trademark of Scitor Corp.

ResSolution is a registered trademark of, and *Project 98 Plus* is a product of, Scheuring Projektmanagement.

@Risk is a registered trademark of Palisade Corp.

Risk+ is a registered trademark of ProjectGear, Inc.

Risk Radar is a product of Software Program Managers Network.

SuperProject is a registered trademark of Computer Associates, Inc.

CHAPTER 16

eBUSINESS PROJECT MANAGEMENT: THE FUTURE IS TODAY

DANEK BIENKOWSKI

For the past 10 or 15 years, we have been hearing that the world is changing dramatically in the following ways:

- Time to market is the critical success factor for business.
- Virtual teams are the way to go.
- Customer focus is number one.
- Organizations without flexible management structures are doomed to fail.
- Responsiveness to changing business conditions is the prerequisite to success.
- The world is becoming projectized.
- Business success rests on the effective application of technology.

All of these diverse trends are true, and they have coalesced around what we have come to call *eBusiness*.

Simply defined, eBusiness is the use of Web-based technology in streamlining business processes throughout the complete and complex supply chain, starting with the suppliers, flowing through all the processes of the enterprise, and ending with the customers. When implemented correctly, this is a radical initiative that asks the following questions for each step in the supply chain:

- Is it a core competency?
- Who is best able to take on this function?
- Should it be performed in-house or outsourced?

Jim Woodward, vice president of Cap Gemini, says, "eBusiness has so much to do with core strategy and company market positioning that CEOs are now taking the time to figure how they're going to use it to restructure along their core competencies in the Internet economy."[1]

General Motors, Ford, and DaimlerChrysler recently announced a "trading hub"—a dramatic example of an eBusiness initiative. This will link more than 30,000 suppliers into a network, allowing them to interact with the three automakers and each other to reduce costs and cut time to market. Jacques Nasser, Ford CEO, says, "This is going to change how we think about the business and the way we conduct business. This is going to reinvent the way the automobile business works."[2] The cost savings alone are expected to run in the billions of dollars. In an analysis of business-to-business (B2B) economy, Bob Austrian of Bank of America Securities says,

> Thanks to the Internet, the go-to-market model for all businesses is changing radically. Every company must be examined with an eye cast towards the ways in which its management succeeds or fails to embrace this new economy. It took the industrialized world at least a few hundred years to evolve its business models and current practices. Over the coming, say, five to 10 years, a comparable magnitude of economic change is likely to be realized, with all parties—employees, managers, investors, professionals, technologists, strategists, educators, etc.—sure to face unprecedented challenges.[3]

eBusiness programs (ePrograms) are different from other major technology initiatives not only in the scope of their impact, but also in that they include three components in roughly equal importance: process change, content, and technology. Processes *must* change for the eProgram to have value. The management of content (product specification, pricing, customers, logistics, and so on) is crucial. And technology is more often acquired than developed. So the term *integration* rather than *development* best describes an eProgram.

Managing ePrograms forces a new management paradigm and corporate culture. This chapter discusses how ePrograms can be managed effectively and how to avoid some major pitfalls. It will cover both how the basic principles of project management can be applied and what tools and techniques are needed to support the process (see Figure 16.1).

The reader should recognize that many of the practices that make an eProgram successful are not totally new, but are applied more intensely and with more of a take-no-prisoners mentality than in more traditional

Figure 16.1
Managing eBusiness Programs

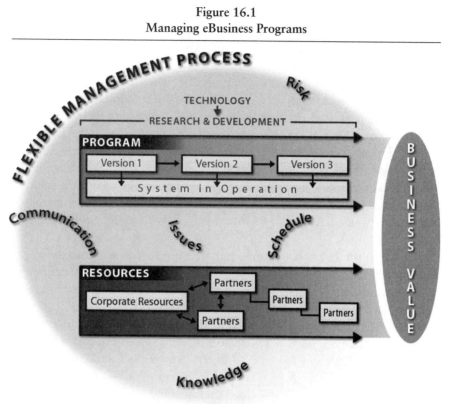

initiatives. "Part 1—eBusiness Management Philosophy" discusses how ePrograms can be structured, how resources can be managed, and how management processes and technology can be applied to achieve success. "Part 2—eBusiness Program Management Systems" explores in more depth the requirements for an effective program management system for ePrograms.

Although the discussion is primarily about eBusiness, it is an obvious extrapolation to say that all business and hence all projects now exist on Internet time. Once business units recognize that they can achieve business value in, say, three months through the type of process applied to eBusiness, they will not want to go back to the more traditional legacy type of project requiring a year or more for implementation. There is now no optional strategy: either successfully "compete in time" or fail (that is, produce the right product, but too late). So, much of what is discussed here has applicability beyond the strict domain of eBusiness.

PART 1—eBUSINESS MANAGEMENT PHILOSOPHY
Structure for Speed and Flexibility

The greatest change in the approach to managing projects and the move into the Internet age has been the dedication—one could even use the word *passion*—to "do it fast" and "turn on a dime." Speed is of the essence, and if we don't get it right the first time (and in most cases we won't), then we try again. These characteristics of speed and flexibility impact not only the process of getting things done but, more importantly, the culture of the team and the organization as a whole. That is why it is so difficult for mature enterprises to move into eBusiness without the injection of Internet culture from the outside.

Project Definition

In yesterday's world, change in both the business environment and technology was slower. Projects could be scoped with some precision, and a year or two could be allowed for development. In today's fast-changing eBusiness environment, a different approach must be adopted. Far-reaching business initiatives, usually called *programs*, are initiated with a broad scope and a broad set of business objectives instead of well-defined deliverables. These programs then generate a series of tightly time-boxed projects that often last no more than three to four months, and whose deliverables are progressive "releases" of the eventual business solution. We will call this process of subdivision *chunking*. The philosophy is to get the first release up and running fast, measure the response, and learn from the experience; then on to the next release, and so forth. While the individual projects have reasonably well-defined beginnings and ends, the overall program may in fact never have a clear end, generating continuing refinements to the business solution.

How this evolution proceeds will depend on the results of the prior release as well as on the changing marketplace and technology. As a release is implemented, it is quickly evaluated as follows:

- Does it support the overall business initiative?
- Is there an appropriate balance between process, content, and technology?
- How has it been received by the business (users, suppliers, customers, and strategic partners)?
- Is the supporting technology sufficient? Will it support the evolution of the business solution?

- What are the most critical changes we need to make? Are they sufficient for the next release?

This more flexible approach has the following benefits:

- The overall program tracks the changing business environment and technology by testing the waters every few months, thereby greatly reducing the risk of delivering a solution that does not work or is too late to market.
- The individual releases deliver business value in a short time frame.
- The eProgram provides the project team (eTeam) with an intense learning experience that could never be duplicated with the more traditional approach.
- The short-term projects focus the eTeam, eliminate all that is nonessential, and encourage a high level of effort. This is very much the Internet culture.

Managing an eBusiness program requires a program manager (let's call him or her the ePM) with some special skills. The ePM must thrive on change, be comfortable with an unstructured environment, be prepared to think and act radically, and be able to focus not only the team but also the myriad stakeholders on the job at hand. The ePM must have the ability to turn on a dime, and as the business or technology changes he or she must redefine the goals, scope, technology, or approach. Anyone who is wedded to the past, even if the past is only a month old, is not the person for the job.

Business Ownership

The eProgram includes not only the various releases, or chunks, of the technology solution, but also the changes in business processes, content, training, possible outsourcing and staff reallocation, and all of the other business-related activities essential for successful implementation. As a result, the role of the ePM is filled from the ranks of business-unit managers who take on responsibility for key decisions such as resourcing, stakeholder management, chunking, risk management, high-level issue resolution, and financial control. This is a full-time position, and the individual filling it moves out from the business units and takes on the full-time role of ePM.

The management of the eProgram inevitably requires a heavy dose of matrixing. While the ePM might own some of the resources required, the majority is likely to be owned by others. They will include business units, information technology (IT), staff functions such as finance and legal, consultants, and last but not least, strategic partners. In each one of these components, an individual becomes the project manager responsible for implementing that part of the program. Depending on the workload, these project managers might either be full-time or wear two hats and still keep their functional responsibilities.

Information technology is a special case because it is usually the major component in terms of resources, funding, and risks. The IT manager responsible for the IT part of the program is often a program manager (while still reporting to the ePM) because the IT solution is made up of a combination of projects. Implementing the IT component typically requires managing Web development, which is often outsourced; making changes to a variety of databases (customer, vendor, product, and so on); making changes to back-end systems; implementing Web servers and communication networks; and so forth. The IT program manager coordinates all of these activities within his or her area of responsibility in a similar manner to that of the ePM, and is also the chief technology officer of the program, advising the ePM on all technology matters.

Get Creative with Resources

In traditional development, most of the resources come from one part of the organization and they are assigned for the duration of the effort. As a result, the project team becomes the primary organizational component providing stability and organizational focus. In eBusiness, that is no longer true. As already indicated, the eProgram requires resources from a variety of sources, both internal and external to the enterprise; and most of them continue to report to their functional managers, not to the ePM. The eTeam composition is constantly changing with resources attaching themselves to the program for short, intensive periods of time to develop a specific deliverable and rarely forming the traditional, stable project team. So, except for a small core, the ultimate continuity resides with the ePM.

So how do we manage resources under these conditions?

Just-in-Time Resources

With new resources joining and leaving the eProgram on a frequent basis for short periods of time, just-in-time staffing techniques need to be adopted to make the resources effective.

These include the following:

- Using automated alerts to communicate the new assignments to the new staff and their management to minimize disruption.
- Setting up an orientation program for new members, effectively using knowledge capital to shorten start-up.
- Organizing the work to minimize handoffs to other team members.

Communication

In all types of projects, effective communication has been a perennial critical success factor. In eBusiness, it is even more so. The eTeam comes from a variety of departments and organizations, and individuals are on board for short periods of time only. They may also be distributed across countries, time zones, and cultures, operating as a virtual team. There is also a high probability that they will never in fact come face to face. So, one of ePM's most important roles is to *communicate, communicate, communicate . . . and then communicate some more.*

However, communicating in today's highly connected enterprise presents special challenges. This is especially true in the case of short-duration eBusiness releases, where relying on traditional reporting mechanisms, such as weekly status meetings or monthly management reports, is almost useless because events simply move too fast. As for the increasingly common cross-enterprise program, with stakeholders spread across two or more organizations, the old ways are nonstarters.

The ePM will have to rely on a variety of communications channels using e-mail, conferencing, work-group tools, web sites, and so on to facilitate long-distance interaction.

The ePM should also recognize and, if appropriate, make use of one possible advantage of programs that span multiple time zones. For example, enterprises doing development work in Asia achieve benefits of a 24-hour day by coding in one time zone, testing in another, and having test results available on the desks of the coders by the next day.

Collaboration

In traditional development, facilitating collaboration usually was not a major problem because the project team typically resided in one location and the team members stayed for the duration of the project. In ePrograms, achieving effective collaboration is a major issue due to the geographic dispersion and fluid nature of the eTeam.

eBusiness project teams are typically composed of fully utilized, expensive specialists who require a frictionless collaboration mechanism if they are to accomplish their objectives within very tight time constraints. This new style of working demands the following:

- Quick decision making and group buy-in without protracted meetings or discussions
- Continuous issue management, risk assessment, and automated alerts
- Removal of project management bottlenecks and bureaucracy
- The ability to work together closely even when geographically dispersed, often across multiple time zones

The payoff for eTeams that implement an effective collaboration is significant. It provides ongoing stakeholder access within the team, across the organization, and across multiple organizations involved in the eProgram, further allowing access to the following:

- Current versions of program and project plans, schedules, deliverables, cost, and other data at additional sites or in other work spaces
- Internal experts (scattered geographically) or experts from the outside to supplement the skills and knowledge of core team members

Knowledge Management

In traditional development, the knowledge content of the project typically resided with the project team. It consisted of documents such as project plans, status reports, scope statements, feasibility studies, requirements, design specifications, best practices, and so forth. With the formal documents kept to a minimum and the fluid nature of the project team, another approach is called for. To move at the speed of eBusiness, the eTeam requires a just-in-time knowledge management infrastructure that both promotes reuse of knowledge capital and facilitates rapid navigation. That means:

- Knowledge must be made easily accessible and provided "just-in-time."
- Best practices and other knowledge elements must be made easy to capture and package.
- Distance learning must be supported.

Effective knowledge management provides an integrated tool, and a deliverable and content-organizing mechanism that promotes a consistent approach across an organization. It also facilitates rapid access to relevant information while avoiding overload.

Partnering

In eBusiness, third parties are typically more fundamental to the success of the initiative than is the case in most other efforts. They often provide business process know-how, as well as applications software, hardware, and communications networks. As already mentioned, outsourcing is a typical solution in technology, and most likely in some of the business processes comprising the supply chain. To ensure that the third parties perform at the peaks of their abilities, we can take one of two approaches:

- Make them sign a tough contract with penalties for violating it.
- Set them up as strategic partners with a vested interest in the successful outcome of the initiative.

Hard-nosed contracts set up a confrontational environment from the start that can put the relationship on a less than ideal basis; they also take a long time to negotiate (longer than Internet time allows). So the preferable route to take is to set up a strategic partnership relationship with the critical vendors—convert them from vendors to partners.

In many cases, primary partners may also use other third parties on the project with multiple relationships between them, in effect forming a mixed hierarchy and network. Without trying to micromanage the situation, the ePM should make sure that these second-level relationships do not unduly raise the program risk.

Apply Dynamic Management Processes

Management processes required to implement a major, technology-based business initiative are comprised of planning and control of the overall program, project life cycle, and a variety of processes, including issues management, configuration management, change management, risk management, and so forth. In traditional development, these management processes were often static and bureaucratic. The plans were often in a rigid format; monthly status reports were verbose and rarely provided any useful information as to where the project stood, and a rigid "waterfall" life cycle was employed, adding overhead to cost and time.

In eBusiness, a dynamic, flexible set of management processes must be adopted to achieve success. The right balance must be struck between providing sufficient control and providing so little structure that control is lost. (Program managers who dislike any level of structure confuse flexibility with a free-for-all, eliminating all controls; these managers are likely to fail on ePrograms as readily as on any other types of programs.)

Another unique facet of ePrograms is that *operations*—the function of running the system on the technology platform and generating business value—is a component of the development program. New releases of the system are not handed over to a separate operations department, as they would be in traditional development, but they remain the responsibility of IT or the outsourcing organization, reporting to the ePM. Management processes for operating the system are quite different from those required to develop it.

Planning and Control

ePrograms demand a flexible level of detail and rigor. For example, plans will often be expressed as a hybrid work breakdown structure (WBS),[4] with portions of the plan "deliverables based" while other WBS components are "process based." If appropriate, the ePM simply enters a list of key deliverables, milestones, or tasks; associates resources with these; assigns target dates; and uses this basic framework as the plan without ever needing to use a scheduling tool.

Similarly, resource assignments in an eBusiness plan may be made at quite different levels within the WBS. In some cases, detailed work-effort estimates, by individual or by task, are required. However, the plan will often only require documenting an overall responsibility by deliverable. Consider a project in which one or more deliverables have been outsourced. For the work being done by employees, the project plan may reflect detailed resource work estimates. For outsourced work, however, the plan may simply reflect a milestone representing the target date, the responsible resource, and perhaps budget information (hours or dollars) allocated to that deliverable.

Fast-moving eBusiness plans will often warrant less detail than traditional project plans. The former may need to be changed frequently as new information is discovered or new technology decisions are made, without much concern for the original baseline. That is, as long as the start and end dates are the same, midstream changes are not formalized. On the other hand, some projects will continue to require the ability to maintain multiple baselines, to avoid losing any of the information associated with these ongoing project corrections.

Tracking is another area where flexibility requirements increase in the world of eBusiness. Often, portions of a project will require using traditional time capture by resource by task, while others require just a completion date per deliverable and an overall percent-complete status.

Project Life Cycle

For ePrograms, the project life cycle of each release is highly iterative, combining a variety of methodologies, such as recursive, prototype-based, and staged delivery. Each release passes through requirements, design, and implementation quickly and perhaps multiple times until it is ready for operations. Prototyping is used extensively, with the prototype sometimes used as a throwaway to test a particular design or concept, and at other times evolving into the actual delivered solution.

Wherever possible, the principles of concurrent engineering are applied by judiciously overlapping phases and accepting the additional risk. However, it is recommended that the team wait until after conceptual design before adopting concurrency. While requirements are being defined, prototypes might be created, vendor contracts negotiated, and hardware and communications ordered.

Change Management

As changes occur in any one project that comprises the eProgram, they need to be quickly reflected throughout all of the components of the eProgram. This implies a seamless and smooth-running, process-based approach for all of the management processes, including change control, risk management, issue management, and configuration management. This process of *change management*—the ability to flow changes throughout the whole program quickly, efficiently, and with minimum bureaucracy—is fundamental to success.

Operational System

The need to run the system in a 24 ×7 operations environment imposes special challenges on the management of ePrograms. It requires an adoption of a factory mentality with strict timetables, provision of uptime and other metrics, and discipline not often found in development organizations.

However, this organizational alignment has a number of benefits. Having operations under the same umbrella as IT development eliminates a large organizational wall. Because the development staff has to "eat what they kill," issues of functionality and performance are surfaced and addressed quickly with minimum finger-pointing and politics. Furthermore, much of the definition of requirements of future releases is made by those closest to the operational system, namely the eTeam. This reduces the need for formality in documenting and approving detailed specifications of required changes. Prototypes can be developed quickly, discussed promptly with the business stakeholders, and often implemented faster than it would take to document the changes.

Innovate with Technology

In yesterday's world, technology was relatively static. Once the selection of the hardware and software was made by the project team, that technology was not changed and was used in the eventual solution. Additionally, the technology that was typically adopted was usually familiar to the project team. That is no longer true in eBusiness as technology is evolving with ever-increasing velocity, and in each case at least some of the technology is new to most of the eTeam.

Also, in eBusiness, technology has a dual role to play. On the one hand, it provides the foundation for the eBusiness solution; on the other, it is the critical tool used to manage the process of development. A discussion of the former is provided in this section; the latter is discussed in "Part 2— eBusiness Program Management Systems."

Anticipate—No, Welcome and Demand—Technology Change
Rather than assuming that technology once selected shall remain constant, we should assume the opposite—that it will need replacement in the near to mid term. In fact, no eBusiness solution is planned with a life span of more than two years because technology and business changes will demand a replacement system. To support the process of ongoing technology evaluation, the IT program manager gives regular technology briefings to the ePM.

This short-term planning horizon and the assumptions that technology might change partway through a project are accepted as normal and are not considered a failure by the team.

Plan to Do Research
With technology changing so fast, some amount of the eProgram budget is allocated to researching technology directions. This gives the team hands-on experience with the new technology, introduces culture change, increases the team's technical competence, and motivates the team—an increasing consideration in times of technical staff shortages. Research activities include attending seminars, reviewing documentation and relevant web sites, and creating prototypes. The prototypes serve to validate new technologies, train staff in their use, and boost morale by showing results quickly.

Research efforts typically are owned by the ePM rather than being centralized. Furthermore, all technical team members get their turn doing research so that there is cross-pollination throughout the organization. As a result, the research project manager is likely to be the only individual permanently assigned to the research effort.

As with all research activities, the research activity related to the eProgram is not expected to achieve concrete results in the short term, but will help achieve the long-term eProgram objectives.

Think Outside the (PC) Box
The long dominance of the Microsoft-Intel model (Wintel) may be over. Even though these two companies will almost certainly continue to be successful, they are being impacted by a variety of technologies where they are not the dominant forces. A more open set of architectures and standards is evolving, and eProgram personnel should give them sufficient consideration. Examples include providing e-mail alerts via cell phone, wireless upload via Palm Pilot, use of the Linux operating system, and use of thin-client workstations. These and other technologies will allow the team to function in a variety of diverse modes, locations, and settings.

Remote Process Execution
Businesses are replacing client-server technology with thin-client, Web-server–based systems. This opens up the possibility of application hosting, where hybrid software-services companies known as *application service providers (ASPs)* take responsibility for renting and delivering the application to the enterprise via the Web. Giga Information Group estimates that by the year 2004, 10 percent of large-company and 75 percent of medium-company applications will be delivered in this manner.[5]

Application hosting has the following significant advantages:

- The ASPs take responsibility for installing, operating, and maintaining the application software, which eliminates a major headache for the organizations.
- Application implementation is quicker, which is a major time-to-market benefit.
- Cost savings result from economies of scale, and costs are more predictable.
- Performance levels will be contractually guaranteed by the ASPs.
- Risks of investing in hardware, software, and communications that might become quickly obsolete (or turn out not to be the optimal solutions) are greatly reduced.

In situations where the thin-client, Web-based technology is brought in-house, every effort should be made not to make long-term commitments. Equipment should be shared or rented (if feasible); software leases should be structured for flexibility; and, if necessary, the ASP should be operated on a shoestring until there is reasonable assurance that the technology platform is sufficient for the purpose.

The Big Caveat

So, what is the downside in moving into the eBusiness world? As with all great endeavors, where the potential benefits are enormous, so are the challenges and risks.

Culture Change

The first and greatest eProgram challenge is to change the culture of the organization. The radical redefinition of business processes throughout the whole supply chain, the need to rely so heavily on strategic partners, and the drastic change in the labor skills mix all demand a change in organizational culture. The biggest investments won't be in technology but in reshaping companies to move at Net speed, says Erik Brynjolfsson, co-director of MIT's Center for eBusiness.[6] Here are the most critical issues:

- Turning the company inside out—focusing on the customer, focusing on core competencies, outsourcing what yesterday may have been seen as a fundamental part of the company (for example, manufacturing)—inevitably causes culture shock.
- While organizations have for many years relied on third parties to supplement their own skill sets, this is now fundamental to eBusiness success. Strategic partners are now expected to provide eBusiness business processes, supply eBusiness technology (applications, hardware, communications), and take on the role of outsourcer—but most importantly, also inject a dose of eBusiness culture.
- It is estimated that costs of purchased materials and services will drop by 10 percent, reducing purchasing staff by a significantly greater percentage. At the same time, web site designers, content providers, systems integrators, and project managers will be in very short supply, causing bottlenecks and even preventing companies from achieving the full benefits of eBusiness. This change in the skills mix causes major staff turmoil.

Now it is the whole organization, not just the ePM, that is expected to turn on a dime. The organization itself is expected to share information instead of hoarding it. Some eBusiness consultants consider corporate bureaucracy to be a bigger block than the technology and estimate that on eProgram as much as 25 percent of their work is involved in cultural issues.

eProgram Characteristics

The second challenge in successfully implementing an eBusiness strategy is the composition of eProgram. As already mentioned, the three legs of the stool consist of process, content, and new technology—all being of roughly equal importance. The focus is on all three and not just "the new system." This requires a different mind-set in the organization, to be able to combine the following into one program:

- Acquisition, customization, and implementation (internally or via outsourcing) of business processes throughout the complete supply chain
- Capture, storage, maintenance, and delivery of content required by the supply chain
- Acquisition of technology (including purchase of a variety of applications); development, modification, and linking of applications; and acquisition of hardware and network communications

All of these must be well integrated to make the eProgram a success.

ePM Skills

The third challenge is the following unique set of skills that the ePM must possess to bring the eProgram to a successful conclusion:

- Thriving in setting up and nurturing alliances
- Being very comfortable with change and being able to operate in an unstructured environment
- Setting up a flexible management process, steering a fine line between too little control and too much
- Having very strong leadership skills and being able to operate at the highest levels in the organization

The role of the ePM is crucial, and only the best individuals (and therefore the most difficult to get) should be considered for the position.

PART 2—eBUSINESS PROGRAM MANAGEMENT SYSTEMS

Managing an eBusiness program at Internet speed requires a powerful, zero-drag technology platform that does the following:

- Allows greatly simplified yet comprehensive *planning and control*
- Encourages continuous, ongoing stakeholder *communication*
- Enables effective *collaboration* across all project stakeholders—core team members as well as external participants

- Provides frictionless *knowledge management* that promotes effective reuse of knowledge capital
- Leverages the standards of *Internet technology*

Let's call this technology platform the eBusiness Program Management System, or ePMS for short (see Figure 16.2). The reader should note that ePMS is a *generic description of a support system for managing eBusiness programs and projects, rather than a description of an actual system in the marketplace.*

Planning and Control

As already mentioned, ePrograms demand a flexible level of detail and rigor in creating the plan, assigning resources, tracking progress, and integrating the various elements of the program. That means that the ePMS must be flexible in supporting the following areas:

- *Plan structures.* Plan by phases, activities, tasks, milestones, and deliverables and any combination thereof.
- *Resource assignments.* Allocate resources as individuals, skills, or simply organizational responsibilities at any level in the plan structure; de-

Figure 16.2
eBusiness Program Management System

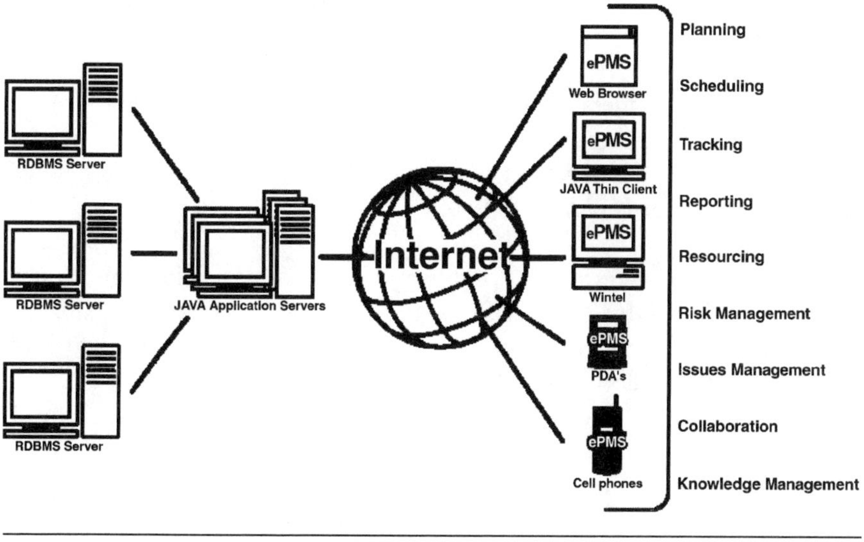

fine work effort (or not, depending on the situation) at any level in the plan structure.

- *Tracking.* Baseline some, but not all, of the plan; track by date, by percentage complete, or by capturing detailed time-sheet data at any level in the plan structure.
- *Integration.* Roll up project plans (or portions of plans) to the overall program (or multiple programs), even when the plans have different owners working for different organizations; the plans reside on different software platforms and are built using different structures.

Communication

The ePMS addresses the communications needs of both core team participants and external stakeholders. In particular, it supports the need to strike a balance between providing sufficient communication versus overloading or distracting the recipients.

The ePMS provides core team members with the following:

- *Project work-space mechanisms,* which issue management, polling, and discussion groups; used for real-time multi-point communications, as opposed to less effective point-to-point communications, such as e-mail
- *Intelligent anti-spam measures,* which automatically generate and push out alerts if specified thresholds (such as schedule, cost, quality, and so on) are exceeded, reducing or removing the need to bombard the entire team with messages relevant to only a few

External stakeholders are generally interested in simplified real-time access to summary program-level, project-level, or portfolio-level data, with the ability to drill down for more detail on an exception basis. The ePMS addresses these needs via the following:

- *Portfolio management capability* that automatically consolidates project data—for example, risk and status—as well as providing the consolidated resource summaries necessary for strategic capacity planning and decision making.
- *Alerts calibrated to the needs of stakeholders* if specified thresholds are exceeded, including intra- or interorganizational notifications. An example might be that when resource shortfalls occur, automatic postings/notifications are sent to resource suppliers.

- *Dynamic data analysis* to further support real-time decision making. For example, a slippage of a key external milestone in one project automatically triggers notification of the downstream ripple effect to all impacted projects, with an analysis of the resource, cost, and schedule impact on these other projects.

A final point about communication: In the past, information-hoarding managers often tried to strictly control visibility into their projects, often to conceal problems. The ePMS philosophy seeks to replace this practice with transparency. The ePMS does this by allowing the real-time auditability of the decision-making process. In the end, the goal of the ePMS is to facilitate real-time decision making by allowing decision makers, either within the core team or external to it, to be connected anytime, anywhere.

Collaboration

The ePMS provides a collaborative project work space to accommodate the new style of working by facilitating both work flow and deliverable life-cycle management for the entire program. The ePMS does this via the following means:

- Shared master lists of common information, such as key milestones, project tasks, or issues
- Best-practices templates that provide structure and leverage without reinventing the wheel
- Real-time polling that frames questions and issues and records participant or stakeholder responses
- Ongoing management and status reporting of deliverables over the entire life cycle
- Maintenance of a document's version and control-revision history, which can provide an audit trail, and, supplemented by a discussion database, can provide insight into the decision-making process that resulted in changes
- Formalized work flow, sharing rules that navigate a deliverable across an organization or multiple organizations, including defined collaboration points, as well as periods of exclusive ownership for deliverables and documents. This formalization allows the following three benefits:
  1. Read-only access to current versions of program and project plans at other sites or in other work spaces

2. Access to master program schedules at any time (up-to-date costs, delivery dates, and so on)
3. Access to internal experts (scattered geographically) or experts from the outside to supplement the skills and knowledge of core team members

Knowledge Management

To move at the speed of eBusiness, the eTeam requires a just-in-time knowledge management infrastructure that both promotes reuse of knowledge capital and facilitates rapid navigation. It should also be obvious that physical, hard-copy documentation is kept to a minimum, with the official versions of program documents (for example, plans, specifications, issues logs, and so on) being maintained in machine-readable form.

The ePMS addresses reuse with a library of best-practices templates, and a library of preconfigured alerts. In addition, via the project collaboration work space, ePMS allows links to subject matter experts and relevant newsgroups. It also provides the ability to link to relevant intranet and Internet sites, allowing content links to sources of useful information, whether within the enterprise, across a supplier network, or from external sources. Examples of useful information could include the following:

- Just-in-time distance learning
- Just-in-time updates from an author—for example, the latest version of a best-practices template

The ePMS has a unified interface and simplified function-oriented design, providing an integrated tool that promotes a consistent approach and facilitates rapid access to relevant information while avoiding overload.

Internet Technology

The ePMS is built upon and leverages the same Internet standards as the ePrograms that it is designed to support. ePMS sits atop an XML (Extensible Markup Language)-enabled repository, for example, which facilitates information sharing with external systems. The ePMS is a thin-client solution with a clean ergonomic design that follows the best web-design principles—that is, a fast and intuitive navigation and layout that doesn't require drilling down through complex menu hierarchies—and requires zero training time to use.

Instead of resource-consumptive applets that are slow to download and require client-side resources to operate, ePMS uses HyperText Markup Language (HTML). Both customizable for the organization and personalizable for the individual, ePMS is intended to provide a seamless user experience. Finally, it is necessarily industrial-strength so that it can handle the largest ePrograms.

The ePMS is also designed to be hostable, offering eTeams the option either to install and run it on an intranet or to access it across the Internet while leaving the implementation and ongoing maintenance/support in the hands of an external service provider, such as an ASP.

NOTES

1. George V. Hulme. "Beyond 2000." *Industry Standard*. November 8, 1999: 142.
2. Jennifer Reingold, Maria Stepanek, and Diane Bundy. "Why the Productivity Revolution Will Spread." *Business Week*. February 14, 2000: 112.
3. Bob Austrian, Craig Wood, and Charlie Chen. *Equity Research*. January 3, 2000, Bank of America Securities: 4.
4. Work breakdown structure (WBS): a deliverable-oriented grouping of project elements that organizes and defines the total scope of the project. Each descending level represents an increasingly detailed definition of the project components (both products and services).
5. Rick Whiting. "Software Morphs into a Service." *Information Week Online*. November 11, 1999.
6. Jennifer Reingold, Marcia Stepanek, and Diane Brady. "Why the Productivity Revolution Will Spread." *Business Week*. February 14, 2000: 112.

REFERENCES

O'Connell, Fergus. 1997. *How to Run Successful Projects, Second Edition*. Upper Saddle River, NJ: Prentice-Hall.
Yourdon, Edward. 1997. *Death March*. Upper Saddle River, NJ: Prentice-Hall PTR.

PART II

THE HUMAN DIMENSIONS TRACK

CHAPTER 17

ORGANIZATIONAL PROJECT
MANAGEMENT: CONCEPT

RICHARD BAUHAUS

$\mathbf{T}$his chapter explores the historically significant move from project management as an *individual competency* to project management as an *organizational competency*. This precedent-setting change is essential in order for us to meet the expectations and needs for projects today and in the future. This discussion of organizational project management begins with a review of the past situation when individual competency was sufficient to do our projects. The second section discusses the present imperative to develop and use an organizational competency to meet today's demands for distributed teams with faster projects to meet requirements on time. The requirements to move to organizational competence, with examples of results where such changes have been made, are presented. Third, we briefly address the lessons learned and the challenge of making the change to project management–based organizational competency.

THE PM INHERITANCE

Historically, project management skills development has focused on the individual project manager. This has led to partial success. Developing PM skills in the entire organization is required in today's PM environment.

Past Perspective of Project Management Competency

Project management largely has been considered in previous times as an individual competency. Individual project managers alone were expected to have the ability and competence to lead individual projects from start to finish. It was incumbent on the individual to manage the logistics, administration, and people in the project to meet the project's goals successfully. Project completion to schedule, budget, and the functionality of the outcome was critical. Finally, the project manager was expected to determine those elements, and gain agreement from the project's sponsor, manager, or customer.

In the high-tech environment that emerged during the 1990s, a competent individual might often become a project manager by accident. The "accidental project manager" is the term coined by Randall Englund and Robert Graham and discussed in their book, *Creating the Environment for Successful Project Management.*[1] That is, due to the technical competence required in fields such as engineering, physics, chemistry, medicine, and so on, individuals possessing those skills might become project managers because they were more organized than their peers and could direct the efforts of a small team to complete a project. A person who became a project manager in this way typically developed an ad hoc style to meet the requirements of delivering the project.

This is not to say that these accidental project managers did not become good at what they did. They learned and performed well, or they failed and someone else became the next project manager. Those who performed well became quite adept at their efforts. Successful projects flowed from their work. They became proficient in a way that was hard to fault. But their methods were unique to them or to a small cadre of project managers around them. Common processes, language, format, and life cycles did not exist very far outside their small project teams, if they existed at all. So as new, larger, program-level efforts became more prevalent, the ability to work across several subprojects became a communications nightmare. But successful practices are hard to supplant. The accidental project managers were prone to keeping their old ways and were resistant to new, consistent, and congruent processes for project management.

Organizational Situations That Inhibit the Project Manager

So what did we observe happening to project managers when they tried to apply their newly trained or developed PM skills within their organizations? Countless anecdotes exist that tell this story. For instance, the project manager who learned or recognized the value of adequately defining the project often tried to apply this knowledge to the work situation. The rigor of developing a clear objective and an understanding of the major deliverables, "is and is nots" (what is in the project, what is not), agreements on trade-offs between requirements, schedule and resources, high-level risks, and the project team's operating norms, all were often lost on the higher management and the project manager's team. Management's response to the project manager was often, "When are you going to start doing something?" Certainly, there is frequently little encouragement to do these definition tasks and to validate them with management and the customer as appropriate.

Then comes the planning and scheduling stage of the project. Too many project managers recount their stories about the resistance from senior management, and often from their own team, to bringing together the team for a couple of days to develop the WBS, dependency diagram, schedule, critical path, resource loading, cost and risk analysis, and change management plan. The admonition is often, "Just go do the project. Why are you wasting time with this planning stuff? It will all change anyway."

In the face of this kind of discouragement to applying sound project management practices to their projects, many project managers will cave in and throw out the very principles that can make their projects successful.

Historical Efforts to Develop Project Managers

As a consequence of this individual project manager focus without organizational and senior management support, there has been a heavy concentration on the education and training of the individual alone to meet these project management competencies. The training also has established processes and methods that developed only the individual project manager in meeting the goal. Those individuals who are project managers or aspire to that position have concentrated on what they need to know and how to apply that knowledge and ability.

This individual competency is essential to the larger picture of successful project management, but it is not sufficient. Even in large companies, the emphasis has been to send individual project managers to PM training and thereby attempt to improve the organization's ability to manage and complete projects. But this training is focused only on the individual project manager, not on how the organization of persons interact and support each other for good PM execution.

I have seen business units lament spending hundreds of thousands of dollars on development and training for the individual project managers without realizing a significant return on their investment for the money spent in terms of faster, more on-time, and less expensive projects to meet the requirements. This is because these organizations have neglected or refused to invest in developing their individual senior management's and the rest of the organization's role in making project management work more effectively. The result is a dysfunctional organization not meeting today's project demands.

Even today, educational and professional project management organizations place much of their focus on training and certification of the project manager. Historically, very little attention has been paid to the ability of the organization to support and indeed accelerate the delivery of projects and produce them on time, less expensively, and in such a way that they meet customer requirements.

THE TRANSITION TO ORGANIZATIONAL PM

Today, PM efforts require a new approach. The PM-based organization provide critical value to the success of today's projects. Increasing evidence is provided by examples of PM-based approaches.

Today's Requirements for Successful Project Management

In today's fast-paced world, which depends on meeting and exceeding customer expectations, the old paradigm for developing and utilizing project managers to successfully project-manage the efforts in an organization is not sufficient or effective. A new model is emerging that is proving to be necessary for effective project management.

The PM-based organization has the following seven critical characteristics:

1. Consistent, congruent processes for managing the projects inside the organization are being used by all levels of the organizational hierarchy.
2. Every manager from the highest level (CEO) to the lowest level (project manager and team members) knows the consistent project management process and uses it.
3. Every manager at every level in the organization has clearly defined roles and responsibilities in the carrying out of the project management efforts in the organization.
4. The common project management principles, language, and expectations are being applied to all kinds of projects in the organization, such as new product development, process improvement, business change initiatives, information technology, and so on.
5. The portfolio of all projects is being managed at the appropriate highest business level (CEO, group business manager, general man-

ager) to assure that the limited set of critical projects is addressed, utilizing the available set of resources. That is, there are not too many projects for the organization actually to address.

6. Projects are clearly linked to the organization's business strategies, with organizational and individual understanding of how each individual's project contributes to meeting that business strategy.

7. A continuing organizational level of attention is placed on maintaining and improving PM practices, and training individuals at all levels of the organization to fulfill their roles in project managing. Change initiatives are run as projects in themselves. Metrics measure progress. This organizational attention can be done in a number of ways: through a project management initiative change team, a project office, a corporate project management executive, a project center of excellence, and so on.

Examples of Organizational PM Changes

Let's explore and expand on the implications of each of these seven critical characteristics.

Congruent PM Processes Are Being Used by All Levels of the Organization

Figure 17.1 shows data from work done at the organizational change level for improving project management (PM) in some specific Hewlett-Packard (HP) businesses.[2] The metric indicates the value placed by individuals in the organization on having a common framework and vocabulary for talking about projects using their project management process. The data shows very consistently that about 92 percent of the participants found the common PM framework and vocabulary gave them major to moderate value in executing their projects.

This common language achieves a few critical objectives. Work can be more easily described and communicated. This is true at the project team level. But it is also true for senior management, for other projects, for vendors or subcontractors, and for business units that are integral to the project. It is also true across the functional boundaries of the business, as congruent product design, design for manufacturability and serviceability, and other features are pursued. Common language and process also allow easier integration of new team members as necessary and easier redeployment of people in the organization (with a benefit of quick start-up), and assist their collective involvement in the project team. All this speeds up project execution and minimizes miscommunication and

Figure 17.1
Initiative Metrics 1: Value of PM Framework and Vocabulary

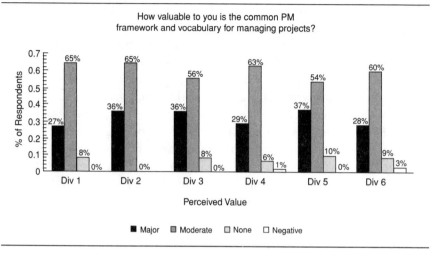

How valuable to you is the common PM
framework and vocabulary for managing projects?

Perceived Value

■ Major   ▨ Moderate   ☐ None   ☐ Negative

misunderstandings. Such practices help avoid the kind of disaster of the recent Mars probe that had subproject teams using mixed metric and English measures, with the result that errors crashed the Mars probe into the planet when the two measures were indiscriminately mixed in the software control program.

All Levels of Management Know the PM Process and Can Use It

This knowledge of PM process is particularly a requirement for senior managers who must also learn the common framework, life cycle, and language for project management in their organizations. This process allows them to use common terminology, set the appropriate expectations, and carry out their essential roles and responsibilities to make any single project successful. It also assists them in making their business portfolios of projects successful.

This critical issue often becomes an inhibitor for establishing the organizational change needed. Senior managers often assume they know these basics. After all, didn't they get to their positions because they successfully led projects in the past? So, through lack of knowledge, arrogance, ignorance, or not realizing the level of their influence, managers exempt themselves from the development of the common skills. Paul Dinsmore addresses the subject of the role of senior managers, pointing out that the PM-based organization with senior management participation is essential because "winning depends on the (whole) team's mastery of the fundamentals. Not even the most brilliant strategy can succeed if the players lack basic skills."[3] So senior managers must become part of the change initiative and the change management education in establishing a PM-based organization.

This issue has been the pivotal point in a successful project management change initiative, and an unsuccessful one. Our experience with group managers, general managers, and ongoing participants who have become part of the learning and implementing process for organizational change initiatives is that their organizations make significant strides toward implementing a working PM-based organization with positive results in their business execution. In those cases where these managers exempted themselves from the learning and implementing process, those initiatives failed to bring about positive results in their business execution. The results from six different project change initiatives carried out in this manner are shown in Figure 17.1 and later in the chapter in Figure 17.4. They show overwhelmingly how valuable and effective those project management change initiatives were to their businesses at all levels of the organizations.

All Levels of the Organization Have Clearly Defined Roles and Responsibilities

Figure 17.2 is from a paper presented at the PMI Philadelphia 1999 conference. The three key roles and responsibilities of senior management as integrators, sponsors, and implementers shown in Figure 17.2 indicate the expanded nature of the task to ensure that effective organizational project management is being accomplished.

Playing the role of integrators, senior managers develop top-down planning, proceeding from business-strategy planning. But integration requires them to go through a cycle or two of getting the bottom-up planning from the projects to ensure that top-down and bottom-up planning are congruent. Otherwise, they get into the common dilemma of having too many projects on their plates, overloading the business units, delaying projects, not meeting customer expectations, and exceeding budgets.

Playing the roles of sponsors, senior managers need to understand thoroughly the project portfolios, the projects, and how each supports the others. Their sponsorship clearly supports the project teams in having the necessary resources when they are needed. Their sponsorship also facilitates escalated decisions that the project managers are unable to address due to cross-organizational issues, or for other reasons.

Playing the roles of implementers, senior managers need to be visible, vocal advocates and champions for their projects. They need to establish

Figure 17.2
Senior Management Roles and Responsibilities in PM Implementation

...as Integrators	...as Sponsors	...as Implementers

• Integrating project environment elements into a whole that is efficiently focused on achieving business objectives
• Ensuring business strategies are implemented
• Linking business strategic objectives to project work of the organization
• Aligning diverse functional units of the organization into a single, coherent project entity
	• Systematically review project plans and project progress
	• Influence project outcome through early and appropriate involvement
	• During project definition, validate:
	  − project objectives
	  − major deliverables
	  − trade-off criteria
	  − target dates
	  − major risks
	  − key project processes (escalation, issues and change management)
	• During planning validate:
	  − detailed optimized plan
	  − risk management plan
	  − project baseline
	• As project is in process, validate:
	  − project schedule status
	  − escalated issues
	  − scope changes
	  − major risks
		• Lead implementation of PM in the organization
		• Set tone for actual use of PM practices in the organization (also for portfolio and product development processes)
		• Establish environment that proactively promotes the use of PM methods
		• Establish clear expectations and job standards
		• Develop/implement a feedback system about performance against job standards
		• Create consequences (+ and −) relative to job standards
		• Provide necessary tools to execute the job standard

Source: Courtesy of Kathy Meikle and Bill Seidman. From Catherine L. Tonne and Richard Bauhaus, "Wisdom of the Wizards: Creating the Framework for Successful New Product Development—The HD Way!" PMI Conference, Philadelphia, October 1999. Reprinted with permission.

an environment that encourages using good PM practices at all levels of the organization. They must set the appropriate expectations and reward appropriately for delivery on those expectations. Lastly, they need to review progress and provide coaching and mentoring as appropriate for the project teams to achieve their objectives.

Figure 17.3 is taken from the same paper, entitled "Wisdom of the Wizards: Creating the Framework for Successful New Product Development—The HP Way!," by Catherine L. Tonne and Richard Bauhaus at the Philadelphia 1999 PMI conference. Figure 17.3 defines various roles in the alignment of the product development process, the project planning and management process, and the portfolio management process. These are clearly organizational activities, not just those of an individual project and project manager. Organizational change initiatives are needed to implant and exercise these activities in their business.

Common PM Framework Is Applied to All Projects in the Business

Many businesses limit application of good project management principles to their new product development efforts. Then, if project manage-

Figure 17.3
Business and Project Alignment Roles

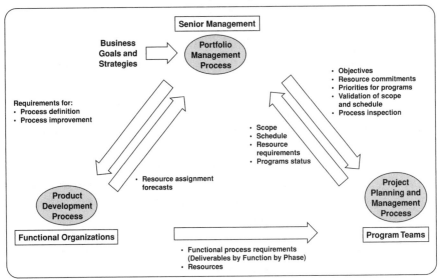

Source: From Catherine L. Tonne and Richard Bauhaus, "Wisdom of the Wizards: Creating the Framework for Successful New Product Development—The HP Way!," PMI Conference, Philadelphia, October 1999. Reprinted with permission.

ment principles are applied to other projects in other parts of the business, they may use inconsistent and incongruent language and framework. An example is that some project methodologies use a project mission statement that usually talks only about the project deliverable. Other methodologies use a project objective statement with scope, schedule, and resources spelled out. This lack of consistency and congruence is a source of confusion, miscommunication, and misunderstanding and has the potential for inefficiency, waste, and failure. The PM principles need to be common across all projects being pursued in a business. There is likely to be some difference in the life cycles used, but the PM practices, terminology, and framework should be consistent. This consistency is critical to the project in order to obtain the speed, lower the cost, and meet client expectations.

In addition, as other partners, vendors, and businesses work on subprojects to complete the primary projects, some relative consistency of terminology and process is vital to defining, planning, and tracking the projects. At the interfaces between subprojects in the different businesses, some consistent interface management must be exercised. That is, the primary project needs a subproject interface manager. The subproject needs a project interface manager. These two managers need to agree on the deliverables and the requirements with metrics. Deliverables from the "supplier" and requirements of the "buyer" must be clearly defined, matched, and "contracted" between the two to meet functionality and schedule. A common language and framework provide the means for this communication to work smoothly.

Relatively common project management terminology and methods are being developed through professional organizations, such as the Project Management Institute (PMI), the Australian Institute of Project Managers (AIPM), and the (European) International Project Management Association (IPMA). Regardless, it is critical for the various project organizations and functions participating in a particular project to have a common language and framework with which to work.

Portfolio of Projects Is Consistent with the Business Resources

When all the managers do not consider all projects going on in their organization, they will find they have overcommitted the resources of their business. In that portfolio of projects, many of the same people and certainly the capital necessary to invest in new product development, business change initiatives, information technology projects, and so forth require a holistic, systems view of the business. The portfolio of projects being undertaken by the business needs input at all levels of the management and staff of the organization. The process is an iteration of planning and execution of projects from the top to the bottom of the entire organization. Two or three iterations of top-down to bottom-up planning will likely be required. Senior management's business strategy planning needs to encompass this systems thinking around projects. So the business strategy goals must be tightly linked to all the projects being done in the organization.

There is a dilemma in this critical characteristic of success: It is often hard to discover all the projects that are being carried out in your particular organization. Some criteria are needed regarding the size of the projects. Often, a project is defined as having three or more people. But some may involve one person on the core team who greatly affects the whole organization. It can be difficult to find these projects because many are "pet projects." However, unless all the projects are identified, resources that you think are available will not be there when needed.

In my experience, too many projects are on the organization's plate; often two to three times too many projects are being attempted. One business was able to trim 30 new product development projects down to 10 in order to have the resources necessary to achieve the projects in the targeted market window. In addition, management had not considered the business and functional change projects in the organization's portfolio and needed to add them to the list. Only after this was done did projects meet function and schedule commitments.

How exactly does this portfolio management work? Too often, I have worked with organizations that have set business strategies, established market segments, and essentially sent teams off doing projects to meet the goals. Even if the project teams managed to do a good job of defining, planning, and tracking their projects, they did not close the loop back to senior management to ensure that the critical minimum set of projects was not overtaxing the resources of the organization. Nor did senior management request this behavior from their project teams.

So how have we seen successful PM-based organizations work? They use an *iterative planning framework*. Business strategies are set, and portfolios of projects are determined from a top-down approach. Then, high-level defining and planning are done for each of the proposed projects. This information is summed up with the required resources. Management then has to determine what's in and what's out of this year's efforts (i.e., a list is made up with a threshold for projects the organization will do; below the cut-off line are projects it won't do). The decision of which projects make the cut is not an easy one; it requires much discussion to identify the critical few that will best carry out the business strategies and yet maximize resources to produce output from projects in the shortest time, with the highest-quality results to meet customer expectations. So the iterative process may take a few cycles at the beginning of each year, and will require review at least quarterly to ensure that the organization is on track.

All Levels Understand How Each Project Delivers to the Business Strategy Goals

I have talked with numerous project managers and project team members who did not have access to the business strategy goals for their organizations. They were not able to tell me, or anyone, how their project fit and contributed into their business strategies. Consequently, they may or may not have been making appropriate decisions on their projects to meet their business needs.

Full disclosure and understanding of the business strategy goals and how a project contributes to the business is essential for each project and the project team. The results will be better-stated project objectives;

better work breakdown structures, schedules, risk analyses, and risk management plans; and better execution of the projects. Individual project team members should be expected to understand how their projects contribute to the organizations' business strategies.

PM-Based Approach to Organizational Change Establishes Good PM Practices

The most critical requirement for leading an organizational change to a PM-based enterprise is that the organizational change project itself is organized, staffed, and run as a project. This demonstrates the power of the project management process. It thereby underlines the power of the process and demonstrates how and why it works.

I recall a typical situation where an organization knew it needed better project management. However, the company was struggling over how to make the change occur. Much discussion and many opinions were heard in numerous meetings. Finally, one day we were able to convince the organization to apply project management principles to the change initiative. After we led them through the steps for defining and planning the project management change initiative, the light dawned. "This is what the whole business needs to be doing," they said. "Now we see what we have to do." They agreed that applying the project management methods to the change initiative would be a powerful demonstration of what project management could do for projects in their organization. The whole experience seems so obvious, yet in the middle of the muddle, this organization had not seen any of it clearly.

In addition, an organizational mechanism has to be put in place to sustain long-term maintenance of strong best practices for project management. This can be done in a variety of ways. Some present-day businesses are identifying a corporate project management officer, and/or there is usually a project management office that is the center for archiving and maintaining good PM practices. A project management center for excellence may exist to develop project management competencies to meet the business needs.[4] Many variations of this sort of theme are evident in today's enterprises that are moving to a PM-based organization.

Figure 17.4 shows the results from six businesses inside HP that took steps to implement an organizational change to become a PM-based business. It shows that 58 percent to 78 percent of the businesses felt they had experienced improvement in meeting commitments to their project deliverables and milestone commitments as a result of implementing good PM practices.

Figure 17.4
Initiative Metrics 2: Improvement Due to PM Techniques

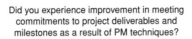

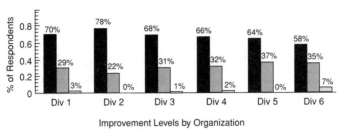

Did you experience improvement in meeting
commitments to project deliverables and
milestones as a result of PM techniques?

Lessons Learned in Organizational PM and the Future Challenge

The benefits of a PM-based organization are to facilitate successful projects. The transition to a PM-based approach is critical and must be project-managed. World-class results depend on this change.

What a PM-Based Organization Does for Project Management

A PM-based organization is essential to making projects work most effectively. With every person, from the CEO to the group presidents, to the general managers, to functional managers, down to the project manager and the individual contributor, there is a crucial role that must be performed. Each is different, and each is essential to achieving our business goals through our project goals. Excellence is still needed in operational efforts in our business. But projects are not operations. There is an excellence in our project efforts that is essential to renewing our business and to developing products or services for our customers that will maintain our business lead and dominance.

This chapter has referred to numerous ingredients that help to develop a maximally functioning PM-based organization. Other chapters in this book provide the other essential ingredients to making project management work effectively for you. But without this organizational approach, the individual project manager is going to be anything from very ineffective

314 THE HUMAN DIMENSIONS TRACK

or even a failure to less effective than he or she could be in making your business a success. So project management requires an organizational commitment and involvement to become world-class.

Today's project manager has become an essential part of the business organization. As numbers of middle management have been eliminated from modern organizations, the project manager's role has risen in importance. Much of what was managed by the middle manager has been moved to the responsibility of the project manager. Therefore, developing the project manager's skills is crucial to project success and business success. Equally crucial has become the role of each level of the management, from the CEO down to the project manager. Developing these managers' skills must be included in the development of the world-class organizational project management business.

How to Make the Change

The change to a PM-based organization with world-class capability can come only through a project-managed organizational approach. Despite the reluctance of senior managers to be involved, their active participation is key to the success of this effort. Managers at every level need to understand their role in this project management process and must be involved in the project management change initiative to improve project management. They also need to set the appropriate expectations for good practices for project management to be carried out in their organizations. Finally, they need to set up and support ongoing project management efforts in their organizations to maintain strong PM practices and build stronger ones as the times dictate.

The Ongoing Work to Maintain Organizational Project Management

Certainly, how project management is applied to our projects will change with the times, depending on our business and on the requirements of the marketplace in which we are playing. For this reason, project management will not simply be something that is injected into an organization, with the expectation that the work is then done.

First of all, there is constant change in personnel in any business organization. New project managers are created, and they need to develop their skills to do their jobs. Concurrently, new senior managers are being promoted, and they need to develop their skills in setting the appropriate expectations and providing the appropriate guidance for projects to be extremely successful. So some ongoing method for ensuring good PM practices will be required in the organization. There are many good alternatives for accomplishing this. Many are described in the other chapters of this book. But the important issue and action is to set up some part of the business organization to watch over and to improve PM practices to meet the current business needs, with an organizational PM-based perspective.

The Future Requirement for a PM-Based Organization

The foreseeable future requires a PM-based organization in order to be a business success. Numerous and increasing efforts are evident in world-class and Fortune 500 companies as well as other organizations. Programs by IBM, Motorola, Lucent, and Hewlett-Packard, to name a few, are evidence of the concern. Some of these programs are well implemented, and some will need added attention and support to make their companies successful.

The Promise of PM-Based Organizations

Success will be dependent on the abilities of senior managers to develop world-class project management in their businesses, using the principles discussed in this chapter and throughout this book. Success will go to those companies that focus the appropriate attention and dedication on their project management efforts. New products, services, and operations will be world-class if world-class project management methods are part of the fiber of those businesses. This must include the organizational approach, in addition to the historical focus on the individual, in building PM competency.

The Call to the Profession to Meet the New Project Management Challenge

Success in implementing the appropriate and necessary PM practices is dependent also on the project management professional field of endeavor. Developing the individual project manager is now no longer sufficient. The whole organization has to be developed into a PM-based organization. This requires a new approach by professionals, trainers, and consultants toward their project management efforts.

The basics have not changed and will remain constant. But how they are applied to the organization becomes critical to establishing project management as one truly necessary means to business success, and probably to human success as well. Curriculum, training, and building the PM competencies will have to change to meet this demand. Institutions, books, associations, and other such media will have to focus more attention on PM-based organizations. This is becoming evident in books such as Paul Dinsmore's *Winning in Business with Enterprise Project Management.*[5]

Increasing evidence of organizational project management discussion is appearing in places such as the Project Management Institute's conferences (see the papers in the PMI 1999 Conference in Philadelphia[6]), which other authors and I have experienced firsthand. Stanford University has just introduced a curriculum (a joint venture between the Stanford University School of Engineering and its partner, Integrated Project Systems/ Epic Edge) in the extended education program that includes two tracks, one for individual and one for organizational project management.

These trends are evidence of the need, emerging recognition, and concern for PM-based organizations. We encourage you and your organization to recognize and implement PM-based organizational change in your efforts toward success.

REFERENCES

1. Randall Englund and Robert Graham. 1998. *Creating the Environment for Successful Project Management.* San Francisco: Jossey-Bass.
2. Adapted from Catherine L. Tonne and Richard Bauhaus. October 1999. "Wisdom of Wizards: Creating the Framework for Successful New Product Development—The HP Way!" PMI Conference, Philadelphia.
3. Paul Dinsmore. 1999. *Winning in Business with Enterprise Project Management.* New York: AMA Publications.
4. Ibid.
5. Ibid.
6 "PMI 99 Seminars and Symposium Proceedings." 1999. Philadelphia: Project Management Institute.

CHAPTER 18

CREATING A PROFESSIONAL PROJECT MANAGEMENT ORGANIZATION: DESIGN

JAMES J. SCHNEIDMULLER

$\mathbf{C}$ompanies base the need to create a professional project management organization on many reasons:

1. The company may be fairly large with a smokestack structure—individual, autonomous departments that don't work together well to meet the needs of clients. Departments such as marketing/sales, product management, operations, billing, and others need to be brought together and focused on a coordinated delivery.
2. Frequently, executive leaders in today's companies seek to utilize better the already scarce resources at their disposal.
3. Many complex product/service offerings that are made available to clients can also dictate the need for overall management and control when these are employed in an interrelated implementation offering. Technological integration of these service offerings into a solution for the client can require a large amount of coordination and effort.
4. In the sales environment, clients are more frequently seeking overall accountability, a single point of contact, for their complex and costly undertaking. Clients do not typically accept multiple interface points into the supplier's company. Requests for proposals (RFPs) in this environment tend to contain a specific section dedicated to how to manage the solution. Experienced, certified, and professional project managers are requested to lead the overall implementation effort to ensure success.

317

5. Companies will also look to position project management as a differentiation of service, hoping it will help them win the business at the expense of their competition.

6. Internally, in today's ever-changing business world, senior leadership will look to project management for the control and management of critical cost containment or reduction efforts to ensure the achievement of the desired results and benefits.

The project managers in these organizations are held accountable for each project under a "the buck stops here" scenario. They are responsible for the successful integration of all of the services involved in the project and their implementation. The client is presented a single point of contact with a view of the project that matches his or her own. This interaction produces a plan with a specific start and a desired end date, and accounts for a set of products and/or services successfully integrated and implemented.

The strategy that can be employed to create a professional project management group will embody several different areas of focus. This chapter will discuss several of the more important areas, which are as follows:

- Clarifying the human resources perspective: Who will become the project managers? How will the group be staffed?
- Creating a process that will guide the project managers as they manage their projects
- Defining education and training for the project managers
- Establishment of standards
- Deciding on a career path for the project managers
- Establishing measurements to enable success

HUMAN RESOURCES

The first area concentrates on the human resources perspective. The organization's sponsor can easily describe his or her vision for the team as a small collection of highly skilled, highly trained professionals, thus imposing limits on the size of the group, its expected skill set, and its capabilities. Several questions immediately come to mind: Which associates are available to perform this function of project management? Do those available possess the right skill sets and experience? What training will they require? Do they have a desire to become professional project managers? Will they be comfortable working in a "the buck stops here" environment? Will others need to be hired? How long will it take the new project managers to become proficient? To what extent will external contractors be employed?

The initial approach should involve a review of existing associates within the company who are performing a project management-like function or have a demonstrated multidisciplinary orientation. While the number of these individuals may be limited, there are advantages associated with the utilization of internal resources. They are already familiar with the company structure, processes, and clients. They will be able to assemble a project team quickly because they already have an understanding of the various departments. Internal morale will not be as negatively impacted as it might be should external contractor resources be acquired.

The risk associated with this alternative is largely based on the ability of a good line manager to become a good project manager. These two jobs have significant differences. The effective line manager can manage a group of specialists for which he or she has job evaluation and compensation authority. The effective project manager typically manages in a matrix environment with little or no impact on the team members' evaluations and compensation. Additionally, the demand and stress levels of the two jobs are very different. While the attainment of a specific set of results is an important part of both, the project manager's job involves less authority and more ambiguity with respect to responsibilities, expected deliverables, and the like.

Nonetheless, time spent in the review of internal candidates is well invested. The resumes of these employees should be reviewed and interviews conducted where necessary. If selected properly, most will be found to have some experience, but will probably be lacking in formal project management training and the application of a project management process. Few will possess the credentials so often associated with a professional project manager. This can be addressed through the education, training, and career path elements discussed later in this chapter.

While a focus on internal candidates is optimal, it will be difficult to succeed at creating a new project management culture within the company unless associates with more project management experience are acquired. Those who have managed projects in the commercial contract arena are of value. Credentials such as a Master's Certificate in Project Management or the coveted certification as a Project Management Professional (PMP) from the Project Management Institute (PMI) should be noted as "strongly desired" in the job requisition. These additional resources are not acquired in great numbers, but are used to seed the project management group with seasoned project managers and to provide a mentoring capability.

The human resources perspective entails the following recommendations:

- Be sure to understand the sponsor's vision. This understanding will help determine the desired size, skill-set capability, and overall strategy for the group. The ongoing, continued support of the sponsor will be required as the group is formed. The sponsor will help create the right environment, assist in building the credibility of the group, and aid in removing roadblocks that are encountered. This sponsor can be determined by an organizational hierarchy or by a demonstrated level of support. The relationship with the sponsor is key to the successful establishment of the group—don't take this lightly!

- Assess both the current capabilities (skill set) and desire of the internal project manager candidates. If skills are currently lacking, emphasis should be placed on the *desire* to become a professional project manager; otherwise the planned investment in training and education will be wasted.

- Try to seed the group with some number of seasoned, experienced project managers. The mentoring opportunity this presents is invaluable. (Actually, each group mentors the other. One mentors in the area of the technology of the projects and the client set. The other mentors in the area of project management.) Coaches or supervisors who are experienced are also invaluable.

- Expect some "storming" to occur as the individuals are identified and brought together. It will take some time to stabilize the group. This will be accomplished through the remaining areas of focus. Be patient! If external resources are employed, expect there to be some clashes with the internal resources. Time must be spent on team building early in the process. Both groups will eventually come to understand that they cannot be successful unless they act as one team.

PROCESS

The next area of focus is applied to the creation of a process that the project managers will follow in the management of their projects. This process will also be shared throughout the larger organization to obtain understanding and buy-in. This will be extremely important as resources are called upon to staff project teams. Should a process already exist, it will need to be reviewed and a decision made to use it as is, modify it, or create a new one. In this case, a review team should be commissioned and charged with the task of making the process decision. This team should be comprised of both internal associates and any external resources that were acquired. Forming the team in this way accomplishes several things:

- It provides an open view of the process for the new environment, which is developed by those who will look to apply it.
- It begins the teaming that is necessary.
- It begins a sharing of ideas and approaches within the group.

Should a process not already exist, one of several options can be investigated. There is a process framework suggested in *A Guide to the Project Management Body of Knowledge*, available from the Project Management Institute. This framework organizes a project management process into five interacting groups:

1. Initiating
2. Planning
3. Executing
4. Controlling
5. Closing

Utilizing this framework as a guideline, with the investment of a relatively small amount of time and resources an overall process can be designed. This initial process will be reviewed and evaluated continually, with revisions applied to better align with the organization's projects, clients, and structure. Additional process information can be obtained from project management textbooks. Another alternative is to use the services of a consultant. A number of consultants will design a process tailored for the company.

The process should provide an end-to-end view of the project management process. The way in which projects will be received, assigned, managed, and closed out will need to be detailed. How the process is initialized—the framework of information required for project manager assignment—should be the first consideration. The scope of the project as well as the target completion date, business case/funding approval, locations, and client information should be a major part of the information requested. After discussion with the requester, an assignment is made and notification is returned.

The next part of the process should be designed to launch the project. This part is aimed at getting the project off to a good start and provides the required up-front planning to ensure project success.

The subsequent part of the overall process is designed to address the standard project management responsibilities of controlling, planning, organizing, scheduling, budgeting, and execution.

The final part of the process, the closeout, typically takes into account the following tasks:

- Closing out all work orders
- Initiation of billing processes
- Notification/declaration of project completion
- Internal and external reviews to determine satisfaction and derive lessons learned
- Client satisfaction determination
- Release of team members

Figure 18.1 diagrams a sample project management process. The determination of client satisfaction is important and can be based on the project scope and schedule (as agreed to), the overall effectiveness of the project manager with respect to the project's implementation, feedback for process improvements as determined by the client, or a combination of all of these. A simple questionnaire can be prepared for this purpose.

Early on, positive reinforcement of the development of project management skills and of the use of the standardized tools and process is highly recommended. This can be accomplished easily through live project reviews. This approach provides the project manager and project team with a proactive, supportive, and professional evaluation of the project to measure the success, or potential success, of the project. Interviews, along with reviews of project documentation and expected process deliverables, should be conducted. The intent is to use these to provide on-the-spot, proactive assistance to the new project managers, and to help them with real project expectations and issues. The more experienced project managers, or the leaders of the group, can conduct the reviews and provide immediate support to the projects, as required.

These are the recommendations associated with the process:

- Where practical, involve the project managers in the process development effort. This will more quickly facilitate their acceptance of the process and will yield a better product. The knowledge they possess related to the work they perform or need to perform provides invaluable input for this effort.
- You don't need to reinvent the wheel. There are numerous sources for obtaining project management process information that can be tailored to fit your needs.
- Training on the process is important. The project managers need to understand the process from start to finish. They also need to

Figure 18.1
A Sample Project Management Process

1.0 Conceptual	2.0 Pre-Approval Planning	3.0 Post-Approval Planning	4.0 Implementation	5.0 Close-Out
1.1 Obtain All Pertinent Documentation	2.1 Review & Summarize Client Requirements	3.1 Review & Summarize Project Requirements	4.1 Manage Project Implementation Plan	5.1 Transition to Life Cycle Management
1.2 Define Project	2.2 Identify & Form Planning Team	3.2 Confirm Project Owner & Gain Acceptance	4.2 Monitor & Control Project for Conformance	5.2 Close Out Project Internally
1.3 Conduct Solution Assurance	2.3 Develop Technical Design	3.3 Identify, Gain Acceptance, & Form Project Team	4.3 Manage Project Variances	5.3 Hold Final Project Team Meeting & Disperse Team
1.4 Determine Project Participation by Organization	2.4 Develop Project Plans	3.4 Establish Vendor Agreements	4.4 Control Changes to Project	5.4 Declare Project Complete
1.5 Develop Preliminary Business Case	2.5 Refine Business Case	3.5 Conduct Internal Kickoff Meeting	4.5 Manage Technical Performance	
1.6 Obtain Decision to Proceed — Yes	2.6 Support Proposal & Contract Negotiation Processes	3.6 Develop Integrated Project Plan	4.6 Manage Contract/ Agreement with Client	
No	2.7 Finalize Bid/No Bid Decision	3.7 Conduct External Project Kickoff Meeting	4.7 Manage Contract/ Agreement with Suppliers	
	2.8 Obtain Approval to Go Ahead — No / Yes	3.8 Establish Integrated Project Plan	4.8 Manage Risk	
1.7 Terminate Project & Capture Lessons Learned			4.9 Manage Test & Acceptance	
1.8 Archive Project Data			4.10 Assess Completion of Project Requirements	
			4.11 Obtain Client Signoff	

understand the organization's expectations with respect to the deliverables.

• The creation of a process-review mechanism should be employed— not in a threatening sense, but rather a supportive one. You want to ensure project success and provide real-time coaching.

• The organization will need to define its own hot spots in the process—those steps that are of particular importance to the organization, your sponsor, and your organizational leaders (e.g., a process hot spot may be the closeout of all work orders or billing initiation).

EDUCATION AND TRAINING— THE PATHS TO PROFESSIONALISM

Special consideration should be applied to this area. It will probably involve the highest investment in terms of expense dollars that will be required. In return, however, it will provide the project managers with the knowledge they will need to be successful. Additionally, it will ultimately provide the project managers and the group with the credentials that have come to be expected of professional project managers.

As a first step, in order to provide a baseline of education and training for all associates, a broad-based training curriculum should be developed. This curriculum can be grouped into modules of project management, technology, management skills, personal development, PCs and software, and quality. An example of a training and development map is provided in Figure 18.2.

Where possible, internally offered courses should be utilized. If no internal training is available, external courses should be investigated. The courses in this initial listing can be denoted as core or elective to provide flexibility while at the same time addressing the varying needs of the project managers. Each internal associate's training history should be reviewed against this curriculum and an individual development/training plan created.

In time, as more of the basic training requirements are met, a movement to a focus on a university Master's Certificate in Project Management program should be employed. The project managers should be strongly encouraged to enroll in the program, as specific budgets allow. Completing the program and obtaining the Master's Certificate can be further encouraged by building it into the career path that will be created for the group. This is discussed later in this chapter.

In addition to the Master's Certificate focus, the organization should

Figure 18.2
Project Manager Training and Development Map

Project Management	Technology	Management Skills	Personal Development	Computer/ Software
Introduction to Project Management	(Applicable Training)	Team Building	Written Communication Skills	PC Software
Contract Management		Problem Solving and Decision Making	Presentation Skills	Word Processing
Team Leadership		Conflict Resolution	Stress Management	Spreadsheets
Risk Management		Negotiation Skills	Conducting Meetings	Presentations
Scheduling Techniques		Building Relationships		Process Management

encourage the attainment of PMP (Project Management Professional) certification. This also can be built into the career path for the project managers. A belief that one important characteristic of the professional project manager is the attainment of PMP certification will soon permeate the group. A competitive phenomenon typically occurs with PMP status. With more and more of the project managers successfully obtaining this status, the remaining potential candidates may become driven to obtain it for themselves.

Lastly, consideration should be given to providing training to support the use of off-the-shelf project management software. This can be obtained through the software company or other in-house training opportunities, if available.

These are the recommendations for this section:

- The organization will need to assess a concentration on a broad-based training curriculum versus a university Master's Certificate program. There is some redundancy. The cost of each will need to be weighed. There may be greater value in the latter.
- Be sure to consider the associates' individual needs. These may be different. Some may need more PC and software knowledge; others

may require more of the project-management basic skills such as leadership, interpersonal, team building, and so on. Be sure to allow for this during the development of your training plans.

• Linking the education/training planning to the career path activity will drive a positive behavior; the project managers will receive the training they need, they will obtain the required competencies needed to perform at the next level, and the group's overall credentials and skill levels will increase.

STANDARDS

Providing standard models and documented methods and procedures will greatly enhance the introduction of the project management process and the likelihood of its use by the project managers. The project managers should be encouraged to refer to and use these as a guide in the management of their projects. Blank forms, completed samples such as meeting minutes, and detailed descriptions supporting each step of the process are made available in this reference documentation. As the project managers become more experienced and familiar with the process deliverables, they will become increasingly less dependent on these references, but during the early stages of group formation, this documentation is typically of high value. The project managers must clearly understand that this material is provided to guide them as they manage their projects. It should not discourage flexibility and creativity on the part of the project managers.

The selection of a standard software package should also be considered. If the group doesn't standardize a specific package, then the handling of project reports, schedules, variances, and other information generated through this mechanism will be difficult. Trade publications, software comparison reports, and individual experience can be used as sources of information regarding the various packages. Over time, the group will typically broaden its perspective relating to software and have the ability to support the use of several commercially available packages.

A standard hardware/software platform is another important consideration for the organization. Most project managers today are equipped with laptop technology to accommodate their travel requirements. Internet access and an e-mail package, along with a word-processing and spreadsheet package, should be a part of the platform.

A final area of standardization can be focused within the administrative area. Certainly, every company has its own administrative requirements. Consideration should be given to providing standards in the areas of attendance tracking, equipment inventory, security, recognition, time reporting and tracking, vacation, expense vouchering, and other appropriate areas. The organizational charts/contact lists, hardware/software platform configuration, and training/certification information can also be included. The intent should be to document key standards or requirements defined as policy and provide a tool for sharing information frequently used by all members of the organization.

These are the recommendations for this section:

- The standards models and the methods and procedures are typically very well received and accepted by project managers. They will be used as reference tools and provide on-the-job learning opportunities.
- The decision relating to the initial selection of the project management software package is not an easy one. The leadership of the group must provide active involvement and interaction in this decision. The leadership must establish a clear set of needs that the software will address in order to facilitate the selection.
- The sponsor should confirm the availability of funds for all acquisitions (hardware, software, and so on). If full funding cannot be immediately obtained, a plan for partial deployment can be created.
- The associates will very much appreciate a single source for key administrative responsibilities. Other organizations will likely use this as a model for their own associates.
- The project managers positively receive standards, once they are documented and communicated. They provide a set of clear expectations and direction.

CAREER PATH

In order to maintain a desire for others to join the group, the leadership of the group must define a career path for the project managers that will *attract, retain, and develop* people who either are project managers already or have the capability to become professional project managers. The leadership will want to ensure the investment already made in the current population. The corporate culture of changing jobs every 18 to 24 months needs to be addressed, especially when a promotional opportunity is offered.

Project managers improve their skills and capabilities with each project they manage. Each project, based on its unique characteristics and its different set of functional team members, provides its own lessons for the project manager. It is only through this cycle of learning, managing another project, learning, managing another project, and so on that the individual project manager begins to maximize his or her capabilities. This repetitive process not only further develops and strengthens the associate's strengths, but it also identifies areas of weakness or unfamiliarity. Solutions to address these areas can be attempted on the next project. Existing internal programs and options that could be utilized as is, or modified to fit varying needs, should be researched. The organization's sponsor can also provide direction and guidance in this area.

The following categories are recommended to be a part of the career-path plan:

- *Personnel data* entails the current and proposed level, total years of experience, past performance appraisal ratings, and so on.
- *Professional orientation* is a direct reflection of the project manager's ability to execute the required technical skills. It involves a numeric score arrived at via a skills matrix that includes software understanding and use, resource utilization, industry standards for project execution, monitoring and control, financial management, and documentation.
- *Education/experience* involves a numeric score based on the defined training and education program and the role of the project manager, as well as the level of performance demonstrated. This is the point at which the Master's Certificate program and PMI certification are tied into the career path. Certain levels require attainment of the certificate, while other, higher levels require PMP certification.
- *Interpersonal skills* are based on their internal and external demonstration.
- *Technical coaching* with respect to project management knowledge involves the ability to provide guidance to others.
- *Business acumen* entails the ability to gain an understanding of the client's needs and an overall understanding of the company.
- *Customer focus* involves the ability to provide complete management of the client's needs throughout the project's life cycle.
- *Technical complexity* entails the ability to manage highly complex and integrated projects, to provide leadership that allows all involved to understand, to develop plans, and to implement complex projects.
- *Complexity of projects managed* deals with the number of processes or organizations involved in the project, the number of projects being managed concurrently by the project manager, or the type of management applied (i.e., direct or through subordinates).
- *Nature of work environment* concerns the ability to manage uncertainty of project activities while maintaining full compliance with the triple constraint (see "Measurements," later in this chapter, for details). The triple constraint refers to the primary focus of the overall

project management process, the success criteria for effective project management—*on time, within budget/cost*, and *according to the requirements/specifications.*

A possible level array, based on these categories, is presented in Figure 18.3.

The process supporting this plan involves the project manager's coach/supervisor, other coaches or supervisors within the organization, and a review panel. The review panel can be comprised of other managers from within the larger organization and other senior project management associates. The panel will receive and review all project manager promotions within the plan. The coach assesses the individual project manager against the career-path criteria as a part of creating the individual's development plan. If the individual is found to be qualified for the next level, the coach completes the required paperwork. This paperwork is reviewed by the project management leadership team, and if agreed upon, is endorsed and forwarded to the review panel. The review panel should review these promotional packages at regularly scheduled meetings held approximately every two months. The review panel has the ultimate responsibility of either accepting or denying the promotion.

These are the recommendations for this section:

- You must identify a career path for the project managers who want to remain in the profession and also desire the increase in stature, along with the recognition and increased salary that promotions carry with them. If the organization is committed to having a cadre of professional project managers, then it must support the establishment of a plan to maintain the group and grow its skills and capabilities, while at the same time rewarding the individual associates. This career plan will have a great impact on the organization's ability to attract, retain, and develop project managers.
- The review panel concept provides an external view and additional grounding for the promotional recommendations. In practice, there should rarely be any conflicts with the panel or their findings.
- The criteria in the career plan should be defined to fit the organization's environment. Be sure to apply the criteria consistently across the associates' universe.
- The plan should be explained to the project managers. This can be done through local coach/team meetings, individual one-on-one sessions, and a total organizational meeting. This explanation will provide the opportunity to ensure associates' understanding, answer their questions, and obtain their feedback.

Figure 18.3
Project Manager Multilevel Career Path

Dimension	Level 1	Level 2	Level 3	Level 4
Education/Experience	• 1 to 2 years of relevant work experience • Undergraduate degree in related field, specialized training or equivalent • Knowledge of project management practices, principles, tools	• 4 to 6 years of relevant work experience • Same • Demonstrated application of project management practices, principles, tools • Master's Certificate (desired) • PMP (desired)	• 6 to 8 years of project/ program work experience • Master's degree (desired) • Significant demonstration of application of project management practices, principles, tools • Master's Certificate (required) • PMP (required) • Studies within the international project management arena • Participation in industry-related activities (articles, papers, and so on)	• 10 to 12 years of project/ program work experience • Master's degree (required) • Mastery of the application of project management practices, principles, tools • Same • Same • Demonstrated knowledge of international project management and/or work experience • Significant participation in industry-related activities (articles, papers, and so on)
Interpersonal Skills	• Effective communication with project team members • Demonstrates good oral and written communication skills • Basic team building and negotiation skills	• Effective communication with project team members, clients, and various levels of management • Demonstrates excellent oral and written communication skills • Strong team building, leading, and negotiation skills	• Excellent communications with project team, owner, functional managers, clients, and executive levels of management • Same • Ability to work with a diverse set of disciplines, adapting leadership style as appropriate	• Exceptional communications with project team, owner, functional managers, clients, and executive levels of management • Demonstrates exceptional oral and written communicational skills • Establishes long-term relationships with team members and customers
Technical Coaching Ability	• Provides high-level guidance regarding process and deliverables to team members	• Provides coaching support to peers and lower-level project managers	• Recognized as subject matter expert • Proactively provides coaching to all levels of peers, team members, and clients • Excellent facilitation skills • Provides consulting support in the areas of project management, financial management, contract management, and resource utilization	• Recognized as subject matter expert by both internal and external peers • Can provide formalized training in project management knowledge • Same • Same • Can influence/develop industry policy
Business Acumen	• Familiarity with organization and process structure • Basic understanding of project objectives	• Knowledge of the organization's goals and objectives • Understanding of the customer's business strategies and goals • Understanding of the impact of the project • Awareness of political environment and the impact on the project's goals	• Applies in-depth knowledge of organization to ensure project/ program success • Possesses an intimate understanding of the customer's business—its strategies and goals • Understands industry trends and practices and their impact on the business • Manages and influences barriers created by the political environment	• Same • Same • Same • Same
Customer Focus	• Forms relationships with customers and suppliers • Sets project objectives	• Forms productive relationships with internal and external customers and suppliers • Recognizes client requirements and develops clear, concise project objectives	• Assumes leadership role in forming productive relationships with internal and external customers and suppliers • Effectively identifies client requirements and develops detailed project objectives	• Same • Same • Provides leadership to ensure the delivery of all project requirements
Project Complexity	• Manages simple, non-complex projects • May be responsible for a portion of a project • Project coordination typically limited to one process or organization	• Manages one or more projects of moderate to high complexity • Typically manages projects across multiple processes or organizations	• Manages multiple projects of moderate to high complexity • Manages projects or programs with significant involvement of multiple processes or organizations	• Responsible for all aspects of multiple, complex business initiatives • Same
Role in Managing Projects	• Manages small project teams • Can provide support to another project manager	• Effectively leads large project teams • Makes project decisions based upon detailed risk assessments	• Effectively leads large, diverse project teams spanning multiple organizations • Effectively formulates risk assessment plans and develops mitigation strategies	• Establishes strategic direction and provides overall leadership to multifunctional, multiorganizational project teams
Nature of Work Environment	• Structured/unstable environment	• New, unstructured/unstable environment • Expertise available	• New, unstructure/unstable environment • Expertise unavailable	• Unstructured, rapidly changing environment

- The plan naturally creates a career structure with an entry-level and career-level position identified.

MEASUREMENTS

The project manager *measures of success* can be easily focused on the industry-standard concept of the triple constraint, which consists of the following:

- Successful delivery of the project's scope of work as documented and agreed to between the project manager and client
- Meeting the project's schedule as documented and agreed to between the project manager and client
- Keeping project costs within budget

Some new thinking submits that there may actually be a fourth constraint to project management, taking into account the *politics* of the environment within which the project is being managed. Some refer to these measures simply as the constraints of time, cost, and performance. Often, "quality" is either attached to or substituted for "performance."

If the project is being done for an external customer, another measure should be considered—customer satisfaction. Effective project management can frequently pave the way for additional business opportunities with the client. In fact, professional project management can often provide a winning differentiation of service among competitors. Items that may be included as additional areas of focus are ease of doing business, overall effectiveness, or other specific areas.

The assessment of performance versus scope and schedule has two important defining criteria. The first of these is the client's perception of the project management performance. A scorecard or satisfaction form can be easily created to obtain the client's feedback for each project. It can be delivered to the customer by the project manager, with a follow-up telephone call or visit from the coach/supervisor to obtain the responses. It can also be delivered via e-mail or Web access. Minimally, questions such as the following should be included:

- Was the agreed-upon scope delivered to the client's satisfaction?
- Was the agreed-upon schedule met?
- How would you rate the project manager's overall effectiveness?

Other appropriate questions reflecting the organization's areas of focus can also be included. In addition to the questions, space should be provided for additional pertinent comments relating to the project delivery, as well as allowing input regarding the support received from other organizations (sales, solution design, and so on). The overall effectiveness item can be broken out into subareas such as providing proactive status and appropriate documentation, issue identification and resolution, and administering a change management plan.

The project manager's coach provides the other input related to performance. The coach assesses scope and schedule performance based on what he or she has learned and observed through interactions with the project manager, the client, and functional team members. The coach's review of project documentation will also provide information for the assessment. Based on predetermined weighting between the client and coach input, an overall assessment is made for each project.

These are the recommendations for this section:

- The triple constraint measures are important. Customers will appreciate the fact that you care about their satisfaction.
- You will need to provide a relative balance between client and coach input to the assessment process. Having an inappropriate slant in either direction can provide an inaccurate or unfair assessment.
- Project managers thrive on feedback. There should never be any surprises.

THE PROJECT MANAGEMENT INSTITUTE

Active participation and involvement with the Project Management Institute (PMI) has been proven to be invaluable. The project managers are able to demonstrate their commitment and dedication to the profession through their support of PMI. Attendance at the PMI annual symposium should be encouraged and funded. The project managers should look to present papers and seminars at either the local chapter or the national level.

Assuming the achievement of success, these are offered as areas of focus:

- You *must* position the successes of your project managers to heighten the awareness of their talent and importance. Look to involve upper-level leaders in recognizing their efforts. Publish project results to these levels to ensure their understanding of the value of the group.
- Maintain linkage with the Project Management Institute. It provides significant opportunities for networking. It is extremely useful for sharing, benchmarking, and obtaining industry information.

SUMMARY

A professional project management organization can provide immeasurable benefit to a company. Disparate departments can be made more congruous, limited resources can be more efficiently utilized, the delivery of technically complex solutions can be better controlled, and a single, accountable interface can be presented to the client. In today's highly competitive business world, professional project management can also be easily positioned as a differentiation of service between companies.

This chapter has examined several areas involved in the development of a professional project management organization. The work within the human resources arena will identify the people who will be called upon to perform the project management function. These people will probably be a mix of internally available candidates as well as external consultants/contractors. The definition of a process is an important activity that not only will provide guidance and instruction for the project managers, but also will serve to assist in the creation of the desired culture within the company.

Dollars invested within the education and training area typically have enormous payback. Motivating the project managers to acquire the professional credentials of Master's Certificate and, more importantly, PMP certification through a tie-in to a progressive career path is extremely important. This will provide a win-win-win situation: The project management organization establishes more professional credibility, the project managers have the ability to receive promotional recognition for their work and skill-set development, and the company is able to ensure its investment in these personnel. Lastly, standards and measurements help the project managers develop a clear idea of what is expected of them in the way of overall performance.

The future is bright for professional project management organizations. Many successful companies have already implemented professional project management and have realized the tangible benefits of better cost control, faster time to market, and improved client relationships.

CHAPTER 19

ORGANIZATIONAL DEPLOYMENT OF PROJECT MANAGEMENT: THE NEXT BIG "AHA" FOR CORPORATE PROJECT LEADERS

ROBERT STOREYGARD

WHAT'S IT ALL ABOUT?

So, what's next for capable project or program leaders? Judicious and competent use of the information, techniques, and disciplines covered in this book should, under most circumstances, net us very successful projects or programs and happy customers, right?

To adequately answer this question, one has to look back at what drives most project leaders (other than *their* managers) to do what they do. At the heart of it for many project leaders is the inborn or learned desire to take a challenging situation and conquer it, and to help an organization or team to succeed through whatever trials it may endure to emerge better and stronger than it was when it started.

This premise gives rise to an answer to the original question, "What's next for capable project or program leaders?" For some, the thrill and/or challenge of continuing to run bigger and tougher projects or programs is answer enough to fuel a career. But I would like to suggest an alternative (or at least additional) direction that could revolutionize the way your organization runs projects.

SOME BASIC ASSUMPTIONS

Let me unveil this new direction by first establishing a few initial assumptions:

- Your organization has many projects/programs to accomplish.
- Your organization has a limited amount of resources to spread across those projects/programs.

334

- Your organization has limited capital to spend on its projects/programs and must make wise decisions about how to spend its money.
- Your organization must balance its workload between new project/program initiatives and essential "keep the train running" daily business functions or activities.

Does this sound at all like your organization? If not, keep reading—it will. Most companies have many more projects and programs than they could hope to complete given their available time, human resources, and budgets. So what does this produce? Heavy infighting, prioritization by whoever screams the loudest or carries the biggest stick, confusion, and chaos. Some companies thrive in an environment like this, but most fail.

WHERE IS THIS LEADING US?

So, where can you as capable, experienced project and program leaders make the biggest long-term difference under these conditions? *The answer lies in helping your sponsoring organizations create and sustain an overall healthful, helpful project management environment.* This will, in turn, help set up the organization's projects and programs for success, not failure.

You will help to replicate the successes you have had on your own projects or programs a *thousandfold* when you enable an organization as a whole to support and sustain a complete project management environment. The rest of this chapter is devoted to helping you know how to do just that.

SOME FUNDAMENTAL QUESTIONS

First off, if an organization is serious about improving its project management practices and deploying PM deeper, further, and faster in their companies, some fundamental questions must be answered:

1. What are the fundamental project management needs of the organization that must be met in order to deliver its products or services better and faster?
2. What changes need to occur within the organization to increase the effectiveness of project results?
3. How do you make sure that the changes in questions 1 and 2 are properly aligned to make their maximum contributions to both the top and bottom lines of the company? (The top line refers to the way the company is managed and structured.)

STEPS TO ADDRESSING THE QUESTIONS

I offer a seven-step process to help answer these three questions, and will expand this process to help give you some solid techniques and models to effectively deploy project management in your organization:

Step 1—Establishing the Need(s)
Step 2—Clarifying/Assessing the Need(s)
Step 3—Modeling/Comparing against the Complete PM Environment
Step 4—Establishing Key Processes and Infrastructures
Step 5—Planning for PM Deployment within an Organization
Step 6—Aligning and Sustaining the Organization
Step 7—Reaping the Benefits

QUESTION 1 (STEPS 1 AND 2): WHAT ARE THE PM NEEDS?

What are the fundamental project management needs of the organization that must be met in order to deliver its products or services better and faster?

Well, it depends on what you need. You know the old saying, "If you don't know where you are going, any road will get you there." So, you first have to establish that indeed there is some real need here (Step 1) and then proceed to clarify and assess those needs (Step 2) to see where you need to start.

Note: For the rest of this discussion, I will be taking the viewpoint as if you, as a consultant, will be providing the assessment and techniques to a client who is coming to you for help. Realize that these can just as easily be applied to you as the client if you are indeed the one with these needs.

Step 1—Establishing the Need(s)

To establish the need(s), most times, it is a matter of gathering information on what the most immediate or obvious needs of your client are (see Figure 19.1, middle column).

Do your clients need help with the following?

- Project planning and Gantt chart production
- Communicating what is going on with their projects/programs
- Coordinating/leading across multiple projects/programs
- Establishing PM standards, roles, methods, and so on

Figure 19.1
Fundamental Project Management Needs

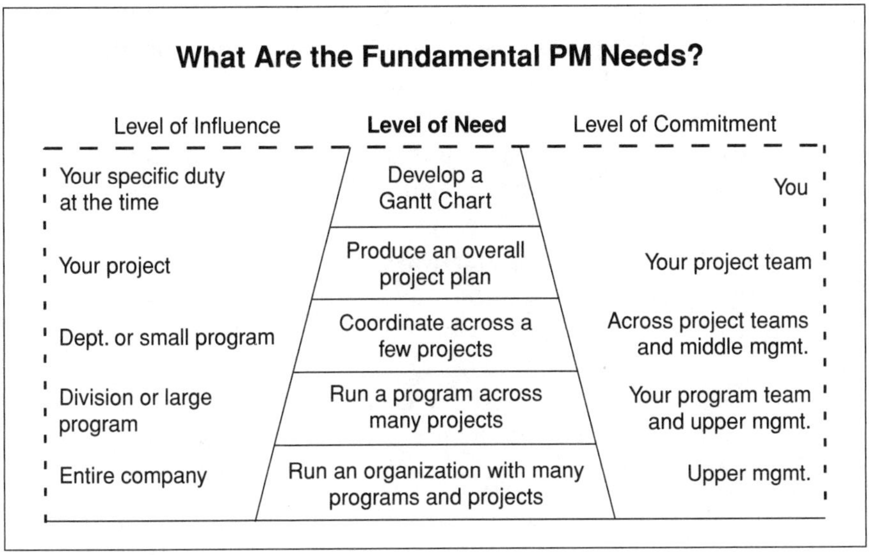

What Are the Fundamental PM Needs?

Level of Influence	Level of Need	Level of Commitment
Your specific duty at the time	Develop a Gantt Chart	You
Your project	Produce an overall project plan	Your project team
Dept. or small program	Coordinate across a few projects	Across project teams and middle mgmt.
Division or large program	Run a program across many projects	Your program team and upper mgmt.
Entire company	Run an organization with many programs and projects	Upper mgmt.

Source: Copyright 3M and Bob Storeygard.

The level of need should really be the driver. View it as an onion that needs to be peeled to see what is the true core need. The client may come to you asking for a Microsoft Project class (a low-level need) when in fact, when you examine their need closely, you may find that this is actually a symptom of not having a good portfolio management process in place (a much higher-level need). You need to find the *systemic need* that is generating the symptom; otherwise, you will always be treating symptoms. *Note*: This usually triggers a more in-depth dialogue, both for the good of the organization or person you are trying to help and for the longer-term health of the company.

Step 2—Clarifying/Assessing the Need(s)

To clarify the true level of need, one has to begin to assess what level of commitment and level of influence will be needed to accomplish the tasks according to the level of need (see Figure 19.1, outer two columns). Sometimes, the needs are very specific and short-term; sometimes, they're not. Regardless, you need to walk into these situations with your eyes wide open so you realize what you are getting into.

This step will enable you to have your first reality check to see if you and/or the requesting organization are adequately positioned to effect the changes that are desired.

The other benefit of this step is to begin to help you scope the magnitude of effort that will be necessary to fulfill the request. Think of the person who walks into a jeweler's shop to ask the time of day, and is instead told how to build a watch. The whole thing is a balancing act. You need to help the organization do the following:

- Meet its immediate needs and deliver value quickly.
- See the whole picture and how short-term solutions, without long-term thinking, effort, vision, and actions, may yet cause defeat.

Once you have clarified what the clients think are their total needs, you are in a position to show the organization the total solution to enable it to assess whether its stated needs go far enough to provide ultimate success.

QUESTION 2 (STEPS 3, 4, AND 5): WHAT CHANGES MUST BE MADE?

What changes need to occur within the organization to increase the effectiveness of project results?

In order to answer this question, the client needs to understand what a solid, healthful, helpful project management environment (complete with the foundation, infrastructure, and processes shown in Figure 19.2) looks like so they can contrast and compare it with their current PM environment (Step 3).

Then, you need to help the clients assess their current situation against that model to see what pieces are adequately in place and which ones are not (Step 4).

Finally, you need to help the client plan for the necessary deployment of those missing pieces that are causing the organization to be less healthy and productive (Step 5). Let's look at each step in more detail.

Step 3—Modeling/Comparing against the Complete PM Environment

The model in Figure 19.2 identifies the components of a complete project management environment. This has affectionately become known at 3M

Figure 19.2
Project Management Environment

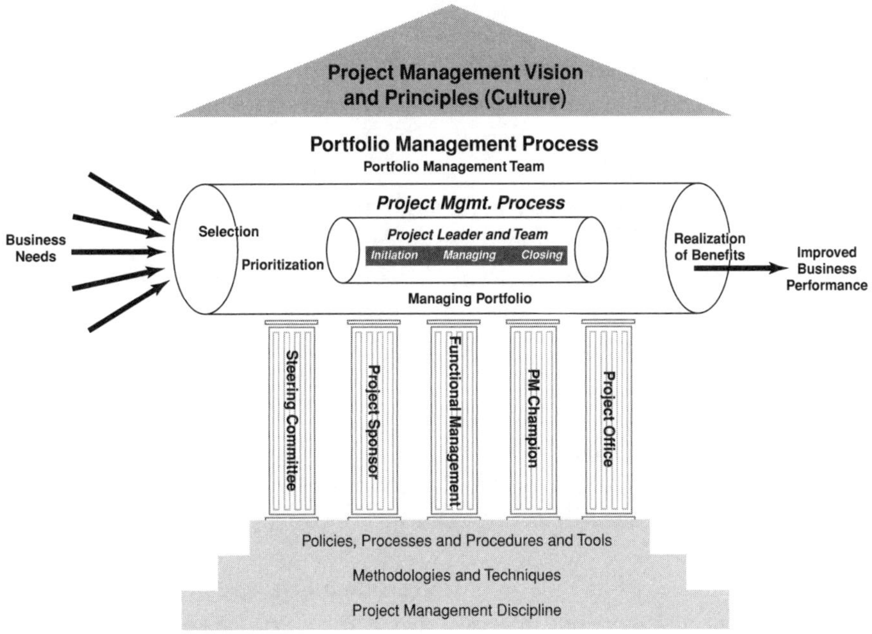

Source: Copyright 3M and Bob Storeygard.

as the "PM Temple" (no religious affiliation intended). I will explain it further using a "house" as a metaphor.

Let's start with the core processes (the small and large "cross beams") that need to provide structure inside the house. There are two fundamental processes at work in the PM environment:

1. The individual project management process (contains the typical life cycle for a given stand-alone project or program)
2. The portfolio management process (contains the higher-level steps to manage multiple project or program initiatives through an organization)

The Processes

The smaller cross beam is where most traditional project management techniques, training, and education focus. This is the core of PMI's *Project*

Management Body of Knowledge (PMBOK), most of this book, and where most project leaders and team members work. This process includes the following:

1. Initiating and Planning the Project/Program
2. Executing and Managing the Project/Program
3. Closing the Project/Program

The larger cross beam is where more traditional management structures take over in shepherding the total workload through an organization. This process begins with some sort of an intake mechanism to look at all the potential work coming in from the larger organization. This, in turn, leads to the following:

1. Selection and Evaluation of the Work
2. Prioritization of the Work
3. Ongoing Management of the Portfolio
4. Realizing the Benefits for the Organization

If an organization has only one project, then obviously there is no need for a portfolio management process. However, as soon as an organization has multiple projects and programs that compete for the same resources, then portfolio management becomes essential.

Organizations with both processes (project and portfolio) effectively functioning will experience a much higher rate or project and program success than those companies coping without these processes. This may seem self-evident, but it is appalling how many organizations attempt to succeed by only deploying good individual project management and forgetting about portfolio management.

The Foundation

Just as a house has to have a foundation, so, too, the complete PM environment must have one (see the bottom three steps). Many project management efforts in companies begin here, by trying to bring some *basic PM discipline* into the organization.

Some organizations try to accomplish this through training and workshops and the institutionalizing of homegrown or purchased *methodologies*. As these methodologies become more accepted and standardized, the organization begins to align other elements with them in terms of *policies, procedures, and common tools*. Together, these lay a firm foundation upon which to build.

The Pillars

The pillars in the model represent the human infrastructure that is necessary to support and sustain the environment. Similar to the walls of a house, these provide the tensile strength for the environment. If any of them are missing, the whole structure is weakened. The following briefly explains the intent of the pillars:

- *Steering Committee.* This is a body of people charged with energizing, directing, and sustaining the portfolio management process. They work to help select, evaluate, prioritize, manage, and follow up on the PM portfolio efforts going through the organization. Note that this committee is differentiated from more traditional "operating committees" that are more concerned with the day-to-day operations of their organizations.
- *Project Sponsor.* Ultimately, this is the person who is paying for and/or has the most to gain or lose from the successful (or unsuccessful) completion of the project or program. I go so far as to say that if you do not have a sponsor, you should not start the project.
- *Functional Management.* These are the people who own the resources that run the business and allocate people to the projects and programs. There needs to be a strong and cooperative relationship between these people and the project/program leaders to share the resources of the organization to both run the business and complete project/program efforts.
- *Project Management Champion.* This is a critical role that should be held by someone who needs to be a visionary/cheerleader/evangelist for the organization in terms of the deployment of the PM discipline. This is somebody who is willing to help keep the effort alive, focused, and well-resourced in the organization. Typically, this person will be in the management ranks and is part of, if not leading, the Steering Committee.
- *Project Office.* This is one of the key functions in sustaining the PM deployment and practice once it has been introduced into an organization. This is a scalable service and should be used to augment, not replace, your existing project leaders. This *is* a personnel investment; however, it may not initially be a full-time person, depending on the size of the organization.

The Roof

The roof of the house represents the organization's declaration and commitment to the good work that has gone on below the roofline. It may take the form of a broader document that states the vision, mission, and guiding principles of the PM environment and can serve to communicate that message to the entire organization. It should be succinct, high-level, and encompass all the components in the house below. This will become the culture of the organization over time.

Once the "PM Temple" is well understood by the organization, it can be used for two primary purposes:

1. To help others understand the main components of a healthful, helpful PM environment
2. To help organizations assess the health of their own areas and plan for necessary interventions to increase their PM effectiveness

Step 4—Establishing Key Processes and Infrastructures

Once there is solid understanding of the whole PM environment, then you can get down to examining the veracity of the existing key processes. Figure 19.3 is an explosion of the two process cross beams from the "PM

Figure 19.3
Project Management Portfolio Process

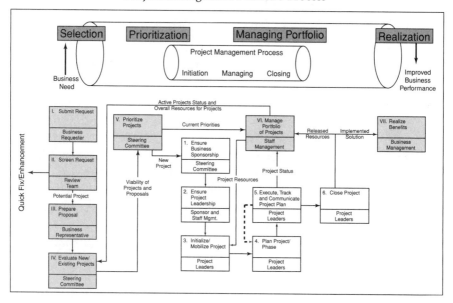

Source: Copyright 3M and Bob Storeygard.

Temple." These provide a more detailed framework of how the components of the individual project and the portfolio management processes should look.

At 3M, we have developed detailed procedures, templates, and specific techniques under each of these boxes that will not be covered in this chapter, but suffice it to say that the key parts of the *portfolio management process framework* (noted in Roman numerals I–VII) are to do the following:

- *Select* from all the possible work requests those potential projects that may be of greatest benefit to the organization. This process entails gathering basic information about the potential projects, screening them for potential size/impact, and then assessing their value and urgency to the organization. The point here is to pick the potential winners for the business.
- *Prioritize* that selected work using the value and urgency criteria, as well as applying dependencies with other projects and potential (macro) resource and budget allocations to arrive at a priority order. This will help to determine the top-priority projects and indicate which ones will wait. Additionally, risk factors can be used as a fine-tuning device to create a balanced portfolio that is challenging, yet attainable.
- *Manage* the portfolio of selected and prioritized work by applying specific resource allocations to projects, then following an iterative loop of reviewing, communicating, and tracking the portfolio. Periodic attention also needs to be given to the selection and prioritization of new work coming into the portfolio. This part of the process should be regularly informed via status reports coming from the project efforts themselves.
- *Realize* the benefits of the overall project or program effort on the business. Specific follow-up needs to happen to make sure that the project or program was not just completed, but that it delivered the intended value to the ongoing business. Many times this step is neglected, resulting in missed opportunities for correction or continuous improvement, celebration of excellent work, and even marketing bonanzas through effective communication of project/program successes and breakthroughs to clients.

Likewise, the *individual project management process* (i.e., the smaller cross beam on Figure 19.3 that is labeled "Initiation—Managing—Closing" and is denoted by Arabic numbers 1–6) represents the process through which each project or program that is part of the portfolio should progress. Again, there is much more detail that could be covered on each of these boxes, but the essence of this process is as follows:

- *Ensure sponsorship and project leadership* for the effort. Without both, projects will meander and usually fail. Part and parcel to this is ensuring thorough training and discussion of the roles that both need to play in the success of project efforts.
- *Initialize and mobilize the project* by getting a solid beginning through the use of classic tools such as problem/opportunity statements, project objectives, scope statements, project charters, and so on.
- *Plan the project or phases* in enough detail to be thorough, realistic, and clear to your team and stakeholders.
- *Execute, track, and communicate the project* through active management of the plan, creating and using a good tracking mechanism, and practicing sound change management procedures.
- *Close the project* by successfully demonstrating the promised results and documenting the post-project review to capture valuable history and lessons learned. Don't forget this step. Without it, companies will not learn from their experiences.

Finally, you need to make sure that the proper *human infrastructure* is in place to support these processes. You can look back to the pillars in the "PM Temple" (Figure 19.2) and to the role designations in the boxes for the portfolio and individual project processes (Figure 19.3) to remind yourself of what key roles and functions are necessary to make these processes and the overall environment work. In particular, I would spend some extra time helping the organization ensure the following:

- Some sort of body is in place to perform the functions of selection and good prioritization discussed here (*steering committee/portfolio management team*) and that they understand their roles.
- *Project sponsors* are clearly identified and understand their active roles regarding the project and what to expect from, and provide to, the project leader/team.
- Qualified and well-trained *project leaders* are put in place or grown/contracted to run the project or program efforts.
- There is provision for a *sustenance mechanism* such as a *project office*, *project champion*, and/or other personnel whose duty is, in part, to keep the PM discipline alive and well and actively contributing to the bottom/top lines.

Step 5—Planning for PM Deployment within an Organization

This step is where "the rubber meets the road" in terms of what has to change in the organization for it to get better and faster. The previous two steps helped to paint the picture of what should be in place to be successful. This step is where the hard work begins.

One of the key roles in deployment, besides yourself as the PM consultant and subject matter expert helping the client, is the PM champion. He or she needs to be at the center of the deployment process. You should also consider putting together a small PM task team to represent the organization and work with the PM champion. This team will be the "actuators" in positioning, customizing, piloting, and rolling out the new processes to the organization.

Figure 19.4 depicts the PM deployment process, which has the following mini-life cycle of its own:

- *Positioning* the organization for the eventual rollout. As a follow-up to the "PM Temple" and the processes, you may need to go more in-depth with the organization to assess its needs; profile their work and current PM practices, issues, and constraints; and make recommendations on how to customize the processes and proceed. Also, senior management needs to buy into the rollout, so the readiness and acceptance of the organization needs to be assessed as well.
- *Customizing* the processes to meet the needs of the organization. The framework is there already, but each organization will put its own spin on the actual processes. This work determines those areas and/or procedures that need to be added/changed or deleted from the original framework processes at an organizational as well as project level.
- *Piloting* the new processes at both the organizational (or portfolio) level and the individual project level, and then assessing the outcome of those pilots. The principle here is twofold: Pick doable, real projects as your pilots; start small and build from success.
- *Rolling out* the new processes to the larger organization. Word will likely spread fast as pilots become visible and successful, and soon all the projects in the organization will desire to follow the new processes. This work also encompasses setting up a continuous improvement loop that feeds back into the deployment process so it can learn from application. The keys here again involve having the PM champion and the project office or sustenance function lead and sustain this continuous improvement effort.

Figure 19.4
Project Management Deployment Process

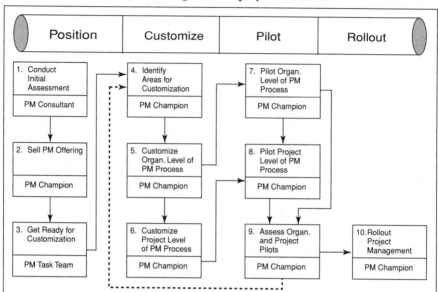

Source: Copyright 3M and Bob Storeygard.

By the completion of this fifth step, you are ready to answer the third fundamental question on how you align and sustain this environment across the organization.

QUESTION 3 (STEPS 6 AND 7): HOW SHOULD CHANGES BE ALIGNED?

How do you make sure that the changes in questions 1 and 2 are properly aligned to make their maximum contributions to the top and bottom lines of the company?

Two remaining steps need to be accomplished to make sure that the new PM environment will have the *thousandfold* effect of which I spoke earlier.

You need to make sure that the organization and the new processes are well aligned and that provisions have been made to sustain the changes (Step 6). Finally, and most importantly, the organization can begin to reap the benefits (Step 7).

Step 6—Aligning and Sustaining the Organization

The key to this step is found back in the overall project management environment model, or the "PM Temple" (see Figure 19.2) that is described earlier. Through understanding both the components of the model and the interdependence of the components, you essentially have the knowledge necessary to ensure that the organization is aligned.

In *The Power of Alignment* by Labovitz and Rosansky (1997), the authors espouse the following concepts about alignment that are relevant to my PM theories:

- "Alignment gives you the power to get and stay competitive by bringing together previously unconnected parts of your organization into an interrelated, easily comprehensible model.
- Alignment gives you the power to create an organizational culture of shared purpose.
- By integrating core business factors, market factors, overall direction, leadership, and culture, alignment gives your organization the power to achieve consistent, defined levels of growth and peak performance."

Proper alignment is key to keeping everything moving forward. Whenever a misalignment occurs (and it will), you can go back to the "PM Temple" to identify where the breakdown occurred and what appropriate interventions are needed in order to get realigned.

The following elements should be in place when assessing the degree of alignment:

- A prescribed methodology that project leaders should follow to run individual projects.
- Portfolio management process to help select, evaluate, prioritize, and manage your project portfolio.
- Adequate and well-understood sponsorship for your projects and programs.
- Designated infrastructure personnel supporting the PM discipline and deployment.
- Foundational PM learning blocks including training, methodologies, and techniques.
- A way to make misalignments visible and painful to your organization, so they get resolved!

This is certainly not an exhaustive list, but it will get you thinking about what things to examine to keep the organization moving forward in the rollout of the new PM environment.

Once the organization is aligned, sustaining the PM environment is a matter of constant vigilance and due diligence on the part of each of the functions, roles, and people involved in it. But the single most important factor in sustaining the organization into the future is the creation of that final pillar in the "PM Temple," the project office function—or, as I called it before, the sustenance function. This can be as simple or sophisticated as the organization needs, but it will serve a key role in keeping the discipline alive, practicing, and flourishing.

Here are just a few benefits that one could expect from an investment in a project office:

- Consistency of effort (standards, procedures, tools, techniques) across the project, program, or organization.
- Better leveraging of scarce resources across a program or organization in an organized manner.
- Consistent and clear metrics to measure project, program, and/or organizational success.
- Better maintenance and centralized repositories of project/program information.
- Potential ability to share and/or swap resources/leaders among projects and programs.
- Better ways to manage and report on interfaces among projects and programs.
- Better visibility for project and program efforts.
- More organizational learning and sharing of best practices.
- Better company competitiveness by continuous improvement via shared and applied learning experiences (good and bad).
- Focus for cultural shift toward better project management and sponsorship.
- More productive teams as similar practices are applied.
- Global recognition as best-practice provider.
- Profitability improvement.

Without this function in your organization, in some form, entropy will eventually set in, the corporate immune system will trigger, and people will go back to "the way we've always done it before." With this in mind, 3M has created another model to help us determine progress in PM deployments to make sure that the signs of a healthy PM environment are present and growing. You will note that it is focused on project management, but can also be used in similar fashion to assess portfolio management.

The model is called the Project Management and Methodology Maturity Model (Figure 19.5). It is intended to be used to view your organization to see whether the items within the stages are present and active. It also reflects a proven sequence in which a company can build an optimal PM environment.

- Stage 1 involves the establishment of competency models, training, and roles to carry forth the discipline. Do you understand the "PM Temple"? Have you established what skills are needed in your organization? Is core training in place?
- Stage 2 contains the sure signs that the discipline is being applied and practiced. Are formal sponsors and teams assigned? Are identifiable pilot projects, published plans, established processes, and the use of consulting (internal and/or external) all in place?

Figure 19.5
Project Management and Methodology Maturity Model

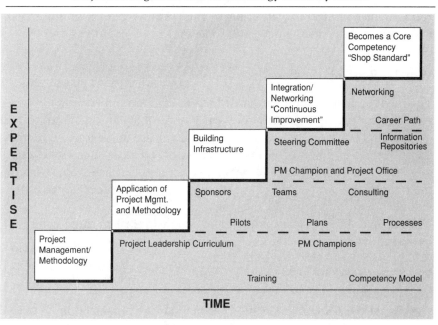

Source: Copyright 3M and Bob Storeygard.

- Stage 3 focuses on building the necessary human and electronic infrastructure. Are steps being taken to build the core pillars of the "PM Temple," such as active and intentional steering committees, an investment in project offices or support functions, and information repositories to capture best practices and methods?
- Stage 4 focuses on making the discipline a profession and establishing continual learning and improvement as the norm. Is PM becoming a career path unto itself? Is networking (internally and externally) in PM becoming an expected part of your job?
- Stage 5 is the stage at which an organization views PM as one of its key core competencies and expects it to be practiced. Is PM no longer considered a "new thing"? Has it become standard operating procedure ("the way we do things")?

The question most organizations ask after reviewing this model is, "How long will it take me to get to Stage 5?" The best and most honest answer is, "It depends." On what? Primarily on the factors of *aggressiveness* and *commitment* of the organization. Additionally, of course, it depends on how many pieces of the overall PM environment you are putting in place. If you are just fine-tuning a pretty good environment, it will not take as long.

Our experience at 3M so far has been that our most aggressive organizations can accomplish quite a bit of the maturity model within a year, while others take much longer, and some may never get there.

Step 7—Reaping the Benefits

This final step is a continuation of Step 6. The more pieces of the complete project management environment you can help an organization put in place and practice, the more benefits you will see in the top and bottom lines. In the top line this means more aligned, creative, innovative, communicative, and productive leadership structures that lead to growth. In the bottom line, you'll realize successful projects and programs that provide the finances to grow the company.

Your investment of time, money, and people in the PM cause will result in the following benefits for your organization:

- Consistent, better-run, faster, and more successful projects and programs.
- Better overall communication throughout the organization (between management and employees, teams and project leaders, sponsors and their projects, and so on).

- Better decision making about what work is critical for the organization to fully resource and budget projects.
- Much clearer roles and responsibilities and thus much less confusion over accountabilities.
- The foundation for continuous learning and thus true continuous improvement.

Clearly, there are many more benefits than can be listed here. But the key to reaping the benefits is to infuse and nurture the PM environment continually wherever you can by encouraging the following individuals in respective ways:

- Project leaders should learn more about PM and how to work with and help their teams.
- Sponsors should communicate regularly and interact with their projects and support them however they can.
- Project teams should apply and follow their methods and share best practices.
- Steering committees should use rigorous selection and prioritization processes, and follow up on completed efforts to see if they really made a difference.
- Everybody should adequately communicate with each other regarding project progress and issues.

CONCLUSION

The elements of the complete, healthful, helpful project management environment (see Figure 19.2) are all intertwined such that together they are much more effective than as stand-alone pieces. The core processes feed on each other (refer back to Figure 19.3). Work continually flows into the portfolio, hopefully influenced by the improved business performance that you realized through previous work. The cycle is also reenergized by resources that are continually coming from completed project or program efforts and will flow back into new efforts as assigned.

This all leads us back to the core challenge, which is that we need to change. Most organizations believe that effective project management is related to how each project is managed versus alignment of the organization to work on and support a few high-priority projects concurrently with their limited human, technical, and financial resources. We need to help our organizations change that long-held paradigm and look instead at the whole

PM environment. Each of the pieces plays an important part in the success of the whole.

Good projects are a start, but if they are going to be focused toward ultimately producing better bottom-line and top-line results, they have to be selected, prioritized, executed, and accomplished within the context of a good portfolio.

A good portfolio strategy and process will certainly help, but without the necessary supporting human infrastructure to supply resources, energy, and focus, "the PM temple will fall."

Both processes and infrastructures need to be well grounded and supported by the core disciplines and methods. Organizations and individuals also need to practice those disciplines and methods in order to achieve project goals and objectives.

And finally, there needs to be vision and direction to create the new path for the culture to follow, for "without vision, the people perish" (Proverbs 29.18).

Our jobs as visionary project and program leaders need to include helping our organizations put these pieces of the complete PM environment in place, and then doing what we can to energize and sustain them.

REFERENCES

Diaz de Leon, Jesus, and Bob Storeygard. 1999[a]."Project Management Deployment Process." Internal 3M document.

————. 1999[b]. "Project Management Portfolio Process." Internal 3M document.

————. 1999[c]. "Project Office Implementation Kit." Internal 3M document.

Labovitz, George, and Victor Rosansky. 1997. *The Power of Alignment*. New York: John Wiley & Sons. Excerpt reprinted by permission of John Wiley & Sons, Inc.

CHAPTER 20

PROFESSIONAL AND PERSONAL DEVELOPMENT MANAGEMENT: A PRACTICAL APPROACH TO EDUCATION AND TRAINING

R. MAX WIDEMAN and AARON J. SHENHAR

This chapter is for the person responsible for project management staff development, but who may not necessarily have a full understanding of project management itself. However, this chapter also offers insights into project management that will be valuable to the individual project management practitioner.

If you are responsible for staff development, perhaps as a member of a human resources (HR) department, your primary concern is to ensure that the right professional development program is available and best suits selected individuals as cost-effectively as possible. For corporate management development, this is relatively simple. Individuals who show consistent promise can be provided with training and experience as they advance in their chosen areas of expertise. This can be provided to these people as needed to improve their contributions to the success of the organization. Because the business environment is consistently established by the culture of the organization, you can provide a development program that is likewise consistent and progressive over an extended time.

However, there are a number of reasons why this is not true for project management. In the private sector, corporate management's responsibility is to improve the bottom line; in the public sector, it is to improve the delivery of services more cost-effectively. Either way, dollars are the measure of organizational success. While it is true that the ultimate measure of success of a project is its contribution to the organization's objectives, this depends on the correct selection of each project in the first place, and this is corporate management's responsibility. At the project manager or project team level, the goal is to conduct a successful project. The difficulty here is that project success can be measured and perceived in different ways, and certainly not by dollars alone.

Setting this issue aside for a moment, we can at least say that the HR professional's goal in project management training is to enable these people to improve the success rate of the organization's projects. Of course, this means improving management skills and style, but this immediately introduces another set of issues for the HR professional. These include the following factors:

- The project management environment and its needs are very different from those of the corporate environment.
- Different types of projects require different management approaches and styles.
- Projects in different periods of their life cycles need different approaches and styles.
- The styles suited to these different periods are sufficiently different that different types of people are more suited to each and, if matched, are more comfortable and hence more effective.
- People with the required personality traits for these different aspects of project work are not evenly distributed throughout the working population, and among this population a significant number are not suited to any aspect of project work at all.

So, for the HR professional to be most effective, he or she must have some understanding of each of these variables. We will examine and briefly describe some of the key aspects of these variables and, in conclusion, provide a simple self-examination test to help determine which aspect of project management best suits an individual.

CORPORATE MANAGEMENT AND PROJECT MANAGEMENT

Some have argued that managing a project simply requires the application of standard management principles to project-type work, that the techniques are similar, and that therefore the difference in the training required is in the details. Certainly, there are similarities and overlaps, but the very definition of the term *project* leads to a dramatically different environment. A well-managed service or production enterprise can be characterized by the following traits:

- Roles and relationships are well understood, having been developed over an extended period.
- Tasks are generally continuous, repetitive, or exhibit substantial similarity.
- Relatively large quantities of services or goods are produced per a given time period.
- Workloads tend to track external demand rather than internal needs.

In contrast, a project may be defined as *a novel undertaking in which a systematic process is followed to create a new product or service, the delivery of which signals completion.*[1] At its simplest, the process followed consists of a series of four broad periods. The first is one in which the goals of the project are conceptualized and validated by comparing alternatives, and priorities and opportunities are assessed. If the results are acceptable and further work is approved, the second is one in which the goals are refined, defined, and planned with specific objectives. Typically, this phase results in a major decision point for corporate management wherein it has the opportunity to review the project and approve the significant funding required for completion of the remainder of the project.

If approval is given, the project moves into an entirely new third period in which the required service or product is actually created. However, that is by no means the end. Once created, a fourth and final period follows. In this period, the service or product must be transferred into the custody of those who will use it, and actions must be taken to ensure customer acceptance and satisfaction. The whole sequence is typically constrained by limited resources. The nature of these four broad periods is significant, and we will return to this later.

Many consider this four-period sequence as the most important difference between corporate management and project management, and the basis of the following features of interest to the HR professional. Project people need training and exposure that emphasize skills and experience to deal with:

- Temporary teamwork and informal relationships within the organization
- A complex management environment in which the work crosses functional boundaries

- Specific time constraints and careful management of shared, limited, and varying resource consumption
- Measurement of progress against plan, which requires looking to the organization of activities and results in the future rather than dwelling on the accomplishments of the past

In a discussion of project resource planning, Marie Scotto has also provided a list of differences between corporate management and project management.[2] Perhaps the most compelling of all is: "The business community believes in understaffing which it can prove is generally good business most of the time." In contrast, projects by their nature are uncertain and hence contain risks for which margins or contingent resources are required. For a project to be underresourced is a recipe for failure. Thus, the very mind-set for project management professional development must be different from that for corporate management training right from the beginning.

THE MEANING OF PROJECT SUCCESS

It is axiomatic that the goal of project management is to be successful; otherwise, the incurring of this management overhead, and the training of staff to do it, is a valueless exercise. Contrary to conventional wisdom, there have been many projects that have been on time and within budget, but the product has not been successful. Similarly, there have been many that have not been on time and within budget, yet by other measures the products have been very successful. Motorola's Iridium is a good example of the former, while the movie *Titanic* is a good example of the latter. From these examples, we can see that just because certain objectives were not achieved does not mean that the project was a failure.

So, project success is much more than just doing what you set out to do. It is also about whether "what you are doing is in fact the right thing to do." Consequently, the ultimate goal of a project, and therefore its measure of success, should be satisfaction with the product on the part of the customer, assuming that the customer is clearly identified. However, project success needs to be defined not only in terms of the acceptability of the project's deliverables (for example, scope, quality, relevance, effectiveness, and so on), but also in terms of its internal processes, such as time, cost, efficiency, and so forth. Finally, and probably most importantly, project success must be assessed in terms of its contribution to the organization that is doing the project—business or otherwise. The timing of the measurement of success may also be critical, as the customer's perception of the product—a measure of customer satisfaction—can also vary considerably as time progresses after the project is completed.

Previous research has shown that project success is a multidimensional construct that inevitably means different things to different people.[3] To be clear, logical, and useful, success criteria by which the relative success or failure of the project may be judged must be expressed at the beginning of a project in terms that are key and measurable. The most important reason is to provide an ongoing basis for management decision making during the course of the project. These key success indicators (KSIs) should reflect the following four dimensions:[4]

1. *Project efficiency*: satisfaction with the project management process—that is, the deliverable is completed on time and within budget, and maybe meets other efficiency measures as well.
2. *Impact on customer*: general acceptance and satisfaction with the project's deliverable on the part of the project's customer and the majority of the project's community at some time in the future. This could include meeting specified performance goals, providing improved service, enhanced reputation, and timely upgrades to the product.
3. *Business and direct success*: key objectives of the project, such as the business objectives of the sponsoring organization, owner, or user. In the case of a not-for-profit project, this could include other direct impacts on the performing organization.
4. *Preparing the future*: To what extent the project contributes to future capabilities and later organizational activities and projects. This may include new technology, new markets, and new organizational infrastructure.

Without agreement on these criteria at the beginning of the project, it will not be possible to measure its success with objectivity. Indeed, the reality of life on many projects is that not everyone has the same aspirations and goals. As a result, the project gets pulled in many different directions by status, pride, or power. Even if this point is a little exaggerated, at the most elementary level the project's owner will be interested in benefiting from the product, while the workers on the project will be interested in benefiting from the process.

However obvious and sensible the setting of project success criteria at the beginning of a project may seem, regretfully, it is not currently a common practice. Without defining these success criteria, how can agreement be reached on a particular project's priorities, the trade-offs involved, the significance of changes, and the overall effectiveness and efficiency of project management post-project? The early definition of a project's KSIs to provide a reference baseline for the correction of divergent activities and progress, as well as how to establish them, should be an essential part of project management professional development.

DIFFERENCES IN PROJECT TYPES AND PROJECT LIFE CYCLE PERIODS

Projects are not only novel undertakings as described earlier in this chapter, but their range in objectives, size, complexity, and technology (areas of project management application) are also almost limitless. To aid in sponsorship planning and decision making, clearly it would be helpful if projects could be categorized into some meaningful and practical classification framework. There have been many approaches to this. Perhaps the most common is the classification by industry.

While this approach is probably the easiest, it is also possibly the least useful, for the number is still large and bears little relationship to the project management methodology involved. For example, a software company could just as easily be involved in a project to extend its office space as a facility owner could be involved in a software project for running its plant. Yet the two projects need to be managed in very different ways.

After conducting a series of studies of more than 250 projects in the early 1990s,[5] Shenhar et al. selected 120 for closer study and proposed a project classification system that is both enlightening and simple. It is included here because it sheds light both on the considerable variation of content for different projects and on where professional development for their staffing might be focused accordingly.

The authors proposed a two-dimensional project typology consisting of project management scope versus technological uncertainty. For practical purposes, the two continuous scales have been reduced to four levels of technological content and three levels of program/project management scope. This matrix is shown in Figure 20.1 and the descriptors along each dimension will now be described briefly.[6]

Figure 20.1
Project Classification

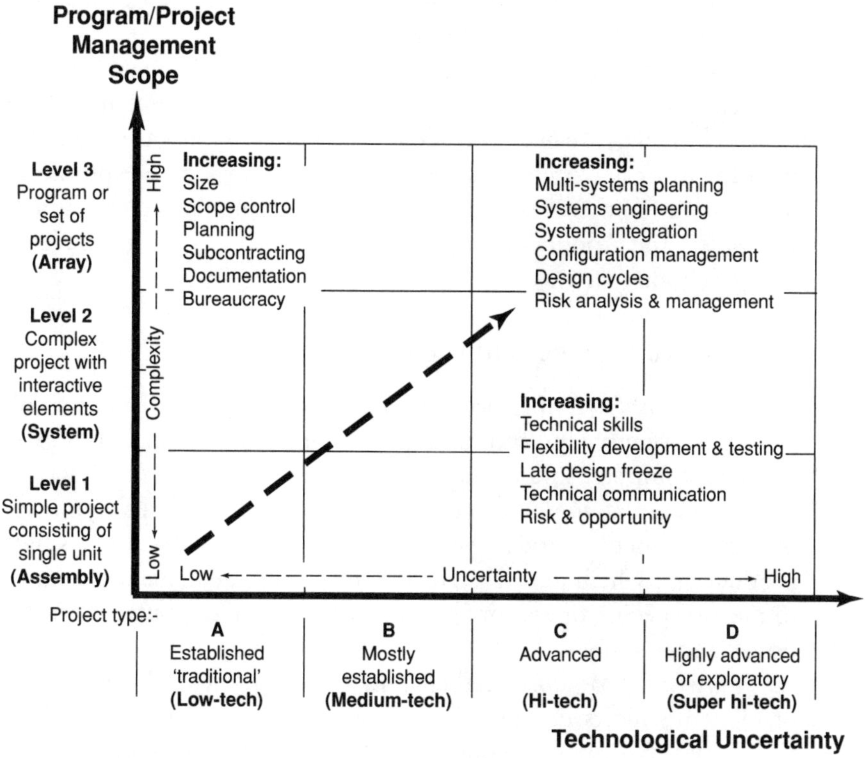

Technological Content

Type A—Low-tech (established technology). These projects rely on existing and well-established base technologies to which all industry players have equal access. They can be very large in scale, but essentially no new technology is employed at any stage. Example: standard building construction.

Type B—Medium-tech (mostly established technology). These projects are similar to Type A, but involve some new technology or feature. While the majority of the work uses existing technology, the new feature provides market advantage but also a higher degree of uncertainty. Examples: new appliance models; concrete construction using advanced carbon fiber reinforcement.

Type C—High-tech (advanced technology). These are projects containing technologies that have been developed prior to project initiation, but which are used together for the first time. Examples: most defense industry projects; new families of computers.

Type D—Super High-tech (highly advanced technology). These are projects that call for the incorporation of technologies that are not entirely existing, are emerging, or even require unknown solutions at the time of project initiation. Such projects incorporate exploratory research and new technology development during project execution. Examples: the Apollo moon-landing project; the Strategic Defense Initiative (Star Wars).

Program/Project Management Scope

Level 1—Assembly (simple project). This is one that consists of a collection of components and modules combined into a single unit. Example: a computer's monitor.

Level 2—System (complex project). This is one that consists of a complex collection of interactive elements and subsystems within a single product, but which jointly perform a range of independent functions to meet a specific operational need. Examples: a computer workstation; a radar system.

Level 3—Array (program). Rather than a single project, this is a series of related projects designed to accomplish broad goals, which produce a widely dispersed collection of systems, which work together for a common mission. Examples: a national communication system; a city; the Internet.

As Figure 20.1 indicates, progression along the technological uncertainty axis leads to the need for increased intensity in technical management. Progression up the program/project management scope axis increases the project management complexity. It also leads to increased intensity and use of project management tools. When both are combined, there is a compounding effect resulting in the need for both added technology management techniques as well as more comprehensive project management techniques. There is also an interaction effect that requires additional attention to systems engineering techniques, system integration, and optimization.

THE NATURE OF PROJECT WORK

The foregoing classification provides a way of categorizing projects and consequently for assessing the extent and type of management techniques required. But what about the different project activities and the people involved? Are there differences in the styles of management that would be most appropriate in managing different project activities and the type of work people do on the project in each case?

It is a common experience that different people respond to different styles of leadership. Some respond better to being told what to do, while others respond better when allowed to think more for themselves. Intuitively, we may suspect that the former aligns more with craft work requiring training, while the latter aligns more with intellectual work where people have more opportunity to educate themselves. Consequently, a more fundamental distinction between or within projects has been suggested for correlation with project management styles.[7]

This distinction has to do with both the type of product emanating from the activity (or work package) and the type of work required to create that product. Depending on the nature of the product, or at least its major element, the effort required to manage the process and to produce the product will require varying degrees of both intellectualism and craftsmanship. From the perspective of management, it is the extent of and balance between these components that provide the distinguishing features.

Thus, we have a simple matrix consisting of two broad types of products—tangible and intangible—and two types of work—craft and intellect. These are defined as follows:

- *Tangible product.* The primary value is in the physical artifact. Examples: a new building; a piece of hardware.
- *Intangible product.* The primary value is in its intellectual property even though there is some tangible product as the vehicle for conveyance. Examples: new software; procedures manual.
- *Craft work.* This work is the result of manual dexterity, has been done before, and essentially requires repetitive effort. Examples: concrete forming; grinding.
- *Intellect work.* This work is the result of applying creative brainpower, has not been done before, and requires new ideas and imagination. Examples: a new design; a new process.

It should be noted that all projects involve intellectual work in their planning, and to this extent all projects appear to be the same. Indeed, this may be the root of a popular misconception that all project management is the same. However, it is the work in the execution period of the project that results in the ultimate product and, as noted earlier, this is what distinguishes one type of project product from another.

At first glance, it might appear that "craft work" is simply the requirement of tangible projects, and that "intellect work" is the requirement of intangible projects. However, a 2×2 matrix introduces the possibility of adding both tangible-intellect projects as well as intangible-craft projects. Figure 20.2 shows the characteristics, results, and some examples of each of all four basic types. More importantly, it indicates the type of education or training required.

We are now ready to connect project management style to personality traits, a vital consideration in selecting staff for project assignments.

PROJECT MANAGEMENT STYLE AND PERSONALITY TRAITS

Kliem and Anderson have pointed out that the project manager's style or approach toward team building is a key variant in managing projects successfully.[8] They observed that "only recently has the influence of the project manager's personality on project performance received recognition." They identified four primary styles regarding how people approach relevant work situations and applied this analysis to the processes of planning, organizing, controlling, and leading. Kliem and Anderson concluded that "knowing the type of [project] environment and the team-building style [required] of the project manager increases the opportunities for selecting the right person for the position."[9] Unfortunately, the descriptors used are not terms familiar to most project-management people.

To bring more recognizable and practical utility to the issue of project-leader selection, we undertook a six-step analysis as follows:[10]

> *Step 1.* A review of 10 years of project management publications was conducted to abstract familiar words or phrases used to describe a project manager's required personal characteristics and skill sets. It excluded words depicting technical experience or know-how. The result was a list of some 200 words or phrases which, not surprisingly, implied that the leader of a project should be a paragon of virtue.
>
> *Step 2.* A literature review of personality typology from which the dominant types most relevant to the project management environment were selected. This was based on two dimensions of focus versus approach as shown in Figure 20.3. This provided four types to which familiar but differentiated project leadership titles could be assigned.

Figure 20.2
Basic Project/Major Element Classification

		Tangible	Intangible
Type of Work or Effort (in the project)	**Intellect** (requires education)	**Characteristic** • Not done before • Subject to linear logic • Requires iterations • Resources less predictable **Result** Development of new physical artifact **Examples** New invention, device; all-new mouse-trap; new product from R&D	**Characteristic** • First of its kind • Creative effort • Nonrepetitive • Resources unpredictable • Exploratory **Result** Development of new piece of intellectual property **Examples** New book, poem, music, movie, etc.; new algorithm, theory, idea; new technology process; new software
	Craft (requires training)	**Characteristic** • Much repetitive effort • Linear logic applies • Learning curve effects • Learn by doing • Resources predictable • Relatively high cost involved **Result** Typical physical artifact **Examples** Typical new physical plant, infrastructure, product, e.g. building, utility, car, appliance	**Characteristic** • Based on previous model • No iterations, only corrections • Learn by repetition • Physical format required only for distribution • Resource predictable • Relatively low reproduction cost **Result** Typical piece of intellectual property **Examples** Typical system, software upgrade, etc.; policies, procedures manual; plan for factory shut-down

Tangible
(Value is in the entity.)

Intangible
(Value is in the content.)

Type of Product (from the project)

Figure 20.3
Four Project Manager Styles

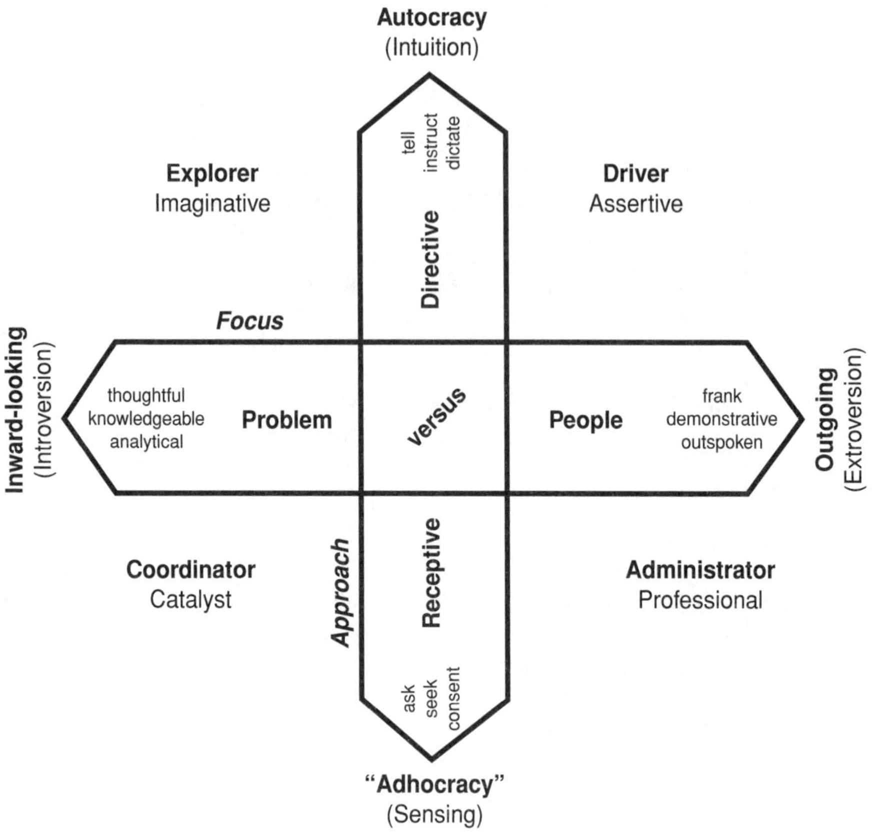

Notes: "Adhocracy" describes a loose, flexible, exploratory project environment. The words in parentheses refer to the well-known Myers-Briggs Type Indicator Grid.

Step 3. Except for those words that plainly referred to all types, each word or phrase in the 200-word list was subjectively assigned to a title.

Step 4. Each group was subdivided into either inherent personality traits or learnable skill sets.

Step 5. Each set was then matched across the four project management types to provide a cross-check and some degree of uniformity.

Step 6. The word groupings were further subdivided into the management processes of planning, organizing, executing, and controlling.

Of course, the propensities and skills of individuals never fit these descriptions exactly. Nor, for that matter, are projects ever that simple. But the arrangement does show a correlation between personal characteristics and the realities of the project management environment. This data provided the basis for the simple "Project Management Style and Skill Sets Questionnaire" self-assessment, which is included as Performance Support Tool 20.1 at the end of this chapter. Figure 20.4 summarizes the project leader types, and the characteristics and skill sets of the four types of project leaders.[11]

Four Types of Project Leaders

The resulting four types of project leaders may be briefly characterized as follows. Bear in mind, however, that all four types should be credible, confident, committed, energetic, hardworking, and self-starting.

The Explorer

The explorer- or entrepreneur-type project leaders have a vision of the future, and projects are the stepping-stones. They are bold, courageous, and imaginative. They search constantly for opportunities and improvements. They are comfortable in the lead, and exude confidence and charisma.

Figure 20.4
Project Leader Types, Characteristics, and Skill Sets

	Explorer	Coordinator	Driver	Administrator
Characteristics:				
Planning	Vision oriented	Mission oriented	Goal oriented	Objective oriented
Organizing	Solution seeker	Conflict mediator	Solution enforcer	Conflict solver
Executing	Inspiring	Understanding	Hard driving	Analytical
Controlling	Determined	Free-form	Rigid	Flexible
Skill Sets:				
Planning	Focus long range	Focus on participation	Focus short range	Focus on solutions
Organizing	Evokes dedication	Obtains willing effort	Gets early results	Harmonizes effort
Executing	Leads by example	Develops commitment	Uses partnerships	Reinforces commitment
Controlling	Makes major decisions	Reaches closure	Makes most decisions	Implements decisions

Note: These words and phrases have been taken from the larger word sets that depict each cell as presented in Tables A and B of Working Paper #5.3, "Dominant Personality Traits Suited to Running Projects Successfully—And What Type Are You?," AEW Services, 1996.

They are good at networking and selling. However, they may have little time for day-to-day problems, which are delegated to others. Their project power derives from past experience, enthusiasm, and superior ability to communicate.

The Coordinator

Coordinators are just as important as explorers when the project period or situation calls for facilitation. They generally take a more independent and detached view of their surroundings. Coordinators are responsive to the views of project team members, who must take responsibility for their own decisions. Therefore, their role is to ensure that team issues surface, and are discussed and resolved to the team's mutual satisfaction. These individuals tend to be humble, sensitive, and willing to compromise. The coordinator's power is derived from his or her ability to persuade others to compromise.

The Driver

Drivers are distinctly action oriented and are both hardworking and hard driving. They are pragmatic, realistic, resourceful, and resolute; their focus is on project mission and precise project goals. They are generally well prepared and self-disciplined, so for those who have similar traits, they are easy to work with. Conflict is likely with those who are not so inclined. Their power is derived from authority, and they are quite prepared to use it.

The Administrator

Administrators recognize the need for stability, typically in order to optimize productivity through maximizing repetition to the extent possible on a project to get the work finished. Often, requisite information must be assembled and carefully analyzed, with thought given to the trade-off and how conflicts and problems can be resolved and disposed of in advance. Work must be carefully scheduled and procedural if potential gains are to be realized and all the pieces carefully put in place. The administrator's power derives from intellectual logic and organizational achievement. Work is highly organized.

In reality, experienced and skilled project managers often find themselves shifting gears to suit current circumstances during the course of a project. Nevertheless, experience and the literature suggest that it is unusual to find all four traits in a single person, and few can switch from one extreme to the other. What is important throughout all four styles is the project manager's force of personality, tenacity, and skill.

Matching Personality Type to Project Type and Project Life-Cycle Period

It would be very satisfying if it were possible to relate these various project management elements into one cohesive pattern. However, project management is multidimensional, apparently with no direct correspondence among elements. Nevertheless, there do appear to be some common trends.

From that database of more than 120 projects mentioned earlier, Shenhar et al. observed that a number of common project variables progress from one form to another across the technological uncertainty spectrum shown in Figure 20.1. For example, from established technology projects to highly advanced or exploratory projects, design cycles and a design freeze progress from only one cycle with a design freeze prior to execution to multiple cycles and late design freeze well into the execution period. Similarly, communications progress from formal and relatively few regularly scheduled meetings to multiple, frequent, and informal interaction.

In the former type of project, the project manager must have good administrative skills and a firm style, and he or she must stick to the initial plan. At the high end, the project manager must be an exceptional technical leader to handle highly skilled professionals, adopt a highly flexible style, and live with continuous change.[12] This suggests that at the low end, a good administrative or driver type is required, while at the high end what is required is a good explorer/coordinator.

Similarly, we might compare the different types of major elements in projects with technological uncertainty and management style. As shown in Figure 20.2, most traditional projects fall into the tangible/craft quadrant and require the driver type of manager for their execution. Conversely, the major elements of many of the high- or super high-tech projects fall into the intangible/intellect quadrant, requiring the explorer/coordinator type of manager for execution.

Matching Style to the Project Life-Cycle Period

We can go further and match the project manager style required on a traditional project with its project life cycle as follows.

Reemphasizing our earlier description of the project management process, every well-run traditional project has four major periods in its life cycle. At this most basic level, a project must first be conceived and articulated as a goal or objective. That goal or objective must then be developed into a viable and doable set of activities. With appropriate approvals and sufficient time and funding, the developed plan can then be executed.

Finally, the project must be properly finished with the product successfully transferred into the care, custody, and control of its new owners.

Figure 20.3 and a moment's thought suggest the allocation of style to period as follows:

- Start out with the explorer type for the concept period.
- Proceed to the coordinator type in the development or planning period.
- Move to an assertive driver type in the execution period.
- Culminate with the administrator type in the clean-up/finishing period.

Obviously, these are oversimplified generalizations, but there can be no question that project leadership style and the need for flexibility to suit particular circumstances must be important determinants of project success. The successful development, production, and testing of the largest and most complex aircraft built to date, the Boeing 777, is an instructive example of the most appropriate style of project management.[13] Conversely, the infamous *Challenger* space shuttle disaster was perhaps the most vivid and tragic example of the application of inappropriate project management style.[14]

Failure to match an appropriate style with the particular project or element can quickly demoralize the project workforce and lead to unsatisfactory project results. Figure 20.5 takes the same period descriptions shown in Figure 20.4 and illustrates vividly what can happen when management assigns to a project a person with an inappropriate style.

Although still tenuous, it is possible to postulate some guiding relationship such as that shown in Figure 20.6. Based on the observations made earlier, this table suggests that to achieve optimum success there must be some correlation between the type of project leader, the type of product, and the period of the project. For example, for established technology-project elements with their shorter-term success goals, a low-key or regular progression through the four project management styles is shown. These compare with those of higher technology, with their relatively longer-term success goals, and in which the styles of the explorer and coordinator types need to drive further down through the project life cycle.

The research cited suggest that the balance between intellectualism and craftsmanship required in producing a major element of a project is what determines the most appropriate management style for producing that element. Hence, to attain the highest potential on a large and complex project, one single management style may not be appropriate throughout the project organization or through all periods of the project life cycle. It is evident that failure to match an appropriate style to project

Figure 20.5
Project Leader's Image When Appropriately and Inappropriately Assigned

Project Leader Type	As seen when appropriately assigned	As seen when not appropriately assigned
Explorer	Vision-oriented Solution seeker Inspiring Determined Focus long range Evokes dedication Leads by example Makes major decisions	Starry-eyed Devious Out of touch Unworkable Far-out Scattered Unrealistic Mischievous
Coordinator	Mission-oriented Conflict mediator Understanding Free-form Focus on participation Obtains willing effort Develops commitment Reaches closure	Impromptu Outsider Sentimental Leisurely Contriving Obtuse Overpersonalizes Stirs up conflict
Driver	Goal-oriented Solution enforcer Hard driving Rigid Focus short range Gets early results Uses partnerships Makes most decisions	Acts first, thinks later Arrogant Domineering Dictatorial Lacks long-range view Ladder climber Self-seeker Untrusting
Administrator	Objective-oriented Conflict solver Analytical Flexible Focus on solutions Harmonizes effort Reinforces commitment Implements decisions	Over zealous Long-winded Overanalytical Indecisive Hidebound Ruling Unemotional Unglamorous

Figure 20.6
Potential Selection of Leader Type or Management Style to Optimize Success,
Given the Project Type and Project Phase

Project type / Project period	Concept C	Development or definition D	Execution E	Close out or finish F
Established technology	Explorer or coordinator	Coordinator or driver	Driver	Administrator
Mostly established (medium-tech)	Explorer	Coordinator	Driver	Driver or administrator
Advanced (hi-tech)	Explorer	Explorer	Coordinator	Driver
Highly advanced or exploratory (super hi-tech)	Explorer	Explorer	Explorer	Coordinator

circumstances can quickly demoralize the project workforce and lead to unsatisfactory project results.

These considerations should be invaluable to management in designing organizational structures for complex projects. It should also prove invaluable to the HR professional in designing project-management development programs for the organization's portfolio of projects. The HR professional can also help to ensure that individuals with the necessary force of personality, tenacity, and skills also have the most suitable leadership styles for maximizing the probability of a successful project outcome.

AVAILABILITY OF DIFFERENT TYPES OF PEOPLE FOR PROJECT WORK

For those familiar with the Myers-Briggs Type Indicator (MBTI), the similarities between the four types of project leaders identified earlier and the four leading types in the MBTI typology will come as no surprise. For those not familiar with the MBTI, it is based on the work of Carl Jung et al. (circa 1920). However, Keirsey and Bates[15] have shown that the concepts bear a marked similarity to Hippocrates' views some 25 centuries earlier. Hippocrates spoke of the four gods Apollo, Dionysus, Epimetheus, and Prometheus, each having a distinct personality temperament.

Thus Jung, reverting to Greek mythology, diverged from the twentieth-century notion that people are fundamentally alike in their motivation, and postulated instead that people are fundamentally different in their personalities. What is important, he suggested, is people's preferences for how they function, and so they may be typed accordingly.

The MBTI postulates that the four temperaments give rise to four separate but interrelated ranges of personal preferences or natural tendencies in a given situation. These ranges may be characterized as follows:

- Information gathering.
- Focus.
- Decision making.
- Orientation.

Combining these four results in 16 possible characteristic types. Presentation is typically in the form of a 4×4 grid, each cell containing descriptive text. Underlying this layout is a primary X-Y cruciform formed by the first two ranges, with each quadrant containing a secondary x-y cruciform formed by the second two ranges. The primary quadrants are mirror images of one another. The two sets together result in the 16 types as shown by the 4×4 grid structure in Figure 20.7.

The personality styles and their preferences represented by each cell in the grid reflect the interaction of various combinations of temperaments, rather than the individual temperaments on their own. The descriptions provided by the MBTI give valuable insight into the differences among normal, healthy people. In project teamwork, these differences can be the source of much difficulty in understanding and communication—a consideration that the HR professional should not overlook in designing professional development programs.

COMPARISON OF PROJECT MANAGER'S STYLE WITH MBTI

Comparison of the two cruciforms shown in Figures 20.3 and 20.7 is very revealing. From Figure 20.3, it will be noted that the X axis, marked *Focus*, corresponds to the Introvert-Extrovert axis of the MBTI grid. Similarly, the Y axis, marked *Approach*, corresponds to the Intuitive-Sensing

Figure 20.7
The MBTI 4×4 Grid Structure

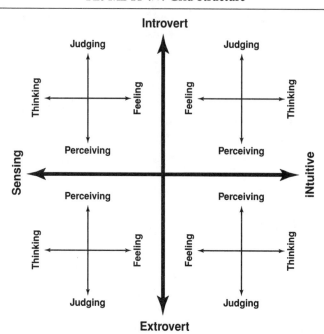

Note: The capitalized characters in the main axis headings are the MBTI reference characters.

axis. Fortunately for us, Keirsey and Bates have indicated approximate percentages of the population that correspond to each of the 16 MBTI types. Possibly, these percentages represent only the North American population, but still the data provide a useful distribution.

Keirsey and Bates indicate the following percentages: Sensing 75 percent, Intuitive 25 percent, Extrovert 75 percent, Introvert 25 percent, Thinking 50 percent, Feeling 50 percent, Perceiving 50 percent, Judging 50 percent.

Just examining the four major quadrants of the grid is instructive. As shown in Figure 20.8, the distribution is heavily weighted toward the extrovert-sensing type (about 55 percent), many of whom are sometimes disparagingly referred to as the "touchy-feely" types. This compares with the much smaller number, in the opposite quadrant, of introvert-intuitive types (only about 5 percent), recognizable as thoughtful but generally unsociable loners. The remaining two quadrants are about equally divided at 20 percent.

To determine which types of people would be suited to some form of

Figure 20.8
Population Distribution in the Primary Quadrants of the MBTI Grid

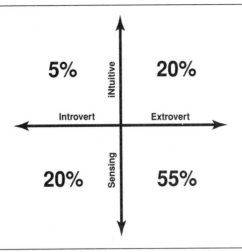

Note: This figure has been reoriented to match the orientation of Figure 20.3.

project work, we conducted a study of the extensive descriptions provided by Keirsey and Bates for each type in the MBTI grid. Of course, few people fall neatly and exactly into a given cell. Even if they do, they probably have a significant bias one way or another. However, for purposes of broad population analysis such as this, the distribution is instructive.

For the analysis, key phrases that appear to be most relevant to the project management team environment were abstracted from these descriptions. A subjective and coarse assessment was then made as to whether the population in the cell fell into the following categories:

- Strongly inclined toward project-management leadership
- More likely a mixture of leader- and follower-suited people
- Probably a mixture of project- and non-project-oriented people
- Unsuited to project management teamwork at all[16]

This enables us to make some assessment of the numbers of different types of project-suited people in the population at large. Figure 20.9 shows a reoriented MBTI grid with a few key words to reflect the flavor of those in each cell and their approximate percentages of the population at large. Each cell in the grid, by the way, is referenced according to its position on each of the four basic MBTI axes shown in Figure 20.7.

Figure 20.10 shows the same grid shaded to reflect six different

Figure 20.9
The MBTI Grid as Seen from the Project Management Perspective

Explorer   **N**   **Driver**

INTJ 1%	INTP 1%	ENTP 5%	ENTJ 5%
Compelling vision Self-confident Strategic Creative Drive	Vision Concentrated Analytical Impatient Not a builder	Alert to next move Analytical Good judge Too many projects Restless	Drive to lead Harnesses people Structured Pushes hard Enjoys responsibility
INFJ 1%	**INFP 1%**	**ENFP 5%**	**ENFJ 5%**
Strong contributor Consistent Looks to future Enjoys problems Good at public relations	Idealistic Prefers values, not goals Perfectionist Impatient with detail	Has influence Skilled with people Likes drama Emotional Gets team off track	Good leader Charismatic Cooperative Organized Good follower
ISFJ 6%	**ISFP 5%**	**ESFP 13%**	**ESFJ 13%**
Service oriented Works hard Dependable/ responsible Likes stability Down-to-earth	Hedonic Impulsive Not a planner Spender, not saver Insubordinate	Adept at selling Excellent at PR Enjoys entertaining Impulsive Conceals problems	Sociable Interacts well Orderly Conscientious Needs appreciation
ISTJ 6%	**ISTP 7%**	**ESTP 13%**	**ESTJ 13%**

Practical, thorough
Persevering
Patient
Decisive
Not a risk taker
	Impulsive
	Thrives on
	  excitement
	Hunger for action
	Irresponsible
	Dislike of authority
		Resourceful
		Manipulative
		Ruthlessly
		  pragmatic
		No follow-through
		Antisocial
			Responsible
			Dependable
			Highly organized
			Loyal, in tune
			Pillar of strength

I   **E**

Coordinator   **S**   **Administrator**

Note: The percentages show the approximate proportion of the type in the total population.

Figure 20.10
The MBTI Grid and Suitability to Project Teamwork

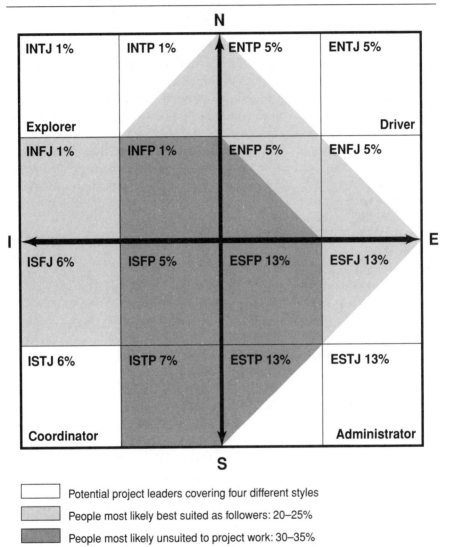

project-personality types. If the analysis is reasonably correct, then we may deduce that the project population is distributed as follows: The explorer (entrepreneur) type makes up only about 1 to 2 percent of the population. Rather more—some 5 to 10 percent—are of the driver (marshal) type. A similar number of coordinator (catalyst) people are available for facilitative-type duties. There are considerably more—25 to 30 percent—administrator (stabilizer) professional types. Another 20 to 25 percent are probably more suited as followers. That still leaves about a third of the population who are most likely not at all comfortable working on projects.

If these relationships are anywhere close to reality, then in a typical large organization contemplating moving to a project-oriented style of management about a third of the workforce may be unsuited to working in the new environment. Thus, we make a mistake if we think that everyone will be highly motivated by working on projects. At the other end of the scale, in a workforce population of, say, 100, only one or two people may be seriously capable of successfully conceptualizing a project, and then, no doubt, only if they have sound project management experience. Indeed, in this size of firm, these could be limited to the CEO and his or her senior vice president.

These are serious considerations for the HR professional, especially one in an organization that is in the process of switching from an essentially functional structure to a management-by-projects structure.

CONCLUSION

It is not difficult to argue that many of the problems experienced on projects in their implementation periods stem directly from ill-considered requirements proposed in the conceptual period of the project. Worse still may be the inappropriate allocation of people whose temperaments do not match the requirements of the type of project and its particular period. Considering the scarcity of people naturally suited to this early work, the rate of unsatisfactory projects should not come as a surprise.

It is up to the HR professional to ensure that these limitations are clearly understood by all concerned and that professional development is provided accordingly.

NOTES

1. "Wideman Comparative Glossary of Common Project Management Terms," V. 2.0; www.pmforum.org/library/glossary/PMG_P07.htm.

2. Marie Scotto. "Project Resource Planning," in *Project Management Handbook*, San Francisco: Jossey-Bass, 1998, Chapter 13.

3. Aaron J. Shenhar, Dov Dvir, and Ofer Levy. "Mapping the Dimensions of Project Success." *Project Management Journal*, Vol. 28, No. 2, June 1997: 5–13.

4. This is a composite of ideas reflected in various success factors and indicators quoted in the "Wideman Comparative Glossary of Common Project Management Terms" at the web site www.pmforum.org/.

5. A. J. Shenhar, "From Low- to High-Tech Project Management," *R&D Management* 23, 3, Oxford, UK: Blackwell Publishers, 1993: 199–214; A. J. Shenhar and D. Dvir, "Toward a Typological Theory of Project Management," *Research Policy*, Vol. 25, 1996: 607–632; A. J. Shenhar, "From Theory to Practice: Toward a Typology of Project Management Styles," *IEEE Transactions on Engineering Management*, 41, 1, 1998: 33–48; D. Dvir, S. Lipovetsky, A. J. Shenhar, and A. Tishler, "In Search of Project Classification: A Non-Universal Approach to Project Success Factors," *Research Policy*, Vol. 27, 1998: 915–935.

6. A. J. Shenhar and R. M. Wideman. "Improving PM: Linking Success Criteria to Project Type." Proceedings of Project Management '96 Symposium, Calgary, Alberta, Canada, May 1996: 71–76.

7. ———. "Towards a Fundamental Differentiation between Projects." Proceedings of PICMET Management and Engineering Conference, Portland, OR, July 1997.

8. Ralph L. Kliem and Harris B. Anderson. "Teambuilding Styles and Their Impact on Project Management Results." *PMI Journal* 27(1), 1996: 41–50.

9. Ibid., 50.

10. R. M. Wideman. "Dominant Personality Traits Suited to Running Projects Successfully—And What Type Are You?" Working Paper #5.3, AEW Services, 1996.

11. Ibid., abstracted from Tables A and B.

12. A. J. Shenhar and Dov Dvir, "Managing Technology Projects: A Contingent Exploratory Approach." Proceedings 28th Annual Hawaii International Conference on System Sciences, 1995, Table 1: 500.

13. K. Sabbagh. "777: First Flight, an Inside Look at the Innovative Production of the Boeing 777." PBS Home Video, Channel 4 London, 1993.

14. R. P. Feynman. *What Do You Care What Other People Think?* New York: Bantam Books, 1989: 113–237.

15. David Keirsey and Marilyn Bates. *Please Understand Me: Character and Temperament Types*, Del Mar, CA: Prometheus Nemesis Book Co., 1984.

16. R. Max Wideman. "Project Teamwork, Personality Profiles and the Population at Large: Do We Have Enough of the Right Kind of People?" Project Management Institute Seminar/Symposium, 1998.

PERFORMANCE SUPPORT TOOL 20.1:
PROJECT MANAGEMENT STYLE AND SKILL SETS QUESTIONNAIRE

A brief self-test designed to highlight your predominant project management style and skill sets. Do they match? What kind are you?

This questionnaire is in two parts. Part A identifies your preferred or instinctive management style associated with each of the four basic project management functions:

- Planning
- Organizing
- Executing
- Controlling

Similarly, Part B assesses your dominant skill-set capabilities as a project manager. Just follow the instructions.

The assessment is based on the following four broad project management styles:

- Explorer (E)
- Coordinator (C)
- Driver (D)
- Administrator (A)

Your own style is revealed upon completing the scorecard that follows the questionnaire. Further information on this typology is provided under the "Interpretation of Results" section on the last page.

A full version is available from:

AEW Services
Vancouver BC
Canada
Voice: 604-736-7025

You can contact me by e-mail at: max_wideman@sfu.ca

Part A—Self-test instructions: Circle one word or phrase in every row that best matches which approach you most prefer, or that makes you feel most comfortable, when working *on a project as the project leader.* Try not to hesitate in making your selections.

	W	X	Y	Z
I feel most comfortable when I am/have (a/an) . . .				
1	ideological	following tradition	Objective	sensitive to personal goals
2	analytical	inspiring	Understanding	hard-driving
3	resolute	precise	Bold, courageous	empathetic
4	power from persuasion	power from authority	Power from intelligence	power from enthusiasm
5	team player	thought provoking	Results-oriented	weighing alternatives
6	conflict solver	solution seeker	Conflict mediator	solution enforcer
7	autocratic	bureaucratic	Charismatic	democratic
8	freewheeling	well planned	Systematic	seemingly chaotic
9	tenacious	in tune	Strong willed	prudent
10	procedure-oriented	value-oriented	Process-oriented	policy-oriented
11	resourceful	reliable	Pioneering	loyal
12	spontaneous	decisive	Reserved	individualistic
13	opportunity driven	team driven	Management driven	information driven
14	objective oriented	vision oriented	Mission oriented	goal oriented
15	rigid	flexible	Determined	free-form
16	sensitive	realistic	Rational	shrewd
17	creative	resilient	Disciplined	organized
18	administrating	in the lead	on the sidelines	have authority
19	risk resolver	risk mitigator	risk-taker	risk avoider
20	good facilitator	good director	Good manager	good leader
21	idealistic	helpful	Emphatic	evaluative
22	professional	opportunist	Probing	pragmatic
23	information distributor	information collector	Information generator	information sharer
24	people-oriented	compliance-oriented	Situation-oriented	stakeholder-oriented

(Continued)

Part B—Self-test instructions: Circle one phrase in every row that best matches what appeals to you most, or you most enjoy, when working *on a project as the project leader*. Try not to hesitate in making your selection.

I most enjoy my work when I am able to . . .

	W	X	Y	Z
1	work around problems	advocate self-correction	Confront problems	generate solutions
2	reinforce commitment	lead by example	Develop commitment	drive using partnerships
3	produce results	produce stability	Produce a vision	produce feedback
4	foster responsive reporting	optimize reporting	Institute effective reporting	minimize reporting
5	delegate	interact	Execute	administer
6	harmonize effort	evoke dedication	Obtain willing effort	get early results
7	give direction	give encouragement	Map out direction	foster self-managed work
8	probe	elaborate	Deliberate	innovate, generate ideas
9	use power by networking	use power by persuasion	use power by authority	use power by consent
10	get things accepted	get things recognized	get things agreed	get things done
11	direct	administer	Inspire	challenge
12	sidestep politics	recognize politics	Manage conflict	use politics
13	enthuse, excite	encourage	Enforce	build confidence
14	focus on solutions	focus long range	Focus on participation	focus short range
15	make most decisions	implement decisions	Take major decisions	reach closure on decisions
16	compromise	coordinate	Collaborate	achieve
17	empower	guide	Constrain	converge
18	use available people	attract the best followers	Coach available people	demand the best people
19	create plans	work with information	Conceptualize plans	build consensus plans
20	foster team building	foster healthy competition	Foster team work	foster personal growth
21	motivate	negotiate	Integrate	summarize
22	keep stakeholder contact	win stakeholder support	Listen to stakeholder	cultivate stakeholders
23	unify by authority	unify by agreement	Unify by enthusiasm	unify by ownership
24	brain-storm	clarify	Analyze and rationalize	envision

Scorecard Scoring instructions:

1. Carefully transfer your selections from Parts A and B by placing an **X** over the corresponding square in the grids below as marked by row number and the column letter in the cell. Note that the cell letters are not all in the same order, so make sure your selections match the cell names in each case.

Part A—Personal Characteristics **Part B—Personal Skill Sets**

Planning					Planning				
1	W	X	Y	Z	1	W	X	Y	Z
3	Y	Z	W	X	3	Y	Z	W	X
8	Z	W	X	Y	8	Z	W	X	Y
14	X	Y	Z	W	14	X	Y	Z	W
19	Y	Z	W	X	19	Y	Z	W	X
24	Z	W	X	Y	24	Z	W	X	Y
Totals:	E	C	D	A	Totals:	E	C	D	A
Organizing					Organizing				
5	W	X	Y	Z	5	W	X	Y	Z
6	X	Y	Z	W	6	X	Y	Z	W
11	Y	Z	W	X	11	Y	Z	W	X
13	W	X	Y	Z	13	W	X	Y	Z
16	Z	W	X	Y	16	Z	W	X	Y
21	W	X	Y	Z	21	W	X	Y	Z
Totals:	E	C	D	A	Totals:	E	C	D	A
Executing					Executing				
2	X	Y	Z	W	2	X	Y	Z	W
7	Y	Z	W	X	7	Y	Z	W	X
12	Z	W	X	Y	12	Z	W	X	Y
18	X	Y	Z	W	18	X	Y	Z	W
20	Z	W	X	Y	20	Z	W	X	Y
22	X	Y	Z	W	22	X	Y	Z	W
Totals:	E	C	D	A	Totals:	E	C	D	A
Controlling					Controlling				
4	Z	W	X	Y	4	Z	W	X	Y
9	W	X	Y	Z	9	W	X	Y	Z
10	X	Y	Z	W	10	X	Y	Z	W
15	Y	Z	W	X	15	Y	Z	W	X
17	W	X	Y	Z	17	W	X	Y	Z
23	Y	Z	W	X	23	Y	Z	W	X
Totals:	E	C	D	A	Totals:	E	C	D	A
Grand totals:					Grand Totals:				

(Continued)

2. Add up the number of **X**'s that you have entered in each column of each of the eight groups. Enter that number in the cells marked E, C, D, or A and circle the highest. If you have a tie, circle both. Also, add up the grand totals as shown. You are now ready to interpret the results.

Interpretation of Results
Part A—Personal Characteristics

Part A of the questionnaire identifies your natural, instinctive or preferred management style under the four basic project management functions of planning, organizing, executing and controlling. The four columns of the scorecard represent four specific project management styles of explorer (E), coordinator (C), driver (D), and administrator (A). These four types are described below.

Circled totals indicate your dominant style for each of the four project management functions.

Note: The following characteristics are required by all:

Being credible, confident, committed, energetic, hardworking, and self-starting.

Part B—Personal Skill Sets

Similarly, Part B assesses your dominant skill-set capabilities as a project manager.

Note: The following skills are required by all:

Ability to communicate well, plan, prioritize, organize, exercise control, and be resourceful.

The highest of the grand totals of all eight sets indicate your overall dominant strength.

Project Manager/Leader Style Typology

The *explorer* is typically an entrepreneur who is bold, courageous, imaginative, and comfortable in the lead. The *coordinator* is responsive to the views of project team members and consequently is a master at achieving results through facilitation. The *driver* is distinctly action oriented and focused on precise project goals. The *administrator* is a master of organization and painstaking detail, one who recognizes the need for stability to get the work finished properly.

For a traditional project involving established technology and in very simplistic terms, the *explorer* is the dominant management style needed in the conceptual period of a project; the *coordinator* is needed in the definition or development period; the *driver* in the execution period; and the *administrator* in the finishing period.

In practice, a project manager may need to adopt a different style to deal with a particular situation. Notwithstanding their dominant styles, most experienced project managers are capable of modifying their styles to an adjacent column as occasion requires. However, it is progressively more difficult to adopt a style that is more than one column removed.

From a project management perspective, the most effective combination is having instinctive style (Part A) and skill sets (Part B) for all four functions, all in the same column, and applying them to the recommended period of a project.

Lack of a dominant style through all four functions in Part A may indicate either limited experience or a higher level of flexibility. Similarly, skill sets that do not fall under your dominant style may indicate areas worth improving by training and experience.

CHAPTER 21

ETHICS MANAGEMENT: ARE YOU REALLY PROTECTED?

CATHERINE DAW

$\mathbf{T}$he *Oxford Dictionary* defines *ethics* as: (1) the science of morals in human conduct; (2a) moral principles; rules of conduct; (b) a set of these (*medical ethics*).

Simply put, ethics involves learning what is right or wrong, and then doing the right thing. However, "the right thing" may not be as clear or straightforward as it seems. Ethical dilemmas in the workplace and on projects are not simply a matter of "Should Jane lie to her boss?" or "Should we award this contract to vendor A?"

The emergence of business ethics over recent years is based on the increasingly complex and dynamic nature of business today. Organizations have realized the need for structure and guidance to ensure the image of supporting the common good and not harming others. Ninety percent of business schools now conduct courses in business ethics. Many corporations have established and implemented codes of ethics, codes of conduct, ethics committees, ethics training, and policies and procedures to resolve ethical dilemmas. Unfortunately, these codes are not always geared toward the practical needs of leaders, managers, and project managers—the people primarily responsible for managing ethics on a day-to-day basis. The Project Management Institute (PMI) has a documented code of ethics for its project management professionals—a good starting point in outlining ethical principles for the project management profession. However, values and ethics that will work on projects within an organization still need to be established.

The Chapter 21 Glossary provides further definitions and explanations of the terms: morality, law, ethics, and values. These definitions provide clarification of the language of right and wrong.

Core Values and Performance Maxims

This chapter will focus on the practical application of an ethical decision-making model and the types of ethical dilemmas faced on projects. In determining how to set the stage for ethics within the context of projects, consider a model of four core values or positive norms (see Figure 21.1) and five performance maxims as described in Vincent Di Norcia's book, *Hard Like Water*, and discussed here. He lays out the need for a base from which organizations can begin to establish not only their own codes of ethics, but also how to ensure their application and performance within the business environment. Business is driven by results, and projects are intended to generate key business deliverables to achieve those results.

Ethical values are supported by a number of performance maxims. These allow individuals and corporations to establish a strong base on which to live by their ethical values and resolve ongoing ethical dilemmas. Di Norcia suggests these five performance maxims:

1. *Do no harm.* No choice is free of risk. When considering options it is important to minimize risk and protect people and life from harm.
2. *Solve the problem.* Identify the ethical dilemma/problem, determine solutions, and implement the best achievable solution.
3. *Enable informed choice.* This includes communication and ensuring knowledge of all potential choices.
4. *Act, learn, improve.* Based on choices made, learn from mistakes and make continuous improvements; ultimately ensure that the right thing is done.

Figure 21.1
Core Values as Presented by Vince Di Norcia—*Hard Like Water*

The Norms ⟶ The Values ↓	The Positive Norms: Do......	The Negative Norms; Don't......
Life	Care for life	Kill
Welfare	Care for welfare	Steal
Honest/open communication	Care for communication	Lie
Civil rights	Care for civil rights	Violate

Source: Vincent Di Norcia, *Hard Like Water: Ethics in Business,* New York: Oxford University Press, 1998. Copyright © Oxford University Press Canada, 1998. Reprinted by permission of Oxford University Press Canada.

5. *Seek the common good.* This is the care of the corporation as a whole, not just one small group; it ensures the welfare of all stakeholders (but does not necessarily mean that we must keep them all happy).

Values and maxims like these can drive the use of ethics within a project context. They also form the basis for developing an ethical decision-making model. These values, maxims, and decision models will be explored more fully in this chapter, both through analysis to major components of project management and via a case study of a project (see Chapter 21 Case Study) with a number of dilemmas both ethical and nonethical.

HOW DO ETHICS FIT WITHIN THE CONTEXT OF PROJECTS?

Projects bring together a diverse group of people to work toward a common goal. Projects today have become increasingly complex, and project teams can include members from a variety of companies. Factors such as culture, distance, organizations, and functions are all aspects faced by a project manager. All projects will confront issues that may include an ethical component. It could be as significant as the delivery of a core component of the product or as small as a decision on an outstanding minor project issue. When examining an ethical issue on a project it must be done within the business ethics and mores of the corporation and the stakeholders of the project.

PROJECTS AS CHANGE AGENTS

Projects by their very nature invoke change within an organization. The development and introduction of a new product, implementation of a new accounting system, or a new marketing campaign are all projects that will have an impact on the way a business will operate and survive in the future.

Ethics, as they pertain to businesses or projects, are critical during times of fundamental change. Values that were previously taken for granted are now strongly questioned as the corporation goes through the change. Many previously held values are no longer followed. For example, the value of open communication may be ignored or not adhered to due to the stress and confusion of the changes. During times of stress, the principles of "doing the right thing" can go right out the door. Consequently, business ethics can be strong preventive medicine and provide moral direction to management. This is also true within the context of projects. Delivery pressures, innovation, time to market, and reduced costs are all reasons for projects to be initiated in the first place. Yet these same drivers can place pressure on the ethical dimension of managing and delivering an end product to the project sponsor or client.

DIFFERENT KINDS OF VALUES

All organizations have ground rules that lay out "how things are done around here." Such values may be stated or implied, written or understood, official or unofficial.

To develop an effective ethics program for the management of projects, it is important not only to clarify an organization's normative ground rules, but also to ensure that practices and policies are in place that neither conflict with nor subvert an organization's desirable ground rules.

As shown earlier in "Core Values and Performance Maxims," one model of classifying values involves the four core values or positive norms presented in Figure 21.1. Although ethicists often differ on classifying types of values, in the project management business we have identified three types:

1. *Administrative values.* Examples include efficiency, effectiveness, and accountability.
2. *Professional values.* Examples include clarity, respect for individuals, clarity of communication, and administrative fairness. Such concepts are often defined by a professional code of conduct (such as for lawyers and accountants). Few fall under the definition of the law. The Project Management Institute (PMI) has such a code that must be signed by all individuals who attain the professional designation of Project Management Professional (PMP) as granted by PMI.
3. *Ethical values.* Examples include honesty, integrity, objectivity, and openness.

The boundaries of these three classifications will overlap, but they are not one and the same. In certain situations, what is right for the employer may not be right for the individual. Project "sniff tests" or ethical decision models should be developed to deal with these dilemmas.

Causes of unethical actions can be systemic. Wrongdoing may occur not so much because people are less than ethical, but because business often gives too little thought to developing and reinforcing an organizational culture in which people can and will act ethically. Corporate ground rules, although often more implicit than stated, are an expression of corporate values and what that organization will do to get what it values.

There are three kinds of ground-rule violations:

1. *Omission errors*—lack of written rules
2. *Remission errors*—pressure by sponsor and/or others to do wrong things
3. *Commission errors*—failure to follow sound, established operational and ethical practices

IMPACT ON PROJECT MANAGEMENT PRACTICES

How do ethics affect the various components of good project management practices? Traversing moral mazes has become the order of the day in dealing with facets of the project management profession and the process of managing projects. Consider the impact of ethics on the following project management practice areas.

Organizational Structure, Roles, and Responsibilities

Organizational structure of a project team and the respective roles and responsibilities become a focal point not only for establishing a performing team, but also for how issues and decisions are going to be made. Projects and operations are often vying for resources across matrixed organizations. With a variety of reporting lines in a matrixed organization, the values that exist in a functional group may be different from those established by a project team. The role of a functional or line manager within the project will also impact how issues are handled or the approach to specific dilemmas that the project team or individual members will face. The Chapter 21 Case Study provides insight into the struggle between managers not directly involved in the project and resources assigned to the project team. A team operating agreement (TOA) or team charter should be used to establish mission, values, and norms. This is an excellent place to begin establishing values, the ethical components of the project and the team's operation in particular.

Quality

Quality is fast becoming a core component of project success. Often, issues related to quality that involve an ethical dilemma will surface during the project cycle. Some quality issues can be buried and not uncovered until long after the project is complete and the product or end deliverable is in use. Shortcuts and inappropriate cost savings are both part of the ethics landscape with regard to quality management. The quality management plan for a project will require thought and procedures that consider the ethical nature of quality. These should include reporting defects, avoiding selection of unqualified resources and shoddy materials, and quality assurance.

Communications

Communications is a key success factor for any project. The team spends a huge amount of time in this untracked activity. Project managers spend on average 70 to 90 percent of their time on communication activities. Honest, open communication values will impact the positioning around any events where those values may become an ethical issue. The Chapter 21 Case Study highlights this specific component. The maze that can be entwined through the use and abuse of communications vehicles in itself becomes a critical factor. Voice mail, e-mail, and other forms of communication can impact the way in which work is interpreted or how a team functions.

Contract Management

Since ethics is not simply ensuring legal compliance, the issues facing a project manager with regard to contract management, award, and maintenance can be extremely challenging. This includes possible favoritism to one vendor over another or allowing bidding on components of a project without opening it to free bidding.

Risk Management

Undertaking any project has inherent risks. What risks are we willing to assume? Has the project determined the risk tolerance of the project sponsor and other key stakeholders? These are all critical components of good risk management and need to be in place with regard to dealing with issues related to handling and managing risk. The level of risk can become a moral issue when there are significantly different levels of tolerance and the consequences are considerable. For example, a moral issue would be the level of objectivity by various stakeholders if one should have a vested interest in a specific decision that carries a sizable risk to the project and corporation.

Constraints of Scope, Time, and Cost

The triple constraints of scope, time, and cost are always competing as the primary objective during the life of a project. There may be pressure to influence or change these depending on what issues and challenges the project may be facing at the time. The project manager and his or her team need to understand not only the core project goal, but also the priority of these three constraints when issues emerge that require action. Dilemmas of an ethical nature may focus on any of these constraints when a project is late, not achieving its scope, or is overrunning its budget.

BENEFITS OF ESTABLISHING AND MANAGING ETHICS ON A PROJECT

There are the universal moral benefits of managing ethics on a project. However, there are other types of benefits as well. The following list describes various types of benefits of managing ethics specifically on projects.

- *Paying attention to ethics on projects improves the overall social structure of the project team and its stakeholders.* The establishment of work standards, common project roles, values, and norms can show there is a high value on fairness and equity. Using instruments such as a team charter or operating agreement will put these types of values up front.
- *Helps maintain a moral course in times of fundamental change.* As noted earlier in this chapter under "Projects as Change Agents," projects themselves can cause fundamental change. Often, there may be no compass to guide project managers through complex conflict and about what is right or wrong. Both the use of business

ethics in an organization and the establishment of standards on projects provide guidance for implementing consistent action as various issues arise.

- *Cultivates strong teamwork and a balance of the project culture.* By establishing a set of team values and norms that take into consideration ethical components, the project team has agreed to alignment not only with the organization, but also with the project. Ongoing dialogue about team values builds openness, integrity, and a strong sense of project-team community.
- *Acts as an insurance policy by ensuring that contracts, policies, and procedures are legal—helps avoid acts of error and omission.* Establishing ethical values tends to detect issues and violations early on so they can be reported and addressed sooner rather than later.
- *Establishes values related to quality and overall strategic positioning of the project within the corporation.* Ethics identify preferred values and ensure that organizational behaviors are aligned. Quality management includes high priority on certain operating values such as performance, reliability, measurement, and feedback. Using ethical values on the quality of project deliverables ensures integrity of the product and meeting the needs of the various stakeholders.
- *It is the right thing to do.*

Resolving Ethical Dilemmas

The need for and benefits of using ethical values within a project environment have been outlined. Because ethics is a matter of values and associated behaviors, establishing a process for ethical decision making becomes essential. The key process components are *reflection* and *dialogue*.

What is considered an ethical dilemma? Often, it is portrayed simply as a matter of resolving conflicts in which one option appears to be a clear choice. However, ethical dilemmas faced by project managers are much more complex, with no clear guidelines or answers. A *dilemma* implies that there are multiple alternatives of which none appear to be desirable. In terms of ethics, Doug Wallace and Jon Pekel of the Fulcrum Group explain that you know when you have a significant ethical conflict because the three following conditions exist:

1. Significant value conflicts exist among differing stakeholders.
2. Significant consequences affect stakeholders in the situation.
3. Real alternatives are ethically justifiable.

Ethical dilemmas will face not only the project manager but all stakeholders in the project (e.g., sponsor, users, clients, team members, community). Consider the following examples of complex ethical dilemmas faced by project teams:

- "The contractor on one of the projects I have worked on before is interested in information on my current project. He hopes to have an opportunity to work with me again. Meanwhile, I know that the project will be hiring a number of contractors, but we are not considering his firm. What should I do?"
- "Our project team has been given a deadline to finish the project. If we do, everyone on the team will get a bonus, scaled based on one's position on the team. Everyone is working flat out, but the bonus arrangement is causing divisiveness in our previously well-performing team. What should we do?"
- "A project within our company has been late for over one year in delivering the system to the client. In the meantime, another project has delivered a new product that makes the other project's deliverable useless. The team is still working to complete the project and is aware of the problems. No one in senior management fully understands the issues and the conflict. The project is over budget by $5 million. What should we do?"

Methods for Resolving Ethical Dilemmas

Project teams should develop and document a procedure for dealing with dilemmas as they arise. Consider having assistance from outside the project team when the ethical issues are very complex. Methods include a checklist, a standard step-by-step process, and a list of key questions. Two decision models or "sniff tests" are outlined next. They both follow the same basic principles:

- Know whom to involve and where they are positioned.
- Determine alternatives.
- Assess against the ethical values established by both the organization (its overall code of ethics and rules of conduct) and those documented by the project team.
- Evaluate an action plan for moving forward.

The first model is simple and focuses the project team on the basics of the ethical dimensions. It requires establishment of values (the values identified earlier could form a basis) and agreement that they will be used for managing ethical dilemmas.

The second model, although more complex, has a number of interesting and useful features. It starts with a preliminary assessment (details in Performance Support Tool 21.1) that is used to determine the ethical dimension and significance of the dilemma and whether you need to go any further. It also provides for the need to consider a preventive component to stop recurrence of the same problem. Finally, it includes a decision-making checklist to evaluate your decisions and action steps. The detailed model is included in Performance Support Tool 21.2 and was developed by Jon Pekel and Doug Wallace.

FOUR-STEP ETHICAL DECISION-MAKING MODEL

This simple model provides the basics for dealing with a potential ethical dilemma. It uses key concepts of problem solving from a values and ethics position.

Step 1—Identify All Stakeholders

The first stage of an ethically tuned decision is to identify all possible stakeholders. This does not mean that an ethical decision is one that satisfies all stakeholders. Rather, a decision that is ethical is one that identifies and considers the needs and wants of all stakeholders.

Often, in the past, major decisions were not seen to be fair, responsible, or appropriate because of a failure to take into account the needs of, or the impacts upon, certain stakeholders.

Step 2—Identify All Possible Alternatives

The second stage of an ethically tuned decision is to identify as wide a range of alternative decisions, actions, or study options as possible. Such alternatives reflect the range of wants and needs of all stakeholders. At this stage, a decision that is ethical tries not to reject an alternative because it has been tried or not been tried before, or to prejudge on the basis of its impact.

The *case study* (see Chapter 21 Case Study) is a tool that takes staff through the exercise of identifying and sorting out the range of possible stakeholders, and analyzing a range of action alternatives in a situation familiar within their work experiences.

Step 3—Apply the Project Sniff Test

The third stage of the ethical decision-making process is to see which options, actions, alternative recommendations, or proposals pass the project "sniff test." A *sniff test* is a question or set of questions used to filter or screen out unethical or unallowable alternatives or decisions. Staff need to know that management has given them the right to say "no" to any action or request that, in the reasonable mind of an employee, violates company and project standards. The tests determine when not to do something—which is when an action, recommendation, or proposal fails to meet (or pass) one or more of the tests. The project team will identify key values by establishing team values, roles, and norms. In addition, the values identified earlier in the "Different Kinds of Values" section of this chapter should be considered as part of the project's sniff-test questions.

Step 4—Allow for and Reinforce the Personal Judgment and Morality of Staff

Many operational decisions may have no ethical dimensions. Even if a proposed action meets the project's sniff test, the behavior may be one that an individual staff member cannot support in good conscience. Some organizations allow for personal standards to be applied, so long as they do not violate the corporate sniff tests. Thus, the fourth characteristic of an ethically tuned decision is one that ensures that a possible decision does not violate the personal integrity standards of staff.

TEN-STEP ETHICAL DECISION-MAKING MODEL

The "Ten-Step Method of Decision-Making" model was developed by Jon Pekel and Doug Wallace and is provided with copyright permission for non-publication organizational use. The detailed process for each step and accompanying forms are provided in Performance Support Tool 21.2. This decision-making model also presumes use of the preliminary assessment instrument outlined in Performance Support Tool 21.1. The preliminary assessment provides three tests to determine to what degree there is an ethical dimension to a particular situation or issue. Completing the preliminary assessment will determine the level of the ethical component of a situation and identify the degree to which the 10-step model should be applied.

The 10-step model at a glance is outlined here with hints for using each step.

Step 1. *Identify the Key Facts*
- Role play key stakeholders to see what *they* see as facts.
- Watch out for assuming causative relationships among co-incidental facts.

Step 2. *Identify the Major Stakeholders*
- Be sure to identify both direct and indirect stakeholders.
- Genuinely "walk in their shoes" to see what *they* value and want as a desired outcome.

Step 3. *Identify the Underlying Driving Forces*
- Think like an M.D.—look for what's beneath the presenting symptoms.
- Use these driving forces to develop your Step 8 preventive component.

Step 4. *Identify/Prioritize Key Operating Values and Ethical Principles*
- Think of this step as determining the up-front design parameters for an effective solution.
- Don't rush this step—building consensus here will pay off later.

Step 5. *Decide Who Should Be Involved in the Decision-Making Process*
- All stakeholders have a right to have *their* best interests considered.
- If you can't actually involve all stakeholders, have someone role play their points of view.

Step 6. *Determine and Evaluate All Viable Alternatives*
- Critical: *All* possible alternatives *must* pass the three-part review-gate criteria (as detailed in Step 6 Performance Support Tool 21.2).
- Imagine consequences of each alternative actually cascading down on each stakeholder.

Step 7. *Test Preferred Alternative with a Worst-Case Scenario*
- This step helps prevent a rush to judgment toward a wrong solution.
- Emphasize this step when all stakeholder interests are *not* being adequately considered.

Step 8. *Add a Preventive Component*
- Problem-solving heroes want to get on to the next problem and won't take time for this step.
- Only immediate-solution decisions usually come back to bite you.

Step 9.   *Decide upon and Build a Short- and Long-Term Action Plan*
- The devil is usually in the details—take the time needed to be detailed and comprehensive.
- Make sure that the means used in your action steps correlate with your desired ends.

Step 10.   *Use a Decision-Making Checklist*
- Become *thoroughly* familiar with this end-point checklist *before* you get started in Step 1.
- Don't allow groupthinking here—make sure everyone involved fills this out *individually.*

TRAINING PROJECT MANAGERS IN ETHICS

So far we have defined ethics within the context of projects, identified the different kinds of values, outlined ethical dimensions within the various components of project management, and provided methods for resolving ethical dilemmas. A key dependency in applying ethics on projects is the knowledge and skill level of project managers and their teams. This means providing training to project managers on how to develop and apply ethical values in a project context and solve dilemmas as they occur on their projects.

The first step in training requires an understanding of ethics, its context within the organization and project, and how to establish values for use by the project team during the life of the project. Values could be developed using the ones outlined in the earlier section titled "Different Kind of Values." Consideration for a code of ethics established by the corporation and any other procedures for handling ethical issues must be incorporated into the training program. The Chapter 21 Glossary outlines standard terms for morality, law, ethics, and values, which provides clarification of the language of right and wrong as part of ethics training.

Practice in applying an ethical decision-making model should also form a major component of a training program. The Chapter 21 Case Study provides a case study that was developed by SPMgroup Ltd. in partnership with EthicScan Canada to train project managers in the issues and values of managing projects where ethical dilemmas would arise. The case study is a composite of real-life scenarios and provides a set of questions to stimulate thought and use of process in resolving the ethical dilemmas posed in the case.

CONCLUSIONS

In this chapter we have provided a foundation of understanding of ethics and values, and how they apply in managing projects. We outlined a basis of values that can be used in developing a common set of ethical values for a project team and its management. The various components of good project management practices were explored in the context of ethics and the benefits of managing issues from an ethical position were also outlined.

The last part of the chapter discussed resolving ethical dilemmas in projects. Two excellent ethical decision-making models were provided—a simple four-step process and a more comprehensive 10-step model. Details of the 10-step model are included in Performance Support Tools 21.1 and 21.2. Training project managers in the use of ethics and the application of a decision-making model was outlined. A case study for use in applying ethical decision-making models to a real-life situation is provided in the Chapter 21 Case Study. Use of the case study and associated training for project managers and their teams will provide a foundation for the process of ethical application.

Ethics is a complex and demanding component of managing projects in today's environment. Project managers are being asked to deliver innovative, competitive, and complex products often in time-pressured and resource-poor environments. Establishing a set of ethical values for the project team and applying a decision-making model when faced with ethical dilemmas provide project managers and their teams with significant support tools. Core values, performance maxims, and a way to navigate the moral mazes of ethical issues successfully are valuable skills that every project manager must be able to apply as ethical dilemmas arise.

GLOSSARY

There is a difference between morality, law, ethics, and values. Because many individuals (erroneously) use values and ethics interchangeably, and because others are confused about the personal versus the public realm of morality, we encourage a brief clarification of the language of right and wrong as part of ethics training. The following distinctions should help.

Morality

The word *morality* comes from the Latin word *mores*, meaning culture or custom. The term does deal with right and wrong, but from a particular cultural perspective. In other words, morality is about culturally determined rights and wrongs. Mores change over time, and may differ from culture to culture as well as vary across geographic regions. For example, attitudes toward gift-giving or same-sex benefits vary in Toronto, Truro, and Teheran, in comparison to Tokyo. The measure is changeable.

Law

Law refers to legally sanctioned behavior. The term does deal with right and wrong, but with a particular perspective, that what the law says is right. But regulations or legal formulations may not exist on a particular topic, or the law may be hopelessly outdated. There may not be enough scientific knowledge, precedent case law, or truth on which to base the law. As a result, compliance with the letter of the law is an imperfect standard, for both individuals and corporations. Organizations should aim to encourage a decision or standard that not only respects the letter of the law but also, more importantly, moves to encompass a higher level—the spirit of the law. What is legal might not be seen to be just in all people's minds. Indeed, individuals have conscientiously objected to what they believe are bad laws.

Ethics

The concept of ethics also deals with right and wrong. However, ethics transcends geography and culture. *Ethics* deals with fundamental issues such as respecting property, human life, the environment, or truth. Such principles are acknowledged by all, even if local or national practices vary. Sniff tests incorporate ethical norms in an attempt to implant or make explicit these notions in a particular organization so that the ethics component behind a decision can be clarified and tested.

Values

Values are not the same as ethics. Values may involve right and wrong, but not necessarily. *Values* involve things we personally hold dear or respect. For instance, one may value an expensive item, such as a house or a car; one might value a friendship or a pet; or, one might value nature and the outdoors. Our large-scale attitudes toward the importance of others versus self, or the importance of money, or doing the right thing are central to our individual character and being. Such values can be as varied as those who hold them. Deep-seated values can change, but this does not happen often over the course of a typical person's lifetime.

REFERENCES

Books

Hard Like Water: Ethics in Business by Vincent Di Norcia, published by Oxford University Press, 1998, is an excellent book studying business ethics with two goals: to show the extent to which ethical values penetrate into business and to stress the social character of business.

Moral Maze: The World of Corporate Managers by Robert Jackall, published by Oxford University Press, 1988, presents an account of how corporate managers think the world works and how big organizations shape moral consciousness.

Articles

"Corporate Ethics Test" by *Ronald E. Berenbeim, Business and Society Review*, Spring 1992, No.81: 77–80.

"Ethics without the Sermon" by L. Nash, *Harvard Business Review*, 1981: 59.

"Prevent Trouble by Improving Ethics" by David R. Francis, *Christian Science Monitor*, June 1991: 9.

Web Sites

www.mapnp.org/library/ethics—an excellent source for basics and how-to of ethics; provides other good sites and references.

www.ubc.ca/resources/business—good resource information on current ethics trends.

Other Sources

"Ten-Step Method of Decision-Making" model, developed and copyrighted by Jon Pekel and Doug Wallace. This excellent decision-making model is a toolkit approach to managing ethical dilemmas; it is used in this chapter in the context of project issues. Copyright permission is granted for nonpublication organizational use.

"A Case Study for Training Project Managers in Ethics," developed and copyrighted by SPMgroup Ltd. in partnership with EthicScan Canada. SPMgroup Ltd., a project management consulting and training firm, determined the need for a corporate and project code of ethics for its consulting practice. As a result the firm developed the case study for training its consultants and clients in the application of ethics within a project context. For use of the case study apply to SPMgroup Ltd., (416) 485-1584, www.spmgroup.ca.

PERFORMANCE SUPPORT TOOL 21.1:

PRELIMINARY ASSESSMENT OF THE ETHICAL DIMENSIONS OF A SITUATION

Before you get started in applying an ethical decision-making model, do a preliminary assessment. The preliminary assessment uses three tests to determine to what degree there is an ethical dimension to a situation.

1. *Value conflicts.* How different are the kinds of values held by different stakeholders?
2. *Consequences.* How significant are the possible consequences?
3. *Ethical justifiability.* How ethically justifiable are the possible solutions?

Test 1—Value Conflicts

Question: How different are the kinds of values held by different stakeholders?

List below some of the different kinds of values in the situation that are in conflict with one another:

1. [Value] _____ vs. [Value] _____

2. [Value] _____ vs. [Value] _____

Check the box that represents the degree of value conflicts in this situation:

Check Below	*Value-Conflict Rating Scale* *In this situation, the kinds of values held by different stakeholders are . . .*
	5. Extremely different
	4. Very different
	3. Somewhat different
	2. Not very different
	1. No major value-conflict differences in this situation

Test 2—Consequences

Question: How significant are the possible consequences?

List below some of the possible consequences in this situation:

1. [Possible consequence] _____

2. [Possible consequence] _____

Check the box that represents the degree of consequences in this situation:

Check Below	Consequences Rating Scale In this situation, the possible consequences are . . .
	5. Extremely significant
	4. Very significant
	3. Somewhat significant
	2. Not very significant
	1. No significant possible consequences in this situation

Test 3—Ethical Justifiability

Question: How ethically justifiable are the possible solutions?
List below at least two ethically justifiable solutions to this situation:

1. [Justifiable solution] _____

2. [Justifiable solution] _____

Check the box that represents the degree of ethical justifiability of the possible solutions:

Check Below	Ethical Justifiability Rating Scale In this situation, the possible solutions are . . .
	5. Extremely ethically justifiable
	4. Very ethically justifiable
	3. Somewhat ethically justifiable
	2. Not very ethically justifiable
	1. Only one solution is clearly ethically justifiable

Preliminary Ethical Dimension Assessment Rating
Total all checked numbers from the three tests and check the appropriate range on the scale:

Consider these answers when determining your decision and action plan.

Check Range	Total	Rating Scale— The Ethical Dimension of This Situation Is:
	13–15	Extremely significant–*Definitely use the Ten-Step Method of Decision Making*
	11–12	Very significant–*Definitely use the Ten-Step Method of Decision Making*
	9–10	Somewhat significant–*Should use the Ten-Step Method of Decision Making*
	6–8	Not very significant–*Should use the Ten-Step Method of Decision Making*
	3–5	Not at all significant–*You may not need the Ten-Step Method of Decision Making*

PERFORMANCE SUPPORT TOOL 21.2:
THE TEN-STEP METHOD OF DECISION MAKING

The following outlines in detail each step in the process and provides forms that can be used to assist in gathering and analyzing the information.

Step 1—Identify the Key Facts

List the most important known facts in the situation:

1.	
2.	
3.	
4.	
5.	
6.	
7.	
8.	
9.	
10.	
11.	
12.	

What else do you need to know to better understand the total situation?

1.	
2.	
3.	

Consider these answers when determining your decision and action plan.

Step 2—Identify the Major Stakeholders

List the major stakeholders (individuals, groups, institutions, and so on) that have a stake in the outcome of the situation. Using "moral imagination," put yourself in their places (walk in their shoes), and identify the key values they would bring to this situation and the desired outcomes they would want from this situation.

Major Stakeholders	What They Value	Their Desired Outcomes
1.		
2.		
3.		
4.		
5.		
6.		
7.		

Stakeholder Values Analysis

What stakeholder values are the *most competing and most different* from one another?

[Stakeholder value] _____ vs. [Stakeholder value] _____

[Stakeholder value] _____ vs. [Stakeholder value] _____

What are the most shared values among all or most of the stakeholders? (Win-win solutions can be crafted out of these shared values.)

[Shared value] _____ [Shared value] _____

[Shared value] _____ [Shared value] _____

Consider these answers when determining your decision and action plan.

Step 3—Identify the Underlying Driving Forces

List the major underlying driving forces creating or exacerbating the situation. Then, describe how each driver is creating or exacerbating the situation. Finally, list what changes in these drivers could help prevent similar situations in the future. Make sure these ideas are included in the preventive component in Step 8.

Major Driver	How is it creating or exacerbating the situation?	What changes could help prevent future situations?
1.		
2.		
3.		
4.		
5.		
6.		
7.		

Consider these answers when determining your decision and action plan.

Step 4—Identify/Prioritize Key Operating Values and Ethical Principles

1. List below any *operating value* (such as maintain profits, customer service, total quality, and so on) that is relevant to the situation and that should be upheld in your decision and action plan.
2. List any *ethical principle* (such as honesty, fairness, respect for the dignity of persons, and so on) that is relevant to the situation and that should be upheld in your decision and action plan.
3. In the far right-hand column, priority rank *together* all operating values and ethical principles by placing a 1 next to the highest-priority operating value or ethical principle; a 2 next to the second highest priority operating value or ethical principle, and so on.

Continue ranking. *Note:* You are to have **one combined ranking list** including both operating values and ethical principles, not two separate ranking lists.

Operating Values Relevant to the Situation	Total Priority Ranking [1 is highest priority]
1.	
2.	
3.	
4.	
5.	
Ethical Principles Relevant to the Situation	
1.	
2.	
3.	
4.	
5.	

Stakeholder Values/Principles Agreement Index

Check the degree of agreement you think there is among the stakeholders with your combined priority-ranking list of operating values and ethical principles.

_____ Great agreement   _____ Some agreement

_____ Little agreement   _____ Virtually no agreement

How could you increase the agreement (or maintain it if already great) throughout the decision-making process?

_____

_____

Consider these answers when determining your decision and action plan.

Step 5—Decide Who Should Be Involved in the Decision-Making Process

List the individuals, groups, or institutions that should definitely have input into the decision and action plan for this situation. Then, indicate how you will obtain this input. [Note: Because of limited time or to protect confidentiality, in some cases you may need to have someone in a decision-making position role play input from this stakeholder rather than receive it directly from that stakeholder.]

Who should have input into this decision and action plan?	*How could this input be obtained?*
1.	
2.	
3.	
4.	
5.	
6.	

Now, list those who should actually make the recommendation and final decision.

Who should be involved in developing the recommended decision and action plan?
1.
2.
3.
4.
5.
6.
7.
Who should actually make or approve the final decision and action plan?
1.
2.
3.

Consider these answers when determining your decision and action plan.

Step 6—Determine and Evaluate All Viable Alternatives

1. Quickly brainstorm a list of possible alternative solutions to this situation.

Alternative 1	Alternative 2	Alternative 3	Alternative 4
Alternative 5	Alternative 6	Alternative 7	Alternative 8

2. Next, evaluate all alternatives using the three review-gate criteria listed below. Only those alternatives that meet all three criteria become viable alternatives.
3. Now, list the major stakeholders identified in Step 2 down the far left hand column. Then, fill in the most important consequences of each viable alternative on each stakeholder.
4. Finally, after having reviewed your list of consequences on each stakeholder, select your preferred viable alternative.

Review-Gate Criteria for an Effective Decision and Action Plan

List below only alternatives that meet all three of these criteria:
1. Prevents or minimizes harm to the major stakeholders listed in Step 2.
2. Upholds the combined prioritized list of operating values and ethical principles from Step 4.
3. Is a good, workable solution to the situation that can actually be implemented.

	Viable Alternative 1	Viable Alternative 2	Viable Alternative 3	Viable Alternative 4
Stakeholders	Consequences of Each Alternative on Each Stakeholder			
1.				
2.				
3.				
4.				
5.				
6.				
7.				

The preferred alternative is viable alternative # _____.

Consider these answers when determining your decision and action plan.

Step 7—Test Preferred Alternative with a Worst-Case Scenario

1. Summarize your preferred viable alternative selected in Step 6 in the box provided.
2. Create in your mind and briefly describe below a worst-case scenario that assumes that if something can go wrong during the implementation of your preferred alternative, it probably will go wrong!
3. Once again, in the far lefthand column, copy the list of major stakeholders from Step 2.
4. Think through and list the consequences of your worst-case scenario on each of your stakeholders. Include other consequences that may not directly relate to a particular stakeholder.
5. Finally, assign a percent likelihood that this worst-case scenario could actually happen. Then, check the degree of concern this percentage gives you. If needed, revise your preferred viable alternative or select another viable alternative.

	Brief description of your preferred viable alternative:
	Brief description of your worst-case scenario:
Stakeholders	*Consequences of Each Alternative on Each Stakeholder*
1.	
2.	
3.	
4.	
5.	
6.	
7.	

Other Consequences Not Directly Related to Particular Stakeholders
1.
2.
3.
4.

Worst-Case Scenario Probability Assessment

What is the percent likelihood that this worst-case scenario could actually happen? _____%

Check the degree of concern this percentage gives you about your preferred alternative:

____ No concern   ____ Some concern

____ Substantial concern   ____ Critical concern

Consider these answers when determining your decision and action plan.

Step 8—Add a Preventive Component

Now, take your preferred alternative (possibly revised, based on your worst-case scenario analysis) and add some action steps that would help prevent the situation from happening again. Usually, preferred alternatives focus only on solving the immediate problem at hand. For ideas on this component, return to Step 3 where you listed the underlying driving forces affecting the situation.

Action Steps That Could Prevent the Situation from Happening Again
1.
2.
3.
4.
5.
6.
7.

Consider these answers when determining your decision and action plan.

Step 9—Decide Upon and Build a Short- and Long-Term Action Plan

List your decision and action steps in two parts—short-term, immediate; and longer-term, preventive.

Short-Term, Immediate-Solution Decision and Overall Strategy
Action Steps to Implement the Short-Term, Immediate-Solution Decision and Strategy
1.
2.
3.
4.
5.
6.
7.
8.

Longer-Term, Preventive-Solution Decision and Overall Strategy
Action Steps to Implement the Longer-Term, *Preventive-Solution Decision and Strategy*
1.
2.
3.
4.
5.
6.

Ethical Justification

List three reasons you think your comprehensive decision and action steps are ethically justified:

1.
2.
3.

Consider these answers when determining your decision and action plan.

Step 10—Use a Decision-Making Checklist

Using the 0 through 6 scale, evaluate your immediate and preventive-solution decisions and action steps against the following eight tests. Circle the most appropriate answers. Then, total all answers and check the appropriate Decision-Making Confidence Scale.

	Rating Scale						
	Not At All			Totally Yes			
Effective Decision-Making Tests	0	1	2	3	4	5	6
				[circle]			
1. *Relevant Information Test.* Have we obtained as much information as possible to make an informed decision and action plan for this situation?	0	1	2	3	4	5	6
2. *Involvement Test.* Have we involved as many as possible of those who have a right to have input into, or have actual involvement in, making this decision and action plan?	0	1	2	3	4	5	6
3. *Consequences Test.* Have we attempted to accommodate the consequences of this decision and action plan on any who could be significantly affected by it?	0	1	2	3	4	5	6
4. *Ethical Principles Test.* Does this decision and action plan uphold the ethical principles that we think are relevant to this situation?	0	1	2	3	4	5	6
5. *Fairness Test.* If we were any one of the stakeholders in this situation, would we perceive this decision and action plan to be fair, given all of the circumstances?	0	1	2	3	4	5	6
6. *Universality Test.* Would we want this decision and action plan to become universal law so it would be applicable to all—including ourselves—in similar situations?	0	1	2	3	4	5	6

	Rating Scale
	Not At All *Totally Yes* 0 1 2 3 4 5 6
Effective Decision-Making Tests	*[circle]*
7. *Preventive Test.* Does this decision and action plan prevent or minimize similar situations from happening again?	0 1 2 3 4 5 6
8. *Light-of-Day (or "60 Minutes" TV Program) Test.* Can our decision and action-plan–including how we made it–stand the test of broad-based public disclosure so everyone would know everything about our actions?	0 1 2 3 4 5 6

Effective Decision-Making Confidence Scale

What is the total of all of your circled numbers? _____ Now, check the box representing the appropriate range. If needed, revise your decision and action plan.

Check Range	*Total*	*How Confident Can You Be of Having Done an Effective Job of Decision Making?*
	44–48	*Extremely confident*—Do not need to revise your decision
	39–43	*Very confident*—Do not need to revise your decision
	33–38	*Somewhat confident*—Should revise your decision
	24–32	*Not very confident*—Definitely revise your decision
	0–23	*Not at all confident*—Definitely revise your decision

APPENDIX 21 CASE STUDY—
A CASE STUDY FOR TRAINING PROJECT MANAGERS IN ETHICS

The following case study was developed for use in training project managers to consider ethical dilemmas and show them how to establish ethical values within the context of a project. The training includes development of a sample set of values that could be used in a project environment. The basis of the values developed is outlined in the section earlier in this chapter titled "Different Kinds of Values."

The participants then role play the case and answer the seven questions provided in the case study. It plays out a typical scenario that a project manager could face on a project, and carries the case in a present state and then eight weeks later. It is provided here and may be used with copyright permission from SPMgroup Ltd.

A Sample Project Dilemma

Ernesta Phillips is a professional project manager working at TycosTel, a telecommunications company. Tom Waterford, the sponsor and executive vice president of operations at TycosTel, has hired her as senior project manager to manage TycosTel's introduction of an automated state-of-the-art customer service system.

The project team consists of 30 people, representing four key business unit areas. All team members have been assigned to the project on a full-time basis. Four key members, including Lindsay Damphuis, report functionally to Tom. Other team members report to functional managers within the other three business units. As an organization, TycosTel is very hierarchical and each division operates in isolation from other divisions: The company is not comfortable with a cross-functional, matrixed project team approach.

Ernesta was brought on board this high-profile project two weeks ago, which was three and a half months after its start. She is now facing two dilemmas, the first of which concerns Lindsay Damphuis, who was the original project manager on this assignment. Early this morning Lindsay, a functional manager, indicated that she was not able to provide Ernesta with a key deliverable—the business architecture strategy paper, due for tomorrow's full-team meeting. The reason she gave was that her draft paper had not yet been vetted by Tom. Without this business architecture strategy paper, the project schedule would be set back at least a couple of weeks.

Ernesta paused before acting. She was aware that Lindsay was a very savvy, upwardly mobile executive with designs on Tom's job. Because of this, and because of resentment on Lindsay's part about having project management responsibility removed from her, Ernesta was reluctant to accept Lindsay's implied suggestion that Tom was delaying the success of his own project.

The second problem concerns Tom Waterford. He seems to be unable to separate his lack of confidence in Lindsay Damphuis from his need to step back and let Ernesta do her job. In Ernesta Phillips's judgment, Tom was typically able to make decisions, but not when it came to the threat that Lindsay presented to his own security.

In the current situation, Ernesta had many unanswered questions. Who was responsible for the delay in Lindsay's report? Did self-protection on Tom's part or blind ambition on Lindsay's part threaten to derail the project? If Ernesta put her foot down on tardiness in meeting agreed-upon deadlines, would this worsen the situation? What should Ernesta do, and why?

Questions
1. *Who are the stakeholders involved?*
2. *What actions and alternatives does Ernesta have?*
3. *Is her dilemma operational, systemic, ethical, or a mix of the three?*
4. *What ethical principles should be at work here, guiding Ernesta's decision?*

Eight Weeks Later

Circumstances over the past few weeks have made the project situation much worse. Tom is not letting Ernesta bring her authority to bear to gain more cooperation from Lindsay. Tom is having discussions with senior executives at TycosTel about the economic fundamentals of the project, stemming from his concern that the payback from the new customer service system may require 15 months rather than the original six to nine months. On her part, Lindsay is seeking every opportunity to undermine Tom's authority. The project is not meeting important internal deadlines. The other team members are beginning to express doubts about the overall project and Tom's increasing inaccessibility.

Questions
5. *In retrospect, should Ernesta have done anything differently two months ago?*
6. *When, if ever, is a project manager justified in going over the head of the sponsor in order to save a project?*
7. *To what extent is this an impossible project, given TycosTel's culture? Should this influence the nature or terms of the professional services contract entered into?*

CHAPTER 22

CONFLICT MANAGEMENT: OPPORTUNITY FOR RELATIONSHIP BUILDING AND EFFECTIVE DECISIONS

GEORGE PITAGORSKY

OVERVIEW

In this chapter we address conflict management. After discussing why conflict management is a mission-critical activity, we discuss strategies and describe effective conflict resolution. We focus on two aspects of conflict resolution—dialogue and decision making.

We define what dialogue is and how it differs from debate. We discuss its importance within conflict management and issues of process awareness, and the conscious identification and handling of assumptions, opinions, and beliefs.

Turning our attention to decision making, we discuss how dialogue provides a solid foundation for coming to effective decisions in a practical and efficient way. Key topics covered are objectives and objectivity, process orientation, creativity and spontaneity, evaluating alternatives, and methods for reaching a decision, with an emphasis on consensus, handling escalation, and arbitration for authority-based decision making.

INTRODUCTION

You have a choice. You can promote and support adversarial advocacy, politics, and division *or* collaboration, synergy, exploration, and excellence. Part of that choice has to do with how you handle conflict. Projects are wonderful opportunities for exercising conflict management skills.

Projects are filled with questions that have multiple right answers, complex issues (with many right responses), and situations that can pit one individual or group against another. Project managers, functional managers, vendors, and performers are often faced with seemingly impossible demands from people with real power—clients, senior managers, project sponsors, and a myriad of content experts.

In fact, if there isn't enough conflict in your projects, you may not be doing them as effectively as you could be. It is by addressing conflict in the early stages of our projects—for example, negotiating realistic schedules, choosing the best vendors, and so on—that we find the right projects to perform, the right way to perform them, the complete requirements, the best designs. Through effective conflict resolution we set the stage for a relatively conflict-free implementation and product life. Through effective conflict resolution we build solid relationships to support teamwork across functional, corporate, cultural, national, and personal boundaries.

WHAT IS CONFLICT?

Conflict, according to the *Oxford American Dictionary*, is, alternatively, (1) a fight or struggle or (2) disagreement between people with different ideas or beliefs. Fighting and struggling are divisive; there have to be winners and losers. Disagreements, on the other hand, are good starting points for learning and for finding optimal action options. Conflict is a positive thing, if it is handled properly.

Differences between people are opportunities for divisiveness or the kind of conflict resolution that ends with people in harmony and with excellent, concrete results.

In this chapter we explore the conflict resolution process, particularly how process awareness, effective communication, and positive intention will help you bring about and continuously improve an effective conflict resolution process.

We can work in a way that fuels project participants while they deliver products and services to the delight of their clients and sponsors by:

- Being consciously aware of the way we and our groups operate (our process).
- Explicitly and regularly acknowledging our values, goals, strategies, objectives, and methods.

THE BLIND MEN AND THE ELEPHANT

The old story of "The Blind Men and the Elephant" is a parable that highlights how *not* to address conflict.

Once upon a time, there was a village populated entirely by blind people. The villagers had heard that an elephant was going to be passing through their vicinity. These people had never encountered an elephant before, so the villagers sent out a small delegation to bring back a report.

The delegation members experienced the beast using their sense of touch. When they returned to the village, everyone gathered in the village center to learn about the elephant.

The first delegate said, "An elephant is like a snake." He was immediately interrupted by another person who said, "That's ridiculous. An elephant is like a tree trunk." Another shouted, "No, an elephant is like a rope with a tuft at the end." And someone else said, "No, an elephant is like a wall."

Soon, all of the delegation members were arguing. Voices were raised. Epithets and insults were flying.

Most of the villagers become frustrated and left. Some people, liking a good argument, stayed to listen. Some began to create logical constructs based on what they heard, adding a few statements of their own based on their opinions. "An elephant should be this," or "Logically an elephant would be that," they said.

Others knew that if their brother-in-law said that an elephant was one thing, it couldn't possibly be the case—and they jumped in. *What* was right didn't matter to them, just *who* was right.

In the end—there is no end to this story. The argument continues to this day. The elephant is replaced by a complex product design, the contents of a meeting, or the cause of a problem. This is what happens when people debate instead of engaging in dialogue with one another.[1]

Of course, the elephant can be a design, a problem definition, the reason for a project failure, whatever.

Imagine if one of the delegation members had said, "It's interesting that we can have such diverse impressions of the elephant," and then followed up with, "Why don't we spend some time exploring how we might explain and even reconcile the differences?" It wouldn't be much of a parable, but chances are the villagers would have been a lot more likely to get an accurate sense of the nature of the elephant. It would have also avoided all the yelling, cursing, and insulting.

DO YOU HAVE DYSFUNCTIONAL CONFLICTS?

How often are you involved in dysfunctional conflicts that may never reach an end, or worse, that reach an end that divides the people on your project and leads to mediocre or ineffective outcomes?

If you are in the real world of project management, it is likely that you have experienced dysfunctional conflict resolution. Arguing, frustration, advocacy based on untested beliefs, and a reticence to be open to the possibility that an opposing idea might be correct are common.

Of course it is also likely that you have experienced *effective* conflict resolution. If you have, then you probably want to continue to do so. If you haven't, you will be delighted to know that you and your colleagues can learn to transform conflict into positive decision making and learning experiences that increase team effectiveness, harmonize relationships, and end in highly effective results. Even as an individual, you can steer your teammates toward collaborative, noncombative conflict resolution.

CONFLICT MANAGEMENT STRATEGIES

We have two alternatives: We can *avoid conflict* or *confront it*. If we choose to confront it, then we choose to do it using a *win-lose* (likely to result in lose-lose) approach or, more effectively, a *win-win* approach. This chapter promotes a win-win approach, even when other parties to the conflict are using win-lose tactics.

Win-win or collaborative conflict resolution does not rule out being forceful and directive. The methods we use depend on who the other parties are, how they approach the conflict, what the issue is, the setting, and so on. Our intention makes the difference. If we intend to make sure all parties' needs are satisfied and that they buy into the resolution, we are choosing the win-win strategy. If our intention is to beat the other guy, win at any cost, then we are choosing the win-lose approach.

WHEN TO AVOID CONFRONTATION

In some situations it is appropriate to avoid confronting the conflict. Perhaps you are familiar with the Serenity Prayer: "Grant me the serenity to accept the things I cannot change, the courage to change the things I can, and the wisdom to know the difference between them." There is wisdom that we need to use to decide when to avoid conflict and when to confront it.

When faced with a conflict (1) that can't be resolved without a significant effort, (2) where there is a likelihood of ruining relationships, and (3) where the stakes are low, it seems that avoiding the conflict may be the best way to proceed. Avoiding conflict means accepting the alternative that the other side is promoting.

I once noted in a workshop, "The stronger, more confident individual will give in more frequently than the weaker." Many in the group questioned this, arguing that the stronger one would push ahead and prevail;

why would he or she give in? My response was that the stronger individual's strength and self-confidence would allow that person more easily to evaluate the different positions objectively. Seeing that the differences weren't significant in terms of ultimately meeting project objectives, this individual would avoid confrontation by accepting the alternative.

But what if the differences are significant, or perceived to be significant? Then the effective individual should confront and work toward a conclusion that satisfies personal, project, and organizational goals and objectives. In effect we seek a consensus in which all parties can at least live with the result. They can live with it because "it works." It promotes successful achievement of objectives.

Motivation for Strategy Choice

Ideally, the only reason for choosing between avoidance and confrontation is because one alternative is an effective way to achieve goals and support values. But we live in the real world. In the real world forces that are not aligned with the achievement of goals and the support of values motivate many people. In fact, many people are unaware of their motivations.

In the context of conflict avoidance, we have experts who remind us that some people choose to avoid or withdraw from a conflict to unnerve their opponent or to win by delay (i.e., to gain time). These are conscious and rational tactics—though we might question the win-lose orientation and the language and intention.

Some people avoid conflict because they have conflict-averse personalities. Others have been conditioned by cultures in which confrontation is not valued or even acceptable. Some avoid confrontation because they fear the possible repercussions. These motivations are not connected to the outcome of the conflict. They are far less rational and may be unconscious.

Consider Tony, the team leader. He is told by his boss, Bob, that the target date is fixed and the design is not to be questioned—"Just do it." Tony feels strongly that the design is flawed and, even if it was perfect, hitting the target date is virtually impossible. Tony may fear that confronting Bob will hurt his chance for a raise or even get him fired. He may have grown up in a family or in a culture where confrontation was met with violence or rejection. If he avoids the conflict, he increases the risk of project failure. If he confronts in the right way, he opens the possibility for success and makes his and his team's lives more pleasant.

Ideally, Bob would be clever enough to avoid creating conflicts like this one—but we know they do exist. If Tony and his boss had some learning in conflict management skills and management skills in general, and if they couldn't avoid the situation, Tony would be more likely to see himself deciding how to deal with Bob's demand. Bob and Tony would probably try to apply techniques that would make it easier for them to acknowledge, confront, and resolve the issue.

Tony, knowing Bob and the organization as well as he does, may consciously choose to temporarily withdraw. He then tacitly or even explicitly agrees to go ahead. He may do some planning, undertake some deeper analysis of the design, document his results, and then confront Bob with facts and well-thought-out assumptions and opinions in hand. This might be his choice if he is relatively mature and disciplined, and is confident that Bob will be open to this approach.

On the other hand, Tony could just avoid the conflict and plunge ahead, miss the deadline, and put out a poor product by implementing the flawed design.

WHAT IS EFFECTIVE CONFLICT RESOLUTION?

Obviously, there are ways to resolve, or at least address, conflicts without the divisiveness and ineffectual outcomes that come from dysfunctional conflict resolution.

In project management, the challenge is to resolve conflict in a way that permits the project to successfully achieve its objectives—delivering a product that achieves the client's goals, within time and cost constraints. We need resolutions that both satisfy the needs of the project and promote harmony among the participants—project stakeholders, including project performers, clients, sponsors, functional managers, content experts, and vendors. And, we usually need these solutions fast.

Resolution can be reached through a consensus among peers or through authority-based decision making. The authority can be a higher-level manager, the client, a board of experts, or others.

As we have said, avoidance is a legitimate strategy for resolving conflict. The alternative, confrontation, requires a well-thought-out and well-executed approach. Once you have decided to adopt a win-win approach, you must hone the skills of dialogue and objective decision making.

DIALOGUE

Dialogue is the foundation for effective conflict resolution. The goal of dialogue is a common understanding through group investigation of all perspectives on a subject. Dialogue is collaborative and allows people to explore differences of opinion to better understand the whole.

In contrast to dialogue we have *debate*. Debate has a winner and a loser. It often leads to unresolved conflict in the long run—not particularly useful in a project. In a debate, the debaters promote their positions and attempt to shoot holes in their opponents' positions. Debates are often based on self-imposed views of how things are or how things are supposed to be. These views harden into beliefs that condition win-lose thinking. What follows is dysfunctional conflict resolution, most often relying on an authority figure to arbitrate the conclusion.

In a dialogue there are no opponents. The participants present their positions along with the underlying reasons for them. They listen. They actively identify assumptions, opinions, and beliefs and open them to individual and group scrutiny. In effect, a dialogue is a thinking process in which the minds of the participants are joined. The individual participants agree to behave as if they are a thinking entity. Their intention is to explore and learn. The process leads not only to a collective understanding of the subject but to a better future collaborative relationship among the participants.

Unfortunately, many education systems and organization cultures value and promote debate as opposed to dialogue. Have you ever heard of a "dialoguing team"? How about dialogues among political candidates? Probably not. Therefore, if we want to change the way we address conflict, we have to consciously retrain ourselves to promote dialogue.

Dialogue Seeks Inquiry, Not Decision

Dialogue does not result in a decision. William Isaacs, in *The Fifth Discipline Fieldbook*,[2] tells us that dialogue won't work if it is done with the intent of making a decision. The reason is that intent will cut off the free flow of inquiry. It is the flow of inquiry that is the objective of dialogue.

"Why," you may be thinking, "have a discussion on a controversial subject without trying to reach a decision? Isn't that just wasting time? We've got a deadline to meet, work to do." This is conventional thinking. In projects we are often time driven. That, coupled with a tendency to be action oriented, causes us to push ahead—like a bulldozer taking down the barriers to its progress.

The bulldozer strategy may be effective in some circumstances, but as a rule it leaves a field littered with rubble and, ultimately, a landscape devoid of the wonderful trees and hills that enrich the environment.

Instead, think "outside of the box." Use some of your valuable time and energy to explore, to inquire, and to investigate. Create a solid foundation for conflict resolution. Open trust among the participants. Think together. Set the stage for collaborative action based on a sense of unity as opposed to an external authority or pressure. The result is to avoid problems, delays, and excess costs later in the project.

Excuses and Failure to Learn from Experience

"We can't afford the time for this kind of luxury. We've got a schedule, cost constraints." This is the principal barrier to effective conflict resolution. It is either an excuse or a failure to learn from experience.

It is an excuse used to avoid the hard work of getting down to a patient and methodical investigation of the facts of the matter. It is an avoidance of the very difficult task of changing one's natural tendency to want to get to the end as quickly as possible. Some groups spend more time and effort arguing about why not to step back and rationally assess an issue than it would have taken to just do it. Sometimes people like to argue. They are comfortable with arguing. It works for them.

What about learning from experience? How many times do we have to experience the "we have the time to do it over but not the time to do it right" syndrome before we get it?

The time and effort it takes to explore an issue before making a decision is a trade-off against the risk of a poor outcome, lack of buy-in, and long-term discord among working groups.

We are not talking about never-ending, touchy-feely rap sessions. We can set limits based on the criticality of the issue and the time available. Over time, as we become familiar with dialogue it becomes a natural part of the way we work.

Process and Process Awareness

Process is the way you do what you do. It can be reduced to a set of steps, like a project life cycle, but it is really much more than that. The process for doing something as complex as a project is multidimensional. It includes the steps to be performed and the underlying factors that influence performance, such as communication, interpersonal relationships, creativity, and organization dynamics (including politics). These underlying factors do not lend themselves to a simple stepwise analysis.

Dialogue is not a simple process. It takes significant learning coupled with effective facilitation to permit a group to have an effective dialogue. The basic skill set is not very different from conventional communication skills—actively listen, don't interrupt, be supportive, stick to the subject, be candid, constructively offer your thoughts, be kind, give openings to others, adapt to the situation, and so on. The difference lies in (1) the group's intention (the intention to explore and learn) and (2) awareness not only of the group process but of your own internal process.

This last part—awareness of your process—is very significant. Here we are talking about what Dr. David Bohm refers to as a conscious collective mindfulness.[3] Mindfulness is the ability to perceive the thinking process as it is occurring—to observe the process while being immersed in it. This mindfulness allows us to see the subtle barriers to collaborative thinking that our habitual thinking process imposes. These barriers are (1) unquestioned assumptions, (2) overanalyzing, (3) either-or thinking, (4) emotionality, (5) lack of respect for others (and, perhaps, ourselves), (6) withholding, and (7) impulsive behavior (for example, outbursts that interrupt another person's statement).

As an individual, learn to be aware of your personal internal process, to see the thoughts as they arise, and to question yourself: What am I thinking? Why am I thinking it? What is my intention at this moment? How do I know what I think I know? Is what I am saying a belief, an opinion, an assumption, or a fact?

Do the same thing in the group: What is our intention here? Why are we discussing this now? What is the basis for this statement? How can we proceed?

As we perceive the process we can choose to modify our behavior to promote inquiry and ultimately to promote the conflict resolution we need to get the project to completion.

Training in Awareness

Some people think they must make a choice—perform the process or be aware of it. But, if one is simply performing the process without awareness there is no opportunity to adjust the process while it is being performed.

We can get stuck. Here are some examples: Someone goes into a monologue about some interesting but tangential issue, and the group is sucked into it. Or, someone keeps coming back to advocate his or her pet point. Or, assumptions and beliefs are being treated as facts, and we go off on a stream of discussion that leads us into a dead end. Or emotions rise, and the discussion gets heated with personal issues that take us away from our purpose.

On an individual level, cultivating process awareness is done through an exercise called mindfulness training. It is a classic meditation technique in which the individual simply observes his thoughts, feelings, and sensations as they arise, bringing her attention back to a point of focus (the breath, for example) when he gets lost.

Did you notice the way the prior sentence switched from "his" to "her" and back to "he"? When did you become aware of it? What went through your mind? How long will it take to return your attention to the rest of the essay?

The previous paragraph was a brief example of a classic inquiry exercise for increasing process awareness.

For the group, facilitated work sessions, process reviews, and specific training in communication skills, meeting skills, problem solving, and/or conflict management are ways to cultivate group process awareness.

Question Assumptions, Opinions, and Beliefs

Questioning assumptions, opinions, and beliefs can be threatening. Assumptions, opinions, and beliefs create barriers between people. Dialogue and other aspects of effective conflict resolution help to bring assumptions, opinions, and beliefs to the surface and identify them for what they are, allowing us to explore them.

By bringing them to the surface, we externalize and objectify them. A belief begins to lose the power it has over the believer as soon as the believer begins to question the belief. Instead of adhering to some idea, the group moves through ideas, consumes them as fuel in a fire, and produces understanding.

This does not mean giving up or devaluing beliefs or opinions. It doesn't mean that we should not make assumptions. It simply means that assumptions, beliefs, and opinions must be identified and explored with the intention of reaching a better understanding among the members of the group.

DECISION MAKING

Dialogue is focused on exploring a subject without the intention of coming to a conclusion. It sets a foundation for conflict resolution on two levels— it builds trust among the decision makers, and it provides the information needed for rationally determining an agreed-upon outcome.

While dialogue is critical, it must be coupled with decision making to permit a project to proceed. Decision making seeks convergence of ideas and beliefs so that the end result is a single accepted way to proceed—a design, an action plan, and so on.

Approaches range from debate decision making to objective decision making. Debate, as noted earlier, is not a particularly good choice. It is based on advocacy for a particular idea. It is adversarial. It promotes division. It is combative. It violates the sense of collaboration we seek to promote by engaging in dialogue. It gives advantage to individuals who are good debaters, and good debaters may not be good designers, planners, or creative thinkers. It inhibits inquiry and analysis.

Objective decision making is much different. It borrows techniques and concepts from dialogue but is very much focused on reaching a conclusion. It is task oriented. In dialogue we can explore the wide variety of divergent views and possibilities that exist around an idea. In objective decision making we consciously seek a convergent outcome—a decision. And, we do it in a way that is methodical, open, and focused on objectives.

Somewhere between the poles of debate and objective decision making are numerous decision-making approaches. Groups often move unconsciously from debate and its advocacy-oriented approach to a more discussion-based approach that fails to really come to grips with the underlying conflict. These middle-ground processes are simply not well engineered to collaboratively reach effective conclusions. They often lead to prolonged discussions, which come to an end only when the time runs out or someone loses patience. These are confused with dialogue-based objective decision making, and give it a bad name.

Negotiation

Negotiation is a form of decision making to resolve a conflict. The adversarial approach is like debate—beat the other guy to get your way. The collaborative, win-win approach is dialogue and objective decision making.

Objective Decision Making

Objective decision making is a disciplined process. Participants agree to reach a conclusion that satisfies mutually accepted objectives or conditions by analytically evaluating alternative possibilities and selecting the one that is most effective at achieving the objectives.

This approach is objective-based in two ways: First, it relies on the idea that the participants have common mutually agreed-upon objectives. Second, it is based on a nonsubjective, unemotional determination of the outcome, which is achieved by measuring the outcome against the objectives. In the first sense, the word "objective" is a noun that means something that is to be achieved, captured, or reached. In the second sense the word "objective" is an adjective that means not based on personal opinions, feelings, or beliefs.

Common Objectives

Without common objectives, resolving a conflict is close to impossible except with external intervention or open warfare. For years the Arab states and Israel have been in conflict. But, when common objectives for economic growth, fewer deaths, less fear, better standards of living, or recognition from world powers are identified as common objectives that overshadow the differences among the parties, conflict resolution becomes possible.

Fortunately, in most project settings finding common objectives is much easier than it is in international diplomacy. Projects are centered on objectives. Once the project begins and the participants agree to take their roles in it, they must buy into the objectives. Perhaps the word "must" is a bit too strong. Certainly there are projects where the participants do not agree with the objectives. These are likely to be failures, or at best they will be dragged to completion by the strength and skill of the project manager. Managing a group of people who do not have a common objective is like herding cats. Cats go off in their own directions and it takes quite some effort continuously to bring them all together.

A Case Example: Clear Objectives Set the Stage for Effective Decision Making

Two designers had opposing designs for a product. Only one design could be used. The division between the designers was clear, and the product development team was polarized around the alternative designs. Meetings were to be held to try to decide which design to use.

The first meeting devolved into a shouting match between the proponents of the competing designs. Its format was to have the design proponents each present their designs, stating strengths and weaknesses. As it turned out, each proponent stated the strengths of one design and the weaknesses of the other. The plan was to quantify strengths and weaknesses in an attempt to reach a decision. But long before the group was able to get to the decision, arguments raged about whether a weakness was in fact a weakness and a strength in fact a strength.

For example, Able put forward the ease of owner maintenance as a strength for his design, while designer Baker viewed it as a weakness and had his design inhibit owner maintenance in favor of factory service maintenance. This maintenance issue and the issue of whether certain features had to be in the initial product offering were at the heart of the conflict.

The product manager, sizing up the situation, ended the session and set a task for the group's next session. They were to back up and review product requirements in light of the firm's product sales and postsales strategies. Then, without regard to any specific designs, they were to agree on strategic objectives. And they were to do it as a single team, collaboratively, by next week.

The designers were forced to address assumptions about what features and functions of the product the firm valued. They had been arguing based on their beliefs, never bothering to validate them with the marketing and product management people. Of course, the conflict might have been avoided in the first place had the product requirements clearly identified these values issues.

What If There Are No Common Objectives?

Sometimes it isn't possible to have common objectives. In project work this may be caused by clashes between the objectives of a single project and organizational objectives or by clashes between individual objectives and project objectives.

Examples of clashes between project and organization-level issues are:

- Resources are needed for the project and to keep up operational activities.
- Two projects are vying for the same resources.
- A functional manager wants to send a person to leadership training during a project assignment.

When these arise it is best to find an authority at the right level of the organization to resolve them, usually by setting priorities. Resolving them among a peer group is very difficult without priorities and direction from above.

Personal objectives may clash with one another or with project objectives. For example, a designer may care less about which design is best for the project or the client and more about getting his or her name on the product credits. To make these matters more difficult to deal with, personal objectives are often only implied—the designer doesn't say, "I want to have my name on this product because it is good for my career."

We try to address the issue from a logical point of view and run into roadblocks. Here we have to bring the motives of the participants to the surface. Are they willing to subordinate their personal objectives to the project and organization objectives? If not, we do well to formalize the decision-making process and bring in outside facilitation, if not authority-based decision making. The "weights and scores" approach discussed later in the chapter helps to cut through the barrier of hidden personal agendas.

Objectivity

Objectivity is basing decisions on something other than personal belief. It relies on the assessment of facts and the evaluation of various perspectives on a subject. Evaluation requires a baseline or benchmark. In objective decision making, the benchmark must be explicit, measurable, and mutually agreed upon. For example, if you were trying to evaluate alternative designs and your benchmark was a "good design," you would probably find that not everyone had the same definition for "good design."

To get to a useful definition of "good design," someone would first have to confront the issue that the mutual assumption—that everyone knows what a good design is—is an assumption. Then the assumption must be validated.

If, upon questioning, the group could not adequately define their understanding of a good design, its attributes would have to be spelled out and quantified so they could be measured to determine if the design was in fact good. These same attributes would become the criteria for deciding which of the design alternatives are acceptable.

Here we are using a dialogue technique—questioning assumptions. Through this open inquiry into the nature of a good design, we take a giant step toward a decision.

Objectivity is a skillful way to avoid the interpersonal strife that is all too common in our project decision-making experience.

The Courage to Raise and Resolve Process Issues

In many projects, it requires great courage to raise a question like "Do we really know what a good design is?" or to tell two opposing design proponents to forget about their designs and validate their assumptions. It requires tenacity and, often, authority to press the question until it is answered and the answer is validated with a concrete and useful definition.

Many project managers, performers, clients, and other stakeholders may feel that we are just spinning our wheels and splitting hairs. "Oh, come on. Let's just get on with it" is an all-too-common mantra. It is as if people like heated, never-ending arguments and/or inadequate results.

Without someone raising the process question (for example, "Are we all using the same definitions and are they correct?"), we have no hope of resolving the content issue (for example, choosing which design is best).

The Decision-Making Process

Objective decision making follows a logical process:

1. Describe the problem and its setting.
2. Set objectives.
3. Identify causes.
4. Identify potential solutions.
5. Decide.
6. Act—implement the solution/decision.
7. Monitor and adjust.

These steps are a model for convenience in discussing and learning about problem solving and decision making. They are a guide through the process, which is really continuous and often requires iterative refinement. There are many models for objective decision making. All of them may be valid and useful. They are describing a complex process. The process always remains the same; the filter (that is, the process steps and definitions) we lay over it changes.

Following this process ensures that there is a solid foundation for deciding (Step 5) before we get to it. But keep in mind that process models are conveniences. They help to align people, and state a value-adding approach to doing something. As the people learn the process intellectually and begin to use it, they begin to embody it—it becomes more natural. As the process becomes more natural, strict orthodox adherence to the model is far less important—though the model, if it is good and truly adds value, should not be forgotten. It remains a reminder of the ideal approach.

Don't be overly attached to the model. The essence is to know what you are to accomplish, and use an approach that is likely to accomplish it well. Open discussion, objectivity, mutually agreed-upon objectives, a logical progression of steps, and respect for other participants are essential.

Creativity and Spontaneity

When an issue arises, the solution that instantly comes to mind is often the best. If there is *really* no time for further analysis, go with your gut feeling.

But, realize that you are taking a risk that could be reduced if you take the time to follow the process. What is at stake? Isn't it better to spend the time analyzing the problem than it is to take the risk of applying a solution that doesn't work or that makes things worse? Is it even possible to implement your decision without justifying it to others?

What is your motivation for moving ahead without due diligence? Is it impatience? lack of a process model? a business need to act without delay?

Objective decision making doesn't disregard creativity and spontaneity. It enhances creativity and permits spontaneity when it is appropriate.

Evaluating Alternatives

One of the most common and powerful decision-making techniques is the "weights and scores" approach. This approach is commonly used in procurement to select among alternative vendors and products and in design selection situations. Underlying the techniques are principles that can be applied in many other situations, perhaps in a less formal way than described here.

The basic principles are:

- Identify and weight or value the criteria for making the decision before you start evaluating alternatives.
- Base your criteria and weights on project or organizational objectives.
- Be analytical and objective.
- Be flexible—don't think the numbers will tell you the right answer. Adjust your criteria and weights and scores to see what happens under different scenarios.

The technique is to determine a "figure of merit" for each alternative by weighting each of the evaluation criteria and then scoring each alternative for each criterion.

While the figures of merit are entirely subjective (they have no units and no intrinsic meaning), they are useful because they permit a comparison based on quantitative measures. Further, the technique forces the decision makers to identify the criteria for the decision before getting caught up in circular arguments based on subjective likes and dislikes.

The weights and scores approach involves the following seven steps:

1. Identify the alternatives being considered.
2. Identify the evaluation criteria that are pertinent to the decision; make sure that this list is complete.
3. Select the single most critical criterion, and give this factor a weight of 10 on a scale of 1 to 10. *Note: This is best done by negotiation between the key stakeholders.*
4. Rank all the remaining criteria in declining order of importance, and assign a weight to each factor on a scale of 1 to 10; this weight is a

rough index of the relative importance of the factor when compared with all other factors.

5. Once a relative weight has been assigned to each factor, score each alternative according to how well it satisfies or realizes the benefit; this scoring may be done on a scale of 1 to 100.
6. Now, compute a weighted score for each criterion, for each alternative, by multiplying the score obtained in Step 5 by its weight assigned in Steps 3 and 4.
7. Finally, sum the weighted scores for each alternative, and obtain a total figure of merit for each alternative.

Since this is not a precise science, it is desirable to reevaluate the criteria, weights, and scores and see what difference they make. This what-if process helps to convince the decision makers that the decision is valid.

Dialogue within Decision Making

Dialogue and decision making are two distinct techniques, but they can be used in an integrated way to confront and resolve conflict, based on a win-win strategy. Dialogue occurs not only as a preparation for decision making but as a communication process that is repeated throughout the decision-making process.

Coming to a Decision

Conflict resolution results in a decision to proceed in a particular direction in a particular way or to not proceed at all. The decision can be tacit or explicit. The behavior or action it puts in place evidences the decision.

There are three ways to come to a resolution or a decision—consensus, majority, and authority. Consensus is where all the parties to the conflict agree that a decision is acceptable to them. Majority is where the largest percentage of the participants—but not all—decide. Authority is where an individual or group with authority decides.

Avoid majority-based decisions in projects. Shoot for consensus within a time limit. If you cannot achieve consensus, escalate the issue and get an authority decision that either gives you more time to come to consensus or resolves the issue.

Majority rule tends to cut off dialogue. It is based on a premise that the majority is more likely to be right than the minority, which may not be correct. To avoid group-think and dictatorship by the majority, avoid taking binding votes on decisions.

Authority-based decisions also cut off the dialogue and the consensus process, but since the participants have bought into the power of the authority they are more likely to accept and work with the result. Of course, we rely on the wisdom of the authority and the notion that the authority will make use of the information that has come out of the attempt to reach consensus. To avoid never-ending conflict you must be ready to escalate resolution to higher authorities for arbitration.

AUTHORITY DECISIONS: ESCALATION AND ARBITRATION

In project management, escalation of issues that cannot be resolved by peers should be an acceptable and planned alternative to leaving the issue unresolved.

The word *escalation* when applied to conflict can have two meanings: (1) increasing the scope or intensity of the conflict, as in escalating a minor issue into a battle or a battle into a war, and (2) raising the conflict issue to a high authority for resolution. We generally want to avoid the first and do the second in a way that minimizes the potential discord that can intensify or broaden the conflict.

Why, you might ask, might escalation to a higher authority cause discord? Often, this is done unilaterally or has a negative connotation ("We failed to come to a conclusion, and now we have to ask someone else for help.")

When one party in a conflict brings the conflict to a higher authority without agreement by the other(s) or does so without notifying the other(s), the conflict escalates in intensity. It shifts from a content issue to a political and interpersonal process issue. Once conflict shifts into political and interpersonal realms, personal feelings intensify, the content is overshadowed, relationships become strained, and so on. Chances are, you've been there.

An Ounce of Prevention

To avoid this unnecessary wasted energy and effort, plan the way conflict will be addressed. When beginning to address a major conflict, clearly identify the criteria for when to escalate to a higher authority. For example, in the case of a design alternative disagreement, the parties should give themselves or be given a time frame and a procedure for how they will engage in the decision-making process.

They should know who would resolve the issue if they do not reach consensus. They should agree that escalation would take place when the time runs out or when they agree that they have reached a deadlock. They should agree that neither party would unilaterally escalate without first notifying the other(s). They should agree in advance how they would escalate—for example, the nature and content of the decision package they will provide to the decision authority.

For issues that are not as clear-cut as design selection, the project participants should agree that notification of the participants would precede any escalation. The intent here is to avoid the embarrassment that comes with being blindsided by someone who informs your boss's boss about some issue that you are responsible for.

Case Example: Shifting from Content to Process and Back Again

What follows is a case that highlights conflict resolution and escalation issues. In particular it shows how lack of planning and inappropriate escalation to higher authority can cause a conflict to expand into the political/process realm.

Vlad worked for a vendor of customization services. His firm had assigned him to a client as a project leader to customize a product supplied by another vendor. After a brief review of the project plan, Vlad informed his management that the target date for his group's work was impossible to meet. The customization work was on the client's project's critical path. The client project manager had committed a target date to her management, a date based in part on the customization vendor's informal proposal.

The customization vendor's account manager mentioned the issue to his contact—the client project sponsor—and the sponsor called the project manager in for an explanation.

Since Louisa, the project manager, was unaware of the issue, she was caught without any explanation. Her embarrassment in front of the sponsor was quickly replaced by anger at the project leader, the account manager, and their firm. At the moment, the content of the issue—whether they could hit the target—was secondary. The foreground was filled with emotions.

Fortunately, Louisa was clever and capable enough to let her anger and embarrassment subside before deciding what to do next. She was aware of her personal process. She was aware of the group process. She knew that both making excuses and lashing out at the vendors would do more harm than good.

So, after a few long breaths she put a subtle smile on her face and told the sponsor that she'd look into the situation and get back to him as soon as possible. As she left his office she said, "And I'll make sure that next time I'll know about any issues on this project before you do."

Louisa set her mind to address two issues—(1) the content issue regarding whether the target date could be met and why and (2) the process issue of how to deal with issues like this one (issues management). Had issues management been addressed properly at the beginning of the project, this escalation and the potential for discord in the project probably would have been avoided.

Louisa addressed the content issue first. She got together with Vlad, the customization vendor's project leader, and simply asked him why he thought the target date was impossible. Ultimately, they engaged the product vendor in a work session and found that some of Vlad's assumptions about the product were incorrect and that by shifting his approach a bit he could easily get the work done with much less effort than he originally thought.

Louisa then took on the process issue. She got Vlad and the account manager together and explained to them how she wanted issues to be handled in the future. She didn't forbid them from going to the sponsor. She just made it clear that she wanted to be notified in advance and that any issues regarding the plan, product definition, or anything else related to the project would be documented and managed through the project's issues management process. She made it clear that she had been put in an embarrassing position and while she could overlook it this time, repetition would not be acceptable.

Louisa also addressed the issue with the sponsor. She asked him to make sure that people coming to him with issues had first gone through her and the issues management procedure. She told him that this would save him time and effort and train the vendors and others to go through the right channels.

Case Example Conclusion

In this case Louisa saved all concerned from an acrimonious and divisive conflict that could have infected the remainder of the project. Louisa chose to take a noncombative approach, even though there was provocation. She went about handling the content (target date) issue in a logical and effective way. She didn't forget about the process issue, but avoided it until she could deal with it without emotionality getting in the way.

Louisa's approach included:

- Process awareness (her own embarrassment and anger, the need for a defined group process, and the impact her intentions and behavior would have on others)
- Dialogue (discussing the issue with Vlad, hearing his reasoning, and questioning his premises) before jumping to the conclusion that a

conflict existed between the two of them. Louisa didn't dig in to her position that the target date was fixed, nor did she raise the point of the vendor's proposal.

- Decision making (involving the right people, addressing the facts of the matter, questioning assumptions, shooting for a win-win resolution, and basing the outcome on concrete considerations such as the effort required to do the work)

This process didn't require an outside facilitator. Louisa facilitated the process while she was an integral player in it. This process did not require that Vlad and his account manager have a course in conflict management. Louisa unilaterally defused the situation and directed it to a mutually acceptable conclusion. The situation was used as an opportunity to set things in order to avoid a recurrence. Louisa learned that it would be to everyone's benefit to put procedures in place for issues management and conflict resolution before a project gets started.

Use the opportunities you have—your conflicts—to build relationships while coming to resolutions that satisfy project, organization, and personal objectives. Engage in dialogue instead of debate and make decisions using an objective decision-making process. Be part of the solution.

SUMMARY

In this chapter we have discussed conflict management with an emphasis on the desirability of dialogue and on the need for effective objective decision making.

Conflict is an inevitable and useful part of project management and performance (as well as life itself). Effective conflict management focuses on conflict resolution that leads to effective resolutions and harmony among participants. We set the stage for relatively conflict-free product implementation and product life.

The keys to effective conflict resolution are process awareness, effective communication, and positive intention.

Dialogue has been identified as a foundation for effective conflict resolution. Dialogue seeks a common understanding through group investigation or inquiry of all perspectives on a subject.

Process awareness involves acknowledging that dysfunctional conflict resolution exists and is probably caused by faulty processes. Awareness permits conscious choice between the strategies of conflict avoidance and confrontation. If we choose confrontation, then we can consciously choose between win-lose and win-win approaches. Awareness allows us to identify and address the assumptions, opinions, and beliefs that often get in the way of conflict resolution or are the underlying causes of conflict. Awareness allows us to address the parts of our process that can be improved.

Once we choose to confront conflict, we need an effective decision-making process. We recommend objective decision making in which mutually agreed-upon objectives are coupled with a nonsubjective, nonemotional approach. Be methodical, rely on facts, question assumptions, and at the same time use creativity and spontaneity as the basis for effective decisions. Shoot for consensus, but be ready to rely on authority-based decision making when time is short and the situation calls for it. Manage escalation so that it does not become a cause for discord.

Remember that you have a choice between adversarial conflict management and the politics and division it brings versus collaboration, synergy, exploration, and excellence. Choose wisely.

REFERENCES

1. Pitagorsky, George. 2000. *Project Management Basics*, New York: International Institute for Learning.
2. Senge, Peter M. 1994. *The Fifth Discipline Fieldbook: Strategies and Tools for Building a Learning Organization*. New York: Currency Doubleday.
3. Bohm, David. 1999. *On Dialogue*. New York: Routledge.

CHAPTER 23

ROLE MANAGEMENT: THE INTEGRATIVE ROLES IN PROJECT MANAGEMENT

RUSSELL D. ARCHIBALD

One way to look at the project management discipline is to view it as consisting of these three basic components:

1. *Integrative project responsibilities*—the integrative roles
2. *Integrative and predictive project planning and control systems*—the project documents, procedures, information processing and communication systems, and their application
3. *Integrative project team*—identifying, integrating, and managing the project team to integrate the efforts of all contributors to the project

This chapter discusses the first of these project management concepts. The other concepts are discussed in detail in other chapters of this book.

THE KEY INTEGRATIVE ROLES

The role of the project manager is obviously a central one, and in fact this role has received considerable attention in the project management literature over the past several decades. However, there are other important integrative roles in project management as shown in Figure 23.1, and these have frequently been ignored. The key integrative roles are:

Executive Level
- *General manager* integrates all projects in the organization's project portfolio with the corporate strategic plans and has overall responsibility for a multifunctional division or an entire company.

Figure 23.1
Generic Relationship of Key Integrative Roles

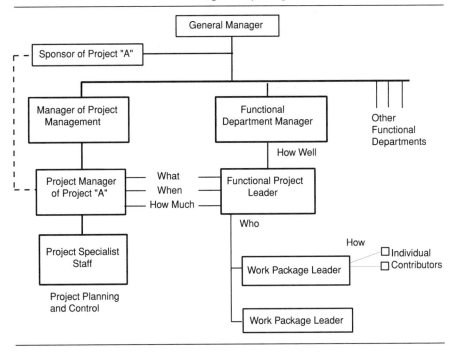

- *Project sponsor* integrates, on the assigned project(s), the ongoing strategic direction of the project, given to the project manager and through him or her to the project team, with the ongoing operations of the organization.

Multi-Project Level
- *Manager* (or *vice president, director,* and so on) *of project management* integrates the operational aspects of the work being done on all projects within the organization, and integrates the development and use of the organization's project management methods and tools on all projects.
- *Multi-project manager* or *program manager* integrates the efforts of all project contributors on his or her assigned projects.

Project Level
- *Project manager* integrates the efforts of all project contributors on his or her project.

Functional Department and Project Contributor Level

- *Functional department managers* integrate the efforts of project contributors on all projects within their individual departments or disciplines, primarily through the allocation of resources available within the departments to the approved, active portfolio of projects.
- *Functional project leaders* integrate the work of all contributors to their specific assigned projects within each of their respective functions.
- *Work package leaders* integrate the work of individual contributors to each of their assigned work control packages within each project.

Other important roles relating to projects include:

- *Project customer*—the person or organization that has authorized the project
- *Project champion*—the person who promotes and keeps the project alive, who may or may not be the general manager
- *Owner of the results of the project*—this person may or may not be the project customer
- *User or operator of the project results*—this person may or may not be the owner

While all of these additional roles are important, they do not carry the same level of *integrative* responsibility as the key roles listed earlier. However, if the project customer organization is a major contributor to the project, performing important tasks on which project completion is dependent, then there is a need to identify the integrative roles listed within the customer's organization as well. The same can be said for all outside organizations that contribute significantly to the project in question.

In the following sections each of the key integrative roles are described and discussed in more detail.

General Manager

The role of the *general manager* in project management is focused on:

- Determining how the organization's portfolio of projects supports the overall business strategies of the organization
- Overseeing the organization's overall project management process
- Monitoring how this process is integrated with all other aspects of the organization
- Assuring that sufficient money, human, and other resources are available to support all of the approved projects

Project Sponsor

The *project sponsor* role is usually held by a senior manager or a "plural executive" in the form of a steering group or committee, acting for the top management of the sponsoring or project executing organization. This role may be held by the general manager of the organization responsible for the project or by a high-level executive, or it may be delegated to someone who reports to the general manager. In some cases, the project sponsor role is held by a steering group comprised of key people from various parts of the organization. Only within the past decade or so has the importance of the project sponsor role been recognized, together with the importance of formally identifying who is assigned to this role for a specific project.

A team of experienced project management professionals concluded that:

> The absence of a specifically assigned project sponsor with well defined and understood responsibilities is the cause of many difficulties for projects and project managers. By focusing more attention on this vital role, the effectiveness of project management practices could be improved in most organizations.[1]

When a project sponsor has not been identified, the project manager often has difficulty in knowing whom to go to, other than the general manager (to whom access is often difficult or inhibited) for the required decisions that are beyond the project manager's assigned authority. Also, when no project sponsor is assigned, some managers (including the project manager at times) may assume that the project manager should act also as the project sponsor. In this case, the project manager may cause problems and conflicts by reaching beyond his or her assigned authority. It is possible to assign one person to both the roles of project sponsor and project manager, but in most circumstances these roles should be separated.

Manager of Project Management

The role of *manager* (or *vice president*, *director*, and so on) *of project management* has emerged in many organizations as these organizations mature in their project management capabilities. This position is a recognition of the project management function as an important capability within the organization, along with the more traditional functions of marketing, engineering, procurement, manufacturing, construction/field operations, finance and accounting, legal, and so on. The manager of project management may also be the project sponsor for specific projects, in some situations.

Some practitioners have predicted that there will soon be a *chief projects officer* in many organizations, on a par with the fairly recent position of chief information officer. This position might combine aspects of the project sponsor and manager of project management roles. It remains to be seen whether this becomes a reality.

Multi-Project Manager

The *multi-project manager* or program manager performs the duties of the project manager on several projects at the same time. These may be several small projects, or a project manager near the end of one project may also be assigned to another project that is in its initial conception phase, for example. Strategically this role differs somewhat from that of the project manager since this person must often resolve conflicts between the two or more projects that she or he is managing. Depending on the number, size, and nature of the projects, this role may take on some of the responsibilities of the manager of project management or the general manager. On some large aerospace programs, for example, a subordinate project manager is usually assigned to each project within the overall program.

Project Manager

The *project manager* role is more operational in nature compared to the more strategic role of the project sponsor. The project manager plans and directs the execution of the project to meet the time, cost, and performance objectives as established by the project sponsor. The project manager integrates the efforts of all persons and organizations contributing to the project.

Functional Department Managers

Because it is usually not feasible to create a totally self-sustaining organization with all the needed specialized skills for any one project, essentially all projects are supported by some kind of functionally specialized or departmentalized organizations. Most organizations are planning and executing a number of projects simultaneously. The result of this matrix management situation is that each specialized department has people assigned to perform various tasks on each of the many current projects. The matrix results from the crossing of two lines of direction, functional and project.

Functional direction (mainly *who* will do the work, *how* and to what *quality level* it will be done) comes down through the functional organization in the traditional manner. Project direction (*what* needs to be done, *when* the task must be completed, and *how much* labor and money is to be expended—initially established in negotiation with the affected department manager) comes from the project manager and usually enters the functional departments through the functional project leaders. Three levels of integrative responsibility exist within each of these departments:

1. Department manager
2. Functional project leaders
3. Work package (or task) leaders

Each *functional department manager* must first provide the needed resources (people and facilities) to support every project on a timely basis, while integrating the often conflicting demands of all active projects within his or her department. The functional department manager integrates the tasks on all projects by working through the functional project leaders assigned to each active project.

The department manager, for example, allocates his or her resources to the various projects' tasks and attempts to reflect the relative priorities of each project, as reported by each affected functional project leader. If the department manager's direction creates schedule, cost, or quality conflicts with the overall project plan, then the functional project leader must either resolve these conflicts or report them to the project manager. These functional project leaders must deal with sometimes conflicting direction from both their functional boss and their project boss, the project manager.

Functional Project Leaders
On any given project there will be several *functional project leaders* whose role is to integrate the project work within their particular functions or subfunctions (marketing, engineering, test operations, manufacturing, production, and so on). Each functional project leader integrates the work being done with the activities of the project team members within their specific function, working through the responsible work package (or task) leaders. The project manager integrates the work of all functions at the project level, and the functional department managers integrate the work of all projects being supported within their departments through their day-to-day direction of the functional project leaders.

Work Package Leaders
A *work package* or *task* is the smallest element of work that is normally planned and controlled within the integrated, overall project plan. Each

work package (or *task*) *leader* integrates the work of the individuals assigned to his or her work package.

Generic Relationship Model of these Integrative Roles

Figure 23.1 illustrates the generic relationships between these integrative roles.

A *project specialist staff* is shown reporting to the project manager of project "A" in Figure 23.1. These persons may be directly assigned to the project office of project "A" or may be located in a functional department responsible for all *project planning and control* support within the organization. In the latter case there will be a project planning and control leader for project "A" within that functional department who takes direction from the project manager.

RESPONSIBILITIES AND AUTHORITY OF THE INTEGRATIVE ROLES

Responsibilities for initiating, defining, planning, executing, controlling, and closing out projects are allocated among the persons assigned to the roles described in the previous section. Assigning authority commensurate with these responsibilities is often difficult, especially when the integrative nature of these roles is not well understood. The project manager role is the most problematic since the person assigned to that role gives direction that cuts across the functional organizational lines of traditional authority. When everyone in the organization understands the nature of this project direction (what, when, and how much), these problems will be minimized. The manner in which these various responsibilities and the related authority are allocated will depend on:

- The size and nature of the project's parent organization
- The size, nature, and priority of a given project and its current life-cycle phase
- The number of projects in progress simultaneously
- The experience and capabilities of the persons involved
- The maturity of the project management function within the organization

The following paragraphs present generally accepted descriptions of the responsibilities associated with each of the integrative roles described earlier, together with comments as appropriate regarding the associated authority of each role.

Responsibilities Retained by the General Manager

All of the responsibilities given to the other integrative roles are delegated either formally or informally by the general manager, but there are certain major project responsibilities that cannot be truly delegated without abdication of the position. Except in rare circumstances, the general manager is not involved directly with the planning and execution of any one project. Generally, the responsibilities retained by the general manager include:

- Assuring that the right projects are selected and approved in the first place
- Providing adequate resources to carry out the approved projects
- Assuring that the project management practices in use within the organization are appropriate and effectively applied
- Monitoring the overall performance on projects and integrating that performance with the other operations of the organization
- Resolving project-related conflicts involving functional department and project managers
- Evaluating project performance of those managers reporting to the general manager
- Evaluating progress on major projects (major milestone accomplishments, forecasts of costs and profits at completion, and so on) periodically

The general manager holds the ultimate authority (as delegated to that position by the board of directors or another higher-level authority) for all aspects of his or her organization. The authority of this position to carry out the responsibilities on projects listed here is rarely, if ever, questioned.

Project Sponsor Responsibilities and Authority

The project sponsor is the focal point for project decisions that are beyond the scope of authority of the project manager. If the project sponsor cannot make a particular decision, he or she is responsible for escalating the decision or conflict to the general manager or other higher-level authority. Typical responsibilities of the project sponsor are:[2]

- Holding accountability for the project investment
- Defining and making the business case for the project (the marketing, economic, technological, and other justification for the project investment)

- Approving the project scope and objectives, including schedule and budget
- Issuing project directives as appropriate (such as release of funds, major changes in project scope, cost, schedule, and so on)
- Appointing or approving the appointment of the project manager and approving that person's organizational charter and reporting location
- Monitoring the project environment and advising the project manager of pertinent strategic changes
- Making and approving major project changes (scope, cost, schedule) and decisions on project requirements
- Being informed of and evaluating project progress periodically and providing strategic direction to the project manager
- Setting strategic priorities and resolving conflicts escalated by the project manager or functional department managers
- Assuring that the products of the project will satisfy the original justification for the project, in light of economic, competitive, and market changes in the environment during the project execution, in close cooperation with the project manager

The charter of the project sponsor should delegate appropriate authority to the person or group of persons assigned to this role to carry out these responsibilities. On large, complex, and high-risk projects the best solution often is to name three or more senior people to act as a "plural executive" in this role, unless the general manager is willing and able to act as the project sponsor. This role is usually not a full-time assignment, whether one or several persons are assigned to it.

Manager of Project Management Responsibilities and Authority

The manager of project management is typically responsible for:

- Providing professional direction and training to the project and multi-project managers. This is usually directed primarily to developing the project managers' skills and the use and application of the organization's project management methods and information systems.
- Developing and improving the organization's project management process, policies, procedures, and practices, including the acquisition and development of needed computer software packages, and assuring that adequate indoctrination and training in all of these areas are provided throughout the organization.
- Providing appropriate project planning, scheduling, estimating, monitoring, and reporting assistance to the project and multi-project managers. What is appropriate assistance varies considerably; at one

extreme, some organizations have established totally centralized support for all projects; at the other extreme, each project manager and project office is self-sufficient in this area.

- Resolving interproject conflicts, in full coordination with the responsible project sponsors, consistent with the scope of authority delegated to this position and to the project sponsors by the general manager
- Assuring project compliance with commitments.

The authority delegated to the manager of project management will vary considerably, depending on the maturity of the project management function within the organization and the self-sufficiency of each project manager, and how his or her project office is staffed. The manager of project management must be a full-time assignment in any organization of reasonable size and complexity.

Multi-Project Manager Responsibilities and Authority

Multi-project managers hold the same responsibilities for their assigned projects as those of the manager of a single project, and are delegated similar authority as a project manager.

Project Manager Responsibilities and Authority

The general manager may delegate very limited or very broad responsibilities and authority to one person to integrate all the work on one project. If very limited responsibility and authority are delegated, that person acts primarily as a project coordinator or expediter, and the general manager (or other higher level person) retains the role of the real project manager.

The project manager, to deserve this title, must be delegated the basic responsibility of overall planning, direction, and control of the project through all of its phases to achieve the specified results within the approved budget and schedule.

The project manager is the general manager of the project in terms of responsibility, accountability for final profit and loss on the project, and meeting the established completion date. The project manager's primary task is the integration of the efforts of all persons contributing to the project. This responsibility does not supplant the responsibility of each functional manager whose people are contributing to the project, but rather overlaps the functional responsibilities, with emphasis on the total project.

The project manager's responsibility may be defined in much greater detail with specific reference to the areas of planning, scheduling, negotiating, communicating, evaluating, controlling, decision making, and reporting.

Table 23.1 presents a typical project manager position description for a complex high-technology project involving product design, manufacture, and field installation. In practice, such position descriptions must be tailored to the specific industry and project. Differences will occur for each category of project (for example, engineering/construction of capital facilities, product development, research, information systems, and so on), as well as for those differences caused by the nature of the parent organization, the industry, and the project itself.

The project manager is delegated *project authority*—the authority to give direction to the functional project leaders (or in their absence, to the appropriate functional managers) required to plan, execute, monitor, evaluate, and control the work to be done on his or her assigned project. As shown earlier in the organization chart in Figure 23.1, this project direction relates to *what* needs to be done, *when* it must be accomplished, and *how much money* or *how many work hours* are to be expended. These are established by negotiation between the project manager and the various functional managers or functional project leaders. Project direction also includes *obtaining the needed information* to plan, monitor, evaluate, and control the overall project. The functional manager or project leader, on the other hand, gives direction concerning *how well* the work is to be done (quality), *who* specifically will do the work, and *how* the work will be accomplished (technical methods). When the project manager tries to give direction to the functional project leaders or the work package leaders regarding how well, who, and how, he or she will generate significant conflicts with the functional people.

The project manager's authority depends to a large degree on his or her ability to earn it, rather than depending entirely on delegated legal authority. The sources of these two types of authority are:

Legal Authority Sources	*Earned Authority Sources*
Organizational charter	Technical and organizational knowledge
Organizational position	Management experience
Position or job specification	Maintenance of rapport
Executive rank	Negotiation with peers and associates
Policy documents	Building and maintaining alliances
Superior's right to command	Project manager's focal position: has more knowledge about the project than anyone
Delegated power	The deliberately created conflict
Hierarchical flow of authority	The resolution of conflict
Control of funds	Being right

Table 23.1
Typical Project Manager Position Description Duties and Responsibilities

Project Start-Up

- Identify key project team members and define their responsibilities.
- Plan and start up the project using project team planning start-up workshops. This should be done rapidly and efficiently.

General

- Assure that all equipment, documents, and services are properly delivered to the customer for acceptance and use within the contractual schedule and costs.
- Convey to all concerned departments (both internal and external) a full understanding of the customer requirements of the project.
- Participate with and lead the responsible managers and key team members in developing overall project objectives, strategies, budgets, and schedules.
- Plan for all necessary tasks to satisfy customer and management requirements, and assure that they are properly and realistically scheduled, budgeted, provided for, monitored, and reported.
- Identify promptly all deficiencies and deviations from the current plan.
- Assure that the required actions are initiated to correct deficiencies and deviations from project plans, schedules, budgets, and deliverable specifications, and monitor execution of such actions.
- Assure that payments are received in accordance with the contractual terms.
- Maintain cognizance over all project contracts with the customer, and assure that proper project team members participate in such contracts.
- Arbitrate and resolve conflicts and differences between functional departments on specific project tasks or activities.
- Maintain day-to-day liaison with all functional contributors to provide communication required to ensure realization of commitments.
- Make or force required decisions at successively higher organizational levels to achieve project objectives, following agreed-upon escalation procedures.
- Maintain communications with higher management through the project sponsor regarding problem areas and project status.

Customer Relations

In close cooperation with the customer relations or marketing department:

- Receive from the customer all necessary technical, cost, and scheduling information required for accomplishment of the project.
- Establish good working relationships with the customer on all levels: management, contracts, legal, accounts payable, systems engineering, design engineering, field sites, and operations.
- Arrange and attend meetings with the customer (contractual, planning, engineering, and operations).
- Receive and answer all technical and operational questions from the customer, with appropriate assistance from functional departments.

(Continued)

Table 23.1 *(Continued)*
Typical Project Manager Position Description Duties and Responsibilities

Contract Administration
- Identify any potential areas of exposure in existing or potential contracts, and initiate appropriate action to alert higher management and eliminate such exposure.
- Prepare and send, or approve prior to sending by others, all correspondence on contractual matters.
- Coordinate the activities of the project contract administrator in regard to project matters.
- Prepare for and participate in contract negotiations.
- Identify all open contract commitments.
- Advise engineering, manufacturing, and field operations of contractual commitments and variations allowed.
- Prepare historical or position papers on any contractual or technical aspect of the project for use in contract negotiations or litigation.

Project Planning, Control, Reporting, Evaluation, and Direction
- Perform, or supervise the performance of, all project planning, controlling, reporting, evaluation, and direction functions (as commonly described in the project management literature) as appropriate to the scope of the assigned project.
- Conduct frequent, regular project evaluation and review meetings with key project team members to identify current and future problems and initiate actions for their resolution.
- Prepare and submit weekly or monthly progress reports to higher management, and to the customer if required.
- Supervise the project controller and his or her staff.

Marketing
- Maintain close liaison with marketing and utilize customer contacts to acquire all possible marketing intelligence for future business.

Engineering
- Ensure that engineering fulfills its responsibilities for delivering, on schedule and within product cost estimates, the required drawings and specifications usable by manufacturing, purchasing, and field operations, meeting the customer specifications.
- In cooperation with the engineering, drafting, and publications departments, define and establish schedules and budgets for all engineering and related tasks. After agreement, release funding allowables and monitor progress on each task in relation to the overall project.
- Act as the interface with the customer for these departments, with their assistance as required.
- Assure the control of product quality, configuration, and cost.
- Approve technical publications prior to release to the customer.

Table 23.1 *(Continued)*
Typical Project Manager Position Description Duties and Responsibilities

- Coordinate engineering support related to the project for manufacturing, installation, legal, and other departments.
- Participate (or delegate participation) as a voting member of the Engineering Change Control Board on matters affecting the project.

Manufacturing
- Ensure that manufacturing fulfills its responsibilities for on-schedule delivery of all required equipment, meeting the engineering specifications within estimated manufacturing costs.
- Define contractual commitments to production control.
- Develop schedules to meet contractual commitments in the most economic fashion.
- Establish and release manufacturing and related resource and funding allowables.
- Approve and monitor production control schedules.
- Establish project priorities in manufacturing.
- Approve, prior to implementation, any product changes initiated by manufacturing.
- Approve packing and shipping instructions based on the type of transportation to be used and the schedule for delivery.

Purchasing and Subcontracting
- Ensure that purchasing and subcontracting fulfill their responsibilities to obtain delivery of materials, equipment, documents, and services on schedule and within estimated cost for the project.
- Approve make-or-buy decisions for the project.
- Define contractual commitments to purchasing and subcontracting.
- Establish and release procurement funding allowables.
- Approve and monitor major purchase orders and subcontracts.
- Specify the planning, scheduling, and reporting requirements for major purchase orders and subcontracts.

Installation, Construction, Testing, and Other Field Operations
- Ensure that installation and field operations fulfill their responsibilities for on-schedule delivery to the customer of materials, equipment, and documents within the cost estimates for the project.
- Define contractual commitments to installation and field operations.
- Define and establish schedules and budgets for all field work, in cooperation with installation and field operations. After agreement, release funding allowables and monitor progress on each task in relation to the overall project.
- Coordinate all problems of performance and schedule with engineering, manufacturing, purchasing, and subcontracting.

(Continued)

Table 23.1 *(Continued)*
Typical Project Manager Position Description Duties and Responsibilities

---

- Act as the customer interface for installation and field operations departments (except for customer contacts related to daily operating matters).

Financial
In addition to the financial aspects of the project planning and control functions:
- Assist in the collection of accounts receivable related to the project.
- Approve prices of all change orders and proposals to the customer that affect the project.

Project Closeout
- Ensure that all required steps are taken to present adequately all project deliverable items to the customer for acceptance, and that project activities are closed out in an efficient manner.
- Assure that the acceptance plan and schedule comply with the customer contractual requirements.
- Assist the legal, contract administration, and marketing or commercial departments in preparation of a closeout plan and required closeout data.
- Obtain and approve project closeout plans from each involved department.
- Monitor closeout activities, including disposition of surplus materials.
- Notify finance and functional departments of the completion of activities and tasks, and of the project itself.
- Monitor payment from the customer until all collections have been made.
- Create a "lessons learned" file to enable continuous improvement in the organization's project management capabilities for use on future projects.

Because the project manager must elicit performance from others who are not under his or her direct control, he or she must rely on interpersonal influence bases other than formal, legal authority. David Wilemon and Gary Gemmill have identified three influence bases that are of major importance to project managers:[3]

1. *Expert power* refers to the ability of the project manager to get project contributors to do what he or she wants them to do because they attribute greater knowledge to that person and believe that she or he is more qualified to evaluate the consequences of certain project actions or decisions.
2. *Referent power* pertains to the responsiveness of project contributors because they are, for some reason or another, personally attracted to the project manager and value both their relationship to him or her and the project manager's opinion of them.

3. *Reward and punishment power* refers to what the project manager can do directly or indirectly to block or facilitate attainment of personal goals of people who balk at his or her requests.

Functional Department Manager Responsibilities and Authority

Each functional department manager holds overall responsibility for planning and executing the specific work (work packages, tasks/activities) to be performed within that function to create the resulting project deliverables (hardware, software, documents, facilities, services) for each active project. The basic technical and management specifications of each work package (result to be achieved, quality, deliverables, schedule, and budget) must be established in a negotiating process between the project manager and the functional manager or his or her representative, namely the functional project leader. Within the limits of these specifications, the functional manager has the responsibility of detailed planning, functional policy and procedure direction, functional quality, and developing and providing an adequately skilled staff.

The authority of the functional department manager is more traditional and better understood than that of the project manager, because the people within his or her department are under the direct control of this manager. However, many functional managers have difficulty becoming accustomed to sharing their responsibilities and authority with project managers, and allowing the project managers to exert project direction within their functional departments.

Functional Project Leader Responsibilities and Authority

The functional project leader (other titles may of course be used for this position) is key to successful operation within a matrix organization. This person is the focal point of all activity on his or her assigned project within the functional organization. The functional project leader is the alter ego of his or her supervisor, usually the functional department manager, and performs all subfunctional tasking. His or her responsibilities cut across all subfunctional lines for the total functional effort on that project, and include actively planning and controlling the functional organization's efforts on the project. In effect, this person is a mini project manager within his or her department.

The authority of the functional project leader is delegated from the department manager and from the organization's project management process documentation. The functional project leader gives project direction to the work package (or task) leaders within the function in question.

Some examples of specific job titles that are in fact functional project leader positions are:

- *Project engineer*—integrating all engineering aspects of all or an assigned part of the project
- *Project controller* (not comptroller)—handling project planning, scheduling, budgeting, monitoring, and reporting
- *Project accountant*—handling financial and resource usage reporting
- *Project cost engineer*—handling project cost control
- *Project contract administrator*—handling all project contractual matters
- *Project purchasing agent*—handling all purchase orders for the project
- *Project manufacturing coordinator*—handling day-to-day contacts with manufacturing departments
- *Project field superintendent*—handling field operations.

Work Package Leader Responsibilities and Authority

Work package leaders (other titles may of course also be used) are responsible for:

- Developing and maintaining work package plans for accomplishments
- Establishing work package technical guidance
- Establishing work package detailed schedules and operating budgets that are properly integrated with the overall project plans, schedules, and budgets
- Controlling and reporting on work package performance.

The authority of work package leaders is delegated from the cognizant functional department manager to carry out these assigned work package leader responsibilities

CONCLUSION

Understanding the integrative roles in project management and implementing them properly are vital to managing complex projects successfully in large organizations. If any of these key integrative roles are left vacant or improperly defined, severe conflicts and significant loss of effectiveness will be encountered. Even the most advanced project management information systems will not compensate for mistakes in defining and assigning qualified people to these roles.

REFERENCES

1. Archibald, Russell D. and Alan Harpham. 1990. "Project Managers' Profiles and Certification Workshop Report," *Proceedings of the 14th International Expert Seminar*, March 15–17, Internet/International Project Management Association, Zurich: 9.
2. Ibid. This list is based on the work of Roland W. Spuhler, a member of the expert working team in Zurich.
3. Wilemon, David L. and Gary R. Gemmill. 1971. "Interpersonal Power in Temporary Management Systems," *Journal of Management Studies*, (October): 319–320.

CHAPTER 24

CULTURALLY DIVERSE MANAGEMENT: A VITAL SKILL FOR MANAGING GLOBAL PROJECTS

VIJAY K. VERMA

Coming together is a beginning; keeping together is progress; working together is success; helping each other win is excellence.
Henry Ford

INTRODUCTION

In tough economic times and under global competition, *management by projects* is now regarded as a competitive way for managing organizations. Time is of great importance to survive in today's dynamic business environment. It is critical that new products are developed and marketed ahead of schedule in order to gain an edge over other competitors. As project management moves into the twenty-first century, project managers face the challenges of operating in a dynamic business environment characterized by high levels of uncertainty, phenomenal growth in technology, cross-cultural project teams, and global competition for competent human resources.

Projects today have dramatically increased in complexity, requiring a culturally and functionally diverse mix of individuals who must be integrated into an effective unit—a *project team*. Effective teamwork is the key to project success during all phases of the project life cycle. Tough global competition has created an acute need for faster, more flexible, and highly competitive operations. These needs can be met only by developing high-performing teams. Effective team building is one of the prime responsibilities of the project manager. The smooth running of project teams becomes more challenging with increased project complexity and a diverse mix of skills and cultural backgrounds of team members.

This chapter focuses on the issues and practical ideas that should help project managers to build, motivate, inspire, and lead project teams to produce high team performance and meet project objectives. Major elements of culture and critical dimensions of cultural differences are described along with practical ideas to manage global projects and achieve cultural synergy. This chapter outlines various issues associated with team building in the project environment, such as the importance of team building, the team building process, and major tasks in building the project teams to suit various phases of the project life cycle. Some practical ideas to achieve excellence through effective team building and to inspire teams for continuous high performance by capitalizing on cultural diversity of team members, cultural synergy, using open communication, resolving conflicts in a constructive manner, building trust, and managing the team morale are presented.

ABOUT THE PROJECT TEAM AND TEAM BUILDING

Pull together; in the mountains you must depend on each other for survival.

Willi Unsoeld, mountain climber

Tough global competition has created an acute need for culturally diverse, fast, flexible, and competitive operations. Developing high-performing teams to meet these needs is a prime responsibility of the project manager. It involves a whole spectrum of management and leadership skills required to identify, organize, commit, and integrate various task groups from functional organizations into a multidisciplinary, cohesive team. Though this process has been known for centuries, it becomes more challenging as vertical bureaucratic hierarchies decline and horizontally oriented teams and work units evolve.

Cultural diversity and the fact that the project team members are physically separated by many time zones pose special challenges in managing global projects. However, it must be recognized that the cultural diversity issues are equally prominent in regional or national projects also, as the project teams are often cross-cultural in terms of their attitudes, beliefs, organizational culture, and physical conditions. Project managers must learn to capitalize on cultural diversity and achieve synergy within a multicultural and cross-functional project team. While belonging to a really successful project team is very satisfactory, it is also very rewarding for the project managers to use their qualities and skills to create such a team. They must provide for the routine care and feeding of team members with diverse cultural backgrounds.

About the Project Team

Some people tend to confuse groups with teams. However, there are some key differences between groups and teams in terms of levels of commitment, interdependencies, and shared responsibility.[1]

What is a team? What makes a good team? These are simple questions and we tend to think we know the answers—until someone asks!

A team is more than just a work group. It is a group of people who are committed to common goals, who depend on each other to do their job (work interdependently), and who produce high-quality results. A team can also be defined as a group of people in which team members have a common aim and in which the jobs and skills of each member fit in with those of others.

The two components of this definition—*a common task* and *complementary contributions*—are essential to the concept of a real team. In general, a project team is a work group of two or more individuals who must interact and work interdependently with each other to accomplish project objectives. Project teams are united by a common purpose and the concept of shared responsibility. An effective team may be defined as one that achieves its goals efficiently and is then ready to take on more challenges if so required.[2] Effective teamwork produces a synergistic effect; that is, the output of the team as a whole is more than the sum of the output from its parts.

About Team Building

Team building is important for many situations. It is especially crucial in a project-oriented work environment where mainly functional specialists and support groups must be integrated to achieve complex multidisciplinary activities. To manage projects with such multidisciplinary activities, project managers and task leaders often have to cross organizational lines and deal with people over whom they have little or no authority. Project managers, in such dynamic environments, must understand the interaction of organizational and behavioral variables in order to create a climate conducive to building an effective team that has a diverse mix of skills and expertise. Such a team, if led and managed effectively, must have the capacity to achieve excellence and innovatively transform a set of technical objectives and requirements into specific products or services that will excel and be superior to other competitive alternatives in the marketplace.

What Is Team Building?

Team building is the process of transforming a collection of individuals with different interests, backgrounds, and expertise into an integrated and effective work unit. It can also be seen as a process of change. In this transformation process, the goals and energies of all team members merge and support the objectives of the team. The team-building process is important for all types of projects but will vary in complexity depending on the project.

Team building as an ongoing process is crucial to project success. While team building is essential during the front end of a project, it is a never-ending process. It must be kept alive. The project manager must continually monitor team functioning and performance to evaluate if any corrective actions are needed to prevent or solve various team problems.

Characteristics of an Integrated Project Team

The interdependence of project team members and the satisfaction and pleasure that they derive from their association with the team are some of the unique characteristics of an integrated project team. Some of the important characteristics of a fully integrated project team are:[3]

- A common reason for working together (commitment to project objectives)
- Pride and enjoyment in group activity (strong sense of belonging)
- Interdependency (members realize that they need each other to succeed)
- Shared interests (helping professional development of everyone)
- Commitment to the team concept (no prima donnas allowed)
- Strong performance norms and results orientation (high expectations of each other to produce quality work)
- Acceptance of group accountability for success or failure (helping each other when needed)
- High degree of intragroup interaction (helping develop mutual understanding)
- Respect for individual differences (listening to and acknowledging different viewpoints)
- Climate of high trust and healthy conflict (expressing ideas, opinions, and disagreements freely)

According to many management practitioners and researchers, team building and team development are some of the most critical leadership qualities that determine the performance and success of multidisciplinary projects. The outcomes of these projects depend on the teamwork and how well many specialists are coordinated and integrated in a dynamic work environment with complex organizational interfaces. Project excellence can be achieved only through a high level of sustained cooperative team effort. Figure 24.1 outlines major elements of teamwork in a nutshell.

Figure 24.1
Teamwork in a Nutshell

T	Trust
E	Encouragement/Effective communication
A	Action orientation
M	Milestones (well defined and agreed upon)
W	Working interdependently
O	Organized (project structure and personally)
R	Resources availability / Recognition for results
K	Knowledge mix

Source: Vijay K. Verma, *Managing the Project Team,* Upper Darby, PA: Project Management Institute, 1997: 149.

CULTURAL DIVERSITY AND PROJECT MANAGEMENT

Learn to recognize cultural differences, for cultural diversity is a reality of life in international projects.

Vijay K. Verma

What Is Culture?

Culture refers to a commonly shared set of values, beliefs, attitudes, and knowledge. It can be created by both people and their environment, and can be transmitted from one generation to the next through family, school, social environment, and other agencies.[4] Culture is difficult to define precisely and is a complex subject because of its several dimensions and elements. Geert Hofstede describes culture simply as a kind of "mental software"—that is "the collective programming of the mind which distinguishes the members of one group of people from another."[5]

Also, culture can be defined as an acquired knowledge that is used to interpret the experiences of a team and which forms the basis of its behavior.[6] To understand a particular culture and its depth, it is useful to study its characteristics. Cultural characteristics demonstrate that cultures are often:[7]

- Learned (through education and experience)
- Shared (by individuals, groups, organizations, and societies as a whole)
- Transgenerational (passed on from generation to generation in terms of its values, beliefs, knowledge, and attitudes)
- Symbolic (based on symbolic representation—e.g., peaceful, warrior, etc.)
- Patterned (based on structure and integration influenced by historical events—e.g., Roman, Chinese, etc.)
- Adaptive (based on capacities of groups, organizations, and societies to adapt themselves to economic, industrial, and environmental changes)

Major Elements of Culture

Today more project managers operate in an environment characterized by cultural diversity. Cultural differences may significantly influence the success in project management, especially for international projects. More business organizations are now investing in educating managers to develop their cultural sensitivity and increase their intercultural commu-

nicating and negotiating skills. To achieve this, it is important to understand and analyze the major elements of culture. M. Dean Martin identified the following seven major elements of culture, which significantly
influence the project management strategy and team development
process:[8]

1. Material culture (refers to physical objects or the results of technology).
2. Language (helps develop better understanding among team members).
3. Aesthetics (encourages informal and open communication).
4. Education (indicates how different team members view the problems).
5. Religion, beliefs, and attitudes (affect general attitudes toward work
   ethics).
6. Social organization (helps in networking and setting informal
   meetings).
7. Political life (relates to approvals of permits, labor laws, import/ex-
   port, and financial transactions).

These cultural elements represent the most important factors for managing joint ventures and international projects (see Table 24.1).[9] Project
managers should be familiar with the self-reference criterion (evaluating
others in terms of own value system) and cultural shock in approaching
another culture.[10]

Critical Dimensions of Cultural Differences

In a multinational project environment, culture is a very dominating variable. Project managers can face serious problems related to project cost,
schedule, quality, and people if they are unable to recognize and deal with
the major elements of culture (described earlier) and appreciate the cultural differences among project stakeholders.

Cultural differences are realities of life in a multinational project. Geert
Hoftstede identified major critical dimensions of cultural differences.[11]
Stephen Owens and James McLaurin described major dimensions of cultural differences with respect to their implications for project managers
and how cultural synergy may be achieved.[12] Each dimension can be described as an aspect of a culture that can be measured relative to other
cultures. An appreciation of these critical dimensions of cultural difference should help project managers understand the dynamics of culture

Table 24.1

Major Cultural Elements Affecting Projects

Cultural Element	What It Means or Implies	Impact on Project	Recommendations/Comments
Material culture	Refers to tools, skills, work habits, and work attitudes	Determines technical and manpower constraints	Formation is needed for planning and negotiations
Language	Medium of communication Words and experiences may differ	Affects communications Influences understanding of beliefs and values	Learning foreign language develops better understanding and rapport
Aesthetics	Arts, music, dance, traditions, and customs	Encourages informal and open communication Influences success indirectly	Relationships are enriched by encouraging informal communication
Education and training	Transmission of knowledge or skills through learning process Approach to problems and people	Affect project planning and negotiations Affect work productivity	Knowledge of education and training helps in determining level of skills and expertise (helpful in project planning and organizing)
Religion, beliefs, and attitudes	Mainspring of culture Affect dress, eating habits, attitudes of workers toward work, punctuality, and work site	Impact promptness and punctuality	Appreciation of religion, beliefs, and values develops mutual trust, and respects, and improves cooperation and team spirit
Social organization	Organizations/groups (labor unions, social clubs) Relates to social classes	Influences formal/informal communication Affects business contacts for negotiating	Social skills can lead to better results than formal meetings
Political life	Government involvement in joint ventures with foreign companies Concerned about treatment of people, jobs, financial aspects, economies, and safety factors	Affects delivery of materials, supplies, and equipment Influences permits and licences	Staying in tune with political life helps identify the strengths, constraints, and areas of risk

Source: Adapted from: M. Dean Martin. 1981. "The Negotiation Differential for International Project Management." *Proceedings of the Annual Seminar/Symposium of the Project Management Institute.* Drexel Hill, PA: Project Management Institute.

and its effect on the project team's behavior. The six critical dimensions of cultural differences are as follows:[13]

1. *Power distance*—evaluates how a particular culture deals with inequality.
2. *Individualism/collectivism*—examines the role of the individual versus the role of the group.
3. *Masculinity/femininity*—describes the relative dominance of male versus female.
4. *Uncertainty avoidance*—focuses on tolerance for ambiguity or uncertainty in the workplace. Project outcomes are not always certain. Depending on the home culture, project team members may feel uncomfortable or even threatened by uncertainties and ambiguities in a project (in terms of project scope, objectives, and overall procedures) and may take particular actions to cope with the uncertainties.
5. *Time horizon*—refers to long-term versus short-term orientation.
6. *Attitude toward life*—refers to quantity (emphasis on materialistic things) versus quality (emphasis on relationships and working interdependently in life).

Cultural Diversity and the Project Manager

Project managers in multicultural projects must appreciate the cultural dimensions described earlier and try to learn relevant customs, courtesies, and business protocols before taking responsibility for managing an international project. Geert Hofstede emphasized the importance of all six dimensions of culture to understand the "mental software" of multicultural members of organizations. His analysis can be summarized as follows.[14]

Out of the six dimensions of national cultural differences, three dimensions—namely, power distance, uncertainty avoidance, and long-term versus short-term orientation—affect one's thinking about organizations. Two other dimensions—individualism/collectivism and masculinity/femininity—help us understand the people in an organization rather than the organization itself, whereas the last dimension—attitude toward life—relates to the value systems of people in different cultures. For example, while organizing a project one should always address four questions:[15]

1. What is the organizational strategy?
2. Who has the power to decide?
3. What rules or procedures will be followed to achieve desired goals and objectives?
4. What do people value the most (relationships or materialistic things)?

The answer to the first question is influenced by the tendency of the organization to plan for the long term or the short term; the answer to the second question is determined by the norms of power distance (high or low Power Distance Index (PDI); the answer to the third question is influenced by external norms about uncertainty avoidance; and the answer to the fourth question is related to the relative value people place on the quality of life (cooperation, relationships, and teamwork) and the quantity of life (competition for achievement and material success).

Project managers must be aware of cross-cultural implications and dimensions of project and organizational culture to better understand expectations of a diverse mix of project participants organized in a team to attain project goals. Project managers must learn to foster cultural synergy within their multicultural teams.

Cultural Synergy

Synergy is defined as a joint or cooperative action and occurs when a diverse mix of people (project team members) work together toward a common goal. Cultural diversity influences project success. Increasing globalization of project work will require project managers to function effectively in cross-cultural project environments. To meet global competition, project teams must aim at increasing their effectiveness by capitalizing on cultural diversity of project team members. The project manager can help a great deal in achieving synergy in a cross-cultural project environment. Philip R. Harris and Robert T. Moran have outlined a set of skills or abilities to achieve team effectiveness in a multinational project, which include: mutual respect, adaptability, empathy, persistence, people orientation, and being nonjudgemental.[16]

Effective application of these skills will increase the level of team synergy. How can a project manager determine if his or her multicultural team is really effective? Harris and Moran suggest a set of questions to evaluate a team's effectiveness, which if addressed and considered will lead to the following essential elements for building cross-cultural teams:[17]

- A common purpose and a commitment to meet that purpose.
- A common language and common ways of doing things (e.g., planning, monitoring, conducting meetings, and reporting procedures).
- Well-accepted and well-supported techniques to solve people problems (e.g., communicating, developing trust, negotiating, and conflict management).

- Team policy to encourage and capitalize on positive ideas, actions, and outcomes.
- Appreciation for, acceptance of, and respect for cultural differences of each other in terms of their habits, beliefs, attitudes, and knowledge. This is one of the most important factors for managing cross-cultural teams and achieving cultural synergy.
- Open-mindedness about other cultures and willingness to deal with, not avoid, the differences.
- Team members recognizing the impact of their own cultural programming and not imposing their own culture and ideas on others
- Having fun. In successful multicultural teams, members enjoy rather than feel frustrated or irritated by the surprises/discoveries arising from cultural differences among team members.

PRACTICAL GUIDELINES FOR EFFECTIVE TEAM BUILDING

I could not have done it without the boys.
Baseball legend Casey Stengel
after winning his ninth American League
pennant in 10 years

Project managers must recognize the importance of an effective project team and the role of team-building activities in optimizing project management performance. They must consider three important factors that determine the need for effective teams.[18]

- In an organization, there are many technical experts whose talents, skills, and strengths must be integrated into an endeavor—a project.
- Today more organizational members want to be involved in their work environments and make useful contributions.
- Teamwork leads to synergy, creativity, and fun.

In fact, the difference between successful and unsuccessful project performance can be attributed to the effectiveness of the project team in terms of its team effort. Global competition, complicated environmental interfaces, and rapidly advancing technology require the development of effective teams. *What's different about projects? What should be done to integrate team building into the life cycle of a project?* Here are 10 guidelines that project managers can use for effective team building and achieving project excellence:[19]

1. *Plan for team building.* A project plan is the first and the foremost thing that the project managers must develop to launch a project on the right foot. The project plan, which addresses the *what* (project goals and objectives), *how* (project procedures), *when* (schedule), and *who* (project roles), becomes the basis for team building.

2. *Negotiate for team members.* Selecting the right team members is crucial to effective team building. Unfortunately, project managers rarely have the luxury of selecting their own team members. However, project managers must try to match interests, team skills, and technical skills while negotiating with functional managers for team members.

3. *Hold a kickoff meeting.* A kickoff meeting is an important element of a team-building process. Since it is at the kickoff meeting that project participants are brought together for the first time, project managers should get everyone involved and build a unity of purpose for accomplishing project objectives.

4. *Obtain commitment of team members.* Project managers must obtain commitment from project team members in terms of their time commitment, role commitment, and priority commitment. It is a necessary but often a frustrating process. Level of commitment may vary from very little to complete dedication. Project managers can best obtain commitments from team members by involving them early in the project life cycle and giving them interesting and challenging assignments.

5. *Build communication links.* Good communication links within and outside the project organization are essential in achieving teamwork. Project managers must recognize both formal and informal communication links in a project. Three basic channels and links of communication in a project environment are:[20]

   - *Upward communication (vertically or diagonally)* with top management and client
   - *Downward communication (vertically or diagonally)* with team members and contractors
   - *Lateral communication (horizontally)* between the project manager and his or her peers

Building and maintaining all communication links is the key to effective team building. It requires diplomacy, experience, and mutual respect. Project managers must encourage openness in communication and expedite the communication process to ensure that project participants understand the intent and real meaning of the information being transferred. They should make sure that the right people interact in a timely manner, participate in meetings, and disseminate the information promptly and accurately.

6. *Obtain top management support.* Top management should emphasize the importance of team building as a means to achieve organizational success. They must demonstrate their commitment to team building by providing extra training and resources.

7. *Utilize ongoing project team development.* Team building is not a one-shot process. It is a major step in the right direction, but it must be recognized as an ongoing process throughout the project life cycle because:
   - New members may join the project team later.
   - Emphasis may change as the project enters a new phase, and key members of that team may change completely (e.g., from research and development to design or from development to manufacturing).
   - The project manager may be replaced due to change in project emphasis.
   - Client representative may be changed or transferred.

   A major concern is to keep up the momentum and morale of the project team, particularly during long projects.

8. *Introduce rewards and recognition.* People are motivated if they feel they are valued in the organization, and this value is demonstrated by the rewards given to them. Generally, money is viewed by most as a very important aspect of any reward system. However, in addition to money, there are several other subtle perks that can be included in the total team reward package. Team rewards are effective motivators, and therefore, if possible, project managers should try to budget funds for team incentives such as team-building exercises, professional training, and paid retreats. Genuine recognition of good performance should be practiced to reinforce the team members positively.

9. *Manage team conflicts effectively.* Conflicts are inevitable in a project environment. It is virtually impossible for people with diverse backgrounds, skills, and norms to work together as a team to meet project objectives without conflict. A rather minor conflict can almost instantly destroy team spirit that may have taken a long time to develop. Managing team conflicts promptly and effectively is one of the prime responsibilities of the project manager. Following are some important issues that project managers should be aware of about managing team conflicts effectively:

- Competition versus conflict (Use competition positively.)
- Team conflict avoidance (Resolve conflict promptly.)
- Conflict resolution styles (Use a win-win strategy.)

Project managers must use an appropriate style for managing conflict because it can have a significant impact on success in team building and overall management of the project. For instance, to resolve conflicts with support personnel, functional managers, and assigned personnel, a forcing and withdrawal technique is least effective, while confrontation, compromise, and smoothing tends to work well. Problem solving and collaborating tend to be very effective in managing conflicts with clients, top management, and regulatory agencies.

10. *Provide good project leadership.* Overall success of project managers depends on the quality of leadership provided to their project teams. Effective teamwork is the by-product of good leadership. During one of the workshops that I facilitated, one participant made the point, *"There is nothing worse than being on a team where communication is not open, no one trusts anyone else, and there is no team leadership."*

The concept of leadership, in terms of expectations from leaders and the relationship between the leader and the followers, varies from culture to culture. Some project managers have a preferred leadership style, while others fit their style to the situation. Instead of using extremes of common leadership styles (autocratic, consultive, consensus, and shareholder), project managers should use *shared leadership* for successful team building and providing effective project leadership.

Shared leadership is more than participatory management. It involves encouraging project teams to assume leadership roles and then letting them actually take over as much of the leadership role as they will accept. Project managers gain wider acceptance and hence commitment of team members to meet project objectives as team members accept responsibilities and feel accountable for the success or failure of the project. Shared leadership even reduces the workload for project managers while team members actually take an increased ownership of project tasks, which usually leads to high performance and quality. It is the most effective route to achieve team commitment and true teamwork.

It is essential that project managers use these 10 guidelines for building and managing effective project teams with emphasis on incorporating essential elements (discussed earlier) to achieve synergy in their multicultural project teams.

SUMMARY

A strong project team is the nucleus of a successful project. When the concept of team building is understood and applied at all levels, it becomes much easier to transform groups into high-performance teams throughout the organization. Building effective project teams in a culturally diverse project environment is one of the prime responsibilities of project managers. Team building involves a whole spectrum of management skills required to identify, commit, and integrate various task groups from traditional functional organizations into a multidisciplinary task management system.

Team building is a process of taking a collection of individuals with different needs, cultural backgrounds, and expertise, and transforming them by various methods into an integrated, effective work unit—*a project team*. In this transformation process, the goals and energies of individual contributors merge and support the overall objectives of the team. Team development is the process of helping a group of individuals, bound by a common purpose, to work more effectively with each other, the leader, external stakeholders, and the whole organization. Team building is also one of the most critical leadership qualities that determines the performance and success in a project environment.

Project managers must appreciate the cultural differences and be aware of six critical dimensions of cultural differences and their implications for the project management process. Project managers must acquire abilities to meet team members on their own cultural grounds and increase team effectiveness by fostering cultural synergy within their project team.

In addition to technical guidance and management expertise, project managers must provide an appropriate atmosphere conducive to teamwork and give their full enthusiasm and support. Project managers must try to identify any problems in the early life of a project and deal with them effectively by maximizing the impact of drivers and minimizing the impact of barriers to effective team building. They must expedite communication, obtain top management support, introduce team rewards and recognition, manage team conflicts promptly, and provide effective team leadership. Special care should be given to respecting cultural differences among team members, emphasizing the importance of teamwork, and building trust and confidence among them. Above all, the process should be fun so that everyone is committed to help each other win.

REFERENCES

1. Verma, Vijay K. 1997. *Managing the Project Team*. Upper Darby, PA: Project Management Institute: 60–63.
2. Ibid.
3. Cleland, David I. 1990, *Project Management Strategic Design and Implementation*. Blue Ridge, PA: Tab Books: 299–322.
4. Martin, M. Dean. 1993. "The Negotiation Differential for International Project Management." Proceedings of Project Management Institute; also published as Chapter 38 in Paul C. Dinsmore, ed., *The AMA Handbook of Project Management*, New York: AMACOM.
5. Hofstede, Geert. 1993. *Cultures and Organizations: Software of the Mind*. New York: McGraw-Hill: 5, 14, 51–67, 82–83, 261–282.
6. Luthan, Fred and Richard Hodgetts. 1991. *International Management*, New York: McGraw-Hill: 35.
7. Owens, Stephen D. and James Reagan McLaurin. 1993. "Cultural Diversity and Projects: What the Project Manager Needs to Know." Proceedings of PMI '93 Annual Seminar/Symposium: 229–236.
8. Martin, op. cit.
9. Ibid.
10. Ibid.
11. Hofstede, op. cit.
12. Owens and McLaurin, op. cit.
13. Hofstede, op. cit.
14. Hofstede, op. cit.: 143.
15. Owens and McLaurin, op. cit.; Verma, op. cit.: 94–100.
16. Harris, Philip R. and Robert T. Moran. 1996. *Managing Cultural Differences (Third Edition)*. Houston: Gulf Publishing Co.: 104–107.
17. Owens and McLaurin, op. cit.; Harris and Moran, op. cit.
18. Wilemon, D. L. and H. J. Thamhain. 1977. "Team Building in Project Management." *Project Management Quarterly* (June): 73–81, 1983; G. H. Varney, *Organization Development for Managers*, Reading, MA: Addison Wesley: 151–152.
19. Verma, op. cit.: 133–148.
20. Verma, Vijay K. 1996. *Human Resource Skills for the Project Manager*, Upper Darby, PA: Project Management Institute: 33–35.

CHAPTER 25

EXPECTATIONS MANAGEMENT: RECONFIRMING ASSUMPTIONS

MARGERY MAYER

Expectations are personal. They determine how we look at things and how we analyze results. Capturing, documenting, and agreeing on expectations are the key to a project's success. If this critical step is missed, the outcome of the project, regardless of whether it is on time or on budget, may be in jeopardy. The execution may not be on time or on budget but must be flawless regardless of time or money.

The standard project management goal of being on time and on budget may no longer apply. The new paradigm for project goals may be flawless execution regardless of time or budget. This expectation must be addressed, understood, and agreed to by all parties throughout the project.

Everyone involved in a project, from the sponsor to each team member, carries expectations about the project. The nature of the project may determine the first expectation that must be identified. Other expectations may concern the following:

- How will the project proceed?
- Who will be responsible for what?
- What are the deliverables and milestones?
- How true *are* the budget estimates and scope?
- What will be the final product?
- What are the important areas of the project?

These questions reflect a few of the initial expectations; there are many more that will come into play as the project continues. Each step, each phase, each deliverable, each issue, and each expenditure carries with it expectations. How can all these expectations be identified and brought together to satisfy the sponsor as well as keep the team focused on the right expectations? Identifying expectations is an ongoing part of managing a project.

Frequent checks with the team and sponsor to reconfirm initial expectations and address new ones is vital in ensuring a satisfactory end result. It should be assumed that expectations change as new requirements are uncovered during all phases of the project. Early identification of expectations is critical in setting the tone and understanding, and these need to be readdressed, reconfirmed, and revised as the project continues.

CLARIFY EXPECTATIONS AT THE BEGINNING OF THE PROJECT

The project begins with a proposal that is approved and funded, usually by a sponsor, who has specific ideas for the project's completion. Project identification and scope development are key to a project's success and will force the sponsor and project manager to finalize exactly what is needed as an outcome from the project.

This exercise identifies exactly what all team members need to contribute in order to achieve the overall project success. It identifies a communication methodology with the project sponsor, determines his or her "hot buttons," and documents agreed-upon expectations up front. It is essential to take time for this clarification in order to develop a rapport with the sponsor, set down criteria for the project and be better able to manage expectations in the future.

Team expectations will differ as project needs and responsibilities evolve. Understanding how everyone perceives the project will enable individual expectations to be identified and addressed. Documenting the project team's expectations is another critical step. Comparing them to the sponsor's expectations could be enlightening, because they may be very different. The project manager must then compare both sets of expectations and come to conclusions for the team. Steering the project to the right end results will be easier if all participants understand, from the beginning, one another's initial project expectations and any discrepancies between them. This effort allows for agreement with the participants to meet or exceed these expectations and be better able to evaluate the project against them.

Finally, Mike Wolfe, who is affiliated with ProSavvy (formerly Pen-

Group), states, "There are three areas for project-specific expectations—general, project, and transactional." They are described as follows:

- *General* expectations pertain to the character and style of the project manager, which come into play in how a team is handled in a crisis. This category also identifies how the project manager handles the issues that must be escalated to a higher authority due to their negative impact to the project.
- *Project* expectations concern the overall goals, objectives, schedule results, costs, and preparations for future support. These involve meeting the stated criteria as well as managing them over time. Most project managers are judged on the way they handle the project in this area.
- *Transactional* expectations are the day-to-day deliverables, reports, analysis, and details of the project.

CONSIDER THE VIEWS OF THE SPONSOR AND STAKEHOLDER

It does not matter whether we think the project has been completed as planned or if it meets our expectations. Meeting the expectations of the sponsor—the one paying for the work—is the true test of completion and actual value. The project may be on time and on budget, but usual completion criteria are often not the criteria for the sponsor.

In addition to the sponsor, there are other critical players involved in the project whose views must be considered as well. This means that the *stakeholders* in various departments, who might benefit or be affected by the project outcome, need to understand the scope of the project, and they should be encouraged to contribute their respective expectations. If their concerns are neglected, duplication of efforts may result; integration with other systems may be compromised; or future support of the project may be jeopardized. It is always best to avoid the syndrome of "throwing the project over the fence" when completed, presenting another department with unpleasant surprises, or having a stakeholder area surprised by the effort in terms of being staffed and prepared for the requirements needed to support the completed project.

The stakeholder must also know about the expectations because he or she may be responsible for support calls for the other organization. The support stakeholder needs to staff accordingly, anticipating heavy call volumes as a result of the project or system implementation. If the stakeholders' needs are not met, they may refuse to provide support that could leave the project completed but not released, or cause additional, unanticipated expense in hiring support personnel. This situation is more common than not; the stakeholder support department is often notified too late to ramp up, and support remains with the team that implemented the project. At this point, transitioning to the support organization is more difficult because trust has been broken. The support organization was not included in any stages of the project and was surprised that it was expected to provide ongoing support. The point at which it was notified of the impending project did not allow it time to plan for resources or systems to accommodate this new work. The support organization may question why it was not brought in sooner and distrust the motives of the project manager and team.

Containing Scope Creep

Often, identifying expectations is a difficult task and one that requires quite a bit of work and tenacity. Most sponsors know what they need the project to do, but expressing the details of their expectations to the project manager is often more difficult. The project manager must spend the extra time identifying these expectations early or will surely fail in some way. However, keep in mind that the expectations gleaned early on may evolve as the project progresses. Inevitably, expectations change and often expand as new needs or concerns are identified over time.

This shifting of expectations, often called *scope creep*, must be identified and discussed as soon as possible to reset expectations and evaluate the effects of change on the existing workload and project commitment. An example might be that these new requirements can be done, but others need to be reduced, or the delivery date will be jeopardized. Another example might be that these new requirements mean rework in areas that have already been completed. They may actually enhance the product, but the risk to the schedule may be too great.

Analyzing new requirements and expectations allows for a more informed approach to accepting or rejecting these changes. As a result, the sponsor or other stakeholders can make decisions from a more realistic and risk-aware perspective. Malcolm McKee from Foreshock Inc. states, "It is preferable to defer the out-of-scope items until the original scope of the project is either completed or modified. If this is not possible, then a change order signed by the customer is needed."

CLARIFYING EXPECTATIONS

It is necessary to identify and document the project objective(s), scope deliverables, milestones, phases, participating team members, and expected completion criteria. This work is usually done in the definition or planning phase of the project before any work is accomplished. Typically, the project sponsor and stakeholders participate in setting these project expectations to ensure that nothing is overlooked or unanticipated. Documenting these details is imperative so that this information can be revisited later to better understand the progress and impact of changes on the original project scope. A template for documenting sponsor expectations is provided as Performance Support Tool 25.1 at the end of this chapter.

All of the clarification tools discussed next enable the project manager to gather, document, and distribute information about the project to a wide audience and gain project support. When questions arise, these documents can be revisited to see whether the situation is addressed or if the issue is new and needs escalation. Setting the tone for a project and determining expectations early on will reap big payoffs down the road. It is always difficult to "re-create the crime" if documentation does not exist.

Conduct Interviews and Make Site Visits

Expectations can be clarified in many ways. Often, questions are prepared and used in individual interviews with key people from the organization. From these interviews, conclusions and expectations should be documented and presented to the sponsor and stakeholders for final confirmation. Site visits often provide a vital understanding of the working environment and often add invaluable information to how projects are done in the organization. Site visits also allow for casual conversation with staff not on the interview list, but who have information that might prove useful sometime during the project.

Develop Questionnaires and Produce Reports or Proposals

Some projects require that questionnaires be developed, distributed, and compiled, and that results be published. These projects often cause major changes within the organization, and surveying the population uncovers needs, requirements, and concerns that otherwise may not be identified. The results are presented as reports or proposals for work to be accomplished.

Use Checklists

Sometimes, developing and distributing checklists makes the difference in identifying expectations and requirements. These tend to help focus thoughts, and trigger needs, concerns, and issues related to the project. Checklists also remind participants of important items that should not be overlooked. Items included in checklists may be the project objectives, the time line for delivery, the names of project participants and a contact list, stakeholders, milestones, deliverables, target dates, related documentation, acronyms, and definitions. Developing and distributing completed checklists enables everyone on the team to have the same expectations of the project.

As project managers and leaders, we assume we are doing a good job until something significant occurs. It is wise periodically to do a self-assessment to ensure that we are on track, as effective as we can be, and providing the best value we can to the project. A Project Manager Self-Assessment checklist is provided for this purpose as Performance Support Tool 25.2 at the end of this chapter.

Document with Project Charters

Project charters are used to document and gain commitment from project sponsors and team members for expectations. These charters, sometimes called *data sheets*, state the overall project objectives. Sometimes, these are related to company objectives, the project scope in terms of what is and what is not included, assumptions and expectations, milestones and key dates, major deliverables, sponsors, stakeholders and team members, and completion criteria. The *completion criteria* clarify how to know when the project is really completed.

DIRECTING THE PROJECT

The project manager's job is that of steering the project in the right direction—that is, toward completion based on objectives and expectations. This requires constant clarification of expectations with members of the project, identifying possible changes in outcomes and expectations, and pointing out unrealistic developments. During the life of a project, new ideas or requirements are identified and evaluated. These developments, though often difficult to broach with the sponsor or stakeholders, must be addressed quickly to avoid impacting the project negatively. Project managers often wait too long, hoping the situation will resolve itself, only to address a bigger and more cumbersome problem later. Timely resolution, even just a simple clarification conversation, often eliminates rework, confusion, or delays.

Many expectations are hidden from the project manager. Expectations such as honesty, integrity, and fairness are always taken for granted. Staying aware and being on top of project developments and communicating about the project are implicit expectations. Some project managers are burdened with actual tasks on the project, which adds to their workloads. Often, this impedes their ability to step up fully to the project manager responsibility and some of the expectations for their performance are neglected. This is unfortunate because the success or failure of the project is often placed on the project manager.

How does a working project manager deal with this extra burden? It must be addressed early on as other expectations and risks are identified. It may become necessary to prove that it is unwise to expect a project manager to fulfill that specific role in addition to performing actual tasks, and make it clear that another less burdened project manager should be named instead.

MANAGING SOFTWARE DEVELOPMENT PROJECTS

Software development projects are notorious for having scope creep, having unclear or incomplete requirements, coming in over budget, and being released with known bugs or problems. Setting expectations on these projects is different from others in that the expectations are often for a usable, not-perfect product upon completion and release. This is a critical expectation that must be addressed and documented if this type of project will ever be successful. In this case, the expectation is on meeting the release date with a usable product that can be patched and upgraded after meeting this date. Quality may not be a factor, and the engineers/developers and project manager need to understand the results and implications. In this instance, the expectation is to release a product and gain market share. The project manager must honor this expectation and not deliver late, or the project will fail to meet the sponsor's expectations.

HOLDING CHECKPOINT MEETINGS

Checking in with the sponsors and stakeholders on a regular basis allows for the early identification of new or changed expectations, thus thwarting surprises later on down the road. These junctures are often called *checkpoint meetings*. Checkpoint meetings occur at critical times in the project, during specific project phases. They usually take place when quite a bit of work has been completed in an area, and review of the issues and progress is critical for understanding the status of the project and continuing its funding. Reconfirming expectations and progress will allow for timely resolution if expectations change or if issues arise that could impact the project negatively.

The checkpoint meeting (or retrospective analysis, discussed in the next paragraph) allows for resetting expectations, reconfirming the project's goals, deliverables, and time line, and addressing concerns before proceeding. This is the time to revisit the changes in the work scope between checkpoints, and review the complexity of issues that need resolution. This is also the time to review all aspects of the schedule, reporting, communication, and any obstacles that exist. During each phase as project work is completed, issues are investigated and assessed, often uncovering related issues. The nature of these new issues requires resolution in addition to addressing the original issues.

A *retrospective analysis*, a review of the events that happened between checkpoints, should occur prior to each checkpoint meeting to allow for better decision making from the team, the stakeholders, and often the sponsor. The checkpoint meeting looks ahead to the next phase of the project and reexamines expectations for estimates, schedule, duration, and workload. Taking the findings from the phase preceding the current checkpoint and the estimates from the following phase, the project manager can better develop realistic expectations for the project.

The analysis and checkpoint meeting results should be documented, identifying participants, issues, risks, changes in expectations and requirements, and resolutions, should questions arise later. Often, action items that require immediate attention and follow-up are identified in these meetings. By applying this technique to subsequent phases, obstacles impeding completion can be identified and resolved early without negative impact to the schedule, resources, or completion criteria.

Between checkpoint meetings, project work is accomplished. Often, the time commitment estimates are way off from the actual work performed. It may be that the work cannot be done in the time frame allotted, and this could be critical in the delivery of the product or the completion of the project. It is critical to notify the sponsor and perhaps stakeholders about this problem as soon as possible. Giving them time to understand the impact and potential delay allows for sound decision making and rapid resolution. The resolution will be analyzed and reviewed at the next checkpoint meeting to ensure the decision was correct, and any additional action will be identified.

MANAGING EXPECTATIONS

Reviewing all aspects of the project on a regular basis is a critical way of managing expectations. Often, developing a questionnaire to formally canvass the organization is the best way to gather feedback. It takes time to develop the questionnaire, conduct the survey, compile results, and take action. Nevertheless, it is a good way to get organizational feedback. However, questionnaires should be used sparingly and they should not be circulated often. Questionnaires are often viewed by recipients as a request for time with no personal benefit. Choosing the appropriate time and length of the surveys is critical in achieving the response required.

Producing a briefing or event is another approach to managing expectations. Executive management may not attend checkpoint meetings or complete questionnaires, but they will attend a briefing with charts and visual analysis to better understand how their expectations have been translated in the project. This is an opportunity to identify new expectations, discuss their impact on the project, and make changes as required and expedient. Briefings are also useful for informing and educating a larger body of participants in the overall project status, as well clarifying the actual deliverables. Often, misinformation is identified in this forum and unnecessary concern is eliminated. It's worth reiterating that clarifying and testing expectations helps to ensure they are identified and met. The more this occurs, the more defined and precise the expectations and requirements will become.

A project manager's role is truly managing expectations during the entire project life cycle. This means uncovering hidden expectations randomly during the project. This task is critical because new expectations may be triggered by events that occur during a project and are as important as discovered expectations.

Monitoring the project and identifying when expectations are met is also quite critical to a project's success. Knowing just how the project is doing against expectations—meeting or even exceeding these—is sometimes as important as staying on schedule. This is the key to sponsor satisfaction and overall project success.

CONDUCT A PROJECT REVIEW AT ITS END

The true test of managing expectations occurs at the end of a project. Knowing when the project is really over is difficult. People often say, "The project is never over." The project should deliver, release, or implement something. At this juncture, a project review is advisable, often facilitated by an outside party, to ensure all aspects from expectations to commitments have been addressed. The participants in this review are usually the team members and the project manager. Analysis of the project occurs and recommendations for future projects are identified.

Here are 15 suggested questions for project review:

1. Were the project goals and expectations clear? Describe which were and which were not.
2. Did the team, stakeholders, and sponsor agree on expectations throughout the project's life cycle? If not, what occurred as a result?
3. Did the project plan reflect estimates to actuals with revisions identified as the project proceeded? If not, how did you keep track? If so, was it helpful?
4. Were the project benefits clearly understood and agreed upon? Describe these benefits.
5. Did the sponsor support the project throughout its life cycle? If not, did this cause problems? Describe this aspect of the project.
6. Were all parties informed of project progress, changes, setbacks, delays, issues, resolutions, and expectations? Did this work well?
7. Were there good project communications? Describe an improvement.
8. Did the sponsor and stakeholders understand the magnitude of project issues and impacts? Did this help in resolution?
9. What could be done or what was done to rectify problems?
10. What changes should be recommended for future projects?
11. What worked and should be continued?
12. Were there outside forces that negatively influenced the project? If so, describe these factors.
13. How did the project outcome meet with expectations established for it? Describe any deviations.
14. Was there any lack of planning, lack of understanding of the entire project, or scope changes that dramatically changed the project?
15. Are there any ways to identify the changes that negatively impacted the project earlier that would be less costly or time-consuming?

Review Past Projects

One way to understand how well other projects' expectations were managed in the past is to review them. Applying the following questions to as many past (and present) projects as possible will provide insight into how well projects met expectations, identify trends in personal project management styles, and recognize improvements that could be made for better project management in the future.

1. How did the project meet sponsor expectations, and what was the level of satisfaction?
2. Which aspects of the project did not meet expectations or result in sponsor satisfaction?
3. How clear and sound were the expectations? Did you assist in their development and clarification?
4. What could be done the next time to better manage expectations?

Conclusion

Expectations management is not easy, nor is it simple. Initial expectations are not always the same as concluding ones. Explicit expectations are necessary and can be identified; implicit ones are harder to grasp and often present themselves only when issues arise. They appear as, "But I thought that was included. . . . We can't possibly release unless we have. . . . I didn't know you weren't going to do that." Often, implicit expectations are hidden as private assumptions and are not uncovered until a design review, checkpoint meeting, or issue analysis and resolution. The key to overcoming these surprises and misconceptions is to communicate expectations clearly and negotiate scope changes as soon as they occur.

A successful project manager not only manages the day-to-day plans and deliverables, but he or she also anticipates obstacles, prepares for them, and manages expectations. The project manager needs to be a visionary—someone who can see ahead and guide the team, sponsor, and stakeholders in the right direction. The project manager can facilitate communications and resolution. He or she can also set, analyze, modify, negotiate, and revise expectations leading to the successful completion of a project. In essence, the project's success resides within the project manager's responsibilities. Managing expectations is one of the most important of these duties.

PERFORMANCE SUPPORT TOOL 25.1:

SPONSOR EXPECTATIONS MANAGEMENT

Sponsor _____ Location _____

Primary contact _____ Function _____

Project title _____ Target date for achievement _____

Stated overall objective(s):

_____

_____

Who are the other stakeholders? What do they expect from this work? Why?

Stakeholders	Input needed?	What they want and why it's important
Executive management		
Engineering		
Purchasing		
Human resources		
Manufacturing		
Quality assurance		
Sales		
Customer service		
Management information systems (MIS)		
Maintenance		
Other		
External stakeholders		

How clearly are the goals, milestones, and deliverables defined?

Goals/events/milestones/ deliverables	Definitions/terms of reference/measures

Do any key goals, milestones, or deliverables require   Y   N
a better definition?

If so, what is the need? _____

What further information is needed to define the sponsor's expectations?

Information needed	From whom	Information gathered	Date

How are the sponsor's expectations documented?

Documentation	Expected? Y/N	Created? Y/N	Received H = Hard, F = Fax E = Electronic	Comments
Request for quotation				
Posting				
Specification				
Proposal				
Purchase order				
Contract				

Project Resource Planning

Resource	Need	Capability	Plan
On-site time at client			
Off-site time			
Equipment			
Software			
Reference sources			
Materials			
Subcontractors			

Risk Analysis

Risk factors	Risk H=High M=Medium L=Low	Prevention actions

Pursue the project?   Y   N

Next steps _____ Start date _____

Additional comments:

_____

_____

_____

PERFORMANCE SUPPORT TOOL 25.2:

PROJECT MANAGER SELF-ASSESSMENT

Managing Expectations

Sponsor name _____ Stakeholder(s) names _____

Project identifier _____ Date initiated _____

Sponsor's objective(s):

_____

Why is it important?

_____

Target date for completion _____

Primary contact _____ Function_____

Input from other functions within the client organization before starting project:

___ Senior management   ___ Purchasing   ___ Engineering
___ Human resources   ___ Manufacturing   ___ Quality assurance
___ Sales   ___ Customer service   ___ Management
                                                       information
                                                       systems (MIS)
___ Other _____

Would it have helped to clarify expectations by getting
    input from others?   Y   N

Input type/information	From whom?

What mechanisms were used to define and clarify the client's expectations?

___ Face-to-face meetings   ___ Telephone conversations
___ Written statement of need   ___ Request for quotation
___ Letters   ___ E-mail messages
___ Consultant proposal   ___ Contract
___ Purchase order   ___ Service-level agreement
___ Other _____

How clearly were sponsor expectations stated?_____

How well were they communicated internally? _____

Overall project objectives	Clarity 1 = Low 5 = High	Communication 1 = Low 5 = High	Comments

Milestones, measures, or deliverables	Clarity 1 = Low 5 = High	Communication 1 = Low 5 = High	Comments

What expectations emerged during the project that were not expressed at the beginning?

_____

_____

Why?

_____

		Y	N
Did the project experience scope creep?		Y	N
Was this anticipated?	By the sponsor?	Y	N
	By the project manager?	Y	N
Was the result of this scope	For the sponsor?	Y	N
creep positive?	For the project manager?	Y	N

What could have been done to identify the likelihood of scope creep and shape the client's expectations accordingly? _____

_____

What obstacles/difficulties were encountered during this project?

_____

_____

Rate how effectively these obstacles were overcome and note any ideas for handling them more effectively in the future.

Obstacles or difficulties	Effectiveness 1 = Low 5 = High	Improving effectiveness

What could have been done to foresee these obstacles and shape the sponsor's expectations accordingly?

_____

_____

How well did you meet the sponsor's expectations?

For each of the project objectives or deliverables, note whether they were delivered on time, and rate your own level of satisfaction with the completed work, as well as your estimation of the client's level of satisfaction with the completed work.

Objectives/milestones/ deliverables	On time? Y / N	Satisfaction PM's view 1 = Low 5 = High	Satisfaction sponsor's view 1 = Low 5 = High
Overall project objectives			
Schedule/timetable			
Individual milestones/ deliverables			

What are the internal processes within project management practice that affect how well we identify and evaluate sponsor expectations? Meet sponsor expectations?

_____

_____

Make a list of internal processes, and rate their relative importance in identifying, evaluating, managing, and meeting sponsor expectations. Then rate the relative performance of each of these processes, in terms of how well they are helping us achieve these objectives.

Processes	Importance 1 = Low 5 = High	Performance 1 = Low 5 = High	Comments
Analyzing sponsor needs			
Generating/submitting proposals			
Training/educating			
Planning with the sponsor			
Responding to requests			
Giving feedback to sponsor			
Monitoring progress			
Generating/delivering reports			
Applying expertise to projects			

Based on the analysis of this self-assessment, what actions should be taken to improve the management of sponsor expectations?

Short term:

_____

_____

Long term:

_____

_____

_____

_____

CHAPTER 26

PARTICIPATIVE MANAGEMENT: GETTING THE MOST FROM YOUR TEAM

PAULA MARTIN and KAREN TATE

George, a project manager for the Happy Shampoo Company (fictitious), is holding a kickoff meeting with his project team. George has been chosen to head up the Clean Curl development project. Clean Curl is envisioned as a shampoo for naturally curly hair. Since Clean Curl is critical to Happy's future success (the competition has just launched a competitive product), George has been given instructions from his sponsor, Leonard, director of product development, that Happy's president wants this product developed in no more than six months. (Happy's competitors are churning out new products at a phenomenal rate, and if Happy doesn't improve its product development cycle time, its future is in the ash heap.) Happy's fastest development time has been nine months, and its average is a year.

George is accountable for the project's success. He works in a matrix structure, and none of the people on the team work for either him or Leonard. George has just gathered the team together for the project kickoff. Let's see how George is handling his kickoff meeting.

THE CLEAN CURL KICKOFF MEETING

Assembled for the kickoff meeting are the key members of the project team: the manager of formulations, the manager of testing, the manager of packaging, the manufacturing manager, the marketing manager, and the purchasing manager. George welcomes everyone and explains the directive he's been given by Leonard. Because George is a very conscientious project manager, he has taken the time to prepare a draft project plan, in-

493

cluding a schedule with six-month time lines. He thinks this will help to streamline both the kickoff meeting and the whole project.

George hands out the preliminary project plan as he explains it to the team. He says, "Now, I know this is a stretch for us. We've never developed a new product this fast, but if we all pull together, we can get it done. We need to do this to save Happy's future." There are groans from around the table as the group flips through the preliminary project plan.

"Where's the project charter?" asks the manager of packaging.

"Well," George responds, "Leonard didn't have time to complete it. I can fill you in on the general direction for the project." Still not satisfied, the manager of packaging asks, "So how do we know this is what the senior leadership team really wants from this project?"

"I've discussed this with Leonard," replies George. "I'm clear on the direction we need to take. The key element here is the time line."

"There's no way we can develop and launch a product in six months," says the manager of formulations. Turning to the manager of testing, he asks, "Do we even have a capability to test curly hair?"

"Not at the moment, and it would take us at least three months to get geared up to test curly hair," replies the testing manager.

George isn't surprised that he is getting this resistance; he's prepared for it. "If you'll turn to page six in your handout, you'll see the project schedule I've put together. You'll note I've scheduled most of the activities concurrently, in order to speed up our development time line. I think if you review it you'll find that with luck we can make the deadline of six months."

"You've got me ordering equipment in month three, and we won't have a process transmittal until month five," says the manufacturing manager. "I can't assume that kind of risk. What if we end up needing different equipment? My head will be on the line."

"I understand your concern," says George, "but if we're going to be successful, we have to do some things differently—take some risks. We all have to take risks." More moans around the table.

George likes the fact that no one says anything. At least then they're not complaining. "Can I get your buy-in on this? The competition is eating our lunch. We have to try something new if we're going to survive." More silence.

The manager of purchasing finally speaks. "It's not that we aren't concerned about our future and it's not that we don't want to do things differently, but I wonder if this is the best way to make the Clean Curl project work. Maybe if we started from scratch and built a new project plan together, we might come up with some creative ideas."

George replies, "That would be great if we had the time, but we're already facing a very difficult time line. If we start all over and have everyone contribute, we'll be here forever and we'll never get done. Since we have a plan that will get us there in six months, I suggest we move on and get to work. Leonard is happy with the plan, and I think it makes sense. What do you say? Can we give it a try?"

WHAT IS THE BEST MANAGEMENT APPROACH?

Is this the appropriate way to lead a project team? Is the project manager supposed to do the planning for the project? Will George be successful with his project management approach? What is the best management approach? What is the role of the project manager?

In order to define the role of the project manager and the best project management approach, we need to clarify the generic role of a manager because a project manager is, in fact, a manager. A manager's job is to act as the trustee of the organization's resources in order to help it reach its vision (by achieving its goals) and fulfill its mission (by creating products and services that serve its customers). In addition, he or she is accountable to develop the human and nonhuman capacity of the organization—this allows the organization to change and grow.

If you're a project manager then, your job is to fulfill the manager's role for a specific project. It doesn't matter whether you're a full-time or a part-time project manager or even whether you have the title of project manager; you're still fulfilling a management role. In the past five to 10 years, we have experienced a major shift in our understanding of how to best fulfill the role of a manager. Let's look at the old approach and why it's obsolete and then look at the new one.

THE OLD MODEL OF MANAGEMENT

The old model of management is based on certain assumptions, one of which is, "You need authority in order to manage." Authority is linked to making a decision and having subordinates to carry out that decision. The other assumption is that you can be accountable only for what is in your circle of control, and your circle includes your own actions and the actions of subordinates. (See Figure 26.1.)

These two assumptions drive most of the old management model. We assume that a manager can't accomplish a goal without authority and

Figure 26.1
Circle of Control—Old Paradigm

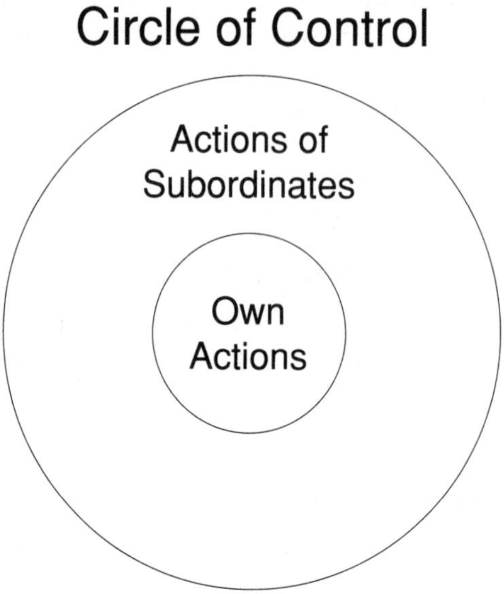

Circle of Control

cannot get things accomplished if decisions are made outside his or her circle of control.

In the old paradigm, project managers must have authority in order to get something accomplished; so must the functional manager. This creates a dilemma—two people need authority. The solution to this dilemma was the creation of the dual reporting structure, which gave authority over subordinates to both the functional manager and the project manager. However, one of the reasons for having a single line of authority is to provide clear, aligned direction within an organization. The dual reporting system makes it very difficult to do that. Dual reporting is the wrong solution to the wrong problem. The problem is not lack of authority; the problem is the management model and approach. The solution is to discard the old management model.

MANAGEMENT BASED ON AUTHORITY

When management is based on authority, people in positions of authority are expected to be the decision makers, because they are expected to be the ones with the most knowledge about their area or project. This style of management is called the directive approach. The project manager (or boss) exercises authority by making planning decisions (sometimes with input from team members)—what the schedule will be, how to allocate the budget, how to minimize risks, and so on. These decisions are relayed to individual members of the project team, who are then expected to carry out their assignments. During execution, the project manager checks up on team members to make sure they are on track. If the project is not on track, the project manager decides what needs to be done to correct the situation. Information flows from individual team members to the project manager and decisions flows from the project manager back down. (See Figure 26.2.)

The old model of managing assumes that the project manager is the best person to make project decisions. He or she is the "superexpert" on the project. It assumes that the role of the people on the team is to carry

Figure 26.2
Directive Management Model

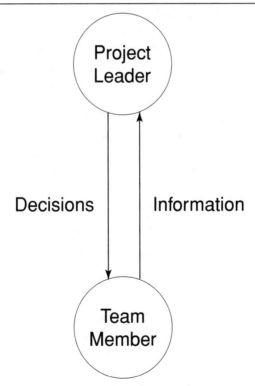

out the decisions made by the project manager. It assumes that the directive style is the most efficient and effective way to get work done. As we'll see, these assumptions are incorrect.

THE DIRECTIVE MANAGEMENT MODEL

In the directive approach, the project manager makes the decisions and hands them down the chain of command to the appropriate team member, who is supposed to carry out the directive. This control/authority model of management doesn't work very well in today's environment. It assumes that human beings are like machines—that they receive orders and then carry them out, like robots. But we know that human beings think, feel, and care about what they do. They want to make a contribution; they want to be a part of something larger than themselves. And people are not just like Pavlov's dogs, responding to external stimuli. People are intrinsically motivated, and their motivation increases when they have ownership of something—a house, an idea, a team.

When we consider the whole human being, we have to begin to question our old directive approach to project management. The directive approach does not produce the best project results. The fundamental assumptions of the old paradigm are flawed. For one, our circle of control is much smaller than we believed it to be in the past. Our true circle of control includes only our own actions and our responses to the actions of others. (See Figure 26.3.) It does not include controlling the actions of others, because we can't control what other people do. We may be able to force compliance, but what we'll get from them is just enough cooperation for them to stay out of trouble. We lose their creativity, their caring,

Figure 26.3
Real Circle of Control

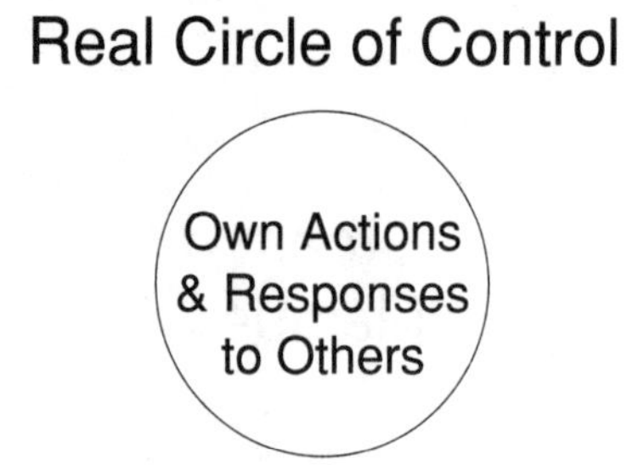

Real Circle of Control

their willingness to go the extra mile—the most valuable gifts that human beings bring to the table.

Although our circle of control is small, our circle of influence is quite large. (See Figure 26.4.) We do not need authority or control in order to get things done. We can get things done using influence. Management in the new paradigm is about working effectively within the circle of influence.

NETWORKED COMMUNICATION

In the old paradigm, everything flowed vertically—information, feedback, inputs, decisions. (See Figure 26.5.) This made horizontal management, which includes process and project management, very difficult.

In the new paradigm, information flow is no longer just up and down. It also flows across, through the network of people involved in an endeavor. In the case of project management, the project manager is the leader of the network. His or her job is to make sure the communication flow within the network is effective. (See Figure 26.6.)

The project manager is also the key person responsible for extending

Figure 26.4
Circle of Influence

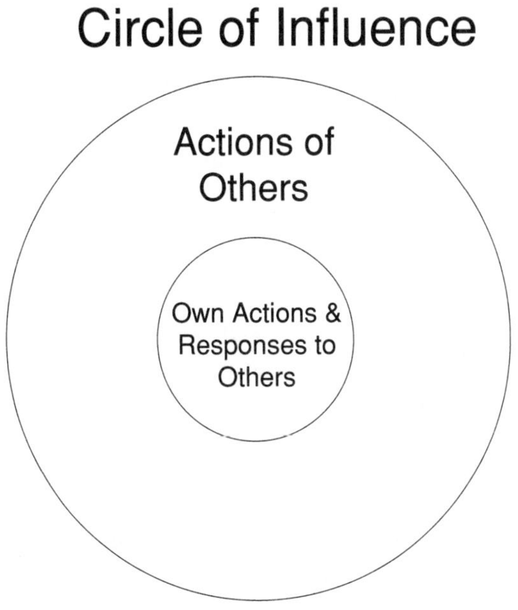

Circle of Influence

Actions of Others

Own Actions & Responses to Others

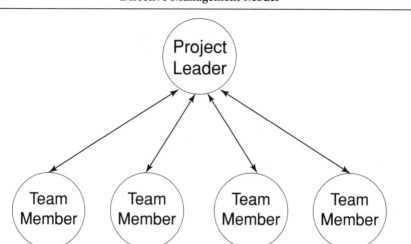

Figure 26.5
Directive Management Model

the network beyond the project team. He or she is the key liaison to the sponsor, the customer, and any other key stakeholders. Members of the project team also act as liaisons, typically to functional managers and other stakeholders.

A key role of the project manager is to ensure that all those who are affected by the project, all project stakeholders, are involved in the project in some way. This may consist of their providing inputs to the project liaison or actually participating on the team. Through involvement, we extend our circle of influence.

OPTIMIZING A SYSTEM

The focus in the old paradigm is on optimizing individual units within the organization—business units, functional departments, and individuals within those departments. Optimization in the old model is achieved by setting functional goals, and then holding individuals accountable for those goals. The organization seeks, through its goal setting and its reward and recognition programs, to reward those individual units that perform the best. This creates a system of competition, and in the old paradigm it is believed that internal competition between units is the best way to optimize organizational performance.

Figure 26.6
Participate Management Model

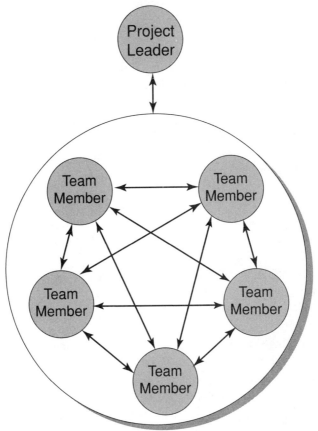

This would be true if an organization were not a system, but unfortunately for the old paradigm, an organization *is* a system, and systems are not optimized through internal competition. They are optimized through internal cooperation.

In a system, all the units are interdependent. That interdependency is shown to us visually if we look at a project PERT diagram. Deliverables are handed off to the next internal customer in the process chain. The parts of a project are interdependent, and thus a project must be managed as a system. In order to do that, we need to do three things:

1. Set goals for the whole system first (the whole project).
2. Define the interdependencies between the parts of the system.
3. Manage those interdependencies.

Setting goals for the whole project means making sure the final deliverable and the customer's acceptance criteria for the final deliverable are clearly defined up front. Schedule and budget targets also must be set for the whole project. Then the project should be decomposed into its parts, determining what each of the subprojects will produce, when, and for how much money.

Second, we need to create a schedule that clearly shows interdependencies. This provides us with a network or process map of the project work.

Third, we have to manage the system as a whole, focusing on the interdependencies. We know that systems usually fail at the handoffs or connections between the parts. This is because the whole does not equal the sum of the parts. You can't manage individual units and expect the whole project or whole organization to be effective and efficient.

That is because the whole depends on how the parts fit together. To illustrate this, he uses the example of building the best possible car. If we try to optimize each part—pick ones that are the best at what they do, such as finding the best transmission, brakes, engine, and so on—and then assemble those parts into a car, what have we got? A heap of parts. Why? Because they don't fit together. You can't connect them properly. They won't work smoothly together. To get an optimized car, we need to create a system of parts—ones that will work together effectively. The same is true of optimizing any system, including project management. If you want a project that is successful, you need to manage the interconnections between the parts.

OWNERSHIP, EMPOWERMENT, AND INTERDEPENDENCY MANAGEMENT

The directive approach to management was designed to direct individual units. The new, participative approach is designed to direct the whole project or system.

Let's look at three key factors in effectively managing in the new paradigm:

1. Ownership
2. Empowerment
3. Interdependencies management

OWNERSHIP

Ownership is created through involvement or participation in the project process. Everyone is asked to participate in making the planning and tracking decisions for the project. Everyone is asked to contribute ideas and to evaluate those ideas. Everyone is asked to bring his or her mind and heart to the project.

Creating involvement does not simply mean asking for input from team members and then having the project manager make the project decisions. It means turning over the project to the team—allowing them to make the decisions on how the deliverables will be produced and when. (It does not mean letting the team decide what should be done—that is for the customer to decide.)

When people are involved, when they participate, they begin to care more about the outcome of what they are involved in. They have a higher level of commitment to making the project succeed.

In order to lead a project team using participation, the project manager will need to use a structured, participative project management process. This process should include tools that allow the team to work through the steps of planning quickly and efficiently. It's up to the project manager to provide the process and to lead the team through it. The role of the project manager thus changes, from decision maker for the project to facilitator of the project process. However, it's still the job of the project manager to assure that good decisions are made. It just so happens that the best decisions are usually made by the team as a whole, because collectively they know more than any individual. In order to make good decisions quickly, the team needs a process to follow with good decision-making tools. It's the job of the project manager to provide the process and the tools.

Characteristics of a structured, participative project management process include the following:

- Uses team-based method
- Has clearly defined steps that the project team members can follow
- Helps the team make decisions

A project manager will need to have the following skills in order to be effective:

- Facilitation skills
- Communication skills
- Effective listening skills
- Constructive feedback skills
- Managing team dynamics skills
- Participative project management skills
- Leadership skills
- Negotiation skills
- Influencing skills
- Selling skills

A project manager will require the following tools:

- Project management tools
- Creativity tools
- Decision-making tools
- Conflict resolution tools
- Team building tools

EMPOWERMENT

Ownership is closely linked to empowerment. Once the decisions are made, people must be empowered to carry out those decisions. Effective empowerment depends on the following basic ingredients:

- *The expectations for the project must be clearly defined.* These expectations are outlined in the charter for the main project and where appropriate in subproject charters. By having clear direction, the person who is being empowered knows what is expected from him or her. That person then has the opportunity to accept or not accept the assignment.
- *Resources are available to do the job requested.* Nothing is more demoralizing to people than asking them to complete a job without adequate resources. Not only is it demoralizing, but it is also an abdication of the role of the project manager. As a manager, the project manager must ensure that adequate resources are provided in order to do the job requested. People cannot create something out of thin air. Creating project results requires time, effort, and money. It's

the job of the project manager, through the sponsor, to ensure these resources are available to the project team members.

- *The person being empowered must have the skills and knowledge to complete the assignment.* It is not empowering to ask someone to complete an assignment that the person doesn't know how to do. The job of the project manager is to make sure people can get the task done. Resource or functional managers are the first source for this type of help.

- *People are involved in the decisions that they are being empowered to carry out.* When people are involved in the decision making, they understand better what is being required of them. They also have had the opportunity to contribute their ideas before the team makes a decision. This creates ownership and a greater willingness to take on the accountability for the results.

- *The results required from the individual should be clearly defined ahead of time.* People should be empowered to create deliverables, not to perform tasks. Tasks are difficult to define or monitor. Deliverables, on the other hand, can be defined (the internal customer provides his or her requirements and customer acceptance criteria), and can be monitored. We can determine whether the deliverable met the customer's acceptance criteria, was on time, and was within the budget. People need to know what is required, and they need to know this before they accept an assignment.

- *Obstacles must be removed that would prevent the person from completing the job.* It is reasonable to ask someone to remove obstacles for himself or herself. However, when there are problems at higher levels of management that the individual cannot remove, it is the responsibility of the project manager, working with the sponsor, to eliminate those obstacles.

- *The person is held accountable for producing results.* Empowerment must be accompanied by clear accountability. When we empower someone, we are letting him or her decide how the deliverable will be created. This power must be accompanied by accountability. Empowerment does not work well with micromanagement. Give people accountability to produce deliverables, have them report back regularly (see next paragraph), and hold them accountable. Then there is no need for micromanagement.

- *Regular reporting is established up front.* Empowerment does not mean hands off entirely. There is an oversight function that must be performed by the project manager and the other team members. Regular reporting is required from the empowered individual back to the team. We don't want to let too much time elapse before we know there is a problem. Empowered individuals have a responsibility to let the team know as quickly as possible when they are running into difficulties and may not be able to meet their accountabilities. This allows the team and the project manager to provide help or make adjustments to the project in order to keep it on track.

INTERDEPENDENCIES MANAGEMENT

As stated earlier, optimization of a system occurs when you manage the relationships or interdependencies between the individual units, making sure they all tie together.

In a directive approach, the project manager is the only one who manages the interdependencies. As a result, project team members work with blinders on. They understand their parts but don't understand how all the parts fit together. Not only does this limit each person's contribution to the whole, but it also demoralizes the individual, as he or she must work in a vacuum, not really understanding how what each does contributes to the whole effort.

Interdependencies are best managed in a collaborative environment. In order to manage a project effectively, the project manager must build collaboration between the team members, and each team member must also understand and manage his or her interdependencies. The project manager can build collaboration and manage interdependencies in the following ways:

- *Focus on building relationships between team members.* Make sure the team members get to know one another, and manage any conflicts that arise between team members. Conflict is a natural stage of team development; however, it's up to the project manager to make sure the team works through the "storming" stage so it can move on to the more productive "norming" and "performing" stages.
- *Have the team members participate in defining the scope of the project.* When team members collaborate in defining the scope and scope boundaries, they have a better understanding of what the end goal of the project is all about. This helps to ensure that everyone is headed in the same direction.
- *Have the team members collaborate in doing the subproject breakdown structure.* Team members should be involved in creating the organizational structure for the project, and because each subproject

will be the accountability of an individual project team member, he or she should be involved in defining what deliverables will be produced within the subproject.

- *Have the team members participate in creating the deliverables schedule.* The deliverables schedule shows what each team member will produce and when, and it will identify the interdependencies. It's important to have the team collaborate in creating the schedule. Each team member then understands where he or she fits into the bigger picture. They know their internal customers and suppliers. They understand the time constraints. They also know what constraints they personally are working under and can factor those into the project schedule. When the team creates the schedule together, they develop an understanding of the overall project and will work harder to make sure the project time lines are met.

THE CASE OF CLEAN CURL

Now that we have explored the basics of the participative approach to project management, we can go back and revisit George at his project team's kickoff meeting.

George has been given instructions from his sponsor, Leonard, director of product development, that Happy's president wants this product developed in no more than six months. (Happy's competitors are churning out new products at a phenomenal rate, and if Happy doesn't improve its product development cycle time, its future is in the ash heap.) Happy's fastest development time has been nine months, and its average is a year.

The first problem is the six-month time line. This is a stretch goal set by the senior management team. Only during planning will the project team be able to determine if it's possible to meet a six-month time line. The project team should begin with the goal of meeting this deadline, if at all humanly possible. But, things that are not humanly possible just aren't possible. So George needs to keep an open mind about the time line and be prepared to go back to Leonard with data about what is possible given the allocated resources and project constraints.

George is accountable for the project's success. He works in a matrix structure, and none of the people on the team work for either him or Leonard, the project's sponsor.

In the old paradigm, the fact that none of the people on the project team work for George or Leonard would be a problem. In the new paradigm, it really doesn't matter. George and Leonard need to make sure that there is buy-in and commitment from the resource managers who are providing people to the project.

George welcomes everyone and explains the directive he's been given by Leonard. Because George is a very conscientious project manager, he has taken the time to prepare a draft project plan, including a schedule with six-month time lines. He thinks this will help to streamline both the kickoff meeting and the whole project.

George is really getting into trouble here. First, he hasn't done anything to attend to the team dynamics. There is no introduction, no icebreaker. Next, he's developed the project plan without participation and, to make matters worse, he obviously hasn't even gotten any input before creating it. George thinks he's speeding up the process, but in fact he's slowing it down. (He may speed up the planning phase, but execution will take longer—which means the whole project will take longer and cost more.) His team members resent him doing the planning without them. In addition, it's doubtful whether George can create a realistic project plan without participation from the people who will have to carry it out.

George hands out the preliminary project plan as he explains it to the team. He says, "Now, I know this is a stretch for us. We've never developed a new product this fast, but if we all pull together, we can get it done. We need to do this to save Happy's future." There are groans from around the table as the group flips through the preliminary project plan.

Being a cheerleader is not a substitute for good project leadership skills. George is not helping to pull the group together. He's taken a directive approach and is using the tack of trying to convince the team to go along with him because of the threats to Happy's existence and their own careers. This is likely to anger the group.

"Where's the project charter?" asks the manager of packaging.

"Well," George responds, "Leonard didn't have time to complete it. I can fill you in on the general direction for the project."

Still not satisfied, the manager of packaging asks, "So how do we know this is what the senior leadership team really wants from this project?"

"I've discussed this with Leonard," replies George. "I'm clear on the direction we need to take. The key element here is the time line."

The manager of packaging has a good point. George should have gotten a charter from the sponsor in order to provide the team with clear expectations and limits regarding the project. It's George's job to review the charter with the team and gather their questions and concerns. Some of those concerns may be addressed during the planning process, but questions about items that are unclear in the charter should be resolved with the sponsor before the team begins planning.

George isn't surprised that he is getting this resistance; he's prepared for it. "If you'll turn to page six in your handout, you'll see the project schedule I've put together. You'll note I've scheduled most of the activities concurrently, in order to speed up our development time line. I think if you review it you'll find that with luck we can make the deadline of six months."

Instead of letting the team work through their difficulties and come up with a solution that everyone has contributed to, George plows ahead, leading them through his project schedule. Again, he's increasing people's resistance to his plan, even if it is a good plan, because they are not being allowed to participate in the development of a solution for the project.

George likes the fact that no one says anything. At least then they're not complaining. "Can I get your buy-in on this? The competition is eating our lunch. We have to try something new if we're going to survive." More silence.

This is a typical response by project managers who don't have team skills—as long as people are not verbally complaining, all is well. All is not well. The team is not committed, and George is pressing for a close. Apparently he thinks he's a salesperson, rather than a project manager.

The manager of purchasing finally speaks. "It's not that we aren't concerned about our future and it's not that we don't want to do things differently, but I wonder if this is the best way to make the Clean Curl project work. Maybe if we started from scratch and built a new project plan together, we might come up with some creative ideas."

George replies, "That would be great if we had the time, but we're already facing a very difficult time line. If we start all over and have everyone contribute, we'll be here forever and we'll never get done. Since we have a plan that will get us there in six months, I suggest we move on and get to work. Leonard is happy with the plan, and I think it makes sense. What do you say? Can we give it a try?"

George is being given the opportunity to change his management style and try a participative approach to accomplishing this project. He might be surprised at the ideas the team would come up with. Instead, he sticks to his directive style and tries to get the team to commit to his plan. They may comply, but it's unlikely the project will run smoothly or get done on schedule.

George is a role model of the old paradigm—of what not to do. If you want to be successful in managing projects, it's time to adopt a new approach. Get the team involved, empower individual team members, and focus on interdependencies. Not only will your projects be more successful, but they'll also be a whole lot more fun for you and the team.

All of the chapters in this part focus on the human dimensions side of the socio-technical model. All of these skills are skills critical in the new paradigm.

CHAPTER 27

VIRTUAL TEAM MANAGEMENT: BUILDING A SUCCESSFUL VIRTUAL TEAM

MARTHA HAYWOOD

In the twenty-first century, virtual teams are becoming the rule instead of the exception. Most project managers don't go out looking for a geographically distributed team. Usually, circumstances force project managers into the position of managing across distance and time zones. There's always the temptation to focus on why "it's more difficult" or why "it doesn't work as well." The reality is that virtual teams do make some things more difficult, but they also make some things easier.

I recently had the experience of working with a worldwide team that *turned down* the opportunity to get together for a face-to-face meeting. The team had members in Japan, Ireland, and the United States. They had developed a very effective process for conducting meetings and resolving issues via an electronic discussion board. The discussion board eliminated problems the team had experienced in previous face-to-face meetings. Accents disappeared on a discussion board. Confusing culturally oriented nonverbal signals were gone. The Japanese team members had time to review postings, so they understood the meeting more clearly. The meeting was completely self-documenting. The geographic distance forced this team to adopt practices that improved their communication. The team turned down the trip because they felt they were communicating just fine and 15 hours on a plane didn't seem appealing.

Virtual teams actually can be more productive and more effective than co-located teams. The project manager plays a key role in setting up the infrastructure to make a virtual team successful. In this chapter, I'll give you a very brief overview of the process of building a successful virtual

511

team. The material presented here is the result of research done by Management Strategies, Inc., between 1995 and 1998. We interviewed 514 managers to find out the best practices for virtual teams. We found that successful virtual teams shared certain key characteristics. We developed a framework called the Maturity Model for Distributed Teams. We've successfully used this model to help many managers assess their teams and develop a plan to improve performance.

It's worthwhile to take a moment to define what we mean by the term *team*. I'm often told by students in my project management classes that "teams are groups of people with a common goal." With that definition, all the competitors at a track meet would be on the same team. Common goals and values don't make a group of individuals into a team. If you think of a hockey team, not only do the team members have a common goal, their tasks are interdependent and they have a common understanding of rules of the game or the process. The people on the team use common tools—they all have skates and hockey sticks. You don't find one player on skates, a second player on a bicycle, and a third riding a horse. In corporate America, companies will give half the team PCs with Microsoft Word and the other half Unix workstations with Framemaker and then wonder why things don't work too well. Each member of the hockey team has the skills required to play his or her position on the team. The hockey players function as a team because they are aligned in four areas:

1. Goals
2. Process
3. Tools
4. Skills

These areas correspond to the parts of a tool called the Alignment Model (Figure 27.1), which is used in conjunction with the Maturity Model for Distributed Teams (Figure 27.2). The Alignment Model helps managers predict team members' performance given the current environment and infrastructure. The Maturity Model is a framework for improving overall team performance. In the following sections, I'll present an overview of these models along with some checklists that you can use in the assessment and planning process. Although a detailed description of either model is beyond the scope of this chapter, the information presented here should point you in the right direction.

Figure 27.1
Using the Alignment Model

Does this person/group fit?

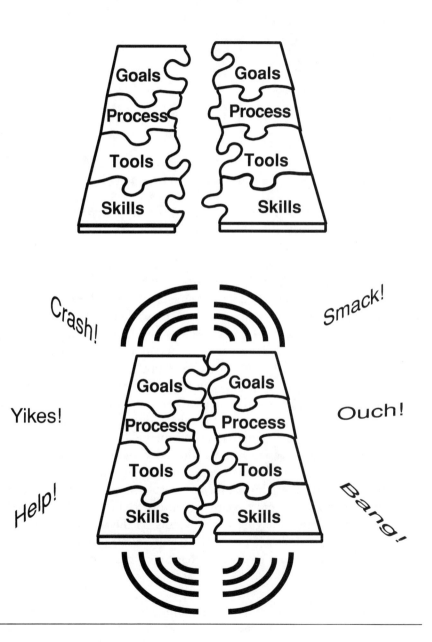

Figure 27.2
Maturity Model for Distributed Teams

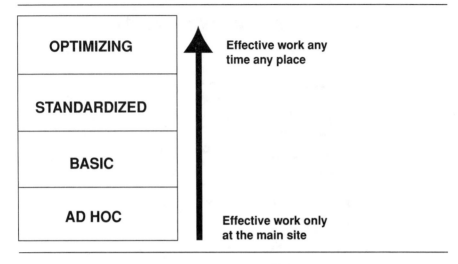

USING THE ALIGNMENT MODEL

The first step in building an effective virtual team is to assess your team to find misalignments. Not only does alignment (or the lack of it) affect the team's ability to perform specific tasks (such as whether I can read the e-mail attachment you sent me), it also has a crucial effect on team cohesiveness and trust. It's a common misconception that building trust is about making people like each other personally. It is perfectly possible to trust someone that you don't like. You trust the airline pilot even though you've never met him. I heard a quarterback once discuss how much he trusted his offensive linemen even though he didn't like them personally and didn't want to associate with them off the field. Trust involves believing that the people on your team are aligned with you in all four of the key dimensions: goals, processes, tools, and skills. Just because people share my goals and values doesn't mean I trust them. I have to believe they know how to do the job and have the resources to do it.

I teach a course in managing virtual teams. In the course, I sometimes give the students the following exercise to explore the nature of trust. The students break into groups to discuss what they would do in the following situation:

You are a scientist working in the rain forest of South America. You've been bitten by an insect whose venom will kill you within 48 hours if you don't receive an injection of the antidote. The antidote is available at the hospital, which is 45 miles from where you are in the rain forest. The antidote costs $5,000 (which is all the money you have). You are feeling so ill that you can't possibly travel. There are only two people available to travel to the hospital to purchase the antidote. The first person is your spouse, who desperately wants you to live but does not know how to drive and doesn't know the way. The second person is your neighbor. Your neighbor has just been released from prison and is known to be a thief. Your neighbor knows how to drive and knows the way to the hospital. The rules of the game are that you can send only one person. What would you have to do to make yourself trust either your spouse or the thief?

Different groups come up with different answers. Some people would give the spouse a driving lesson and a map; others try to think of ways that they could motivate the thief, such as telling him they'll get him a job when he returns. In either case, the group recommends a process to bring the messenger into alignment in all four areas. Neither person can be trusted until they have been aligned. When managers tell me their teams don't work because the team members don't trust each other, I tell them to look for the misalignments. It is not always about goals and values. Maybe your East Coast team doesn't trust your West Coast team because they don't believe the West Coast team has enough resources or training to do the job. As project manager, you need to show that adequate resources are available or (if you find the distrust is well founded, because there really aren't enough resources) you need to get more resources allocated to the project.

I am sometimes asked why values aren't included as a piece of the Alignment Model. Goals are different from values. A *goal* is the objective of a specific project (for example, writing a computer program, winning a war, and so on). Goals change with time and are usually negotiable. A *value* is a deeply held belief, such as the importance of honesty or equality. Values are very difficult to change; as a project manager, it is not usually worth your time to try. People who have different values can work well together for a specific project if they are aligned in the other four areas. The classic example of this would be the partnership of the United States and the Soviet Union in World War II. Team members with very dissimilar values will not have aligned goals often enough to work together on multiple projects over the long term.

To do a detailed assessment, you need to pose different types of questions to various types of team members. However, there are some high-level checklists that you can apply to all team members. I'll review those briefly in the next section.

ASSESSING GOALS WITH A HIGH-LEVEL CHECKLIST

Any project management course will tell you the first order of business is to define the project's goals. When you evaluate a deeply troubled project, it is not surprising to find that not only is the project manager confused about the goals of the team members, he or she has also done a poor job of defining and communicating the goals of the project and the team. It may sound obvious, but if you don't create a written statement of the project goals, you are going to have a lot of difficulty evaluating team members for alignment. In assessing goals, it is important to consider more than just dates and deliverables. Determining a remote team member's other commitments and priorities is key. For example, one of my partners was managing a project that was a joint venture between a California company and a Japanese company. As the project progressed, she found that the true goal of the Japanese partner was not to finish the current project on time, but to establish relationships with vendors and suppliers in the United States.

The following checklist should help you evaluate the goals and values of distributed team members:

- What is their reason for participating in the project?
- How are the team members compensated? (By the hour? By the deliverable?)
- What is their attitude toward processes, tools, and skills?
- What are their competing priorities?
- What is their level of commitment to schedule and quality goals?
- What is their attitude toward decision making?
- What is their attitude toward communication?
- Are there cultural issues?

ASSESSING PROCESSES WITH A HIGH-LEVEL CHECKLIST

The area where we see the largest number of misalignments is work process. Project managers working in companies that have experienced mergers or acquisitions get hit hard with this issue. It is also crucial when evaluating contractors and third-party development organizations. If your team is accustomed to a rigorous development process that includes writing specifications, conducting design reviews, and executing extensive testing, you need to select team members who understand that process and are comfortable with it. Hiring a contractor who has worked only at start-up companies and has never participated in a design review is probably asking for trouble, regardless of how skilled that contractor may be in a particular technical area. The converse is also true. It you're working at a start-up company and you need to ship some kind of product next month or you're out of business, you don't want to work with a team member who requires a lot of structure. The following checklist will help you in assessing the process of potential distributed team members:

- Do they understand what a process is?
- Have they documented their own process?
- What is their process maturity level?
- Do they understand your team's process?
- Do they have direct experience with a process similar to your team's process?
- How willing are they to adapt to the team's process?
- Do they have the tools available to feed into your team's systems for corporate memory?
- Do they have acceptable availability standards? Are they willing to commit to yours?

ASSESSING TOOLS WITH A HIGH-LEVEL CHECKLIST

How many times have you gotten an e-mail attachment that you can't read? Either you don't have the software application required to open it or you have the wrong version. How many times do you need to communicate with a team member who doesn't have a fax machine or an e-mail address? A little bit of up-front planning and communication about team standards for tools can greatly affect how quickly your project is completed. Tool misalignments create delays that can add 50 percent to the overall project duration.

Large companies that have experienced mergers and acquisitions have the most difficulty aligning tools. It is simply not economically feasible to throw out legacy hardware and software when companies as large a Lockheed and Martin Marietta merge. Alignment of tools does not necessarily mean that everyone has the same computer and software on their desktops (although that is one way to do it). It means that all the team members have equal ability to access shared resources and communicate information to the team.

A Web-based infrastructure is an excellent solution for companies needing to align large legacy systems. Most of the commonly available word processors allow documents to be saved in HTML. Adobe's distiller and PDF format are excellent for making the outputs of platform-specific software readable by other team members. By *platform-specific software*, I mean a special-purpose application, such as a computer-aided design (CAD) program that may run only on a Sun workstation.

The following checklist should help you align the tools of potential distributed team members:

- What tools (software applications, hardware platforms) will they have available for the work? If the tools are not identical, is there a common data interchange format?
- What tools (e-mail, fax, voice mail, FTP, remote LAN access) will they have available for communication? Are the communication tools compatible?
- What tools will they have available for documentation? If the tools are not identical, is there a common data interchange format?

ASSESSING SKILLS WITH A HIGH-LEVEL CHECKLIST

Most managers already do a pretty good job of assessing skills. It's the way they have selected their co-located team members for years. For distributed team members, managers may want to examine a somewhat broader skill set. Distributed team members need to have better communication skills and also need to be able to do a better job of managing themselves.

When you assess team members for alignment in the area of skills, make certain you don't limit your assessment to technical skills. Although it is certainly necessary to use separate checklists for the technical skills required for each functional area represented on your team, the following high-level checklist can help you broaden your perspective.

- What is their level of technical skill and how can they demonstrate it?
- What is their track record for:
    Delivering quality work?
    Delivering work that meets specifications?
    Producing documentation?
- What is their level of management experience?

- What is their track record for:
  Delivering on time?
  Delivering on budget?
  Using the process?
- How strong are their communication skills?

THE RELATIONSHIP BETWEEN THE ALIGNMENT MODEL AND THE MATURITY MODEL

The Alignment Model is a tool for helping managers predict performance of team members in an existing team environment. How does a manager go about improving overall team performance? In our studies of distributed teams, we found that some teams were much more likely to meet their objectives than others. We decided to do some formal surveys and try to determine which characteristics were common to successful distributed teams and how those characteristics could be measured. These surveys resulted in the Maturity Model for Distributed Teams. This four-level model (Figure 27.2) gives managers a framework for assessing their team's maturity level and provides assistance in determining the next steps to improve their team's effectiveness. The Maturity Model works well in conjunction with the Alignment Model.

Our experience showed that companies had a tendency to overemphasize improvements in tools and underemphasize improvements in processes and skills. One company that we worked with spent over $3 million designing and rolling out a sophisticated Lotus Notes implementation. The software was intended to facilitate the work of their newly distributed teams. When we became involved, the company was in the process of abandoning the tool because team members were unable or unwilling to use it. The problem was not with the tool or the team members; Lotus Notes can be a great collaboration tool. The problem was with the way the management went about implementing their distributed teams. Installing expensive collaboration tools without spending time on training and processes is a waste of money. The research showed that teams were more successful when they gradually improved all four factors (goals, processes, tools, and skills).

UNDERSTANDING THE CHARACTERISTICS OF SUCCESSFUL DISTRIBUTED TEAMS

Before I can present the characteristics of successful distributed teams, I need to explain a few key terms and concepts.

Availability Standards

Many distributed team members are frustrated and panicked by not knowing when and how to expect responses to their communications with distant team members. Managers of distributed teams need to set up *availability standards* appropriate for their teams. For example, voice mail will be checked once a day and acknowledged within 24 hours, or e-mail will be checked twice a day and acknowledged within four hours. Putting these standards in place replaces the nine-to-five de facto availability standard that provides co-located team members with a feeling of security. This de facto standard has been such a fundamental part of our business process that without it team members feel like the rug has been completely pulled from underneath them.

The truth is that having people work in the same building does not necessarily make them available to one another. Most office workers are at their desks less than 25 percent of the time. Availability and presence are two different things. In this day and age, pagers and cell phones can make your distributed team member more available than the person in the next cubicle. Typically, this extreme is not necessary or appropriate. However, some new standards and structure involving availability are absolutely necessary for distributed team members to communicate effectively and trust one another.

Corporate Memory

Corporate memory refers to whatever systems your team has in place to retain the knowledge to repeatedly manufacture your product or perform your service. Historically, co-located teams have been able to get away with relatively informal systems for corporate memory. The corporate memory for some companies literally resides in the heads of certain long-term employees. "Old Joe" has always been there. He's seen how everything has been done. If you have a question, you can ask him. Unfortunately, the Old Joe method doesn't work for distributed teams. Old Joe didn't see the manufacturing process that your overseas partner used or the design process that your consultant created.

Distributed team members need to feed into a formal system for corporate memory. Examples of systems for corporate memory include project repositories, document control, source control, Lotus Notes, and so on. The systems and tools that would be appropriate for you would depend on your industry.

Pushing versus Pulling Information

The amount of information that each of us is expected to process each day is increasing. When information is presented to us in a manner that allows us little control over when and how we process it, that information is *pushed* at us. Examples of pushed information include phone calls, pages, voice mail, and unprioritized, unfiltered e-mail. Examples of *pulled* information include electronic bulletin boards, intranets, Lotus Notes, source control systems, and document control systems. Several of the new means of electronic communication make it much easier for us to broadcast information to a large number of users. Poorly trained users of electronic communication enslave their co-workers in an overload of pushed electronic information.

The Key Characteristics of Successful Distributed Teams

We found that there was a high degree of correlation between the following characteristics and a team's ability to meet its objectives:

- The existence of availability standards
- The reliability of electronic communication
- The existence of performance metrics
- Process definition, maturity, and alignment
- The existence of corporate memory systems
- The existence of written goals, objectives, and project specifications
- Managers and team members possessing a better-than-average ability to estimate requirements for time and resources accurately
- A lower-than-normal ratio of pushed-to-pulled information
- Communications are prioritized by the sender
- Team member proficiency at distance communication

USING THE MATURITY MODEL FOR DISTRIBUTED TEAMS

The Maturity Model for Distributed Teams consists of the four levels shown in Figure 27.2. Teams operating at each level have certain characteristic and key problem areas. One of the things we have found most valuable about the model is that it helps set the expectations of both managers and team members with regard to how long it takes to move from one level to the next. In large organizations (500 members or greater) it typically takes between nine months and a year to move up one level. However, it is not unusual for expectations to be completely unrealistic at all levels of an organization. Simply declaring yourself a virtual organization does not make it so. Team members, managers, and executives need to look at the implementation of a virtual team as a process that will take some time. For the purposes of this model, *effectiveness* is defined as a team's record for meeting project or organizational objectives on time and on budget.

Teams performing at the ad hoc level are typically outperformed by their co-located counterparts. Teams at the basic level typically achieve performance comparable to their co-located counterparts. Teams at the standardized and optimizing levels consistently outperform co-located teams.

The following sections describe some of the characteristics and key problem areas associated with each level and give recommendations for moving to the next level. The key to the successful implementation of a distributed team is to move forward the goals, processes, tools, and skills of the team *together*.

Implementing a sophisticated process without necessary tools and training in supporting skills is useless. Likewise, implementing level 4 tools in a team with level 1 process is a waste of money.

At the lowest levels of maturity, there are a multitude of issues in each area (goals, processes, tools, and skills). After an assessment, project managers and team members may feel overwhelmed. It is important not to try to fix everything at once. The purpose of the model is to help you determine which problems to target first. In the following sections, you may notice a problem or characteristic is identified a level 1 but no action is recommended until the team has progressed to level 2. This is because you need to focus your resources and energy on the characteristics that are most strongly correlated with success first. Every team's problems and issues are unique. The recommendations need to be taken within the context of your environment. If no action is recommended at a specific level, but you have a simple, inexpensive solution, by all means move ahead.

Teams at Level 1 (Ad Hoc Level)

Teams at the ad hoc level consistently underperform co-located teams. Some of the characteristics and key problem areas of teams at this level are listed here, along with some recommendations. At this level, teams are lacking the two characteristics that are the most strongly correlated to success: (1) the existence of availability standards and (2) the reliability of electronic communication. If these two issues are not addressed, your team will always underperform a co-located team.

Goals

Characteristics/Problems	Recommendations for Moving to Next Level
Unstated or unclear objectives	Develop a written mission statement for the company or organization. Develop written high-level project specifications and high-level objectives for team members.

Processes

Characteristics/Problems	Recommendations for Moving to Next Level
No availability standards	Institute availability standards.
Misaligned and undefined business processes	
Nonexistent or poor systems for corporate memory	
Communication is primarily push.	
Management is by observation or "walking around."	

Tools

Characteristics/Problems	Recommendations for Moving to Next Level
Nonexistent, unequal, or unreliable access to communication	Stabilize the electronic communication in your electronic organization. You must have *reliable* e-mail, voice mail, fax, and file transfer facilities.
Misaligned and incompatible tools	At this level, focus on aligning communication tools. Deal with applications tools misalignment by partitioning work.
Unreliable or nonexistent performance metrics for team members	Begin performance logging to facilitate the development of metrics and standards for team performance.

Skills

Characteristics/Problems	Recommendations for Moving to Next Level
Team members are untrained and inexperienced in required modes of electronic communication.	Develop team member proficiency in the specific required vendor implementations of modes of electronic communication: e-mail, voice mail, and fax.
Communication is unprioritized.	Develop a policy of having senders prioritize communications.
Team members have not been exposed to the principles of effective distance communication.	Institute training on effective distance communication concepts.
Team members and managers have limited ability to estimate resources and time accurately.	Institute training for managers and team members in estimating and scheduling.

Teams at Level 2 (Basic Level)

Teams at the basic level achieve a performance level similar to their co-located counterparts. Although they have begun to derive some of the benefits of a virtual organization, problems with infrastructure rob the team of time and efficiency. Some of the characteristics and key problem areas of teams at this level are listed here, along with some recommendations:

Goals

Characteristics/Problems	Recommendations for Moving to Next Level
Lack of detailed project specifications and team member objectives	Develop detailed project specifications and team member objectives.

Processes

Characteristics/Problems	Recommendations for Moving to Next Level
Availability standards are in place. Business processes are misaligned.	Define, document, and align business processes.
Communication is primarily push.	Analyze information flow with the company—target a subset of the

The transition has begun from management by observation to management by objective.

Corporate memory systems are inadequate or nonexistent.

information to transition from push to pull (coordinated with selected tools).

Institute processes for building corporate memory (coordinated with selected tools).

Tools
Characteristics/Problems

Electronic communication is reliable and all team members have access (communication tools are aligned).

Application tools continue to need alignment.

Performance metrics for team members are not yet stabilized, although performance histories are being maintained.

Recommendations for Moving to Next Level

Select tools for implementing corporate memory systems and processes.

Align application tools or select translation mechanisms.

Develop performance metrics based on work history.

Skills
Characteristics/Problems

Team members have been trained in the specific implementations of e-mail, voice mail, fax, and so on.

Team members have a limited understanding of distance communication concepts.

The majority of communications are assigned a priority by the sender.

Managers and team members have begun to improve estimating, scheduling, and objective writing.

Recommendations for Moving to Next Level

Reinforce distance communication standards with training and performance monitoring.

Reinforce project management skills with training and performance monitoring.

Teams at Level 3 (Standardized Level)

At the standardized level, the benefits derived from operating as a virtual organization outweigh the problems. Some of the characteristics and key problem areas of teams at this level are listed here, along with some recommendations:

Goals

Characteristics/Problems	Recommendations for Moving to Next Level
Organizational, project, and team members' objectives are defined, documented, and aligned.	

Processes

Characteristics/Problems	Recommendations for Moving to Next Level
Business processes are defined and aligned.	Optimize business processes.
Processes and systems for building corporate memory are installed.	
Information flow is transitioning from push to pull.	Continue to analyze/optimize information flow.

Tools

Characteristics/Problems	Recommendations for Moving to Next Level
Performance metrics, corporate memory systems, electronic communication tools, and tools for information flow are in place and reliable.	Refine performance metrics.

Skills

Characteristics/Problems	Recommendations for Moving to Next Level
Distance communication skills are well understood and practiced.	Develop team-member awareness of business processes.

Teams at Level 4 (Optimizing Level)

Teams at level 4 are characterized by the ability to have team members working anytime, anyplace. New team members are easily integrated and released. At this level, a team should continue to measure and optimize performance. The primary method for improving performance at this level is the incorporation of new technology and business-process reengineering.

CONCLUSION

Increasing your virtual team's effectiveness requires commitment from all the team members. You should be prepared to devote time to building stakeholder support and setting appropriate expectations. If your team has no experience working virtually, performance may drop before it improves. It is important that your team members understand that the process takes time. Just because it isn't perfect two weeks after you've begun isn't a reason to surrender and move everyone back to the main office. Your competitors have not given up. In the new millennium, successful organizations will not be bound by geography or time zones. By using the models outlined in this chapter, you can create a project plan that will move your team forward. Working with virtual teams creates an exciting and rewarding environment. Once you have experienced the benefits of the new work style, it's hard to conceive of returning to the restrictions of traditional work arrangements.

CHAPTER 28

TEAM INFRASTRUCTURE MANAGEMENT: PROJECT TEAM PLANNING AND PROJECT START-UP

DANIEL P. ONO and RUSSELL D. ARCHIBALD

$\mathbf{A}$s discussed elsewhere in this book and in the voluminous project management literature, many tools and methods have been developed to carry out the important jobs of project planning, scheduling, estimating, budgeting, and the many other planning aspects of project management. Too frequently, these planning tasks have been assumed to be the responsibility only of the project manager, or even delegated entirely to specialized project schedulers and cost estimators.

This chapter presents the need for collaborative project team planning and describes methods that have been developed to carry this out in an effective manner. It further describes the planning deliverables that the project team can produce and identifies the important benefits that can be obtained by using the project team planning approach. The use of intensive project start-up planning workshops over the past 14 years on Lucent Technologies (previously AT&T) communications projects in the United States and other countries is described in some detail together with the important benefits that have been obtained from using this approach.

COLLABORATIVE PROJECT TEAM PLANNING—AN ANSWER TO INTERNET SPEED

In recent years, the importance of the multidisciplinary project team has been recognized more widely, and the power of project team planning has been discovered by many practitioners. This is becoming evident in the increased emphasis on systematic project start-up using team planning workshops at the beginning of each phase of the project life cycle.

Additionally, as the world immerses itself into the "Internet New World" way of doing business, the imperative for speed—Internet speed—has intensified. This imperative adds more significance to using the project start-up process because it sets the requirement for collaborative planning. The usual approach to speeding up things is to eliminate or overlap numerous activities. Unfortunately, with each dropped and overlapped activity, an increase in project risk occurs. Instead of dropping activities, the proper approach is to reduce the number of times each activity is done. For instance, consider a typical planning scenario between a subcontractor, a prime contractor, and an end-user client. The subcontractor or supplier drafts a proposed plan and presents it to the prime contractor, then the prime asks for changes and the sub goes back and replans in those areas. The sub submits the amended plan for approval; the prime approves and presents the plan to the end-user client. The end-user client asks for some changes, then the prime delivers the end-user client changes to the sub; the sub makes the changes and resubmits to the prime, and the prime resubmits to the end-user client. This process represents three iterations of this plan. Collaborative planning will get this plan done once through.

THE NEED FOR COLLABORATIVE PROJECT TEAM PLANNING

Recognition of the need for project team planning has grown out of the increased awareness of the following:

- Weaknesses in the more traditional project-planning approaches
- Difficulties in getting functional managers and team members to be committed to a plan that has been created by others
- Need to accelerate the project-planning and team-building processes at the very beginning of a project, or at the beginning of a new phase of a project

Team planning can also be used effectively when any major change in scope is required, or when a major, unforeseen problem is encountered.

Traditional Project Planning Approaches

Traditionally, project-planning activities are considered to be a primary function of the project manager. On smaller projects and within organizations that have relatively little experience in formalized project management, the project manager is typically expected to put together whatever plans and schedules may exist for the project.

In larger organizations, especially when they have considerable experience in project management and have formalized their approaches to managing their projects, project-planning specialists often create the project plans, schedules, and budgets. The basic tools used by such specialists are described in the project-management literature. Ideally, these project-planning specialists (planners, schedulers, cost estimators, cost engineers, and software and computer operations specialists) will carry out their work for a specific project under the direction of the project manager assigned to that project. In other situations, they may work rather independently of the project manager, as discussed later in the chapter.

Weaknesses in the Traditional Approaches

Several critical weaknesses often can be observed in the traditional approaches just described:

- *Project plans, schedules, and budgets do not reflect the realities of how the work will actually be done.* There are always many ways to plan and execute a project; even the best plans will not be followed if they do not reflect the methods that the people doing the work will actually use.
- *The functional managers and other team members, and even at times the project manager, are not committed to the plans and schedules.* If the plans do not reflect how the work will actually be done, the people doing the work obviously will not have a sense of commitment to the plans, with the result that they will not be committed to the project itself.
- *More than one plan exists.* Given these points, it is not surprising to find many situations where more than one plan exists, either for the entire project or for many portions of it. The project manager who does not believe in and is not committed to the official plans and schedules produced by a central planning department will produce

his or her own real plans as a result. Many functional managers and project leaders often do the same thing.

- *The planning process is inefficient in the use of key persons' time.* A project manager or the planning specialists who recognize the need for involvement of the key project team members in creating the plans will often meet with each individual team member one-on-one to obtain the needed information. After meeting with other team members, a second round or even several more rounds are usually needed to work out various conflicts or discrepancies. This "honeybee" or "round robin" process is inefficient and consumes much time of all concerned, compounding the dislike most people have for planning in the first place. This approach slows down the critical start-up period of the project, and does not enhance teamwork or communication.

- *Plans created either without involvement of the key people or with their involvement through the "round robin" or "honeybee" approach just described will generally be based on a bottom-up view of the project.* This bottom-up approach results in project plans and schedules that are often poorly integrated and harbor unrecognized conflicts that will be identified later when there is insufficient time to avoid them through more integrated, top-down planning.

- *Standardized project templates are used improperly.* Corporate attempts at templating project plans generally do not work. Using overall project templates contradicts the definition of a project— namely, that each project is unique. However, the use of templates for lower-level, specific, repetitive functional tasks within the overall unique project plan can be a useful technique, if properly used.

These weaknesses have led to a growing realization that there is a better way. That is the use of project-team planning during intensive project start-up workshops.

PROJECT START-UP WORKSHOPS AND THE PROJECT TEAM PLANNING PROCESS

Many organizations regularly hold project kickoff meetings to inform key participants that a particular project is being launched (contract or go-ahead received, project proposal approved, and so on). Often such meetings are limited to rather formal presentations—giving the good news and marching orders to the troops. However, by integrating the concept of project team planning with the kickoff announcement, significant benefits can be realized, as described in the remainder of this chapter.

Project Start-Up Workshops

Although the importance of getting a project off to a good, well-planned start has long been recognized, it has only been within the last 15 years that the concept of systematic, intensive, well-planned project start-up (also called project kickoff) workshops has been widely accepted and used. The Committee on Project Start-Up of the International Project Management Association has been instrumental in promulgating and documenting this concept. The Committee's 1989 *Handbook of Project Start-Up* provides detailed information on the concept, the methods, and many examples of experience in its application in various industries and geographic areas.[1] Claudio Pincus, in a 1989 paper, presents a persuasive case for using the intensive workshop approach to developing execution plans on a team basis for design and construct projects.[2] Hector Valencia Franco, in his 1997 paper, emphasizes the importance of using a systematic start-up planning process for new projects at Bombardier-Concarril in Mexico.[3]

The fundamental essence of these systematic project start-up workshops is *project team planning*. Start-up workshops, when properly conducted, provide the setting and well-planned process that enable the project team to work together effectively to produce integrated plans and schedules in a very short time period.

With functional groups handling multiple projects simultaneously, often in different parts of the world, the project team must focus on and use common processes, communication methods, and standards.

The phrase "project start-up" may be misleading because the concept applies not only to the very first start-up—say, at the beginning of the conceptual phase of a project—but also to the beginning of each subsequent phase: definition, planning, or proposal; execution or implementation; and project closeout. The term "project phase transition workshop" may be more appropriate than "project start-up workshop." This is not to be confused with starting up the facility, system, or product being created by the project.

The Team Planning Process

The basic elements of an effective team planning process are:

- Adequate preparation
- Identification of the key project team members
- Interactive exchange of information
- Physical setting conducive to the process

- Capturing the team memory
- Appropriate planning aids
- Use of a planning process facilitator

Each of these is discussed in the following sections.

Adequate Preparation
Prior to bringing together a project team for a team planning session, it is vital to prepare adequately for the meetings. This preparation includes the following:

- Defining the specific objectives of the team sessions and the results to be achieved
- Establishing a well-planned agenda for each session
- Preparing sufficient project planning information in preliminary form (project objectives, scope definition, top levels of the project/work breakdown structure (PBS/WBS), team member list, established target schedules if any, and so on)
- Setting the session date sufficiently in advance to ensure that all team members can attend
- Announcing the session through appropriate authoritative channels to ensure higher management interest and support, and to assure that all team members show up
- Defining and understanding the planning process to be used, and the roles and responsibilities of the project manager and the planning process facilitator
- Arranging for a suitable meeting facility and related logistical support

Pincus states, "The workshop approach should not be considered without the full endorsement and participation of the project manager. The project manager must control the planning and decision-making."[4]

Identification of the Key Project Team Members
It seems obvious that in order to have a project team planning session, it would be necessary to identify the team members. However, this is often not a simple task. Who are the *key* project team members? Which functions must be included, and what level of manager or specialist from each function should be identified and invited to the team planning session? How many people can participate effectively in such a session? The following basic rules can be helpful in answering these questions:

- Each of the important functional specialties contributing to the project must be represented. This may include people from within and outside of the organization (contractors, consultants, major vendors, and so on) and often the customer.

- The persons holding responsibility and accountability for the project within each functional area (the "functional project leader") must be present.
- If a functional project leader cannot make commitments of resources for his or her function, that person's manager (who *can* make such commitments) should also be invited to participate in the team planning session, or at least be available by telephone when resource decisions are required.
- If the key team members number more than 20 people, special efforts are needed to assure appropriate interaction (such as plenary sessions combined with breaking into smaller working team sessions).
- The project manager obviously plays a vital role in the team planning sessions, and, if available and assigned, project planning, scheduling, and estimating specialists should also participate in—but not dominate—the sessions.

Interactive Exchange of Information

Central to the collaborative project team planning concept is the need for intensive interaction between the team members during the planning process. The session preparation, the information provided, the physical setting, and the methods of conducting the planning sessions must be designed to promote, not inhibit, this interaction. If the project manager goes too far in preparing planning information prior to the meeting and presents this information as a fait accompli to the team in a one-way presentation, there will be little or no interaction, and the objectives of the team planning session will not be met.

Robert Gillis has pioneered the development of such sessions over several decades in his work in Canada, the United States, and Europe. Figure 28.1, from one of his papers, illustrates several important factors in achieving the interactive exchange of information that is needed for effective project team planning.[5] As indicated in Figure 28.1, the interaction process is based on the following:

- Immediate recording of keyword abstracts of what is said (recall trigger)
- Immediate display of the group memory
- Exploration of what the group memory means (through interactive discussion)
- Fitting the keyword card in the right information structure
- Continuing the process until the objectives of the session have been reached

Figure 28.1
Project Team Planning Using a Planning Theater

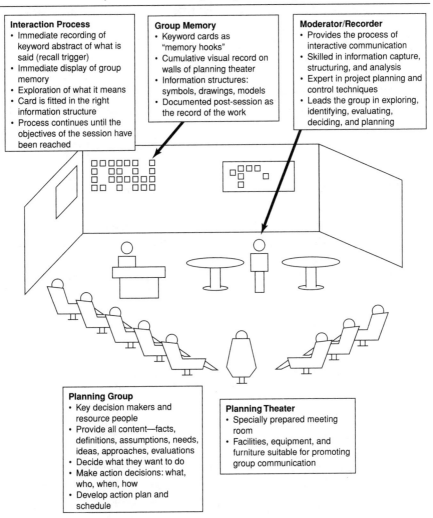

Interaction Process
- Immediate recording of keyword abstract of what is said (recall trigger)
- Immediate display of group memory
- Exploration of what it means
- Card is fitted in the right information structure
- Process continues until the objectives of the session have been reached

Group Memory
- Keyword cards as "memory hooks"
- Cumulative visual record on walls of planning theater
- Information structures: symbols, drawings, models
- Documented post-session as the record of the work

Moderator/Recorder
- Provides the process of interactive communication
- Skilled in information capture, structuring, and analysis
- Expert in project planning and control techniques
- Leads the group in exploring, identifying, evaluating, deciding, and planning

Planning Group
- Key decision makers and resource people
- Provide all content—facts, definitions, assumptions, needs, ideas, approaches, evaluations
- Decide what they want to do
- Make action decisions: what, who, when, how
- Develop action plan and schedule

Planning Theater
- Specially prepared meeting room
- Facilities, equipment, and furniture suitable for promoting group communication

Source: Reprinted with the permission of Robert B. Gillis, "Strategies for Successful Project Implementation," *Handbook of Project Start-Up*. Internet/International Project Management Association, 1987.

In developing the project master schedule on the wall of such a planning theater, for example, using the PBS/WBS and the major milestones and interface events that have been identified, very effective integration of all functional tasks can be achieved. Serious conflicts are quickly revealed and become the subject of later, more detailed planning and analysis involving only the specific parties concerned.

Physical Setting Conducive to the Process

As shown in Figure 28.1, Gillis uses the term *planning theater* for the room in which the interactive team planning sessions are held. Such a facility is an important factor in achieving the interaction desired. It does not have to be an elaborate design, but it must provide the following:

- Plenty of wall space with good lighting for display of the team memory and planning results
- Open access to the walls by the team members (elimination of large tables and other impediments to individual movement and interaction to fill in keyword cards and place them on the walls)
- Sufficient space to enhance individual comfort, movement to view other walls, and open communication

Capturing the Team Memory

The *group* or *team memory* is based on the following:

- Using the keyword cards as "memory hooks" to recall specific ideas
- Creating a visual record on the walls of the planning theater or meeting room
- Proper information structures that are appropriate to the planning work being done: models, matrices, drawings, symbols, and charts

The team memory resulting from capturing and structuring the information exchanged and produced during the planning sessions provides an agreed, understood, post-session record of the plans created by the team.

Appropriate Planning Aids

These include:

- Notebook computers and LCD projectors to enable interactive team planning by joint viewing of all information, capture of the team memory, and instant analysis of proposed plans
- Preformatted output files in PowerPoint, Excel, MS Project, and so on, for the following:
  PBS/WBS responsibility matrix
  High-level schedule in selected areas

Contact/team member lists

Agendas and minutes

- Portable color printers to produce usable hard copies for all team members during the planning sessions
- Whiteboards that can produce xerographic copies of what is written on them
- Plastic-coated, adhesive paper for wall-planning work with marker pens
- Preprinted adhesive forms (symbols, calendars, and so on)

Use of a Planning Process Facilitator

The facilitator (moderator/recorder in Figure 28.1) is a crucial player in the project team planning process. This person does the following:

- Supports and enables the process of interactive communication
- Is skilled in information capture, structuring, and analysis
- Is expert in the application of project planning, control methods, and techniques; and other aspects of project management
- Leads the team during the planning sessions in the processes of exploring, identifying, evaluating, decision making, and planning
- Maintains the process discipline to adhere to the established agenda for the planning session

The Project Manager's Role in Team Planning

It is widely recognized that the key characteristic of the project manager's role is that of *integration*. In project team planning, the integrative role of the project manager becomes quite obvious. The project manager must assist the project team members in developing acceptable plans and schedules that achieve the objectives of the project and reflect the plans and available resources of the various team members. The project manager usually holds the lead responsibility for preparing for the team planning sessions, as discussed earlier.

The project manager plays a vital role in the project start-up team planning sessions, to accomplish the following:

- Establish his or her leadership position
- Create the paradigm (or management model) that the project team will use on the project

- Establish the proper focus of the project team
- Make the project special among the contributing functional managers

In today's environment, where most functional groups are handling multiple projects, the project manager has to create some type of distinction for his or her project to get the proper attention.

During the planning sessions, the project manager must be alert to real or potential conflicts in plans, and bring these to the surface for resolution. He or she must concentrate on identification of the key project interface events, or those points of transition of responsibility from one team member to another. This is because one of the key tasks of the project manager is to manage these interfaces properly. The project manager begins to establish discipline within the project team by maintaining the schedule for the project start-up meetings. Finally, he or she starts to build an effective project team during these planning sessions.

The key role of the process facilitator can also be taken by the project manager. However, experience shows that it is much more effective for another person to carry out the facilitator's role, especially when an organization is just beginning to use this approach.

SETTING THE STAGE FOR
DETAILED PLANNING

The plans, schedules, and other planning documents created during a team planning session should be limited to integrated plans at the overall project level. These will, of course, require definition of the project down to the major functional task level, so that responsibilities can be assigned, agreed-upon, and understood among the team members. The team-produced project master schedule will show the agreed-upon target dates for key milestones, reflecting the team's judgment on the overall allocation of time to accomplish the intermediate and final objectives.

Team planning sessions are not intended to produce detailed, functional task plans, schedules, or budgets. To attempt to do so would be an extravagant waste of valuable time. Rather, these team sessions are intended to set the stage for truly effective detailed planning, scheduling, and budgeting. The stage is set very effectively for the ensuing detailed planning needed to validate the team's efforts and prove whether its collective judgments are correct. This outcome is based on the results of the top-down planning performed by the project team, under the integrating influence of the project manager and guided by the planning process facilitator.

After completion of the start-up sessions, the project manager, often with the assistance of planning, scheduling, and estimating specialists, can proceed with the more detailed, integrated planning that is necessary to assure effective monitoring and control of the project. The top-level project plans produced by the team can be entered into the computer software to be used on the project, often during the team planning sessions themselves. The more detailed functional task plans and schedules can also be entered in the planning and control system, usually shortly after the team planning sessions, to the extent that this is warranted and practical.

PROJECT START-UP WORKSHOPS IN THE TELECOMMUNICATIONS INDUSTRY— A CASE STUDY

The experience in the use of project team planning and project start-up workshops over the past 14 years within what is now the Business Communications Systems (BCS) strategic business unit of Lucent Technologies (formerly a unit within AT&T) is described in this case study. With sales of over $6 billion per year, and 29,000 employees around the world within this business unit, there is a wide variety of projects of all sizes and of diverse degrees of risk, complexity, and character of the end result. For the projects involved here, Lucent Technologies has agreed, under fixed-price contract to companies, institutions and agencies, that it will:

- Design and manufacture hardware
- Develop software
- Install, test, and cut over into operation complex, high-technology voice/data/video communications and related systems together with required training and documentation

Such projects usually must be completed within a few months to perhaps one year, although some multi-project contracts cover several years. These projects involve global voice/data/video networks, call center technologies, and global voice messaging networks.

Within Lucent Technologies, there are many projects of this type under way at any one time, ranging from small implementations to systems covering an entire state government. There are also a small number of mega-projects for federal, state, and local government agencies or nationwide and multinational corporate facilities. Such projects must be executed so that the new facilities are in place and tested to enable a rapid cutover from the old to the new, usually over a weekend, with minimum disruption to the ongoing operations of Lucent's customer. Achieving the agreed cutover date is almost always of extreme importance to the customer, and once the cutover date has been agreed upon, it is very difficult to change. Cost is of course fixed by the contract, but changes in project scope often affect the total system cost. The technical and functional performance specifications to be met by the system are spelled out in great detail in the contract terms.

Project Management in Lucent Technologies' Business Communications Systems (BCS)

Over a number of years, Lucent-BCS had been moving toward more formalized project management practices. In the 1980s a national director of project management held responsibility for the management of all contractual projects. The national project director had three project directors (each responsible for a region of the United States) and specialized staffs reporting to him. The three project directors had a number of program and project managers, and project scheduling specialists reporting to each of them. A full-time project manager was assigned to a project when its value exceeded a few million dollars. Some projects exceeded a value of $100 million. In some cases, a project manager was assigned for smaller contracts if the project was unusually complex, either technically or organizationally. Other exceptions were made for smaller projects that are parts of a larger program. A program manager held responsibility for multi-project contracts with one customer, and usually had several project managers or site managers (a step below project manager) reporting to him or her.

In 1988, because of the rapid growth of this business segment, a cadre of experienced project managers was not available. There was a continual need to indoctrinate and train new people, who were experienced within other parts of the company, in the requirements of the project manager assignment and project planning and control principles, practices, and tools. As a result, the AT&T forerunner of Lucent-BCS established a broad-ranging education and training program in project management, and has for a number of years stressed the certification of its project managers and supporting staff as project management professionals (PMPs) with the Project Management Institute (PMI). This broad program has continued with the divestment of Lucent Technologies in the mid-1990s.

Two important points regarding the project management challenges within Lucent-BCS are the following:

- *Detailed performance specifications.* These are spelled out in the project contract. They consist of both technical and functional specifications. While the technical specifications are still important, the functional specifications are more critical to customer satisfaction and willingness to pay. In today's environment, customers expect vendors to provide systems that do what the customers need in order to achieve their strategic objectives. Customers rarely care about the type of equipment or the technical aspects of the systems, as long as the systems provide the functionality that will create a competitive advantage.
- *Schedule achievement is dependent on customer actions.* These communication systems are deeply intertwined with the customer operations and physical facilities. The customer must carry out significant actions during the life of a project, which directly affect schedule achievement. Therefore, to be successful, the project schedules must be developed collaboratively with the customer. If the project is positioned correctly with the customer and the other vendors, the people involved with the project from all aspects will realize that the biggest challenge is for the project team to overcome the difficulties provided by the environment—and not by each other.

Today, the Lucent Technologies project manager continues to operate within a classic matrix organization, usually as a one-person project office, but using specialized staff support as required. In very large projects, the project manager has several people on his or her direct staff. Many different parts of Lucent, located in different geographic regions, contribute to each of these projects, which include several engineering and technical disciplines, purchasing, manufacturing, field installation and testing, provisioning and logistic support, software development, training, and various other services and operations departments. The project manager is charged with providing full project management deliverables in order to mitigate risk as much as possible. There is a continuing need to train new people, and a project coordinator group has been established as a feeder pool for project managers.

Identifying the Need for Project Start-Up Improvement

In the mid-1980s, the Lucent-BCS (then a part of AT&T) director of projects for Southern California and Hawaii identified a need for ways to accelerate the planning, learning, and team-building processes that take place on every project. He saw this need for his own project managers as well as the functional managers who carried out the specific tasks on each project. Very importantly, he also saw this need within the customer's people who were involved with the project. In addition to this acceleration, he wanted to prevent or quickly resolve any adversarial attitudes that may be encountered at the start of a project with the customer's assigned people or among the BCS project team. Such attitudes, when encountered, took some time to overcome and had sometimes caused delays and avoidable added costs.

Typically, after a new project had been under way for a few months, good teamwork emerged. The director of projects wanted to achieve that teamwork in a few days or weeks, due to the short duration of many of his projects.

Finally, the projects were not meeting financial and customer satisfaction objectives.

Satisfying the Need with Project Start-Up Workshops

The projects director decided to initiate project start-up workshops on his new projects to see whether these needs could be met in this manner. The workshops were structured as discussed next.

Approach
A three-meeting start-up workshop format was designed. The first two meetings, usually spaced at least a week apart, involved only BCS people. The third meeting, following the second by at least a week, included the customer people who were involved directly in the project, and also involved senior customer managers.

Workshop Objectives
The start-up workshop objectives were as follows:

1. To apply proven project management methods to the project, and develop—as a team—jointly agreed-upon project plans, schedules, and control procedures
2. To assure good understanding of the roles and responsibilities of all BCS and customer project team members, thereby enhancing effective teamwork
3. To identify additional steps needed to assure project success

While team building is not stated specifically as an objective, it obviously is one of the most important results to be achieved.

Start-Up Workshop Planning Deliverables
Emphasis throughout the workshop sessions was on the deliverables to be produced by the team. These were as follows:

- Agreed list of key project team members
- List of key concerns and major open issues
- A well-defined project/work breakdown structure (PBS/WBS)
- A task/responsibility matrix based on the PBS/WBS and reflecting all identified contributors to the project, including the customer and outside agencies (such as the involved local telephone operating companies)
- A list of key project interface events, linked to the PBS/WBS and showing the initiator and receiver(s)
- A project master schedule, based on the PBS/WBS, reflecting the key project interface events and the consensus of the project team on the overall allocation of time
- Agreed procedures for project monitoring and control, including dates for periodic project review meetings
- A mutually agreed-upon escalation plan that states how key problems or conflicts will be escalated through organizational channels for prompt resolution
- Action items resulting from the start-up workshop discussions, with assigned responsibility and agreed-upon due dates for each

Continued Application of Project Start-Up Workshops in Lucent Technologies-BCS

Since the initial application of this approach in the mid-1980s, the aforementioned objectives and deliverables have remained essentially unchanged. The approach has been embedded as a key element of the Lucent-BCS project management process.[6]

Results Achieved

The most direct indication of the overall benefits of using a well-organized process for starting up projects is that the system *cutovers*—project completions—are on schedule more often and of better quality on projects using this approach than on projects that did not.

Better Project and Functional Planning
The start-up workshops get the project team started quickly, with a good understanding of *what* needs to be done, *who* does each of the many

tasks, and *when* each must be completed. This approach gets all of the functional organizations thinking about what kind of planning is required—before getting into the thick of the action. Previously, some functional managers would leave the planning to the last minute, or would not do any planning at all.

Improved Financial Performance

From the corporate viewpoint, the primary benefit achieved was improved financial performance. When the job was done on schedule and met the customer requirements without rework to correct quality problems, the payoff in financial terms became very obvious.

Better Communications and Teamwork

After the start-up workshops, all project team members use the same semantics and planning terms. By jointly working through the planning deliverables, good teamwork is achieved much earlier on each project. This joint planning shows each team member that everyone on the team has important tasks to perform, and how these tasks are interrelated. There is a better realization that they all need to be involved in the planning effort to assure project success. The success achieved during the start-up meetings gets the team working together in an effective way that is immediately carried into the actual work on the project.

Improved Customer Relations

There are very positive reactions from customer team members and higher management to the start-up workshop sessions and the resulting deliverables. Lucent Technologies marketing managers give similar positive reactions, and point to the fact that the workshops provide a vehicle for the company's team members to work closely with the customer team members very early in the project. This has avoided the adversarial attitudes that were experienced previously on some projects. An important result of the external meeting with the customer team members and managers is quick escalation and resolution of open issues that threaten to delay the cutover.

Benefits to the Project Manager

Several important benefits to the project manager are the following:

- *Positioning the project manager.* Typically, the marketing people work on the sale to a particular customer for months if not years, preparing the proposal and negotiating the contract. The project manager, who is often involved during the proposal preparation stage, takes over implementation when the contract is signed. Before using the start-up workshops, it would usually take the project manager some time to establish his or her position with both the customer and the internal team members, especially the marketing people who naturally felt a strong proprietary interest in the project. By the end of each start-up workshop process, all team members have a good understanding of the need for a project manager, and are ready to give him or her the required support.

- *Detailed planning and scheduling.* Another benefit to the project manager is that she or he can immediately use the project breakdown structure, the project master schedule, and the project interface event lists produced by the team as the basic framework for the detailed PERT/CPM network plan and schedules.
- *Project manager as project interface manager.* A key benefit is that the team members understand the project manager's role as the project interface manager. By getting the team to identify the key project interface events and explaining to the team members how the project manager manages these project interface events while each functional manager manages his or her assigned tasks between these events, good acceptance of the project manager role is achieved. The functional managers quickly realize that this is a valuable asset to their getting the job done successfully to specification, on schedule, and within budget.
- *Earlier establishment of the project manager as the leader of the project.* The start-up sessions provide the project manager with the opportunity to demonstrate that he or she is the real leader of the project. Previously, it would take a number of weeks or even months for this to be established in the minds of the project team members.

Hidden Agenda Items within the Start-Up Workshop Process

In addition to the deliverables and other results described previously, there are several important hidden-agenda topics and related results involved in the start-up workshop process. The most important of these—not listed necessarily in order of importance—are as follows:

- Introducing uniform, proven industry project management practices with common terminology
- Providing hands-on training to all project team members in effective project planning and control methods
- Tapping the wisdom of the group to develop the best overall project plan

- Creating a shared vision of the total scope of the project, its challenges, and objectives at several levels
- Demonstrating and gaining the power and benefits of open team planning and communications
- Establishing early project discipline and the management model for the project
- Exchanging experience and developing planning skills and understanding among the team members of all aspects of what goes into a complex communications/information systems project
- Building a working team and getting individual team members to commit to, and be enthusiastic about, the project through involvement, understanding, and promises made to the peer group and not just to the project manager

Learning and Development at Four Levels

The approach used—short presentations, small team assignments, and team reports to the full group—has proven to be effective in exchanging and transferring knowledge and experience. Using this approach, individual and team development takes place at the four following levels:

1. The facilitator and project manager convey a certain level of knowledge with the initial presentation on a given topic.
2. The members of the small teams work together for periods of one or more hours, and interchange ideas and experience; there will always be diverse levels and types of experience and knowledge in each small team, and the team members learn from each other.
3. As each team reports its results to the full project team, exchange and learning take place as the team members see what their peers have done. Team members also get the experience of making presentations to the full team.
4. The workshop facilitator and the project manager add to and expand on the information presented, or show where it may need further improvement. Additional knowledge and development occur during these discussions.

After completion of the three project start-up/kickoff meetings, the project team has been put through several experiences that provide firsthand demonstration of the team's ability to work together effectively and to produce valuable deliverables that will be used for the life of the project.

Modifications Made for Smaller Projects

In order to achieve the same objectives on smaller projects, and on larger projects that are very similar to or use the same team members as other recent projects, the following modifications have been made to the procedures described earlier:

1. Reduce the duration of the internal sessions from two days to approximately four hours.
2. Condense the formal presentations to fit the reduced time.
3. Prepare more detailed drafts of the project breakdown structure, the task/responsibility matrix, the interface event lists, and the project master schedule before the workshop is started, and incorporate any changes introduced by the team members during the workshop sessions.
4. Shorten the client workshop to four hours or less.
5. Address only areas of relatively high risk.

The objectives, preparation, invitations, and workshop deliverables for smaller projects do not vary from large projects. However, on some smaller projects the full set of project planning deliverables may be limited to the areas of greatest risk. If the small project workshops are conducted with the same professionalism as those for large projects, the project manager can instill the same team spirit, generate the same quality plans, and use the same monitoring of progress and quality while demonstrating sensitivity to the functional managers' workloads.

BENEFITS AND LIMITATIONS OF PROJECT TEAM PLANNING

The basic benefits of project team planning are as follows:

- Plans produced are based on how the work will actually be accomplished.
- Persons responsible for performing the work have a greater sense of commitment to the plans and to the project.
- Only one set of plans exist: the one that the project team has created and is following.
- The overall time required for planning by the key project team members is reduced.

- The project plans reflect a top-down approach using the total wisdom of the project team, which then sets the stage for more effective, detailed, bottom-up validation and elaboration of the plans.
- The project manager gets an early indication of where to spend his or her time to begin mitigating the risks of the project.

The decision to use project team planning should be based on the characteristics of the project in question. The following factors may indicate some limitations to project team planning. It would not be appropriate to insist on the type of project team planning described if projects:

- Are of the type that is very well known to the organization.
- Are very repetitive of many previous projects.
- Have project team members who are all experienced in this type of project.
- Have planners available who can produce plans and schedules that are valid and acceptable to all concerned.
- Satisfy top management with their financial and technical results.

There appears to be no upper limit in project size for the use of the project team planning approach. At the top of a massive mega-project, as one extreme, the objective of the top-level project team planning session would be to do the following:

1. Define the appropriate major subprojects into which the mega-project should be divided.
2. Identify the key milestones and interface events that will link these subprojects.
3. Assign responsibilities as appropriate.
4. Lay out the target project master schedule.
5. Identify and assess the key risk areas.

At each subordinate level, the project team must recognize the appropriate level of detail below which they must not attempt to develop plans and schedules. Each team must concentrate on handing down the structured plans and schedules within which the next-level teams must in turn develop their plans.

The primary limitation in project team planning is probably the time required of the project team members to devote to the team planning sessions. Although planning should be given a high priority in any organization, frequently planning is viewed as unproductive and even wasteful;

hence it is difficult to convince the project team members that they should devote even a few days to developing the project plans. Top management understanding and support is required to overcome these ingrained attitudes and habits. A successful project team planning session can also do a lot to demonstrate the power and usefulness of this approach.

In order for team planning as described here to be most successful, the project manager must have a thorough understanding of the project start-up process and its objectives, as well as the project's objectives, political attributes, and the personal aspirations and motivations of the project team members.

REFERENCES

1. Fangel, M. editor. 1989. *Handbook of Project Start-Up*. Saettedammen 4, Hilleroed, Denmark: International Project Management Association.
2. Pincus, Claudio. 1989. "A Workshop Approach to Project Execution Planning." In *Project Management, A Reference for Professionals*, Robert L. Kimmons and James H. Loweree, eds., New York: Marcel Dekker: 349–355.
3. Ing, Hector Valencia Franco. 1997. *"Procediento para la Preparation y Arranque de un Nuevo Proyecto."* Proceedings of the PMI *Foro Nacional*, PMI Mexico City Chapter, November 13–14, *Ponencia 17*.
4. Pincus, op. cit., 351.
5. Gillis, Robert. 1987. "Strategies for Successful Project Implementation," *Handbook of Project Start-Up*. Internet/International Project Management Association: Section 4.
6. For more details regarding the agenda and conduct of these project start-up workshops see Dan Ono and Russell D. Archibald, "Project Start-Up Workshops: Gateway to Project Success," Proceedings of the Project Management Institute Seminar/Symposium. Newtown Square, PA: Project Management Institute, September 17–21, 1988: 50–54.

CHAPTER 29

TEAM MANAGEMENT: WORKING EFFECTIVELY

HANS J. THAMHAIN

Teamwork is the frontier in today's competitive business world. More than 70 percent of managers in our organizations consider effective cross-functional teamwork a key determinant of business performance and success. Virtually all managers recognize the critical importance of effective teamwork and strive for continuous improvement of team performance in their organizations. Yet only one in 10 of these managers has a specific metric for actually measuring team performance.[1] Obviously, this creates some tough challenges, especially in project-based environments where teamwork is crucial to business success. In these organizational environments, work teams must successfully integrate multidisciplinary activities, unify different business processes, and deal with cross-functional issues such as innovation, quality, speed, producability, sourcing, and service.

Furthermore, managerial principals and practices have changed dramatically. Not too long ago, project management was to a large degree considered "management science." Project leaders could ensure successful integration for most of their projects by focusing on properly defining the work, timing, and resources, and by following established procedures for project tracking and control. Today, these factors are still crucial. However, they have become threshold competencies that are critically important but unlikely to guarantee by themselves project success.

Today's complex business world requires *project teams* that are fast and flexible and can dynamically and creatively work toward established objectives in a changing environment (Cusumano and Yoffie 1998; Engel 1997; Thamhain 1998b; Thamhain and Wilemon 1999). This requires effective networking and cooperation among people from different organizations, support groups, subcontractors, vendors, government agencies, and customer communities. It also requires the ability to deal with uncertainties and risks introduced by technological, economic, political, social, and regulatory factors. In addition, project leaders have to organize and manage their teams across organizational lines, dealing often with resource personnel over whom they have little or no formal authority. Resource sharing, multiple reporting relationships, and broadly based alliances are as common in today's business environment as e-mail, flextime, and home offices. Managing project teams effectively in such dynamic environments requires task leaders to understand the *interaction of organizational and behavioral variables*. These project leaders must develop their multidisciplinary task groups into unified teams and foster a climate conducive to involvement, commitment, and conflict resolution, in spite of these organizational challenges.

WHAT WE KNOW ABOUT TEAMWORK IN PROJECT ORGANIZATIONS

Teamwork is not a new idea. The basic concepts of organizing and managing teams go back in history to biblical times. In fact, work teams have long been considered an effective device to enhance organizational effectiveness. Since the discovery of important social phenomena in the classic Hawthorne studies (Roethlingsberger and Dickerson 1939), management theorists and practitioners have tried to enhance group identity and cohesion in the workplace (Dyer 1977). Indeed, much of the *human relations movement* that followed Hawthorne is based on the group concept. McGregor's (1960) theory Y, for example, spells out the criteria for an effective work group, and Likert (1961) called his highest form of management *the participating group* or *system 4*. However, the process of team building becomes more complex and requires more specialized management skills as bureaucratic hierarchies decline and horizontally oriented teams and work units evolve.

Modern Concepts and Processes

In today's more complex multinational and technologically sophisticated environment, the work group has reemerged in importance as the *project team* (Wellins, Byham, and Wilson 1991; Fisher 1993; Nurick and Thamhain 1993; Shonk 1996; Thamhain and Wilemon 1999). *Team building* can be defined as the process of taking a collection of individuals with different needs, backgrounds, and expertise and transforming them into an integrated, effective work unit. In this transformation process, the goals and energies of individual contributors merge and focus on specific objectives. When describing an effective project team, managers stress consistently that high performance (although ultimately reflected by producing desired results, and being on time and within budget) is a derivative of many factors that are graphically shown in Figure 29.1.

Team building is an ongoing process that requires leadership skills and an understanding of the organization and its interfaces, authority, power structures, and motivational factors. This process is particularly crucial in environments where complex multidisciplinary or transnational activities require the skillful integration of many functional specialties and support groups with diverse organizational cultures, values, and intricacies. Typical examples of such multidisciplinary activities requiring unified teamwork for successful integration include:

- Establishing a new program
- Transferring technology
- Improving project-client relationships
- Organizing for a bid proposal
- Integrating new project personnel
- Resolving interfunctional problems
- Working toward major milestones

Figure 29.1
Traits of High-Performing Project Teams

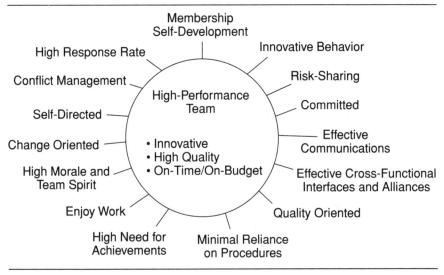

- Reorganizing mergers and acquisitions
- Transitioning the project into a new activity phase
- Revitalizing an organization

Because of their potential for producing economic advantages, work teams and their development have been researched by many. Starting with the evolution of formal project organizations in the 1960s, managers in various organizational settings have expressed increasing concern with and interest in the concepts and practices of multidisciplinary team building. As a result, many field studies have been conducted, investigating work group dynamics and criteria for building effective, high-performing project teams. These studies have contributed to the theoretical and practical understanding of team building and form the fundamental concepts discussed in this chapter.

Prior to 1980, most of these studies focused just on the behavior of the team members, with limited attention given to the organizational environment and team leadership. While the qualities of the individuals and their interaction within the team are crucial elements in the teamwork process, they represent only part of the overall organization and management system that influences team performance, which was recognized by Bennis and Shepard as early as 1956. Since 1980, an increasing number of studies have broadened the understanding of the team work process (Tichy and Ulrich 1984; Walton 1985: Dumaine 1991). These more recent studies show the enormous breadth and depth of subsystems and variables involved in the organization, development, and management of a high-performing work team (Gupta and Wilemon 1996). These variables include planning, organizing, training, organizational structure, nature and complexity of task, senior management support, leadership, and socioeconomic variables, just to name the most popular ones (Shaw, Fisher, and Randolph 1991; Thamhain and Wilemon 1987, 1997, 1999; Thamhain 1990a, 1998a).

Even further, researchers such as Dumaine (1991), Drucker (1996), Peters and Waterman (1987, 1997), Moss Kanter (1989), Ouchi (1993), and Thamhain (1990a and b) have emphasized the nonlinear, intricate, often chaotic, and random nature of teamwork, which involves all facets of the organization, its members, and environment. These teams became the conduit for transferring information, technology, and work concepts across functional lines quickly, predictably, and within given resource restraints.

Toward Self-Direction and Virtual Teams

Especially with the evolution of contemporary organizations, such as the matrix, traditional bureaucratic hierarchies have declined, and horizontally oriented teams and work units have become increasingly important

---

Self-Directed Teams

Definition: A group of people chartered with specific responsibilities for managing themselves and their work, with minimal reliance on group-external supervision, bureaucracy, and control. Team structure, task responsibilities, work plans, and team leadership often evolve based on needs and situational dynamics.

Benefits: Ability to handle complex assignments, requiring evolving and innovative solutions that cannot be easily directed via top-down supervision. Widely shared goals, values, information, and risks. Flexibility toward needed changes. Capacity for conflict resolution, team building and self-development. Effective cross-functional communications and work integration. High degree of self-control, accountability, ownership, and commitment toward established objectives.

Challenges: A unified, mature team does not just happen, but must be carefully organized and developed by management. A high degree of self-motivation, and sufficient job, administrative, and people skills must exist among the team members. Empowerment and self-control might lead to unintended results and consequences. *Self-directed* teams are not necessary *self-managed*; they often require more sophisticated external guidance and leadership than conventionally structured teams.

---

to effective project management (Fisher 1993; Shonk 1996). Increasingly, the team leader's role as supervisor has been diminished in favor of more *empowerment and self-direction* of the team, as defined in the box above. In addition, advances of information technology have made it feasible and effective to link team members over the Internet or other media, creating a *virtual team* environment, as described in the box on the following page. *Virtual teams* and *virtual project organizations* are powerful managerial tools, especially for companies with geographically dispersed project operations, including contractors, customers, and regulators.

Teams of this contemporary nature exist in nearly all of our organizations, ranging from dedicated venture groups, often called *skunk works*, to product development teams, process action teams, and focus groups. These team concepts are being applied to different forms of project activities in areas of products, services, acquisition efforts, political election campaigns, and foreign assistance programs. For these kinds of highly multifunctional and nonlinear processes, researchers stress the need for

---

Virtual Teams

Definition: A group of project team members, linked via the Internet or media channels to each other and various project partners, such as contractors, customers, and regulators. Although physically separated, technology links these individuals so they can share information and operate as a unified project team. The number of elements in a virtual team and their permanency can vary, depending on need and feasibility. An example of a virtual team is a project review conducted among the team members, contractors, and customers over an Internet web site.

Benefits: Ability to share information and communicate among team members and organizational entities of geographically dispersed projects. Ability to share and communicate information in a synchronous and asynchronous mode (application: communication across time zones, holidays, and shared work spaces). Creating unified visibility of project status and performance. Virtual teams, to some degree, bridge and neutralize the culture and value differences that exist among different task teams of a project organizations.

Challenges: The effectiveness of the virtual team depends on the team members' ability to work with the given technology. Information flow and access is not necessarily equal for all team members. Information may not be processed uniformly throughout the team. The virtual team concept does not fit the culture and value system of all members and organizations. Project tracking, performance assessment, and managerial control of project activities are often very difficult. Risks, contingencies, and problems are difficult to detect and assess. Virtual organizations often do not provide effective methods for dealing with conflict, power, candor, feedback, and resource issues. Because of the many limitations, more traditional team processes and communications are often needed to augment virtual teams.

---

strong integration and orchestration of cross-functional activities, linking the various work groups into a unified project team that focuses energy and integrates all subtasks toward desired results.

Further, the life cycle of these teams often spans the complete project, not just the phase of primary engagement. For example, the primary mission of the product development team may focus on the engineering phase. However, the team also supports activities ranging from recognition of an opportunity to feasibility analysis, bid proposals, licensing, and subcontracting, while transferring technology to manufacturing, distribution, and field service. While these realities hold for most team efforts in today's work environment, they are especially pronounced for efforts that are associated with risk, uncertainty, creativity, and team diversity such as high-technology and/or multinational projects. These are also the work environments that first departed from traditional hierarchical team structures and tried more self-directed and network-based virtual concepts (Fisher 1993; Ouchi 1993).

MEASURING PROJECT TEAM PERFORMANCE

"A castle is only as strong as the people who defend it." This Japanese proverb also applies to organizations. They are only as effective as their unified team efforts. Although team performance is difficult to measure, research agrees on specific metrics for characterizing winning teams, as graphically shown in Figure 29.1.[2] More specifically, Table 29.1 breaks these characteristics of high-performing project teams into four categories:

1. Work and team structure
2. Communication and control
3. Team leadership
4. Attitudes and values

These broad measures can provide a framework for benchmarking. Teams that score high on these characteristics are also seen by upper management as most favorable in dealing with cost, quality, creativity, schedules, and customer satisfaction. They also receive favorable ratings on the more subtle measures of high team performance, such as flexibility, change orientation, innovative performance, high morale, and team spirit.

A MODEL FOR TEAM BUILDING

Figure 29.2 provides a simple model for organizing and analyzing the variables that influence the team's characteristics and its ultimate performance, as baselined in Figure 29.1 and Table 29.1. The influences shown in Figure 29.2 are divided into three sets:

1. Drivers and barriers toward high team performance
2. Managerial leadership style, including components of authority, motivation, autonomy, trust, respect, credibility, and friendship

Table 29.1
Benchmark Your Team Performance

Project Performance Metrics
1. Agreed-on results and performance
2. Innovative, creative solutions
3. Concern for quality
4. On-time and within budget delivery

Work and Team Structure
- Team participates in project definitions; work plans evolve dynamically
- Team structure and responsibilities evolve and change as needed
- Broad information sharing
- Team leadership evolves based on expertise, trust, respect
- Minimal dependence on bureaucracy, procedures, politics

Communication and Control
- Effective cross-functional channels, linkages
- Ability to seek out and process information
- Effective group decision making and consensus
- Clear sense of purpose and direction
- Self-control is stimulated by visibility, recognition, accomplishments, autonomy, accountability, and ownership

Team Leadership
- Minimal hierarchy in member status and position
- Internal team leadership based on situational expertise, trust, and need
- Clear management goals, direction, and support
- Inspires and encourages

Attitudes and Values
- Members committed to established objectives and plans
- Shared goals, values, and project ownership
- High involvement, energy, work interest, need for achievement, pride; self-motivated
- Capacity for conflict resolution and resource sharing
- Team building and self-development
- Risk sharing, mutual trust, support
- Innovative behavior
- Flexibility and willingness to change
- High morale and team spirit
- High commitment to established project goals
- Continuous improvement of work process, efficiency, quality
- Ability to stretch beyond agreed-on objectives

Figure 29.2
Model for Analyzing Team Performance

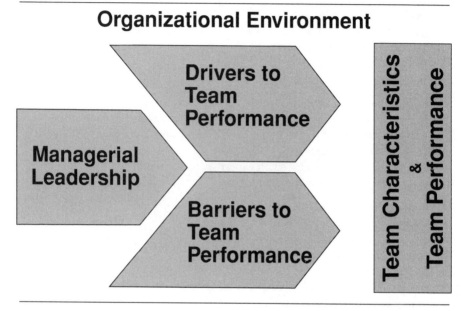

3. Organizational environment, including working conditions, job content, resources, and organizational support factors, as well as the social, political, and economic factors of the firm's external business environment

All three sets of variables are intricately interrelated. However, using the systems approach allows researchers and management practitioners to break down the complexity of the process of analyzing team performance and defining managerial strategies for transforming resources into desired results.

Drivers and Barriers to High Team Performance

Management tools such as benchmarking and root-cause analysis can be helpful in identifying the drivers and barriers toward effective teamwork. *Drivers* are factors that influence the project environment favorably, such as interesting work and good project leadership. These factors are perceived as enhancing team effectiveness, and therefore correlate positively with team performance. *Barriers* are factors that have an unfavorable influence, such as unclear objectives and insufficient resources, therefore impeding team performance. Table 29.2 breaks down the characteristics that can impose barriers to team performance into four categories: people, tools and processes, leadership, and organization. Based on field re-

Table 29.2
Major Barriers to Team Performance

People
- Different objectives, interests, viewpoints
- Role conflict, confusion, anxiety
- Fear of failure
- Personal conflict and power struggles
- Mistrust, collusion
- Work is not enjoyable
- No sense of achievement and recognition
- Little flexibility and change orientation
- Little mutual trust, respect, competence
- Groupthink

Tools and Process
- Unclear technology transfer process
- Weak project management system
- Unclear channels of communication, responsibility, control
- Weak administration support
- Inability to track progress

Leadership
- Insufficient direction and leadership
- Inappropriate leadership style and motivation
- Inability to assist in problem solving
- Inability to assist in conflict resolution
- Inability to develop can-do atmosphere, risk sharing
- Inability to attract and hold quality people
- Inability to create intrinsic rewards
- Inability to create effective work environment

Organization
- Changing work environment, instability
- Changing business objectives
- Poor interfunctional linkages and communications
- Inadequate functional support and resources
- Improper command control structure (too rigid, too flat, and so on)
- Insufficient rewards, growth potential, and mobility

search, the six strongest drivers and 13 strongest barriers are summarized as follows.[3]

These are the six strongest drivers to project team performance:

1. Good interpersonal relations
2. Professional growth potential
3. Professionally interesting and stimulating work
4. Proper technical direction and team leadership
5. Qualified project team personnel
6. Recognition of accomplishment

These are the 13 strongest barriers to high team performance:

1. Communication problems
2. Competition over team leadership and power struggle
3. Conflict among team members or between team and support organizations
4. Different outlooks, objectives, and priorities perceived by team members
5. Insufficient qualification of poor credibility of project leader
6. Insufficient resources
7. Insufficient rewards and lack of interest in project
8. Lack of senior management support, interest, and involvement
9. Lack of team definition, role conflict, and confusion
10. Lack of team member commitment
11. Poor project team/personnel selection
12. Shifting goals and priorities
13. Unstable project environment, poor job security, and anxieties

These drivers and barriers have the highest association to team performance and explain over 85 percent of the variance in team and project performance.

It is interesting to note that many of these factors are, to a large degree, based on the perception of team members. That is, team members *perceive* "good personal relations" or "communication problems." Because this perception is the reality that influences the team behavior, management must deal with the conditions as seen by the people and foster a project environment conducive to the needs of the team. Such a favorable work environment not only enhances the drivers and minimizes the barriers to project performance, but is also associated with the *15 indirect measures of team performance* shown in Figure 29.1.

The Critical Importance of Managerial Leadership

Creating a climate and culture conducive to quality teamwork involves multifaceted management challenges and skills that increase with the complexities of the project and its organizational environment. No longer are technical expertise *or* good leadership alone sufficient, but excellence across a broad range of skills and sophisticated organizational support systems are required to manage project teams effectively. It is critically important for project leaders to understand, identify, and minimize the various barriers to team development identified earlier. Further, team leaders must know when in the life cycle of the project these barriers are most likely to occur, so that they can take preventive actions early and foster a work environment that is conducive to team building as an ongoing process.

Work challenge seems to be a particularly strong catalyst toward effective teamwork. Formal research on best practices consistently and measurably shows a favorable correlation between (1) interesting, professionally stimulating work with opportunities for recognition and accomplishments and (2) effective teamwork and high project performance. Professionally stimulating and challenging work seems to affect team member motivation, commitment, and cross-functional communications. It also leads to a favorable perception of leadership effectiveness, such as enhanced trust, respect, credibility, and ability to influence decisions.

The effective team leader is usually a social architect who understands the interaction of organizational and behavioral variables and can foster a climate of active participation and minimal dysfunctional conflict. This requires carefully developed skills in leadership, administration, organization, and technical expertise. It further requires the project leader's ability to involve top management and to ensure organizational visibility, resource availability, and overall support for the project throughout its life cycle.

Organizational Environment and Team Performance

The organizational environment, its culture and values add yet another dimension and challenge to the management of project teams. Since team members are often selected from hierarchically organized resource departments, team leaders have to deal with dual accountability of their team members. They also have to deal with the realities of resource and power sharing, and an organizational environment that is likely to foster internal competition rather than cooperation. In fact, at the contributor level, many of the highly innovative and creative people are highly individualistically oriented and often admit their dislike for team involvement and cooperation.

For project managers, this represents a challenge, integrating these individuals into teams that produce innovative results in a systematic, coordinated, and integrated way. Many of the problems that occur during the project life cycle, and especially during the team formation stage, are normal and predictable. However, they present barriers to effective team performance that must be quickly identified and dealt with. In addition, project teams experience the pressure from the broader organizational environment that includes new and changing goals, contractor relations, regulatory requirements, mergers and acquisitions, as well as the social, political, and economic influences.

While all of these factors are part of the organizational ambience and its business realities that the team has to deal with, effective project managers have the ability to foster a team environment that is responsive to these challenges, yet can shield team members from excessive pressures and unnecessary anxieties. Many project-oriented companies are matrixed all the way from external contractors down to the individual contributor. Yet, what holds it all together is the network of people and its local culture. Outside of this team network, the organization or its business does not have much value! Effective project leaders can match the impedance between the organizational environment, including its senior management, and the local team environment at the project level. They find ways to balance the tensions and values of external competitiveness with local team effectiveness and responsiveness.

BUILDING HIGH-PERFORMING TEAMS

What does all this mean to managers in today's work environment with high demands on efficiency, speed, and quality? With increasing technical complexities, cross-functional dependencies, and the need for innovative performance, project leaders are experiencing great difficulties in managing the team from the top down. More and more, managers have to rely on information and judgments by their team members for developing solutions to complex problems. Therefore, with decision processes distributed throughout the team and solutions often evolving incrementally and iteratively, power and responsibilities are shifting away from management toward the project team members.

Team members, both individually and collectively, are taking higher levels of responsibility, authority, and control for project results. That is, these teams become *self-directed*, gradually replacing the more traditional, hierarchically structured project team. These emerging team processes are seen as a significant development for orchestrating the multifunctional activities that come into play during the execution of today's complex projects. These processes rely strongly on group interaction, resource and power sharing, group decision making, accountability, self-direction, and self-control.

Leading such self-directed teams also requires a great deal of team management skills and overall guidance by senior management. In addition, managers must realize the organizational dynamics involved during the team's formation, start-up, and integration process,[4] as graphically shown in Figure 29.3. No work group comes fully integrated and unified in its values and skill sets, but it needs to be skillfully nurtured and developed. Understanding how teams evolve provides some guidelines for managerial leadership.

Realizing the changing professional needs, as well as changing levels of conflict, anxieties, and need for communication effectiveness that can be anticipated as the team goes through the various stages of integration provides some insight into which managerial leadership style works best at what stage of the team development process. Early stages, such as the team formation and start-up, usually require a predominately directive style of team leadership. Providing clear guidelines on the project mission, its objectives, and its requirements, and creating the necessary infrastructure and logistics support for the project team, are critically important in helping the team pass quickly through the first two stages of their development.

Figure 29.3
Four-Stage Team Development Model

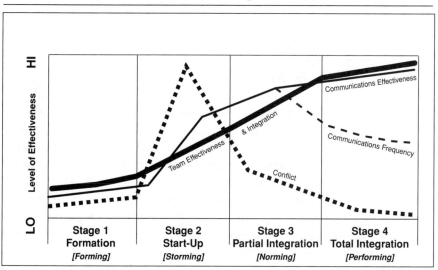

During the third stage, often called *norming* or *partial integration*, the team still needs a considerable amount of guidance and administrative support, as well as support in dealing with the inevitable human issues of conflict, power and politics, credibility, trust, respect, and the whole spectrum of professional career and development. This is the stage where a combination of *directive and participative leadership* will produce most favorable results.

Finally, a team that reaches the fully integrated stage, by definition, becomes *self-directed*. That is, such a fully integrated, unified team can work effectively with a minimum degree of external supervision and administrative support, as profiled earlier. While at this stage, the team often appears to have very little need for external managerial intervention. However, it requires highly sophisticated external leadership to maintain the delegate balance of self-directed forces in a highly dynamic, intricate organizational environment.

RECOMMENDATIONS FOR EFFECTIVE TEAM MANAGEMENT

A number of specific recommendations may help managers in cultivating productive working conditions for multidisciplinary task integration and in building high-performing project teams. The recommendation section follows to some degree the team development process flow shown in Figure 29.3.

Negotiate the Work Assignment

At the outset of any project, team leaders should discuss with their team members the overall task, its scope, and its objectives. Involvement of the people during the early phases of the assignment—such as bid proposals, and project and product planning—can produce great benefits toward plan acceptance, realism, buy-in, personnel matching, and unification of the task team. A thorough understanding of the task requirements comes usually with intense personal involvement that can be stimulated through participation in project planning, requirements analysis, interface definition, or a producibility study. In addition, any committee-type activity, presentation, or data gathering will especially help to involve new team members and facilitate integration. It also will enable people to understand their specific tasks and roles better in the overall team effort. Senior management can help develop a priority image and communicate the basic project parameter and management guidelines.

Communicate Organizational Goals and Objectives

Management must communicate and update the organizational goals and project objectives. The relationship and contribution of individual work to overall business plans and goals, as well as individual project objectives and their importance to the organizational mission, must be clear to all team personnel.

Plan the Project Effectively

An effective project definition and involvement of potential team members early in the life cycle of a project or specific mission will have a favorable impact on the work environment, enthusiasm of the team toward the assignment, commitment toward the project objectives, team morale, and, ultimately, team effectiveness. Because project leaders have to integrate various tasks across many functional lines, proper planning requires the participation of all stakeholders, including support departments, subcontractors, and management. Modern project management techniques, such as phased project planning (PPP) and stage-gate concepts (SGC) provide the conceptional framework and tools for effective cross-functional planning and organizing the work toward effective execution.

Staff and Organize the Project Team

Project staffing is a major activity, usually conducted during the project formation phase. Because of the pressures on the project manager to produce a final product, staffing is often done hastily and prior to defining properly the basic work to be performed. The results are often personnel poorly matched to the job requirements, conflict, low morale, suboptimum decision making, and, in the end, poor project performance. For best results, project leaders should define the project organization, the tasks, and the work process before starting to interview candidates. These interviews should always be conducted one-to-one.

Define the Project Organization, Interfaces, and Reporting Relations

The keys to building a successful new project organization are clearly defined and communicated responsibilities and organizational relationships. The tools for systematically describing the project organization come, in fact, from conventional management practices, including the following:

- Charter of the program or project organization
- Project organization chart, which defines the major reporting and authority relationships
- Responsibility matrix or task roster
- Job description

Make Everyone a Full Player

Team leaders who build an effective project team, unified and committed to the project, make sure that every team member is fully involved and accountable. Individual roles and responsibilities should be clear and agreed on from the start, at least in principle. Today's flatter organizations with focus on empowerment put a premium on self-direction and self-control. Managers must foster a sense of community among team members. Every member should be expected to contribute to both, the agreed-to individual part of the project and the team as a whole, and be evaluated on both components.

Build a High-Performance Image

Building a favorable image for an ongoing project in terms of high-priority, interesting work, importance to the organization, high visibility, and potential for professional rewards is crucial for attracting and holding high-quality people. Senior management can help develop a priority image and communicate the key parameters and management guidelines for specific projects. Moreover, establishing and communicating clear and stable top-down objectives help in building an image of high visibility, importance, priority, and interesting work. Such a pervasive process fosters a climate of active participation at all levels, helps attract and hold quality people, unifies the team, and minimizes dysfunctional conflict.

Define Work Process and Team Structure

Successful formation and development of a project team requires an infrastructure conducive to teamwork. The proper setup and communication of the operational transfer process—such as concurrent engineering, stage gate process, CAD/CAE/CAM,[5] and design-build—is important for establishing the cross-functional linkages necessary for successful project execution. Management must also define the basic team structure for each project early in its life cycle. The project plan, task matrix, project charter, and operating procedure are the principal management tools for defining organizational structure and business process.

Build Enthusiasm and Excitement

Whenever possible, managers should try to accommodate the professional interests and desires of their personnel. Interesting and challenging work is a perception that can be enhanced by the visibility of the work, management attention and support, priority image, and the overlap of personnel values and perceived benefits with organizational objectives. Making work more interesting leads to increased involvement, better communication, lower conflict, higher commitment, stronger work effort, and higher levels of creativity.

Ensure Senior Management Support

It is critically important that senior management provide the proper environment for a project team to function effectively. At the onset of a new development, the responsible manager should negotiate the needed resources with the sponsor organization and obtain commitment from management that these resources will be available. An effective working relationship among resource managers, project leaders, and senior management critically affects the perceived credibility, visibility, and priority of the engineering team and their work.

Define Effective Communication Channels and Methods

Poor communication is a major barrier to teamwork and effective project performance. Management can facilitate the free flow of information, both horizontally and vertically, by work-space design, regular meetings, reviews, and information sessions. In addition, modern technology—such as voice mail, e-mail, electronic bulletin boards, and conferencing—can greatly enhance communications, especially in complex organizational settings.

Build Commitment

Managers should ensure team member commitment to their project plans, specific objectives, and results. If such commitments appear weak, managers should determine the reason for such lack of commitment of a team member and attempt to modify possible negative views. Because insecurity is often a major reason for low commitment, managers should try to determine why insecurity exists, then work to reduce the team members' fears and anxieties. Conflict with other team members and disinterest in the project may be other reasons for the lack of commitment.

Conduct Team-Building Sessions

A mixture of focus team meetings, brainstorming sessions, experience exchanges, and social gatherings can be powerful tools for developing the work group into an effective, fully integrated, and unified project team. Such organized team-building efforts should be conducted throughout the project's life cycle. An especially intensive team-building effort may be needed during the team formation stage. Although formally organized and managed, these team-building sessions are often conducted in a very informal and relaxed atmosphere to discuss critical questions such as these:

- How are we working as a team?
- What is our strength?
- How can we improve?
- What support do we need?
- What challenges and problems are we likely to face?
- What actions should we take?
- What process or procedural changes would be beneficial?

Ensure Project Leadership

The project management and team leadership positions should be carefully defined and staffed at all projects levels. To build and lead a project team, especially in a dynamic or self-directed work environment, requires credibility, trust, and respect of the project leader—a quality that usually comes from the image of a sound decision maker with a good track record.

Create Proper Reward Systems

Personnel evaluation and reward systems should be designed to reflect the desired power equilibrium and authority/responsibility sharing of an organization. A *quality function deployment* (*QFD*) philosophy helps to focus efforts toward desired results on company internal and external customers, and helps to foster a work environment that is strong on self-direction and self-control.

Manage Conflict and Problems

Project managers should focus their efforts on problem avoidance. That is, managers and team leaders, through experience, should recognize potential problems and conflicts at their onset, and deal with them before they become big and their resolutions consume a large amount of time and effort.

Ensure Personal Drive and Involvement

Project managers and team leaders can influence the team environment by their own actions. Concern for their team members, the ability to integrate personal needs of their staff with the goals of the organization, and the ability to create personal enthusiasm for a particular project can foster a climate of high motivation, work involvement, open communication, and ultimately high engineering performance.

SUMMING UP BEST PRACTICES

The increasing complexities of today's project environment, both internally and externally, prompt enormous managerial challenges for directing, coordinating, and controlling teamwork. Especially with the expansion of self-directed team concepts, additional managerial tools and skills are required to handle the burgeoning dynamics and infrastructure.

Effective teamwork is a critical determinant of project success and the organization's ability to learn from its experiences and position itself for future growth (Senge 1990). To be effective in organizing and directing a project team, the leader must not only recognize the potential drivers and barriers to high-performance teamwork, but also know when in the life cycle of the project they are most likely to occur. The effective leader takes preventive actions early in the project's life cycle and fosters a work environment that is conducive to team building as an ongoing process. The new business realities force managers to focus also on cross-boundary relations, delegation, and commitment, in addition to establishing the more traditional formal command and control systems.

The effective team leader is usually a social architect who understands the interaction of organizational, technological, and behavioral variables, and can foster a climate of active participation and minimal dysfunctional conflict. This requires carefully developed skills in leadership, administration, organization, and technical expertise. It further requires the project leader's ability to foster an ambiance conducive to change, commitment, self-direction, and top management involvement, ensuring organizational visibility, resource availability, and overall support for the project throughout its life cycle. Four major conditions must be present for building effective project teams:

1. Professionally stimulating work environment.
2. Good project leadership.
3. Qualified personnel.
4. Stable work environment.

Building effective project teams involves the whole spectrum of management skills and company resources, and is the shared responsibility between functional managers and the project leader. To be effective in such a complex environment, the manager must understand the interaction of organizational and behavioral variables. This understanding will facilitate a climate of active participation, minimum dysfunctional conflict, and effective communication. It will also foster an ambiance conducive to change, commitment, and self-direction necessary for effective teamwork and continuous organizational improvement.

NOTES

1. Source: Field survey on team leadership, conducted between 1999 and 2000, involving a sample of 560 managers in 38 technology-oriented companies; Working Paper, H. J. Thamhain, 2000. One survey question was "What factors and conditions do you consider most critical for effective business performance?" Seventy-two percent of the respondents ranked teamwork among the top three factors crucial to success.
2. For more detailed discussions of the field research see H. J. Thamhain and D. L. Wilemon, "A High-Performing Engineering Project Team," *The Human Side of Managing Innovation* (R. Katz, editor). New York: Oxford University Press, 1997.
3. Studies by Nurick and Thamhain (1993) and Thamhain and Wilemon (1997) into work group dynamics clearly show significant correlation and interdependencies among work environment factors and team performance. These studies indicate that high team performance involves four primary factors: managerial leadership, job content, personal goals and objectives, and work environment and organizational support. Kendall-tau rank-order correlation was used to measure the actual correlation of 60 influence factors to the project team characteristics and team performance. Statistical significance was defined at a confidence level of 95 percent or better.

4. The four-stage model is a common framework used by management researchers and practitioners to analyze team development processes. Its roots go back to the pioneering research work by Hersey and Blanchard (1996).
5. These acronyms stand for: CAD, computer-aided design; CAE, computer-aided engineering; CAM, computer-aided manufacturing.

REFERENCES

Bennis, Warren G., and Herbert A. Shepard. 1956. "A Theory of Group Development." *Human Relations*, No. 9: 415–437.

Cusumano, Michael A., and David B. Yoffie. 1998. *Competing on Internet Time*. New York: Free Press.

Drucker, Peter F. 1996. *The Executive in Action: Managing for Results, Innovation and Entrepreneurship*. New York: Harper & Row.

Dumaine, Brian. 1991. "The Bureaucracy Buster." *Fortune* (June 17).

Dyer, W. G. 1977. *Team Building: Issues and Alternatives*. Reading, MA: Addison-Wesley.

Engel, Michael V. 1997. "The New Non-Manager Manager." *Management Quarterly*, Vol. 38, No. 2 (Summer): 22–29.

Fisher, Kimball. 1993. *Leading Self-Directed Work Teams*. New York: McGraw-Hill.

Gray, Clifford F., and Erik W. Larson. 2000. *Project Management*. New York: Irwin McGraw-Hill.

Gupta, A. K., and D. L. Wilemon. 1996. "Changing Patterns in Industrial R&D Management." *Journal of Product Innovation Management*, Vol. 13, No. 6 (November): 497–511.

Hersey, Paul, and Kenneth H. Blanchard. 1996. *Management of Organizational Behavior*. Upper Saddle River, NJ: Prentice Hall.

Likert, R. 1961. *New Patterns of Management*. New York: McGraw-Hill.

McGregor, D. 1960. *The Human Side of Enterprise*. New York: McGraw-Hill.

Moss Kanter, Rosabeth. 1989. "The New Managerial Work." *Harvard Business Review* (November–December).

Nurick, A. J., and H. J. Thamhain. 1993. "Project Team Development in Multinational Environments." In *Global Project Management Handbook* (D. Cleland, editor). New York: McGraw-Hill.

Ouchi, William G. 1993. *Theory Z*. New York: Avon Books.

Peters, Thomas J., and Robert H. Waterman. 1987, 1997. *In Search of Excellence*. New York: Harper & Row.

Roethlingsberger, F., and W. Dickerson. 1939. *Management and the Worker*. Cambridge, MA: Harvard University Press.

Senge, Peter. 1990 (audiocassette, 1994). *The Fifth Discipline: The Art and Practice of the Learning Organization*. New York: Doubleday/Currency.

Shaw, J., C. Fisher, and A. Randolph. 1991. "From Maternalism to Accountability." *Academy of Management Executive*, Vol. 5, No. 1 (February): 7–20.

Shonk, J. H. 1996. *Team-Based Organizations.* Homewood, IL: Irwin.

Thamhain, H. J. 1990[a]. "Managing Technologically Innovative Team Efforts towards New Product Success." *Journal of Product Innovation Management,* Vol. 7, No. 1 (March): 5–18.

————. 1990[b]. "Managing Technology: The People Factor." *Technical and Skill Training* (August/September).

————. 1998[a]. "Managing People." Chapter 68 in *Mechanical Engineer's Handbook* (M. Kutz, editor). New York: John Wiley & Sons.

————. 1998[b]. "Working with Project Teams." Chapter 18 in *Project Management* by David I. Cleland. New York: Van Nostrand Reinhold.

Thamhain, H. J., and D. L. Wilemon. 1987. "Leadership, Conflict and Project Management Effectiveness." *Executive Bookshelf on Generating Technological Innovations, Sloan Management Review,* (Fall).

————. 1997. "Building High Performing Engineering Project Teams." In *The Human Side of Managing Technological Innovation* (R. Katz, editor). New York: Oxford University Press.

————. 1999. "Building Effective Teams in Complex Project Environments." *Technology Management,* Vol. 5, No. 2 (May).

Tichy, Noel, and David Ulrich. 1984. "The Leadership Challenge—Call for the Transformational Leader." *Sloan Management Review.* (Fall): 59–69.

Walton, Richard. 1985. "From Control to Commitment in the Workplace." *Harvard Business Review* (March–April).

Wellins, Richard S., William C. Byham, and Jeanne M. Wilson. 1991. *Empowered Teams.* San Francisco: Jossey-Bass.

Zenger, John H., Ed Musselwhite, Kathleen Hurson, and Craig Perrin. 1994. *Leading Teams.* Homewood, IL: Business One Irwin.

CONCLUSION

CHAPTER 30

PROJECT MANAGEMENT: THE FUTURE

JEFFREY K. PINTO

INTRODUCTION

When we look at the future of project management, it is important to distinguish between project management as a philosophy and project management as a series of techniques. Clearly, the techniques of project management will undergo substantial changes over the coming years. New technological breakthroughs, new approaches in operations management, and changing organizational demographics are all likely to render important and useful changes in the processes by which we manage projects down the road. Our techniques for running projects are open to change and, indeed, require constant updating in order to gain the maximum potential from our people and processes.

The philosophy of project management is likely to change dramatically as well. In fact, the decade of the 1990s has served as an important step in inaugurating an era of growth in the project management field. Consider some of the evidence: Professional project management associations, such as the Project Management Institute and the International Project Management Association, have had their membership double and redouble in the past decade. Corporations in industries as diverse as insurance, heavy and light manufacturing, banking and finance, utilities, infrastructure management, and software development have embraced project management as the new operating paradigm for managing their businesses. Project management has become the technique of choice for new product introductions, system implementation, corporate reorganizations—the list goes on and on. When we suggest that project management has come of age, we are not engaging in hyperbole.

What, then, is the future of project management? Although I cannot claim the gift of prognostication, I can offer some suppositions based on my experience and the state of the industrial world at the millennium. I am convinced that the importance of project management for organizational success will expand rather than wane in the years to come.

In this chapter I will discuss in detail some of the reasons why I see a proliferation in project management and subsequent increasing demand for project management skills in the years to come. Finally, I will suggest that companies need to become more systematic in their approach to developing project managers who have the tools and abilities to get the job done.

In the larger context of international business, attempts to make projections regarding the future are often met with skepticism, wariness, and even amusement, as in cases when these gurus are confronted with their guesses years later. Peter Drucker, the well-known management consultant and writer, is particularly leery of organizations becoming overly infatuated with the future, arguing that those who forecast the future and make strategic decisions on the basis of probabilities and present-day trends are generally unlikely to succeed in the long term (Drucker 1992). Nevertheless, although the future itself is a murky proposition, there is compelling evidence to support the fact that the future does hold out some tremendous opportunities in addition to its threats and uncertainty. For project-based organizations, in particular, there are a number of encouraging signs that point to the likelihood of a tremendous upsurge in market demand for their services and techniques.

THE AGE OF PROJECT MANAGEMENT

"The Age of Project Management" derives from the title of an article by a well-known project management scholar (Cleland 1991). In his article, Cleland painted a convincing portrait of the state of project management in the international sphere and demonstrated the basis for supposing that project management will increase in importance in years to come. There are a number of reasons behind the expectation that project management techniques will gain in popularity, including:

1. Dramatically shortened market windows and product life cycles.
2. Rapid development of third world and "closed" economies.
3. Increasingly complex and technical products.
4. Heightened international competition.
5. The pressures of an economy operating under low inflation.
6. The environment of organizational resource scarcity that has led to downsizing and streamlining operations.

Let us consider each of these reasons in turn.

Shortened Market Windows and Product Life Cycles

The speed at which products become obsolete is evidence of the turbulent changes affecting the business world. Traditionally, in many industries, product launches could be carefully crafted and planned because companies knew that they had a comfortably wide window of opportunity to develop, test, and market new products. For example, the IBM System 360, which so revolutionized mainframe computing, continued as a viable product for nearly a decade. A more recent example concerns the IBM personal computer, the PC. This benchmark 64K RAM microcomputer, launched in the early 1980s, continued to be the industry standard for almost five years. Such lengthy product life cycles, particularly in the computer hardware and software industries, are a thing of the past. Indeed, the technology is moving so rapidly today that year-old PCs are often literally passé. (See Figure 30.1.)

Figure 30.1
Product Life Cycles—Traditional versus Modern

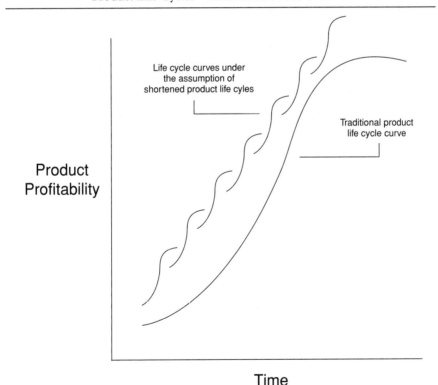

Life cycle curves under the assumption of shortened product life cyles

Traditional product life cycle curve

Product Profitability

Time

These time-to-market pressures and shortened product life cycles have a significant impact on organizations as they seek to counter such threats through the use of project teams. Cross-functional teams and project management techniques have a major impact on companies and their ability to deliver new products within significantly shorter time frames. For example, in 1989 Honda was touted by *Fortune* magazine for its "superfast" approach to new product innovation. Using team approaches, Honda had shortened the time frame for new automobile development from five years to three years. While a significant achievement, Honda's team approach was just the beginning of innovative process changes in the automotive industry. By 1994, Chrysler president Robert Lutz was able to announce that the Viper platform (cross-functional) team had designed, developed, engineered, and produced a new prototype in 18 months. Less than six years later, the cycle time has dropped to approximately 12 months.

The other by-product of shortened life-cycles has been the narrowing of new product launch windows. Firms routinely plan for product launches in the same way they plan for new product development. The timing of product launches has become highly sophisticated in the past decade. For example, even as new products in the software industry hit the store shelves today, firms are already gearing up for product upgrades and support products. Because of the tremendous competition, it is imperative that new products be timed to take advantage of very narrow launch windows. As one executive in the computer industry put it to me, "If the new product is not out the door within a four-week period next year, we might just as well not bother developing it this year." At the beginning of new product development is an understanding that to be successful, timing is key. If the project is late, it is useless because a rival will have exploited the opening and offered a substitute product. Embedded in this realization has been the increased use of project teams and project management techniques to maximize organizational resources and creative processes while giving development teams the freedom from bureaucracy and red tape that can often strangle innovation.

Rapid Development of Third World and Closed Economies

One of the astounding by-products of the growth of free-market capitalism and economic expansion in Russia, Eastern Europe, and Asian countries has been the explosion in pent-up demand within these societies for all manner of consumer goods and infrastructure development. Wherever one turns in the developing sectors of the international economy, there are numerous large-scale projects either underway or about to begin. Vietnam has recently opened its borders to a number of foreign corporations and has begun a massive program of infrastructure development and industrial expansion. The People's Republic of China, while nominally the world's largest communist state, is poised to join the list of World Trade Organization (WTO) countries and is increasingly eager to encourage consumerism and pockets of capitalism within its largest cities. Further, project management groups from major industrial construction firms in the United States, Europe, and Japan are in serious negotiations with the Chinese government for a number of large-scale development projects of every sort.

Eastern Europe, likewise, stands poised to take advantage of project management in the drive to modernize industries in the wake of a democratic revolution that has replaced the centralized, command economies with market-driven capitalism. Old, inefficient factories are being closed and torn down or upgraded to turn out new products. While there are very real limits on funding for revitalization of their industries, the nature of the economies of Eastern Europe is such that capital development is likely to continue, albeit slowly at first, for several decades.

Despite the current recession in some international economies, the construction industry continues to boom in Asia, which now accounts for over 60 percent of worldwide construction and continues to grow rapidly. This development has been a positive windfall for Japanese, European, and American contractors (*Asian Review* 1994). Project management will continue to play a key role in this expansion (Cleland 1991).

An issue of the *Asian Wall Street Journal* (April 18, 1994) carried a 14-page supplement entitled, "Asian Infrastructure—Asia Transforms Itself." The article examines Asia's most pressing demands for major infrastructure development. This situation holds enormous opportunities to exploit these needs for private firms, both local and foreign.

To illustrate the level of development currently being undertaken in these Asian countries, consider some of the examples summarized in Table 30.1, each representing a mega-project forecast to cost in excess of $1 billion.

This is just a cursory list of the more exciting mega-projects in the Asian world. There is no question that in spite of recent economic downturns in the economies of several Pacific Rim countries, huge infrastructure projects are the continuing wave of the future. These countries realize that the quickest road to economic recovery and prosperity lies in a determined policy of development and growth.

Increasingly Complex and Technical Products

Many of the products that are being created today in a variety of industries, from children's toys to automobiles, are becoming more technically

Table 30.1
Recent/Current Asian Mega-Projects

Country	Number of Projects	Cost Range ($ Billions)	Largest Project
China	7	1–77	Dam and hydropower station
Hong Kong	5	1–20	New airport
India	2	1–2	Enron power plant
Malaysia	5	1–5.6	Dam and hydropower station
Philippines	1	1.3	Elevated rail system
South Korea	6	1–20	Superhighway system
Taiwan	5	5–17	Rapid mass transit system

complex to develop, manufacture, and use. Technologically driven innovation presents a tremendous challenge for organizations in the areas of engineering and design, production, and marketing. As a result, many organizations are relying on project teams to efficiently create and move their products to market.

The need to redesign is often the result of poor internal communication (Cooper 1998). Many departments must cooperate to bring a new product to market. In many instances, when done wrong, the new product introduction process consists of a series of cycled loops from one functional area to another. (See Figure 30.2.) Consider a simplified case in which a new consumer electronics product is slated for introduction. Typically, some sort of causal chain would be set in motion. Engineering would first design the product and send specifications to production. The production department may object to certain aspects of the product's design (perhaps

Figure 30.2
"Over the Fence" Product Development

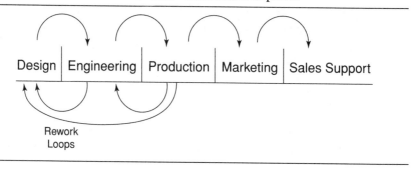

Design | Engineering | Production | Marketing | Sales Support

Rework
Loops

due to manufacturing limitations) and will then return the product plans to engineering for rework.

Following this loop, engineering may or may not make enough modifications to satisfy production. Perhaps a couple of iterations of this loop will be needed before production agrees to the design and begins prototype development. At this point, in many organizations, marketing personnel are finally brought on board and given the opportunity to comment on the prototype. With their knowledge of competing products, they may offer suggestions that will restart the cycle between engineering and production, all the while holding up development and new product launch.

The reader can readily see how unwieldy such a causal chain is when an organization is faced with the pressures of new product introduction. Consequently, companies are scrapping this strategy and employing cross-functional teams from the beginning. There is ample supporting evidence that allowing all relevant departments immediate access and the ability to influence new product designs,will significantly shorten time-to-market delivery.

Heightened International Competition

In our undergraduate economics courses, we learned the nature of choices. These choices, often called "guns or butter" decisions, were based on a zero-sum assumption of a fixed pie. The fixed-pie view said that there was only so much to go around; choosing more guns meant less butter was available. As we enter the new millennium, we see a "pie" that continues to expand. The global economic climate is not one of shrinkage or even zero-sum stability; it represents incredible opportunity on a scale never before imagined. During the 1990s' stock market boom times, it was routine for firms to be valued at 70, 80, even 90 times projected future earnings. Analysts are taking a look at the potential for future development and drawing the obvious conclusions: There is a gold mine out there for the companies that can exploit it. Project management firms, aiming at market agility while keeping a disciplined hand on costs and development times, are ideally poised to reap the benefits of the global marketplace.

Competition drives innovation. It is only in the face of substitutable products that organizations are compelled to upgrade, alter, or develop new and innovative products of their own. In the past, American manufacturing has had the economic playing field to itself for a variety of reasons, many associated with the impact of World War II on other industrialized nations and the slow industrial advance of developing countries. During this period, U.S. companies had enormous domestic markets to exploit, leading to a sense of hubris that sowed the seeds for later problems. On the other hand, foreign manufacturing was in its infancy and suffering from the teething problems associated with new start-up companies: poor quality, lack of name recognition, uncertain marketing strategies, and so forth. While truly a golden age for American business, clearly this was not a state that could continue indefinitely, in spite of many companies' belief that, in fact, it would.

It was not until the late 1960s that any appreciable inroads were made into traditional American markets such as automobiles. However, during the 1970s, the oil shocks and Japanese manufacturing skills, combined with lower unit prices, served to seriously threaten many strategic and consumer industries, such as steel, computers, electronic data systems (copiers), and electronic consumer goods (television). These economic attacks, while painful, offered a blessing in disguise in that they served finally to shake many U.S. companies out of the inertia and sense of complacency into which they had sunk.

In many industries, domestic counterattacks have been spurred on by increased use of project management. One of the fortunate side effects of the pressures placed on American firms was in forcing them to develop innovative processes for survival in a new, international marketplace for which they were underequipped and which they did not foresee with accuracy. Project management has a long history in certain industries, such as airframe development at Boeing, Lockheed, and McDonnell-Douglas. However, one of the effects of the end of American corporate lethargy was to convince other companies, many of which had no experience in project management, to look upon it as a new and useful tool for competitive advantage. Properly trained and schooled in its techniques, these firms stand to reap substantial benefits within the international marketplace through speedier product development and greater efficiency of operations.

An Economy Operating under Low Inflation

Most of us, as consumers, look at low inflation with delight. Our money goes further, products remain affordable, and expense forecasting is easier. Businesses, however, see low inflation as a mixed blessing. On the one hand, they have the same reactions we consumers do: Manufacturing and operating expenses stay low, it makes cost projections easier, negotiations with suppliers and vendors are based on better information, and so forth. On the other hand, low inflation creates a challenge to maintaining a state of profitability. Profit essentially derives from one of two sources: raising prices or cutting costs. In the past, many organizations maintained their profitability through some combination of the two. The idea was to keep costs under control while passing along regular price increases to consumers. The public, used to a steady rise in prices for goods, generally did not object.

In the current economic climate, particularly in the United States, these old rules no longer hold. Corporations no longer have the luxury of increasing profit through price increases and are forced to find ways to improve operating margins, cut costs, and enhance internal efficiency in order to maintain profitability. Jack Welch, former CEO of General Electric, took a hard look at this problem during a recent speech in Boca Raton, Florida, and suggested that when wages are added in, we are actually in a period of deflation, in which prices are diminishing. The implication is that successful companies of the future will be those that find their profits through streamlining internal processes, saving money by doing this better than their competition. Project management is a tool to realize these goals of internal efficiency and profit in a low-inflation time.

The Environment of Organizational Resource Scarcity

Obviously, companies have always been forced to operate in pursuit of a variety of scarce resources: money, skilled personnel, plant and equipment, and so forth. Nevertheless, the uncertain economic conditions of the current decade have led to a new management philosophy, the need to do more with less. This new approach leads to downsizing and streamlining of operations in pursuit of cost savings and efficiency.

The impact of such corporate downsizing has been to create increased demands on those who remain to perform as effectively as possible within a resource-scarce atmosphere. Some of these organizations (e.g., Kodak) are increasingly relying on project management to achieve the dual benefits of rapid product development and reduction of time to market under the constraints of greater cost controls and budgetary limitations. These companies, some using project management for the first time in a formal manner, have discovered one of the important features of these techniques: Their use gives project teams the ability to be both externally effective in getting products to market as well as internally efficient in their use of organizational resources.

Project management is predicated on the ability to use resources carefully: In effect, the techniques are themselves "resource constrained." Consequently, in an atmosphere of efficiency and streamlining operations, project management offers a valuable tool for companies to employ, as many currently are doing.

These are some of the more compelling reasons why we are likely to continue to witness an increase of interest in and use of project management in international businesses. As Cleland (1991) noted, the strategic thrusts of many businesses and, indeed, many countries point to a continued drive to improve, upgrade, modernize, and develop their infrastructures, markets, and capital and natural resources bases. In this context, the benefits of project management are substantial and clearly equipped to provide these countries and their business organizations with a powerful tool for effective and efficient operations.

CLOUDS ON THE HORIZON

At the same time as we can look with hope to an expansion in the use of project management, it is important to point out the dangers in creating overly optimistic expectations about project management as a business technique. It is true that project management is the management of change, versus traditional functional management, which often solidifies the status quo. As a result, project management is ideally situated to serve as a platform upon which many organizations can achieve the degrees of flexibility and efficiency needed for long-term survival and prosperity. Nevertheless, I would point to a few potential clouds on an otherwise upbeat horizon for the future of project management. These clouds are in the form of:

1. Current poor project management training programs
2. Lack of understanding by top management of what project management can and cannot do
3. Need to avoid the bandwagon effect

Let us consider these concerns in order.

The Need for Training

In my research, teaching, and consulting experiences, one issue comes through very clearly with a number of the corporations with whom I work: the lack of clear, systematic training in project management techniques. Project managers are often trained by the oldest (and worst) method: They are tossed into a project without any advance warning, almost no training, and little on-the-job guidance. To say that many companies' training programs are ad hoc is to put it mildly. We need to instill a better sense of systematic training across functional disciplines, get everyone speaking the same language of project management, and establish protocols and procedures with which everyone within an organization, regardless of functional position, is familiar. Until we do so, project will continue to operate in selected pockets within organizations, rather than working across the corporation.

Understanding the Strengths and Limitations of Project Management

Top management has an important role to play in this process. As the key individuals who set the tone for the rest of their company, people at the top can do much to infuse a sense of purpose to project-based work. The key is improving their understanding of the sorts of things project management can and cannot do for them. Unrealistic expectations or fundamental misunderstanding of the project management process have a tendency to create the assumptions of sky-high results. When they are not achieved to the degree expected, there is often a call to dismantle the process and try something newer and even more different. The key to making project management work lies in training top managers in understanding its uses and how best to support it. Time spent training top management can yield huge dividends downstream. Like any other useful management tool or technique, project management will work to the degree that organizations employ it in a measured and thoughtful approach, understanding its strengths and weaknesses.

Avoiding the Bandwagon Effect

Finally, because much is expected from the project management movement, it is also helpful to consider some reasoned words of warning on how to avoid the "flash in the pan" sobriquet so often attached to the latest management technique. As Barnes and Wearne (1993) write:

> Project management is the management of uncertainty, and its future must itself be uncertain. . . . No technique with a distinctive name achieves what its enthusiasts hope for it or lasts as long as they expect. The same could be true of project management itself.

While we may hope that the authors' concerns are overstated, nevertheless, they strike an appropriate note of caution that must be considered. The worst future for project management would be to create a new organizational buzzword out of the technique, leading too many companies with too high expectations to begin jumping on the bandwagon in hopes of achieving quick and painless solutions to their problems. Overly ambitious programs without the necessary level of commitment, support, and training could do the worst possible damage to the project management profession. Let's not turn an invaluable discipline into simply another fad tried by ill-informed and unprepared companies that fails predictably and is then dismissed as ineffective.

CONCLUSION

In an arena of controlled costs, rapidly increasing complexity, calls for greater quality, and diminishing natural resources, organizations find themselves confronted with the specter of having to make do with less and less. Corporate profitability and long-term survival is predicated on the ability to grow, offer new and innovative products and services, and find competitive niches. In today's supercompetitive world, it is those firms that have taken the time to learn and use well the techniques of project management that will get the competitive advantage.

Project management is a philosophy and technique that enables its practitioners to perform to their maximum potential within the constraints of limited resources, thereby increasing profitability. The rapid expansion of Asian, Eastern European, and Latin American economies will continue to drive a concomitant expansion in development, building, and infrastructure repair and improvement, as well as within the industrial sectors of these economies. Many of these pushes for expansion will be fueled by project management techniques (Kovanen, Artto, and Arenius 1998).

With the future bright for expanding the role of project management on a worldwide basis, the only potential clouds on the horizon concern the ability of governments and businesses to use these techniques well. The lack of formal training for many future project managers is worrisome and must be corrected. We must continue our efforts to develop a common skill set and body of knowledge so that these techniques can be used to their maximum potential.

REFERENCES

Asian Review. 1994. "Construction Industry Remains Buoyant." 31.

Barnes, N. M. L., and S. H. Wearne. 1993. "The Future of Major Project Management." *International Journal of Project Management,* 11: 135–142.

Cleland, D. I. 1991. "The Age of Project Management." *Project Management Journal,* XXII (1): 19–24.

Cooper, K. G. 1998. "Four Failures in Project Management." In J. K. Pinto (editor), *The Project Management Institute Project Management Handbook.* San Francisco: Jossey-Bass: 396–424.

Drucker, P. 1992. "Planning for Uncertainty." *Wall Street Journal* (July 22), A12.

Kovanen, V., K. A. Artto, and M. Arenius. 1998. "Project Management of the Future: Developing the Project Business Field." In A. Hauc et al. (editor), *Proceedings of the 14th World Congress on Project Management:* 754–761.

INDEX